Evolutionary Design by Computers

Wherever then all the parts came about just as they would have been if they had come for an end, such things survived, being organized spontaneously in a fitting way; whereas those which grew otherwise, perished and continue to perish . . .

Aristotle, approx. 350 BC
Physicae Auscultationes (Physics, book 2, part 8)
Translated by R. P. Hardie and R. K. Gaye

. . . I think it would be a most extraordinary fact if no variation ever had occurred useful to each being's own welfare, in the same way as so many variations have occurred useful to man. But if variations useful to any organic being do occur, assuredly individuals thus characterised will have the best chance of being preserved in the struggle for life; and from the strong principle of inheritance they will tend to produce offspring similarly characterised.

Charles Darwin, 1859
The Origin of Species by Means of Natural Selection, 1st Edn.
Penguin Classics

It is raining DNA outside. On the bank of the Oxford canal at the bottom of my garden is a large Willow tree, and it is pumping downy seeds into the air. . . . It is raining instructions out there; it's raining programs; it's raining tree-growing, fluff-spreading, algorithms. That is not a metaphor, it is the plain truth. It couldn't be any plainer if it were raining floppy discs.

Richard Dawkins, 1986
The Blind Watchmaker
Longman Pub

'. . . a computer of such infinite and subtle complexity that organic life itself shall form part of its operational matrix. . . . Yes! I shall design this computer for you. . . . And it shall be called . . . The Earth'.

Deep Thought
The Hitch Hiker's Guide to the Galaxy
Douglas Adams, 1979
Pan Books

Evolutionary Design by Computers

Peter Bentley

Department of Computer Science
University College London
Gower Street
London, UK

Developed by Academic Press, published by Morgan Kaufmann Publishers

Morgan Kaufmann Publishers, Inc.
San Francisco, California

This book is printed on acid-free paper

Morgan Kaufmann Publishers, Inc.
Editorial and Sales Office
340 Pine Street, Sixth Floor
San Francisco, CA 94104-3205
USA

Telephone	415-392-2665
Facsimile	415-982-2665
Email	*mkp@mkp.com*
WWW	http://*www.mkp.com*

Order toll free 800-745-7323

ISBN 1-55860-605-X

A catalogue record for this book is available from the British Library

Typeset by J&L Composition Ltd, Filey, North Yorkshire
Printed in Great Britain by The Bath Press, Bath

99 00 01 02 03 04 BP 9 8 7 6 5 4 3 2 1

Contents

The colour plate section is located between pages 208 and 209.

Acknowledgements

My thanks to the following people:

Bridget Shine, my editor for Academic Press, for her enthusiasm, her invaluable support and her wicked sense of humour.

Tamsin Cousins, Gioia Ghezzi, Emma Roberts and all the staff at Academic Press for their exceptional work in producing this book.

Denise Penrose, Meghan Keeffe, Sheri Dean, Brent Emerson and all the staff at Morgan Kaufmann Publishers for their on-going work in distributing and marketing this book.

Phil Treleaven and Suran Goonatilake for encouraging me to start this monstrous project, and for providing useful advice and criticism.

All of the contributors to this book, who gave up their time to help make this book the definitive work in the area.

All of the contributors to the CD-ROM, which will be invaluable to readers because of their support.

Richard Dawkins for writing the foreword and providing his Biomorph program for the CD-ROM.

Andy Hindle's five art students: Dominic King, Daniel King, Kate Tarpey, Finn Smith and Tom Caumont from St. Helena School in Colchester, for providing the artwork on the five section title pages.

The 'famous blokes' for not only agreeing to read chapters from the book, but for saying nice things about them as well – see the cover!

Tina Yu for her help and enthusiasm.

My Ph.D. students Hugh Mallinson and Jungwon Kim, for putting up with me being constantly distracted from them.

All the members of UCL's Design Group, and all of the people at the numerous conferences and workshops around the world who have inspired me or made useful suggestions for the book.

The contributors and speakers for my workshops and journal special issues on evolutionary design, for helping me to promote research in this exciting area.

My friends and family for their support and excitement in this endeavour, and for providing welcome distractions.

And finally (as usual), I would like to thank the cruel and indifferent, yet astonishingly creative process of natural evolution for providing the inspiration for my work. Long may it continue to do so.

About the Editor

Peter Bentley is an award-winning Research Fellow at the Department of Computer Science, University College London.

He is well known for his prolific research which covers all aspects of evolutionary computation, including multiobjective optimisation, constraint handling, variable-length chromosomes, speciation and artificial immune systems. Dr Bentley has applied genetic algorithms and genetic programming to a diverse range of applications, such as floor-planning, control, fraud-detection and music composition (which has been the subject of a television documentary). His work in creative evolutionary design has been described as 'ground-breaking', 'impressive' and 'exceptionally interesting'.

Peter is a regular speaker at international conferences, and is the author of numerous research papers and book chapters on evolutionary design. He is a respected consultant, chair and reviewer for workshops, conferences and journals on evolutionary computation. Peter is the convenor of international symposia on evolutionary design and creative evolutionary systems. He is the guest editor of the series of special issues on evolutionary design in the international journal *Artificial Intelligence in Design, Analysis and Manufacturing*.

Foreword

What might Charles Darwin have done if he had had a computer at his disposal? What, indeed, would he make of this book? Of course he'd first have to get to grips with the astonishing power of the digital computer as an amplifier of human intelligence, and this might be initially shattering to an elderly Victorian gentleman. But having penetrated that barrier, I suspect that he'd have found here a cathartic rounding off of his 'one long argument': an elegant closure.

In Darwin's own time, the idea he had to offer was just as shattering to his contemporaries. In the first chapter of *The Origin of Species*, he wisely softened up his readers with a weakened, almost homeopathic, dose of the medicine. Not natural selection – not the real thing – but a familiar and non-threatening analogue of natural selection. Artificial selection helped the Victorian mind in something like the same way computer models and 'artificial life' help ours. You want to design a new breed of pigeon with a long neck, in a way analogous to nature's way? The obvious engineering solution might seem to be direct mechanical manipulation: hang weights from the neck to stretch it, or put increasing numbers of rings round the neck like a fashionable tribeswoman? But this is not the Darwinian way. Instead, you wait for spontaneous genetic variation and breed from the longest necked individuals in successive generations. This is the principle by which we have engineered faster horses, or tamer wolves reshaped into poodles and weimeraners. This is how we have rejigged cows into milk machines, hens into mass production egg machines. A human designer can imagine a desired animal or plant shape, and set about achieving that goal generations later. This is evolutionary design of domestic animals and plants.

Darwin's original readers understood this process. The sticking point for them was when he took the designer out of the equation, replacing the deliberate human will of the breeder by unconscious natural selection: the survival of the fittest in the struggle for life. A hundred and forty years on, we have got used to natural selection. Today, our problem is the opposite, and Darwin would have enjoyed the irony. Deliberate, creative human design, which Darwin used as his starting point because it is apparently so easy to understand, is today our mystery. How did the simple, mechanical, automatic process of survival of the fittest generate a brain powerful enough to engage in this novel – by evolutionary standards – kind of design process? For that matter, how did it produce a brain capable of painting pictures, of writing music or proving Fermat's last theorem? When an Eddison designs the electric light, or a Whittle the jet engine, what goes on inside the brain? Is it a kind of Darwinian survival of a minority of good ideas from a population of wild inspirations welling up inside the head? If so, what is the population of varying entities that are selected, and by what criteria do they survive? Are they memes, as suggested by Derek Gatherer in Chapter 3? The meme was originally defined as a unit of cultural inheritance, but is the transfer of memes from brain to brain just the tip of the iceberg? Does most of the struggle for survival among memes, most of the cut and thrust of population memetics, go on inside individual brains? Do only the winners of an internal struggle see the light of day and enter the wider competition to jump to another brain?

Darwin would surely have been fascinated by such questions, not least in the context of art. As a masterwork takes shape, is each brushstroke – or some larger unit of creativity? – the winner of a Darwinian struggle for existence inside the artist's head? If so, should we define the survival criterion as 'taste', or is that still too anthropomorphic and empty? Is it rather that the artist's brain, before he even begins the painting, is already swarming with memes, and new ones gain a foothold only if they are compatible, in complicated ways, with the existing population? If so, the analogy with genetic Darwinian selection is closer than many people realise, for the most important part of the 'environment' in which genes survive is the other genes of the gene pool, as encountered in the cells of successive generations of bodies within the species. In any case, the possibility of using Darwinian selection explicitly in making computer art is a fascinating one, as we learn from some of its leading practitioners, in Section 3.

Most of all, Darwin would enjoy this book for its repeated demonstrations of the emergent, creative power of his principle of selection, the non-random survival of randomly varying manufacturing instructions, with or without something equivalent to sexual recombination. Here, Darwin would surely feel, is the experimental demonstration he really needed; a fully transparent manifestation of natural selection, not artificial selection, albeit in the artificial environment of the computer. Karl Sims' creatures, evolved to swim, walk, jump or follow, are sufficiently similar to real life to strike an instant chord with Darwin. But so, in their different ways, are the productions of many of these authors. It only remains, Darwin might feel, to release such virtual creatures into an artificial ecosystem to prey on each other, run away from each other, coevolve in lockstep like antelopes and big cats. Easier said than done, of course. Meanwhile, I think we can be confident that Darwin would love this book.

Richard Dawkins
Charles Simonyi Professor of the
Public Understanding of Science
at Oxford University

Contributors

David Andre
Division of Computer Science,
University of California, Berkeley,
California 94720, USA
dandre@cs.berkeley.edu
http://www.cs.berkeley.edu/~dandre

Ronald Averill
Dept. of Materials Science and Mechanics
Michigan State University, East Lansing,
MI 48824 USA
averill@egr.msu.edu

Forrest H Bennett III
Chief Scientist, Genetic Programming Inc.,
Los Altos, California 94023, USA
forrest@evolute.com

Dr. Peter Bentley
Intelligent System Group,
Department of Computer Science,
University College London,
Gower St., London WC1E 6BT, UK
P.Bentley@cs.ucl.ac.uk
http://www.cs.ucl.ac.uk/staff/P.Bentley/

Terence Broughton
Centre for Environment and Computing in Architecture,
University of East London,
School of Architecture,
Longbridge Rd.,
Dagenham, Essex RM8 2AS, UK

Paul Coates
Centre for Environment and Computing in Architecture,
University of East London,
School of Architecture,
Holbrook Rd.,
Stratford, London E15 3EA, UK
coates@uel.ac.uk
http://ceca.uel.ac.uk

Prof. Richard Dawkins
Charles Simonyi Professor of the Public Understanding of Science,
Oxford University, UK

Dr. David Eby
Department of Materials Science and Mechanics
Michigan State University, East Lansing,
MI 48824 USA
ebydavid@egr.msu.edu
http://web.egr.msu.edu/~ebydavid/

Mohammed A. El-Beltagy
Evolutionary Optimisation Group,
Department of Mechanical Engineering,
University of Southampton, Highfield,
Southampton SO17 1BJ, UK
M.A.El-Beltagy@soton.ac.uk
http://www.soton.ac.uk/~elbeltag/

Prof. Emeritus Michael French
Engineering Department,
Lancaster University,
Lancaster LA1 4YR, UK.
m.french@lancaster.ac.uk

Pablo Funes
Computer Science Department,
Volen Center for Complex Systems,
Brandeis University,
Waltham,
MA 02454–9110, USA
pablo@cs.brandeis.edu

Dr. Hugo de Garis
Brain Builder Group,
Evolutionary Systems Department,
ATR Human Information Processing
Research Labs,
2–2 Hikaridai, Seika-cho, Soraku-gun,
Kansai Science City,
Kyoto-fu, 619–02, Japan
degaris@hip.atr.co.jp
http://www.hip.atr.co.jp/~degaris

Dr. Derek Gatherer
School of Biomolecular Sciences,
Liverpool John Moores University,
Liverpool L3 3AF, UK
DEREK-GATHERER@USA.NET

Prof. Mitsuo Gen
Intelligent Systems Lab.,
Dept. of Indust. & Systems Engg.,
Graduate School of Engineering,
Ashikaga Inst. of Technology,
Ashikaga, 326-8558 Japan
gen@ashitech.ac.jp

Prof. John Gero
Professor of Design Science,
Co-Director, Key Centre of Design
Computing,
Dept. of Architectural and Design Science,
University of Sydney, NSW 2006 Australia
john@arch.usyd.edu.au
http://www.arch.usyd.edu.au/~john/

Prof. David Goldberg
Director of Illinois Genetic Algorithms
Laboratory (IlliGAL),
Professor, General Engineering
Department,
University of Illinois at Urbana-
Champaign,
117 Transportation Building, MC-238,
104 S. Mathews Ave., Urbana IL 61801,
USA
deg@uiuc.edu
http://www-illigal.ge.uiuc.edu/

Prof. Erik D. Goodman
Director of the Case Center for Computer-
Aided Engineering and Manufacturing,
Co-director of Genetic Algorithms
Research and Applications Group
(GARAGe),
Case Center, 2325 Engineering Building,
Michigan State University East Lansing,
MI 48824–1226, USA
goodman@egr.msu.edu
http://web.egr.msu.edu/~goodman/

Helen Jackson
Dept. of Architecture,
University of Edinburgh,
20 Chambers Street,
Edinburgh EH1 1JZ
hjackson@caad.ed.ac.uk
http://homepages.uel.ac.uk/0483p/

Prof. Andy Keane
Head, Dept. of Mechanical Engineering,
Director of Computational Engineering and Design Centre (CEDC),
University of Southampton, Highfield,
Southampton SO17 1BJ, UK
Andy.Keane@soton.ac.uk
http://www.soton.ac.uk/~ajk/welcome.html

Dr. Martin A. Keane
Econometrics Inc.,
111 E. Wacker Dr.,
Chicago, Illinois 60601, USA
makeane@ix.netcom.com

Jong Ryul Kim
Intelligent Systems Lab.,
Dept. of Indust. & Systems Engg.,
Graduate School of Engineering,
Ashikaga Inst. of Technology,
Ashikaga, 326-8558 Japan
jrkim@genlab.ashitech.ac.jp

Dr. John Koza
Section on Medical Informatics,
Department of Medicine,
School of Medicine,
Stanford University,
Stanford, California 94305, USA
koza@stanford.edu
http://smi.stanford.edu/people/koza

William Latham
Artist and M.D. of Computer Artworks,
14 Stanhope Mews West,
South Kensington,
London SW7 5RB,
latham@artworks.co.uk
http://www.artworks.co.uk/

Dr. William Scott Neal Reilly
Zoesis Inc., 3 Billings Way,
Framingham, MA 01701, USA
scott@zoesis.com

Dr. Ian Parmee
Director, Plymouth Engineering Design Centre,
University of Plymouth,
Drake Circus, Plymouth,
Devon PL4 8AA, UK
iparmee@hebe.soc.plym.ac.uk
http://techweb.see.plym.ac.uk/soc/research/edc/

Prof. Jordan Pollack
Computer Science Department,
Volen Center for Complex Systems,
Brandeis University,
Waltham, MA 02454–9110, USA
pollack@cs.brandeis.edu

Prof. William F. Punch III
Co-director of Genetic Algorithms Research and Applications Group (GARAGe),
Michigan State University East Lansing,
3115 Engineering Building,
Dept. of Computer Science,
E. Lansing MI, 48824, USA
punch@egr.msu.edu
http://web.cps.msu.edu/~punch/

Dr. Gordon Robinson
Evolutionary Optimisation Group,
Department of Mechanical Engineering,
University of Southampton, Highfield,
Southampton SO17 1BJ, UK
Gordon.Robinson@soton.ac.uk
http://www.soton.ac.uk/~gmr2/

Dr. Michael Rosenman
Senior Research Fellow,
Key Centre of Design Computing,
Department of Architectural and Design Science,
University of Sydney NSW 2006 Australia
E-mail: mike@arch.usyd.edu.au
http://www.arch.usyd.edu.au/~mike/

Andrew Rowbottom
9 Melland Ave,
Chorlton-cum-Hardy,
Manchester M21 7HZ, UK
rummy@snaffle.demon.co.uk
http://www.netlink.co.uk/~snaffle/

Karl Sims
Genetic Arts, Inc.
8 Clinton St.,
Cambridge, MA 02139, USA
ksims@media.mit.edu

Prof. Stephen Todd
IBM UK Scientific Centre M.P.137,
Hursley Park, Winchester,
Hampshire SO21 2JN, UK
stephen_todd@uk.ibm.com

Dr. Michael Witbrock
Principal Scientist
Lycos Inc.
400–2 Totten Pond Road,
Waltham, MA 02154, USA
mwitbrock@lycos.com

Chapter 1

An Introduction to Evolutionary Design by Computers

By Peter Bentley

1.1 Introduction

Computers can only do what we tell them to do. They are our blind, unconscious digital slaves, bound to us by the unbreakable chains of our programs. These programs instruct computers what to do, when to do it, and how it should be done.

But what happens when we loosen these chains? What happens when we tell a computer to use a process that we do not fully understand, in order to achieve something we do not fully understand? What happens when we tell a computer to evolve designs?

As this book will show, what happens is that the computer gains almost human-like qualities of autonomy, innovative flair, and even creativity. These 'skills' which evolution so mysteriously endows upon our computers open up a whole new way of using computers in design. Today our former 'glorified typewriters' or 'overcomplicated drawing boards' can do everything from generating new ideas and concepts in design, to improving the performance of designs well beyond the abilities of even the most skilled human designer. Evolving designs on computers now enables us to employ computers in every stage of the design process. This is no longer computer aided design – this is becoming computer design.

The pages of this book testify to the ability of today's evolutionary computer techniques in design. Flick through them and you will see designs of satellite booms, load cells, flywheels, computer networks, artistic images, sculptures, virtual creatures, house and hospital architectural plans, bridges, cranes, analogue circuits and even coffee tables. Out of all of the designs in the world, the collection you see in this book have a unique history: they were all evolved by computer, not designed by humans.

1.1.1 Evolutionary Tools

This may sound a little alarming to the designers and artists amongst us, but it should not be. In fact, these are the people who should feel most excited and optimistic by these advances, for it is the designer and artist who are the main beneficiaries of this field of research. Evolutionary design systems are advanced software tools which are intended to be used by people, not to replace people. They are the latest in a number of computer software advances created to improve the productivity, quality, speed and reduce the expense of designing.

EVOLUTIONARY DESIGN BY COMPUTERS
ISBN 1-55860-605-X

Today, designers recognise the usefulness of computers for data management and drawing – most art and design departments use graphics software or computer aided design (CAD) packages to draw, manipulate and store their designs. These software tools are becoming more and more advanced, with many having the ability to render designs with photorealism, produce animations, or even generate stereoscopic virtual reality worlds. Analysis tools that can simulate and measure the performance of designs are also becoming more common, with much of engineering design relying on software analysis to test designs before prototypes are built.

Evolutionary design builds on these software tools by actually taking over part of the design process. It allows designers to improve the performance of their designs automatically, judged by analysis software. It allows a designer to explore numerous creative solutions to problems (overcoming 'design fixation' or limitations of conventional wisdom) by generating these alternative solutions for the designer. It can use knowledge from designers to generate new solutions, based on many separate ideas. It can even suggest entirely new design concepts, or new ways of using existing technology. Evolutionary design can and does achieve all of this with the blinding speed and low cost of the computer.

However, although the field of evolutionary design is showing some impressive results, the computers are not fully autonomous. People are required to work out what function the design should perform, and how a computer should be applied to the problem. As this book describes, there are many complex issues involved in getting a computer to evolve anything useful at all. And although the 'design skills' of the computer are surprisingly good, they are still no match for the human brain.

1.1.2 The Unconscious Power of Evolution

In reality, evolutionary design by computers does not involve conscious design at all. How could it, for today's computers are incapable of independent conscious thought, and evolution has no consciousness of its own. Evolutionary design is simply a process capable of generating designs, it can never truly be called a designer. This can be difficult to understand – surely an intricate design must be designed? The answer is no, an intricate design can arise through slow, gradual, mindless improvement. Evolutionary biology has taught us this harsh lesson – and there are no designs more complex than those evolved in nature.

Natural evolution is, of course, the original and best evolutionary design system. Designs have been evolving in nature for hundreds of millions of years. Biological designs that far exceed any human designs in terms of complexity, performance, and efficiency are prolific throughout the living world. From the near-perfection of the streamlined shape of a shark, to the extraordinary molecular structure of a virus, every living thing is a marvel of evolved design. Moreover, as biologists uncover more information about the workings of the creatures around us, it is becoming clear that many human designs have existed in nature long before they were thought of by any human, for example: pumps, valves, heat-exchange systems, optical lenses, sonar. Indeed, many of our recent designs borrow features directly from nature, such as the cross-sectional shape of aircraft wings from birds, and velcro from certain types of 'sticky' seeds. As Ray Paton observed: 'A very good example of how biology can inspire engineering solutions is the work of Professor O. H. Schmitt who introduced the term "biomimetic" (emulating biology) into the US literature over a decade ago. It is fascinating to see how, following his Ph.D. thesis on the simulation of nerve action, four well-known electronic devices emerged: Schmitt trigger, emitter-follower, differential amplifier and heat pipe.' (Paton, 1994, p. 51).

1.1.3 Evolutionary Design by Computers

So it is clear that evolutionary design in nature is capable of generating astonishingly innovative designs. This book demonstrates how evolutionary design by computers is also capable of such innovation. To achieve this, the highest achievers in evolutionary design have come together for the first time to contribute chapters and provide a showcase of the best and most original work in this exciting new field. The book promotes the use of the word 'Design' in its broadest sense, allowing all aspects of evolutionary design to be explored, including: evolutionary optimisation, evolutionary art, evolutionary artificial life and creative evolutionary design. Of course the number of pages available for such a volume is finite, and so not every researcher in this field can be a contributor of a chapter. As the editor of this book I have tried my hardest to ensure a coherent and definitive selection of significant developments in evolutionary design is included, but there will always be omissions, and for that I apologise.

The contributors all have considerable technical expertise in this area, but beginners to this field should take heart, for the concept of evolution is a simple one, and the simpler forms of evolutionary design do not require years of study to achieve. Indeed, to help budding evolutionary designers get started, the CD-ROM included with this book contains code from many of the contributors of the chapters, including some demonstration evolutionary design systems. Perhaps one of the primary barriers to understanding is the terminology, which often seems to be an impenetrable tangle of words such as *meiosis*, *allele*, *epistasis* and *embryogeny*. Never fear: even the most experienced of us sometimes forget what the latest term to be stolen from biology means, so do not be afraid to consult the glossary included in the book!

And finally: before we open up evolutionary design by computers and explore its gory innards, a warning. This has been an area of computer science which has fascinated and thrilled me for some years. Like any researcher with a 'pet subject', I cannot pretend to hold unbiased views in this area. But I still find the excitement of my computer evolving an innovative design is undiminished, despite the hundreds I have already been privileged enough to see evolving before my eyes. I hope I can transfer some of my enthusiasm to you, my perceptive reader, so sit back and enjoy the ride!

1.1.4 What's to Come

This chapter gives an introduction to evolutionary design by computers. It is structured into three major sections: first, a general summary of evolutionary computation and the dominant evolutionary algorithms is given. Second, definitions and reviews of the significant aspects of evolutionary design are provided, to place the contents and structure of the rest of the book into context. Finally, some important technical issues in evolutionary design are explored.

However, before we explore these more detailed aspects of evolutionary design by computers, there is a question which must be tackled:

1.2 Why *Evolve* Designs?

This is an important and fundamental question, asked by many people. There are a number of reasons why we choose to use evolution, most which boil down to: 'because it seems to work rather well'. In more detail, there are perhaps four main reasons why the choice of evolutionary algorithms (EAs) is appropriate for design problems:

REASON 1: *Evolution is a good, general-purpose problem solver.*

Evolutionary algorithms are just one of many types of method known in computer science. It is currently not possible to define exactly which of these methods is best for which problem or even class of problems (Fogel, 1997), except in a very broad sense. However, it is possible to identify methods that consistently produce improved results (compared to results produced by other techniques) for a wide range of different problems. Indeed, as will be explained later, the evolutionary algorithms fall into this category, having been demonstrated successfully with hundreds of different types of problem. Table 1.1 lists some of these types of application. (It should be noted that there are literally hundreds of researchers working in each of the areas listed, all developing their own evolutionary systems.)

Researchers and software developers apply computers to a wide variety of design problems. Rather than spending time, effort and money developing new specialised computational techniques for every new problem, most developers prefer to use an algorithm proven through extensive trials to be reusable and robust – such as an evolutionary algorithm.

REASON 2: *Uniquely, evolutionary algorithms have been used successfully in every type of evolutionary design.*

Although there are contenders to the throne of computational design, evolutionary algorithms are, without doubt, the leading techniques at present. Hill-climbing, simulated annealing, Tabu search and other techniques have all been applied successfully in certain areas, but only evolutionary algorithms such as the genetic algorithm have been used successfully in all types of automated design system. Indeed, the popularity of genetic algorithms in engineering design

Table 1.1 Examples of types of applications tackled successfully by evolutionary computation.

Control systems	(Husbands et al., 1996).
Data mining	(Radcliffe and Surrey, 1994b).
Fault-tolerant systems	(Thompson, 1995).
Game playing	(Axelrod, 1987).
Machine learning	(Goldberg, 1989).
Ordering problems	(Schaffer and Eshelman, 1995).
Scheduling	(Yamada and Nakano, 1995).
Set covering and partitioning	(Levine, 1994).
Signal timing	(Foy et al., 1992).
Strategy acquisition	(Greffenstette, 1991).

has led to workshops, conferences, and books devoted entirely to this subject (Fleming et al., 1995; Gen and Cheng, 1997; Bentley, 1998b).

REASON 3: *Evolution and the human design process share many similar characteristics.*

Some researchers claim that natural evolution and the human design process are directly comparable (Fogel et al., 1966; Goldberg 1991; French 1994). It is clear that our designs have evolved, as flint hand-axes became arrowheads, as the first primitive computers have become the powerful supercomputers of today. The 'arms race' which is known to dramatically increase the complexity of our designs is thought by biologists to be responsible for the development of the complexity in living creatures (Dawkins, 1982). Comparative studies of our own designs also reveals the development of 'species' of designs which fit within clearly defined 'niches' (French and Ramirez, 1996).

Indeed, Goldberg actually attempts to formally define human design in terms of evolution by the genetic algorithm (Goldberg, 1991). He compares the recombination of genetic material from parent solutions when forming a new child solution, with a human designer combining ideas from two solutions to form a new solution. (These ideas and others are explored further in the first section of the book.)

REASON 4: *The most successful and remarkable designs known to mankind were created by natural evolution, the inspiration for evolutionary algorithms.*

Natural evolution has been creating designs successfully for an unimaginable number of years. Even a cursory study of the myriad of extraordinary designs in nature should be sufficient to inspire awe in the power of evolution. Indeed, conceivably the most complex and remarkable miracle of design ever created – the human brain – was generated by evolution in nature. Not only is it an astonishing design in its finished form, but equally astonishingly, its huge complexity grew from a single cell using instructions contained in one molecule of DNA. This is perhaps the most conclusive demonstration of all that the evolution-based techniques of evolutionary computation are highly suitable for design problems.

1.3 Evolutionary Computation

Evolutionary computation is all about *search*. In computer science, search algorithms define a computational problem in terms of search, where the *search-space* is a space filled with all possible solutions to the problem, and a point in that space defines a solution (Kanal and Cumar, 1988). The problem of improving parameter values for an application is then transformed into the problem of searching for better solutions elsewhere in the solution space, see fig 1.1. There are many types of search algorithm in existence, of which evolutionary search is a recent and rapidly growing subset.

Evolutionary search algorithms are inspired by and based upon evolution in nature. These algorithms typically use an analogy with natural evolution to perform search by *evolving* solutions to problems.[1] Hence, instead of working with one solution at a time in the search-space, these algorithms consider a large collection or *population* of solutions at once.

Although evolutionary algorithms (EAs) do make computers evolve solutions, this evolution is not explicitly specified in an EA, it is an *emergent property* of the algorithm. In fact, the

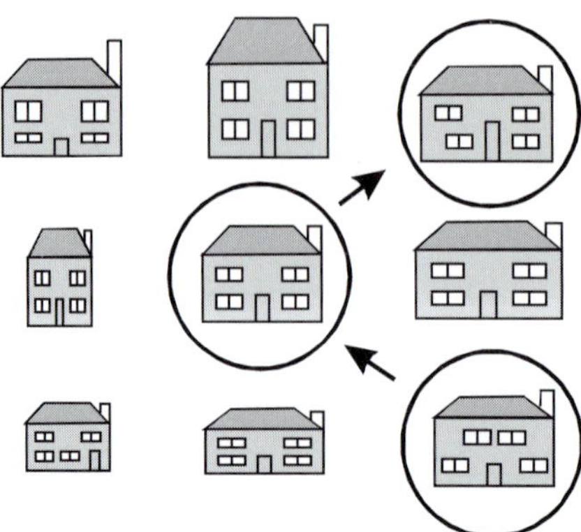

Figure 1.1 Searching for a solution in an example search space of house designs.

computers are not instructed to evolve anything, and it is currently not possible for us to explicitly 'program-in' evolution – for we do not fully understand how evolution works. Instead, the computers are instructed to maintain populations of solutions, allow better solutions to 'have children', and allow worse solutions to 'die'. The 'child solutions' inherit their parents' characteristics with some small random variation, and then the better of these solutions are allowed to 'have children' themselves, while the worse ones 'die', and so on. This simple procedure causes evolution to occur, and after a number of generations the computer will have evolved solutions which are substantially better compared to their long-dead ancestors at the start, see fig. 1.2.

By considering the search space, it is possible to get an idea of how evolution finds good solutions. Figure 1.3 shows the search space for the example shown in fig. 1.2. It should be clear that evolution searches the space in parallel (in the example, it considers four house

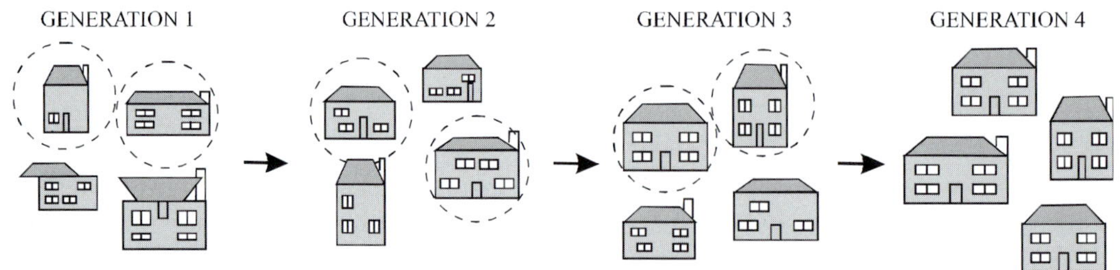

Figure 1.2 Four generations of evolving house designs using a population size of four. Parents of the next generation are circled.

---

[1] It must be stressed that evolution is not simulated in these algorithms, *it actually happens*. While EAs may simulate natural evolution, to call this process simply 'simulated evolution' is incorrect – an EA no more simulates evolution than a pocket calculator simulates addition, or a typewriter simulates text. (Indeed, it could be argued that compared to our pocket calculators, we are the ones who simulate addition, for we often rely on memory to provide us with answers, but the calculator must always calculate the sum.) Evolutionary search generates evolution in a different medium compared to evolution in nature, but both are equally valid forms of evolution.

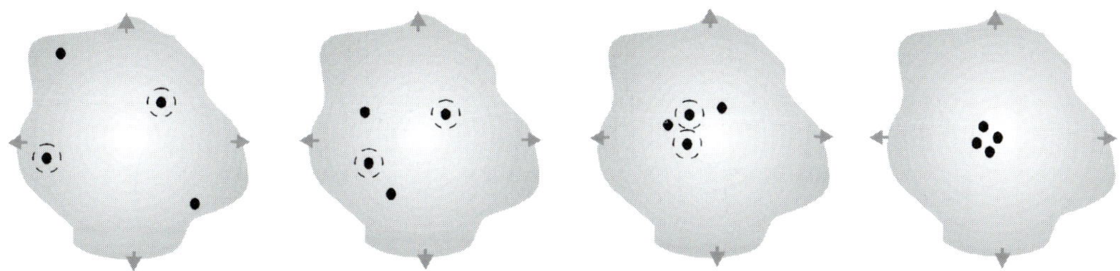

Figure 1.3 The location of the evolving houses in the space of house designs, each generation. Better solutions are found in the centre of this example space.

designs at a time). It should also be clear that evolution quickly 'homes in' on the best area of the search space, resulting in some good designs after only four generations.

All EAs require guidance to direct evolution towards better areas of the search space. They receive this guidance by *evaluating* every solution in the population, to determine its *fitness*. The fitness of a solution is a score based on how well the solution fulfils the problem objective, calculated by a *fitness function*. Typically, fitness values are positive real numbers, where a fitness of zero is a perfect score. EAs are then used to minimise the fitness scores of solutions, by allowing the fitter solutions to have more children than less fit solutions. In the 'house' example, the problem objective might be to find a house design which has four evenly placed windows, a door in the centre, a chimney, and so on. The fitness function would take a solution as input and return a fitness value based on how well the solution satisfies these objectives, e.g. when evaluating the number of windows, the fitness score could simply be incremented by:

$$| 4 - \textit{no. of windows in solution} |.$$

Fitness values are often plotted in search spaces, giving mountainous *fitness landscapes*, where a high peak corresponds to solutions in that part of the search space which have optimal fitnesses (i.e., low fitness scores). If the problem has many separate optima (i.e., if the fitness function is *multimodal*), finding a globally optimal solution (the top of the highest mountain) in the landscape can be difficult, even for an EA.

There are four main types of evolutionary algorithm in use today, three of which were independently developed more than thirty years ago. These algorithms are: the **genetic algorithm** (GA) created by John Holland (1973, 1975) and made famous by David Goldberg (1989), **evolutionary programming** (EP) created by Lawrence Fogel (1963) and developed further by his son David Fogel (1992), and **evolution strategies** (ES) created by Ingo Rechenberg (1973) and today strongly promoted by Thomas Bäck (1996). The fourth major evolutionary algorithm is a more recent and very popular development of John Koza (1992), known as **genetic programming** (GP). The field of evolutionary computation has grown up around these techniques, with its roots still firmly in evolutionary biology and computer science, see fig. 1.4. Today researchers examine every conceivable aspect of EAs, often using knowledge of evolution from evolutionary biology in their algorithms, and more recently, using EAs to help biologists learn about evolution (Dawkins, 1986).

Evolution-based algorithms have been found to be some of the most flexible, efficient and robust of all search algorithms known to computer science (Goldberg, 1989). Because of these

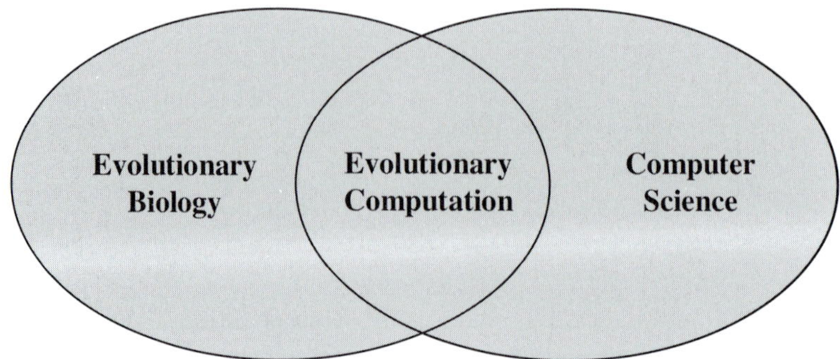

Figure 1.4 Evolutionary computation has its roots in computer science and evolutionary biology.

properties, these methods are now becoming widely used to solve a broad range of different problems (Holland, 1992).

The following sections briefly summarise the four dominant types of EA, and then a general architecture for EAs is introduced, to show how these separate techniques follow a common evolutionary paradigm.

1.3.1 Genetic Algorithms

A Summary

The genetic algorithm is perhaps the most well known of all evolution-based search algorithms. GAs were developed by John Holland in an attempt to explain the adaptive processes of natural systems and to design artificial systems based upon these natural systems (Holland, 1973, 1975). (Precursors of GAs were developed by Alex Fraser in 1957 and Hans Bremermann in 1962.[2]) Whilst not being the first algorithm to use principles of natural selection and genetics within the search process, the genetic algorithm is today the most widely used. More experimental and theoretical analyses have been made on the workings of the GA than any other EA. Moreover, the genetic algorithm (and enhanced versions of it) resembles natural evolution more closely than most other methods.

Having become widely used for a broad range of optimisation problems in the last fifteen years (Holland, 1992), the GA has been described as being a 'search algorithm with some of the innovative flair of human search' (Goldberg, 1989). GAs are also very forgiving algorithms – even if they are badly implemented, or poorly applied, they will often still produce acceptable results (Davis, 1991). GAs are today renowned for their ability to tackle a huge variety of optimisation problems and for their consistent ability to provide excellent results, i.e. they are *robust* (Holland, 1975; Goldberg 1989; Davis 1991; Fogel 1994).

Genetic algorithms use two separate spaces: the search space and the *solution space*. The search space is now a space of *coded* solutions to the problem, and the solution space is the space of actual solutions. Coded solutions, or *genotypes* must be mapped onto actual solutions, or *phenotypes*, before the quality or *fitness* of each solution can be evaluated, see fig. 1.5.

---

[2] This information was kindly provided by David Fogel, private communication.

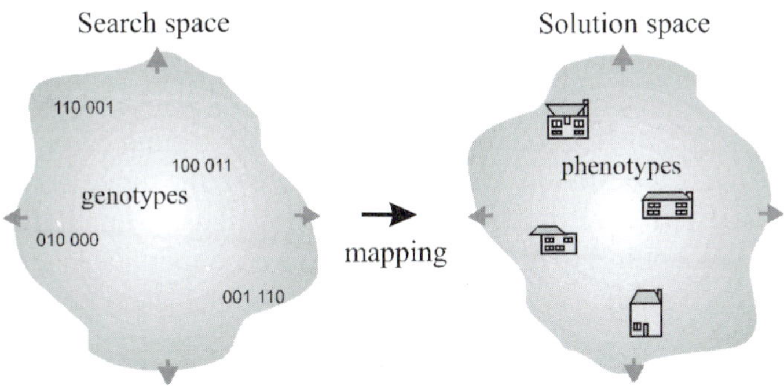

Figure 1.5 Mapping genotypes in the search space to phenotypes in the solution space.

GAs maintain a population of *individuals* where each individual consists of a genotype and a corresponding phenotype. Phenotypes usually consist of collections of parameters (in our 'house' example, such parameters might define the number and position of windows, the position of the roof, the width and height of the house, and so on). Genotypes consist of coded versions of these parameters. A coded parameter is normally referred to as a *gene*, with the values a gene can take being known as *alleles*. A collection of genes in one genotype is often held internally as a string, and is known as a *chromosome*.

The simplest form of GA, the *canonical* or *simple* GA, is summarised in fig. 1.6. This algorithm works as follows: The genotype of every individual in the population is initialised with random alleles. The main loop of the algorithm then begins, with the corresponding phenotype of every individual in the population being evaluated and given a fitness value according to how well it fulfils the problem objective or fitness function. These scores are then used to determine how many copies of each individual are placed into a temporary area often termed the 'mating pool' (i.e. the higher the fitness, the more copies that are made of an individual).

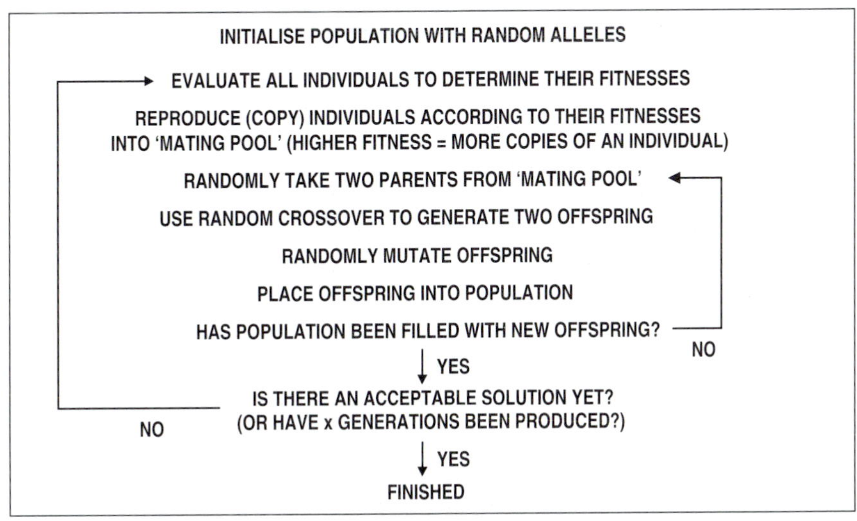

Figure. 1.6 The simple genetic algorithm.

Two parents are then randomly picked from this area. Offspring are generated by the use of the crossover operator, which randomly allocates genes from each parent's genotype to each offspring's genotype. For example, given two parents: 'ABCDEF' and 'abcdef', and a random crossover point of, say, 2, the two offspring generated by the simple GA would be: 'ABcdef' and 'abCDEF', see fig. 1.7. (Crossover is used about 70% of the time to generate offspring, for the remaining 30% offspring are simply clones of their parents.) Mutation is then occasionally applied (with a low probability) to offspring. When it is used to mutate an individual, typically a single allele is changed randomly. For example, an individual '111111' might be mutated into '110111', see fig. 1.8.

Using crossover and mutation, offspring are generated until they fill the population (all parents are discarded). This entire process of evaluation and reproduction then continues until either a satisfactory solution emerges or the GA has run for a specified number of generations (Holland, 1975; Goldberg, 1989; Davis, 1991).

The randomness of the genetic operators can give the illusion that the GA and other EAs are nothing more than parallel random search algorithms, but this is not so. Evolutionary search has a random element to its exploration of the search space, but the search is unquestionably *directed* by selection towards areas in the search space that contain better solutions. Unless the genetic operators are very badly designed, an EA will always 'home-in' on these areas, and because the search is performed in parallel, these algorithms are rarely fooled by local optima, unlike many other search algorithms (Goldberg, 1989).

However, the simple GA is just that – very simple and a little naïve. This GA is favoured by those that try to theoretically analyse and predict the behaviour of genetic algorithms, but in reality, typical GAs are usually more advanced. Common features include: more realistic

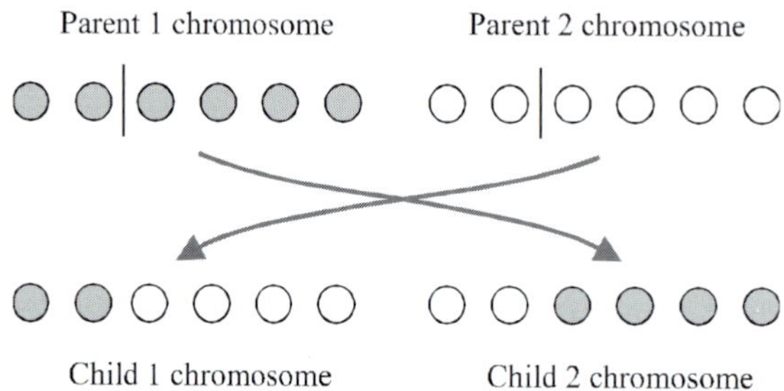

Figure 1.7 The behaviour of the crossover operator. The vertical line shows the position of the random crossover point.

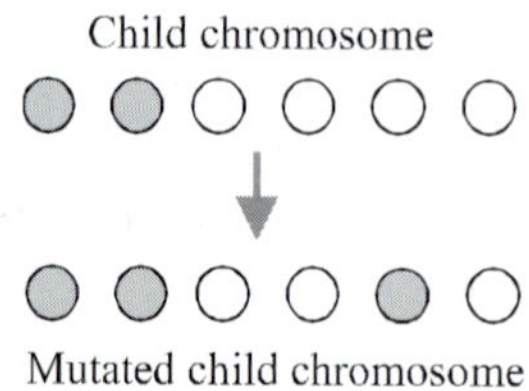

Figure 1.8 The behaviour of the mutation operator.

natural selection, more genetic operators, ability to detect when evolution ceases, and overlapping populations or elitism (where some fit individuals can survive for more than one generation) (Davis, 1991). Because of this improved analogy with nature, the term *reproduction* is normally used as it is in biology to refer to the entire process of generating new offspring, encompassing the crossover and mutation operators. (This is in contrast to the somewhat confusing use of the word 'reproduction' to mean an explicit copying stage within the simple GA.)

GA Theory

Whilst there is no formal proof that the GA will always converge to an acceptable solution to any given problem, a variety of theories exist (Holland, 1975; Kargupta, 1993; Harris, 1994), the most accepted of these being Holland's Schema Theorem (Holland, 1975) and the Building Block Hypothesis (Goldberg, 1989).

Briefly, a *schema* is a similarity template describing a set of strings (or chromosomes) which match each other at certain positions. For example, the schema *10101 matches the two strings {110101, 010101} (using a binary alphabet and a metasymbol or *don't care* symbol *). The schema *101* describes four strings {01010, 11010, 01011, 11011}. As Goldberg (1989) elucidates, in general, for alphabets of cardinality (number of alphabet characters) k, and string lengths of l characters, there are $(k + 1)^l$ schemata.

The *order* of a schema is the number of fixed characters in the template, e.g. the order of schema *1*110 is 4, and the order of schema *****0 is 1. The *defining length* of a schema is the distance between the first and last fixed character in the template, e.g. the defining length of 1****0 is 5, the defining length of 1*1*0* is 4, and the defining length of 0***** is 0.

Holland's Schema Theorem states that the action of reproduction (copying, crossover and mutation) within a genetic algorithm ensures that schemata of short defining length, low order and high fitness increase within a population (Holland, 1975). Such schemata are known as building blocks.

The building block hypothesis suggests that genetic algorithms are able to evolve good solutions by combining these fit, low order schemata with short defining lengths to form better strings (Goldberg, 1989). However, this still remains an unproven (though widely accepted) hypothesis.

GA Analyses

Experimental results show that for most GAs (initialised with random values), evolution makes extremely rapid progress at first, as the diverse elements in the initial population are combined and tested. Over time, the population begins to converge, with the separate individuals resembling each other more and more (Davis, 1991). Effectively this results in the GA narrowing its search in the solution-space and reducing the size of any changes made by evolution until eventually the population converges to a single solution (Goldberg, 1989). When plotting the best fitness value in each new population against the number of generations, a typical curve emerges, fig 1.9 (Parmee and Denham, 1994).

Theoretical research to investigate the behaviour of the various varieties of GAs for different problems is growing rapidly, with careful analyses of the transmission of schemata being made (De Jong, 1975; Kargupta, 1993). The use of Walsh function analysis (Deb et al., 1993)

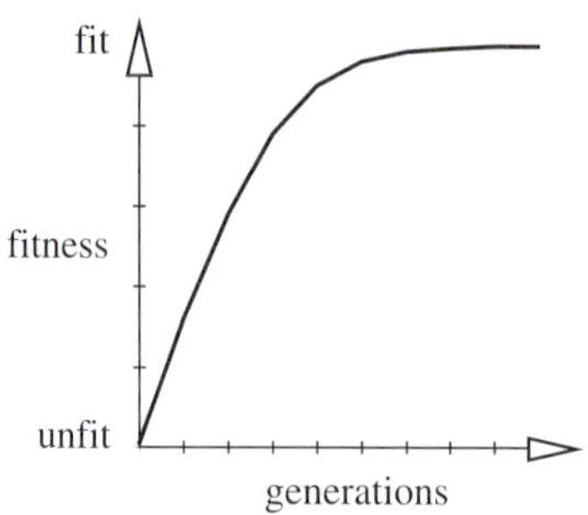

Figure 1.9 Typical curve of evolving fitness values over time.

and Markov chain analysis (Horn, 1993) has led to the identification of some 'deceptive' and 'hard' problems for GAs (Deb and Goldberg, 1993). Chapter 4: *The Race, the Hurdle, and the Sweet Spot* by David Goldberg summarises some of the significant advances in the understanding of GAs made to date.

Advanced Genetic Algorithms

When applying GAs to highly complex applications, some problems do occasionally arise. The most common is *premature convergence* where the population converges early onto non-optimal local minima (Davis, 1991). Problems are also caused by deceptive functions, which are, by definition, 'hard' for most GAs to solve. In addition, noisy functions (Goldberg et al., 1992) and the optimisation of multiple criteria within GAs can cause difficulties (Fonseca and Fleming, 1995a). In an attempt to overcome such problems, new, more advanced types of GA are being developed (Goldberg, 1994). These include:

- **Steady-state GAs**, where offspring are generated one at a time, and replace existing individuals in the population according to fitness or similarity. Convergence is slower, but very fit solutions are not lost (Syswerda, 1989).
- **Parallel GAs**, where multiple processors are used in parallel to run the GA (Adeli and Cheng, 1994; Levine, 1994).
- **Distributed GAs**, where multiple populations are separately evolved with few interactions between them (Whitley and Starkweather, 1990)
- **GAs with niching and speciation**, where the population within the GA is segregated into separate 'species' (Horn, 1993; Horn and Nafpliotis, 1993; Horn et al., 1994).
- **Messy GAs (mGA)**, which use a number of 'exotic' techniques such as variable-length chromosomes and a two-stage evolution process (Deb, 1991; Deb and Goldberg, 1991).
- **Multiobjective GAs (MOGAs)**, which allow multiple objectives to be optimised with GAs (Schaffer, 1985; Srinivas and Deb, 1995; Bentley and Wakefield, 1997c).
- **Hybrid GAs (hGAs)**, e.g. memetic algorithms, where GAs are combined with local search algorithms (George, 1994; Radcliffe and Surrey, 1994a).
- **Structured GAs (sGAs)**, which allow parts of chromosomes to be switched on and off using evolveable 'control genes' (Dasgupta and McGregor, 1992; Parmee and Denham, 1994).

- **GAs with diploidy and dominance**, which can improve variation and diversity in addition to performance (Smith and Goldberg, 1992).
- **Mutation-driven GAs**, such as Harvey's SAGA (Harvey and Thompson, 1997), which uses converged populations modified primarily by mutation to allow the constant 'incremental evolution' of new solutions to varying fitness functions.
- **GAs with 'genetic engineering'**, which identify beneficial genetic material during evolution and prevent its disruption by the genetic operators (Gero and Kazakov, 1996).
- **Injection Island GAs (IIGAs)**, which evolve a number of separate populations ('islands') with representations and fitness functions of different accuracy, and occasionally 'inject' good solutions from one island into another (Eby et al., 1997).

Most of these advanced types of GA are described further in the chapters of this book.

Recommended Books for GAs:

Adaptation in Natural and Artificial Systems.
by John Holland (1975).

Genetic Algorithms in Search, Optimization & Machine Learning.
by David Goldberg (1989).

The Handbook of Genetic Algorithms.
edited by Lawrence Davis (1991).

Genetic Algorithms + Data Structures = Evolution Programs.
by Zbigniew Michalewicz (1996).

Practical Handbook of Genetic Algorithms.
edited by Lance Chambers (1995).

An Introduction to Genetic Algorithms.
by Melanie Mitchell (1996).

Evolutionary Computation: Toward a New Philosophy of Machine Intelligence.
by David B. Fogel (1995).

The Design of Innovation: Lessons from Genetic Algorithms
by David Goldberg (1998).

1.3.2 Genetic Programming

A Summary

Genetic programming is not, strictly speaking, a separate evolutionary algorithm in its own right. It is a specialised form of genetic algorithm, which manipulates a very specific type of solution using modified genetic operators.

GP was developed by Koza (1992) in an attempt to make computers program themselves (i.e., perform *automatic programming*) by evolving computer programs. Perhaps because of this application, or perhaps because of the higher conceptual level at which the algorithm operates, GP has become immensely popular amongst computer scientists, and it seems likely that the number of publications on this new evolutionary technique will soon approach the wealth of publications in its parent field, genetic algorithms. Practitioners of GP are beginning to move away from the original application of evolving computer programs, with GP now being applied in alternative areas, evolutionary design amongst them. John Koza describes one such application in his chapter *The Design of Analog Circuits by Means of Genetic Programming*, in the last section of the book.

GP follows essentially the same procedure as described previously for GAs. Populations of individuals are maintained. These individuals are initialised randomly, evaluated and parents are selected for reproduction based on fitness. Offspring are generated using crossover and mutation operators, and these offspring replace some or all of their parents in the population. The individuals are then evaluated, parents are selected for reproduction, and so on.

However, unlike GAs, GP does not make a distinction between the search space and the solution space. In GP, genotypes are the same as phenotypes, i.e. GP does not manipulate coded versions of the solutions, it manipulates the solutions themselves. This means that for GP, the search space and solution space are identical. In addition, unlike GAs (which use almost any conceivable representation), GP represents solutions in a very specific, hierarchical manner. Figure 1.10 shows an example solution for GP.

A strong motivation in the use of such hierarchical representations was the problem of applying crossover to variable-length chromosomes. Computer programs are obviously of variable sizes – they can be anything from a few characters to thousands of lines long. The standard crossover operator for GAs simply cannot cope with performing recombination with two chromosomes that are of different lengths. To illustrate this, consider two chromosomes: 'A+B/C' and '~A/B+C'. Using the simple crossover of GAs, if the random crossover point happened to be 1, the two child chromosomes would be: '~+B/C' and 'AA/B+C'. These are clearly meaningless and invalid expressions. The solution suggested by Koza for GP is to arrange its solutions in hierarchical tree-structures, and then crossover can be used to interchange randomly chosen branches of the parents' trees without the syntax of the programs being disrupted, as shown by fig. 1.11. (In fact, this is just one solution to the problem of variable-length crossover. There are many types of GA which use a number of alternatives (Bentley and Wakefield, 1996c).)

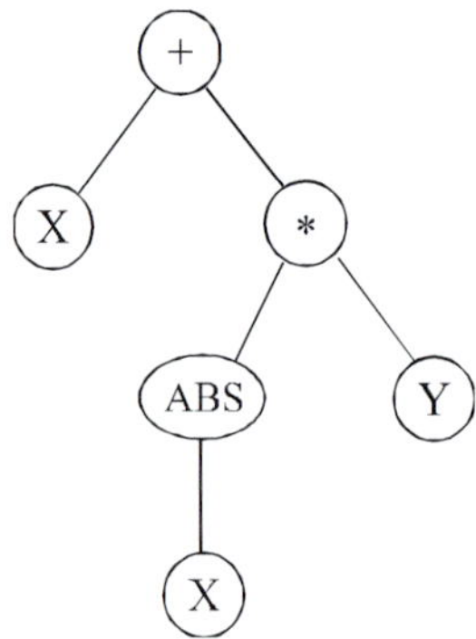

Figure 1.10 A simple computer program defined by GP's hierarchical representation.

GP also has a modified mutation operator. This operator picks a random point in a tree and deletes everything below it, replacing it with a randomly generated subtree, see fig. 1.12. However, because the crossover operator plays a similar role to mutation in GP, mutation is often considered unnecessary (Koza,1992).

The other major distinction between GAs and GP is in the evaluation of solutions. As described previously, GAs require the genotypes of individuals to be mapped onto the phenotypes before evaluation. Phenotypes are then analysed by fitness functions. In standard GP, there is no mapping process – because GP evolves phenotypes directly – and the evaluation process is very different. To calculate the fitness of solutions, these evolved programs must be *run* to find out what they do. Normally a series of input values and desired output values are provided, and the fitness of the program is based on how closely actual output values match the desired output values, for each set of input values. GP terminates evolution when a solution has been evolved which has a satisfactory fitness value (or after a predefined number of generations).

GP normally evolves symbolic expressions (S-expressions) in languages such as LISP – a computer programming language which uses combinations of functions written as lists. For

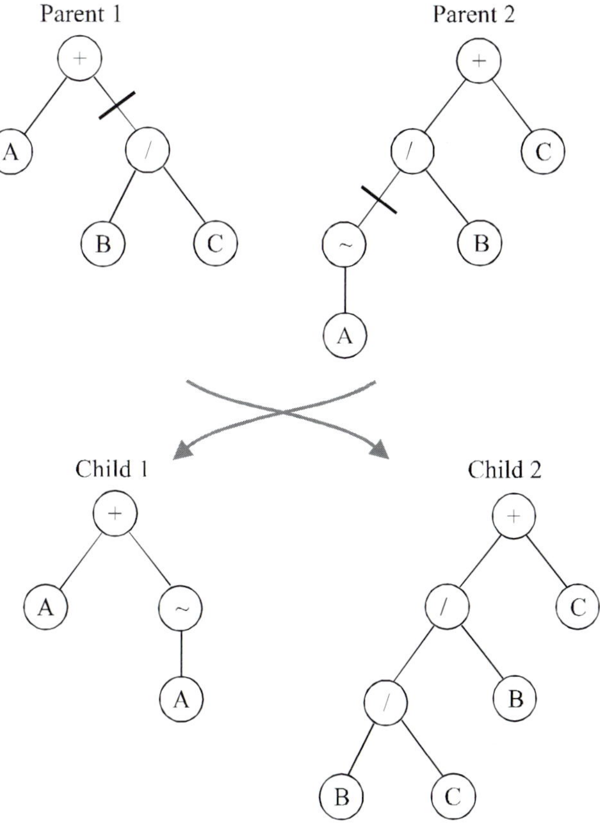

Figure 1.11 The behaviour of the crossover operator in GP. The thick lines show the positions of the random crossover points.

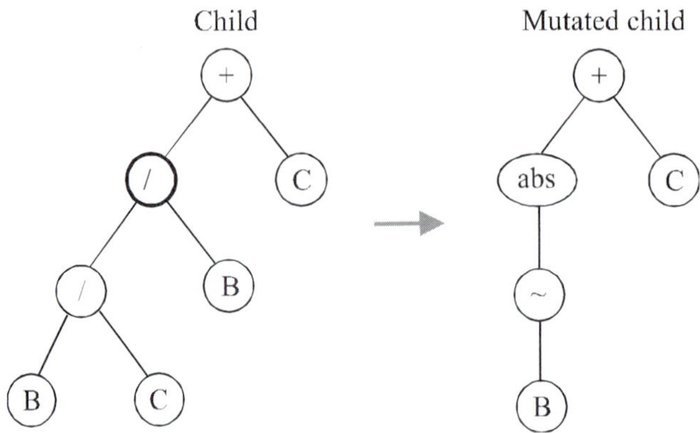

Figure 1.12 The behaviour of the GP mutation operator.
The random mutation point is shown in bold.

example, the two parent solutions used to illustrate the crossover operator in fig. 1.11 would be written in LISP as:

(+ A (/ B C))   and
(+ (/ (~ A) B) C).

LISP allows the usual high-level programming operators, including conditional operators, to be applied in the same way. For example, the following LISP S-expression tells the computer to add 1, 2 and 3 (if *time* is greater than 10) or 4 (if *time* is less than 10):

(+ 1 2 (IF (> time 10) 3 4))

Because solutions can contain such conditional statements, it is possible for evolving solutions to contain redundant code which is never executed. For example, the following S-expression will always return the result of A+B. The sub expression (− A (/ B C)) will never be executed by the computer:

(IF (5 > 0) (+ A B) (− A (/ B C)))

Solutions with redundant code in them are said to contain *junk* or *introns*. Such solutions are common in GP, with most solutions steadily increasing in size as evolution progresses. This tendency is known as *bloat* (Langdon and Poli, 1997). The effects of bloat can be reduced by penalising the fitness of any solutions that become oversized.

Conditional statements in GP allow a simple form of implicit *dominance* to occur in evolving S-expressions. Normally implementations of dominant and recessive alleles in EAs require diploid chromosomes (pairs of chromosomes) where the value of a gene is the combined meaning of both alleles from the twin chromosome. Certain alleles are defined to be dominant and others recessive, ensuring that the phenotypic effect of a gene is caused by dominant alleles in preference to recessive ones. GP allows a simpler version of this with conditional statements. For example, if in the following S-expression, *X* can only take the values 0, 1, or 2, then the result A could be regarded as being dominant to the result *B*:

(IF (> X 0) A B)

Conditional statements in GP also resemble the operons and regulons found in our own DNA, used to switch on and off other genes during the development of the organism (Paton, 1994).

GP Theory

Because there are significant differences between the representation and operators of GP and GAs, it is not clear whether the Schema Theorem and Building Block Hypothesis described previously can be applied to GP. Koza (1992) attempts to achieve this by defining a schema to be the set of all individual trees from the population that contain, as subtrees, one or more specified subtrees. So for GP, disruption is smallest and the deviation from the optimum number of trials is smallest when the schema is defined in terms of a single compact subtree (Koza, 1992). As long as crossover is not too disruptive, the fittest of such compact subtrees should exponentially grow within the population, and be used as building blocks for constructing fit new individuals.

Unfortunately, it seems that crossover in GP is often too disruptive for such theories to be applicable. Definitions of schema and the Schema Theorem are still the subject of much research in the GP community (O'Reilly and Oppacher, 1995; Poli and Langdon, 1997b).

Advanced GP

Just as GAs have many other advanced genetic operators, GP has a number of specialised operators. These include: *permutation*, which swaps two characters in a tree; *editing*, which allows the optimisation and reduction of long S-expressions; and *encapsulation* which allows a subtree to be converted into a single node, preserving it from disruption by crossover or mutation.

One commonly used technique, which is a more advanced version of encapsulation, is the evolution of *automatically defined functions* (ADFs). Typically, the GP system is set up to evolve a predetermined number of functions in addition to the main program. Each function can then be called in the program, allowing the multiple use of code without the need to re-evolve it each time, and also minimising the danger of disruption by crossover or mutation. The use of ADFs has been shown to enhance the performance of GP (Koza, 1992).

Figure 1.13 shows an example solution with two ADFs. The first ADF (ADF0) takes a single argument and returns its cube, the second (ADF1) takes two arguments and returns 1/(ARG0*ARG1). The main program (at the right of the tree) adds the result of calling both ADFs with parameters A and B. When expanded into a single LISP S-expression, the solution becomes:

(+ (* (* A A) A) (/ (1 (* A B))))

Should it be necessary, hierarchical ADFs can be employed to allow one ADF to call another (Koza, 1992). Researchers are now exploring other styles of function creation, e.g. Yu

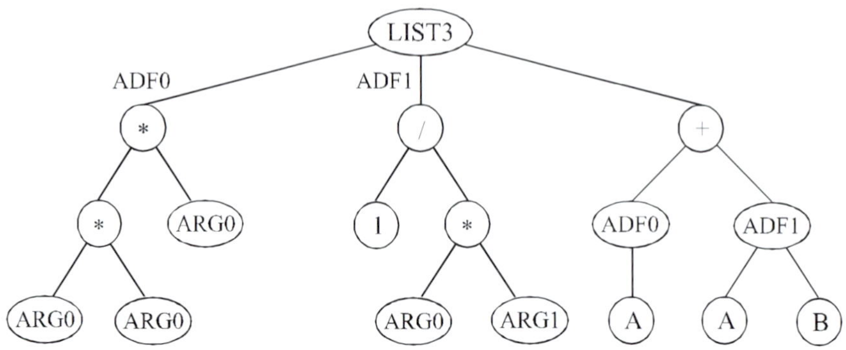

Figure 1.13 A solution with two ADFs (the two left branches of the tree). Note the function calls within the program in the right branch of the tree.

evolves anonymous functions known as λ-abstractions, which are reused through recursion (Yu and Clack, 1998a,b). Current research also investigates the automatic creation of iterations (ADIs), loops (ADLs), recursions (ADRs), and various types of memory stores (ADS), see (Koza et al., 1999).

The hierarchical tree representation used by GP allows crossover and mutation to manipulate solutions whilst preserving the syntax of LISP S-expressions. However, there are problems of excessive disruption with these genetic operators (O'Reilly and Oppacher, 1995). In GAs, the operators tend to be constructive: many offspring generated using crossover or mutation from fit parent solutions will be at least as fit as their parents. In GP, the reverse is true: the operators tend to be destructive, with many offspring less fit than their parents. This sorry state of affairs has led to the development of new crossover operators, designed to minimise the disruption of good solutions. Most of these new operators limit the use of crossover to the recombination of similarly structured parent solutions (Poli and Langdon, 1997a).

Recommended Books for GP:

Genetic Programming: On the Programming of Computers by Means of Natural Selection
by John Koza (1992).

Genetic Programming II: Automatic Discovery of Reusable Programs
by John Koza (1994).

Genetic Programming III
by Koza, Andre, Bennett and Keane (1999).

Advances In Genetic Programming
Edited by Kenneth E. Kinnear Jr. (1994).

Advances In Genetic Programming 2
by Peter Angeline and Kenneth E. Kinnear Jr. (Eds) (1996).

Genetic Programming – an Introduction
by Wolfgang Banzhaf, Peter Nordin, Robert E. Keller and Frank D. Francone (1998).

Genetic Programming and Data Structures
by Bill Langdon (1998)

1.3.3 Evolution Strategies

A Summary

Evolution strategies (or *evolutionstrategie*) were developed in Germany in the 1960s by Bienert, Rechenberg and Schwefel (Bäck, 1996). Evolutionary design was one of the very first applications of this technique, involving shape optimisation of a bent pipe, drag minimisation of a joint plate and structure optimisation of nozzles. However, these early experiments were not performed using computers. Instead, actual physical designs were built, tested and mutated by changing the joint positions or adding and removing segments.

The first ES computer algorithm was demonstrated initially by Schwefel (1965), and then developed further by Rechenberg (1973). This simple form of ES, known as the *two membered* ES, used only two individuals: a parent and child. Like GP, it made no distinction between genotype and phenotype, each individual being represented as a real-valued vector. It has a simple operation: the child solution is generated by randomly mutating the problem parameter values of the parent. Mutation is performed independently on each vector element by aggregating a normal-distributed random variable with zero mean and a pre-selected standard deviation value. The child is then evaluated, and if its fitness is better than the fitness of its parent, the child survives and becomes the parent solution. Otherwise, the child is discarded and the original parent is mutated once again to produce another child solution. This selection scheme is known as $(1+1)$-selection.

Unfortunately, there were a couple of drawbacks to the $(1+1)$-ES: the point-to-point search made the procedure susceptible to stagnation at local optima, and the constant standard deviation for each vector element made the procedure slow to converge on optimal solutions.

Advanced ES

Other ES selection schemes followed, incorporating the idea of populations of solutions. By the early 1980s, the current state-of-the-art evolutionary strategies had been developed (Bäck, 1996), known as the $(\mu+\lambda)$-ES and (μ,λ)-ES (where μ is the number of parents and λ is the number of offspring). These new types of ES now strongly resemble the genetic algorithm, by maintaining populations of individuals, selecting the fittest individuals, and using recombination and mutation operators to generate new individuals from these fit solutions.

There are some significant differences between ES and GAs, however. For example, although ES maintains populations of solutions, it separates the parent individuals from the child individuals. In addition, as mentioned above, ES does not manipulate coded solutions like GAs. Instead, like GP, the decision variables of the problem are manipulated directly by the operators. Also unlike the probabilistic selection of GAs and GP, ES selects its parent solutions deterministically.

The $(\mu+\lambda)$-ES picks the best μ individuals from both child and parent populations. The (μ,λ)-ES picks the best μ individuals from just the child population. In order to ensure that a selection pressure is generated, the number of parents, μ must always be smaller than the number of offspring, λ. Bäck (1996) recommends the use of the (μ,λ)-ES with a parent:offspring ratio of 1:7.

Figure 1.14 shows the operation of the population-based evolutionary strategy. The ES is initialised with a population of random solutions, or from a population of solutions mutated from a single solution provided by the user. Parent solutions are chosen randomly from the 'parent population', and a number of random recombination operators are used to generate child solutions, which are placed in the 'child population'. These operators may recombine the values within two parents like the crossover operator of GAs, or they may use a parent for every decision variable in the solution. New solutions are then mutated using *strategy parameters* within each solution.

Mutation plays an important role in ES, and is regarded as the primary search operator. Unlike the entirely random mutation of simple GAs and GP, the mutation of ES follows a *normal distribution*. The distribution of possible mutated values is guided by two types of strategy parameter: standard deviation σ and rotation angle a for each decision variable in the solution. (In fact, ES does not require these two parameters for every variable in the solution – it permits the use of the same strategy parameters for multiple variables.) The strategy parameters influence the direction of search in the search space taken by mutation, and by modifying the values of σ and a. for each variable, the ES is able to use mutation to follow the contours of the search space and quickly find the optimal solutions, see fig. 1.15.

But the ES has another trick up its sleeve. Not only does it have directed mutation, it actually *evolves* this direction. ES achieves this by placing the strategy parameters for each

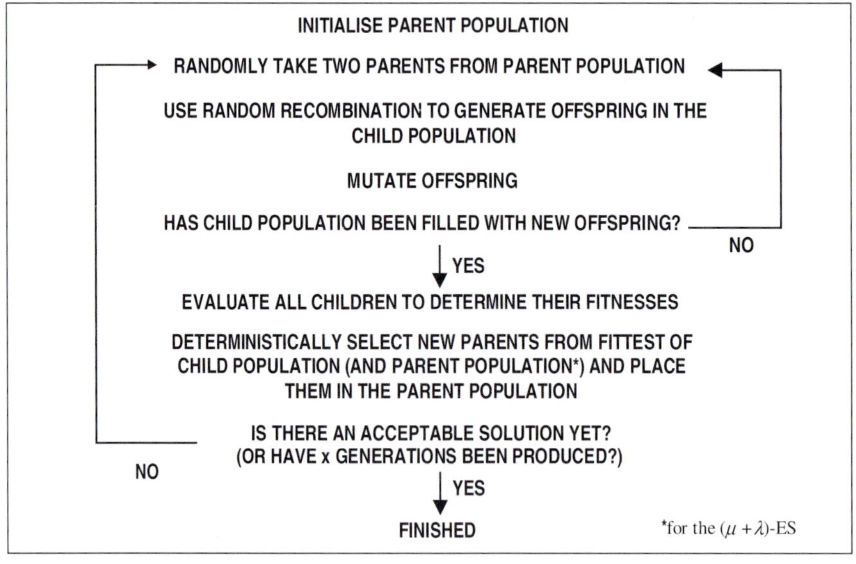

Figure 1.14 The evolutionary strategy.

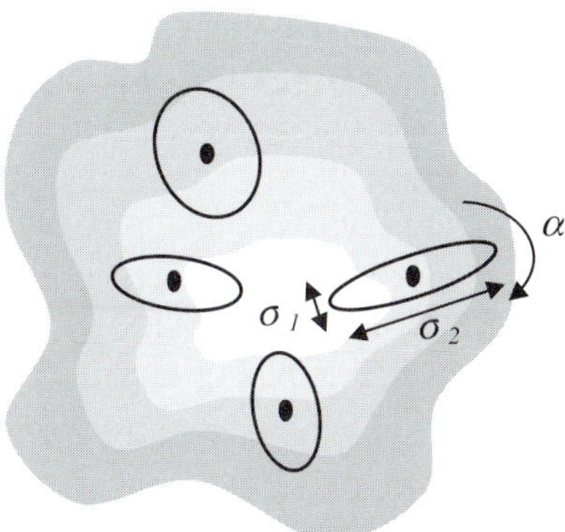

Figure 1.15 Mutation hyperellipsoids defining equal probability density around each solution. In this example, each solution has two σ parameters and one α parameter to guide mutation. Note how mutations towards the better area of the search space are encouraged.

variable within the individual solution. The operators of ES are then able to modify the strategy values in addition to the values of the variables within individuals, and hence optimise the direction of mutation in parallel to the optimisation of the variables. This important feature (which has only been introduced into advanced GAs in the last 5 years or so) is known as *self-adaptation*.

Once mutation and recombination has generated enough new individuals to fill the child population, these individuals are evaluated to obtain fitness measures, as described earlier for GAs. The fittest offspring are then deterministically selected to become parents and these are placed into the parent population.

With the parent population filled with (mostly) new individuals, the ES randomly picks parents from this population to generate new child solutions, which are then evaluated, and so on. Evolution terminates after a predefined number of generations, or when a solution of sufficient quality has been generated.

ES Theory

Like GA theory, the theory of ES was developed in the 1970s, and applies to the simplest form of the algorithm, in this case the (1+1)-ES with no self-adaptation. Rechenberg analysed the convergence rates of this two-membered ES for two objective functions, and calculated the optimal standard deviation and probability values for a successful mutation. From this he formulated the *1/5 success rule*:

The ratio of successful mutations to all mutations should be 1/5. If it is greater than 1/5, increase the standard deviation, if it is smaller, decrease the standard deviation. (Rechenberg, 1973.)

In order to apply the 1/5-success rule, the ES keeps track of the observed ratio of successful mutations to the total number of mutations, measured over intervals of $10 \times n$ trails, where n is the number of variables in the individual. According to this ratio, the standard deviation is increased, decreased, or remains constant. Born (1978) subsequently formally proved that this simple form of (1+1)-ES will result in global convergence with a probability of one under the condition of a positive standard deviation. Other theoretical analyses have shown that the introduction of populations in ES causes a logarithmic speed-up in evolution, compared to the (1+1)-ES.

As Bäck (1996) describes, Schwefel derived an approximation theory for the convergence rate of the simplified (μ,λ)-ES and ($\mu+\lambda$)-ES (one standard deviation for all object variables; no crossover nor self-adaptation). More recently, Rudolph (1996, 1997, 1998) has used Markov chains to investigate the convergence theory in EAs.

Recommended Books for ES:

Evolutionstrategie: Optimierung Technischer Systeme nach Prinzipien der Biologischen Evolution
by Ingo Rechenberg (1973).

Numerical Optimization of Computer Models
by H.-P. Schwefel (1981).

Evolution and Optimum Seeking
by H.-P. Schwefel (1995).

Evolutionstrategie'94 (volume 1 of ***Werkstatt Bionik und Evolutionstechnik)***
by Ingo Rechenberg (1994).

Evolutionary Algorithms in Theory and Practice
by Thomas Bäck (1996).

Evolutionary Computation: Toward a New Philosophy of Machine Intelligence
by David B. Fogel (1995).

1.3.4 Evolutionary Programming

A Summary

Evolutionary programming resembles evolutionary strategies closely, although EP was developed independently (and earlier) by Lawrence Fogel in the 1960s. The early versions of EP were applied to the evolution of transition tables of finite state machines[3] (FSMs), and the fitness of individuals was based on how closely the output sequence of letters generated by each individual matched a target sequence. A single population of solutions was maintained, and reproduction used mutation alone (Fogel et al., 1966).

---

[3] In fact, EP was proposed as a procedure to generate machine intelligence. Intelligent behaviours were viewed as the ability to predict one's environment and to provide a suitable response in order to achieve a given goal.

For the sake of generality, the behaviours were represented in finite state machines (FSMs). For each state of an FSM, each possible input symbol has an associated output symbol and next-state transition. A sequence of input symbols such as 010001 is given to an FSM as an observed environment. A behaviour is then considered to be 'intelligent' if it predicts what the next symbol will be and satisfies a pay-off function.

Unfortunately, despite many theses written on EP at New Mexico State University during the 1970s, this algorithm was either misunderstood or overlooked for many years. It was only when Lawrence Fogel's son, David Fogel, redeveloped EP in the late 1980s, that this technique was rediscovered by the research community.

Advanced EP

David Fogel extended the original EP, which could only evolve discrete parameterisations, to allow it to be used for continuous parameter optimisation (fixed-length real-valued vectors). Another important addition to EP was self-adaptation – the use of evolveable strategy parameters to guide mutation in a very similar way to ES.

There are three main types of EP in use: *standard EP*, *meta-EP*,[4] and *Rmeta-EP*. These three types differ by the level of self-adaptation employed. Standard EP uses no self-adaptation, meta-EP incorporates mutation variance parameters in individuals to allow self-adaptation, and Rmeta-EP incorporates mutation variance and covariance parameters into individuals to permit more precise self-adaptation (Fogel, 1995). Figure 1.16 shows the working of a general evolutionary program.

Like ES, EP operates on the decision variables of the problem directly (i.e. the search space is the same as the solution space). During initialisation, these variables are given random values, often with a uniform sampling of values between predefined ranges. These solutions are then evaluated to obtain the fitness values (which in EP may involve some form of scaling or the addition of a random perturbation). Next, parents are picked using *tournament selection*. This type of selection is commonly used in GAs, and involves a series of tournaments between

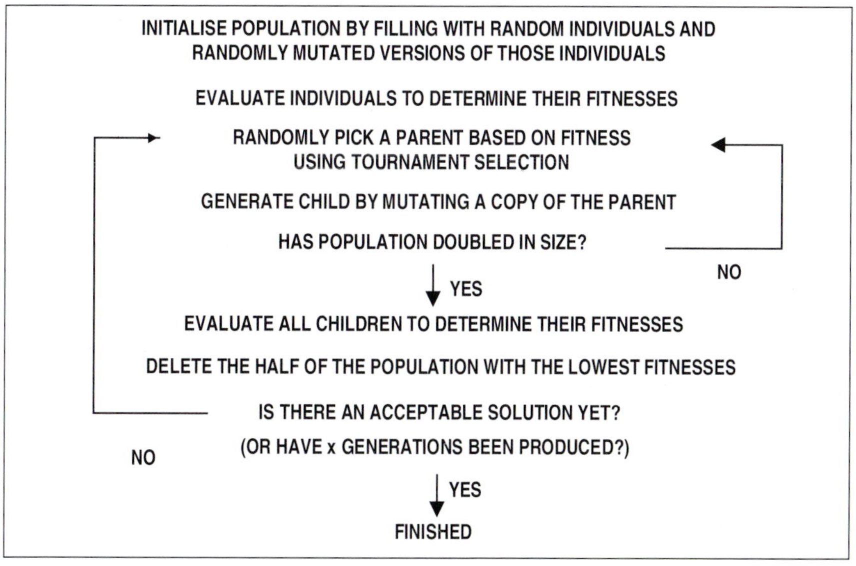

Figure 1.16 The evolutionary programming algorithm.

[4] Meta-EP is now the standard form of EP in use today, and is usually called simply EP.

each individual and a group of randomly chosen individuals. The probability of being selected for reproduction is then based on how many other individuals the prospective parent has managed to beat during the tournament (i.e., a solution with a better fitness than most of the others it 'played' in the tournament has a higher probability of being selected than a solution with a worse fitness compared to its competitors). The number of individuals in each tournament is a global parameter of the algorithm.

Children are generated asexually, by simply creating a copy of the parent and mutating it. In a similar way to ES, meta-EP and Rmeta-EP ensure that mutation will favour the search towards the areas of the search space containing better solutions, by the use of variance and covariance strategy parameters held within individuals for each variable. EP allows mutation to modify these parameters, thus permitting self-adaptation to occur. Unlike any of the evolutionary algorithms mentioned so far, EP does not use any form of recombination operator. All search is performed by mutation, following the assumption that mutation is capable of simulating the effects of operators such as crossover on solutions (Fogel, 1995).

Child solutions are generated and placed into the population until the population has doubled in size. All new solutions are evaluated, and then the half of the population with the lowest fitnesses are simply deleted. Parents are then picked, offspring generated, and so on. Evolution is typically terminated after a specific number of generations have passed.

All three types of EP can also be *continuous* (Fogel and Fogel, 1995), where instead of generating offspring until the population size has doubled and then deleting the unfit half, a single individual is generated, evaluated, and inserted into the population, replacing the least fit individual. This *replacement* method strongly resembles that used by steady-state GAs (Syswerda, 1989).

New advances in EP continue, as this EA is applied to new types of problem. Chellapilla (1997) has recently expanded EP to allow it to evolve program parse trees. Various subtree mutation operators were designed in solving four benchmark problems. He reported that the experiment results showed the technique compares well with EAs which use the crossover operator.

EP Theory

Although ES theory can be applied with little modification to EP (Bäck, 1996), Fogel has performed independent analyses of various forms of EP, including the case where the population size = 1 (in which case EP strongly resembles the (1+1)-ES (Bäck, 1996)). He calculated that mutations should increment or decrement the value of a decision variable by no more than the square root of the fitness score of the solution.

Fogel proved that the simple EP will converge with a probability of one, however convergence rates (time taken to converge) and other significant features of EP remain unsolved. Complete details of the proofs are beyond the scope of this chapter; interested readers should consult (Fogel, 1992b).

Yao and Liu (1996) proposed a Cauchy instead of Gaussian mutation operator as the primary search operator in EP. In (Yao, Lin and Liu, 1997), an analysis based on the study of neighbourhood and step size of the search space is performed to compare these two mutation operators. Their work provides a theoretical explanation, supported with empirical evidence, of when and why Cauchy mutation is better than Gaussian mutation in EP search. The long jumps provided by Cauchy mutation increase the probability of finding a near-optimum when the distance between the current search point and the optimum is large. The Gaussian mutation, on the other hand, is a better search strategy when the distance is small.

A study by Gehlhaar and Fogel (1996) also indicates that the order of the modifications of object variables and strategy parameters has a strong impact on the effectiveness of self-adaptation. It is important to mutate the strategy parameters first and then use them to modify the object variables. In this way, the potential of generating good object vectors that are associated with poor strategy parameters can be reduced. Thus the likelihood of stagnation can be reduced.

Experimental comparisons between the different types of EP are ongoing. For example, EP with self-adaptation has now been reapplied to the original task of evolving FSMs (Fogel et al., 1995; Angeline and Kinnear, 1996). Each state in an FSM was associated with mutation parameters to guide which component of the FSM was to be mutated and how to perform the mutation. Angeline and Kinnear (1996) reported that EP with self-adaptation performs better than a standard EP when solving a predication problem.

Recommended Books for EP:

Artificial Intelligence through Simulated Evolution
by L. J. Fogel, A. J. Owens and M. J. Walsh (1966)

System Identification through Simulated Evolution: A Machine Learning Approach to Modeling
by David B. Fogel (1991).

Evolutionary Computation : Toward a New Philosophy of Machine Intelligence
by David B. Fogel (1995).

Evolutionary Algorithms in Theory and Practice
by Thomas Bäck (1996).

1.3.5 A General Architecture for Evolutionary Algorithms (GAEA)

Sadly, the four major types of evolutionary algorithm are rarely considered in unison. Most researchers are genetic algorithmists, genetic programmers, evolutionary strategists, or evolutionary programmers – there are very few evolutionary computationists. Researchers in the field of evolutionary computation spend considerable time and energy exploring their favourite EA, and usually no time at all on considering the general concepts behind EAs.[5] This is unfortunate, because it should be clear that these algorithms are hardly different at all. Consequently, rather than dwell on the differences between the four major types of EA summarised previously, it is perhaps more appropriate to stress the similarities of these techniques.

---

[5] As the editor of this book, I cannot claim to be any different. My first venture into this field was when, as a teenager, I wrote a program called Evolve, which I discovered years later was essentially both a real-coded steady-state genetic algorithm, and a continuous standard evolutionary program, except that all evolutionary pressure was exerted using negative selection. Despite being yet another 'independent discoverer' of an evolutionary algorithm, it will be apparent to any knowledgeable reader that today I am a genetic algorithmist at heart.

In general, as suggested by the theory of Universal Darwinism (Dawkins, 1983), for evolution to occur, the following criteria must be met (where 'transmission' has been expanded to 'reproduction' and 'inheritance' for clarity):

reproduction **inheritance** **variation** **selection**

In other words, as long as some individuals generate copies of themselves which inherit their parents' characteristics with some small variation, and as long as some form of selection preferentially chooses some of the individuals to live and reproduce, evolution will occur. As Chapter 3: *The Memetics of Design*, describes in this book, this is true regardless of what the individual is, be it an ant, an artificial creature, or an idea.

Evolutionary search algorithms are no exception. All EAs perform the **reproduction** of individuals, either directly cloning parents or by using recombination and mutation operators to allow **inheritance** with **variation**. These operators may perform many different tasks, from a simple random bit inversion to a complete local search algorithm. All EAs also use some form of **selection** to determine which solutions will have the opportunity to reproduce, and which will not. The key thing to remember about selection is that it exerts *selection pressure*, or *evolutionary pressure* to guide the evolutionary process towards specific areas of the search space. To do this, certain individuals must be allocated a greater probability of having offspring compared to other individuals. Selection is often misunderstood by developers of EAs, who often regard it to mean simply 'selection of parents'. As will be shown, however, selection does not have to mean parent selection – it can also be performed using fertility, replacement, or even 'death' operators. It is also quite common for multiple evolutionary pressures to be exerted towards more than one objective in a single EA.

Unlike natural evolution, evolutionary algorithms also require three other important features:

initialisation **evaluation** **termination**

Because we are not prepared to wait for the computer to evolve for several million generations, EAs are typically given a head start by **initialising** (or *seeding*) them with solutions that have fixed structures and meanings, but random values. In our earlier 'house' example, each solution might consist of 'number of windows', 'position of roof', 'height' and 'width' parameters.

Evaluation in EAs is responsible for guiding evolution towards better solutions. Unlike natural evolution, evolutionary algorithms do not have a real environment in which the 'survivability' or 'goodness' of its solutions can be tested, they must instead rely on simulation, analysis and calculation to evaluate solutions.

Extinction is the only guaranteed way to **terminate** natural evolution. This is obviously a highly unsuitable way to halt EAs, for all the evolved solutions will be lost. Instead, explicit *termination criteria* are employed to halt evolution, typically when a good solution has evolved or when a predefined number of generations have passed.

There are two other important processes, which although not necessary to trigger or control evolution, will improve the capabilities of evolution enormously. These processes are:

mapping **moving**

Currently only the genetic algorithm separates the search space (containing genotypes) from the solution space (containing phenotypes), and has an explicit **mapping** stage between the two. This is unfortunate, for embryogeny and ontogeny are known by biologists to be highly significant, allowing highly complex solutions to be specified using a compact set of instructions, incorporating constraint handling and error checking.

Using EAs to evolve more than one population or *species* concurrently and separately is becoming an important tool in the optimisation of difficult or multimodal functions. **Moving** (or *migrating* or *injecting*) individuals from one population to another, or from one species to another, allows separately evolving individuals to occasionally share useful genetic information, reducing premature convergence within species, reducing the number of evaluations needed, and improving the quality of solutions evolved.

Figure 1.17 shows the general architecture of evolutionary algorithms (GAEA). This architecture should be regarded as a general framework for evolutionary algorithms, not an algorithm itself. Indeed, most EAs use only a subset of the stages listed. For example, EP uses: *initialisation*, *evaluation*, *selection*, *reproduction*, *replacement* and *termination*. Alternatively, a simple GA uses: *initialisation*, *mapping*, *evaluation*, *selection*, *fertility*, *reproduction* and *termination*. (Each optional stage in the architecture is marked as such.)

To help give the reader a more general view of using computers to perform evolution, this introductory section of the chapter will now briefly examine each of the stages in GAEA.

Initialisation

Evolutionary algorithms typically seed the initial population with entirely random values (i.e., starting from scratch). If, like the genetic algorithm, a distinction is made between the search space and the solution space, then the *genotype* of every individual will be filled with random alleles. Evolution is then used to discover which of the randomly sampled areas of the search space contain better solutions, and then to converge upon that area. Sometimes the entire population is constructed from random mutants of a single user-supplied solution. Often random values are generated between specified ranges (a form of constraint handling). It is not uncommon for explicit constraint handling to be performed during initialisation, by deleting any solutions which do not satisfy the constraints and creating new ones.

More complex problems often demand alternative methods of initialisation. Some researchers provide the EA with 'embryos' – simplified non-random solutions which are then used as starting points for the evolution of more complex solutions. John Koza describes such an approach in Chapter 16. Some algorithms actually attempt to evolve representations or low-level building blocks first, then use the results to initialise another EA which will evolve complex designs using these representations or building blocks. John Gero and Michael Rosenman describe this approach in Chapter 15.

Although most algorithms do use solutions with fixed structures (i.e. a fixed number of decision variables), some, like GP, allow the evolution of the number and organisation of parameters in addition to parameter values. In other words, some evolve *structure* as well as *detail*. For such algorithms, initialisation will typically involve the seeding of solutions with both random values and random structures.

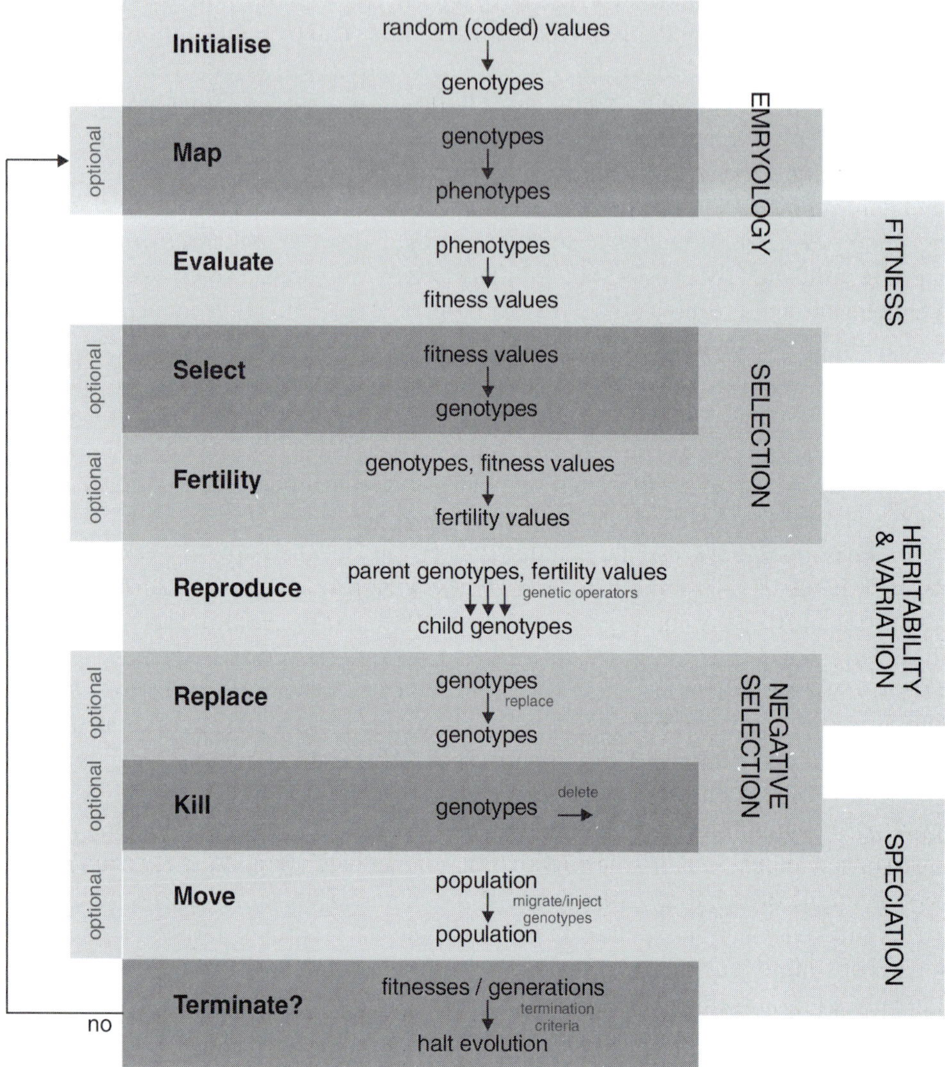

Figure 1.17 The general architecture of evolutionary algorithms (GAEA).

Map

Only algorithms which make a distinction between the search space and the solution space require a mapping stage to convert genotypes into phenotypes. Consequently, the genetic algorithm is the only major EA which uses mapping. This mapping stage is often trivially simple, e.g. converting a binary allele in the genotype to a decimal parameter value in the phenotype. However, as some chapters in this book describe, this mapping stage can also be very complex.

So why bother with it? This is a difficult question which neatly divides evolutionary computation into two camps: those who believe the effects of genetic operators can be simulated on phenotypes without needing to resort to storing, modifying, and mapping genotypes, and those who prefer to 'do it properly' and actually perform search at the genotype-level. There can be no doubt that evolution will occur whether genotypes are maintained or not, but most genetic algorithmists would argue that evolutionary search is improved if genotypes are employed. Certainly the latest advances in the understanding of natural evolution are from the level of the gene, not of the organism (Dawkins, 1976, 1986, 1996).

But the mapping process should not be viewed as a time-consuming side-effect of maintaining genotypes. Quite the opposite – this process, known by biologists as *embryogeny*, is highly important in its own right. Indeed, the advantages of embryogeny have caused some researchers to introduce genotypes into traditionally 'phenotype-only' algorithms such as GP (Banzhaf, 1994).

There are many good reasons to use a mapping stage in an EA. These include:

- **Reduction of search space**. Embryogeny permits highly compact genotypes to define phenotypes. This reduction (often recursive, hierarchical and multifunctional) results in genotypes with fewer parameters than their corresponding phenotypes, causing a reduction in the dimensionality of the search space, and hence a smaller search space for the EA.
- **Better enumeration of search space**. Mapping permits two very differently organised spaces to coexist, i.e. a search space designed to be easily searched can allow the EA to locate corresponding solutions within a hard-to-search solution space.
- **More complex solutions in solution space**. By using 'growing instructions' within genotypes to define how phenotypes should be generated, a genotype can define highly complex phenotypes. Chapter 14 gives an excellent example of this, using a Lindenmayer system as the embryogeny process.
- **Improved constraint handling**. Mapping can ensure that all phenotypes always satisfy all constraints, without reducing the effectiveness of the search process in any way, by mapping every genotype onto a legal phenotype.

The use of simple mapping stages is increasing, but research in artificial embryogenies is still in its infancy, with most researchers designing their own. Many of the chapters in the last two sections of this book describe approaches for evolutionary design. The design of artificial embryogenies is not trivial, so it seems likely that researchers will attempt to evolve them in the future (just as our own embryogeny evolved in nature). Section 1.5.2 in the final part of this chapter describes embryogenies in more detail.

Evaluation

Every new phenotype must be evaluated to provide a level of 'goodness' for each solution. Often a single run of an EA will involve thousands of evaluations, which means that almost all computation time is spent performing the evaluation process (most EAs use negligible processing time themselves). In evolutionary design, evaluation is often performed by dedicated analysis software which can take minutes or even hours to evaluate a single solution, so there is often a strong emphasis towards reducing the number of evaluations during evolution. Chapters 5, 6 and 7 describe various advanced techniques in EAs to reduce evaluation times.

Evaluation involves the use of fitness functions to assign fitness scores to solutions. These fitness functions can have single or multiple objectives, they can be unimodal or multimodal, continuous or discontinuous, smooth or noisy, static or continuously changing. EAs are known to be proficient at finding good solutions for all these types of fitness function, but specialised techniques are often required for multimodal, multiobjective, noisy and continuously changing functions. Some of these are summarised at the end of this chapter.

Evaluation is not always performed by explicit fitness functions. Some EAs employ human evaluators to view and judge their solutions – the chapters on evolutionary art describe this approach. Fitness can also be determined by competition between solutions (for example, each solution may represent a game playing strategy, and the fitness of each strategy depends on how many other solutions in the population the current strategy can beat (Axelrod, 1987)).

Once fitness values have been calculated, some form of scaling is common. For example, if multiple species of individuals are being evolved, *fitness sharing* reduces the fitness of any individuals in large groups to encourage the development of more groups containing smaller numbers of individuals (Goldberg, 1989). Fitness scores are also commonly scaled as part of multiobjective optimisation (Bentley and Wakefield, 1997c) or to prevent unwanted biases during parent selection (Goldberg, 1989).

Parent Selection

Parent solutions are always required in an EA, or no child solutions can be generated. However, the *preferential selection* of some parents instead of others is not essential to evolution. (If parent selection is not present in the EA, then all solutions are permitted to generate offspring with equal probability.) Every one of the major EAs does perform parent selection, but evolution will still occur without it, as long as evolutionary pressure is exerted by one of the three other selection methods: *fertility*, *replacement* and *death*.

Choosing the fitter solutions to be parents of the next generation is the most common and direct way of inducing a selective pressure towards the evolution of fitter solutions. Typically, one of three selection methods are utilised: fitness ranking, tournament selection, or fitness proportionate selection. Fitness ranking sorts the population into order of fitness and bases the probability of a solution being selected for parenthood on its position in the ranking. Tournament selection bases the probability of a solution being selected on how many other randomly picked individuals it can beat (see the section on EP). Fitness proportionate selection (or roulette wheel selection) bases the probability of a parent being selected on the relative fitness scores of each individual, e.g. a solution ten times as fit as another is ten times more likely to be picked as a parent (Goldberg, 1989). This method also incorporates the *fertility* selection method, see below.

Although fitter parents are normally selected, this does not have to be the case. It is possible to select parents based on how many constraints they satisfy, or how well they fulfil other criteria, as long as a fitness-based selection pressure is introduced elsewhere in the algorithm. The selection of pairs of parents is usually limited by EAs with speciation or multiple populations (i.e. two parents from different species or different populations/islands will not be permitted to generate offspring together). In algorithms that record the age of individuals, parent selection may be limited to individuals that are 'mature' or individuals which are below their maximum lifespans. Any individual that is sterile (see below) should not be selected for parenthood.

Fertility

The *fertility* of a parent solution is the number of offspring that parent can have, e.g. a parent with a high fertility will have more offspring than a parent with low fertility. The fertility of parent solutions is often confused with the selection of parent solutions. For example, fitness proportionate selection not only selects parents based on their relative fitnesses, it also increases the fertility of fitter parents based on fitnesses. This confusion is unfortunate, because in reality, changing the fertility of parents is an independent and separate way to exert selection pressure in EAs.

The separation of parent selection and fertility is perhaps clearest in natural evolution. A peahen *selects* the most attractive peacock it can find (perhaps based on the size and pattenation of the tail) to be the parent of its offspring (Dawkins, 1986). Conversely, the *fertility* of the two parents is an innate characteristic of the parents, based on their fitness, their age, and, for some birds, the number of other birds sharing the same neighbourhood (Dawkins, 1976). Because unhealthy birds tend to have lower fertilities than healthy birds,[6] an evolutionary pressure is exerted towards healthy birds, in addition to the selective pressure towards birds with ornate tails.

Currently the use of fertility to induce selection pressures towards explicit goals in EAs has been limited to constraint handling. Experimental results have shown that selecting parents based on fitness, and setting fertility values based on how many constraints each solution satisfies, can be a very effective method of performing twin-objective optimisation using EAs (Yu and Bentley, 1998).

Individuals in the population may have reduced fertilities, or may even be sterile (i.e., have a fertility of zero) if immature or too old. Two parents from different species are typically regarded as having very low fertilities (e.g., a one in twenty chance of generating any offspring). EAs that do not employ fertility ensure that every parent has a fixed, unchanging number of offspring – usually with each parent producing one child.

Reproduction

Reproduction is the cornerstone of every evolutionary algorithm – it is the stage responsible for the generation of child solutions from parent solutions. Crucially, child solutions must *inherit* characteristics from their parents, and there must be some *variability* between the child and parent. This is achieved by the use of the genetic operators: recombination and mutation.

Recombination operators require two or more parent solutions. The solutions (or the genotypes, if the algorithm distinguishes between search and solution spaces) are ‘shuffled together’ to generate child solutions. EAs normally use recombination to generate most or all offspring. For example, ES often uses recombination to generate offspring, GAs typically use recombination with a probability of 0.7, with the remaining offspring being clones of their parents. Only EP uses no recombination at all.

---

[6] This is an oversimplification: in nature most creatures have an optimal fertility rate – if it is too low, none may survive predation, if too high, the excessive cost of rearing all the offspring may cause all to die of malnutrition. If the creature is unfit, it may have too many or too few offspring, with the net result that fewer survive (Dawkins, 1976).

Recombination is normally performed by crossover operators in EAs. Examples of the working of various types of crossover were provided in the previous sections on specific EAs.

Mutation operators modify a single solution at a time. Some EAs mutate a copy of a parent solution in order to generate the child, some mutate the solution during the application of the recombination operators, others use recombination to generate children, and then mutate these children. In addition, the probability of mutation varies depending on the EA. For example, GAs use low probabilities, often between 0.01 and 0.001 per bit in the genotype, whereas EP always uses mutation.

There are huge numbers of different mutation operators in use today. Examples include: bit-mutation, translocation, segregation, inversion (GAs), structure mutation, permutation, editing, encapsulation (GP), mutation directed by strategy parameters (ES and EP), and even mutation using local search algorithms (memetic algorithms) (Goldberg, 1989; Koza, 1992; Radcliffe and Surrey, 1994a; Bäck, 1996). The previous sections on EAs described some of these further.

An important feature of both recombination and mutation is *non-disruption*. Although variation between parent and child is essential, this variation should not produce excessive changes to phenotypes. In other words, child solutions should always be near to their parent solutions in the solution space. If this is not the case, i.e. if huge changes are permitted, then the semblance of inheritance from parent to child solutions will be reduced, and their position in the solution space will become excessively randomised. Evolution relies on inheritance to ensure the preservation of useful characteristics of parent solutions in child solutions. When disruption is too high, evolution becomes no more than a random search algorithm.

This is the reason why researchers are trying to improve the crossover and mutation operators of GP – the existing operators disrupt so many of the offspring that most are less fit than their parents. This is also the reason why ES and EP use a normal distribution to guide their mutation operators – the distribution encourages smaller mutations.

Replacement

Once offspring have been created, they must be inserted into the population. EAs usually maintain populations of fixed sizes, so for every new individual that is inserted into the population, an existing individual must be deleted. The simpler EAs just delete every individual and replace them with new offspring. However, some EAs (such as the steady-state GA and continuous EP) use an explicit replacement operator to determine which solution a new child should replace. Replacement is often fitness-based, i.e. children always replace solutions less fit than themselves, or the weakest in the population are replaced by fitter offspring. Indeed, the use of fitness-based replacement exemplifies the famous Darwinian phrase 'survival of the fittest', for by replacing all the less-fit solutions, the fittest literally have an increased chance of survival.

Replacement is clearly a third method of introducing evolutionary pressure to EAs, but instead of being a selection method, it is a *negative selection* method. In other words, instead of choosing which individuals should reproduce or how many offspring they should have, replacement chooses which individuals will die. (Negative selection also takes place within immune systems; recent work using computers to evolve artificial immune systems uses negative selection as the sole purveyor of evolutionary pressure (Forrest et al., 1995)).

Replacement need not be fitness-based, it can be based on constraint satisfaction, the similarity of genotypes, the age of solutions, or any other criterion, as long as a fitness-based evolutionary pressure is exerted elsewhere in the EA. Replacement is also limited by speciation within EAs: a child from two parents of one species/population/island should not replace an individual in a different species/population/island.

Kill

The fourth and final way to induce evolutionary pressure in an EA is very similar to the replacement method. It involves 'killing' individuals based on some criterion, and consequently is also a negative selection method. 'Kill' is related to replacement, but is subtly different. Replacement involves the comparison of a child with the solution it may replace. 'Kill' operates on a single solution – if the solution does not fulfil the criterion, it is removed from the population. Also unlike replacement, the 'kill' operator is usually used for constraint satisfaction rather than to help generate fit solutions. (Non-continuous EP is the exception to this – 'kill' is used to remove the weakest half of the population after the generation of offspring.)

Typically, the child solution is 'killed' before it has a chance to reproduce. This may happen during initialisation or during reproduction, but in either case, once a solution has been deleted, another attempt will be made to generate a solution (possibly using the same parents). If every child that does not fulfil the criterion is deleted without exception, the maximum possible level of negative selection is exerted, i.e. every solution will always satisfy the criterion. Simply deleting solutions in an EA is very much a brute-force method, often used to enforce hard constraints. As will be described later in this chapter, this approach suffers from significant drawbacks such as reduced diversity and increased difficulty of search for the EA.

'Kill' can also be used as a 'die of old age' operator. This is normally achieved by recording the number of generations each individual has been in the population in the EA and 'killing' solutions when they reach a maximum lifespan (although most will have been replaced by fitter offspring long before then). Deleting older individuals can be a useful method of preventing very fit individuals from becoming 'immortal' and corrupting evolution by filling the entire population with their numerous progeny – particularly if the immortal individual only received a good fitness score because of random noise in the fitness function (Bentley, 1997).

Move

All evolutionary algorithms search populations of solutions in parallel, but most converge onto a single point in the search space after a number of generations. If the fitness function has a single optimal solution, this behaviour is acceptable, but if the fitness function is multimodal (i.e., it has multiple optima), then it is often desirable to use an EA to converge on as many of the separate optima as possible. This is achieved by evolving a number of separate, non-interbreeding groups of individuals (sometimes referred to as separate populations, species, islands, or *demes*), and allowing each of these groups to converge onto potentially different optima. Such EAs are often termed *parallel* or *distributed*. Other motivations for the use of these EAs include the reduction of evaluation times and improvement of solution quality (Eby et al., 1997).

If the separate groups of individuals evolving in the EA never interact in any way, this becomes equivalent to running multiple EAs at the same time, or running one EA many times. However, by permitting the occasional migration or injection of an individual from one group to another, the behaviour becomes distinct.

'Move' encompasses such operators in EAs. 'Move' operators allow characteristics evolving in one group of individuals to be passed to another group of individuals, to help propagate the best independently evolving features. Typically only a single individual is moved (or migrated, or injected) at a time, and usually this occurs infrequently. Individuals may be randomly chosen, or, more commonly, selected according to fitness. The 'movement' may also involve a translation from one representation to another. Chapter 7: *The Optimization of Flywheels using an Injection Island Genetic Algorithm* describes this process in more detail.

Termination

Evolution by an EA is halted by termination criteria, which are normally based on solution quality and time. Most EAs use quality-driven termination as the primary halting mechanism: they simply continue evolving until an individual which is considered sufficiently fit (or for GP, until a program with hits for every exemplar) has been evolved. Some EAs will also reinitialise and restart evolution if no solutions have attained a specific level of fitness after a certain number of generations.

For algorithms which use computationally heavy fitness functions, or for algorithms which must generate solutions quickly, the primary termination criterion is based on time. Normally evolution is terminated after a specific number of generations, evaluations, or seconds. In order to reduce the number of unnecessary generations, some algorithms measure the convergence rates during evolution, and terminate when convergence has occurred (i.e. when the genotypes, phenotypes or fitnesses of all individuals are static for a number of generations). Many EAs also permit the user to halt evolution – an option often misused by more impatient users.

Some EAs do not use explicit termination criteria. These rare beasts are used to continuously adapt to changing fitness functions, and so must evolve new solutions unceasingly. Experiments have shown that EAs with self-adaptation (such as ES and EP) seem to provide the best results when trying to evolve solutions towards a 'moving target' (Bäck, 1996). Harvey and Thompson (1997) describe a GA created for this purpose. Nevertheless, even these EAs are subject to the most fundamental of termination criteria: a power failure.

1.3.6 From Evolutionary Algorithms to Evolutionary Design

This section of the chapter has introduced the concept of using computers to *search* for good solutions in a *search space*. The parallel searching mechanism used by evolutionary algorithms was described, and the four major EAs were summarised: genetic algorithms, genetic programming, evolution strategies, and evolutionary programming. The section concluded by describing the general architecture of evolutionary algorithms, showing that all EAs are fundamentally the same.

Having now explained how computers are used to perform evolution, the following section describes how computers perform evolutionary design.

1.4 Evolutionary Design

Evolutionary design has its roots in computer science, design, and evolutionary biology. It is a branch of evolutionary computation, it extends and combines CAD and analysis software, and it borrows ideas from natural evolution, see fig. 1.18.

The use of evolutionary computation to generate designs has taken place in many different guises over the last 10 or 15 years. Designers have optimised selected parts of their designs using evolution, artists have used evolution to generate aesthetically pleasing forms, architects have evolved new building plans from scratch, computer scientists have evolved morphologies and control systems of artificial life.

In general, these varied types of evolutionary design can be divided into four main categories: *evolutionary design optimisation*, *creative evolutionary design*, *evolutionary art*, and *evolutionary artificial life forms*, see fig. 1.19. As is usually the case with any kind of classification system, the work of a few researchers does not fall neatly within one category, but may be included in two or more categories. Such work comprises four 'overlapping' types of evolutionary design: *integral evolutionary design*, *aesthetic evolutionary design*, *artificial life-based evolutionary design*, and *aesthetic evolutionary AL* (Bentley, 1998a). Figure 1.19 shows all of these areas of research and how they relate to each other.

This middle section of the chapter summarises the scope of research in each area of evolutionary design. The aims and objectives of researchers in each area are described, and some key contributions to the fields of research is examined. For each of the four major aspects of evolutionary design, examples are provided of how designs are represented, which evolutionary algorithms are used and what designs have been evolved.

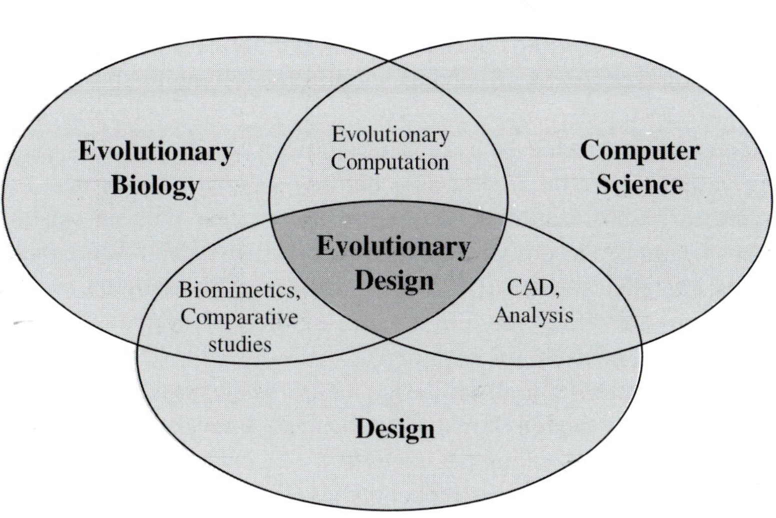

Figure 1.18 Evolutionary design has its roots in computer science, design, and evolutionary biology.

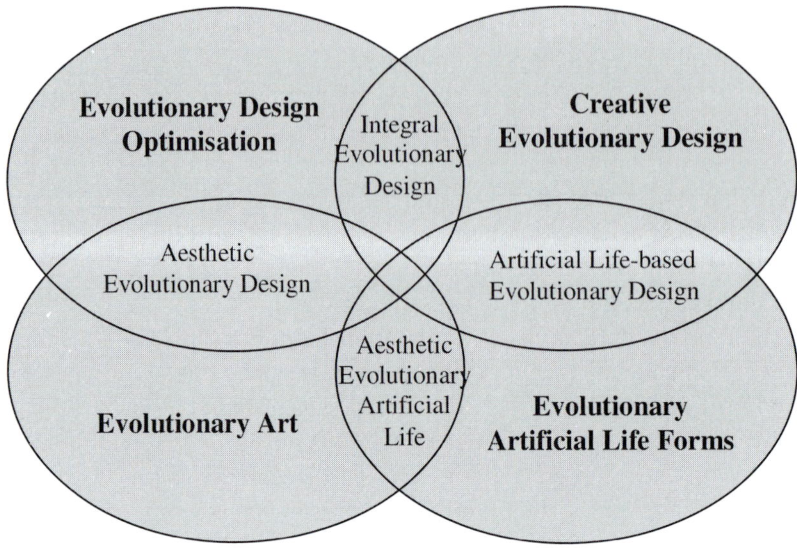

Figure 1.19 Aspects of evolutionary design by computers.

1.4.1 Four Aspects

Evolutionary Design Optimisation

The use of evolutionary computation to optimise existing designs (i.e., perform *detailed design* or *parametric design*) was the first type of evolutionary design to be tackled. Over the last fifteen years, a huge variety of different engineering designs have been successfully optimised (Holland, 1992; Gen and Cheng, 1997), from flywheels (Eby et al., 1997) to aircraft geometries (Husbands et al., 1996). Other more unusual types of evolutionary design optimisation include reliability optimisation (see Chapter 8) and techniques for solving the protein folding problem (Canal et al., 1998).

Although the exact approach used by developers of such systems varies, typically this type of evolutionary design cannot be classed as *generative* or *creative* (see next section). Practitioners of evolutionary optimization usually begin the process with an existing design, and parameterise those parts of the design they feel need improvement. The parameters are then encoded as genes, the alleles (values) of which are then evolved by an evolutionary search algorithm. The designs are often judged by interfacing the system to analysis software, which is used to derive a fitness measure for each design.

Phenotype representations for these design optimisation problems are application-specific, consisting of existing designs for that application, with the evolved parameter values simply inserted into the corresponding parameterised elements. Artificial embryogenies (mapping or 'growth' stages from genotypes to phenotypes (Dawkins, 1989)) are often rudimentary or non-existent, simply because they are not necessary for such evolutionary design. Because of this, genotype representations may match phenotype representations closely, often with a one-to-one mapping between genes and parameters. Consequently, the addition or deletion of genes in genotypes, and parameters in phenotypes, is usually not performed by the evolutionary algorithm for evolutionary design optimisation.

To illustrate this form of evolutionary design, consider the design of a four-legged table. A typical approach to evolutionary design optimisation would be to parameterise part of the table design – for example, the position and length of the legs – and use an EA to optimise the values of those parameters for some criteria – for example, maximise the stability of the table (Bentley and Wakefield, 1996b). As fig. 1.20 shows, phenotypes could consist of eight parameters, with genotypes being 64 bits.

In this trivial example, the optimal solution is clearly a table design with all four legs the same length, and with the legs placed at the four corners of the table top, fig. 1.20 (right).

As the example illustrates, evolutionary optimisation finds functionally optimal (or at least functionally good) permutations of the form of existing designs. However, it is incapable of changing the design concept (i.e. a table top resting on a single pedestal with a wide base will never be 'invented').

Evolutionary optimisation places great emphasis upon finding a solution as close to the global optimal as possible – perhaps more so than for any other type of evolutionary design. Often designs that are already of good quality are to be improved, and it can be a challenge to improve them at all. Because of this motivation towards global optimality, researchers tend to concentrate on methods for evolutionary search which reduce any tendencies towards convergence upon local optima. In addition, because the analysis software used to provide fitness functions for solutions can have heavy computational demands, there is often a strong emphasis towards reducing the number of evaluations required before a final solution is found.

Numerous techniques have been tried to achieve these goals. To improve performance, sometimes multiple genetic representations are used in parallel (see Chapter 7). Many complex types of genetic algorithm are used (Gen and Cheng, 1997). For example, Husbands et al. (1996)

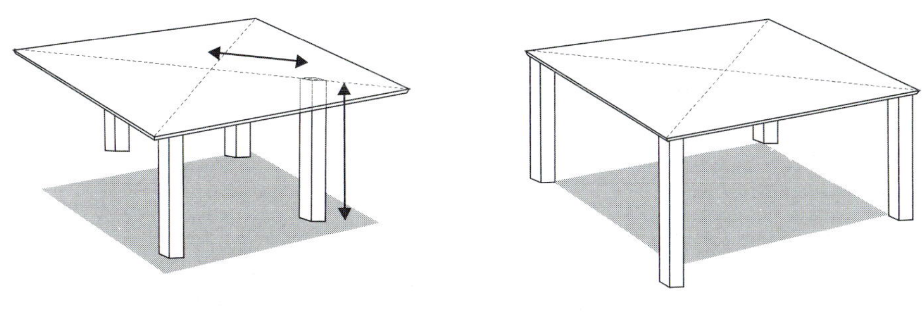

Phenotype:
Table consisting of fixed top and four legs defined by:
Length of leg 1, Distance of leg 1 from centre
Length of leg 2, Distance of leg 2 from centre
Length of leg 3, Distance of leg 3 from centre
Length of leg 4, Distance of leg 4 from centre

Genotype:

11010110	10101101	10101110	10011010	01101010	10001010	11110010	00101110
Length 1	*Distance 1*	*Length 2*	*Distance 2*	*Length 3*	*Distance 3*	*Length 4*	*Distance 4*

Figure 1.20 Evolutionary optimisation of a table.

describes the use of a distributed GA and a distributed GA hybridized with gradient descent techniques to evolve the cross-section of optimal aircraft wingboxes. The research found that hybrid GAs outperformed many other search algorithms for this problem (Husbands et al., 1996).

The *Evolutionary Optimization* section in this book provides two chapters on 'classic' evolutionary optimisation. In Chapter 6, Andy Keane descibes the minimisation of the structural vibration of designs such as satellite booms, using a GA to minimise fitness values returned by a statistical energy analysis package. Gordon Robinson also describes his work to optimise strain in load cells. In Chapter 7, Erik Goodman describes the optimisation of flywheels using GAs. Cross-sections of flywheels are parameterised (into a collection of height parameters) and evolved, see fig. 1.21. Evaluation of structure is performed using multiple finite element models (Eby et al., 1997). In Chapter 8, Mitsuo Gen and Jong Ryul Kim describe a more unusual application for evolutionary optimisation: reliabity design. For more examples of evolutionary optimisation of designs, see Gen and Cheng's recent book: *Genetic Algorithms and Engineering Design* (Gen and Cheng, 1997).

Creative Evolutionary Design

Calling anything generated by computer 'creative' is fraught with ambiguity and controversy, so this section will begin by attempting to define, for the purposes of evolutionary design, what 'creative' actually means.

Writing about this very subject in his paper 'Computers and Creative Design', Gero (1996) makes the distinction between cognitive and social views, i.e. an individual can display creativity when designing, and a design can have characteristics which may be regarded as being creative. Gero concentrates on the former definition, and concludes that a computer is designing creatively when it explores the set of possible design state spaces in addition to exploring parameters within individual design spaces. In other words, Gero indicates that by evolving the

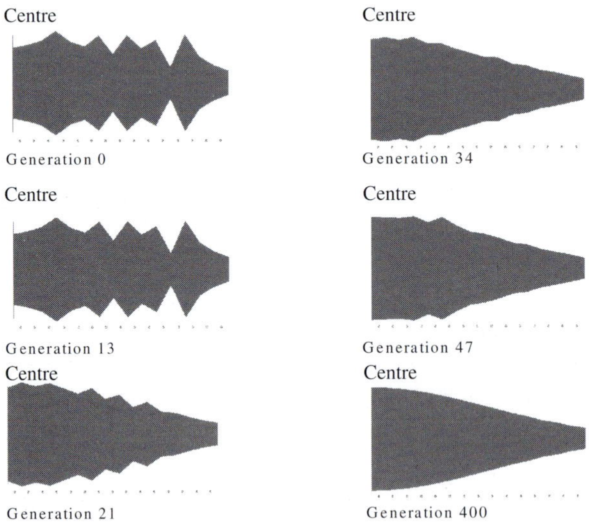

Figure 1.21 Goodman's evolutionary optimisation of flywheels.

number of decision variables in addition to evolving the *values* of those variables, a computer is being creative (Gero, 1996). In a similar vein, Boden (1992) suggests in her book *The Creative Mind*, that creativity is only possible by going beyond the bounds of a representation, and by finding a novel solution which simply could not have been defined by that representation. Boden, however, does not feel that computers are capable of such creativity (Boden, 1992).

Other definitions for creative design include: the transfer of knowledge from other domains (see Chapter 4), having the ability to generate 'surprising and innovative solutions', or the creation of 'novel solutions that are qualitatively better than previous solutions' (Gero and Kazakov, 1996). However, for the purposes of this book, Rosenman's description seems most apt:

> *The lesser the knowledge about existing relationships between the requirements and the form to satisfy those requirements, the more a design problem tends towards creative design.*
> (Rosenman, 1997).

Consequently, the main feature that all creative evolutionary design systems have in common, is the ability to generate entirely new designs starting from little or nothing (i.e. random initial populations), and be guided purely by functional performance criteria. In achieving this, such systems often do vary the number of decision variables during evolution (Bentley and Wakefield, 1997b; Rosenman, 1997). They can often generate surprising and innovative solutions, or novel solutions qualitatively better than others (Bentley and Wakefield, 1997a; Harvey and Thompson, 1997). Whether this means that these systems are really 'designing creatively', or whether they simply generate 'creative designs', will be left for the reader to decide.

Research in the field of creative evolutionary design is concerned with the preliminary stages of the design process. There are two main approaches. Both involve the use of evolutionary computation to generate entirely new designs from scratch, however the level at which these designs are represented is different:

Conceptual evolutionary design
– *the production of high-level conceptual frameworks for designs.*
In this type of evolutionary design, the relationships and arrangements of high-level design concepts are evolved in an attempt to generate novel preliminary designs. A good example of this is the work of Pham, who describes his preliminary design system known as TRADES (TRAnsmission DESigner) (Pham and Yang, 1993). TRADES uses a genetic algorithm to evolve the organisation of a set of conceptual building blocks (such as rack and pinion, worm gear, belt drive). When given the type of input (e.g. rotary motion) and the desired output (e.g. perpendicular linear motion), the system generates a suitable conceptual transmission system to convert the input into the output.

In these systems, evolution is used to search through the possible networks of interconnected conceptual building blocks. The genotype and phenotype representations of these systems are often simple, with rudimentary embryogenies, if any. Returning to our 'table' example, the typical approach to conceptual evolutionary design would be to devise a number of conceptual building blocks, each having a specific behaviour, and use evolution to find a suitable organisation of the blocks to ensure that the whole design behaves as a table, see fig. 1.22.

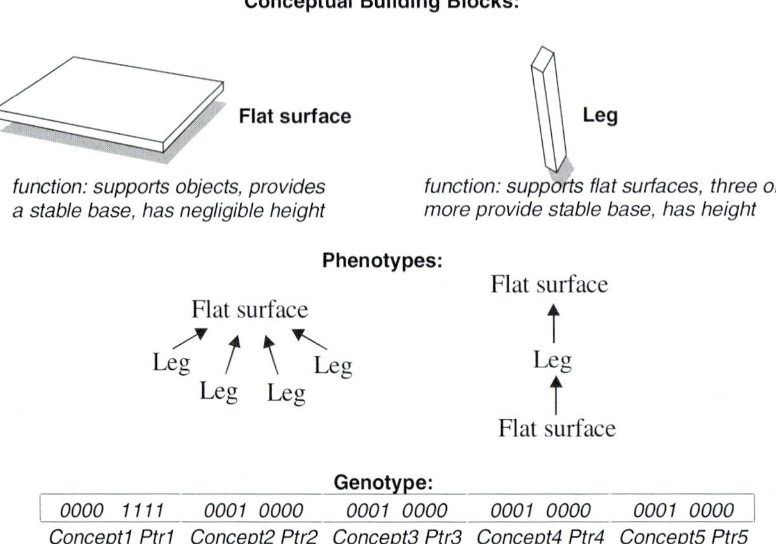

Figure 1.22 Conceptual evolutionary design of a table.

The example uses only two conceptual building blocks: *flat surface* and *leg*, each of which have their behaviours predefined. Phenotypes consist of networks of these concepts. Figure 1.22 shows the phenotype representation of a four-legged table (middle left) and a table with its table top resting on a single pedestal with a wide base (middle right). If GP is used to evolve these designs, the phenotypes could be directly modified, and the number of concepts would be variable. If a GA is used to evolve the designs, a genotype representation similar to the one shown in fig. 1.22 (bottom) would be required. It should be clear that, unlike evolutionary optimisation, conceptual evolutionary design is capable of generating new design concepts. However, such systems are inevitably limited to the building blocks and their functions which have been provided by the designer.

Basic evolutionary algorithms are usually sufficient for conceptual evolutionary design. There are always exceptions to every rule, however, and the work of Parmee provides such an exception. Parmee (1996) describes the use of structured GA to evolve a large-scale hydropower system (this is intended to take place at the feasibility/bid stages of the design process, after the conceptual design stage). His advanced GA manipulates a design hierarchy of 'sites', 'dam types', 'tunnel lengths', 'modes of operation', etc., and allows appropriate elements to be switched on or off by control genes during evolution (Parmee, 1996a). This work is mentioned by Ian Parmee in Chapter 5.

Generative evolutionary design (or genetic design)
– the generation of the form of designs directly.
Using computers to generate the form of designs rather than a collection of pre-defined high-level concepts has the advantage of giving greater freedom to the computer. Typically such systems are free to evolve any form capable of being represented, and the evolution of such forms may well result in the emergence of implicit design concepts (Bentley and Wakefield,

1997a; Harvey and Thompson, 1997). However, the difficulty of this type of creative evolutionary design is severe, since it often involves the creation of dynamically specified representations and complex evaluation routines (see below).

Often involving just the preliminary stages of design, the emphasis for this type of evolutionary design is on the generation of novelty and originality, and not the production of globally optimal solutions. Representations of form vary tremendously, but they do all share certain features. Because the emphasis is on the generation of new forms, phenotype representations are typically quite general, capable of representing vast numbers of alternative morphologies (this is in contrast to representations for optimisation, which can only define variations of a single form). Representations range from direct spatial partitioning (e.g. voxels), which have one-to-one mappings between genes in genotypes and elements of phenotypes (Baron et. al., 1997), to highly indirect representations which use shape grammars or cellular automata (CA) with some advanced embryogenies to map genotypes to phenotypes (Frazer, 1995; Coates, 1997; Rosenman, 1997).

Figure 1.23 shows how a generative evolutionary design system approaches the task of evolving a table. The initial population begins with randomly shaped 'blobs' (fig. 1.23, left), and evolution is used to gradually fine-tune these shapes until they function as tables (fig. 1.23, right). The representation is crucial for such systems – every part of the design must be alterable. In this example, designs (phenotypes) are represented by a number of blocks, defined by their 3D position and size. Genotypes define *desired* 3D position and size genes. As alleles are mapped to parameter values, the values may change slightly (i.e. two overlapping blocks are 'squashed' until they touch rather than overlap). Genotypes may define partial designs, which are subsequently reflected to form symmetrical phenotypes (fig. 1.23, right). These simple mapping processes mean that there is no longer a direct one-to-one mapping between genes

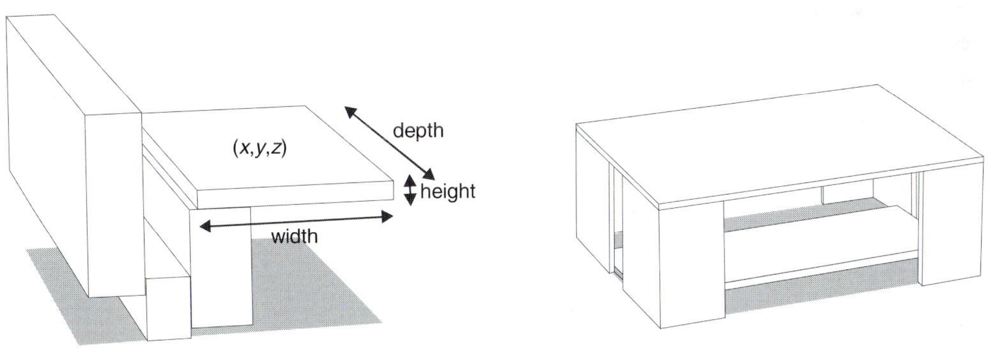

Phenotype:

x, y, z, width, height, depth of block 1 *x, y, z, width, height, depth of block 2*
x, y, z, width, height, depth of block 3 *x, y, z, width, height, depth of block 4*
x, y, z, width, height, depth of block 5 *...x, y, z, width, height, depth of block 16*

Genotype:

11010110	10101101	10101110	10011010	01101010	01101010	...	10001010	10001010	10001010
desired xpos 1	*desired ypos 1*	*desired zpos 1*	*desired width 1*	*desired height 1*	*desired height 1*	...	*desired width 4*	*desired height 4*	*desired depth 4*

Figure 1.23 Generative evolutionary design of a table.

and parameters – the form of designs is affected by interactions between different genes. More details of this type of representation and how it can be used in a generic evolutionary design system are provided in Chapter 18.

Because designs are generated 'from the bottom up', generative evolutionary design has yet to be used for the evolution of complex designs with moving parts. Nevertheless, this type of creative evolutionary design is capable of greater creativity than conceptual evolutionary design, as it uses only the fitness functions to provide guidance. It also overcomes potential limitations of 'conventional wisdom' and 'design fixation' by evolving forms without the use of knowledge of existing designs or design components.

The final section of this book explores this exciting type of creative evolutionary design. For example, Mike Rosenman describes the use of a GA to evolve house plans, using a design grammar of rules to define how polygons should be constructed out of edge vectors (Chapter 15). John Koza uses genetic programming (GP) to evolve novel analogue circuits (Chapter 16). John Gero attempts to evolve new higher-level representations of form, suitable for subsequent evolution of house plans in a specific architectural style (Chapter 15).

Simple evolutionary algorithms are often sufficient for the design systems that employ simpler representations (Baron et al., 1997). However, for creative evolutionary design systems with advanced representations and corresponding embryogenies (e.g. to 'grow' phenotypes from a set of shape-grammar rules defined in the genotypes), more advanced EAs are essential. Typically, these EAs are used to evolve the larger structure of the representation (e.g. number and organisation of shape-rules) in addition to the detail (e.g. type and content of the individual rules). In other words, these EAs are capable of evolving designs which have representations of variable length – they explore new and different search spaces in addition to the parameter values within each space (Bentley and Wakefield, 1996a). Typically, GAs and GP are used to evolve these highly variable forms (Frazer, 1995; Bentley and Wakefield 1997b; Coates, 1997), usually beginning from random, simple forms, and gradually improving the structure and detail of these designs until some functional criteria are met. The objective of this type of research is not normally to use computers to generate a single global optimal solution, but rather to generate a number of 'creative' alternatives. The evaluation of designs can be more difficult, since most off-the-shelf analysis packages are limited to judging specific types of designs – when presented with some of the initially random forms generated by these systems, they simply generate errors. Consequently, many of these systems rely on simplified custom-written evaluation routines, which can analyse everything presented to them, but perhaps not always with the desired accuracy (Bentley and Wakefield, 1997b).

However, this is one of the most recent and exciting types of evolutionary design, and is already showing great potential in a number of application areas. Chapter 18 describes the evolution, from scratch, of a number of unusual and inventive designs for numerous applications, such as tables, heatsinks, optical prisms, aerodynamic and hydrodynamic forms, etc., see fig. 1.24. In Chapter 17, Jordan Pollack demonstrates the use of a GA to evolve novel bridge and crane structures, which are subsequently built as LEGO™ models. An application area currently receiving much media attention is 'evolveable hardware', where new logic circuits are evolved and evaluated in real silicon using FPGAs. Evolution is also now being used to generate analogue circuits (described by John Koza in Chapter 16). Already some surprising and novel electronic solutions have been found using these techniques (Harvey and Thompson, 1997).

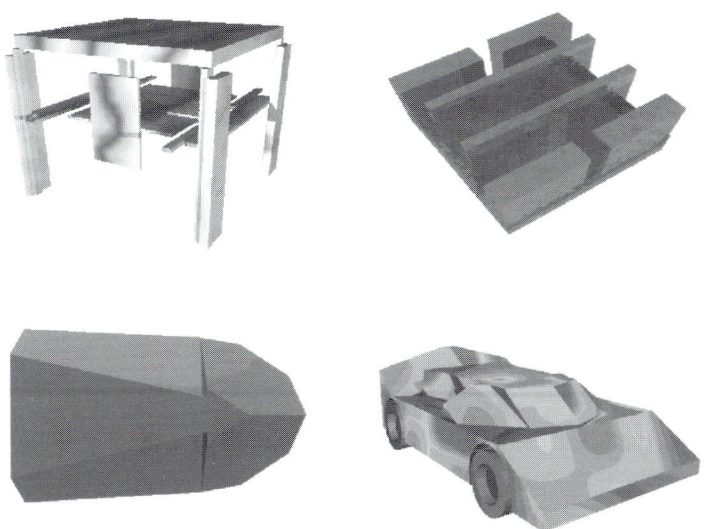

Figure 1.24 Examples of creative evolutionary design.

Evolutionary Art

Evolutionary art is perhaps the most commercially successful type of evolutionary design. Although academic research in this area is less common than in the other fields, there are more evolutionary art products available today than any other type of evolutionary design system (see Chapter 11 for a review).

Most evolutionary art systems tend to resemble each other closely. They all generate new forms or images from scratch (random initial populations). They rely completely upon a human evaluator to set fitnesses for each member of the population – normally based on aesthetic appeal. Population sizes are usually very small (often less than ten individuals), to allow them all to be quickly judged every generation. User-interfaces are often similar, with members of the current population shown on the screen in the form of a grid, allowing the user to rank them, or assign fitness scores by clicking on them with a mouse.

The main differences between these systems lie in their phenotype representations. A large variety of alternative representations have been employed, from fractal equations (such as John Mount's 'Interactive Genetic Art', which is shown on-line at http://www.geneticart.org/), to recursive grammar-rules using constructive solid geometry (Todd and Latham, 1992).

These representations are created with different intentions. For example, Dawkins' recursive tree-like structures were intended to resemble the recursive embryogenies found in nature, in the hope that natural looking forms would emerge (Dawkins, 1986, 1989). Todd and Latham's representation was based upon repeated elements such as spheres and tori, used to form 'horns' and 'ribs' out of which images are constructed (Todd and Latham, 1992). Colour and texture can also be incorporated into these representations (Dawkins, 1989; Sims, 1991; Todd and Latham, 1992).

Perhaps surprisingly, many of the representations are evolved with fixed structures (e.g. Todd and Latham (1992) hand-designed the structures of forms, then evolved the detail within these structures). Allowing evolution to vary structures (e.g. change the number of rules or primitive shapes), as is done in creative evolutionary design, could possibly increase the creativity of such systems.

Returning once again to the 'table' example, fig. 1.25 (left) shows the type of primitive shapes an evolutionary art system might use to represent forms. Figure 1.25 (right) shows an 'artistic table' generated from such shapes. As this example shows, it is quite common for the artist to employ a shape description language to specify the fixed structure of the designs to be evolved. In the example, each 'artistic table' must be constructed from an ellipse and a variable number of differently positioned and rotated swirls. This structure then defines how many genes will be evolved by the system, and how the values of the genes will be used to generate the phenotypes, i.e. the shape description language defines the genome and embryogeny for evolutionary art systems. By evolving the values of the genes, a number of unusual and hopefully aesthetically pleasing designs (some of which may behave as tables) will emerge.

Evolutionary art is an effective way of creating highly original and unusual pieces of art, but it is rarely used to generate anything as practical as a table. Since forms are not analysed

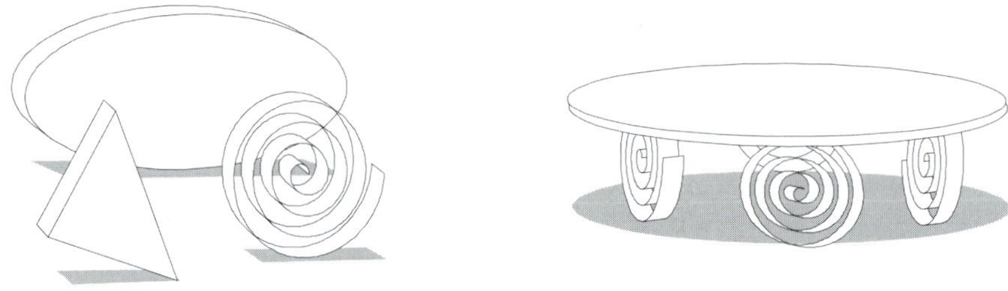

Phenotype:

Ellipse, *width 80, height 50, depth 4, rotated by 90 degrees*
Spiral, *radius 40, curliness 4, depth 6, shifted horizontally by 50, vertically by -20*
Spiral, *radius 40, curliness 4, depth 6, shifted horizontally by 50, vertically by -20, rotated 90 degrees*
Spiral, *radius 40, curliness 4, depth 6, shifted horizontally by 50, vertically by -20, rotated 180 degrees*
Spiral, *radius 40, curliness 4, depth 6, shifted horizontally by 50, vertically by -20, rotated 270 degrees*

Fixed structure (embryogeny) using Shape Description Language:

Table = { Ellipse (*width, height, depth*)
YZ_Rotate (*angle*) }
{ Leg
X_Shift (*distance*)
Y_Shift (*distance*)
Rotate & Duplicate (*angle, #duplicates*) }
Leg = Spiral (*radius, curliness, depth*)

Genotype:

80	50	4	90	40	4	6	50	-20	90	4
width	*height*	*depth*	*angle*	*radius*	*curliness*	*depth*	*distance*	*distance*	*angle*	*#duplicates*

Figure 1.25 Evolving 'artistic tables'.

for their functionality (although users may be able to choose forms which appear more functionally valid than others), the output from evolutionary art systems is usually attractive, but non-functional.

One undesired side-effect of many of these representations is that they generate pieces of art which have very distinct styles. Often the style of form generated using a particular representation is more identifiable than the style of the artist used to guide the evolution. This can cause problems if the artist wishes to take the credit for the piece. The cause of this 'style problem' is perhaps due to the initial preconceptions and assumptions of the designer of the representation. By limiting the computer to a specific type of structure, or a specific set of primitive shapes and constructive rules, it will inevitably always generate forms with many common and identifiable elements.

Because evolution is guided by a human selector (i.e. the 'fitness function' is an artist), the evolutionary algorithm does not have to be complex. Evolution is used more as a continuous novelty generator, not as an optimiser. The artist is likely to score designs highly inconsistently as he/she changes his/her mind about desirable features during evolution, so the *continuous* generation of new forms based on the fittest from the previous generation is essential. Consequently, an important element of the EAs used is *non-convergence*. If the populations of forms were ever to loose diversity and converge onto a single shape, the artist would be unable to explore any further forms. Because of this, most evolutionary art systems do not employ crossover within their EAs. Typically only mutation is used, with all offspring being mutated copies of their parents (and often only a single parent is used per generation). This mutation-driven evolution is similar to the approach used in EP and ES, which are known to be excellent for finding solutions to problems with continuously changing fitness functions (Bäck, 1996).

Examples of such systems include Dawkins' biomorphs program (included on the CD-ROM) (Dawkins 1986, 1989), Todd and Latham's evolutionary art (described in Chapter 9), Rowbottom's Evolutionary Art (described in Chapter 11, and shown in fig. 1.26) and Sims' evolved computer graphics (Sims, 1991). Today, numerous evolutionary art systems are available on-line (see Chapter 11).

Evolutionary Artificial Life-forms

Evolutionary computation plays a significant role in many aspects of the new field of computer science known as artificial life (AL). Artificial 'brains', behaviour strategies, methods of communication, distributed problem solving and many other topics are commonly explored using genetic algorithms and other evolutionary search techniques (Cliff et al., 1994).

Although all types of evolved AL could be described as aspects of evolutionary design, it is clear that certain topics within AL fall into the 'evolutionary design' category more comfortably than others. For the purposes of this book, AL research that can be readily categorised as an aspect of evolutionary design will be defined as research which aims to evolve 'artificial life-forms'. Examples of evolutionary AL-forms include: Lohn's cellular automata (CA) evolved to be capable of self-replication (Lohn and Reggia, 1995), Harvey's evolved layout and structure of neurons (Harvey, 1997), and the evolved plant-like and animal-like morphologies of Dawkins (1986, 1989) and Sims (1994a,b)

Motivations for the creation of evolutionary AL-forms are usually theoretical. The goals of such research are often to discover more about the mechanisms of natural evolution, to find

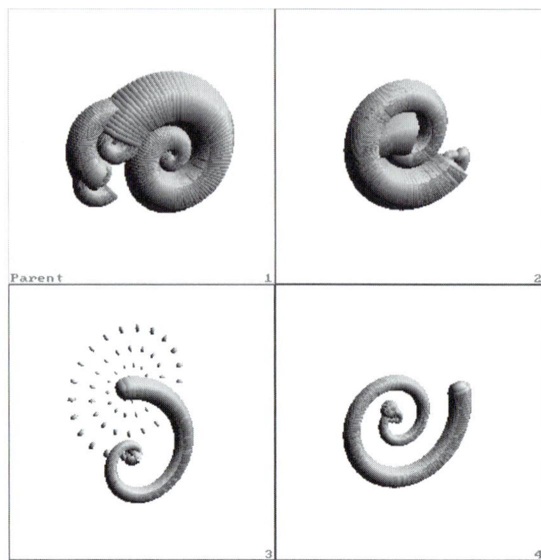

Figure 1.26 Rowbottom's evolutionary art.

explanations of forms observed in nature, or to exploit the solutions proven in nature by attempting to duplicate them. Often the evolved AL-forms show the enormous potentials of this type of evolutionary design, but as yet, practical applications are still scarce.

To illustrate this type of evolutionary design, we return to the 'table' example one final time. However, instead of a static table, we now require a robot/virtual creature/animat capable of carrying objects around – a robot waiter, perhaps. Figure 1.27 shows the dual nature of these designs: evolutionary AL-forms typically involve the evolution of the form (or some aspect of the form) and the brain. In this example, the form, or 'body' is defined by a collection of variable-sized blocks (which may be 'sensors', 'body' or 'muscles'). The 'brain' is defined by a network of neurons which receive input from 'sensory blocks' and produce output to the 'muscle blocks'. Each part of the phenotype is encoded as a variable-length chromosome in the genotype. The fitness function judges phenotypes on their ability to move whilst keeping the flat upper surface level. Over time, evolution will co-evolve both chromosomes in individuals to generate a virtual creature capable of supporting objects and movement in a virtual world.

Figure 1.27 shows just one example of how such animats can be represented. In reality, representations are typically specific to each system. For example, Lohn and Reggia (1995) use CA 'rule tables' within the chromosomes of their GA. Sims (1994a,b) uses a hierarchical chromosome structure to define both 'brain' and 'body'. Ventrella (1994) combines ordered morphology and control parameters of his animats in a flat chromosome structure, as does Harvey et al. (1993) for his evolved robots. Many of these representations are inspired by the genotype structure of natural organisms, and some researchers have attempted to evolve AL-forms with complex embryogenies. Other researchers invent their own intricate coding schemes (Cliff et al., 1994). Most such representations are highly flexible and of variable length, requiring complex genetic operators with the EAs.

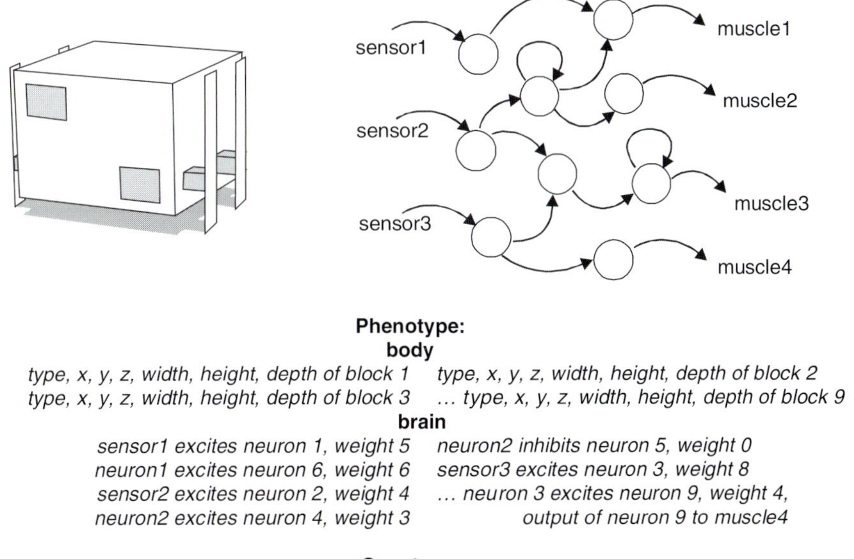

Genotype:
Chromosome 1

11	11010110	10101101	10101110	10011010	01101010	01101010	...	10001010	10001010	10001010
type1	*xpos 1*	*ypos 1*	*zpos 1*	*width 1*	*height 1*	*depth 1*	...	*width 9*	*height 9*	*depth 9*

Chromosome 2

0000	10	1001	1	0110	1	...	1110
neuron1 marker	*neuron1 type (in/intl/out)*	*neuron1 link1*	*neuron1 link1 type (ex/inhib)*	*neuron1 link2*	*neuron1 link1 type (ex/inhib)*	...	*neuron9 link2*

Figure 1.27 Evolutionary artificial life form.

Because research in this field is still very much at the 'blue-sky' stage, evolutionary techniques are often used as exploration tools, in a similar way to evolutionary art. These algorithms can be used to generate multiple solutions, incorporating niching, speciation, parasitism, competition, co-operation and other advanced methods (Cliff et al., 1994). Evaluation usually consists of analysing behaviour in simulated virtual worlds (although some researchers do test solutions using real robots (Harvey, 1997)), and can be very time-consuming. To try to shorten evolution run-times, advanced methods are commonly used, e.g. steady-state GAs, parallel GAs, hybrid GAs (Cliff et al., 1994). Many systems that evolve AL-forms also use changing fitness functions, which necessitate the use of other specialised genetic search techniques (Harvey, 1997). Most systems evolve the forms from scratch (the initial population is random), however some occasionally seed initial populations with the fittest individuals from previous runs (Sims, 1994b). Figure 1.28 shows perhaps the most notable work in this field: Sims' evolved virtual creatures (see Chapter 13 for full details).

1.4.2 Combining Good Ideas by Merging the Boundaries

Many researchers confine themselves to one of the four aspects of evolutionary design mentioned above, and seem loath to consider alternative approaches. However, more recently, some have begun to combine ideas from one or more of these areas in their work. This is

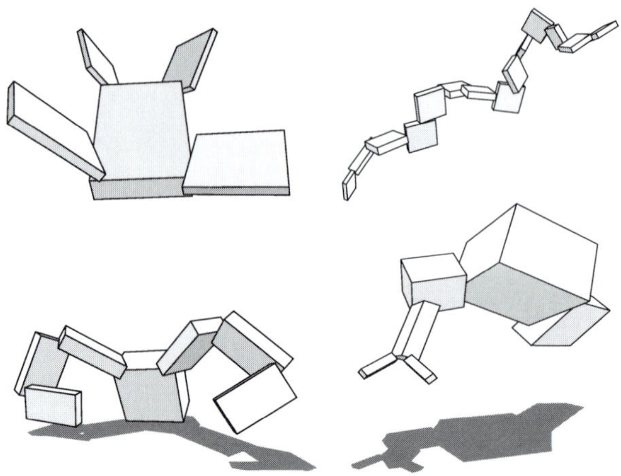

Figure 1.28 Sims' evolved artificial life forms.

leading to four more (still very new and relatively unexplored) 'overlapping' areas of research in evolutionary design (see fig. 1.19).

Integral Evolutionary Design

The evolution of engineering designs is becoming widespread today, with numerous academic engineering design centres exploring these ideas. Although most research seems to fall into either the evolutionary optimisation category, or the creative evolutionary design category, some work does attempt to combine the two into unified, or *integral* evolutionary design systems.

For example, Parmee suggests that computers can be used within the entire design process, both the early conceptual design stages and the later, detailed design stages, by using a number of adaptive techniques. He discusses how the use of several different systems, each dedicated to a specific stage of design could be used in combination, thus 'integrating adaptive search at every stage of the design process' (Parmee, 1996a). Ian Parmee gives more details of these ideas in Chapter 5.

Alternatively, Chapter 18 describes the investigation of the use of a single generic evolutionary design system, to perform the complete design process without making any distinction between the stages of design. (It is 'generic' because it is capable of evolving designs for multiple different design tasks.) This work has shown that it is possible to use a computer to evolve new designs from scratch, and optimise them, such that they fulfil specific functional criteria (Bentley and Wakefield, 1996b, 1997a,b).

With many optimisation systems beginning to be applied to more and more detailed parameterisations of designs, and many creative design systems beginning to be used to optimise the designs they generate, the field of integral evolutionary design looks set to grow rapidly.

Artificial Life-based Evolutionary Design

Work in artificial life has generated forms of astonishing diversity and creativity, so some researchers are now using some of the techniques from AL in their creative evolutionary design systems, in an attempt to improve the quality and originality of evolved engineering designs. For example, Parmee (1996b) borrows distributed agent methods from AL to increase performance of search, in his 'ant colony' method, which he combines with evolutionary search. Coates (1997) employs L-systems with GP to evolve new architectural forms (described in Chapter 14).

Many other unexplored possibilities still exist in this area. For example, Bonabeau et al. (1994) describes an AL computer simulation of a swarm of artificial wasps, which build intricate three-dimensional nest architectures. One future avenue of research may be to evolve artificial wasps capable of building new engineering designs between them.

Aesthetic Evolutionary Artificial Life

The evolution of aesthetically pleasing AL was perhaps first performed by Dawkins (1986), who hand-selected his artificial 'biomorphs' for reproduction in exactly the way artists select their forms using evolutionary art systems. Ventrella (1994) has taken this one step further, and has evolved aesthetically pleasing animats which resemble animated stick-men. These are evolved for their ability to walk naturally in a virtual world, and evolution is also guided by the aesthetic judgement of the user. Alternatively, Lund et al. (1995) and Tabuada et al. (1998) describe neural networks which judge the aesthetics of evolving images.

Although to date there have been few applications to benefit from this area of research, the use of computers to evolve amusing or attractive animated characters may well be lucrative in the computer games industry, or for television advertisements.

Aesthetic Evolutionary Design

The evolution of aesthetic designs is an area of research with obvious importance, which should perhaps receive more attention than it does. Few designs are purely functional, most are chosen partly because of their aesthetics, and some functionally outstanding designs are discarded purely because of their ugly appearance. Furuta et al. (1995) describes an approach in which bridge designs can be optimised using GAs, based on their appearance, using 'psychovectors' to quantify the aesthetic factors of the structures. Frazer (1995) describes his substantial and pioneering research on the evolution of architectural forms, using a combination of formal analysis and aesthetic guidance from designers. Husbands et al. (1996) describes the evolution of 3D solid objects resembling propellers, using a superquadric shape-description language and guided by 'the eye of the beholder'.

1.4.3 Recommended Reading for Evolutionary Design

Advances in Design Optimization
by Hojjat Adeli (Ed) (1994).

Genetic Algorithms and Engineering Design
by Mitsuo Gen and Runwei Cheng (1997).

Artificial Intelligence in Design '94, '96 & '98
by John Gero and Fay Sudweeks (Eds) (1994, 1996, 1998).

Modeling Creativity and Knowledge-Based Creative Design
by John Gero and Mary Lou Maher (Eds) (1993).

An Evolutionary Architecture
by John Frazer (1995).

The Creative Mind: Myths & Mechanisms
by Margaret Boden (1992).

Evolutionary Art and Computers
by Stephen Todd and William Latham (1992).

The Blind Watchmaker
by Richard Dawkins (1986).

Climbing Mount Improbable
by Richard Dawkins (1996).

Artificial Life: an Overview
by Chris Langton (Ed) (1995).

Artificial Life: Grammatical Models
by Gheorghe Paun (Ed) (1995).

Modern Heuristic Search Methods
by Victor Rayward-Smith et al. (Eds) (1996).

Soft Computing in Engineering Design and Manufacturing
by P. K. Chawdhry, R. Roy and R. K. Pant (Eds) (1997).

Advances in Soft Computing – Engineering Design and Manufacturing
by R. Roy, T. Furuhashi and P. K. Chawdhry (Eds) (1998).

1.4.4 From Perusals to Problem Solving

In summary, this middle section of the chapter has described how computers are used to perform evolutionary design. The four main aspects: *evolutionary design optimisation*, *creative evolutionary design*, *evolutionary art*, and *evolutionary artificial life forms*, were surveyed in detail. In addition, the four 'overlapping' types of evolutionary design: *integral evolutionary design*, *aesthetic evolutionary design*, *artificial life-based evolutionary design*, and *aesthetic evolutionary AL* were introduced.

Having now explained both evolutionary computation and evolutionary design by computers, the final major section of this chapter discusses some of the significant technical issues faced by developers of evolutionary design systems.

1.5 Enumerations, Embryogenies and other Problems

There are a number of common problems encountered when attempting to perform evolutionary design using computers. As is usual when applying the techniques of evolutionary computation to anything, there are issues related to the fitness functions, such as noisy functions, discontinuous functions, and multimodal functions (Bentley and Wakefield, 1996c; Parmee, 1996a). Ian Parmee discusses some of these in Chapter 5. There are, however, some more specific problems that typically arise more often with evolutionary design (Roston, 1997).

1.5.1 Enumerating the Search Space

Before an evolutionary algorithm can be applied to a problem, a suitable genotype and phenotype representation must be created. The genotype representation enumerates the search space of the problem, i.e. it defines which genotypes should be next to each other in the search space. The phenotype representation enumerates the solution space, i.e. it defines which phenotypes should be next to each other in the solution space. Both spaces must be carefully designed to ensure that the task of finding good solutions is not made any harder than it needs to be. The key thing to remember when developing these representations is that two genotypes which are *close* to each other in the search space should map onto two solutions which are *similar* to each other in the solution space. In other words, *a small change in the genotype should produce a small change in the phenotype*. (If the EA makes no distinction between genotypes and phenotypes, this equates to: *a small change in the value of any decision variable should produce a small change in the design*.)

To illustrate this concept, consider the problem of evolving a two-dimensional rectangle of specific size. Figures 1.29 and 1.30 show two ways in which the genotypes and corresponding phenotypes can be represented for this problem. In fig. 1.29, the genotype representation defines the path of a turtle using the three instructions: 'forwards' (F), turn right 'R', and 'turn left' (L). The rectangle phenotype is defined by the starting and ending positions of the turtle. It should be clear from the example that this is a very poor genotype representation – a small change in the genotype will often cause a big change in the phenotype. Alternatively, fig. 1.30 shows a genotype representation which defines the corners of a rectangle using angle and length parameters. This representation is far more conducive to search – a small change in the genotype will usually produce a small change in the phenotype.

The first genotype representation is worse than the second because its enumeration of the search space is very discontinuous: genotypes that map onto very dissimilar phenotypes are

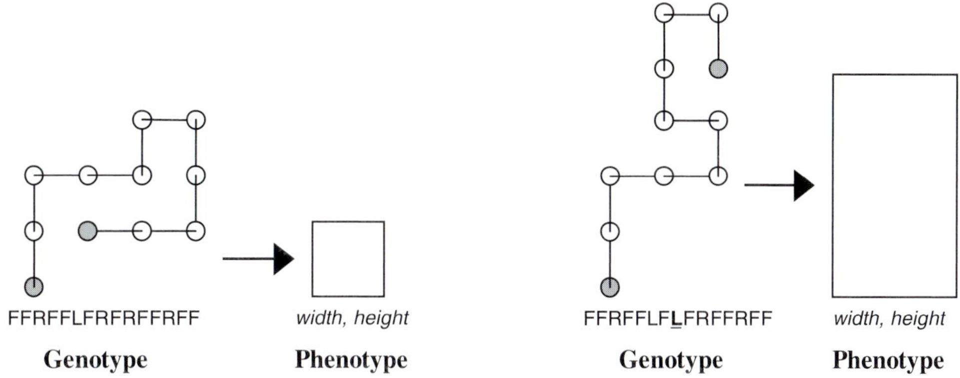

Figure 1.29 Representing rectangles using the start and end points of a turtle trail. Note how the smallest possible change in the genotype causes a very large change to the phenotype.

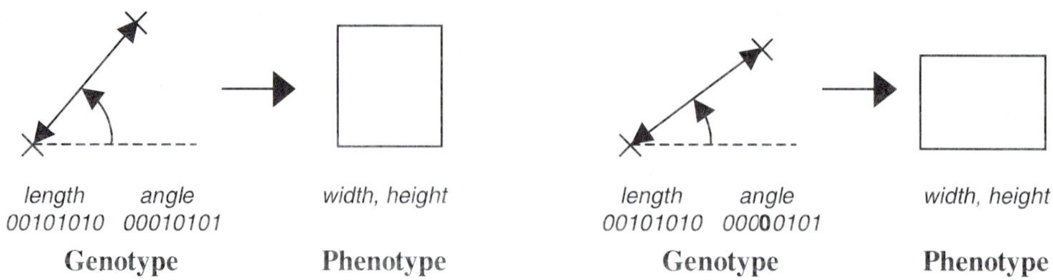

Figure 1.30 Representing rectangles using length and angle parameters. Note how a small change in the genotype causes a small change to the phenotype.

placed next to each other in the search space. Evolution relies on inheritance with a small degree of variation to ensure that most offspring resemble their parents and thus have similar fitnesses to their parents. If the search space is too discontinuous, then every application of crossover or mutation will generate offspring which hardly resemble their parents at all. This reduces the effectiveness of traversing from parent solution to child in the search space, and the search deteriorates into random exploration. As mentioned earlier in the chapter, this effect is caused by the genetic operators disrupting the parent solutions too much. It should now be clear that the level of disruption is often determined by the representations employed in the EA (a poor representation will be disrupted by all standard operators – and may require the creation of specially designed 'non-disruptive' operators).

Poorly designed representations are most problematical towards the end of an evolutionary run. As the population converges onto a small area of the search space, fine-tuning these solutions becomes nearly impossible if every minor change in the genotype causes a major change in the phenotype. Consequently, to ensure the successful evolution of good designs, all representations should be created with care.

Often, the hardest type of representation to design is a genotype representation which incorporates some form of *embryogeny* to 'grow' phenotypes from the genotypes. Such representations often use chains of rules which are epistatically linked – removing or altering one rule can radically alter the action of many others, resulting in major phenotypic changes.

1.5.2 Designing Embryogenies

As mentioned earlier, an embryogeny is an advanced form of mapping, from genotypes to phenotypes. Embryogenies have a number of advanced features:

- **Compression**. Because of their ability to allow simple genotypes to define complex phenotypes, many of these mappings resemble compression techniques, with genes performing more than one function during the development of the phenotype.
- **Repetition**. Properly designed embryogenies can improve the ability of evolution to generate solutions with repeating structures such as symmetry, segmentation, and subroutines.
- **Adaptation**. This is one of the most significant features of the use of embryogenies. It is possible to 'grow' phenotypes from genotypes adaptively, allowing constraints to be satisfied (Yu and Bentley, 1998), improvement to variable conditions, and correction of

malfunctions in designs (Sipper, 1997). Such adaptation seems likely to play significant roles in future applications of evolutionary design. For example, if the problem was to evolve a building which had good access to fire exits, various simulations modelling 'virtual people' trying to escape fires could be performed during the 'growth' of each building, thus ensuring that the final design was developed to maximise access (and satisfy the constraint).

Unfortunately, embryogenies can suffer from some drawbacks:

- **Hard to design**. All types of embryogeny require careful design, and to date, only those few researchers capable of performing this difficult art have demonstrated successful results.
- **Hard to evolve**. Many embryogenies introduce problems for evolutionary algorithms. Bloat, epistasis and excessive disruption of child solutions is common, resulting in the need for carefully designed genetic operators.

In nature, embryogenies are defined by the interactions between genes, their phenotypic effects and the environment in which the embryo develops. In evolutionary design by computers, we can define embryogenies in three main ways: *externally*, *explicitly*, and *implicitly*.

External (non-evolved) Embryogenies

Embryogenies are, in a very real sense, complex designs in their own right. Most embryogenies are hand-designed and are defined globally and externally to genotypes. For example, evolutionary optimisation systems usually use very simple, fixed, non-evolveable mapping procedures to specify how the genes in the genotype are mapped to the parameters in the phenotype. Evolutionary art systems often use more complex embryogenies defined by fixed, non-evolveable structures which specify how phenotypes should be constructed using the genes in the genotypes (see section 1.4.1, and Chapter 9). The advantage with such external embryogenies is that the user retains more control of the final evolved forms, and can potentially improve the quality of evolved designs by careful embryogeny design. In addition, this type of embryogeny produces the fewest harmful effects for evolution, and requires no specialised genetic operators. The disadvantage of this approach is that these embryogenies are not evolved, so they remain static and unchanging during the evolution of genotypes. This does not necessarily imply that the evolved designs will be any less fit, but it does mean that the designer of the embryogeny must take care to ensure that this complex mapping process will always perform the desired function. Figure 1.31 provides a simple example of an external embryogeny.

Explicit (evolved) Embryogenies

If each step of an embryogeny is explicitly specified in a data structure, the embryogeny resembles a computer program. Designs are 'grown' by following the instructions in this program, and these instructions may contain conditional statements, iteration, and even subroutines.

Although it is possible to hand-design such 'programs', genetic programming allows us to evolve them. Typically, the genotype and embryogeny are combined, allowing the evolution of both simultaneously. Clearly, this approach avoids the need to hand-design embryogenies, and

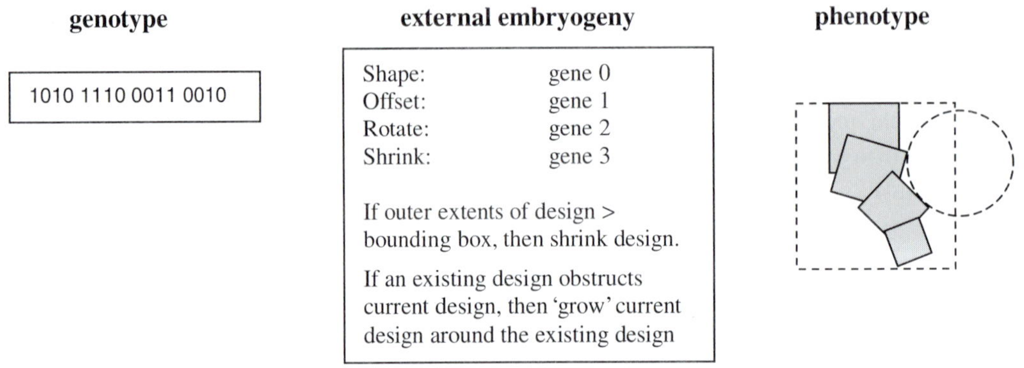

genotype | **external embryogeny** | **phenotype**

1010 1110 0011 0010

Shape: gene 0
Offset: gene 1
Rotate: gene 2
Shrink: gene 3

If outer extents of design > bounding box, then shrink design.

If an existing design obstructs current design, then 'grow' current design around the existing design

Figure 1.31 An example of an external embryogeny. Note how the embryogeny is adaptive, ensuring that the phenotype fits within a bounding box, and forcing the phenotype to 'grow' around a circular obstacle.

allows the emergence of adaptive mapping from genotype to phenotype (i.e., different initial conditions acting on conditional statements could trigger the growth of different phenotypes). There are some disadvantages, however. The creation of suitable representations can be difficult. Successfully evolving such representations can also be difficult (often specialised genetic operators are required to ensure disruption is minimised (Koza et al., 1998)). In addition, because the complete embryogeny process must be defined explicitly, advanced features such as iteration, subroutines and recursion must be manually added to the GP system – they cannot emerge spontaneously (see below).

Figure 1.32 gives a simple example of an explicit embryogeny. For a more detailed example of the use of explicit embryogenies, readers should consult Chapter 16, which summarises the use of David Andre's cellular encoding embryogeny to evolve analogue circuits using GP.

Implicit (evolved) Embryogenies

Natural evolution does not use externally defined embryogenies, nor does it explicitly represent embryogenies in our genes. Instead, natural evolution uses highly indirect chains of interacting 'rules' to generate complex embryogenies, which result in the development of living creatures. The flow of activation is not completely predetermined and preprogrammed, it is dynamic, parallel and adaptive.

To summarise in very simple terms, natural embryogenies use chemicals surrounding each cell to activate or suppress genes within the chromosomes of the cell, triggering patterns of cellular growth. Cellular death, differentiation, and the production of chemicals is also triggered by genes. Living creatures are grown in wombs or eggs with chemicals carefully placed to guide the early development of the embryo. As embryos develop, complex chains of gene activation occur, cells grow and die to form the appropriate shapes, and cells are differentiated to perform specialised functions. Even the movement of the developing muscles of the embryo affects the development and placement of cells.

Few researchers have explored the use of implicit embryogenies for evolutionary design, and yet the potential advantages of this approach are significant. Because of the way in which

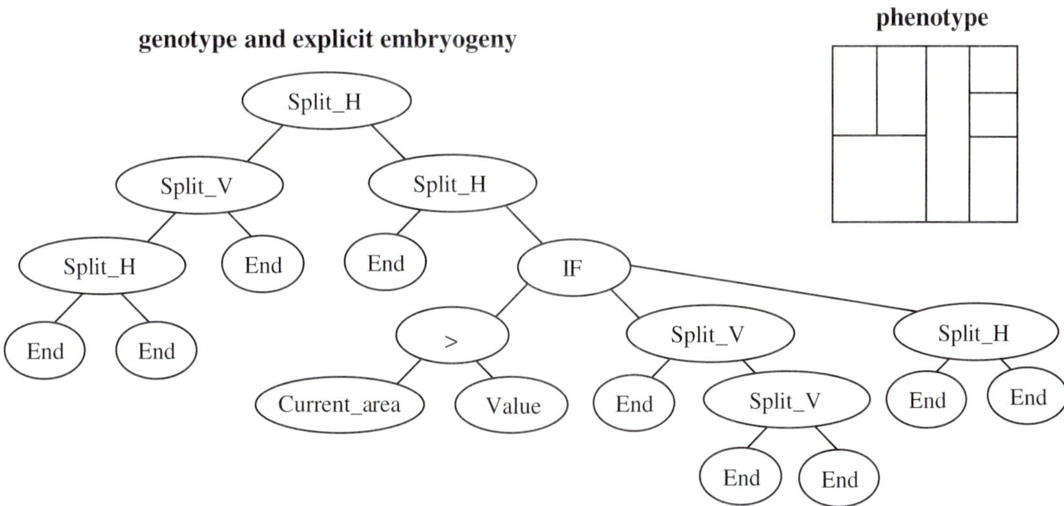

Figure 1.32 An example of an explicit embryogeny, incorporated into the genotype. Note how the embryogeny is adaptive, varying the phenotype depending on 'Value'. Also note that the same evolved embryogeny will generate different phenotypes if provided with a different initial starting shape.

genes can be activated and suppressed many times during the development of phenotypes, because the same genes can be used to specify multiple functions, and because of the inherent parallelism of gene activation, such implicit embryogenies go far beyond today's genetic programming. Through emergence during evolution, these implicit embryogenies incorporate all concepts of conditional iteration, subroutines, and parallel processing which must be manually introduced into explicit GP embryogenies. There is a serious disadvantage with the use of implicit embryogenies, however. Currently, the design of suitable genetic representations is proving prohibitively difficult, with very few useful designs having been evolved using this approach. Figure 1.33 shows a simple example of an implicit embryogeny. For some more detailed examples, readers should consult Chapter 12 by Hugo de Garis.

From Embryogeny to Ontogeny

Embryogeny defines the growth of a phenotype from zygote to new-born baby. Ontogeny defines the growth (as specified by its genes) throughout the life of the phenotype. In nature, our genes continue to affect our bodies and behaviour throughout our lives, defining when we become sexually mature, how we grow, which diseases we will be immune to, and even affecting aspects of our personalities and behaviour tendencies. To date there has been little research performed on evolving and growing adult designs from child designs (basing fitness on the life-time functionality of the design). Yet it is clear that our designs do often go through such growth and change. For example a mature 'adult' building can be very different from the 'child' building designed by an architect, as walls and facades are added and removed, roofs replaced, extensions added. If approximations of such phenotype growth were also incorporated into the genetic description (as an ontogeny) it might be possible to evolve designs

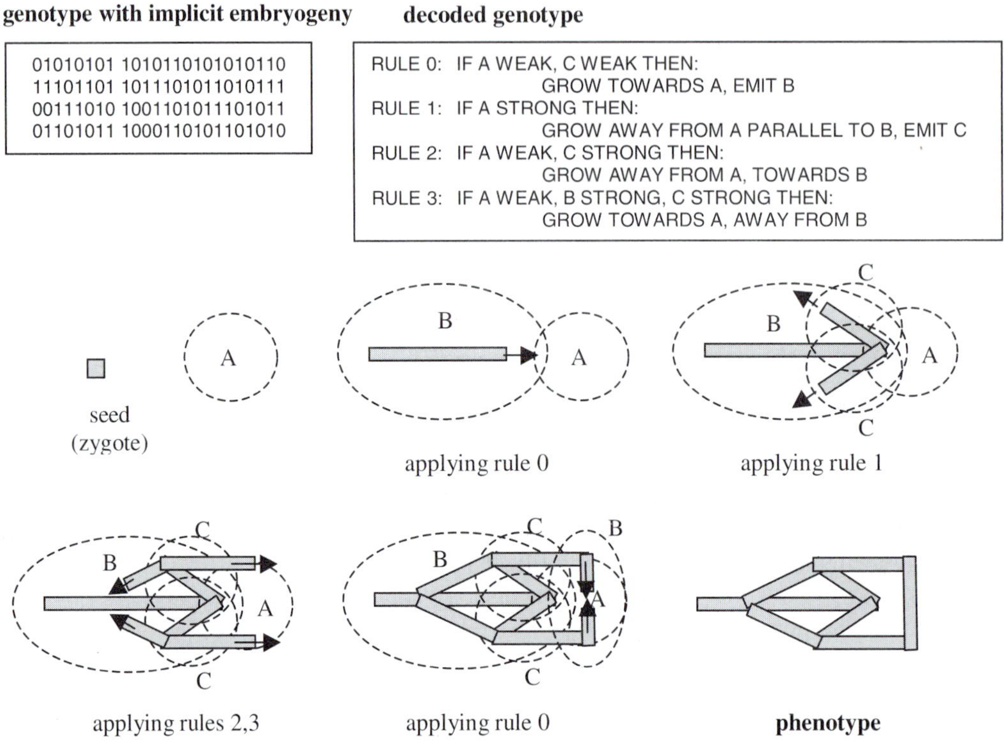

genotype with implicit embryogeny

```
01010101 1010110101010110
11101101 1011101011010111
00111010 1001101011101011
01101011 1000110101101010
```

decoded genotype

```
RULE 0:  IF A WEAK, C WEAK THEN:
                    GROW TOWARDS A, EMIT B
RULE 1:  IF A STRONG THEN:
                    GROW AWAY FROM A PARALLEL TO B, EMIT C
RULE 2:  IF A WEAK, C STRONG THEN:
                    GROW AWAY FROM A, TOWARDS B
RULE 3:  IF A WEAK, B STRONG, C STRONG THEN:
                    GROW TOWARDS A, AWAY FROM B
```

seed (zygote)

applying rule 0

applying rule 1

applying rules 2,3

applying rule 0

phenotype

Figure 1.33 An example of an implicit embryogeny in a genotype. The decoded genotype provides an English description of the rules defined by the genes. Various components of the phenotype are grown towards and away from the chemicals A, B and C, by switching on and off rules. Note the reuse of rule 0.

which remain useful for many years, instead of simply evolving designs which satisfy certain criteria at 'birth'.

Our genes also control aspects of our bodies' repair mechanisms: continuously defining where cells should grow, and what type of cells they should be, to replace dying cells. By evolving designs which have self-repair mechanisms defined in their genes, the possibility of designs that can automatically correct faults within themselves becomes conceivable. Moshe Sipper (1997) is leading research in this area, by attempting to evolve electronic hardware capable of surviving 'injury'.

1.5.3 Epistasis

Epistasis means the 'degree of dependency' between multiple genes in a chromosome. Significantly, epistasis is all about *genes* acting in combination to produce *solutions*. Consequently, epistasis is defined by the genotype (and embryogeny) representation, and not by the fitness function.[7] A genetic representation with high epistasis may have many genes whose

[7] Epistasis causes confusion in the GP community, as practitioners of GP make no distinction between genotypes and phenotypes, so the epistatic properties of conditional statements in the evolved programs only

phenotypic effect relies to a large degree on the alleles of other genes. For example, a single shape-rule in a rule-based representation may have very different phenotypic effects, depending on which other shape-rules precede and succeed it. Conversely, a representation with low epistasis has few or no genes whose phenotypic effect relies on the alleles of other genes. For example, a simple voxel representation in which every gene switches on or off a single voxel in a grid has zero epistasis.

Experiments investigating whether epistasis should be high or low have so far been inconclusive (Schoenauer, 1996). However, a simple thought experiment can help explain this dilemma. Consider a (fictional) representation which uses, say, ten genes to represent the entire form of designs, and the phenotypic effect of every gene is *completely dependent* on all of the other genes through some embryogeny process. With this (maximum) amount of epistasis, these ten genes effectively become elements of a single overall gene. So our ten-gene representation with complete epistasis could be considered as a single-gene representation. Consider what effect varying any part of that gene would have on the phenotype. With every part of the design epistatically linked to every other part, any attempt to improve just one small area would result in changes to all of the rest of the design (*pleiotropy*) – making evolution to acceptable designs very difficult, if not impossible.

Alternatively, consider a representation with zero epistasis (e.g. a voxel representation using a 3D array). This requires no embryogeny, since every gene maps directly onto a specific area of the phenotype, and only that area of the phenotype. It should be clear that such a representation is well suited for evolution of small-scale detail, but evolution of large-scale characteristics becomes immensely difficult, e.g. the scaling of the entire form in one dimension, or the duplication or mirroring of an existing feature in the design. (To duplicate or mirror an existing feature in the way segmentation or symmetry does, each new duplicate part would have to be re-evolved in entirety – highly unlikely to occur (Bentley and Wakefield, 1996b).

Having examined the two extreme cases, it should be clear that both too much epistasis and too little epistasis in a representation is undesirable. Perhaps the ideal representation for evolutionary design should have a 'middling' amount of epistasis. However, it seems likely that the best tutor on this subject will be natural evolution, which seems to use varying degrees of epistasis in a single living creature, with recombination of DNA carefully controlled to avoid disruption, and the harmful effects of pleiotropy minimised (Altenberg, 1995).

1.5.4 Incorporating Knowledge in Evolutionary Design

Experience, insight and judgement make a good designer. Evolutionary design often relies only on the last of these attributes, for evolutionary algorithms are usually guided solely by the fitness function. In other words, design knowledge is provided in terms of an objective which must be met. As described in the previous section, this can be a significant strength of evolutionary design, allowing the generation of creative designs, art and artificial life by the

---

seem to appear during the evaluation of those programs. The confusion can be avoided if the hierarchical program structure is considered to be the genotype, and the *result of the action of the program as it runs* is considered to be the phenotype. This corresponds nicely with nature: we are the result of the action of our DNA – a continuously running program which builds and repairs us throughout our lives.

computer. However, the use of a single fitness function to guide the evolution of designs does prevent the computer from benefiting from the substantial knowledge of designers.

It is possible to add further knowledge to EAs by using more than one fitness function. In this way, multiple design objectives can be specified, including partially or fully contradictory objectives. These fitness functions need not define desired functionality – they can be used to compare evolving designs with a database of different good designs, allowing evolution to be guided by the case-based knowledge contained within each example design. Additional knowledge can also be used to constrain evolution, and prevent it from generating designs which are known to be unsatisfactory. (Handling multiple objectives and constraints in EAs is discussed later in this section.) There are also two other ways to provide additional knowledge to an evolutionary design system:

Knowledge-rich Representations

As described in the previous section, evolutionary optimisation uses EAs to optimise parameterised portions of existing designs. In other words, within the phenotype representation, the EA is provided with knowledge of the general form or structure of a rough design, which it then fine-tunes using the judgement provided by the fitness function. This is one way to incorporate knowledge into the representation of an EA. Another method is to provide a series of building blocks from which designs can be constructed. Conceptual evolutionary design uses this approach, allowing designers to use EAs to 'juggle' with their knowledge and find new ways of using it in combination. Alternatively, as John Gero illustrates in the first part of Chapter 15, it is possible to use evolution to *learn* representations which incorporate knowledge in the form of architectural styles, and then evolve new designs using such knowledge-rich representations.

Knowledge Seeding

Evolutionary algorithms are often initialised with random values, but this is not a prerequisite to evolutionary design. A common practice by some researchers is to seed the initial population with non-random values, i.e. give the EA some examples of good designs to work from. The advantage of this case-based design approach is the simplicity of introducing knowledge into the system. Unfortunately, the disadvantages are two-fold: firstly a pair of very fit, but very different parent designs provided by a designer may well generate nothing but unfit malformations because of the large differences in their structures. Secondly, if one example design is substantially fitter than the others provided by the designer, evolution will quickly seize upon it, and base almost all future generations on that single design – disregarding the knowledge contained within the other, less fit designs. Nevertheless, when performed with care, seeding populations with designs (whether they are designed by human or previously evolved) can provide a boost to the quality of designs evolved by computers (Bentley and Wakefield, 1997a).

1.5.5 Multiple Objectives

A substantial proportion of evolutionary design problems involve the evolution of solutions to problems with more than one criterion. More specifically, such problems consist of several separate objectives, with the required solution being one where some or all of these objectives are satisfied to a greater or lesser degree. Perhaps surprisingly then, despite the large numbers of these multiobjective applications being tackled using EAs, only a small proportion of the literature explores exactly how they should be treated with EAs.

With single objective problems, the evolutionary algorithm stores a single fitness value for every solution in the current population of solutions. This value denotes how well its corresponding solution satisfies the objective of the problem. By allocating the fitter members of the population a higher chance of producing more offspring than the less fit members, the EA can create the next generation of (hopefully better) solutions. However, with multiobjective problems, every solution has a number of fitness values, one for each objective. This presents a problem in judging the overall fitness of the solutions. For example, one solution could have excellent fitness values for some objectives and poor values for other objectives, whilst another solution could have average fitness values for all of the objectives. The question arises: which of the two solutions is the fittest? This is a major problem, for if there is no clear way to compare the quality of different solutions, then there can be no clear way for the EA to allocate more offspring to the fitter solutions.

The approach most users of EAs favour to the problem of ranking such populations, is to weight and sum the separate fitness values in order to produce just a single fitness value for every solution, thus allowing the EA to determine which solutions are fittest as usual. However, as noted by Goldberg: '. . . there are times when several criteria are present simultaneously and it is not possible (or wise) to combine these into a single number'. (Goldberg, 1989). For example, the separate objectives may be difficult or impossible to manually weight because of unknowns in the problem. Additionally, weighting and summing could have a detrimental effect upon the evolution of acceptable solutions by the EA (just a single incorrect weight can cause convergence to an unacceptable solution). Moreover, some argue that to combine separate fitnesses in this way is akin to comparing completely different criteria; the question of whether a good apple is better than a good orange is meaningless.

The concept of Pareto optimality helps to overcome this problem of comparing solutions with multiple fitness values. A solution is Pareto optimal (i.e., Pareto minimal, in the Pareto optimal range, or on the Pareto front) if it is *not dominated* by any other solutions. As stated by Goldberg (1989):

> A vector $\mathbf{x}$ is partially less than $\mathbf{y}$, or $\mathbf{x} < p\ \mathbf{y}$ when:
>
> $$(\mathbf{x} <p\ \mathbf{y}) \Leftrightarrow (\forall_i)(\mathbf{x}_i <= \mathbf{y}_i) \wedge (\exists_i)(\mathbf{x}_i < \mathbf{y}_i)$$
>
> $\mathbf{x}$ *dominates* $\mathbf{y}$ iff $\mathbf{x} <p\ \mathbf{y}$.

However, it is quite common for a large number of solutions to a problem to be Pareto optimal (and thus be given equal fitness scores). This may be beneficial should multiple solutions be required, but it can cause problems if a smaller number of solutions (or even just one) is desired.

For example, consider the multiobjective function (to be minimised):

$$\begin{aligned} f_1 &= (x + 50)^2 \\ f_2 &= (x - 50)^2 \qquad \text{where } -64 \leq x \leq 64. \end{aligned}$$

For this twin-objective function, the Pareto minimal solutions range from -50 to 50 – so almost every allowable value of x is Pareto optimal, see fig. 1.34. Although this is an extreme

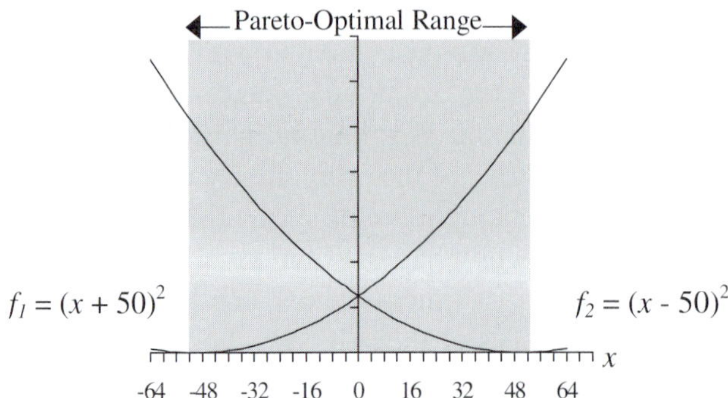

Figure 1.34 The Pareto optimal range of solutions for some multiobjective functions can include almost all allowable solutions to the problem.

case, it does illustrate a fundamental flaw with the concept of Pareto optimality: the Pareto front can be so large that it becomes infeasible to use the non-dominance of solutions as the sole fitness measure for solutions in an EA.

Hence, for many problems, the set of solutions deemed acceptable by a user will be a small subset of the set of Pareto optimal solutions to the problems (Fonseca and Fleming, 1995b). Manually choosing an acceptable solution can be a laborious task, which would be avoided if the EA could be directed by a ranking method to converge only on acceptable solutions (Bentley and Wakefield, 1997c).

So why do multiobjective problems cause such difficulties for EAs? Fundamentally, successful multiobjective optimisation is all about *range-independence*.

Range-Independence

Throughout the evolution by the EA, every separate objective (fitness) function in a multiobjective problem will return values within a particular range. Although this range may be infinite in theory, in practice the range of values will be finite. This 'effective range' of every objective function is determined not only by the function itself, but also by the domain of input values that are produced by the EA during evolution. These values are the parameters to be evolved by the EA and their exact values are normally determined initially by random, and subsequently by evolution. The values are usually limited still further by the coding used, for example 16 bit sign-magnitude binary notation per gene only permits values from −32768 to 32768.

Although occasionally the effective range of all of the objective functions will be the same, in most more complex multiobjective tasks, every separate objective function will have a different effective range (i.e., the function ranges are non-commensurable (Schaffer, 1985)). This means that a bad value for one could be a reasonable or even good value for another, see fig. 1.35. If the results from these two objective functions were simply added to produce a single fitness value for the EA, the function with the largest range would dominate evolution (a poor input value for the objective with the larger range makes the overall value much worse than a poor value for the objective with the smaller range).

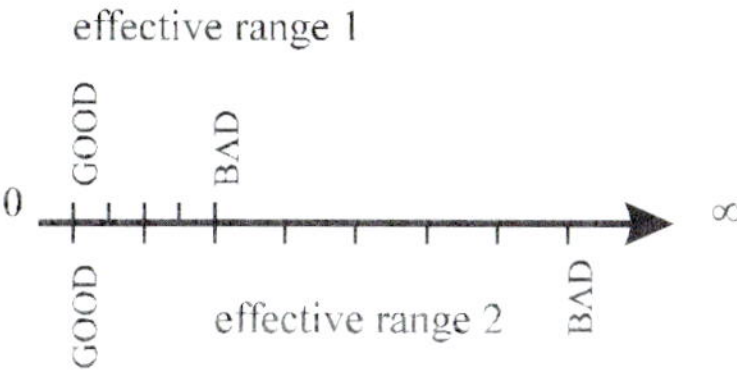

Figure 1.35 Different effective ranges for different objective functions (to be minimised).

For example, consider the two objective functions:

$$f_{11} = x^2$$
$$f_{12} = (x - 2)^2 / 1000$$

(both to be minimised).

Given a non-optimal input value, the output value from f_{11} will normally be three orders of magnitude worse than that from f_{12} (i.e., the second function will be approximately one thousand times closer to the minimum of zero). As can be seen in the simplest of tests, if the outputs from both were simply summed, the first function would completely dominate the second, resulting in the effective evolution of a good solution only to the first function.

Thus, the only way to ensure that all objectives in a multiobjective problem are treated equally by the EA is to ensure that all the effective ranges of the objective functions are the same (i.e., to make all the objective functions commensurable), or alternatively, to ensure that no objective is directly compared to another. In other words, either the effective ranges must be converted to make them equal, and a range-dependent ranking method used, or a range-independent ranking method must be used (Bentley and Wakefield, 1997c). Typically, range-dependent methods (e.g., 'sum of weighted objectives', 'distance functions', and 'min-max formulation') require knowledge of the problem being searched to allow the searching algorithm to find useful solutions (Srinivas and Deb, 1995). Range-independent methods require no such knowledge, for being independent of the effective range of each objective function makes them independent of the nature of the objectives and overall problem itself. Hence, a ranking method should not just be independent of individual applications (i.e., problem independent), as stated by Srinivas and Deb (1995), it should be independent of the effective ranges of the objectives in individual applications (i.e., range-independent).

For example, the standard 'sum of weighted objectives' method favoured by so many, uses the weights to make the effective domains of each objective equal, then provides a single fitness value by summing the resulting values. This is a range-dependent method, for it relies completely on the weights being set precisely for every problem. Should any of the objectives be changed, or the allowable domain of input values be changed (perhaps by a change in coding, or seeding the initial population with anything other than random values), then these weights may have to be changed.

Alternatively, the non-dominated sorting method, and variants of it, is a range-independent method. It requires no weighting of the objective values, for the fitness values from each objective function are never directly compared with each other. Only values from the same objective are ever compared in the process of determining the non-dominance of solutions (Goldberg, 1989). For complex multiobjective problems, this range-independence is extremely advantageous: good results do not depend on the ability of the user to fine-tune weights correctly. However, a disadvantage of non-dominated sorting is that all Pareto optimal solutions are considered equally good, regardless of what the user actually regards as being acceptable.

For a detailed review, analysis and investigation of six different multiobjective handling methods for GAs, see Bentley and Wakefield (1997c).

1.5.6 Constraints

Constraints form an integral part of every problem, and yet they are often overlooked in evolutionary algorithms (Michalewicz, 1995, 1996). It is vital to perform constraint handling with care, for if evolutionary search is restricted inappropriately, the evolution of good solutions may be prevented.

A problem with constraints has both an objective, and a set of restrictions. For example, when designing a VLSI circuit, the objective may be to maximize speed and the constraint may be to use no more than 50 logic gates. When writing a computer program, the objective is to generate a program which performs a specific task and a constraint is not to violate the syntax of the language. A good problem solution must both fulfil the objective and satisfy these restrictions.

In the same way that phenotypes are evaluated for fitness, not genotypes, it is the phenotypes which must satisfy the problem constraints, not the genotypes (although their enforcement may result in the restriction of some genotypes[8]). However, unlike the fitness evaluation, constraints can be enforced at any point in the algorithm to attain legal phenotypes. As is described by Yu and Bentley (1998), they may be incorporated into the genotype or phenotype representations, during the seeding of the population, during reproduction, or handled at other stages.

There are two main types of constraint: the *soft constraint* and the *hard constraint.* Soft constraints are restrictions on phenotypes that should be satisfied, but will not always be. Such constraints are often enforced by using penalty values to lower fitnesses. Illegal phenotypes (which conflict the constraints) are permitted to exist as second-class, in the hope that some portions of their genotypes will aid the search for fit phenotypes (Michalewicz, 1995). Hard constraints, on the other hand, must always be satisfied. Illegal phenotypes are not permitted to exist (although their corresponding genotypes may be, if the constraints are enforced in the mapping stage).

Just as evolution requires selection pressure to generate phenotypes that satisfy the objective function, evolution can have a second selection pressure placed upon it in order to generate phenotypes that do not conflict the constraints. However, using *pressure* in evolutionary search to evolve legal solutions is no guarantee that all of the solutions will always be legal (i.e., they are soft constraints).

Constraints can also be handled in two other ways: solutions that do not satisfy the constraints can be *prevented* from being created, or they can be *corrected.* Such methods can have significant drawbacks such as loss of diversity and premature convergence. Nevertheless, these

---

[8] There are other types of constraints, e.g. minimisation of the number of evaluations, which may be applied to the evolutionary algorithm as a whole. This section focuses on evolving solutions which satisfy constraints, not on handling constrained evolutionary algorithms.

Table 1.2 Classification of constraint handling.

Prevention	HARD
Correction	HARD
Pressure	SOFT

two types of constraint handling ensure that all solutions are always legal (i.e., they are hard constraints). Table 1.2 shows the three conceptual categories for constraint handling.

As is typical in evolutionary computation, researchers typically investigate constraint handling from the perspective of a single evolutionary algorithm. For a general analysis and investigation of constraint handling in evolutionary algorithms, see Yu and Bentley (1998).

1.5.7 Evolving Designs with Interdependent Elements

Opponents of Darwin's theory of natural selection often give the example of the eye as a structure 'impossible to occur by evolution'. They state that the eye consists of many interdependent parts: the iris, the retina, the cornea, the lens, with each element relying on the correct functioning of all the other elements for the eye to work as a whole. Dawkins (1986) convincingly argues that there does exist a series of gradual evolutionary steps from *no eye* to *eye*, and that not only has the eye evolved, but it has evolved many times independently in different species. However, although it is clear that such intricate designs have been evolved in nature, it is also clear that using evolutionary computation to generate designs with interdependent elements is a very difficult task.

For example, Bentley and Wakefield (1997a) describe (amongst other things) the evolution of a Penta prism. This design must bounce light twice using total internal reflection within its solid glass structure in order to reflect an image through 90 degrees whilst keeping the output image the right way up, see fig. 1.36. Although it is a single component, it does have two interdependent elements: the two reflective parts. If either of these internally reflective sides are imprecisely oriented, or omitted, the design will not function correctly. Not only that, but the first reflection must direct the light in a direction almost opposite to the final, desired direction: so a design without the second reflective part is actually worse than a design with no reflective parts at all (Bentley and Wakefield, 1997a).

Evolution 'prefers' to begin with a single functional element that performs the function to some extent, however small, then slowly and incrementally build up the complexity of the

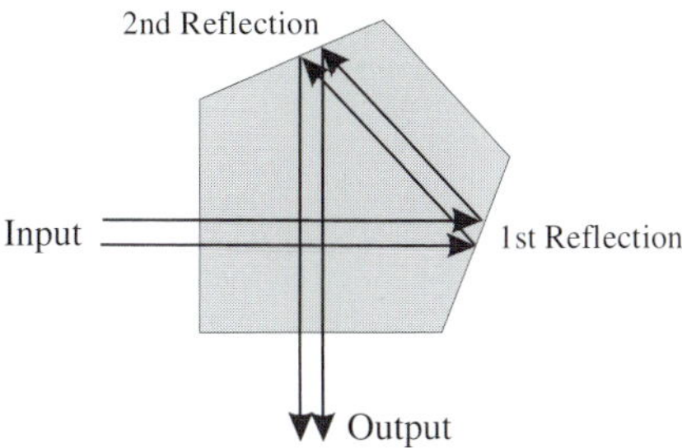

Figure 1.36 A Penta prism uses two interdependent internal reflections.

design, adding new elements *if they improve the fitness of the design* (Dawkins, 1989). However, if care is not taken in the design of the representation and operators, evolution may commit itself too early to simple approximations of the desired design. In the example of the Penta prism, evolution normally began by evolving a simple right-angle prism (using a single reflection), which directed the light in the correct direction, but oriented the wrong way up, fig. 1.37. Having committed itself to this simple, but unsatisfactory type of solution, evolution was then unable to proceed to the more complex Penta-prism design. Perhaps because of limitations of the representation, the only way that evolution could be forced to abandon this unsatisfactory local optimum was by penalising all such designs with a fitness constraint (Bentley and Wakefield, 1997a).

Such examples of evolutionary design illustrate that design problems requiring solutions with many interdependent elements can have large numbers of local optima – some of which do not resemble the functionally correct designs at all. Penalising all such unsatisfactory designs is not always a practical solution, so for design problems of this type, very careful consideration should be given to the creation of a representation and genetic operators that will always permit evolutionary paths from local optima to global optima.

1.5.8 Evolving Structure and Detail

As described in previous sections, some types of evolutionary design allow evolution to explore the *structure* (e.g. number of parameters/rules/primitive shapes) of designs in addition to the *detail* (e.g. parameter values) of designs. In most representations, varying the structure of designs has considerably more impact on the fitness of these designs, compared to varying the detail. Because of this, evolution typically converges on suitable design structures long before converging on design details. (This effect is also evident in the convergence of most significant bits before least significant bits in a binary coded genotype.) Although this is not always a disadvantage (e.g. the skeletal structure of all mammals seems to permit sufficient diversity, as does the cellular structure of plants), in some instances evolution may prematurely converge onto an inappropriate structure. If this happens, the evolution of detail around this structure may be insufficient to allow the production of an acceptable design.

There are two potential solutions to this problem. First, an improved representation capable of allowing changes in structure without disastrous fitness changes would allow structure and detail to converge simultaneously. This could be accomplished if the evolution of detail

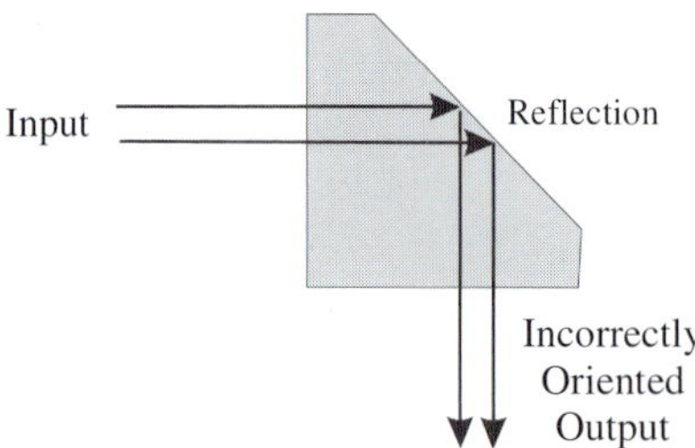

Figure 1.37 A right-angle prism is an easily found solution which does a similar job to the Penta prism, but there is no easy evolutionary path from a right-angle prism to a Penta prism.

could directly affect the degree to which changes in structure affected fitnesses. For example, in nature, a superfluous bone will be gradually reduced in size by evolution (a change in design detail), whilst at the same time improving other aspects of the organism because of that change. This reduction continues until at some point the bone becomes sufficiently small and redundant that evolution can remove the entire bone (structure mutation), without decreasing the fitness of the organism.

The second way to prevent premature convergence of structure is to reduce selection pressure once in a while, and permit less-fit designs to propagate. Dawkins (1989) suggests that certain landmark mutations in structure such as the development of segmentation may have initially resulted in solutions with worse fitnesses. It seems likely that some of the more gross mutations are more likely to survive during 'good times' where food is plentiful, predators are scarce, and hence selection pressure low (Dawkins, 1989). By reducing selection pressure in our evolutionary design systems in a similar way, we may well permit changes in structure to occur at later stages of evolution.

1.5.9 Summary

The final major section of this chapter has explained eight significant issues which prospective evolutionary designers should consider: enumerating the search space, designing embryogenies, epistasis, incorporating knowledge, handling multiple objectives, handling constraints, interdependent elements in designs, and the evolution of structure and detail. Not every evolutionary design system is affected by all of these issues, but most will be affected by some. More solutions to these and other problems are discussed in the other chapters of this book.

1.6 Summary of Chapter

This introductory chapter has attempted to explain the fundamental issues surrounding evolutionary design by computers. The technical jargon and equations have deliberately been minimised in the chapter in an attempt to provide a gentle introduction and an intuitive *feel* of evolutionary design. Beginning with a justification of why evolution is used to generate designs, the chapter then explored the techniques and ideas of evolutionary computation, reviewed the different types of evolutionary design, and discussed the problems faced by creators of evolutionary design systems.

The stress throughout has been the promotion of *understanding*. This chapter does not provide a set of instructions for, or results of, performing evolutionary design. It provides instead a series of explanations of how evolutionary design can be performed, in the hope that you, the reader, will create your own original evolutionary design system. And remember: this is still a new and rapidly growing field. There are no hard and fast rules which must always be followed. As the following chapters of this book show: the results of evolutionary design are limited only by our imagination – and the unlimited imagination of evolution.

1.7 Organisation of the Book

The book has five major sections, intended to cover the major aspects of evolutionary design by computers.

The first section, **Evolution and Design**, describes and explores the relationships between the design process and evolution. The four chapters discuss whether our own method of design bears any resemblance to evolution, whether insight and creativity can be achieved by evolution, and how evolution should be used in the design process.

The second section, **Evolutionary Optimisation of Designs**, provides examples of design optimisation using genetic algorithms. The three chapters describe detailed investigations of how satellite booms, load cells, flywheels and reliable networks can be optimised using evolution.

The artistic side of evolutionary design is shown by the third section, **Evolutionary Art**. The three chapters in this section give very graphic illustrations of the artistic capabilities and creativity of evolutionary design.

The fourth section of the book, **Evolutionary Artificial Life Forms**, explores the exciting use of evolutionary design to generate astonishing virtual creatures, and investigates the use of biologically inspired embryogenies and other techniques to evolve forms.

The fifth and final section, **Creative Evolutionary Design**, examines the creative potential of evolution to generate novel and useful designs. The chapters in this section show the remarkable diversity of original designs that are now being evolved, and give clues to the future of evolutionary design.

The books ends with a glossary of commonly used terms.

Acknowledgements

Thanks to Tina Yu, who provided help, time, and some of the text for the GP, ES and EP summaries. Thanks to Suran Goonatilake and Phil Treleaven for their advice, and to David Fogel, Laura Decker and Tina Yu for proof-reading sections of this monstrosity of a chapter. Thanks to Jonathan Wakefield, Sanjeev Kumar and all the members of UCL's Design Group for providing stimulating discussions and helpful criticism. Thanks also to Ying Li for the idea of including 'recommended reading' sections, and to Jim Viner for the title of section 1.4.4. Portions of the middle section of this chapter have appeared as the chapter 'Aspects of Evolutionary Design by Computers' in *Advances in Soft Computing – Engineering Design and Manufacturing*, Springer-Verlag, London, 1998, reprinted with permission.

References

Adeli, H. (ed.) (1994). *Advances in Design Optimization*, Chapman and Hall, London.

Adeli, H. and Cheng, N. (1994). Concurrent Genetic Algorithms for Optimization of Large Structures. *ASCE Journal of Aerospace Engineering* **7:3**, 276–296.

Alternberg, L. (1995). Genome Growth and the Evolution of the Genotype-Phenotype Map. In *Evolution and Biocomputation: Computational Models of Evolution*. Springer-Verlag, pp. 205–259.

Angeline, P. and Kinnear Jr., K. E. (eds) (1996). *Advances in Genetic Programming 2*. MIT Press, Cambridge, MA.

Axelrod, R. (1987). The Evolution of Strategies in the Iterated Prisoner's Dilemma. In Davis, L. (ed.), *Genetic Algorithms and Simulated Annealing*, Pitman, London, pp. 32–41.

Bäck, T. (1996). *Evolutionary Algorithms in Theory and Practice*. Oxford University Press, New York.

Banzhaf, W. (1994). Genotype-Phenotype-Mapping and Neutral Variation – A Case Study in Genetic Programming. In Davidor, Y., Schwefel, H.-P. and Mnner, R. (eds), *Parallel Problem Solving From Nature*, 3. Springer-Verlag, pp. 322–332.

Banzhaf, W., Nordin, P., Keller, R. E. and Francone, F. D. (1998). *Genetic Programming – an Introduction*. Morgan Kaufmann Publishers, San Francisco.

Baron, P., Fisher, R., Mill, F., Sherlock, A. and Tuson, A. (1997). A Voxel-based Representation for the Evolutionary Shape Optimisation of a Simplified Beam: A Case-Study of a Problem-Centred Approach to Genetic Operator Design. *2nd On-line World Conference on Soft Computing in Engineering Design and Manufacturing (WSC2)*.

Bentley, P. J. (1997). The Revolution of Evolution for Real-World Applications. *Emerging Technologies '97: Theory and Application of Evolutionary Computation*, 15th December, University College London.

Bentley, P. J. (1998a). Aspects of Evolutionary Design by Computers. In *Proceedings of the 3rd On-line World Conference on Soft Computing in Engineering Design and Manufacturing (WSC3)*.

Bentley, P. J. (ed.) (1998b). *Proc. of the Workshop on Evolutionary Design, 5th International Conference on Artificial Intelligence in Design '98*, Instituto Superior Técnico, Lisbon, Portugal, 20–23 July 1998.

Bentley, P. J. and Wakefield, J. P. (1996a). Generic Representation of Solid Geometry for Genetic Search. *Microcomputers in Civil Engineering* 11:3, Blackwell Publishers, 153–161.

Bentley, P. J. and Wakefield, J. P. (1996b). The Evolution of Solid Object Designs using Genetic Algorithms. In Rayward-Smith, V. (ed.), *Modern Heuristic Search Methods*, Ch. 12, John Wiley and Sons Inc., pp. 199–215.

Bentley, P. J. and Wakefield, J. P. (1996c). Hierarchical Crossover in Genetic Algorithms. In *Proceedings of the 1st On-line Workshop on Soft Computing (WSC1)*, Nagoya University, Japan, pp. 37–42.

Bentley, P. J. and Wakefield, J. P. (1997a). Conceptual Evolutionary Design by Genetic Algorithms. *Engineering Design and Automation Journal* 3:2, John Wiley and Sons, Inc, 119–131.

Bentley, P. J. and Wakefield, J. P. (1997b). Generic Evolutionary Design. In Chawdhry, P. K., Roy, R. and Pant, R. K. (eds), *Soft Computing in Engineering Design and Manufacturing*, Springer Verlag, London, Part 6, pp. 289–298.

Bentley, P. J. and Wakefield, J. P. (1997c). Finding Acceptable Solutions in the Pareto-Optimal Range using Multiobjective Genetic Algorithms. In Chawdhry, P. K., Roy, R. and Pant, R. K. (eds), *Soft Computing in Engineering Design and Manufacturing*. Springer Verlag, London, Part 5, pp. 231–240.

Boden, M. A. (1992). *The Creative Mind: Myths and Mechanisms*. Basic Books.

Bonabeau, E., Theraulaz, G., Arpin, E. and Sardet, E. (1994). The Building Behaviour of Lattice Swarms. In Brooks, R. and Maes, P. (eds), *Artificial Live IV*, Proc. of the 4th Int. Workshop on the Synthesis and Simulation of Living Systems, MIT Press, Cambridge, MA, pp. 307–312.

Born, J. (1978). *Evolutionstrategien zur Numerischen Lösung von Adaptationsafgaben*. Dissertation A, Humboldt-Universität, Berlin.

Canal, E., Krasnogor, N., Marcos, D. H., Pelta, D. and Risi, W. A. (1998). Encoding and Crossover Mismatch in a Molecular Design Problem. In Bentley, P. J. (ed.), *Proceedings of the AID '98 Workshop on Evolutionary Design*, July 19, 1998, Lisbon, Portugal.

Chambers, L (1995). *Practical Handbook of Genetic Algorithms*, CRC Press, Boca Raton.

Chawdhry, P. K., Roy, R. and Pant, R. K. (eds) (1997). *Soft Computing in Engineering Design and Manufacturing*. Springer-Verlag, London.

Chellapilla, K. (1997). Evolutionary Programming with Tree Mutations: Evolving Computer Programs without Crossover, In Koza, J., Kalyanmoy, D., Marco, D., Fogel, D., Garzon, M., Hitoshi, I. and Rick, R. (eds), *Genetic Programming 1997: Proceedings of the Second Annual Conference*. Morgan Kaufmann, San Francisco, CA.

Cliff, C., Husbands, P., Meyer, J. and Wilson, S. W. (eds) (1994). *From Animals to Animats 3. Proceedings of the Third International Conference on Simulation of Adaptive Behaviour*, MIT Press, Cambridge, MA.

Coates, P. (1997). Using Genetic Programming and L-Systems to explore 3D design worlds. In Junge, R. (ed.), *CAADFutures '97*, Kluwer Academic Publishers, Munich.

Dasgupta, D. and McGregor, D. R. (1992). Nonstationary Function Optimization using the Structured Genetic Algorithm. In *Parallel Problem Solving from Nature 2*, Elsevier Science Pub., Brussels, pp. 145–154.

Davis, L. (1991). *The Handbook of Genetic Algorithms*. Van Nostrand Reinhold, New York.

Dawkins, R. (1976). *The Selfish Gene*. Oxford University Press.

Dawkins, R. (1982). *The Extended Phenotype*. Oxford University Press.

Dawkins, R. (1983). Universal Darwinism. In Bendall, D. (ed.), *Evolution from Molecules to Men*. Cambridge University Press.

Dawkins, R. (1986). *The Blind Watchmaker*. Longman Scientific and Technical, Harlow.

Dawkins, R. (1989). The Evolution of Evolvability. In Langton, C. G. (ed.), *Artificial Life. The Proceedings of an Interdisciplinary Workshop on the Synthesis and Simulation of Living Systems*, vol. VI, September, 1987, Los Alamos, New Mexico. Addison-Wesley Pub. Corp, pp. 201–220.

Dawkins, R. (1996). *Climbing Mount Improbable*. Penguin Books, Harmondsworth.

De Jong, K. A. (1975). *An Analysis of the Behaviour of a Class of Genetic Adaptive Systems*. Doctoral dissertation, University of Michigan, Dissertation Abstracts International.

Deb, K. (1991). *Binary and Floating Point Function Optimization using Messy Genetic Algorithms*. Illinois Genetic Algorithms Laboratory (IlliGAL), report no. 91004.

Deb, K. and Goldberg, D. E. (1991). *mGA in C: A Messy Genetic Algorithm in C*. Illinois Genetic Algorithms Laboratory (IlliGAL), report no. 91008.

Deb, K. and Goldberg, D. E. (1993). Analyzing Deception in Trap Functions. In *Foundations of Genetic Algorithms 2*, Morgan Kaufmann Pub.

Deb, K., Horn J. and Goldberg, D. E. (1993). Multimodal Deceptive Functions. *Complex Systems* 7:2, 131–153.

Eby, D., Averill, R., Gelfand, B., Punch, W., Mathews, O. and Goodman, E. (1997). An Injection Island GA for Flywheel Design Optimization. In 5th *European Congress on Intelligent Techniques and Soft Computing EUFIT '97*, vol. 1, Verlag Mainz, Aachen, pp. 687–691.

Fleming, P., Zalzala, A., Bull, D., Fonseca, C. and Patton, R. (1995). *Proceedings of the Genetic Algorithms in Engineering Systems: Innovations and Applications (GALESIA '95)*, Sept. 1995, Sheffield. IEE, London.

Fogel, D. B. (1991). *System Identification through Simulated Evolution: A Machine Learning Approach to Modeling*. Ginn Press, Needham Heights.

Fogel, D. (1992a). Evolving Artificial Intelligence. PhD thesis, University of California, San Diego, CA.

Fogel, D. (1992b). An Analysis of Evolutionary Programming. *Proc. of the 1st Annual Conf on Evolutionary Programming*, San Diego. Evolutionary Programming Society, San Diego, CA, pp. 43–51.

Fogel, D. B. (1994). Asymptotic Convergence Properties of Genetic Algorithms and Evolutionary Programming: Analysis and Experiments. *J. of Cybernetics and Systems* **25**, Taylor and Francis Pub., 389–407.

Fogel, D. B. (1995). *Evolutionary Computation: Towards a New Philosophy of Machine Intelligence*. IEEE Press.

Fogel, D. B. (1997). The Advantages of Evolutionary Computation. *Biocomputing and Emergent Computation (BCEC97)*.

Fogel, G. B. and Fogel, D. B. (1995). Continuous Evolutionary Programming: Analysis and Experiments. *J. of Cybernetics and Systems* **26**, Taylor and Francis Pub., 79–90.

Fogel, L. J. (1963). *Biotechnology: Concepts and Applications*. Prentice Hall, Englewood Cliffs, NJ.

Fogel, L. J., Owens, A. J. and Walsh, M. J. (1966). *Artificial Intelligence through Simulated Evolution*. Wiley, New York.

Fogel, L., Angeline, P. and Fogel, D. (1995) An Evolutionary Programming Approach to Self-adaptation on Finite State Machines.In J.R. McDonnell, R.G. Reynolds and D.B. Fogel (eds), *Proceedings of the Fourth International Conference on Evolutionary Programming*, MIT Press, Cambridge, MA.

Fonseca, C. M. and Fleming, P. J. (1995a). An Overview of Evolutionary Algorithms in Multiobjective Optimization. *Evolutionary Computation* 3:1, 1–16.

Fonseca, C. M. and Fleming, P. J. (1995b). Multiobjective Genetic Algorithms Made Easy: Selection, Sharing and Mating Restriction. *Genetic Algorithms in Engineering Systems: Innovations and Applications*, Sheffield. IEE, London, 45–52.

Forrest, S., Perelson, A. S., Allen, L. and Cherukuri, R. (1995). A Change-Detection Algorithm Inspired by the Immune System. Submitted to *IEEE Transactions on Software Engineering*.

Foy, M. D. et al. (1992). Signal Timing Determination using Genetic Algorithms. *Transportation Research Record #1365*, National Academy Press, Washington, DC, 108–113.

Frazer, J. (1995). *An Evolutionary Architecture*. Architectural Association, London.

French, M. J. (1994). *Invention and Evolution: Design in Nature and Engineering*, 2nd Edition. Cambridge University Press.

French, M. and Ramirez, A. C. (1996). Towards a Comparative Study of Quarter-turn Pneumatic Valve Actuators. *Journal of Engineering Manufacture*, part B, 543–552.

Funes, P. and Pollack, J. (1997). *Computer Evolution of Buildable Objects*. Brandeis University Computer Science Technical Report CS-97-191.

Furuta, H., Maeda, K. and Watanabe, W. (1995). Application of Genetic Algorithm to Aesthetic Design of Bridge Structures. In *Microcomputers in Civil Engineering* 10:6, Blackwell Publishers, MA, 415–421.

Gehlhaar, D. K. and Fogel, D. B. (1996). Tuning Evolutionary Programming for Conformationally Flexible Molecular Docking. In L. Fogel, P. Angeline and T. Back (eds), *Proceedings of the Fifth International Conference on Evolutionary Programming*, MIT Press, Cambridge, MA.

Gen, M. and Cheng, R. (1997). *Genetic Algorithms and Engineering Design*, John Wiley and Sons.

Gero, J. S. (1996). Computers and Creative Design, In Tan, M. and Teh, R. (eds), *The Global Design Studio*, National University of Singapore, pp. 11–19.

Gero, J. S. and Kazakov, V. (1996). An Exploration-based Evolutionary Model of Generative Design Process. *Microcomputers In Civil Engineering* 11, 209–216.

Gero, J. S. and Maher, M. L. (eds) (1993). *Modeling Creativity and Knowledge-Based Creative Design*, Lawrence Erlbaum, Hillsdale, NJ.

Gero, J. S. and Sudweeks, F. (eds) (1994). *Artificial Intelligence in Design '94*, Kluwer, Dordrecht.

Gero, J. S. and Sudweeks, F. (eds) (1996). *Artificial Intelligence in Design '96*, Kluwer, Dordrecht.

Gero, J. S. and Sudweeks, F. (eds) (1998). *Artificial Intelligence in Design '98*, Kluwer, Dordrecht.

Goldberg, D. E. (1989). *Genetic Algorithms in Search, Optimization and Machine Learning*. Addison-Wesley.

Goldberg, D. E. (1991). Genetic Algorithms as a Computational Theory of Conceptual Design. In *Proc. of Applications of Artificial Intelligence in Engineering* **6**, pp. 3–16.

Goldberg, D. E. et al. (1992). Accounting for Noise in the Sizing of Populations. In *Foundations of Genetic Algorithms* **2**, Morgan Kaufmann Pub., pp. 127–140.

Goldberg, D. E. (1994). Genetic and Evolutionary Algorithms Come of Age. *Communication of the ACM*, 37:3, 113–119.

Goldberg, D. (1998). *The Design of Innovation: Lessons from Genetic Algorithms*. (in press)

Greffenstette, J. J. (1991). Strategy Acquisition with Genetic Algorithms. Ch. 12 in *The Handbook of Genetic Algorithms*. Van Nostrand Reinhold, New York, pp. 186–201.

Harris, R. A. (1994). An Alternative Description to the Action of Crossover. In *Proceedings of Adaptive Computing in Engineering Design and Control – '94*. University of Plymouth, Plymouth. pp. 151–156.

Harvey, I. (1997). Cognition is Not Computation: Evolution is Not Optimisation. In Gerstner, W., Germond, A., Hasler, M. and Nicoud, J.-D. (eds), *Artificial Neural Networks – ICANN97*, Proc. of 7th International Conference on Artificial Neural Networks, 7–10 October 1997, Lausanne, Switzerland, Springer-Verlag, LNCS 1327, pp. 685–690.

Harvey, I., Husbands, P. and Cliff, D. (1993). Issues in Evolutionary Robotics, In J.-A. Meyer, H. Roitblat and S. Wilson (eds), *From Animals to Animats 2: Proc. of the Second Intl. Conf. on Simulation of Adaptive Behavior, (SAB92)*, MIT Press/Bradford Books, Cambridge, MA, pp. 364–373.

Harvey, I. and Thompson, A. (1997). Through the Labyrinth Evolution Finds a Way: A Slicon Ridge. In Higuchi, T. and Iwata, M. (eds), *Proceedings of the 1st Int. Conf. on Evolveable Systems: From Biology to Hardware (ICES96)*. Springer Verlag, LNCS 1259, pp. 406–422.

Holland, J. H. (1973). Genetic Algorithms and the Optimal Allocations of Trials. *SIAM Journal of Computing* 2:2, 88–105.

Holland, J. H. (1975). *Adaptation in Natural and Artificial Systems*. University of Michigan Press, Ann Arbor.

Holland, J. H. (1992). Genetic Algorithms. *Scientific American*, 66–72.

Horn, J. (1993). Finite Markov Chain Analysis of Genetic Algorithms with Niching. In *Proceedings of the Fifth International Conference on Genetic Algorithms*, Morgan Kaufmann Pub., pp. 110–17.

Horn, J. and Nafpliotis, N. (1993). *Multiobjective Optimisation Using the Niched Pareto Genetic Algorithm*. Illinois Genetic Algorithms Laboratory (IlliGAL), report no. 93005.

Horn, J., Goldberg, D. E. and Deb, K. (1994). *Implicit Niching in a Learning Classifier System: Nature's Way*. Illinois Genetic Algorithms Laboratory (IlliGAL), report no. 94001.

Husbands, P., Jermy, G., McIlhagga, M. and Ives, R. (1996). Two Applications of Genetic Algorithms to Component Design. In Fogarty, T. (ed.), *Selected Papers from AISB Workshop on Evolutionary Computing*. Springer-Verlag, Lecture Notes in Computer Science, pp. 50–61.

Kanal, L. and Cumar, V. (eds) (1988). *Search in Artificial Intelligence*. Springer-Verlag.

Kargupta, H. (1993). *Information Transmission in Genetic Algorithm and Shannon's Second Theorem*. Illinois Genetic Algorithms Laboratory (IlliGAL), report no. 93003.

Keane, A. (1994) Experiences with Optimizers in Structural Design. In I. C. Parmee, *Proceedings of the Conference on Adaptive Computing in Engineering Design and Control '94*. University of Plymouth, Plymouth, pp. 14–27.

Kinnear, Jr., K. E. (ed.) (1994). *Advances In Genetic Programming*. MIT Press, Cambridge, MA.

Koza, J. (1992). *Genetic Programming: On the Programming of Computers by Means of Natural Selection*. MIT Press, Cambridge, MA.

Koza, J. (1994) *Genetic Programming II: Automatic Discovery of Reusable Programs*. MIT Press, Cambridge, MA.

Koza, J., Bennett, III, F. H., Andre, D. and Keane, M. A. (1999). *Genetic Programming III*. Morgan Kaufmann, San Francisco.

Langdon, B. (1998). Genetic Programming and Data Structures: *Genetic Programming + Data Structures = Automatic Programming!* Kluwer, Boston.

Langdon, B. and Poli, R. (1997). Fitness Causes Bloat. *2nd On-line World Conference on Soft Computing in Engineering Design and Manufacturing (WSC2)*.

Langton, C. (ed.) (1995). *Artificial Life: an Overview*. MIT Press, Cambridge, MA.

Levine, D. (1994). A Parallel Genetic Algorithm for the Set Partitioning Problem. D. Phil. dissertation, Argonne National Laboratory, Illinois, USA.

Lohn, J. and Reggia, J. (1995). Discovery of Self-Replicating Structures Using a Genetic Algorithm. *1995 IEEE Int. Conf. on Evolutionary Computation (ICEC '95)*, vol. 1, Perth, Western Australia, pp. 678–683.

Lund, H., Pagliarini, L. and Miglino, O. (1995). Artistic Design with GA and NN. *Proc. of the* 1st *Nordic Workshop on Genetic Algorithms and Their Applications (1NWGA)*, University of Vaasa, Finland, pp. 97–105.

Michalewicz, Z. (1995). A Survey of Constraint Handling Techniques in Evolutionary Computation Methods. *Proc. of the* 4th *Annual Conf. on Evolutionary Programming*, MIT Press, Cambridge, MA, pp. 135–155.

Michalewicz, Z. (1996). *Genetic Algorithms + Data Structures = Evolution Programs*. 3rd extended edn, Springer, Berlin.

Michalewicz, Z., Dasgupta, D., Le Riche, R. G. and Schoenauer, M. (1996). Evolutionary Algorithms for Constrained Engineering Problems, *Computers and Industrial Engineering Journal*, 30:2, September, 851–870.

Mitchell, M. (1996). *An Introduction to Genetic Algorithms*. MIT Press, Cambridge, MA.

O'Reilly, U.-M. and Oppacher, F. (1995). The Troubling Aspects of a Building Block Hypothesis for Genetic Programming. In Witley, L. D. and Vose, M. D. (eds), *Foundations of Genetic Algorithms*. Morgan Kaufman, San Fransisco, CA, pp. 72–88.

Parmee, I. (1996a) Towards an Optimal Engineering Design Process using Appropriate Adaptive Search Strategies. *Journal of Engineering Design*, 7:4, Carfax Pub.

Parmee, I. (1996b) The Development of a Dual-Agent Strategy For Efficient Search Across Whole System Engineering Design Hierarchies. 4th *Int. Conf. on Parallel Problem Solving From Nature*, Berlin, Germany, September 22–27.

Parmee, I. C. and Denham, M. J. (1994). The Integration of Adaptive Search Techniques with Current Engineering Design Practice. In *Proc. of Adaptive Computing in Engineering Design and Control '94*, University of Plymouth, Plymouth, pp. 1–13.

Paton, R. (1994). Enhancing Evolutionary Computation using Analogues of Biological Mechanisms. In *Evolutionary Computing, AISB Workshop*. Springer-Verlag, pp. 51–64.

Paun, G. (ed.) (1995). *Artificial Life: Grammatical Models*. Black Sea University Press, Romania.

Pham, D. T. and Yang, Y. (1993). A Genetic Algorithm Based Preliminary Design System. *Journal of Automobile Engineers*, 207:D2, 127–133.

Poli, R. and Langdon, B. (1997a). Genetic Programming with One-point Crossover. In Chawdhry, P. K., Roy, R. and Pant, R. K. (eds), *Second On-line World Conference on Soft Computing in Engineering Design and Manufacturing*. Springer-Verlag, London.

Poli, R. and Langdon, B. (1997b). A New Schema Theorem for Genetic Programming with One-point Crossover and Point Mutation. In Koza, J., Goldberg, D., Fogel, D. and Riolo, R. L. (eds), *Genetic Programming 1997: Proceedings of the Second Annual Conference on Genetic Programming*. Morgan Kaufmann, San Francisco, CA, pp. 278–285.

Radcliffe, N. J. and Surry, P. D. (1994a). Formal Memetic Algorithms. *Edinburgh Parallel Computing Centre*.

Radcliffe, N. J. and Surry, P. D. (1994b). Co-operation through Hierarchical Competition in Genetic Data Mining. (Submitted to) *Parallel Problem Solving From Nature*.

Rayward-Smith, V., Osman, I. H., Reeves, C. R., Smith, G. D. (1996). *Modern Heuristic Search Methods*. John Wiley and Sons, London.

Rechenberg, I. (1973). *Evolutionstrategie: Optimierung Technisher Systeme nach Prinzipien der Biologischen Evolution*. Frommann-Holzboog Verlag, Stuttgart.

Rechenberg, I. (1994). *Evolutionstrategie '94*, volume 1 of *Werkstatt Bionik und Evolutionstechnik*. Frommann-Holzboog, Stuttgart.

Rosenman, M. (1997). The Generation of Form Using an Evolutionary Approach. In Dasgupta, D. and Michalewicz, Z. (eds), *Evolutionary Algorithms in Engineering Applications*, Springer-Verlag, pp. 69–86.

Roston, G. (1997). Hazards in Genetic Design Methodologies. In Dasgupta, D. and Michalewicz, Z. (eds), *Evolutionary Algorithms in Engineering Applications*, Springer-Verlag, pp. 135–154.

Roy, R., Furuhashi, T. and Chawdry, P. K. (eds) (1999). *Advances in Soft Computing – Engineering Design and Manufacturing*. Springer-Verlag, London.

Rudolph, G. (1996). Convergence of Evolutionary Algorithms in General Search Spaces. *Proceedings of the Third IEEE Conference on Evolutionary Computation*, Piscataway, NJ. IEEE Press, pp. 50–54.

Rudolph, G. (1997). Convergence Rates of Evolutionary Algorithms for a Class of Convex Objective Functions, *Control and Cybernetics* 26(3), 375–390.

Rudolph, G. (1998). Local Convergence Rates of Simple Evolutionary Algorithms with Cauchy Mutations, *IEEE Transactions on Evolutionary Computation* 1(4).

Schaffer, J. D. (1985). Multiple Objective Optimization with Vector Evaluated Genetic Algorithms. *Genetic Algorithms and Their Applications: Proceedings of the First International Conference on Genetic Algorithms*, pp. 93–100.

Schaffer, J. D. and Eshelman, L. (1995). Combinatorial Optimization by Genetic Algorithms: The Value of Genotype/Phenotype Distinction. In *Proc. of Applied Decision Technologies (ADT '95)*, April 1995, London, pp. 29–40.

Schnier, T. and Gero, J. S. (1996). Learning Genetic Representatrions as an Alternative to Hand-coded Shape Grammars. In Gero, J. and Sudweeks, F. (eds), *Artificial Intelligence in Design '96*, Kluwer, Dordrecht, pp. 39–57.

Schoenauer, M. (1996). Shape Representations and Evolution Schemes. *Proc. of the* 5th *Annual Conf. on Evolutionary Programming*, MIT Press, Cambridge, MA, pp. 121–129.

Schwefel, H.-P. (1965). *Kybernetische Evolution als Strategie der experimentellen Forschung in der Strömungstechnik*. Diplomarbeit, Technische Universität, Berlin.

Schwefel, H.-P. (1981). *Numerical Optimization of Computer Models.* Wiley, Chichester.

Schwefel, H.-P. (1995). *Evolution and Optimum Seeking*, Wiley, New York.

Sims, K. (1991). Artificial Evolution for Computer Graphics. *Computer Graphics*, 25, 4, 319–328.

Sims, K. (1994a). Evolving Virtual Creatures. In *Computer Graphics*, Annual Conference Series (SIGGRAPH '94 Proceedings), July 1994, 15–22.

Sims, K. (1994b). Evolving 3D Morphology and Behaviour by Competition. In Brooks, R. and Maes, P. (eds), *Artificial Life IV Proceedings*, MIT Press, Cambridge, MA, pp. 28–39.

Sipper, M. (1997). A Phylogenetic, Ontogenetic, and Epigenetic View of Bio-Inspired Hardware Systems. *IEEE Transactions On Evolutionary Computation*, 1:1.

Smith, R. E. and Goldberg, D. E. (1992). Diploidy and Dominance in Artificial Genetic Search. *Complex Systems* 6, 251–285.

Srinivas, N. and Deb, K. (1995). Multiobjective Optimization Using Nondominated Sorting in Genetic Algorithms. *Evolutionary Computation*, 2:3, 221–248.

Syswerda, G. (1989). Uniform Crossover in Genetic Algorithms. In Schaffer, D. (ed.), *Proc. of the Third Int. Conf. on Genetic Algorithms*. Morgan Kaufmann Pub,

Tabuada, P., Alves, P., Gomes, J. and Rosa, E. A. (1998). 3D Artificial Art by Genetic Algorithms. In Bentley, P. J. (ed.), *Proc. of the Workshop on Evolutionary Design*, 5th International Conference on Artificial Intelligence in Design '98, Instituto Superior Técnico, Lisbon, Portugal, 20–23 July 1998.

Todd, S. and Latham, W. (1992). *Evolutionary Art and Computers*. Academic Press,

Thompson, A. (1995). Evolving Fault Tolerant Systems. In *Genetic Algorithms in Engineering Systems: Innovations and Applications*, IEE Conf. Pub. No. 414, pp. 524–529.

Ventrella, J. (1994). Explorations in the Emergence of Morphology and Locomotion Behaviour in Animated Characters. In Brooks, R. and Maes, P. (eds), *Artificial Life IV*, Proc. of the 4th Int. Workshop on the Synthesis and Simulation of Living Systems, MIT Press, Cambridge, MA, pp. 436–441.

Whitley, D. and Starkweather, T. (1990). GENITOR II: A Distributed Genetic Algorithm. *Journal of Experimental and Theoretic Artificial Intelligence* 2:3, 189–214.

Yamada, T. and Nakano, R. (1995). A Genetic Algorithm with Multi-step Crossover for Job-shop Scheduling Problems. In *Genetic Algorithms in Engineering Systems: Innovations and Applications*, IEE Conf. Pub. No. 414, pp. 146–151.

Yao, X. and Liu, Y. (1996). Fast Evolutionary Programming, In Fogel, L., Angeline, P. and Back, T. (eds) *Proceedings of the Fifth International Conference on Evolutionary Programming*, MIT Press, Cambridge, MA.

Yao, X. Lin, G. and Liu, Y. (1997). An Analysis of Evolutionary Algorithms Based on Neighbourhood and Step Sizes. In Angeline, P., Reynolds, R., McDonnell, J. and Eberhart, R. (eds), *Proceedings of the Sixth International Conference on Evolutionary Programming*. Springer, pp. 298–307.

Yu, T. and Bentley, P. (1998). Methods to Evolve Legal Phenotypes. *Fifth Int. Conf. on Parallel Problem Solving From Nature*. Amsterdam, Sept 27–30. Springer.

Yu, T. and Clack, C. (1998a). Recursion, Lambda Abstractions and Genetic Programming, *Genetic Programming 1998: Proceedings of the Third Annual Conference*. Morgan Kaufmann, San Francisco.

Yu, T. and Clack, C. (1998b). PolyGP: A Polymorphic Genetic Programming System in Haskell (ed.), *Genetic Programming 1998: Proceedings of the Third Annual Conference*. Morgan Kaufmann, San Francisco.

1 EVOLUTION AND DESIGN

What does evolution have to do with design? Do our designs really evolve? Can evolution teach us about our own design process? How should we harness evolution in design?

This section explores these questions of evolution and design from four different viewpoints. *The Interplay of Evolution and Insight in Design* by Emeritus Prof. Michael French of Lancaster University gives the designer's view. He believes that our designs did evolve in the past, but today our own design process has more to do with insight than evolution. *The Memetics of Design* by Dr. Derek Gatherer, of Liverpool John Moores University, provides the starkly contrasting view of a memeticist. (Memetics is a controversial, but growing field which tries to explain our culture in terms of the evolution of ideas and concepts, or *memes*.) In his chapter, Derek suggests that, according to the theory of memetics, design is entirely an evolutionary process, and even our own creativity and inventiveness may be illusory. *The Race, the Hurdle, and the Sweet Spot* by Prof. David Goldberg, director of the Illinois Genetic Algorithms Laboratory (IlliGAL) gives the opinion of a computer scientist (and dedicated Genetic Algorithmist) by examining the development of genetic algorithms to throw light on our innovative and creative abilities. He suggests that a truly creative algorithm needs the ability to use knowledge from other domains. Finally, *Exploring the Design Potential of Evolutionary Search, Exploration and Optimisation* by Dr. Ian Parmee, head of the Plymouth Engineering Design Centre, gives the practical viewpoint of a computational designer, exploring how evolution can and should be integrated within our own design process.

Chapter 2

The Interplay of Evolution and Insight in Design

By Michael French

2.1 Introduction

Within our knowledge, the designed world consists of living things, produced by evolution through natural selection, and artifacts, which apart from a few things like nests, beaver dams, termite hills and honeycombs, are produced and designed by humans, using imagination and reasoning.

There is one kind of human design that is without any parallel in nature, and that is artistic design. All natural design is purely functional in purpose, even the forms and colours of flowers and birds, since there must have been some evolutionary pressure to produce it, some way in which it contributed to survival of the kind. That we find beauty in nature says something about the origins of our aesthetic sensibility, not about evolution directly (although the question of how our aesthetic sense evolved is an important and interesting one which will not be discussed here).

It is convenient to refer to all design that is not purely artistic as functional (meaning, strictly, having functions other than the aesthetic) because most of the methods and reasoning which help in functional design do not apply in the arts. There are, of course, many fields, such as architecture, in which both kinds of design are present.

In functional design, there are a number of functions to be performed and the designer selects or invents means to perform them. In a car, for example, the functions of prime mover, transmission, suspension and braking are performed by petrol or diesel engine, gears and shafts, links, springs and dampers and brakes, all of various kinds. The same structure of functions and means is present in living things, and so it is convenient to describe them also as functional designs, even though a purist might object that no purpose is involved. It is convenient also to adopt the anthropomorphism of 'nature' as the 'designer' of living organisms, but it must always be remembered that this is a figure of speech. The alternatives to this figment are an intolerable burden of circumlocution or some new terminology, and neither is attractive.

Many functions are needed in both living organisms and human designs, for instance, the circulation of fluids such as blood, oil and air. It is not surprising that in many cases the means developed by nature and by engineers to provide them are similar. Thus nature has evolved, and engineers have devised, pumps, fins, wings, jaws, hands and so on. Parallels might be expected to arise in such circumstances, and many have. Sometimes engineers have copied

EVOLUTIONARY DESIGN BY COMPUTERS
ISBN 1-55860-605-X

from nature, but more often they have simply found that their own ideas are already to be found in living organisms. It is only recently that serious attempts have been made to search deliberately for ideas from nature, in the field called 'biomimetics'. At present, there is particular interest in 'smart materials', an area where we may have a lot to learn from nature.

Since nature has produced very good engineering by natural selection, it is sensible to ask if engineers might do the same, in a new evolutionary design process, retaining all we have learnt from engineering science. The techniques used in this book are a partial answer to that question.

2.2 The Human Designer and Nature

2.2.1 Common Solutions to Common Problems

Striking parallels are to be found in the solutions to design problems reached by nature and by humans. For example, we developed our understanding of optics by the use of our sight. We then went on to develop other ways of 'seeing' using high frequency sound, only to discover that nature had also developed such senses. We developed radar, and found that some of the sophisticated techniques we devised for military purposes were already used by bats in their sonar. We invented leading-edge slots to delay stall in aircraft wings, and then found that the alula on the leading edge of a bird's wing appears to supply the same function. More recently we discovered just how far ahead birds were in the control of circulation, the flow of air round a wing that provides lift, and so on.

2.2.2 Learning from Nature

Sometimes we have learnt directly from nature, perhaps most importantly about how to fly. A few inventors were led astray by the flapping wing means of propulsion, but birds gave us plenty of free demonstrations of the regimes of flight and how to turn and land. Their form gave us hints about aerodynamic form and aspect ratio. We should have found it all much harder without the lessons they taught us.

Besides such clear examples, there are many cases in which our debt is less obvious. For example, the first robots used in manufacture mostly resembled a human arm, and while this form would probably have been chosen anyway because of its intrinsic advantages, it is natural it should come to mind. This is only what we should expect: common problems lead to common solutions.

In many cases, however, we have adopted different means to those of nature.

2.2.3 Different Solutions

Sometimes the solutions are different, because some of the means available to us are not available to nature. For instance, to convert chemical energy to mechanical energy, we use steam and gas turbines which require temperatures that living organisms cannot sustain. Nature uses muscle, in which the change from chemical to thermal energy is not made. Given the difficulties of direct chemical routes to mechanical energy, it is not surprising that we can achieve much higher efficiencies than nature. However, it is interesting to note that the fuel cell, in which chemical energy is converted to electrical energy without passing through the intermediate form of heat, is capable of higher efficiencies still. This is because, not using heat, this route is not limited in efficiency by the second law of thermodynamics.

There are other cases where human designs are not paralleled in nature. For instance, unlimited unidirectional rotation presents difficulties in animals, so there are no wheels and only minute propellers. Also, nervous systems ought surely to have buses, channels each carrying multiplexed signals to many destinations, rather than the 'one wire, one signal' design we used to use. Nature cannot use metals, with their desirable properties of strength and energy-absorption. But nature has used the rather unpromising structural materials that organisms can make to great advantage in elegant composites like bone and wood, from which we are currently drawing lessons. In this respect, we go more and more down the routes of nature, as we do also in our growing use of flexible constructions.

2.2.4 A Limitation of Natural Selection

The scope of natural selection is limited to forms attainable by viable routes, that is, series of forms each of which is viable in itself and subject to the pressure of natural selection to change in the direction of the next.

The air-breathing, viviparous, young-suckling whales are a large group of successful natural designs. It might have been expected that such creatures would have evolved from sharks, an old and successful range of designs occupying adjacent, and in many cases overlapping, niches, but that is not what happened. The whales came about through an enormous evolutionary detour, via other, bony, kinds of fish which took to the land, from which sprang amphibians, reptiles and eventually mammals. This devious route involved the adoption of legs and fur, later to be lost. An adaptation to swimming via flexing the body about a vertical axis was lost, to be replaced after a long interval on land by one involving flexure about a horizontal axis. Presumably this detour of evolution came about because either no direct route from fish to whale-like creature was viable (it is difficult to imagine, for example how air-breathing could have developed in a wholly marine creature) or else, if such routes existed, the evolutionary pressure along them was too weak. The one development which does look viable, that of becoming viviparous, did take place in the sharks.

This limitation of natural selection as a means of automatic design, that it can only proceed in viable directions, and cannot become less 'fit' in order subsequently to become even fitter, has resulted in some very circuitous paths.

2.2.5 The Remarkable Achievements of Natural Selection

In all comparisons, though, two aspects of nature above all command the admiration of the designer and make us recognize how far behind we are. First, there is the marvel of reproduction and growth. The flight of birds is magnificent to watch, but to think that this creature has grown from a single cell caps it all. The second is that nature has developed the human brain, that is itself able to design after a fashion, an ability no computer yet comes near, despite the grand term, 'artificial intelligence'.

2.3 The History of Design by Humans

2.3.1 Overview

Functional design is the means by which we have built up the material aspects of civilization. The beginnings of technology were tentative and resembled natural evolution in several ways, in the role of accident, in the selection of what proved good or fit and perhaps in the expansion from one niche to another. They were very slow, for example, taking many millennia to achieve slight refinements in stone tools.

As language improved, so the transfer of knowledge from one person to another became more accurate and complete. As observation led to understanding and experience accumulated, what started as a very slow process gathered pace. The advent of science improved the design process itself, and progress came to be expected and later planned. In the last two centuries, the role of trial and error has been progressively reduced: experiments on components and later, computer simulation, have brought us to a stage where many products are designed to be 'right first time', or at worst, right with a minimum of development.

Recently, evolutionary techniques in design have been reintroduced, on the computer, and these are the subject of this book. Although at present they are used for a small category of design problems, in this growing field design might be said to have come full circle.

2.3.2 The Early Evolutionary Phase

It seems probable that the idea of consciously designing useful artifacts from scratch was a long time in dawning, although certainly it had arrived two millennia ago. The beginnings of functional design in prehistory can only be guessed at. The discovery that the sharp edges left on certain stones when fractured were useful for cutting, the deliberate fracturing of stones to produce such edges, the development of the skill of knapping, the recognition of the most suitable forms for different purposes, are stages we can only conjecture at. We know from the different types of tool characteristic of different ages that the process was very slow, although it did accelerate. It was a kind of evolution, with even a trace of natural selection in it. A man making a scraper, for example, might copy examples found to be good, a kind of selective reproduction of the fittest for purpose.

This mechanism must have been present in historic times as well, and to some extent can be traced today. For example, the scythe is a strange tool, unlikely to be hit upon in one inventive burst, because of the dynamics of its use, with the user swinging regularly from one foot to the other in a way very economical of energy. Evolutionary development is the most likely way of arriving at such a form. 'I find Jack's scythe easier to use, please make me one like it.'

While it is usual to call this sort of development 'evolutionary', it is important to note that it does not proceed by random variations and natural selection. The selection is by observed performance and the variations are deliberately chosen in the belief they will prove beneficial. In this respect, evolutionary design was like breeding rather than evolution, where the breeder selects stock to be mated in the belief the offspring would be nearer to some imagined ideal.

As engineering developed and we acquired science, variations could be selected with more and more confidence and the results of changes became more predictable. Engineering design gradually became more deliberate, and progress more rapid. The violin is a fine piece of pre-scientific technology. It is a remarkable example of rapid 'trial and error' evolution, where an understanding of the required properties was far beyond the mechanics of the day, but a very good solution was achieved in a relatively short time historically. Only a decade or so ago we acquired the engineering understanding to analyse the remarkably complicated acoustic behaviour of a violin and its relation to its structural form. Perhaps one day we shall have fully engineered violins, superior to any Stradivarius made.

2.3.3 Examples from the History of Weapons

Spear-thrower

An early example of prehistoric engineering was the spear-thrower. This was a short stick, slightly worked at one end to fit the butt of a spear. The user held the other end, and flung the spear with it. The spear-thrower enabled force to be applied to the spear through a longer distance, so achieving a greater initial velocity and greater range and penetration.

It is difficult to see how such a device arose. It seems unlikely that it was an invention, because it is not an easy device to use and the technique is difficult to acquire. It seems more probable to the writer that it arose in play and developed as an informal game, throwing a spear with a stick. To begin with, range would be reduced, accuracy greatly reduced, and muffed throws common. Moreover, the ideal spear would be lighter than one for simple throwing, a further obstacle to developing the kind of performance that would be necessary before the spear-thrower was a valuable innovation in hunting technology. But eventually throwing spears with improved sticks, now evolved to suit their function well, might have come to be recognized as having potential for hunting.

A role as a plaything may have provided a niche in which the spear-thrower was developed.

If that was how it happened, there is a parallel with the way in which the land provided ecological niches in which the mammals developed the attributes which made possible the whales.

The Bow

The bow is a very elegant design, appearing with the Neolithic age, although it was not until the late 17th century that we knew enough mechanics to be able to appreciate it. It converts energy stored as strain energy into kinetic energy of the arrow, but to begin with, much of the energy goes into the tips of the bow. As the string straightens late in release, however, the ratio of the velocity of the bow tips to that of the arrow becomes small, and kinetic energy is actually fed back from the tips of the bow to the arrow.

The chief types of bow were the reflex, where the chief spring material was animal sinew, and the wooden long-bow. The reflex bow was a subtle combination of materials, in the most advanced form sinew, wood and horn, and its construction was understood throughout most of Asia and North America, and in the Mediterranean countries. For example, both the Turkish bowyers and the North American Indians used the sinew in pieces like short spaghetti, and glued layers of them to the underlying wood until they had built up the required thickness. The glues were animal or fish glue, so that basically they were making a composite of collagen in a matrix of collagen.

The bow, almost certainly of wood in the first instance, may have started as a toy and a game as suggested in the case of the spear-thrower, but it is conceivable that some Neolithic genius saw its potential and developed it with hunting in view.

Many millennia later, it is conceivable also that some unknown genius thought to try the effect of sticking sinew to the back of a wooden bow, in the expectation that it might improve the performance. It is difficult to see how the reflex bow can have been entirely an evolutionary development: it must surely have involved invention. Certainly the ideas of invention and innovative development were around early in written history, as the next section shows, even though it took a long time for them to gain general currency.

Ancient Greek Catapults

The bow had a remarkable descendant in the Greek and Roman catapults which were an important arm in warfare from the fourth century BC to well into the fall of the Roman Empire. In the Middle Ages only more primitive projectile weapons were used.

We know a great deal about the Greek weapons, probably more than we do about any other area of technology of the time, because three artillery manuals survive, in the form of later copies, those of Bito, Hero, and Philo. These books contain, not only instructions for building these machines to any specification, but some of the rationale of their design, notes on the history of their development and details of particular or novel designs (including a repeating catapult and designs using bronze and air for springs). Moreover, Philo noted, quite correctly, the shortcomings of the standard design and invented a form intended to overcome them.

The first Greek catapults were huge crossbows, based on sinew, wood and horn like the hand bows, but the torsion type soon displaced them. The torsion catapult was like the crossbows except that instead of the spring element being a bent beam it consisted of a frame carrying two tight bundles of cord made from sinews (the springs), through which passed two arms (fig. 2.1). Pulling back the string of the 'bow' twisted the bundles, storing energy which on release impelled the arrow forward, just as the straightening beam of a bow does.

The Spanish windlass, a device consisting of a bundle of cords tightened by twisting, using a bar thrust through it, was well known in the ancient world. It had been used centuries earlier by the Egyptians to tighten ropes to pull up the sagging ends of their ships, and the Greeks may have tightened a rope encircling their warships by the same means.

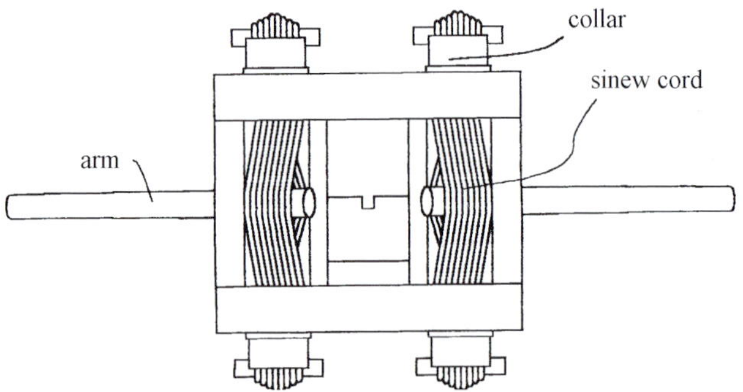

Figure 2.1 Greek catapult, 'bow' part only: front elevation.

A remarkable feature of these catapults was that they were of modular design. The Greek engineers arrived at fixed proportions for their machines, all expressed as multiples of the diameter ***D*** of the holes through which passed the bundles of sinew. The value of ***D*** was derived from the length (arrows) or mass (stones) of the projectiles it was intended to use. For stones, ***D*** in dactyls was given by 1.1 times the cube root of the weight of stone in drachmae. The cube root was found by drawing the construction for two mean proportionals. The width of the frame was then made 6.5***D***, the side stanchions were 3.5***D*** high, and so on. All this was sound engineering, justifiable in terms of our modern engineering science. The proportions were arrived at on a basis of experiment, and calculations by the author suggest that the structural design was well-balanced, that is, the different parts would fail at about the same overload. The Greek engineers were then probably the most advanced designers in the world.

Sinew is a good material for storing energy, with about twenty times the capacity per unit mass that spring steel has, but it must be stretched by about 6% to be effective. The bundles were too slender to develop such a large strain. If no special measures had been taken, the stretch in even the outermost cords would have been only 0.3%, which would store a mere 0.25% of the possible energy. To overcome these problems two measures were adopted, pre-twist and pre-tension. The bundle was wound under tension, each half turn being held under tension by a temporary stop driven home by a mallet, thus 'crushing and tearing the cord', as Philo observed (Marsden, 1971). The bundle was then pre-twisted by turning the collars supporting its ends about its axis: this twisting introduced further pre-tension as well as increasing the additional strain on turning the arm.

Philo

Philo is eloquent about the effects of both pre-tension and large pre-twist, which makes the machine 'hard to draw back and weak in shooting' (a consequence of friction between the strands). In his design winding was done in the slack state, and then pre-tension was introduced by driving the top and bottom of the frames apart by hammering in wedges. It seems nothing came of his ideas and with modern understanding of mechanics that is what one might expect. Nevertheless, Philo looked at the current design, was aware of its defects and worked out a possible way round them. The stage had certainly been reached at which progress by innovative design was expected, by then if not earlier.

Philo did not know how right he was. This writer has shown that the Greeks were using about fifty times as much sinew as was necessary, and their catapults were much heavier and more expensive than they need have been (French, 1989).

Summary of the History of Design of Ancient Weapons

This survey of ancient weapons has shown the development of functional design (largely based on hypothesis in the prehistoric section) from processes having a large element of accident and bearing some resemblance to natural selection, to deliberate innovation based on the observation of defects and the invention of alternatives by the third century BC. The Greek engineers even used some science in their designing, correctly in the case of rules for finding ***D*** from the calibre of missile. They were the leading edge, however, and the Romans who came after improved the designs only marginally. It took another two millennia for approaches like Philo's to become commonplace.

It is significant that to begin with, development was so slow. Wallace, co-originator with Darwin of the theory of evolution, held that natural selection could not account for the human brain, because it had abilities far beyond the needs of survival. The late appearance of the spear thrower and the bow, however, show that they must have been at the limit of human creative power. Those remote ancestors of ours, in the primitive state of their culture, were only just equal to the tasks, which undoubtedly had value for survival. With our great accumulated knowledge and understanding, it is difficult to recognise the height of such intellectual hurdles for them.

Such reasoning does not entirely dispose of Wallace's argument. It could be held that there are whole areas of our mental faculties that are irrelevant to technical progress. This writer believes they are all related by-products of the development of high-level, general-purpose thinking, as distinct from the low-level, high-capacity, specialised data processing, associated, for instance, with vision and language.

By Philo's time, and probably earlier, the idea of deliberate innovative design was established, among engineers at least. Nevertheless, progress only gathered pace slowly.

2.3.4 Why did Innovative Functional Design Take so Long to Become Accepted?

Progress in functional design was very slow until the nineteenth century. Opportunities were there on every side, but innovations came only slowly. It seems extraordinary, for example, that the use of cartridge ammunition came so late, or that there were over fifty years between the early steam engines (1712 on) and Watt's invention of the separate condenser (patented in 1769).

A number of causes can be suggested. First, the expectation of material progress was not widely shared. Secondly, many of the more influential in society would be hostile to any new idea, seeing it as a threat, however remote, to a status quo out of which they were doing very well. Thirdly, there was the spear-thrower problem, the development gap: it may take prolonged trials and large investments before a new idea, however sound, is fit for the market-place. The designer may have faith in the idea, but his backers may not be willing to continue. Moreover, one advance often depends on another, without which it is impractical. The use of ammunition with the bullet fixed in a cartridge increases the rate of fire of infantry to several times that possible in the Napoleonic wars, but without developments in manufacturing methods it would have been prohibitively expensive for armies.

The thought of making a fortune produces inventors, and the thought of stripping a rich fool of some of his fortune attracts charlatans, so the sound proposal has to struggle with both the unsound (which may none the less have merit) and the simply fraudulent. Unfortunate experiences in innovation are always likely to outnumber the fortunate, developing a profound scepticism in the public. Swift expresses this in *Gulliver's Travels*. In Laputa, a scientist was working on storing sunbeams in cucumbers for release in bad weather (which in a way is what the Swedes do now, except they use willows instead of cucumbers) and other schemes of like ingenuity.

2.3.5 Acceleration

But the tally of very successful innovations grew and grew, and with the growth of science, it became easier to distinguish the feasible from the impossible. Improvements in manufacturing, improved materials and a better appreciation of their properties made life easier for the designer and progress more predictable. One industry laid the foundations for another. Steam power required improved machine tools which stimulated a virtuous cycle of more accurate instruments and gauges and better products, culminating in the interchangeability necessary to avoid hand fitting and opening the door to mass production. Bicycles demanded light strong components of types soon to be needed in cars and aircraft. The typewriter was made possible by the invention of type and itself led to improvements in production methods which contribute to many modern products. Photography in the nineteenth century paved the way for the production methods which were to be used later to make microchips, and so on.

It is often said that innovation is ever accelerating, but perhaps we have done the easier things and those that remain are mostly difficult and take longer. We first flew in 1903, and aircraft were extensively used in the 1914–18 war. The first fuel cell was demonstrated in 1880, but it is still not an everyday commercial reality, though its day looks very near. The first car with a continuously variable transmission (CVT) came on the market around 1930, and at the time of writing they are still rare, though very desirable on environmental grounds. Nuclear fission power was on stream in the UK less than twenty years after the first working pile, yet fusion power is anticipated to be still at least forty years away. Perhaps technical progress peaked around 1900, with the steam turbine, electrical power, the telephone, radio, the car, and flight. In the middle of the nineteenth century we had the gas turbine, television, nuclear power, the computer and computer-controlled machines, but none except the computer have had such impact as the first group.

Now we are at a stage when ideas run well ahead of achievements. Prediction of performance at the drawing stage becomes more and more reliable, even for novel products where there is no directly relevant experience to draw upon. Engineering is done increasingly on a 'right first time basis'. Perhaps the most spectacular success of engineering so far, the landing of men on the moon, had to be done on a 'right first time' basis.

There still remains a role for the trial and error process: it is often a matter of cost. In some fields, it is relatively cheap and quick to build a prototype and try it out, and sometimes that may still be the best way. However, in much innovative design, it is very expensive to try out an idea in hardware, and so it is highly desirable to make extensive calculations and simulations so as to 'get it right first time'.

2.3.6 How Design Progresses: Insight and Evolution

How is progress made in design? Engineering designers work, whether consciously or not, by deciding the functions to be performed and the best means of performing them. In general, the means they choose are what are described in patents as 'known means', drawn from the design repertoire. The design repertoire is just the collection of all those means of performing commonly or uncommonly needed functions that have been evolved or invented in the past, together with the ways of suiting them to different circumstances and requirements. It is a vast body of knowledge, and any individual is only familiar with parts of it.

All this sounds very simple, but it is really nothing of the kind. The possibilities are endless: it is not practicable to evaluate all the alternatives and judgement must be used to select from them. Most known means need some adaptation to suit them for use in a particular design, and often this adaptation is far from trivial. A pump for a washing machine is an application of a known means. Only a modest performance is demanded, it is not difficult to see that a kinetic type of pump is most suitable, and there are hundreds of examples available. Nevertheless, there may remain scope for a great deal of original design, to keep down the cost of manufacture and make assembly easy while maintaining reliability. A pump of this kind may be just competently designed, or it may be a brilliant piece of work, recognizable from some innovative feature with real advantages, displaying qualities not different in kind from those of much more important inventions.

Insight

How does outstanding design come about? It usually happens because of some clarification of understanding that leads to old thinking being revised, an insight after which problems appear changed and new approaches to a solution are suggested. Torroja, the great Spanish civil engineer, wrote that a designer should understand the working of a structure as fully as he understood the fall of a stone or the discharge of an arrow from a bow. With such deep insight comes the ability to spot the possibilities for new approaches, of the kind which by hindsight appear obvious.

Watt

One of the great engineering inventions was the separate condenser, with which Watt reduced the fuel consumption of the steam engine to about one-third. By hindsight, nothing could be more obvious. But it was Watt's insight into the working of the engine, developed by experiment, that showed him what to do.

In 1784 Watt wrote to his partner Boulton, who was concerned that the steam turbine, upon which some people were working, might prove a rival to their engine. He wrote that the turbine could not be a practical machine 'without god makes it possible for things to move at 1,000 ft pr', an entirely sound insight. Dickinson and Jenkins, 1981, write of Watt 'It was a curious trait in Watt's character that no sooner did anyone suggest an application of steam than he at once seized on it, and by calculation and reasoning carried the matter on paper to a stage much farther than the original suggestion.' It is exactly this insight and direct grasp of essentials that show the genius of the man.

Other Examples of Insight

Other examples of insight are the letter in which Sir Robert Watson-Watt indicated the practicability of radar detection of enemy bombers by a few back-of-an-envelope calculations, and the extraordinary guess about the essential nature of the genetic code made by Schrödinger. Schrödinger argued that the only means which could store information compactly enough and yet be robust enough to survive thermal excitation was a non-repeating crystalline molecule, whose composition would be the code. This was very much an engineering style of argument, with its review of possible means of achieving a function. The 'aperiodic crystal', as Schrödinger called it, turned out to be DNA.

Those are grand examples of insight. Here is another, not nearly so grand, but important in its own way.

Large alternators such as are used in power stations used to be made with the rotor winding housed in parallel slots in the armature, so that the 'teeth' left between the slots were tapered, wider at the outside than at the inside (fig. 2.2). The insight concerned was the recognition of the value of space in the annular region of the teeth and slots, which is where all the work goes on. The outer diameter of the rotor is severely restricted by the centrifugal stresses and the inner diameter of the teeth must be enough to accept the magnetic flux, so there was little scope for increasing the cross-sectional area. Consequently, to improve performance the first option to examine was that of using this valuable space to better advantage.

The material in the space has several functions, resisting centrifugal forces, providing magnetic or electrical flux paths, providing passages for coolant (hydrogen) and so on. The material of the teeth provides magnetic flux path and centrifugal strength, but the amount of both is limited to that which can be carried by the narrow section at the root of a tooth (AA in fig. 2.2). It follows that the overhangs of the teeth, shown shaded in fig. 2.2, are a waste of valuable space, and a great advance can be made by giving the shaded part over to more slot, with more electrical conduction path and so on. In outline, that is what was done, the improvement being cashed in, as it were, partly as increased output per metre length of rotor and partly as increased efficiency (French, 1971).

There are snags. The conductors, which are not wires but machined bars with coolant ways cut in them, must now be of several different widths and so the parts count is increased. But this extra cost is small compared with the gains. A rough calculation to compare these factors numerically, a small *insight-developing study*, can be done in hours and will return a clear answer in favour of parallel-sided teeth.

The insight here was just to recognize the value of regarding the problem as one of using to the most advantage a valuable commodity, here that of space in way of the teeth, what the writer calls a problem of disposition. This insight provides a simple way of improving the design substantially.

Aids to Insight

In cases like the last, insight is readily within the scope of the human brain. It often requires a little separate *insight-developing study* to bring it out. Even elaborate or recondite systems will often yield clear insights, but sometimes only after long study and with great difficulty. Understanding fractional distillation processes is no easy matter, but it is done. Diagrams

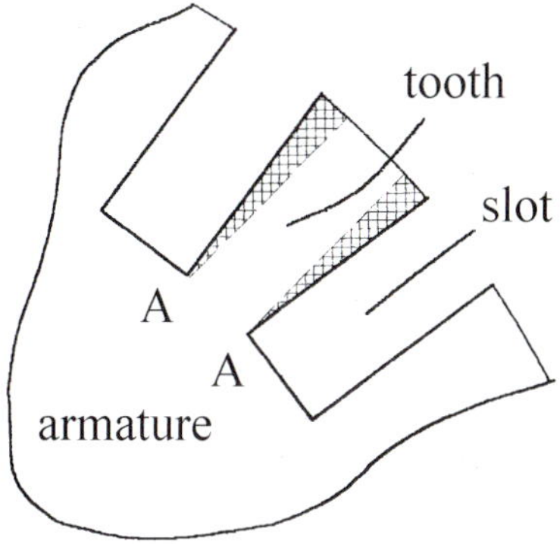

Figure 2.2 Part of alternator rotor.

have been devised which enable the initiated to develop a deep understanding and a measure of intuition about the relationships between the concentrations in the phases (e.g., Ruhemann, 1940). Other examples could be quoted from electrical machines, steam turbines, control theory, and so on. For a method developed purely to improve insight in a particular case, applied to the extraction of energy from sea waves, see French (1996).

The human mind can generate thinking aids of these sorts to achieve insight in what appear at first daunting situations. When this has been done, we see order in the confusion. The mist clears, we see everything entire and know just how to proceed. The insight provides an informing principle and progress is often rapid, with piece after piece falling into place.

The insight must be sound, however. Philo had great familiarity with the shortcomings of the Greek catapults, but insufficient mechanics to recognize the real weakness in the design (the bundles were too tall and thin). Had he known Hooke's Law he could have seen this defect and addressed it directly, and so have arrived at a very successful new version.

2.3.7 When Insight Fails

But some problems do not yield insights that make the way clear for the designer in this way. There is no simple elegant key to their complexity that leads to the heart of the problem. The violin probably belongs to that class. How then are such problems to be approached? The answer for Stradivarius and his forerunners was trial and error, by building hundreds of instruments and gradually learning how to achieve what was sought, keeping what was good and avoiding what proved unsuccessful, the evolutionary way.

Today, the availability of massive computing power may provide a route to insights of the kind that lead to progress. By working out and comparing results for families of designs obtained by varying a number of important parameters we may be able to spot important effects and so arrive at insights. Even when clarifying insights do not come, whether because they do not exist or because we are unable to spot them, we can simply persist with our calculations until we have found the design which performs best, according to whatever criteria we choose. Stradivarius today could 'build' that violin with increased curvature of the belly and a little less thinning round the edges of the back on the computer, calculate its elastic properties and hence its performance and then decide whether it was worth building it in wood.

2.3.8 The Computer in Engineering Design

The computer has made possible these heavy calculations, analyses and simulations, and has put the means of performing them into the hands of the individual designer. In addition, the computer has now become the sole medium for making finished drawings, and handling the vast amount of information they contain. The problem of keeping track of design information on modern aircraft, for example, has become difficult even with the computer. In its several roles in manufacturing, the computer has increased the demands the designer can make on production, such as special shapes, tighter tolerances, short runs and customized combinations of features. Most recently, contributions to rapid prototyping and tooling of complex forms have become an important resource for the designer, and these depend upon the computer, among other advances.

Nevertheless, none of these have touched deeply on the work of designing itself. There have now emerged, however, computer aids in which the man and the machine work almost in partnership. An example is that of computer-aided conceptual design (CACD) where the normal procedure followed by the designer (the conceptual and embodiment stages; French 1971 Pahl and Beitz 1977) is greatly expedited by the computer automatically carrying out the necessary calculations, offering advice from the repertoire on possible means which can be used for a particular function, keeping a record of the current state, warning of problems and simulating performance. Embedded in such tools is a great deal of engineering knowledge. An example is Schemebuilder, a CACD tool for mechatronic engineering which the writer started in 1990 and is now usable (see Porter, 1998). Others are more specialized, for instance, several for the conceptual design of aircraft based on existing designs (case-based approaches).

Where the parameters are numerous and the calculations related to performance heavy, however, the search for the optimum design can be a massive task even for the prodigious computing power we dispose of today. Some economical search procedure is needed, and in many cases this may be found in the techniques with which this book deals, modelled on evolution by natural selection.

So it is that some design by humans has come full circle. An evolutionary search today is not unlike the evolution of human design in the past, by trial and error. The differences are, first, that the designs are not constructed, but simulated, and secondly, that the selection and evaluation of models is systematic. In nature, favourable mutations may be unlucky and die before they reproduce, while equivalent accidents can be prevented from occurring with genetic algorithms. Also, unlike evolution by natural selection, it is possible to jump through regions that would correspond to non-viable forms. In evolution on the computer, the whale could evolve from the shark without the detour through land creatures.

It remains to be seen how important this new form of evolutionary design will prove, whether it will be limited to a technique that is useful in a rather rare kind of problem or whether it will extend in scope to become a tool regularly used in design offices everywhere.

References

Dickinson, H. W. and Jenkins, R. (1981). *James Watt and the Steam Engine*, Encore Editions, London.

French, M. J. (1971). *Engineering Design: the Conceptual Stage*, Heinemann, London.

French, M. J. (1989). The design of torsion catapults, *Design Studies*, **10;** 208–213.

French, M. J. (1996). Tadpole: a design problem in the mechanics of sea wave energy, *Proc Inst Mech E* **210;** 273–277.

Marsden, E. W. (1971). *Greek and Roman Artillery*, Clarendon, Oxford.

Pahl, G. and Beitz, W. (1977). *Konstruktionslehre*, Springer, Berlin.

Porter, I. (1998). Schemebuilder mechatronics, *Engineering Design Conference*, Brunel University.

Ruhemann, M. (1940). *The Separation of Gases*, Clarendon, Oxford.

Chapter 3

The Memetics of Design

By Derek Gatherer

3.1 The Evolution of Designed Objects

Does the history of human technology reveal an evolutionary process at work? In other words, does design evolve? If so, can we take the considerable repertoire of conceptual techniques developed in the field of biological evolution, and adapt them to study of the evolution of design?

As an illustration of this way of thinking about design processes, one might consider the history of the commercial combustion engine vehicle over the last century. A series of mass production 'saloon' vehicles, from the Ford Model T onwards, is reminiscent of the familiar school biology diagram of human evolution from the knuckle-walking *Proconsul* through the heavy-browed muscularity of *Australopithecus* to *Homo sapiens*, looking sleek if a little naked in front of a line of more hirsute ancestors.

Such evolutionary trees are often extensively branched; for instance the tree of the vertebrates shows both terrestrial mammals and deep sea fishes to be descended from primitive chordates which lived some 400 million years ago. Likewise, the Formula 1 racing car and the Honda Civic are both 'descendants' of the Benz Motor-Wagen of the 1890s. Like the cod and the kangaroo, they have adapted in the meantime to perform quite distinct roles, to fit into very different evolutionary niches. Similar evolutionary sequences may be constructed, with a little imagination, for almost any human artefact. Thus in addition to the evolution of the motor car, we may visualise the evolution of the television, the evolution of the refrigerator, a far longer evolutionary series from Palaeolithic hand axe to the latest kitchen knife, and even a short but rapid evolution of the personal computer.

Other parallels between biological evolution and the history of technological change also spring to mind. For instance, some designs, such as the Beetle or the Mini, have considerable longevity whereas others last scarcely a few years. Similarly, in biology, most species last a few million years at most before extinction or evolution into som ething else, but there are the Beetles and Minis of the animal kingdom, such as horseshoe crabs and sharks, which seem to have been perennially successful over hundreds of millions of years. In design as in biology, we have our evolutionary successes as well as our extinct species.

However, are these processes of change really evolutionary processes? Evolution, as we shall see, is not a synonym for *any* kind of change, but requires the three linchpins of transmission, variation and selection. Identifying these factors in human culture, and formulating evolutionary explanations of cultural change is the domain of a cross-disciplinary effort termed 'memetics'.

EVOLUTIONARY DESIGN BY COMPUTERS
ISBN 1-55860-605-X

3.2 Memetics is Not (very) Difficult

The term 'memetics' is now over twenty years old, and the general concept of cultural evolutionism has deeper roots going back well into the 19th century and even earlier (rev. Gatherer, 1997). Nevertheless, its progress has been tortuous and slow. One of the reasons for this is that a sound understanding of evolution is helpful, and this is usually only obtained through pursuit of a degree in biology. Even that is no guarantee – in the words of the great evolutionist Theodosius Dobzhansky: 'the problem with evolution is that everybody thinks he understands it, but few do'. In any case, most trained biologists are more interested in purely biological problems, and tend to see the study of culture as at best a secondary issue. On the other hand, the humanists and social scientists who are well versed in culture can be a little suspicious of arrivistes from biology. However, these fears are unjustified. Culture is biologically interesting, as one of the principal ways in which we humans adapt to our environment, and humanists need not fear an invasion of philistine reductionists onto their intellectual territory – evolutionary theory has come a long way since the days of Herbert Spencer and the Social Darwinists. More importantly, Dobzhansky's jaundiced comment incorrectly implies that it must be a virtually insurmountable problem to make evolution comprehensible – if even those who claim to understand evolution really do not, then what hope can there be? In fact, the pedagogical difficulty with evolution is that it is often made more complex than it need be. Evolutionary theory is like learning to ride a bicycle, simple but just a little tricky at the beginning. It is certainly easier than some of the concepts that are regarded as de rigueur in a humanist education, such as dialectics, structuralism or the synthetic a priori. Whatever our disciplines, we should all make the effort to understand evolutionary principles. If memetics is correct, then all human culture – science, art, technology and religion – falls within the remit of evolutionary theory. The first step in this process is to consider the nature of evolutionary change, in other words what a process must be like in order to be described as evolutionary.

3.3 What is Evolutionary Change?

Evolution is a much used, and abused, word. Sometimes it is taken to be virtually synonymous with change of any variety, sometimes restricted to a specific set of changes that occur in genetic systems, i.e. biological evolution. The former is certainly too loose a definition, and the latter probably too narrow, but there is no absolute consensus. One influential theory is that of Universal Darwinism (Dawkins, 1983). This proposes that *any* informational system that fulfils certain criteria is potentially an evolving system. These criteria are:

a) **heritability** – the information must be transmissible in some way.

b) **variability** – although fidelity is important, there must be some scope for errors to creep in, a perfectly replicating system cannot evolve.

c) **selection** – some variants may be more efficiently replicated or more durable than others; those variants will tend to increase in frequency in the system as a whole. Selection need not be continuous; a variable hereditary system may drift for long periods between episodes of selective pressure, without necessarily losing any of its potential to respond to selection should the situation demand.

Provided, therefore, that selection can act on some variable transmitted information, evolution will occur. In biological systems, as Darwin perceived, these conditions are satisfied. Creatures reproduce themselves, but seldom perfectly; the resulting variability is raw material for the quality-control processes of natural selection. Geneticists of the 20th century went on to demonstrate that heritability in biology is provided by the encoding of structural information in DNA, and that variability is a consequence of the processes of mutation and recombination in that DNA. The exact nature of selective pressures can be difficult to identify, but Darwin's successors have pursued his intuitions and focused on such factors as competition for food and mates or avoidance of predators. Darwin's contribution is all the more remarkable in that it was achieved with little or no understanding of the mechanisms of either heritability or variation.

Dawkins' concept of Universal Darwinism was framed in the form of a thought experiment concerning how life might evolve, assuming that there are conditions sufficiently benign, elsewhere in the universe. Dawkins' purpose is not so much to make a contribution to the search for extraterrestrial life as to suggest that evolution is *not* dependent on specifically biological elements such as DNA or organisms, but may apply to any other informational systems where heretability, variability and selection occur. The other informational system that Dawkins has specifically in mind is human culture.

Examples of cultural selection pressures spring to mind without too much difficulty. To return to the evolution of the motor car: first the car must run adequately. Secondly, economics requires the product to be affordable by the target consumer. Fuel prices may result in the development of engines designed to maximise efficiency. Legislation or public demand may push for more environmental friendliness. General stylistic tastes may influence vehicle shape, etc. Variability is even less of a problem, numerous designs are in the showrooms and on the road at any one time, all competing for a larger future slice of the market. These two factors are relatively straightforward. Heritability, however, is a different matter. Motor cars obviously do not reproduce in the way that organisms do. They need to be constructed by humans, and also designed by humans. There can be little doubt that *Proconsul* (or a similar species) is the ancestor of *Homo sapiens*, through thousands of generations of replication, variation and selection. Apes are *literally* our distant grandparents. However, to consider the Ford Model T the ancestor of the Ford Probe is considerably more problematic.

3.4 The Reproduction of Information

Since cultural artefacts such as motor cars or refrigerators do not directly reproduce themselves, where does the information for their (re-)production lie? The obvious answer would seem to be in the blueprints upon which their physical form is based. In biological systems the blueprint is present in every genome as DNA (or in a few systems the related molecule RNA), in culture these blueprints are very distant from the objects they encode. In some cases, before production of the artefact has begun, the blueprint may only be in the mind of the designer, or may lie diffusely in the minds of several members of a design team, each of whom is employed to make a contribution to the final form of the object that they are about to create. The implications of this separation of cultural artefact and cultural blueprint need to be spelled out, as they are pivotal to the whole attempt to construct an evolutionary analysis of design.

In biological evolution the 20 million year sequence from *Proconsul* to modern humans represents the evolution of both physical form and also the informational blueprint, since that information is contained *within* the physical form of the organism, sequestered as DNA in the nucleus of each cell, and passed to the next generation in the gametes. The evolutionary sequence of the physical form of the motor car in the 20th century contains no such tangible evolution of information, but nevertheless hints at a corresponding evolution of the blueprints in the minds of the designers. Parallel to the apparent evolution of the artefact, we can begin to form a notion of the evolution of the ideas behind the artefact. In short, evolutionary processes in human cultural artefacts imply an evolutionary process in the human mind.

This enables us to proceed to analyse the evolution of the motor car in terms of parallel evolutionary processes. The vehicles themselves, although created by people, are independent physical objects in what we might call the real world. The ideas that resulted in the production of any particular vehicle are abstract notions of form. In the process of design and production, these abstract notions were first created in the minds of the designers, and then used as templates from which the physical form of the motor car was constructed. The mental concept was thus expressed in physical terms. Any individuals looking at the new vehicle, observing its shape, examining its engine or driving it, will develop an abstract idea of that vehicle in their minds, based on the physical form with which they are presented. There need not even be a first-hand interaction with the artefact, the concept may be passed purely by word of mouth, with or without the aid of a few sketches or photographs. If the individuals involved are themselves designers, they may use some of that concept in the production of their own new designs. There is thus a continual interaction between the conceptual and the physical, between vague ideas in designers' heads and the final physical manifestation of those ideas. Conceptual evolution can also occur on its own, as ideas are passed from individual to individual without ever taking material form as a finished motor car or refrigerator, but nevertheless existing in the mind as vague plans and dreams. The physical evolution of artefacts, however, cannot be independent, as there must always be a conceptual design for any artefact. Refrigerators per se do not evolve, but the design of a refrigerator does.

3.5 Memetics and Cultural Replicators

The evolutionary analysis of human culture was given a further twist by Dawkins' (1976) coining of the term *meme*. This was originally posited as *any* 'cultural replicator', implying that both mental blueprints and artefacts are memes, but was later (Dawkins, 1982) restricted to a replicating informational pattern in the brain. Any resulting artefacts or behaviours are considered to be physical manifestations of those memes, part of the 'extended phenotype' of the organism. The memetic informational unit in the brain is not defined other than by its ability to replicate, that is to find itself instantiated in another brain. It therefore need not be precisely the same in any two individuals. A meme for tying a Windsor knot, for instance, will not involve *exactly* the same pattern of neurological activity in any two individuals tying the knot. However, there must presumably be some neuronal correspondence in order for the behavioural activity of Windsor knot tying to be effectively replicated. The meme is the mental blueprint for the knot. It is not a rigid unit of mental structure, but a functional definition of transmitted, variable cultural information. Transmission and variation will, as we have seen,

produce evolution when subjected to selective pressure. Memetic evolution is the evolution of mental blueprints for physical objects or behaviours.

If this was all there was to it, the meme concept would simply have restated the old case for cultural evolution. However, by deliberately punning 'meme' on 'gene', Dawkins suggests that the range of analytical approaches developed in post-war genetics should also be applicable to the renovation of the 19th century edifice of cultural evolutionism. The principal thesis of the memetic approach is that we should focus on the memes themselves rather than on the people who have the memes in their minds, just as evolutionary geneticists now focus on the genes themselves rather than the organisms that are their temporary vehicles. Valid questions which may be posed within a memetic framework are such things as: why is one idea transmitted more rapidly and efficiently than another? Why are some ideas long-lived and others rapidly dated? How does variability appear in our ideas? What selective factors cause some ideas to spread and others to disappear?

A more precise definition of the meme, beyond saying that it is simply a replicating unit of culture either physical or mental, is not available, nor is it easy to see how one might be formulated. This is often seen as a weakness of the theory, but it need not be. Since the gene is no longer atomistically defined but has, in the era of molecular biology, acquired a flexibility in both size and form, neither is it necessary that a term like the meme should imply any rigid inheritance of indivisible units of culture. The meme-gene analogy is to a certain extent simply the revival of the bio-cultural analogy of 19th-century anthropology, but it is also much more than that. It is the bio-cultural analogy refurbished in the light of a century of genetics and molecular biology. Part of that refurbishment package is the realisation that the unit of selection *can* be very small – in genetic terms a gene rather than the organism that carries it, in memetic terms a meme rather than the individual mind that carries it. However, another part of the package is the reassurance that units of selection are of *variable* size and need not be rigidly atomistic. Just as modern molecular genetics can deal with any entity between a single nucleotide informational 'bit' to an entire genome, so can memetics consider everything from the simplest proposition to an entire religion. Memetics is also more than the old bio-cultural analogy in that the meme is taken *literally* to be a replicator. Therefore memeticists do not merely say that culture is *like* biology, but that both are genuine evolutionary systems in their own right. It might equally be maintained that biology is like culture. If this seems too absurd a claim, it is worth recalling that Darwin may have had precisely this thought when he pondered Sir William Jones's work on 'homology by descent' in the Indo-European languages. It was as a consequence of this study that Darwin was persuaded to entertain the same notion concerning the relationships of species (Darwin, 1985, p. 406).

Geneticists were quick to turn their theoretical tools onto the processes of memetics, and an impressive body of mathematical theory rapidly developed (e.g. Richerson and Boyd, 1978; Cavalli-Sforza and Feldman, 1981; Lumsden and Wilson, 1981). Many of these authors took issue with some parts of the meme concept, and all coined their own alternative terminologies; for instance *culturgen*, divided into *mentifacts* and *artifacts*, by Lumsden and Wilson or *culture-types* by Richerson and Boyd, but their ideas contain more points of agreement than disagreement (rev. Ball, 1984). However, empirical attempts to verify or deny some of the predictions of memetic theory have been a little slower in appearing. The major part of this work has been carried out on animals, whose cultural repertoire is more limited and thus less

confusing to study. One particularly fruitful area has been birdsong (Payne et al., 1988; Lynch et al., 1989; Lynch and Baker, 1993, 1994; Ficken and Popp, 1995). Human memetics has been energetically examined by Cavalli-Sforza and colleagues (Cavalli-Sforza et al., 1982, 1983; Cavalli-Sforza and Feldman, 1983; Hewlett and Cavalli-Sforza, 1986; rev. by Cavalli-Sforza, 1986) from whose school comes the most thorough study to date (Guglielmino et al., 1995). This examines several dozen memes in a wide variety of West African populations, demonstrating that transmission of memes is mostly within a local context, e.g. family or village groups, and that accumulation of variability is quite slow. Only a small proportion of the traits were correlated with the environment, which was taken to be indicative of selective pressures. Identification of genuine cultural adaptation seems to be the greatest current challenge to any empirical memetics on humans. Perhaps the Cavalli-Sforza school would find more obvious selection pressures if they were to confine their analysis to technology instead of attempting to analyse cultures in their entirety. The very breadth of their approach means that they are forced to consider aspects of culture such as religion, art and language, where selection may be only intermittent at best.

For Pocklington and Best (1997) the solution to this problem is to limit the field of study, to extract a single aspect of human culture that is easily analysable. These authors concentrate on the statistical properties of word usage in NetNews (the 'noticeboard' of the Internet, where users can 'post' text contributions in lists sorted by field of interest). They demonstrate that certain words or combinations of words appear to replicate with high efficiency from one news posting to another.

3.6 Memetics and the Design Process

One of the differences, so the classic argument runs, between a design process and an evolutionary process is the apparent autonomy of the designer, who is able to make direct decisions about the form a design will take. The designer can, at least in theory, rip up the basic design and seek to produce something entirely novel. Design is thus apparently both directional and able to take enormous leaps (in evolutionary jargon, 'saltatory'). This is very far from the random generation of diversity and slow phenotypic change in biological evolutionary processes. Only two mechanisms are generally considered available for the generation of evolutionary variability. One is *mutation* and the other *recombination*. The latter may be likened to the shuffling of a pack of cards. The order of the units is changed, new combinations are generated, but the individual units stay the same. Mutation, by contrast, is the piecemeal alteration of the units, such as taking a card and changing it from a jack to a queen or from clubs to spades. In a memetic context, recombination can be seen in, for instance, the fusion of two artistic styles, and mutation in small changes in technique and taste within those styles.

Crucially, memetics requires these processes to occur *at random*, just as the analogous processes are random in biological systems. There is no Grand Designer in biological evolution – hence the religious furore that surrounded Darwin's work in the 19th century. It would therefore appear that there is no space for designers in memetic evolution. Since there obviously are people who describe themselves as designers, artists, composers or creators of diverse kinds, the conclusion is often reached that Darwinism is therefore strictly biological and cannot be applied to culture (e.g. the terse comment of O'Hear (1995) in *The Oxford Com-*

panion to Philosophy). But are we ascribing an originality to ourselves in our design functions which is not justified by an objective examination of the way culture evolves? This author here proposes that the apparent directionality and saltationality of design are consequences of the selective process, and occur several steps downstream of the generation of memetic diversity. It must be remembered that design *is* apparent in nature as well, i.e. in genetic systems; however, this 'design' is a consequence of selection, the underlying generation of novel genetic variation is random. The same is true in memetics. To declare, as some would, that culture is different to a genetic system because it exhibits directional change (because, as O'Hear maintains, it is teleological) is to misunderstand both culture and biology. What then is the mechanism by which memetic variation appears?

The memetic model proposes that the brain is a generator of random novelty. The resources for this factory of cultural innovation are drawn from the total cultural heritage available to the individual. This may be seen as the *meme pool*, by analogy to the corresponding gene pool of genetics. No single person holds this entire meme pool in the mind at any one time. Rather, we are immersed in it. It is all around us in the material world of our cultural artefacts, in books and libraries and increasingly on computers, and also in the discourse we have with our fellow human beings. Our individual minds are thus continually drawing memes from this pool and using them to throw up novel memes. Because of the randomness of this process, much of this new memetic variability may often be bizarre, irrelevant or banal. Here we are very close to the territory of William James and the 'stream of consciousness'. Occasionally, however, perhaps very occasionally, useful novelty is generated by mutation and recombination and it can then be transformed into objective cultural innovation or transmitted to other individuals. We therefore return memes to the meme pool just as we siphon them off. The often fragmentary and incoherent nature of the stream of consciousness now appears more purposeful as its primary aim is to generate random novelty rather than to reinforce the familiar, the comprehensible or the regular. It is precisely because we only tend to efficiently remember that which is comprehensible and has useful memetic novelty, that the process appears to have a direction.

When a problem presents itself to the designer, it is often possible immediately to see the answer. This may be taken to infer that the problem has in fact already been solved, that cultural resources in the meme pool are available to deal with the problem. Alternatively it may be that only a small memetic mutation or recombination is sufficient to produce the required novelty. The resulting design solution may be very well suited to the problem in hand, and subsequently spread rapidly through the material world of things – perhaps as a mass-produced problem-solving artefact, and rapidly through the meme pool as a new meme available to all. The designer is here acting as a generator of memetic diversity, a filter of that diversity (the first selective force acting on new memes), and finally a transmitter of those novel memes that have passed that first selection test.

The second of these three points merits further consideration. One popular technique for problem solving is the 'brainstorming' session, which was developed by Alex Osborn in 1938 (rev. Holt, 1996). Ideas are poured forth onto paper, often by groups of highly imaginative and intelligent individuals, with the strict rule that no criticism be offered at this initial productive stage of the process. Once the flow of novelty has begun to flag, the brainstorming group begins to process its creations, discarding the trivial and the absurd, weighing up the more

plausible options and hoping for a consensus in the production of 'a good idea'. Brainstorming as thus described is simply a group technique. However, memetics proposes that this is in fact what the individual brain is doing *all the time*. The first selective pressure that a new meme is exposed to is whether it makes sense to the individual who 'thought of it'. Many a brilliant idea is probably consigned to oblivion because that test is failed. The function of the designer is not to *produce* novel memes in the sense of increasing the memetic mutation and recombination rate, not to be an individual super-brainstormer, we are all doing that all the time anyway, but to be the first step in the application of selective pressure to those ideas. (Memeticists, with our evolutionary background and pretensions to hold onto our scientific stance, generally have little positive to say concerning Freud. However, in this context, it seems that the borderline between the unconscious and the conscious may be found in the moment that a novel meme passes its first selection test and enters the domain of comprehensibility.)

Some designers may feel that this belittles their individual contribution to culture. Some philosophers may feel that it fails to deal with 'intentionality', i.e. the fact that thought is always 'about something' rather than merely thinking-in-itself. Outside of some forms of meditational practice which are designed to cultivate what may be termed a non-specific awareness, it does seem as if thought always consists of a thinker-as-subject having thoughts about some object. A designer thus thinks about the artefact under construction and makes decisions regarding this structure, etc. However, memetics insists that this intentionality, this sense of subjectivity, is *an illusion produced by selection*, just as the notion of design in nature is an illusion produced by selection. The impression of intentionality may be produced by the rapid sequence of problem and solution. However, the solution was not so much derived by the sheer effort of the designer as intentional subject, but as a meme extracted from the meme pool, quickly mutated and recombined in the brain of the designer, and the results of the process applied to the problem in hand. The designer may protest: 'But *I* solved it', but the memeticist would reply: 'No, you were the brain/processing unit in which the cultural solution to the problem arranged itself'. Furthermore, the constant process of memetic shuffling and mutating in our minds is continually producing solutions to problems that have not yet been posed ("But what is it for?", as Napoleon is reputed to have said to Alessandro Volta). The moment of design is the moment that solution comes together with problem for the first time. If this seems implausible, it may be worth considering those situations where problems are not readily forthcoming. Often the most unusual thought processes give rise to the solution: the "Eureka!" of Archimedes as the water flowed over the sides of his bath, or Kekulé's solution to the benzene ring problem in a dream of a snake eating its own tail. Here the random diversity generator of the brain is on more open display and its capriciousness is more evident.

Why then are some individuals more talented designers than others? The memetic answer would be that different brains have a greater information sifting and pattern recognition capacity. Some algorithms are more efficient than others, but nevertheless an algorithm exhibits no intentionality. Our varying talents are frequently a reflection of the breadth of culture to which we have been exposed. The more of the meme pool we can download, the more material our minds have to work on and the greater the range of options they can generate. This has some implications for educationists, as it certainly suggests that as far as 'creativity' is concerned, breadth of education is preferable to narrow training in specific tasks.

3.7 Some Concrete Examples (or, Edison Designs Furniture)

Thomas Alva Edison (1847–1931) provides an interesting case history in design 'genius' (Lutyk, 1989). Edison's Menlo Park laboratory was run on a combination of his own idiosyncratic originality and the technical prowess and practicality of the engineers and scientists with whom he surrounded himself. Ideas thrown out by the maestro were left to the underlings to troubleshoot and optimise. However, Edison himself had little academic training and an aversion to mathematics. The secret of his phenomenal success seems to have been the practical application of earlier scientific developments, in particular those of Michael Faraday, by whom he was profoundly influenced. Edison displayed an openness to memes that were already in circulation, making to a large extent discoveries that were waiting to be made. It may seem churlish to speak of a great inventor in this way, but only to those who are wedded to the idea of the designer as demiurgic auteur.

Edison's determination to exhaust the possible applications of 19th-century physics is revealed by the inventions that failed. Some, like the electric car powered by an alkaline storage battery, were well-formed memes ('good ideas') that nevertheless failed under strong memetic selection pressures – in this case economic ones. Others, like concrete furniture, were truly memetic mutants. Only an imagination devoted to the expression of every possible memetic variant could have produced such a bizarre concept. At other times, the randomness of his approach resulted in superb innovations that were not followed up. For instance, despite discovering the vacuum tube, Edison seemed scarcely to comprehend the enormous potential of this breakthrough, and left it to others to develop the electronics industry, which he despised to his dying day. At his death he left 3.5 million pages of notebooks and 1,093 patents. Memetic success, like success in any evolutionary system, relies upon selection, and the more variability the higher the likelihood that an advantageous mutant will be found.

The memetic theory also helps to explain how some discoveries tend to happen simultaneously, often in different parts of the world. Many individuals will have similar memes appearing in their brains at any one moment. Only when these memes are in a situation where there is potential for them to be selected, which initially simply means that they must make sense, will they transfer efficiently into the public domain. Cultures often arrive at stages where there are discoveries 'waiting to happen'. What is then required is less a supreme creative inspiration than the clicking into place of the final meme necessary for the technical innovation to be produced. A good example of this is the independent development of photography by William Henry Fox Talbot and Louis-Jacques-Mandé Daguerre. The crucial point, as it was also with the work of Edison discussed above, was that the basic science had already been developed. In the case of photography, the relevant preceding memes were the study of the properties of sodium thiosulphate by Sir John Herschel, and of light-sensitive chemicals by Joseph Niepce. With these two memes already in place, it was simply a matter of memetic recombination to bring them together and produce the principle of photography. Another salient example is provided by Frank Whittle and Hans von Ohain, who were able to develop jet engines simultaneously and independently.

3.8 Junk Memes and the Recycling of Knowledge

Often, old memes can make a comeback. Even when an idea is no longer part of the everyday usage of a culture, the information may well still be stored in libraries and other repositories, and can be recycled when conditions are again favourable. There is a clear parallel between the retrieval and refurbishment of old memes and Susumu Ohno's (1970) concept of 'junk DNA'. This theory, which is well supported by molecular evidence, posits that random duplicational events in the genome create copies of genes. These copies are functionally redundant, and may accumulate mutations to become non-functional 'pseudogenes'. Ohno observed that a substantial proportion of the genome may be composed of such junk DNA in varying states of post-duplicational 'decay', and proposed that it may occasionally return to functionality by random mutation. If this novel function is advantageous to the organism, it will be selected. Vestigial, or 'junk' genes are thus important potential sources of new function for the organism. Similarly, vestigial, half-forgotten or rarely thought, memes can persist in the long-term storage of a culture, in libraries or in oral folklore, waiting for their contents to be cannibalised in the construction of new memes.

There are dozens of examples of cases where 'junk memes', mere curiosities of the history of ideas, have been dusted off and returned to use in a new context. This happens again and again in both the arts and the sciences. For instance, the cosmology formulated by Copernicus in the 15th century was derived in part from pre-Aristotelian cosmologies which had been obsolete for some 1800 years. More recently, Mendelian genetics languished in obscurity for some forty years before its 'rediscovery' by Bateson, Correns and De Vries at the turn of the century. The development of the computer has provided three very good examples of this phenomenon, where three hitherto obscure 19th-century intellectuals were found to have made key discoveries; the concept of the higher-level programming language extracted from the work of Augusta Ada Lovelace (whose contribution is honoured by naming one language ADA), the general design and conception of the computer based on the work of Lovelace's collaborator Charles Babbage, and the mathematical logic required for programming based on the work of George Boole. Of course these three junk memes were processed through the hands of Grace Murray Hopper, John von Neumann and Claude Shannon, respectively, before they were quite ready for contemporary use, but once again the role of the designer is in handling memetic resources rather than inventing afresh.

3.9 Culture as a Communal Enterprise

Anyone who relishes the grand concept of the designer as creator, solving insuperable technical difficulties by sheer force of concentrated intellectual power, will find the picture presented in this chapter difficult to accept. However, it must be appreciated that such a characterisation of design genius is very much a product of the growth of individualism during the Renaissance (Cassirer et al., 1948). This individualism, a growth in importance of the ego, is itself a meme that would merit further study. Life in the pre-individualist world had some aspects that seem strange today. For instance, prior to around 1300, it was not uncommon for philosophers to attribute their works to Aristotle or some other giant of the past, in order to ensure a wider readership. Such a selfless elevation of the meme above its 'creator' indicates a relationship between thinker and thought, very different to that which exists today. Modern intellectuals are

usually so involved in promoting their own achievements (and who can blame them if unemployment is the alternative?) that such a voluntary surrendering of credit would be unthinkable nowadays. No late 20th-century mathematician who thought she had solved Fermat's Last Theorem would fancifully claim to have found the solution in Turing's lost notebooks. Indeed, if such a notebook did exist, with the solution inside, it would probably be destroyed by its discoverer after the immortality-granting solution had been safely copied onto a fresh sheet of paper.

This process of the deification of the 'creative individual' became apparent in the arts as well as in philosophy. Ludwig van Beethoven was the first truly monstrous ego in music, who turned the stereotype of the composer from skilful, obliging artisan to difficult, tormented genius virtually overnight, and his self-regard has been turned into a model of what artistic genius should be. Nevertheless, he carried a notebook with him everywhere, in order to annotate the musical fragments that sporadically appeared in his mind, before they vanished from his memory. If he had really created them, they would surely have had the decency to remain with their originator a little longer before evaporating. Sometimes even Beethoven had to admit that the music seemed to compose itself, but his solution to this apparent conundrum was divine inspiration – a convenient alternative to modesty. Scientists, too, are often inspired by examples of creative genius, in their case by the intense brooding figure of Isaac Newton, whose method involved thinking about problems 'for a long time', not eating for several days, etc. However, Louis Pasteur, surely in his own way scarcely a lesser figure than Newton, was able to say that 'chance favours the prepared mind'. Like his contemporary Edison, Pasteur had a superbly prepared mind, but the engine of creativity in both cases (as indeed with Beethoven), was chance, as Pasteur recognised. Mutation is always random, in memetics as much as in genetics.

3.10 Conclusions

Memetics seeks to provide a Darwinian framework for the evolution of culture. The art and science of design are elements of that total evolving culture, and therefore as subject to Darwinian precepts as any other aspect of that culture. As this chapter has shown, in order for a process to be truly Darwinian, the following criteria need to be fulfilled:

- *Cultural information must be transmitted.* This presents no particular problem, as verbal communication, writing and electronic media all qualify as transmission. All of these media are used in the design process.

- *Some selection pressures must operate on that cultural information.* Most culture may well be free from such pressure, or only exposed to it intermittently. However, as far as technology is concerned, the material advantages it can bring seem to have ensured consistent selection pressure for design improvements. Memetics has pretensions to explain all culture, but the memetics of engineering is certainly more approachable than the memetics of art.

- *Variation, in other words cultural novelty, must be random.* This is the most difficult point, but a close examination of most episodes in the history of technical innovation will demonstrate the stumbling, coincidental, indeed accidental, nature of our material progress.

Combining the above we arrive at the general statement:

- If the design process begins with the production of novel ideas generated from random combinations and mutations of existing ideas, continues with selection of those ideas for applicability to the problem in hand, and then proceeds to the (not necessarily accurate) transmission of those ideas, then the conditions necessary for an evolutionary process exist. That, in a nutshell, is the basis for an evolutionary theory of the design process.

Those who are disturbed by the implication of this theory, that creativity is a more random and messier process than we might care to admit, may console themselves with the thought that the dignity of the designer is not entirely forfeit. The meme pool is something to which all are capable of contributing, even if our contributions are more accidental than we may realise. Our memes are derived from the meme pool, pass through us in a brief moment and return to the meme pool. Human culture is a seething mass of memes which belongs to all of us. Bickering over originality, and regret over lost opportunities, are understandable human feelings, but the memes are what matter. Descartes' 'cogito, ergo sum', was recast by Lichtenberg as: 'es denkt', it thinks (Vesey, 1964). In fact 'it thinks' in all of us. The trick of creativity to recognise the novelty of our own thoughts.

References

Ball, J.A. (1984). 'Memes as replicators.' *Ethology and Sociobiology* **5;** 145–161.

Cassirer, E., Kristeller, P.O. and Randall, J.H. (eds) (1948). *The Renaissance Philosophy of Man.* London: The University of Chicago Press Ltd.

Cavalli-Sforza, L.L. (1986). 'Cultural evolution.' *American Zoologist*, **26;** 845–855.

Cavalli-Sforza, L.L. and Feldman, M.W. (1981). *Cultural Transmission and Evolution: A Quantitative Approach. Monographs in Population Biology*, **16**. Princeton: Princeton University Press.

Cavalli-Sforza, L.L. and Feldman, M.W. (1983). 'Cultural versus genetic adaptation.' *Proceedings of the National Academy of Sciences*, **80;** 4993–4996.

Cavalli-Sforza, L.L., Feldman, M.W., Chen, K.H. and Dornbusch, S.M. (1982). 'Theory and observation in cultural transmission.' *Science*, **218;** 19–27.

Cavalli-Sforza, L., Feldman, M., Dornbusch, S. and Chen, K.H. (1983). 'Anthropology and cultural transmission.' *Nature*, **304;** 124.

Darwin, C. (1985). *The Origin of Species*, reprint of 1st edition (1859). Burrow, J.W. (ed.), London: Penguin.

Dawkins, R. (1976). *The Selfish Gene*. Oxford: Oxford University Press.

Dawkins, R. (1982). *The Extended Phenotype*. Paperback edition 1983. Oxford: Oxford University Press.

Dawkins, R. (1983). 'Universal Darwinism.' In Bendall, D.S. (ed.), *Evolution from Molecules to Men*. Cambridge: Cambridge University Press.

Ficken, M.S. and Popp, J.W. (1995). 'Long-term persistence of a culturally transmitted vocalization of the black-capped chickadee.' *Animal Behaviour*, **50;** 683–693.

Gatherer, D. (1997). 'Macromemetics: towards a framework for the reunification of philosophy'. *Journal of Memetics – Evolutionary Models of Information Transmission 1* (http://www.cpm.mmu.ac.uk/jom-emit/)

Guglielmino, C.R., Viganotti, C., Hewlett, B. and Cavalli-Sforza, L.L. (1995). 'Cultural variation in Africa – role of mechanisms of transmission and adaptation.' *Proceedings of the National Academy of Sciences*, **92;** 7585–7589.

Hewlett, B.S. and Cavalli-Sforza, L.L. (1986). 'Cultural transmission amongst Aka pygmies.' *American Anthropologist*, **88;** 922–934.

Holt, K. (1996). 'Brainstorming – from classics to electronics.' *Journal of Engineering Design*, **7;** 77–82.

Lumsden, C.J. and Wilson, E.O. (1981). *Genes, Mind and Culture: the Co-evolutionary Process*. Cambridge, MA: Harvard University Press.

Lutyk, C.B. (1989). 'Thomas Alva Edison'. In: Newhouse, E.L. (ed.) *Inventors and Discoveries: Changing Our World*. Washington DC: National Geographic Society, pp. 56–61.

Lynch, A. and Baker, A.J. (1993). 'A population memetics approach to cultural evolution in chaffinch song – meme diversity within populations.' *American Naturalist*, **141;** 597–620.

Lynch, A. and Baker, A.J. (1994). 'A population memetics approach to cultural evolution in chaffinch song – differentiation among populations.' *Evolution*, **48;** 351–359.

Lynch, A., Plunkett, G.M., Baker, A.J. and Jenkins, P.F. (1989). 'A model of cultural evolution of chaffinch song derived with the meme concept.' *American Naturalist*, **133;** 634–653.

O'Hear, A. (1995) 'Darwinism.' In: Honderich, T. (ed.), *The Oxford Companion to Philosophy*. Oxford: Oxford University Press.

Ohno, Susumu (1970). *Evolution by Gene Duplication*. Springer-Verlag, Berlin/New York.

Payne, R.B., Payne, L.L. and Doehlert, S.M. (1988). 'Biological and cultural success of song memes in indigo buntings.' *Ecology*, **69;** 104–117.

Pocklington, R. and Best, M.L. (1997). 'Cultural evolution and units of selection in replicating text.' *Journal of Theoretical Biology*, **188;** 79–87.

Richerson, P.J. and Boyd, R. (1978). 'A dual inheritance model of the human evolutionary process I: basic postulates and a simple model.' *Journal of Social and Biological Structures* **1;** 127.

Vesey, G.N.A. (ed.) (1964). *Body and Mind*. London: George Allen and Unwin Ltd.

Chapter 4

The Race, the Hurdle, and the Sweet Spot:

Lessons from Genetic Algorithms for the Automation of Design Innovation and Creativity

By David Goldberg

4.1 Introduction

Design is a complex human activity involving a dizzying array of interconnected activities. None the less, it seems natural to divide those activities in design that lend themselves to fairly rote algorithmic solution from those that don't. In the former category, we might include activities such as the selection of a standard component (a beam, a transistor, or a carburettor, for example), almost all formal analysis activities related to design (mathematical modelling or computational modelling and simulation), and many activities of configuration, staging, and planning. In the latter category, are activities that go by a variety of names – words such as *innovation* and *creativity* come to mind – but the important characteristic to keep in mind here is that these activities are often *thought* to be beyond the reach of computation, and some might go so far as to reserve these activities for members of our or some other sentient species. In this chapter, I will argue rather strongly that computational innovation – at least certain important facets of the processes of innovation – has been achieved, and that computational creativity is plausibly within our sights. Specifically, I will argue that modern research in *genetic algorithms* – search procedures based on the mechanics of natural selection and genetics – is showing us the way toward computational innovation, thereby possibly paving the way toward a computational theory of the creative.

These are fairly bold claims, and I should confess that I didn't start out by trying to do anything as highfalutin as the construction of computational models of innovation and creativity. In fact, I first invoked (Goldberg, 1983) the term 'innovation' as a simple metaphor to help explain how such simple mechanisms as genetic algorithms might plausibly do useful search. In this chapter, we retrace those steps by first reviewing the mechanics of simple genetic algorithms and then invoking the *fundamental metaphor of innovation* as an *explanation* for GA power of effect. Thereafter, I reverse the argument, by setting out to construct *competent* GAs – GAs that solve hard problems quickly, reliably, and accurately – through a combination of effective: (1) design methodology; (2) design theory; and (3) design. While, we won't have the opportunity to review the technical lessons in detail, the chapter does examine three crucial qualitative issues:

1. the key *race* between selection and the innovation operators,

EVOLUTIONARY DESIGN BY COMPUTERS
ISBN 1-55860-605-X

2. the idea of a *control map* that helps us understand the genetic algorithm's *sweet spot*, and
3. the primary *hurdle* or impediment to competent GA design, a hurdle that has been overcome by three different algorithms that obey the same principle: the need to identify important substructures before deciding among them.

Finally, I conclude with some speculation about what lies beyond the realm of the simply innovative and suggest that a computational theory of the creative will one day be developed using the ideas herein as springboard.

4.2 The One Minute Genetic Algorithmist

Elsewhere, I have written at length (Goldberg, 1989) about GA basics, and in this section we quickly review the fundamental mechanics by discussing what GAs process and how they process it.

Suppose we are seeking to find a *solution* to some *problem*. To apply a genetic algorithm to that problem, the first thing we must do is *encode* the problem as an artificial *chromosome* or chromosomes. These artificial chromosomes can be strings of 1s and 0s, parameter lists, or even complex computer codes, but the key thing to keep in mind is that the genetic machinery will manipulate a finite representation of the solutions, not the solutions themselves.

Another thing we must do in solving a problem is to have some means or procedure for discriminating good solutions from bad solutions. This can be as simple as having a human intuitively choose better solutions over worse solutions, or it can be an elaborate computer simulation or model that helps determine what good is. But the idea is that *something* must determine a solution's relative *fitness to purpose*, and whatever that is will be used by the genetic algorithm to guide the evolution of future generations.

Having encoded the problem in a chromosomal manner and having devised a means of discriminating good solutions from bad ones, we prepare to *evolve* solutions to our problem by creating an initial *population* of encoded solutions. The population can be created randomly or by using prior knowledge of possibly good solutions, but either way a key idea is that the GA will search from a population, not a single point.

With a population in place, *selection* and *genetic operators* can process the population iteratively to create a sequence of populations that hopefully will contain more and more good solutions to our problem as time goes on. There is much variety in the types of operators that are used in GAs, but quite often: (1) *selection*; (2) *recombination*; and (3) *mutation* are used.

Simply stated, selection allocates greater survival to better individuals – this is the survival-of-the-fittest mechanism we impose on our solutions. This can be accomplished in a variety of ways. Weighted roulette wheels can be spun, local tournaments can be held, various ranking schemes can be invoked, but however we do it the main idea is to *prefer better solutions to worse ones*. Of course, if we were to only choose better solutions repeatedly from the original database of initial solutions, we would expect to do little more than fill the population with the best of the first generation. Thus, simply selecting the best is not enough, and some means of creating new, possibly better individuals must be found; this is where the genetic mechanisms of recombination and mutation come into play.

Recombination is a genetic operator that *combines bits and pieces of parental solutions* to

form, new, possibly better offspring. Again, there are many ways of accomplishing this, and achieving competent performance does depend on getting the recombination mechanism designed properly; but the primary idea to keep in mind is that the offspring under recombination will not be identical to any particular parent and will instead *combine parental traits in a novel manner*. By itself, recombination is not all that interesting of an operator, because a population of individuals processed under repeated recombination alone will undergo what amounts to a random shuffling of extant traits.

Where recombination creates a new individual by recombining the traits of two or more parents, mutation acts by simply modifying a single individual. There are many variations of mutation, but the main idea is that the offspring be identical to the parental individual except that *one or more changes is made to an individual's trait or traits* by the operator. By itself mutation represents a 'random walk' in the neighbourhood of a particular solution. If done repeatedly over a population of individuals, we might expect the resulting population to be indistinguishable from one created at random.

4.3 The Fundamental Intuition

The previous section described the mechanics of a genetic algorithm, but it gives us little idea of why these operators might promote a useful search. To the contrary, individually we saw how the operators acting alone were ineffectual, and it is something of an intellectual mystery to explain why such individually uninteresting mechanisms acting in concert might together do something useful. Starting in 1983 (Goldberg, 1983), I have developed what I call the *fundamental intuition of genetic algorithms* or the *innovation intuition* to explain this apparent mystery.

Specifically, I liken the processing of selection and mutation together and that of selection and recombination taken together to *different facets of human innovation*, what I will call the *improvement* and *cross-fertilizing* types of innovation. We start first with the combination of selection and mutation and continue with the selection-recombination pair.

4.3.1 Selection + Mutation = Continual Improvement

When taken together, selection and mutation are a form of hillclimbing mechanism, where mutation creates variants in the neighbourhood of the current solution and selection accepts those changes with high probability, thus climbing toward better and better solutions. Human beings do this quite naturally, and in the literature of total quality management this sort of thing is called *continual improvement* or as the Japanese call it, *kaizen*. When I first introduced the innovation intuition, it was largely based on introspection, but others have had similar thoughts, for example the British author and politician Bulwer-Lytton (Asimov and Shulman, 1988):

> *Invention is nothing more than a fine deviation from, or enlargement on a fine model. . . . Imitation, if noble and general, insures the best hope of originality.*

Although this qualitative description is a far piece from an algorithmic one, we can hear the echo of mutation and selection within these words. Certainly, continuing to experiment in a

local neighbourhood is a powerful means of improvement, although it will have a tendency to be fairly local in scope, unless a means can be found for intelligently jumping elsewhere when a locally optimal solution is found.

4.3.2 Selection + Recombination = Innovation

One way of promoting this kind of intelligent jumping is through the combined effect of selection and recombination, and we can start to understand this if we liken their effect to that of the processes of human cross-fertilizing innovation. What is it that people do when they are being innovative in a cross-fertilizing sense? Usually they are grasping at a notion – a set of good solution features – in one context, and a notion in another context and juxtaposing them, thereby speculating that the combination might be better than either notion taken individually. Again, my first thoughts on the subject were introspective ones, but again others have written along similar veins, for example, the French mathematician Hadamard (1945):

> *We shall see a little later that the possibility of imputing discovery to pure chance is already excluded. . . . Indeed, it is obvious that invention or discovery, be it in mathematics or anywhere else, takes place by combining ideas.*

Likewise, the French poet-philosopher Valéry had a similar observation:

> *It takes two to invent anything. The one makes up combinations; the other chooses, recognizes what he wishes and what is important to him in the mass of the things which the former has imparted to him.*

Once again, verbal descriptions are far from our more modern computational kind, but something like the innovation intuition has been clearly articulated by others.

With a basic understanding of the mechanics of genetic algorithms and an intuitive understanding of their power, we now examine some of the technical lessons of modern GA design and what those lessons can teach us about the processes of innovation.

4.4 Down and Dirty: Some of the Technical Lessons of GA Design

The primary difficulty of using innovation as an *explanation* or *design metaphor* for GAs is that the processes of innovation are themselves not very well understood. The more interesting possibility is that the design of more effective GAs should shed mechanistic light on one or more facets of innovation itself. In fact, the last decade has seen great strides in GA design theory and GA design to the point where it is reasonable to assert this claim. In the remainder of this section, we briefly review some of the key lessons of GA design. Here, I will abandon my concern above for the facet of innovation I called continual improvement and instead will focus entirely on the cross-fertilizing type of innovation by briefly discussing five key facets of selectorecombinative GA design.

What do GAs process? The primary idea of selectorecombinative GA theory is that genetic algorithms work through a mechanism of *quasi-decomposition* and *reassembly*. John Holland

(1975), one of the great early pioneers of genetic and evolutionary computation (GEC), called well-adapted sets of features that were components of effective solutions *building blocks* (BBs). The basic idea is that GAs (1) implicitly identify building blocks or subassemblies of good solutions and (2) recombine different subassemblies to form very high performance solutions.

BB growth and timing. Another key idea is that BBs or notions exist in a kind of competitive *market economy of ideas*, and steps must be taken to ensure that the best ones (1) grow and take over a dominant market share of the population and (2) the growth rate can be neither too fast, nor too slow.

BB decision making. Understanding selectorecombinative GAs helps us understand that the decision making among different, competing notions is *statistical* in nature, and that as we increase the population size, we increase the likelihood of making the best possible decisions.

BB identification and exchange. Perhaps the most important lesson of current research in GAs is that the *identification and exchange of BBs is the critical path* to innovative success. First generation GAs, usually fail in their ability to promote this exchange reliably. The primary design challenge to achieving competence is the need to identify and promote effective BB exchange.

Hard problems are BB challenging. A final lesson of GA theory for cross-fertilizing innovation is that problems that are hard from the standpoint of innovation are problems whose BBs are hard to acquire. This may be because the BBs are deep or complex, hard to find, or because different BBs are difficult to separate, but whatever the difficulty, it may be understood in strictly mechanistic terms.

In hindsight, one wonders why it took so long to enunciate these principles, because individually they are so sensible and almost unremarkable. But before 1991 (Goldberg, 1991) there was no integrated understanding of selectorecombinative GA operation, and it wasn't until 1993 (Goldberg, Deb and Thierens, 1993) that all the quantitative pieces of the puzzle were in place. Decomposing the facets of selectorecombinative GAs and devising quantitative design theory for each of the facets resulted immediately in two key developments: (1) the determination of the limits of first-generation selectorecombinative GAs, and (2) the design and implementation of adaptive and self-adaptive recombination mechanisms that overcome those limitations. To better understand these developments, we examine the race, the sweet spot, and the hurdle.

4.5 The Race

This synopsis of the hard fought design lessons for selectorecombinative GAs hardly does them justice, and the first key to greater insight is to understand the critical race that goes on in a competitive innovating system. This can be seen in fig. 4.1, a schematic that illustrates the main idea. In an evolving system acted upon by selection alone, we would expect to see an S-shaped time history of the market share of the best individuals in the population. Such curves

can be computed exactly for selection schemes of various types (Goldberg and Deb, 1991), but here qualitative understanding suffices. If we understand the growth of market share under selection alone, it is a straightforward matter to calculate a characteristic *takeover time* or t^* as the time it takes to go from a single good individual (a proportion $P = 1/n$, where n is the population size) to a population all but filled with good individuals (containing $n - 1$ superior individuals or a market share $P = (n - 1)/n$ in proportion). This takeover time is shown approximately on the schematic. This observation may seem somewhat pedestrian, and by itself it is none too useful, because real genetic algorithms use operators other than selection. What difference could it possibly make to understand the behavior of a competitive system under selection alone?

The answer to this question comes quickly and convincingly if we *imagine another characteristic time*, call it the innovation time t_i, which we shall define as the mean time for a recombination or innovation operator to achieve a solution better than any achieved to this point. With such a characteristic time in mind there are two basic situations that we must be concerned with: the situation where the takeover time is greater than or equal to the innovation time, $t^* \geq t_i$, and that where the innovation time exceeds the takeover time $t^* < t_i$.

In thinking about these two situations, we immediately wonder which is the more advantageous for a selectorecombinative GA, and the answer is apparent with some straightforward reasoning as follows. The condition where innovation time leads (is less than or equal to) the takeover time is most advantageous for continuing innovation, because prior to the best individual dominating the population, recombination *creates a better individual.* Thereafter this better individual starts to dominate the population, and in essence, the innovation clock is reset. This cycle of partial takeover and continued innovation is repeated over and over again, resulting in the happy condition I have dubbed *steady-state innovation.*

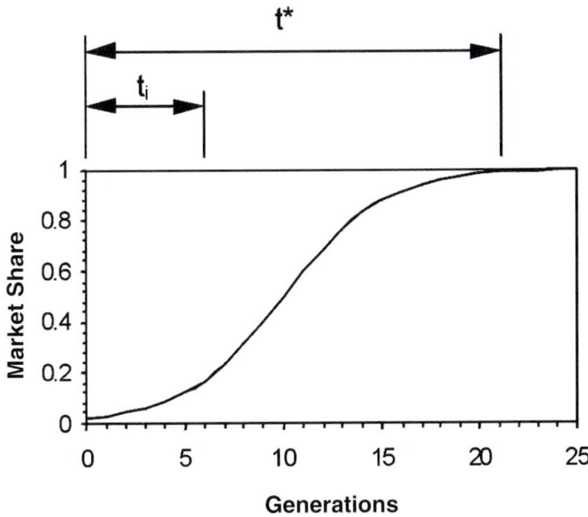

Figure 4.1 A schematic of the race between innovation and selection.

Contrast this virtuous setting with the condition where innovation time lags (is greater than) takeover time. In such a situation, the current best guy continually increases in market share without serious competition and ultimately takes the population to substantial convergence. At the point where recombination and associated mechanism might inject something good, it is now too late, because *diversity is a necessary condition of selectorecombinative success*. To understand this, we simply need to recognize that if we, for example, have a population full of strings converged to 11111 that 11111 crossed with 11111 is 11111 almost regardless of how and where we cross. As a result, when innovation lags takeover, the population is stalled from making progress on the basis of selection and recombination alone. This situation was called *premature convergence* (De Jong, 1975) fairly early in the GA literature, but until the introduction of the above *time scales* argument (Goldberg, Deb and Thierens, 1993), there was no means of analysing the boundary between innovative success and failure. With the understanding of the crucial role of time scales and the race, rational analysis and design of competitive innovating GAs has advanced quite rapidly.

4.6 The Sweet Spot

One of the tools critical to these rapid advances is the so-called *control map*, which helps us delimit a genetic algorithm's *sweet spot*. Technical details of these developments are in the original papers (Goldberg, Deb and Thierens, 1993; Thierens, 1995; Thierens and Goldberg, 1993), but here we strive for qualitative understanding of the key points. These can best be obtained by focusing on the schematic of the sweet spot of a genetic algorithm operating on an easy problem as shown in fig. 4.2. In this map, we plot the feasible settings of the GA's control parameters, s, the selection pressure, and p_c, the probability of crossover. The selection pressure is simply the number of copies that are given to the best individual in the population under selection alone. The crossover probability is the frequency with which mated chromosomes actually undergo the exchange of crossover.

The first assumption we make in creating an s-p_c control map is that we are using a population size n somewhat in excess of that needed to make good decisions on those building blocks necessary toward an effective solution of our problem. In the original work, we used population sizes that grew linearly as a function of the number of decision variables in the problem (Goldberg, Deb and Clark, 1992), although more recent results (Harik, Cantú-Paz, Goldberg, and Miller, 1997) suggest that the population sizes need only grow as quickly as the square root of the number of decisions variables. Interested readers should consult the original papers for detailed sizing formulas, which can be remarkably accurate guides in sizing populations. In any event, the key thing to keep in mind is that we must size the population to ensure high quality statistical decisions. If the population is sized in this way, then success or failure is determined primarily by the outcome of the race, but secondarily by whether we have allowed conditions called drift or cross-competition to occur. We discuss each of these quite briefly.

In the previous section, we discussed the race between innovation and selection, and here we quantify that race somewhat better, although the most technical of details must be left to the original literature. Most of the schemes in common usage have takeover times (in numbers of generations) that are proportional to the log of the population size n and inversely proportional

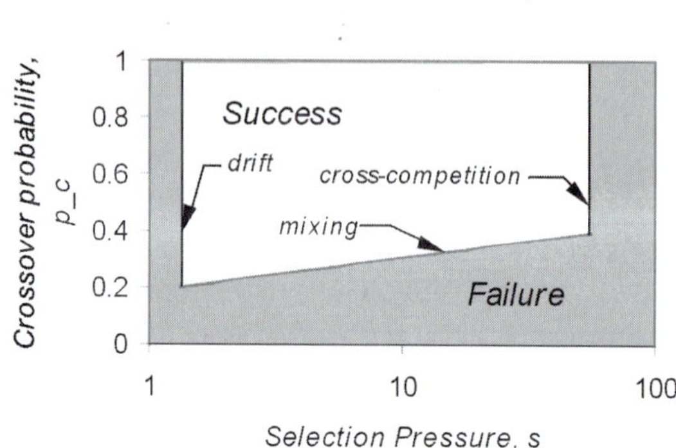

Figure 4.2 A control map shows the GA's sweet spot or zone of success for setting GA control parameters.

to the log of the selection pressure s. Innovation time for crossover is inversely proportional to the product of the population size n and the crossover probability p_c. Recognizing that the boundary between premature convergence and steady state innovation – we will call this the innovation boundary – occurs mathematically when the takeover time and innovation or mixing time are of the same order of magnitude, we conclude that the crossover probability should grow as the log of the selection pressure times some function of the population size. Moreover, values of the crossover probability larger than this value are the ones for which we should expect steady state innovation (success) to occur, and values less than this are those where we should expect premature convergence to occur, and this is the state of affairs shown in the schematic. Specifically, for the boundary labeled 'innovation,' we see that the critical value of crossover probability grows as the log of the selection pressure and the region of success is *above* the innovation boundary.

To the left we see the region of success bounded by the so-called *drift boundary*. Biologists have long known about the possibility of convergence in small populations as a result of the vagaries of stochastic fluctuations, and genetic algorithmists have been aware of these results for some time (De Jong, 1975; Goldberg and Segrest, 1987). Formal analysis is beyond our mission here, but intuitively when the selection pressure is small enough, stochastic variations overpower selective pressure for or against an individual's increase or decrease in population market share. In such circumstances, a trait or an individual can be expected to dominate a finite population on the basis of these stochastic fluctuations alone.

To the right, we see the region of failure dominated by what we call *cross-competition*. When selection pressures are low, we expect the competition for trait or building-block market share to be held relatively independently across the genotype. In other words, conflicting traits will compete against one another, but not against non-conflicting traits. For example, we would expect different eye-colour traits to compete against one another, but we would not expect an eye-colour gene combination to compete with a hair-colour building block. When the selection pressure is raised to very high values (values near the population size) semantically independent traits do compete with one another. To understand this intuitively, imagine what would happen if we had a selection pressure of 99 in a population size of 100. The action of selection would make 99 copies of the best individual in the population leaving only one slot for a lesser individual, and this action would reduce diversity so severely as to cripple even the most effective recombination mechanisms. A coarse analysis is given elsewhere (Goldberg, Deb and Thierens, 1993), but here it is sufficient to recognize that when selection pressure values are raised to values near the population size there is a threshold value above which failure should be expected because of this kind of cross-competitive interference.

4.7 The Hurdle

The previous section paints a somewhat rosy picture of selectorecombinative GA life. After all, in our figure the boundaries are well spaced, and it is a fairly easy thing for the GA user to empirically or theoretically choose a set of GA parameter values to give us good results. On the other hand, we need to question whether this state of affairs will always be the case, and unfortunately it depends on the difficulty of the problem we are trying to solve. As demonstrated theoretically and empirically elsewhere (Goldberg, Deb and Thierens, 1993), problems that may be solved through bitwise exchanges, have large sweet spots, and almost any selectorecombinative GA with any reasonable choice of crossover operator can be expected to do well with almost any serious choice of s and p_c. We can have no objections to this, and in fact the size of the sweet spot may be taken as a measure of the robustness of the algorithm.

On the other hand, as a problem becomes more difficult – that is as a problem has building blocks larger than single bits – the size of the sweet spot shrinks even as the population size is increased nominally to account for the increased noise of the more difficult problem instance. This is problematic and results ultimately in the sweet spot vanishing. Another way to view the same problem is to ask the question what size population is required to solve problems of increasing difficulty and length. Both theoretically and empirically it has been shown (Thierens and Goldberg, 1993; Thierens, 1995) that population sizes must grow exponentially to accommodate increased difficulty and length.

This leaves us with a split decision regarding the efficacy of simple GAs. If a problem is bitwise solvable, modest population sizes may be used and accurate, reliable solutions may be expected in small numbers of function evaluations, and we should expect those numbers to scale well, growing no more quickly than a subquadratic function of the number of decision variables or bits. On the other hand, with a more difficult problem instance, simple recombination operators scale badly, requiring a superexponential number of function evaluations to get reliable answers to even boundedly difficult problems, and therein lies the rub, the hurdle to the design of competent GAs. Is there some way to design crossover mechanisms that allow solutions to hard problems to scale more like those of easy problems?

4.8 Competent GA Design

Remarkably, the answer to this question is a resounding 'yes,' and the trick of the endeavour goes back to our discussion of the fundamental intuition. Recall that earlier we likened the processing of selection and crossover to that of human cross-fertilizing innovation. As loose metaphor this seemed reasonable enough, but if we think of our own episodes of innovation the action of simple recombination operators seems *much less directed* than the human kind. Oftentimes when human beings innovate, the building blocks being exchanged are chunked whole, consciously or subconsciously, and the human recombinative process is far from the willy nilly exchange of the simple crossover operators discussed earlier. This observation makes us wonder whether there is some way of building a crossover operator that can *identify* and *exchange* clusters of genes appropriate to solving a problem without the need for human intervention or advice.

A line of work dating back to 1989 (Goldberg, Korb and Deb, 1989) has set this as its goal, and succeeded in achieving this goal for the first time in 1993 (Goldberg, Deb, Kargupta and Harik, 1993) with the creation of the *fast messy genetic algorithm* (fmGA). Two other mechanisms have also achieved competence in the sense of solving boundedly hard problems quickly, reliably, and accurately, and these are Kargupta's (1996) *gene expression messy genetic algorithm* (gemGA) and Harik's linkage learning GA (LLGA) (Harik and Goldberg, 1997; Harik, 1997). Detailed descriptions are beyond the scope of this treatment, and the mechanisms are surprisingly different from one another in their details of operation. Despite these differences, the need to tame the race between selection and crossover pushes the GA designer to do one thing above all else: *identify building blocks before deciding among them.* Stated this way, this condition sounds straightforward enough, but achieving it is a difficult design challenge, because the natural tendency of most naive design choices is to promote decision prior to identification, thereby delaying or even prohibiting the identification of the best groupings of variables. If this happens, and the problem is even partially misleading, the tendency will be for genes to fix on the wrong values, whereupon the algorithm will be led to the wrong solutions.

Figure 4.3 shows the results from the first competent GA, the fast messy GA (Goldberg, Deb, Kargupta and Harik, 1993). In a problem with order-5 difficult building blocks, the fast messy GA is able to find global solutions in times that grow as a subquadratic function of the number of decision variables as expected. By contrast, the original messy GA, and mutation-oriented hillclimbing (Mühlenbein, 1992), have numbers of function evaluations that grow as a quintic function of the number of decision variables. Of course, quintic growth is superior to the expected exponential growth required of a simple GA using a recombination operator of fixed structure. But the subquadratic growth expected on all problems of fixed difficulty is exactly the kind of robust solution genetic algorithmists have been seeking for so long.

The problems that can be solved via this mechanism are quasi-decomposable ones, but they are by no means easy. Straightforward hillclimbing mechanisms will be defeated on relatively easy instances of such problems, and it is not an exaggeration to claim that a competent selectorecombinative GA is *innovating* in a cross-fertilizing sense to quickly find global or very near global solutions. Although most GA implementations do not use such recombination operators yet, the research reported herein has asked and answered the right questions, and it is only a matter of time before such mechanisms are incorporated into everyday GA practice. While this integration may yet take some time, and the exact combination of mechanisms to use in practice is still open to refinement, I will assume in the remainder that the problem of computational cross-fertilizing innovation is solved or at least well on its way to a solution. In what remains, I speculate on the possibility of a computational theory of the creative.

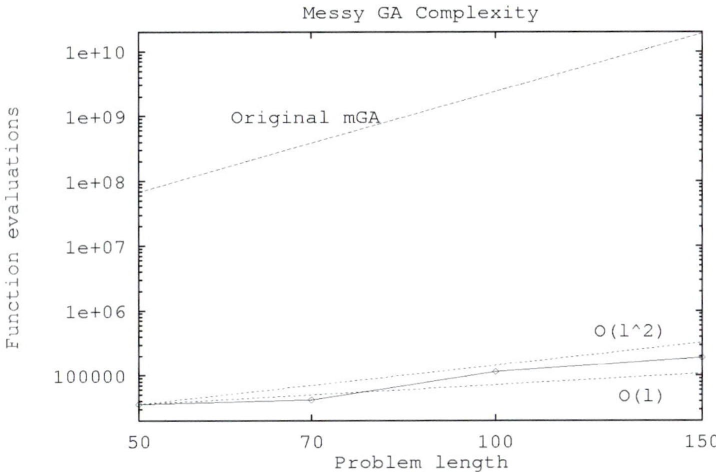

Figure 4.3 The fast messy GA results reported in Goldberg et al. (1993) demonstrate subquadratic growth in the computation time compared to the original messy GA and simple mutation-based hillclimbers, which grow as the fifth power of the number of variables and are much slower across the board than the fmGA.

4.9 From Competence to Creativity

The progress made in developing competent selectorecombinative GA whets our appetites for more. One way to consider what lies beyond competent GAs is to appeal to the innovation intuition one last time to see if it might help us imagine mechanisms that go beyond the 'merely innovative.'

Thinking informally and linguistically, one word that we often use to describe thinking processes that go beyond the innovative is 'creative.' What does it mean to be creative? Well, it probably means more than one thing[1] – just as innovation has meant at least two different things in this chapter – but it is helpful to examine what we mean more closely when we say that a piece of art, for example, is creative. Oftentimes, creativity in art (or literature or science or engineering) can be understood as a certain *richness of association* with different, perhaps seemingly unrelated disciplines. Much great art alludes to prior art, literature, culture, history, and many more sources besides, and all of this can understood as a form of *knowledge transfer* from those disciplines to the subject at hand.

In the same way, a more *creative* algorithm would act to go beyond *innovation* by transferring useful information from other domains. Seen in this way, innovative mechanisms involve exchange or discovery from *within* a discipline, whereas creative computation requires a transfer from *without*. There are a number of mechanical ways of imagining how to do this,

[1] In fact, the definition herein differs from that used in this volume for the section entitled 'Creative Evolutionary Design'. None of these perspectives should be viewed as 'correct,' and if we were to have convergence in the population of definitions at this early stage in our quest for innovating and creating machines, it would almost certainly be premature.

either through the transfer of deep, whole building blocks from other fields, or through the transfer of knowledge about better knowledge representation. At this juncture, the key to keep in mind is that whatever mechanisms we devise should borrow the *implicitly parallel* style of selectorecombinative GAs and avoid the one-at-a-time explicit calculation of symbolic artificial intelligence or similar disciplines. Doing so will maximize the exploitation of local processing, minimize the utilization of global mappings, data structures, and processing at the same time it gives us competent creativity that solves even harder problems, more quickly, more reliably, and more accurately. Designing and implementing such mechanisms is a tall order, but the methodological, theoretical, and implementation example of selectorecombinative GAs gives us more than a little hope that a vision of computational procedures that surprise and delight us is nearer than we thought.

4.10 Conclusions

This chapter started by distinguishing between tasks in design that lend themselves to rote computation and those that don't. It has ended by undermining that very categorization and by suggesting that the processes surrounded in the most mystery – processes that go by the names 'innovative' and 'creative' – are yielding to computational modelling and mechanistic understanding. Specifically, work in genetic algorithms has been reviewed in the light of the so-called innovation intuition, and this has led to a more detailed consideration of five of the key technical lessons of selectorecombinative GA design. In turn these lessons have led us to consider the race between innovation and selection, the sweet spot of GA control parameters, and the primary hurdle to effective GA design, which have both exposed the weakness of first-generation GAs and shown us how to make them competent.

It is yet unclear how this work will impact the practice of GAs on the one hand and the state of knowledge on the other, but it seems reasonable and unassailable to assume that fast, accurate solutions to very hard search and optimization problems are useful and desirable across the spectrum of human endeavor. It also seems reasonable to assume that a more mechanistic understanding of the categories 'innovative' and 'creative' is something that the humanities, the social sciences, and physical sciences could all benefit from. But the assertion that genetic algorithms offer useful models for the understanding of such things will no doubt remain controversial for some time to come. None the less, even if these models only illuminate small nooks and crannies of intelligent innovation and creativity they will have performed a large service. Certainly having at least one line of consistent methodology, theory, and design practice that has already made important strides through such difficult territory should give others reason for reflection, imitation, and hypertrophy to see how far these ideas can go.

Acknowledgements

This chapter was written mainly because Peter Bentley is a persistent guy. I thank him for urging me to write this paper until I actually did so. It was written while I was on sabbatical at the Section on Medical Informatics at Stanford University. I am grateful to Mark Musen, Russ Altman, and John Koza for inviting me to lovely, albeit somewhat soggy, Palo Alto.

My contribution to this study was sponsored by the Air Force Office of Scientific Research, Air Force Materiel Command, USAF, under grants F49620-94-1-0103, F49620-95-1-0338, and F49620-97-1-0050. The US Government is authorized to reproduce and distribute reprints for Government purposes notwithstanding any copyright notation thereon.

The views and conclusions contained herein are my own and should not be interpreted as necessarily representing the official policies or endorsements, either expressed or implied, of the Air Force Office of Scientific Research or the US Government.

References

Asimov, I. and Shulman, J. (eds) (1988). *Isaac Asimov's book of science and nature quotations*. New York: Weidenfeld and Nicolson.

De Jong, K. A. (1975). An analysis of the behavior of a class of genetic adaptive systems. Doctoral dissertation, University of Michigan, Ann Arbor (University Microfilms No. 76–9381).

Goldberg, D. E. (1983). Computer-aided pipeline operation using genetic algorithms and rule learning. Doctoral dissertation, University of Michigan, Ann Arbor.

Goldberg, D. E. (1989). *Genetic algorithms in search, optimization, and machine learning*. Reading, MA: Addison-Wesley.

Goldberg, D. E. (1991). A tutorial on genetic algorithm theory. A presentation given at the Fourth International Conference on Genetic Algorithms, July 1991, University of California at San Diego, La Jolla, California.

Goldberg, D. E. and Deb, K. (1991). A comparative analysis of selection schemes used in genetic algorithms. *Foundations of Genetic Algorithms*, **1,** 69–93. (First published in 1990 as IlliGAL Report No. 90007.)

Goldberg, D. E., Deb, K. and Clark, J. (1992). Genetic algorithms, noise, and the sizing of populations. *Complex Systems*, **6,** 333–362. (First published in 1991 as IlliGAL Report No. 91010.)

Goldberg, D. E., Deb, K., Kargupta, H. and Harik, G. (1993). Rapid, accurate optimization of difficult problems using fast messy genetic algorithms. *Proceedings of the Fifth International Conference on Genetic Algorithms*, 56–64. (First published in 1993 as IlliGAL Report No. 93004.)

Goldberg, D. E., Deb, K. and Thierens, D. (1993). Toward a better understanding of mixing in genetic algorithms. *Journal of the Society of Instrument and Control Engineers*, **32(1),** 10–16. (First published in 1992 as IlliGAL Report No. 92009.)

Goldberg, D. E., Korb, B. and Deb, K. (1989). Messy genetic algorithms: Motivation, analysis, and first results. *Complex Systems*, **3(5).** 493–530. (First published in 1989 as TCGA Report No. 89003.)

Goldberg, D. E. and Segrest, P. (1985). Finite Markov chain analysis of genetic algorithms. *Proceedings of the Second International Conference on Genetic Algorithms*, pp. 1–8.

Hadamard, J. (1945). *The psychology of invention in the mathematical field*. Princeton University Press: Princeton, NJ.

Harik, G. (1997). Learning gene linkage to efficiently solve problems of bounded difficulty using genetic algorithms. Doctoral dissertation, University of Michigan, Ann Arbor. (Also published as IlliGAL Report No. 97005.)

Harik, G., Cantú-Paz, E., Goldberg, D. E. and Miller, B. L. (1997). The gambler's ruin problem, genetic algorithms, and the sizing of populations. *Proceedings of the 1997 IEEE International Conference on Evolutionary Computation*, 7–12. (First published in 1996 as IlliGAL Report No. 96004.)

Harik, G. and Goldberg, D. E. (1997) Learning linkage. *Foundations of Genetic Algorithms*, **4,** 247–262. (First published in 1996 as IlliGAL Report No. 96006.)

Holland, J. H. (1975). *Adaptation in natural and artificial systems*. Ann Arbor, MI: University of Michigan Press.

Kargupta, H. (1996). *SEARCH, evolution, and the gene expression messy genetic algorithm* (Unclassified Report LA-UR 96-60). Los Alamos, NM: Los Alamos National Laboratory.

Mühlenbein, H. (1992). How genetic algorithms really work: I. Mutation and hillclimbing. *Parallel Problem Solving from Nature*, pp. 15–25.

Thierens, D. (1995) Analysis and design of genetic algorithms. Doctoral dissertation, Katholieke Universiteit Leuven, Belgium.

Thierens, D. and Goldberg, D. E. (1993). Mixing in genetic algorithms. *Proceedings of the Fifth International Conference on Genetic Algorithms*. Morgan Kaufmann, Urbana-Champaign, pp. 38–45.

Chapter 5

Exploring the Design Potential of Evolutionary Search, Exploration and Optimisation

By Ian Parmee

5.1 Introduction

This chapter discusses the potential of evolutionary and adaptive search (ES/AS) techniques when applied to complex engineering design problems or integrated with engineering design processes and current design team practice. The real potential of these technologies within the engineering design domain is only now becoming apparent even though the foundations of the technology were established some thirty years ago. The relatively long gestation period has been largely due to the computational expense associated with such population-based/multi-start search and optimisation strategies. Recent developments in powerful desktop computing capability, however, is now allowing their realistic application to real-world problems and their integration with day-to-day engineering design practice although computational requirement still represents a significant obstacle in some application areas.

Common attributes of the various stochastic search techniques of particular relevance to engineering design processes requiring extensive search and optimisation capabilities include:

- requirement for little, if any, a priori knowledge relating to the search environment – no gradient information is needed;
- excellent search capabilities due largely to a population-based approach that efficiently samples the space of possible design solutions;
- ability to avoid local optima; the stochastic nature of the various algorithms combined with continuing random sampling of the search space can prevent convergence upon a local sub-optimum;
- ability to handle high dimensionality; successful application to problems described by greater than four hundred variable parameters can be found in the literature (Parmee and Vekeria, 1997);
- robustness across a wide range of problem class; the techniques can generally outperform more deterministic optimisation algorithms across a wide range of problem class where high modality/high dimension are evident;
- the provision of multiple good solutions; if required, ES/AS strategies can be developed that identify multiple high-performance solutions from complex design spaces;

EVOLUTIONARY DESIGN BY COMPUTERS
ISBN 1-55860-605-X

- ability to locate the region of the global optimum solution; ES/AS algorithms will generally locate the region of a globally optimum solution although extensive local search may be required to isolate the optimum.

There are many examples of the application of evolutionary and adaptive search algorithms to specific well-defined problems from the engineering design domain. Little research effort, however, has been expended in moving from these well-defined problems to investigate the generic integration of ES/AS with each stage (i.e. conceptual, embodiment and detailed) of the engineering design process as a whole. Both design exploration and search represent major components of such an integration in addition to solution exploitation and system optimisation. Individual designer and design team interaction with evolutionary and adaptive machine-based processes is a major requirement during the early exploratory stages of design where such exploration involves off-line processing of initial results which will likely lead to a redefinition of the design environment. Although not a definitive list the following aspects must be considered if successful integration is to be achieved:

- the ability to efficiently sample complex design spaces described by differing model representation/simulation (e.g. quantitative, qualitative, linguistic, crisp, fuzzy, etc.);
- the addition, removal and/or variation of constraints, objectives and variable parameter bounds;
- the rapid identification of multiple high-performance solutions/regions of complex spaces;
- the development of search/exploration systems that can capture specific design knowledge through extensive designer interaction;
- the on-line processing of information relating to multiple design criteria concerning design, manufacturing, economic and marketing requirements;
- the ability to access regions of design feasibility, to define such regions to some extent and to identify optimal solutions within them;
- the autonomous and efficient manipulation of complex design analysis software leading to the identification of optimal detailed design solutions;
- the minimisation of required calls to the fitness evaluation and thus a minimisation of the computational expense associated with population-based search;

The importance of such aspects has become evident from recent research relating to the integration of evolutionary and adaptive computing with all stages of design. These requirements are discussed in the following sections and strategies that satisfy them to a varying extent are introduced and supported by experimental results from their application within a range of industrial design domains.

Entirely machine-based evolutionary design processes are not suggested here nor are they considered currently viable except perhaps in single component domains as described in section 5.3. The belief is that, particularly during the higher levels of the design process, advanced computational search and optimisation techniques can be utilised within a design team environment to support the engineer across a wide range of design activity and that best utility can be achieved by developing systems that enhance the inherent capabilities of the engineering designer. A problem-oriented approach to such ES/AS integration is essential due to the complex iterative processes and human centred aspects evident during these higher levels of design in particular. Continuous interaction with designers and design team activity is an essential element of the research process to enable identification of those areas where ES/AS strategies would be of most benefit and to recognise specific problems relating to their successful integration. Experience suggests that such an approach can result in the development of prototype evolutionary design tools that offer considerable potential as powerful extensions of design team activity allowing rapid, extensive exploration and stimulating innovative reasoning at the higher conceptual levels of the design process; providing diverse, high-performance solutions to support decision-making during embodiment design and acting as powerful global optimisers that can operate efficiently within complex, computationally intensive domains during detailed design.

The information processing capabilities of population-based evolutionary and adaptive computing systems support powerful exploration, search and optimisation capabilities. However, as stand-alone processes they can only operate within the variable bounds imposed by the operator/engineering designer. In order to achieve true exploration of an overall design domain such bounds need to be adaptive to allow design solutions, which offer utility but are not described by the initial problem definition, to be assessed. Such adaptability can be achieved via designer interaction where information gained from evolutionary search solutions contributes to the developing knowledge-base relating to design requirements and possible structure. This information will contribute to design change by prompting the addition, removal and/or variation of variables/variable bounds, soft/hard constraint values and objectives/objective weightings during an iterative designer/evolutionary search process thereby altering the position and nature of the fitness landscape in terms of variable space, objective space and constraint space. Recent research indicates that co-operative frameworks involving a number of search strategies/optimisation techniques operating concurrently within single or multi-level environments can offer significant utility (Parmee and Denham, 1994; Parmee, 1997) within this complex, changing environment. The additional integration of complementary computational intelligence (CI) techniques with such strategies can result in overall search and processing capabilities that can significantly support the engineer at each level of engineering design. Fuzzy technologies (Zadeh, 1965) for example, when integrated with evolutionary search, may best handle the uncertainties inherent in high-level design (Brehm, Kriese and Sebastian, 1997; Otto and Antonsson, 1995). The emerging intelligent agent technologies (Clearwater et al., 1992; Talukdar et al., 1993; Wooldridge and Jennings, 1995) also offer considerable potential for co-evolutionary state recognition and subsequent reactive or proactive involvement in addition to providing appropriate communication and constraint satisfaction protocols. However, in order to establish meaningful, coherent designer/machine-based systems significant research is also required relating to the human-centred aspects of the iterative information feedback loop which forms the essential component of an overall evolutionary exploratory framework.

The various evolutionary/adaptive search algorithms are well suited to the concurrent manipulation of models of varying resolution and structure due to their ability to search non-linear space with no requirement for gradient information or a priori knowledge relating to model characteristics. These capabilities, when combined with complementary CI techniques, enable feature/knowledge-based modelling approaches to be utilised alongside more quantitative, mathematically-based design descriptions. It is therefore possible to emphasise those design features that have the most significance in terms of manufactureability, economic feasibility and marketing considerations and to promote the emergence of design spaces that contain solutions that best satisfy criteria relating to product design, realisation and utilisation. Co-operative, adaptive design strategies have the potential to provide an optimal definition process in terms of such multi-disciplinary requirements. Concurrent manipulation of both qualitative and quantitative models to provide an initial design definition is an area of research now attracting increasing interest. The initial objective is to achieve optimal stage designs which do not involve detailed analysis but contain a considerable amount of information relating to a wide range of design/manufacturing considerations.

The following sections describe strategies that utilise evolutionary and adaptive computing as a foundation for design exploration, search and optimisation whilst also utilising more deterministic optimisation procedures when appropriate. In addition, complementary computational intelligence technologies are introduced to enhance the information processing capabilities of the evolutionary search. The aim is to develop/extract those search characteristics in the form of operators and low-level strategies that offer utility to generic design requirements and integrate these with a number of other techniques/technologies to achieve the required level of designer support. We can therefore look upon the various evolutionary and adaptive search algorithms as a rich source of operators, structures and low-level strategies whilst also introducing and experimenting with new search concepts. These can be combined in an appropriate manner to address specific design issues when integrated with other more deterministic optimisation methods and/or computational intelligence technologies. Appropriate combinations that may better handle the complexities of human/computer design processes during the higher levels of design will likely be radically different to those required during the far more deterministic procedures of low-level detailed design analysis.

5.2 Design Decomposition

5.2.1 Region Identification

A significant area of evolutionary computing research concerns the development of multi-modal optimisation (MMO) techniques that are able to identify and maintain solutions upon local sub-optima in addition to identifying a near-global optimum solution. Thus a number of high-performance solutions from diverse regions of the design space are evident in the final population of an evolutionary MMO process. Such techniques generally rely upon crowding (De Jong, 1975; Mahfoud, 1992) and sharing (Goldberg and Wang, 1997) concepts and most assume some a priori knowledge relating to the modality of the search space in order to determine factors relating to niche radii and population sample size. Techniques that require such knowledge to a lesser extent are Spear's SSS technique (Spears, 1994), Goldberg's adaptive niching strategies (Goldberg and Wang, 1997) and Roy and Parmee's ARTS algorithm (Roy and Parmee, 1996).

Much of the research discussed in this section however, concerns the identification of high-performance *regions* as opposed to single solutions. The reasoning here is that, generally, during the preliminary stages of design, models defining the system under design are coarse representations involving a significant degree of assumption and partially dependent upon empirical data. Results from such models must be treated with caution. Expending significant computing resource isolating single, local optima is therefore not justified as such solutions have a high probability of proving erroneous when subjected to more rigorous analysis at a later stage. Such solutions may, at best, merely indicate to the engineer that their immediate locality or region may offer utility in design terms whereas, at worst, they could prove seriously misleading to those unfamiliar with the shortcomings of the design model. Thus techniques that utilise natural evolutionary clustering tendencies to identify regions of high performance as opposed to single solutions within complex design spaces are being developed as designer-interactive, problem decomposition strategies (Parmee and Denham, 1994; Parmee, 1996a,b).

These strategies for design decomposition/problem reduction involve the identification of high performance (HP) regions of conceptual/preliminary design spaces and the subsequent extraction of relevant information regarding the characteristics of the designs within those regions. HP regions are rapidly identified during a coarse-based evolutionary search with maximum region cover in terms of number of solutions being a major objective. Subsequent qualitative and quantitative evaluation of the solutions of each region can provide information for overall off-line evaluation by the designer. Such information should enhance domain knowledge and support the definition of 'good' designs in terms of specific features of each region and 'design commonalities' between regions. This leads, through an iterative designer/machine-based process, to the improvement of system representation/fitness function through the refinement of inherent heuristics and approximations; the introduction/removal of constraints and variables and a modification of objective weightings. The integration of prototype experimental software supporting such region identification with current design team practice is providing information as to the required development of these interactive systems to support radical changes of the design environment which may lead to innovative or perhaps even creative design solutions.

Simple variable mutation regimes that encourage diversity during the early stages of a GA search promoting the formation of solution clusters in the better areas of the design space were initially introduced (Parmee, 1996a). Populations from selected generations are extracted and stored in a final clustering set thereby removing the need to maintain such clusters through successive generations. The objectives of these initial COGAs (cluster-oriented genetic algorithms) have been to identify a maximum number of regions; maximise set cover in terms of number of solution across each region; improve the robustness of the techniques and minimise the number of test function evaluations. An adaptive filter has been introduced to prevent low-performance solutions passing into the clustering set (i.e. the final set comprising of the extracted populations of pre-selected generations). Extracted solutions are first scaled and a threshold value (Rf) is introduced as shown in fig. 5.1. Solutions are either rejected or accepted into the clustering set depending upon their scaled fitness in relation to Rf which can be preset or varied at each of the selected generations. Varying Rf introduces an investigatory aspect in initial experimental runs which can provide information concerning the relative nature of differing regions of the design space. The adaptive filter is dependent upon the relative fitness of solutions within the extracted populations and there is no requirement for a priori knowledge relating to the nature of the fitness landscape nor any need to introduce niche radii or population sampling metrics. Figure 5.2 shows the application of COGA to a two-dimensional test function and the resulting identification of distinct regions of high performance. Figure 5.3 shows application to an eight-dimensional model relating to the primary elements of preliminary military aircraft airframe design (research currently in progress with British Aerospace). A two-dimensional hyperplane relating to two of the eight variable parameters is shown. In this case only one cluster/region is in evidence and the sequence illustrates the degree of exploration and problem reduction that can be achieved by varying the Rf value. Such variation allows the engineer to explore the extent of the high-performance region/regions. Relative solution fitness is normally represented by colour variation of the points. The introduction of high values of Rf results in the identification of individual solutions of very high performance as shown in the final graph. Figure 5.4 illustrates the decomposition of an eleven-dimensional space relating to the design of gas turbine blade cooling hole geometries. Again, a two-dimensional slice of the entire space is shown and three regions of high performance are defined each relating to particular discrete internal geometry configurations that exist in addition to the eleven continuous variable parameters defining the overall system.

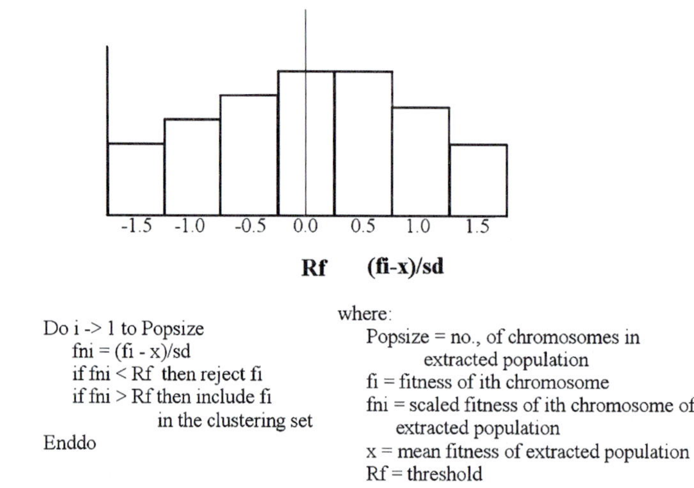

Figure 5.1 Scaling the fitness of solutions.

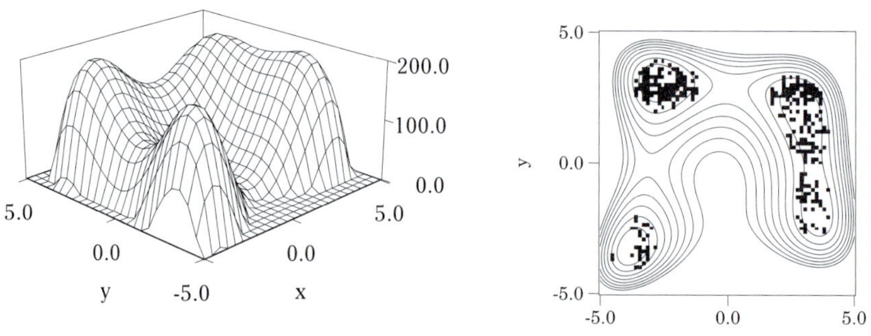

Figure 5.2 COGA decomposition of two-dimensional test function.

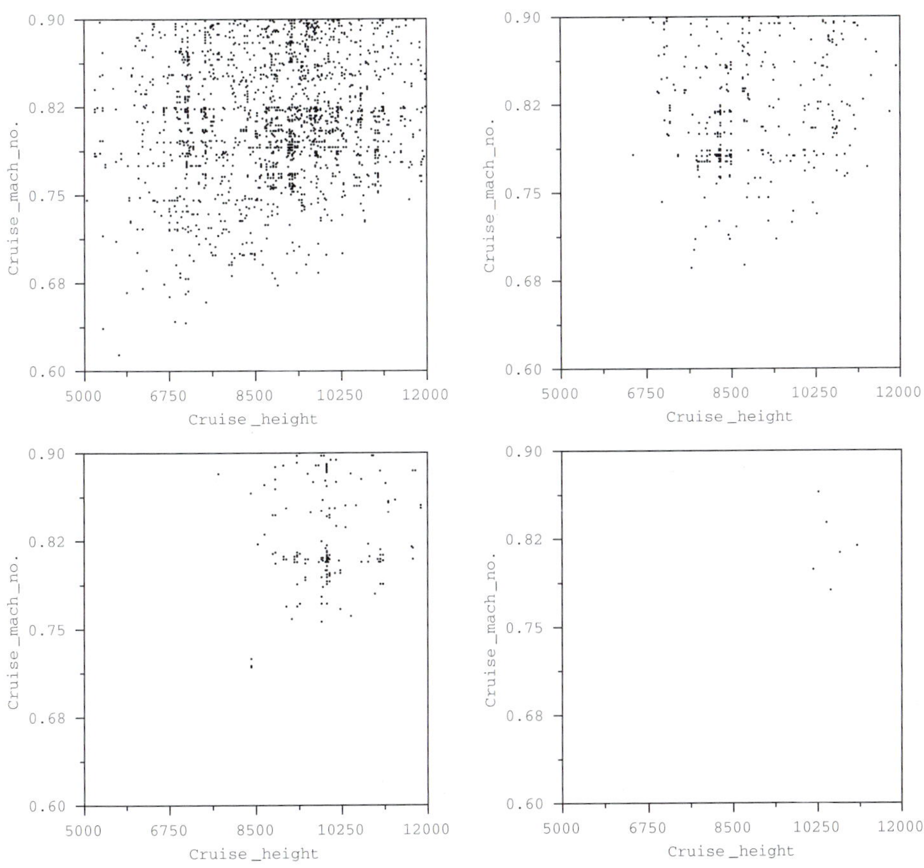

Figure 5.3 The application of COGA to preliminary military aircraft airframe design.

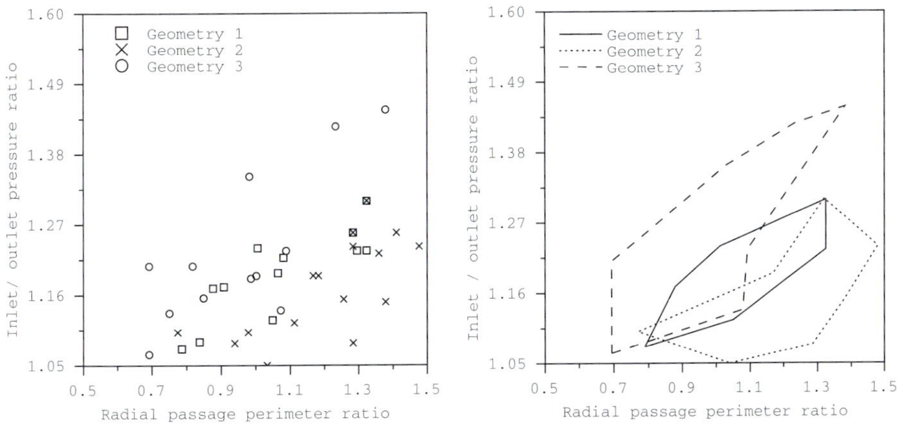

Figure 5.4 High-performance regions relating to differing discrete gas turbine blade cooling internal geometries.

As the preliminary design models used here incur little computational expense the engineer can rapidly explore the defined space generating graphical representations of two and three dimensional hyperplanes showing high-performance regions. Information relating to individual regions can support variable bound and constraint penalty variation in addition to the variation of objective weightings. Subsequent runs thus allow the engineer to rapidly explore beyond the initially defined bounds. Comparative information relating to identified diverse HP regions can also be extracted. Such information may relate to solution sensitivity and degree of multi-criteria/constraint satisfaction and can lead to the recognition of the common design characteristics of widely differing (in terms of the defining variable values of the solutions within them) regions of the design space. Common aspects of such seemingly different regions may alter the engineer's overall perception of the problem and result in changes to initial concepts leading to the generation of innovative solutions or even creative solutions. It is also possible to define feasible regions by setting the minimisation of degree of constraint violation as a primary objective. Alternatively, current research is investigating the introduction of several objectives and the concurrent identification of high-performance regions relating to each. Initial results from this work indicate that the variation of objective weightings rapidly allows the identification of a common region that satisfies all objectives thereby resulting in the rapid decomposition of the design space into succinct regions of multi-objective satisfaction.

Other current research in this area concerns alternative strategies involving the adoption of geographically structured GAs (Parmee and Beck, 1997) after Davidor (Davidor and Yamada, 1993) and also investigating the integration of the adaptive filter with a number of other evolutionary algorithms that support search diversity and cluster formation.

5.2.2 Whole System Design

Related problem decomposition research concerns search across design hierarchies of discrete design configurations which are further described by dependent continuous variable sets. Achieving an efficient search across such hierarchies is not a trivial task. Many discrete paths have differing sets of dependent variables as illustrated in fig. 5.5. The search space therefore comprises differing continuous design spaces each related to a discrete design option. A search strategy is required that efficiently samples each continuous design space in order to rapidly determine the discrete design paths of high potential. The objective is to provide a more extensive search of available design alternatives within budget and time constraints. This results in the identification of regions containing competitive solutions that may have been overlooked during the problem decomposition processes of traditional heuristic design. The developed strategies should enable the engineer to rapidly survey the potential of diverse regions of the hierarchy thus avoiding premature concentration of search effort within previously known regions.

A dual agent strategy (GAANT) has been developed that maintains the combination of discrete and continuous variables within a single chromosome but only permits crossover between solutions with identical discrete configurations (Parmee, 1996b,c). In order to maintain the information exchange evident during traditional crossover it is necessary to speciate the populations in terms of like discrete configurations and restrict crossover to members of the same species. Elements of the Ant Colony metaphor (Bilchev and Parmee, 1995) have

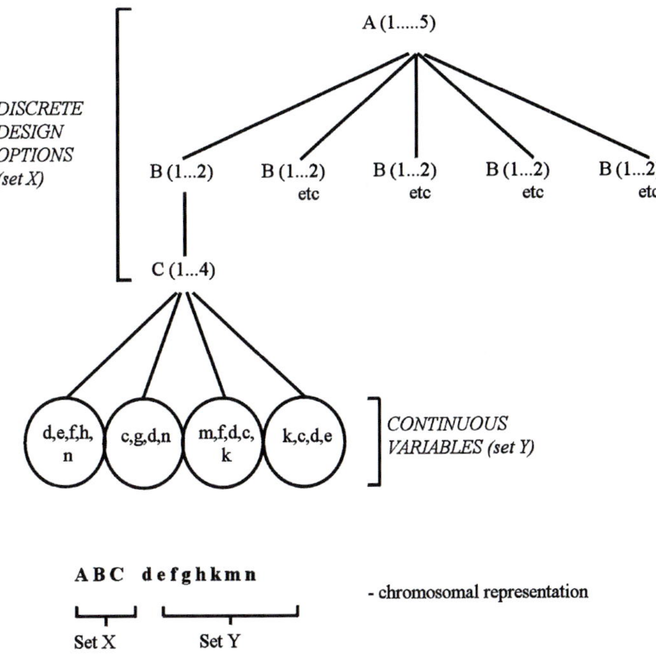

Figure 5.5 Simple design hierarchy.

been integrated for the manipulation and continuous improvement of the discrete set whereas a genetic algorithm concurrently operates within the continuous variable sets. Speciation prevents disruption of high-performance parameter sets in earlier generations as a result of crossover of the continuous variables between differing discrete configurations. Such disruption leaves little opportunity for the evolution of better continuous variable sets for any particular configuration. Appropriate communication between the two search agents results in overall improvement of the whole system solutions. Results from this co-operative strategy show satisfactory robustness and significant improvement in search diversity and solution fitness when compared to other fixed-length structured representations. Of equal importance is the simplicity of the chromosomal representation which is essential if complex, real-world design hierarchies are to be considered.

A flow chart describing the GAANT process is shown in fig. 5.6. Although the GA manipulation of the continuous variable set, Y, is apparent throughout, the values of the parameters of the discrete parameter set, X, are held constant for a set number of generations (epoch). The overall chromosome fitness is then calculated from a ratio of average fitness over the epoch (fitn) and mean fitness of the current generation (fitall). Relative fitnesses (rfit) are then scaled in terms of numbers of standard deviations from the mean. Upper and lower bounds (Rf1 & Rf2) are then introduced and the chromosomes are manipulated in the manner shown dependent upon their scaled fitness in relation to Rf1 & Rf2.

GAANT and variations of the algorithm have been utilised in two design domains. The first concerns the initial design stages of large-scale hydropower systems (Parmee, 1996c) where several potential sites exist with a number of discrete options relating to mode of operation and

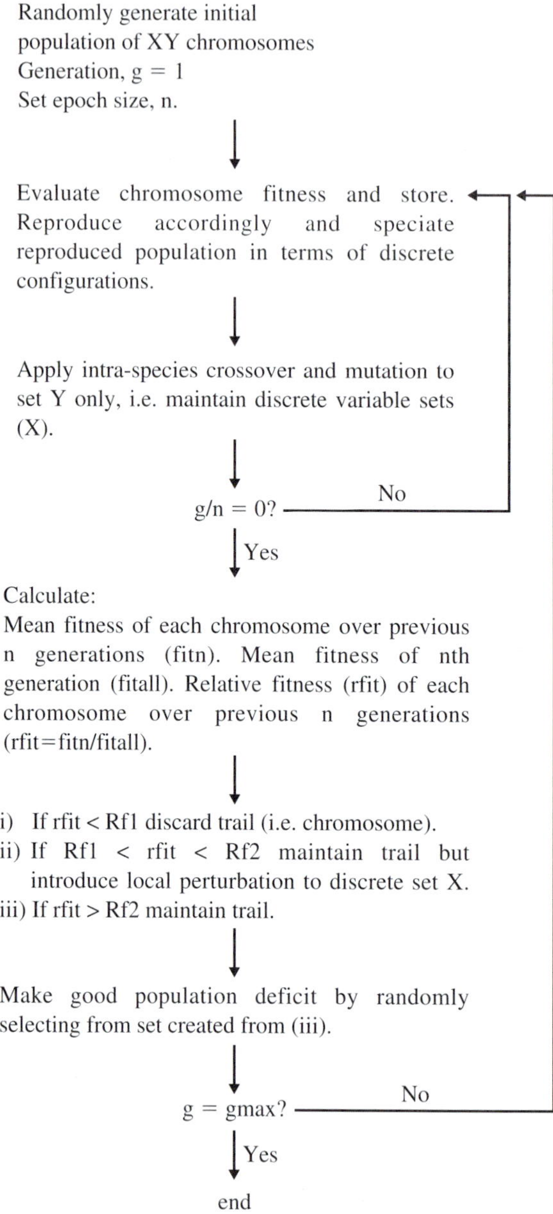

Figure 5.6 GAANT flow chart.

major components. Continuous variables include pressure tunnel lengths, dam height, generation period, powerhouse depth, etc. This relatively simple hierarchy contains twenty possible discrete paths with related continuous design spaces described by five to seven variables. Results shows that GAANT can provide an efficient search across the hierarchy and can identify a number of high-performance design solutions at an acceptable level of computational expense. The second domain concerns the redesign of certain aspects of thermal power systems (Chen and Parmee, 1998). In this case discrete parameters relate to feed heater number and layout and steam line tapping points and configuration. Continuous variables include friction coefficients, heat conductances and parallel feed heater fractional flow rate. In addition there are eight control setting variables related to various feed water and gas flow rates, turbine control, pressures, etc. Again the GAANT strategy achieves an efficient diverse search across this discrete/continuous design hierarchy and very significant improvements in predicted power outputs have been achieved. Of equal importance, however, are the significant reductions in design lead time that have been achieved in both cases.

Results so far indicate that GAANT can provide a search capability that allows the design engineer to rapidly explore the potential of complex discrete/continuous design hierarchies to a far greater extent than is currently possible within time and budget constraints. Research is now underway to further improve overall performance and to assess the scaleability of the strategy. Far more complex hierarchies exist and further development of the basic GAANT concept may be necessary to ensure that satisfactory performance is maintained. GAANT may also be integrated with the cluster oriented approaches of section 5.2.1 to better provide an interactive exploratory system that can be integrated with design team activity.

5.2.3 Variable Length Hierarchies

The concepts behind the GAANT representation have also been applied to the manipulation of variable-length multi-level mathematical function representations. The objective has been to improve the calibration of preliminary design models to empirical data or to results from a more in-depth analysis (FEA or CFD). This is achieved by identifying those areas of coding where insufficient knowledge or the requirement of keeping computational expense to a minimum has resulted in unavoidable function approximation. A contributing factor may be the inclusion of empirically derived coefficients (i.e. discharge, drag, etc). The objective is to evolve improved coding within these areas in order to achieve a better calibration with existing empirical data or results generated from a more in-depth, computationally expensive analysis. If this is possible then the element of associated risk would be correspondingly lessened whilst rapid design iteration can still be achieved utilising these simple, but more representative models. Initial research indicated that genetic programming (GP) (Koza, 1992, 1998) when utilised for system identification can achieve these objectives to a certain extent. GP manipulation of engineering relationships has provided some reasonable results related to the generation of formula for pressure drop in turbulent pipe flow and also energy loss associated with sudden contraction or sudden expansion in incompressible pipeflow (Watson and Parmee, 1996). However, it soon became apparent that the problems associated with the crossover of continuous coefficients between differing discrete functional structures was causing similar problems to those identified in the previous section relating to the successful crossover of useful information within the fixed-length design hierarchies. As previously noted the exchange of information from continuous design spaces to unrelated discrete design configurations does not promote the formation of high performance variable parameter combinations.

The success of the GAANT strategy stimulated experimentation to assess the benefits of a similar approach to the manipulation of the variable length 'design' hierarchies describing the mathematical functions. A classification system relating to the functional forms within the variable length hierarchies that would subsequently allow useful exchange of information between similar representations is required The variable lengths of the discrete decision trees and the related number of possible discrete system/function configurations eliminates possible classification in terms of identical structure. A classification in terms of complexity by arbitrarily ranking the mathematical functions and real numbered terminals has therefore been introduced, i.e. terminals = 1.0; addition or subtraction = 1.1; multiply or divide = 1.2. Individual node complexity (NC) is then calculated from the weighted values of the nodes/terminals below it. The complexity of the tree decreases with depth and the root node NC(0) gives an overall rating of the whole tree. Trees can now be classified in terms of similar complexity and appropriate crossover regimes can be introduced between similar subtree classes to reduce semantic disruption. In a similar manner to that of the GAANT model elements from two search algorithms are introduced. A genetic programming operator manipulates the discrete functional structure whilst a genetic algorithm searches the continuous coefficient space (Watson and Parmee, 1997).

A return to the engineering problems previously addressed with the canonical GP form indicates a significant improvement in performance relating to a reduction of overall population size and required calls to the fitness function resulting in a much reduced CPU time; a reduction in computer memory requirement; better accuracy in terms of correlation with empirical data or data generated from more complex analysis techniques and an ability to fit higher-dimensional surfaces (Watson and Parmee, 1998). Although encouraging, further improvement is required in order to generate meaningful multi-variable models. It is expected that further improvement will be achieved as research continues relating to the GAANT concept and the successful manipulation of design grammars.

5.3 Co-operative Strategies for Detailed Design

The requirements of the search strategies change considerably as we progress to detailed design or introduce low-level analysis to verify results from preliminary design tools. The emphasis is now generally upon the identification of a single high-performance solution as opposed to the achievement of a number of alternative designs. The major problem is the considerable computational expense associated with complex analysis and population-based search. It is essential that the number of calls to the system model for fitness evaluation is minimised if extensive integration is to be considered feasible.

There are many examples of parallel processing/distributed computing strategies where members of a population are distributed across a number of processors for evaluation in an attempt to address this computational expense problem (e.g. Cai and Thierauf, 1996; Leite, 1996). Although significant speed-up can be achieved in this manner further radical improvement is possible by the co-evolution of mathematical representations of differing resolution and the establishment of appropriate communication regimes between such co-evolving representations as in Michigan State's 'injection island' strategy (Lin et al, 1994; Goodman et al., 1996). The co-operative co-evolution of differing representations of a design problem distributed across a number of separate 'evolution islands' results in a significant reduction in the number of required calls to the evaluation function. Good lower resolution solutions are 'injected' into higher resolution evolution processes. This co-evolutionary, multi-level approach offers great potential as a framework for the support of single component design through both preliminary and detailed stages. Parmee and Vekeria (1997) have been investigating the combination of computationally inexpensive preliminary design models with more highly definitive finite element techniques within a single injection island framework. The intention is to evolve a design from initial configuration through to product realisation (Parmee and Vekeria, 1998).

Work in this area has concentrated upon the structural analysis of concrete flat plates where a finite element analysis (FEA) is ultimately required to provide a low-risk design solution. The problem domain is high-dimensional with circa 400 elements of the plate being able to vary in depth and has conflicting objectives, i.e. the minimisation of stress violation and the minimisation of weight. Initial research concentrated on the sequential introduction of plate representations of increasing resolution during an evolutionary search process. Various adaptive search techniques were introduced but the CHC GA (Eshelmann, 1991) provides best performance across the range of plate resolutions. However, satisfactory convergence was initially only possible with plate representations of up to 80 varying elements. This was sufficient to allow the evolution of specific areas of the plate and the achievement of improved plate designs. The research relates to a real-world domain and is supported by an international manufacturer of building components. Integration of the initial techniques has led to the evolutionary design and subsequent mass manufacture of related building products.

Introduction of the injection island techniques whilst still utilising the CHC GA has subsequently led to successful concurrent search of several plate resolutions culminating in the required 400 element variable depth representation. A very significant reduction in the overall number of calls to the plate model is evident in addition to further significant reductions in plate weight. Early comparison of the various AS algorithms upon this plate problem indicated better performance from certain AS techniques during the earlier generations than from others and this has led to the establishment of a multi-agent approach with appropriate search agent introduction/removal strategies within the framework of the injection island architecture.

Two simple strategies have been assessed. In the first the CHC algorithm manipulating a 5×5 grid representation co-evolves with a PBIL manipulation of a 10×10 representation. Migration is allowed every 200 evaluations with the better solutions from the CHC process updating the probability vector of the PBIL process. When the CHC ceases to provide sufficiently high-performance solutions for injection the process is killed and replaced by a second PBIL process manipulating a 20×20 grid representation. This continues to co-evolve with the lower resolution PBIL process receiving injected solutions every n generations. The reasoning here is that the more diverse search of the CHC which leads to higher performance on the coarser resolutions interacts with the more rapid convergence characteristics of PBIL to provide an optimal starting population for the final PBIL-based search. The objective is a higher-performance solution within a lesser number of function evaluations than would be attainable using the CHC alone within a DiiGA architecture. Results from a single load-case representation are shown in fig. 5.7 (left) and compared to the results from a three load-case representation, fig. 5.7 (right). The second configuration involves a PBIL manipulation of the 5×5 grid co-evolving with a CHC manipulation of the 10×10 grid. The 5×5 PBIL process is killed as it ceases to pass useful information to the CHC process and at this point the CHC algorithm is replaced by PBIL which now manipulates the 10×10 resolution. A further 20×20 CHC process is introduced and co-evolves with the 10×10 PBIL representation. This strategy

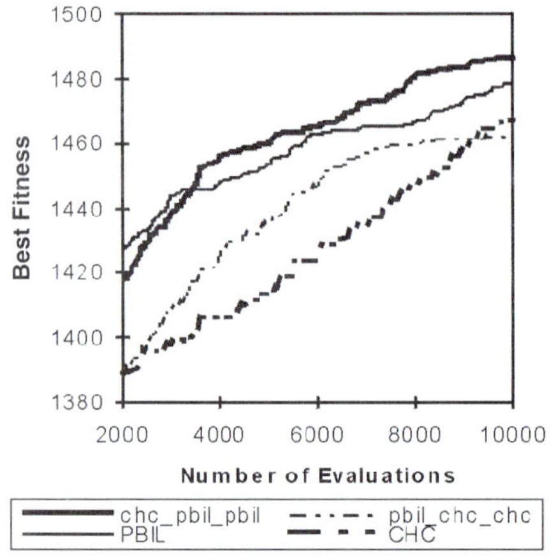

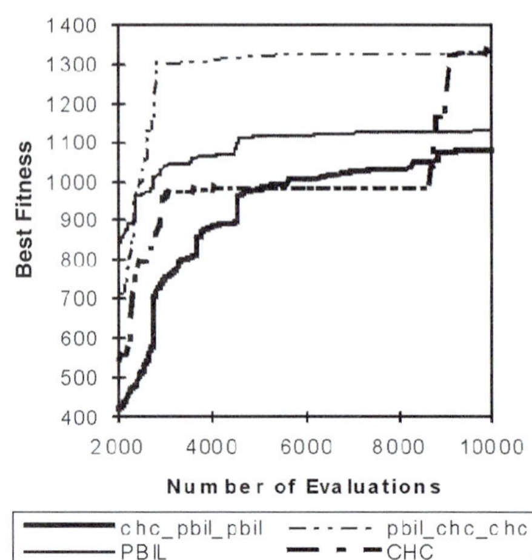

Figure 5.7 Results from a single-load case representation (left) and a three-load case representation (right).

therefore investigates an alternative dynamic where PBIL injects locally high-performing solutions into the more diverse search processes of CHC.

The chc-pbil-pbil (c-p-p) co-evolution results in increased performance both in terms of reduced calls to the evaluation function and improved overall fitness in the single load case situation. However, as a more realistic three-load case problem is introduced the c-p-p is very significantly out-performed by the pbil-pbil-chc (p-p-c) co-evolution. The single-load case promotes the generation of material concentrations in one area of the plate and it is suggested that the convergence characteristics of the c-p-p are better suited to this less complex distribution of material. With three-load cases material is distributed across a wider area of the plate to best satisfy stress characteristics. A more detailed discussion of these results can be found in the literature (Parmee and Vekeria, 1997). Initial investigation does suggest significant utility in the introduction of a number of search techniques within an injection architecture although further research is required to investigate the interaction between the differing search agents.

The injection island/CHC approach is now being integrated with industrial design practice and it is expected that this will result in a machine-based, stand-alone process that can take single components from preliminary through detailed design to manufacture within an acceptable period of time and with significant improvement in component performance. Research related to multi-agent integration is continuing.

5.4 Qualitative Criteria, Constraint and Multi-objective Satisfaction

Although many criteria may be represented quantitatively many will be qualitative in nature, e.g. those relating to in-house design and manufacturing preference, etc. Many multi-objective optimisation techniques rely upon a clear quantitative representation of the criteria and assume a high confidence in their validity whereas other approaches fuzzify quantitative criteria in order to soften the objectives and lead the search to satisfactory solutions. In general however, such strategies only consider quantitative criteria. There remains a requirement to include the designer in the assessment loop to both provide qualitative judgement and to assess the relevance of the included criteria. One attempt to achieve this utilises a niching approach to first identify good solutions before introducing a fuzzy logic interface which assesses the solutions in terms of designer-generated qualitative rules concerning relationships between the defining parameters (Roy and Parmee, 1996). The result is a quantitative evaluation from the GA generated solutions which is enhanced by a crisp qualitative rating from the fuzzy interface. Additional information concerning solution and variable sensitivity and degree of constraint violation is also extracted and presented to the engineer.

We must consider however the validity of single solutions identified from preliminary design models that are coarse representations of the system under design. This could prove to be a too specific approach at this stage as subsequent, more in-depth analysis could prove such solutions erroneous. An alternative is to return to the regional identification procedures introduced in section 5.2.1. In this case the characteristics of high-performance bounded regions can be assessed by the designer with the assistance of complementary soft computing techniques such as the fuzzy interface already mentioned. This approach has already been utilised for the identification of regions characterised by low gradient and thus providing robust design solutions (Parmee and Denham, 1994; Parmee, 1996a). Research is continuing in this area to further assess the extent and nature of relevant engineering information that can be extracted from these regions.

Much research is evident in the evolutionary constraint satisfaction/constrained optimisation area (see Michelewicz et al., 1996). There are, in general, two cases; the first concerning explicit constraints that directly affect the structure of chromosomal representation. In this case various specialised crossover operators, repair algorithms and chromosome templates may be required to ensure that feasible representations are maintained after the chromosomal disruption caused by crossover and mutation (Michalewicz, 1996). The second case concerns implicit constraints, i.e. those represented by some function of the mathematical simulation of the system under design and their values therefore being returned as part of the objective function. The introduction of penalty functions (Siddall, 1982) that draw the evolutionary search into regions of feasibility is a common strategy when handling such implicit constraints

It is very unusual for an industrial design problem to be free of constraint and the extent of such constraints may often be poorly defined. Although the effectiveness of penalty functions can be well illustrated on a range of mathematical test functions the development of a generic approach that is effective across a wide range of real-world design problems is extremely difficult. One approach that has proved to be effective in a number of diverse design environments is to utilise the exploratory capabilities of evolutionary search to identify regions of high solution feasibility, i.e. the objective function becomes the minimisation of constraint violation. Once the search has converged upon such a region/solution then crossover and mutation operators may best be avoided as, in those situations involving non-convex or even disjoint feasible regions, such operators can translate feasible points into non-feasible space. A better strategy is to introduce other, more localised search procedures initiated from the identified points of minimum constraint violation. One example of this approach is Bilchev and Parmee's work (1996) concerning heavily constrained problems relating to whole system configuration and flight trajectories of air-launched space vehicles (British Aerospace). A co-operative strategy involving an initial GA search for feasibility followed by an ant colony-based local search has enabled the identification of feasible design solutions from design spaces that have defied heuristic approaches combined with more deterministic optimisation techniques. In this instance, the noisy nature of the fitness landscape required the introduction of an ant colony algorithm, which again avoids premature convergence upon local optima through the utilisation of communicating multiple search agents. An inherent characteristic of the ant colony algorithm for constrained, continuous space search is its tendency, once feasible space has been accessed, to remain within that feasible space. The use of a secondary adaptive search technique was not required in the case of Parmee et al.'s (1996d) work with Nuclear Electric where, again, the exploratory capabilities of the GA have been utilised to locate feasible points from which a linear programming optimiser can be initiated. This approach has totally automated a design process that formerly required significant engineer-based heuristic search in order to locate a feasibility point.

The reader is directed to Michalewicz (1996) for a comprehensive cover of evolutionary methods for handling explicit constraints. However, another practical example involves the development of an evolutionary strategy for the optimal generation of codes for the testing of electronic circuitry. Research within this field has been supported by Rolls Royce Associates (RRA) and has resulted in strategies for handling explicit constraint in a highly discrete search domain (Bilchev and Parmee, 1996). The problem is decomposed into variable parameter subsets and an overall solution is generated from successive evolutionary search of each subset. Preliminary results indicate very significant reductions in design lead times are possible using this strategy and further development is underway.

Again, significant research investigating evolutionary-based multi-objective satisfaction/optimisation (MOO) is evident in the literature (Fonseca and Fleming, 1995). Various MOO techniques lend themselves to integration with evolutionary algorithms whilst others specifically rely upon an evolutionary population-based search framework. Well-established techniques include weighted sums (Osyczka, 1984), Pareto optimisation (Horn and Nafpliotis, 1993) and lexicographic methods (Ben-Tahl, 1979) whereas Schaffer's vector evaluated genetic algorithm (Schaffer, 1985) is an early example of an evolutionary-based strategy. A comparison of such techniques applied to a preliminary airframe design problem with nine main objectives (Cvetkovic and Parmee, 1998) illustrates the sensitivity of solutions to the utilisation of differing multi-objective optimisation methods and differing combinations of objectives. Such comparisons show that on the whole the techniques not only rely upon well-defined objectives but also a good understanding of the degree of interaction between various objectives and of their relative importance. In machine terms no result returned from one technique can be considered better than another; such judgements ultimately remain with the design engineer. There is obviously a need to include some qualitative measure of the 'goodness' of returned solutions. The fuzzy interface introduced earlier in this section attempts to quantify the quality of a solution through the application of engineer generated interactive rules. Other approaches involving the introduction of rule-based preferences are available (Antonsson, 1997; Brehm et al., 1997) and in some cases such techniques have been integrated with evolutionary techniques with some significant success.

Most techniques relating to both constraints and multi-objectives, however, assume a fixed, relatively well-defined design environment. This may be appropriate when dealing with routine design tasks but is likely not appropriate when operating in poorly defined conceptual and preliminary design environments. A very high degree of flexibility may be required when dealing with both constraints and objectives. It may be difficult to distinguish between the two, for instance, a constraint could be considered an objective when penalty functions are introduced and evolutionary search struggles to minimise degree of violation. A hard constraint may soften as the engineer's knowledge base expands or the constraint may even disappear as the design environment shifts and its perceived importance diminishes against possible gains. Early objectives may seem trivial as concepts firm-up and more significant goals become possible. Such changes relating to the design space may initially be prevalent but diminish as high-performance configurations become established. Instigating such change and therefore maintaining extensive exploration of the design domain whilst minimising design lead time presents a major challenge that can be significantly addressed by the development of interactive engineer/evolutionary systems. The following section is speculative in nature investigating appropriate structures/strategies involving both evolutionary search and other CI techniques that may ultimately support such interactive processes.

5.5 Co-operative Evolutionary/Computational Intelligence Systems

A common element of the PEDC research described in the preceding sections is the utilisation of co-operative strategies that utilise two or more search techniques to overcome the complexities related both to the various design spaces and to the structure of the problem representation. The research described indicates that such co-operative strategies can be of significant benefit within the adaptive search domain. PEDC research has shown that such co-operation can overcome problems related to constraint satisfaction (Bilchev and Parmee, 1996), mixed discrete/continuous variable design hierarchies (Parmee, 1996c), design space decomposition (Parmee, 1996a,b) and computational expense related to complex analysis during detailed design (Parmee and Vekeria, 1997). In addition, although each of the related computational intelligence technologies offer potential in their stand-alone application to specific design problems, far greater utility in the form of their satisfactory integration with current design practice can be achieved by an investigation of overall co-operative structures that utilise their particular characteristics in a more generic manner. This integration of co-operating CI techniques offers major potential especially in achieving meaningful designer/machine interaction.

It is suggested that a major role of machine-based agent technologies (Clearwater et al., 1992; Talukdar et al., 1993; Wooldridge and Jennings, 1995) within the design domain will relate to this communication aspect. As the utilisation of ES/AS techniques moves to meaningful integration with the design process and current design team practice so the need for co-operative strategies will increase. This will involve co-evolving processes each of which may describe:

- individual elements of the engineering system
- aspects related to individual disciplines (i.e. multi-disciplinary co-evolution)
- high-level aspects of design, manufacture and marketing, etc. (i.e. integrated product development).

Irrespective of the level at which processes operate there will be a requirement for communication both between each process and with the design team. Such communication may relate to, for instance, the degree of constraint/criteria satisfaction in each domain or degree of convergence. A capability for state recognition will be required to identify the need to:

- redistribute search resources
- terminate search or instigate new search processes
- relax, harden, eliminate or introduce constraints and criteria
- communicate current status or seemingly relevant data to the design team or conversely collect and distribute relevant data via the design team interface
- in the same manner, archive relevant information to an on-line database or extract data required by the search processes in order to continue.

This suggests an intelligent agent approach integrated both with machine-based and design team activities and a structure similar to that shown in fig. 5.8. The structure of fig. 5.8b is aimed primarily at high level concept formation to establish an initial design brief that takes into account the many factors relating to overall product development. Figure 5.8a describes the manipulation of relatively simplistic preliminary design representations in order to establish an overall feasible domain. Although ambitious, the development of such overall co-evolutionary strategies may support meaningful integration with design team practice. The designers themselves can be regarded as external agents extracting information from the system and processing such information off-line. Such off-line processing allows the dynamic re-definition of the problem domain via the re-introduction of reformed constraint, criteria and objective functions.

In many ways this suggested combination of evolutionary/CI techniques and strategies relates more to current design practice rather than natural evolution by attempting to model design team interaction, information exchange and processing. With appropriate design team interaction this will result in concurrent, iterative improvements in system/product design. The objective is to provide an interactive facility which results in a far broader search of design and manufacturing alternatives within an acceptable time frame during all stages of design. A greater range of variable design parameters can be combined with manufacturing objectives and constraint to significantly increase the probability of achieving an optimal, acceptable design definition within a shorter time span and with the added possibility of competitive innovation. The design team can rapidly assess design concepts by utilising the search and decision support capabilities of the suggested adaptive search engine as illustrated in fig. 5.9. Off-line discussion based upon solutions generated by the search processes redefines the problem space whilst increasing the engineer's knowledge-base with regard to the overall design problem. It is intended that initial establishment of such frameworks will be restricted to the simpler design representations utilised during conceptual design. Having established basic feasibility then future work will address more complex co-evolutionary design tasks.

5.6 Summary

It was suggested in section 5.1 that a number of requirements need to be satisfied by any ES/AS system if meaningful integration with design team activities is to be achieved. It is

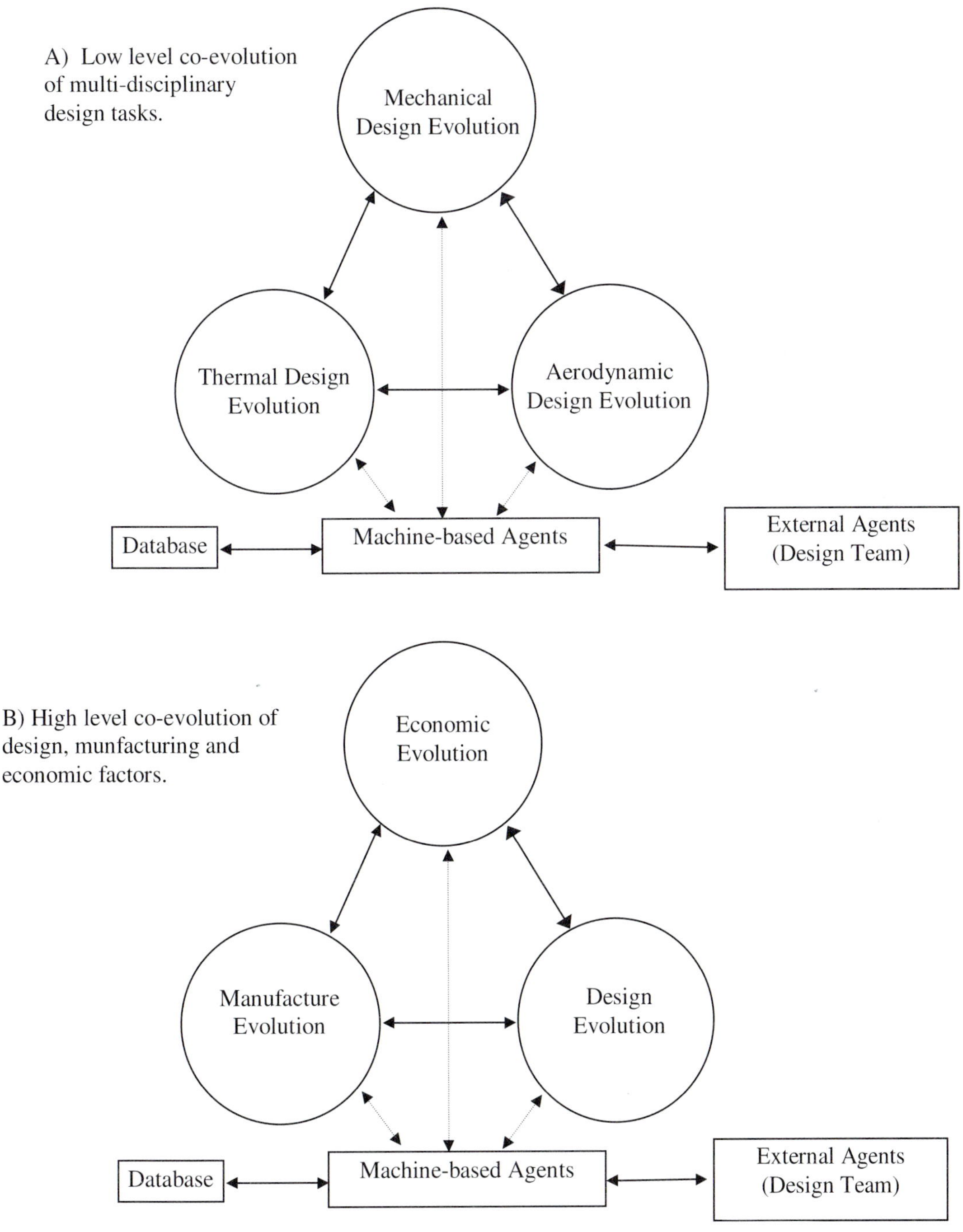

Figure 5.8 High and low level co-evolutionary processes.

interesting, in the light of the information contained within subsequent sections, to ascertain to what extent such requirements can be satisfied at this point in time and speculate as to future potential. Commencing with model representation, research relating to the utilisation of various model types for fitness function evaluation is relatively well-advanced with many examples in the literature describing the EC and AS manipulation of neural network, response surface and fuzzy representations of engineering systems. There are several reasons why such representations are required, for instance, no analytic model of the system may be available due to complexity issues but sufficient empirical data is present to train a neural or fuzzy representations or to develop acceptable response surface representations. Alternatively complex analytic models may be available but their utilisation is not acceptable due to related computational expense incurred when manipulated by population-based stochastic search techniques.

At the higher levels of design, initial specification may be so ill-defined and initial knowledge so poor that a more qualitative model is required to first establish initial design direction. Such qualitative models may be fuzzy rule based, simple correlations or developed from

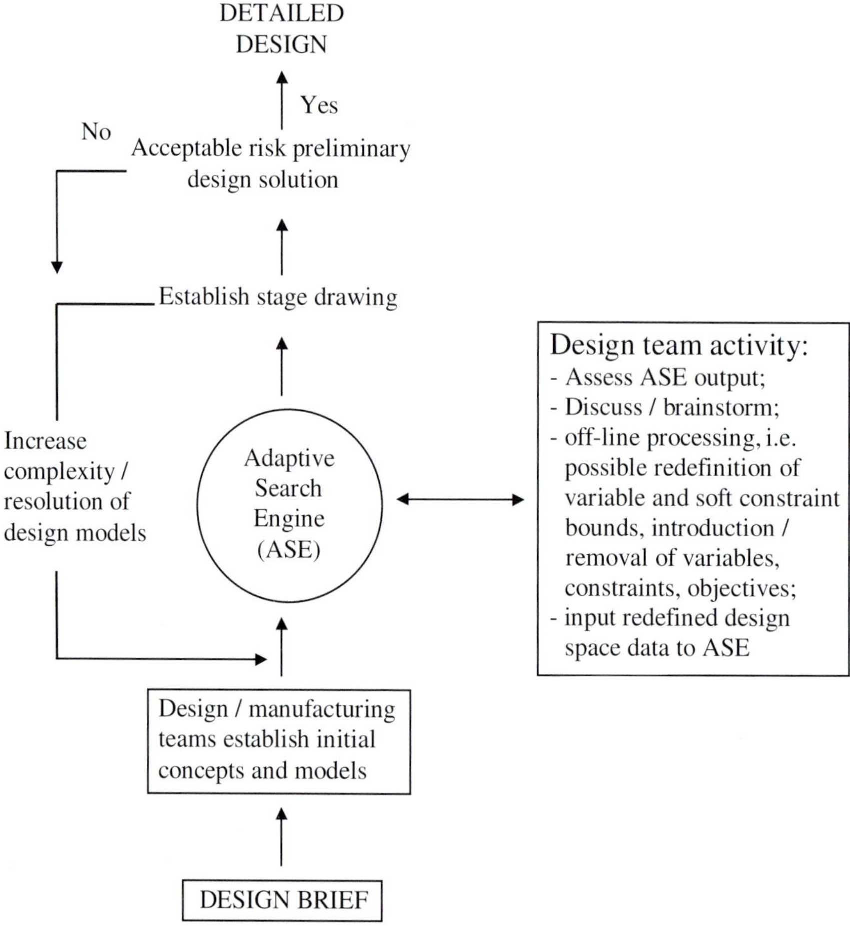

Figure 5.9 Utilising the search and decision support capabilities of the adaptive search engine.

empirical formulae, calculated assumption and empirical data. They will be utilised during the preliminary design stages to support the definition of an initial system (or subsystem) configuration. It is during this process that a true exploratory capability involving the on-line addition, removal and/or variation of constraints, objectives and variable parameter bounds is required. Research involving evolutionary/adaptive systems which support such exploration either within a machine-based environment (Gero et al., 1994) or through extensive designer interaction is now apparent. The strategies described in section 5.2 attempt to provide an exploration framework by introducing problem reduction strategies that can be used in a highly interactive manner to enable the engineer to rapidly survey available design options both within and outside of an initial predefined design space. These strategies are now available as prototype design tools and are currently being assessed in an industrial design environment. Further, more fundamental research is concurrently investigating the underlying dynamics of design space sampling and region formation in order to further improve the techniques in terms of number of identified regions, region set cover, on-line extraction of information, multi-objective satisfaction and the definition of feasible space. It is now intended to investigate the integration of both machine-based emergence (Gero, 1998) and human/computer-based emergence with a view to long-term development of interactive systems that take best advantage of the dynamics of both approaches.

In the case of whole system design of section 5.2.2 the designer would ordinarily be forced to significantly decompose the design hierarchy to create design subsets of sufficiently small dimension to allow meaningful heuristic search. Previous experience will lead the engineer to those regions that have a high-confidence rating, i.e. regions from which the engineer is likely to find satisfactory solutions within strict time constraints. The powerful search capabilities of the AS techniques however, result in very rapid, concurrent multi-level search of the entire hierarchy eliminating the need for decomposition and opening up new areas warranting further investigation. Using these techniques perhaps in conjunction with a more traditional approach, may result in the generation of higher performance, competitive solutions within a similar or reduced timescale.

It is suggested that it is these higher levels of design (which constitute a very large proportion of overall design effort, expense and incur high levels of risk) that can benefit to the greatest extent from the development of adaptive exploratory, search and optimisation systems. The foreseen benefits are twofold: a reduction in design lead time allied with a much higher degree of design exploration leading to extremely competitive, innovative/creative design solutions.

The utilisation and further development of multi-level, multi-resolution distributed evolutionary systems offers significant utility during the lower-level stages of detailed design and analysis. Such systems, allied with still rapidly increasing computational processing capabilities may form the foundation of evolutionary detailed design optimisation. The research described in section 5.3 illustrates how, for single component design, such systems have the potential to provide a fully automated design capability. Although the introduction of differing search agents operating either concurrently or sequentially appears to offer significant utility in terms of introducing exploration and exploitation capabilities at appropriate stages of the overall search process we should view this at the operator level as opposed to manipulating differing adaptive search techniques. The concurrent introduction of operators that promote exploration and exploitation and the on-line control of the level of resource available to them within an overall adaptive search framework offers a more economic and probably more efficient approach. Such on-line resource balancing is a feature of the ant colony models (Colorni et al., 1981; Bilchev and Parmee, 1996) where increasing numbers of search agents explore high potential paths whilst resource to poor performance paths is penalised and such paths are eventually evaporated. Manipulation at operator level is also probably preferable to the sequential exploration and local search procedures described in section 5.4 relating to the identification of disjoint feasible regions of complex, highly constrained spaces.

It is interesting to note that the co-evolutionary injection island approach with the integration of both preliminary and detailed design models provides an overall progression through preliminary and detailed stages in single component design. In a simplistic manner this models the design process and provides us with an indication of the basic co-operative framework required to achieve a continuous ES/AS environment to support design activity as a whole. More complex interactive systems obviously require co-operative elements concerning human/machine interaction, the integration of design heuristics and the relationship between machine-based search and design team practice. The strategies presented in sections 5.2 and 5.4 address such requirements whilst the speculative systems of section 5.5 suggest co-operative, interactive systems to support overall design activity. It is quite apparent that considerably more research effort is required to achieve meaningful working prototypes of such co-operative systems. An approach must be adopted that initially investigates relatively simplistic design problems which are then developed to address scaleability aspects. However, in general, the CI technologies are available, although some are significantly more mature than others. Research should therefore concentrate upon the structure of such overall systems and the development of architectures that provide the essential elements that support interactive working and integration with design and manufacturing team practice. If engineering design and manufacture is to take advantage of the computational processing capabilities that are available at the moment and which can only increase very significantly even in the near future, significant research resource must address investigation and experimentation relating to the utility of advanced computational procedures such as those described here. Industry must also contribute to ensure that designer requirements are fully understood and addressed within developed prototype systems. Collaborative working is essential.

Acknowledgements

The chapter relates to research supported by the UK Engineering and Physical Science Research Council and by several UK industrial organisations including Rolls Royce plc, British Aerospace and Nuclear Electric. The author thanks these organisations for their continuing support. The author also wishes to thank the researchers that have contributed so much to the complementary concepts and strategies described in the chapter, namely Harish Vekeria, Andrew Watson, George Bilchev, Kai Chen, Raj Roy, Chris Bonham, Martin Beck and Dragan Cvetkovic.

References

Adeli, H. and Kummar, S. (1995). Concurrent Structural Optimisation on Massively Parallel Supercomputers. *ASCE Journal of Structural Engineering*, **121,** no. 11, pp. 1588–1597.

Antonsson, E. K. (1997). Imprecision in Engineering Design. *Proceedings of IDEA '97 – Intelligent Design in Engineering Applications Symposium, 5th European Congress on Intelligent Techniques and Soft Computing*, Elite Foundation, Aachen, Germany, pp. 13–22.

Baluja, S. (1994). Population Based Incremental Learning: A Method for Integrating Genetic Search Based Function Optimization and Competitive Learning. Technical Report, School of Computer Science, Carnegie Mellon University, Pittsburgh, CMU-CS-94-194.

Ben-Tahl, A. (1979). Characterisation of Pareto and Lexicographic Optimal Solutions. In *Proceedings of the Third Conference on Multiple Criteria Decision Making Theory and Applications*, West Germany, Lecture Notes in Economics and Mathematical Systems, Springer-Verlag.

Bilchev, G. and Parmee, I. C. (1995). Constrained Optimisation with an Ant Colony Search Model. In *Proceedings of 2nd International Conference on Adaptive Computing in Engineering Design and Control*, PEDC, University of Plymouth.

Bilchev, G. and Parmee, I. C. (1996). Constraint Handling for the Fault Coverage Code Generation Problem: An Inductive Evolutionary Approach. In *Proceedings of Parallel Problem Solving from Nature IV*, Lecture Notes in Computing 1141, Springer-Verlag, pp. 880–899.

Brehm, R., Kreise, T. and Sebastian, H.-J. (1997). Fuzzy Sets in Engineering Design. *Proceedings of IDEA '97 – Intelligent Design in Engineering Applications Symposium, 5th European Congress on Intelligent Techniques and Soft Computing*, Elite Foundation, Aachen, Germany, pp. 1–6.

Cai, J. and Thierauf, G. (1996). Structural Optimisation of a Steel Transmission Tower using Parallel Evolution Strategy. *Procs. Adaptive Computing in Engineering Design and Control '96*, University of Plymouth, UK, ISBN 0 905227 61 1, pp. 18–25.

Chen, K. and Parmee, I. C. (1998). A Comparison of Evolutionary-based Strategies for Mixed-discrete Multilevel Design Problems. In *Proceedings of Adaptive Computing in Design and Manufacture*, Dartington Hall, Devon, UK, Springer-Verlag.

Clearwater, S., Hogg, T. and Hubermann, B. (1992). Cooperative Problem Solving. Computation: The Micro and Macro View. B. A. Hubermann, (ed.), World Scientific, pp. 33–70.

Colorni, A., Dorigo, M. and Maniezzo, V. (1981). Distributed Optimisation by Ant Colonies. In *Proceedings of First European Conference on Artificial Life*, Paris.

Cvetkovic, D., Parmee, I. C. and Webb, E. (1998). Multi-objective Optimisation and Preliminary Air Frame Design. In *Proceedings of Adaptive Computing in Design and Manufacture*, Dartington Hall, Devon, UK, Springer Verlag.

Davidor, Y. and Yamada, Y. N. (1993). The Ecological Framework: Improving GA Performance at Virtually Zero Cost. In *Proceedings of the Fifth International Conference on Genetic Algorithms*, Morgan Kaufmann.

De Jong, K. A. (1975). *An Analysis of the Behaviour of a Class of Genetic Adaptive Systems*. (Doctoral dissertation, University of Michigan), Dissertation Abstracts International.

De Jong, K. A. (1978). An Analysis of the Behaviour of a Class of Genetic Adaptive Systems. PhD Dissertation, University of Michigan, Dissertation Abstracts International, 36 (10), 5140B (Uni. Microfilms No 76–9381).

Eshelman, L. J. (1991). The CHC Adaptive Search Algorithm: How to Have Safe Search When Engaging in Non-traditional Genetic Recombination. In *Foundations of Genetic Algorithms and Classifier Systems*, Morgan Kaufmann.

Fonseca, C. M. and Fleming, P. J. (1995). An Overview of Evolutionary Algorithms in Multi-objective optimisation. *Evolutionary Computation*, **3,** pp. 1–16.

Gero, J. S. (1998). Adaptive Systems in Designing: New Analogies from Genetics and Developmental Biology. In *Adaptive Computing in Design and Manufacture*, Dartington Hall, Devon, UK, Springer Verlag, pp. 193–206.

Gero, J. S., Louis, S. J. and Kundu, S. (1994). Evolutionary Learning of Novel Grammars for Design Improvement. *Artificial Intelligence for Engineering Design, Analysis and Manufacturing*, **8,** pp. 83–94.

Goldberg, D. E. (1989). *Genetic Algorithms in Search, Optimisation and Machine Learning*. Addison-Wesley Publishing Co.

Goldberg, D. E. and Wang, L. (1997). Adaptive Niching via Coevolutionary Sharing. In *Genetic Algorithms and Evolution Strategies in Engineering and Computer Science*, Quagliarella D. et al. (eds), John Wiley, pp. 21–37.

Goodman, E. D., Averill, R. C., Punch, W. F., Ding, Y. and Malott, B. (1996). Design of Special-purpose Composite Material Plates via Genetic Algorithms. In *Proceedings of Adaptive Computing in Engineering Design and Control '96*; University of Plymouth, UK, ISBN 0 905227 61 1, pp. 3–9.

Horn, J. and Nafpiotis, N. (1993). Multiobjective Optimisation using the Niched Pareto Genetic Algorithm. Technical ILLiGAL Report No. 93005, Illinois Genetic Algorithm Library.

Koza, J. R. (1992). *Genetic Programming – on the Programming of Computers by Means of Natural Selection*. MIT Press.

Koza, J. R. (1998). Evolutionary Design of Analog Electrical Circuits Using Genetic Programming . In *Adaptive Computing in Design and Manufacture*, Dartington Hall, Devon UK, Springer-Verlag, pp. 177–192.

Leite, J. P. B. (1996). Parallel Adaptive Search Techniques for Structural Optimisation. Ph.D. thesis, Dept. of Mechanical and Chemical Engineering, Heriot-Watt University, Edinburgh, UK.

Mahfoud, S. W. (1992). Crowding and Preselection Revisited. *Proceedings of Parallel Problem Solving from Nature II*, Elsevier Science Publishers, pp. 27–36.

Lin, S. C., Punch, W. F. and Goodman, E. D. (1994). Coarse-grained Genetic Algorithms: Categorisation and New Approach. *Procs 6th IEEE Conference on Parallel and Distributed Computing*, pp. 28–37.

Michalewicz, Z. (1996). *Genetic Algorithms + Data Structures = Evolution Programs*, Springer-Verlag, 3rd Edition.

Michalewicz, Z., Dasgupta, D., Le Riche, R. G. and Schoenauer, M. (1996). Evolutionary Algorithms for Constrained Engineering Problems. *Computers and Industrial Engineering Journal*, vol. 30, no. 4, pp. 851–830.

Osyczka, A. (1984). *Multicriterion Optimisation in Engineering with Fortran Programs*. Ellis Horwood Series in Engineering Science, Ellis Horwood.

Otto, K. N. and Antonsson, E. K. (1995). Propagating imprecise engineering design constraints. In *Proceedings of 1995 IEEE International Conference on Fuzzy Systems*, vol. 1. IEEE, New York, NY. pp. 375–382.

Parmee, I. C. (1996a). The Maintenance of Search Diversity for effective Design Space Decomposition using Cluster-oriented Genetic Algorithms (COGAs) and Multi-agent Systems (GAANT). In *Proceedings of 2nd International Conference on Adaptive Computing in Engineering Design and Control*, PEDC, University of Plymouth, pp. 128–138.

Parmee, I. C. (1996b). Cluster-Oriented Genetic Algorithms (COGAs) for the Identification of High-Performance Regions of Design Spaces. *Proceedings of EvCA96 Conference*, Moscow, pp. 66–75.

Parmee, I. C. (1996c). The Development of a Dual-Agent Strategy for Efficient Search Across Whole System Engineering Design Hierarchies. In *Proceedings of Parallel Problem Solving from Nature IV*, Lecture Notes in Computing 1141, Springer-Verlag, pp. 523–532.

Parmee, I. C. (1997). *Strategies for the Integration of Evolutionary/Adaptive Search with the Engineering Design Process*. In Dasgupta, D. and Michelewicz, Z. (eds), *Evolutionary Algorithms in Engineering Applications*; Springer-Verlag, pp. 453–478.

Parmee, I. C. and Beck, M. A. (1997). An Evolutionary, Agent-Assisted Strategy for Conceptual Design Space Decomposition. In *Proceedings of AISB Workshop on Evolutionary Computing*, Springer Lecture Notes in Computer Science, No. 1305, Springer-Verlag, pp. 275–286.

Parmee, I. C. and Denham, M. J. (1994). The Integration of Adaptive Search Techniques with Current Design Practice. *Proceedings of Adaptive Computing in Engineering Design and Control*, University of Plymouth, UK, pp. 1–13.

Parmee, I. C., Gane, C., Donne, M. and Chen, K. (1996d). Genetic Strategies for the Design and Optimal Operation of Thermal Systems. In *Proceedings of Fourth European Congress on Intelligent Techniques and Soft Computing*, Elite Foundation, Aachen, Germany.

Parmee, I. C. and Vekeria, H. (1997). Co-operative, Evolutionary Strategies for Single Component Design. In *Proceedings of Seventh International Conference on Genetic Algorithms*, pp. 529–536.

Parmee, I. C. and Vekeria, H. D. (1997). Evolutionary/Adaptive Search Strategies and Model Representation in Engineering Design. In *Proceedings of the 15th IMACS World Congress on Scientific Computation, Modelling and Applied Mathematics*, Berlin, August 1997.

Parmee, I. C. and Vekeria, H. D. (1998). Reducing Lead Time for Single Component Design via Appropriate Adaptive Search Strategies. In *Journal of Engineering Valuation and Cost Analysis, Special Issue on Engineering Valuation and Computational Intelligence*, (in Press).

Roy, R. and Parmee, I. C. (1996). Adaptive Restricted Tournament Selection for the Identification of Multiple Sub-optima in a Multi-modal Function. *Lecture Notes in Computer Science (Evolutionary Computing)*; Fogarty T. C. (ed.), Springer-Verlag, pp. 236–256.

Roy, R, Parmee, I. C. and Purchase, G. (1996). Integrating the Genetic Algorithm with the Preliminary Design of Gas Turbine Cooling Systems. *Proceedings of 2nd International Conference on Adaptive Computing in Engineering Design and Control*, PEDC, University of Plymouth.

Schaffer, D. (1985). Multiple Objective Optimisation with Vector Evaluated Genetic Algorithms. In *Proceedings of the First International Conference on Genetic Algorithms*, Lawrence Erlbaum Associates.

Siddall, J. N. (1982). *Optimal Engineering Design – Principles and Applications*. Marcel Decker.

Spears, W. M. (1994). Simple Subpopulation Schemes. In *Proceedings of Evolutionary Programming*, World Scientific, pp. 296–307.

Talukdar, S., de Souza, P. and Murthy, S. (1993). *Organisations for Computer-based Agents*. Engineering Design Research Centre, Carnegie Mellon University, Pittsburgh, USA.

Vekeria, H. D. and Parmee, I. C. (1996). Reducing Computational Expense Associated with Evolutionary Detailed Design. In *Proceedings of International Conference on Evolutionary Computing '97*, Indianapolis.

Watson, A. H. and Parmee, I. C. (1996). Identification of Fluid Systems using Genetic Programming. In *Proceedings of Fourth European Congress on Intelligent Techniques and Soft Computing*, Aachen, Germany.

Watson, A. H. and Parmee, I. C. (1997). Steady State Genetic Programming with Constrained Complexity Crossover Using Species Sub-population. In *Proceedings of Seventh International Conference on Genetic Algorithms*, Michigan State University, USA.

Watson, A. H. and Parmee, I. C. (1998). Improving Engineering Design Models using an Alternative Genetic Programming Approach. In *Adaptive Computing in Design and Manufacture*, Dartington Hall, Devon, UK, Springer-Verlag, pp. 193–206.

Wooldridge, M. and Jennings, N. R. (1995). Intelligent Agents: Theory and Practice. *Knowledge Engineering Review*, vol. 10(2).

Zadeh, L. A. (1965). Fuzzy Sets. *Journal of Information and Control*, vol. 8, pp. 29–44.

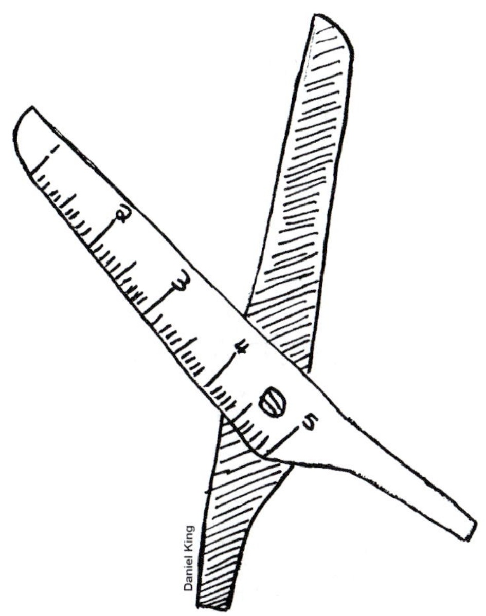

2 EVOLUTIONARY OPTIMISATION OF DESIGNS

How can evolution be used to improve our designs? What kinds of design can be optimised? How should the designs be represented? Can the abilities of evolution to find global optima be improved?

This section tackles these and other questions in evolutionary optimisation, by providing detailed case studies of successful evolutionary optimisation from three well-respected research groups in England, USA, and Japan. ***Optimization in Mechanical Design*** by Dr. Gordon Robinson, Mohammed El-Beltagy and Prof. Andy Keane, of the *Evolutionary Optimisation Group, University of Southampton*, describe how the structural vibration and strain of designs such as satellite booms and load cells can be minimised by evolution. They suggest the use of multi-level GAs which use representations with different levels of accuracy. A similar idea is then explored in ***The Optimization of Flywheels using an Injection Island Genetic Algorithm*** by Dr. Erik Goodman and his team at *Michigan State University's A. H. Case Center for Computer-Aided Engineering and Manufacturing*. They describe the use of multiple co-evolving populations of designs, using representations and analyses of different complexities, to optimise flywheels. Finally, Prof. Mitsuo Gen and Jong Ryul Kim of the *Ashikaga Institute of Technology* describe the use of genetic algorithms to evolve network designs optimised for reliability, in their chapter, ***A GA-based Approach to Reliability Design***.

Chapter 6

Optimization in Mechanical Design

By Gordon Robinson, Mohammed El-Beltagy and Andy Keane

6.1 Introduction

This chapter discusses the place of evolutionary search methods in the design of mechanical engineering systems. It is illustrated by reference to the design of two rather different engineering structures where working prototypes have actually been manufactured and tested. The work described is therefore very much concerned with using evolutionary methods in a realistic engineering setting. This fact means that rather severe restrictions have to be placed on the computational effort that can be considered, since all real engineering problems lead to rather expensive calculations if modern state-of-the-art analysis methods are to be used (it is the authors' experience that unless real engineering codes are used to evaluate designs it is very difficult to gain the trust of practising designers in using evolutionary techniques).

The chapter then goes on to discuss how the inevitable limitations of computing power available to designers influences the direction in which evolutionary design methods will need to go if they are to be more widely adopted by the mechanical engineering and related communities. An evaluation of some simple approaches to tackling this difficulty is then described before the chapter closes with some final remarks.

6.2 Case Study 1: Vibrations in Satellite Booms

In the design of practically all engineering structures and machines it is desirable to minimize mechanical noise and vibrations. The subject of this case study is the improvement of the vibration response of booms for satellite applications. These lattice beams are used to support sensors remote from the main payload or, in the case of interferometric instruments, to locate two or more sensors at fixed separations. The response of the booms to vibrational excitation critically influences the performance of the sensors.

When considering solutions to vibration and noise problems at least three possible strategies may be considered. The first, and presently most popular, option is to incorporate some form of vibration absorbing material into the design of the structure. For example, one might elect to coat structural elements with a heavy viscoelastic damping material. Similarly, pieces of vibration isolating material could be placed at mounting points, as is the case with most automobile engines. However, this method has rather significant weight and cost penalties. In the design of aerospace structures this is a major concern, since any increase in weight results in subsequent increases in the cost of deploying the structure or reductions in payload. The

EVOLUTIONARY DESIGN BY COMPUTERS
ISBN 1-55860-605-X

second method is so-called 'active' vibration control. This method employs the use of 'anti-noise' to cancel out unwanted vibrations and hence block noise propagation. However, active vibration control methods are inevitably complex and expensive.

A third option is passive vibration control. In this method, the design of the structure is modified so that it has intrinsic noise filtration characteristics. For example, it may be shown that the frequency response of a specific structure can be considerably improved by making changes to the structure's geometry. The geometric regularity or irregularity of a structure affects its vibrational response. In the case of a satellite boom, a geometrically regular structure would be one in which the lengths of beam elements and the angles between them were repeated numerous times along the length of the structure. An irregular geometry would be one in which no two beam lengths or angles were equal. By considering a large number of different geometries using an evolutionary algorithm, a design with superior noise performance can be achieved. Here, genetic algorithm (GA) optimization methods are combined with an energy flow analysis to produce new structural geometries with improved noise performance.

Energy approaches are commonly used to predict the flow of vibrations around structures. In this work, the vibration analysis is carried out using matrix receptance methods based on the Green functions of the individual beam elements. By combining these receptance methods with the well-known characteristics of Euler–Bernoulli beams, it is possible to solve directly for the energetic quantities of interest (Shankar and Keane, 1995). As has already been noted a GA is then used to select the design geometries with the best noise performance. The GA used here (Keane, 1994a) is fairly typical of those described by Goldberg (1989), being binary coded with a version of the McQueen's KMEAN clustering/niching algorithm (Anderberg, 1975) and progressive constraint application (Fiacco and McCormick, 1968).

The work detailed in this first case study concerns optimization of the frequency response of a three-dimensional satellite boom (Keane and Brown, 1996). This optimization was carried out in two stages: first a two-dimensional version of the structure was designed and tested and then, having established that the method was viable, attention was turned to the full three-dimensional case. The principal reason for adopting this approach was one of computational effort: the analysis of the two-dimensional case, with one third the number of elements, takes rather less than one tenth of the computational effort needed for the full structure (even so, such analyses still take minutes rather than seconds).

In applying this analysis procedure the following steps have been taken: first, the initial boom design (i.e., a geometrically regular design) was modelled using a commercial FEA computer-aided design package (Igusa, 1994). Next, the natural frequencies of the structure were calculated using finite element analysis. A force was then applied to the boom, and a frequency response curve obtained. A second frequency response curve was then calculated using receptance methods (Shankar and Keane, 1995). Upon confirmation that the frequency response curves produced by the two methods were similar, the receptance method code was used in conjunction with suitable optimization software to carry out the search for new geometries with superior noise performance. Throughout this research, the frequency response curves produced by FEA were used to support and confirm those obtained from the receptance code.

6.2.1 Geometric Optimization

The two-dimensional boom was formed by taking one side of the basic structure shown in fig. 6.1, i.e. from 40 individual Euler–Bernoulli beams connected at 20 joints. Each of the 40 beams had the same properties per unit length.

This regular geometric design was then manipulated using the OPTIONS suite of optimization software (Keane, 1994b). The goal of the optimization was set as minimizing the frequency averaged response of the end beam in the range 150–250 Hz. The optimizer was allowed to generate new geometries by varying the coordinates of the inner 18 joints of this simplified structure. Upon applying the GA using various values for the population size, number of generations, and limits on the joint positions, the most improved frequency response curve was obtained using 15 generations with a population size of 300 and a $\pm 25\%$ constraint on the joint positions (Keane, 1995).

To test the validity and value of these results, physical models of both the original and final 2D boom designs have been built and tested (Keane and Bright, 1996). These models were mounted and the forces applied in the same manner as in the theoretical analysis. The energy levels in the beams of interest were measured using appropriate transducers. The resulting frequency responses (as characterized by velocity squared) from testing the physical models correlated well with those from the theoretical predictions.

Having proven the technique for two-dimensional structures the same procedure was then applied to the three-dimensional problem. In this case the initial structure to be optimized consisted of all 90 Euler–Bernoulli beams of the original structure, once more with all elements having the same properties per unit length, see again fig. 6.1 (which also shows the forcing and response points used in this case). Once the three-dimensional boom had been set up an initial frequency response curve was again produced using the commercial FEA package. The output obtained from the receptance method could again be compared against the finite element results to confirm that accurate results were still being obtained.

The finite element computation was solved to mode 500 (1090 Hz) and to mode 800 (2170 Hz). Solving for 800 modes takes approximately 12 hours of c.p.u. time here using a Silicon Graphics R4400-based machine. In the range of interest (150–250 Hz), no noticeable discrepancy was seen between the frequency response curves obtained during the 500 mode solution and the 800 mode solution. Thus, confidence could be expressed in the results obtained for this range.

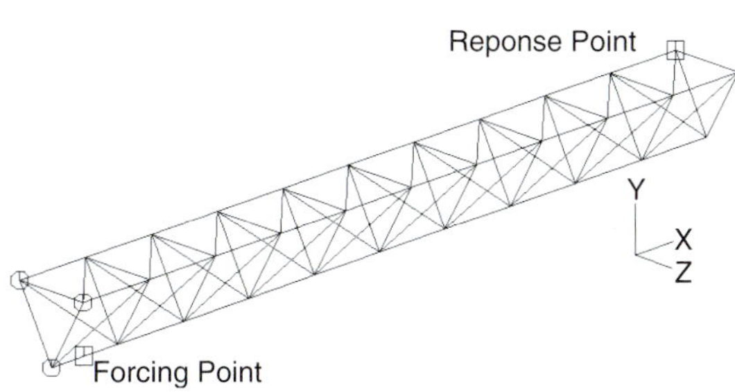

Figure 6.1 A simplified satellite boom.

The next step in this study was to produce frequency response curves using receptance theory. To produce a curve that could be compared with that produced by the finite element analysis, the program was run for a frequency range of 150–250 Hz using 101 data points. This calculation took about four and a half hours to complete. On comparison with the results of the finite element analysis the two curves proved virtually identical.

It should be noted that the time taken to carry out the FEA analysis is dominated by the number of elements used while the receptance method is influenced strongly by the number of frequency points to be studied (it is, of course, also affected by model size). Thus, although the FEA takes around twice as long to carry out as the receptance code when examining 101 frequencies, it takes roughly ten times as long when dealing with the reduced set of frequencies needed for optimization (here a 21-point integration rule is applied to assess band averaged frequency response). The receptance method's principal attraction over FEA is therefore the speed with which an individual design can be analysed for its band-averaged performance. Moreover, the receptance code used can be interfaced more easily to the optimization software used here and can readily be run in parallel on multiple processors when carrying out design searches.

6.2.2 Optimization

Given that the reliability of the receptance code had been proven, it was then interfaced with the optimization software and a GA optimizer selected to produce superior designs. For this particular run of the GA, the number of generations was set as 10 and the population size as 100. In the creation of a new geometry, the coordinates of all joints in the structure (with the exception of those at the extreme left and right-hand ends of the boom) were varied within some specified maximum deviation from their original positions, again ±25%. The search through ten generations took approximately 2000 c.p.u. hours which, using parallel processing, took around 20 days. This extremely large c.p.u. effort explains why so few generations were used and why only 100 members were allowed for each one. Clearly, with $3 \times 27 = 81$ variables, a rather larger population size would have been desirable, as would more generations. None the less, as will be seen, significant performance improvements were obtained.

Figure 6.2 shows the change in the mean, standard deviation, and minimum value of the objective function of the GA over the ten generations used. The initial value of the objective function (i.e. before generation 1) was 0.0365. At the conclusion of the first generation, the value of the objective function for the best design was 0.000650, an improvement of over 5000%. This was followed by less dramatic, but none the less substantial improvements, with the final objective function being 0.000173, a reduction of a further 380%. Figure 6.2 also shows that the generational mean steadily decreased across all generations and that the generational normalized standard deviation showed a generally downward trend. The fact that the deviation was still roughly equal to the mean at the last generation indicates that the populations had by no means become stagnant and that further generations could have been expected to improve the design still further. It is unlikely that any massive additional improvement would be made to the objective function value, but it should be possible to further tune the designs so that the generational mean and minimum started to converge and the standard deviation dropped to significantly lower levels.

This behaviour (a huge initial improvement followed by more modest refinements) reflects

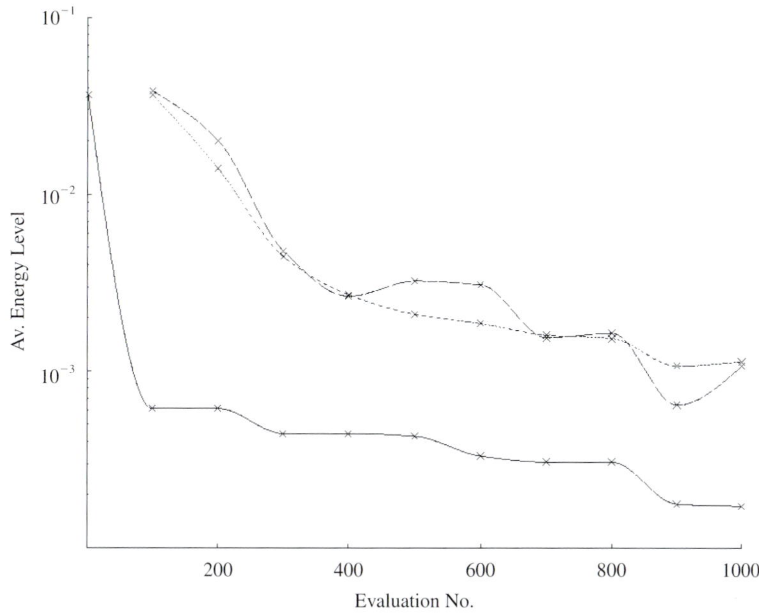

Figure 6.2 Variation of objective function with evaluation number, with generational mean shown dotted and generational normalized standard deviation dashed.

what one would expect. It is well known that a geometrically regular design does not produce a particularly favourable frequency response curve. Conversely, an irregular geometry has the potential to produce significant improvements in the frequency response (however, many irregular designs are, in fact, worse). This knowledge represents the foundation of this research. Therefore, it is not surprising that a very large improvement has been achieved by choosing the best out of 100 irregular geometries. During subsequent generations, this irregular geometry is then 'fine tuned'. With the first generation, a good base design is found. Subsequent generations provide steady, but less dramatic, improvements of a similar magnitude throughout the run. This is a direct consequence of the limited number of trials allowed by the time consuming analysis underpinning the work. In such cases it is unrealistic to aim at achieving globally optimal designs, instead good improved designs have to be sufficient. Even so, dramatic performance improvements have been obtained, see fig. 6.3, which shows the frequency response for the final design, along with that for the initial regular design. Figure 6.4 shows the final geometry achieved, c.f., fig. 6.1. Although this modified geometry may appear extreme when compared to the original design, it does provide the required noise isolation characteristics. Clearly, it would not be simple to build or deploy, but then neither are 'active' control systems. In fact, a combined approach might well offer the best of both worlds. Construction and testing of this final design is currently in progress.

6.2.3 Discussion

This first case study shows that significantly improved frequency responses may be obtained for three-dimensional beam structures using genetic algorithm optimization procedures.

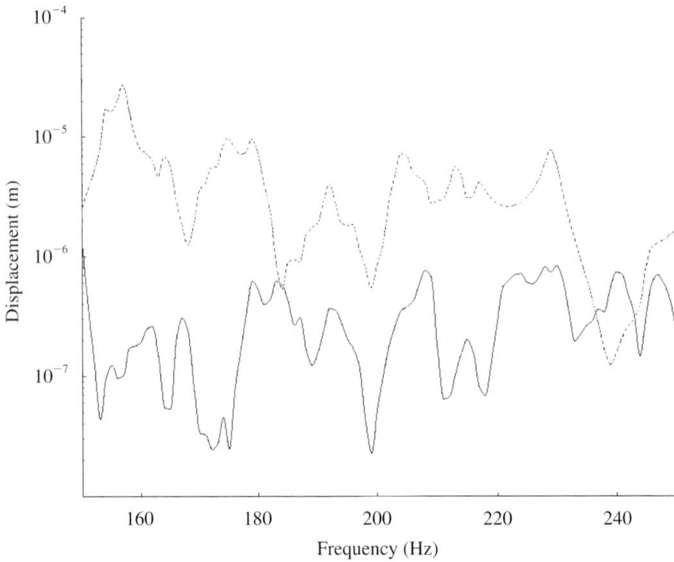

Figure 6.3 Frequency response of final three-dimensional design, with that for the original regular design shown dotted.

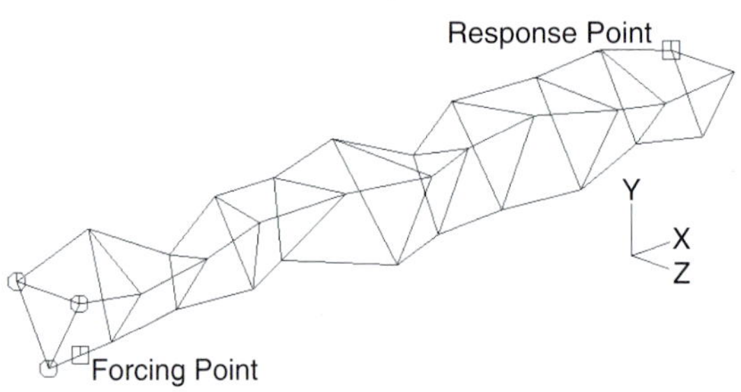

Figure 6.4 Geometry of the final three-dimensional design (diagonal elements omitted for clarity).

However, in order to accurately assess the designs considered by the GA, very significant computations are required, even when using a highly tuned and customized code to carry out these calculations. This leads to very long run times, necessitating the use of parallel processing if realistic studies are to be undertaken. Although only at an early stage, the work presented shows that improvements of over 20 000% in frequency averaged energy levels can be obtained following this approach. Most of this improvement is seen to be due to the selection of promising design types during the first, randomly selected, generation of the GA. However, further calculations over succeeding generations then allow another 380% reduction in the energy transmitted through the structure. The nature of these changes suggests that, despite the massive improvements obtained, the GA is not likely to have found the globally optimum design in this study. This would seem to be an inevitable result of dealing with a problem with 81 variables using only 1000 function evaluations. As such, it once again demonstrates that, in many cases of engineering interest, global optima cannot be found with current levels of computing power applied directly to engineering analysis codes.

6.3 Case Study 2: The Design of an Improved Load Cell

Almost all areas of engineering require accurate and traceable measurements of force, the majority being carried out using strain gauge force transducers commonly referred to as load cells. Applications include tensile testing of materials, proof testing of components and performance testing of machines and engines. Load cells consist of a steel or aluminium body (the elastic element) upon which a number of strain gauges are bonded. The strain gauges are connected as a Wheatstone bridge, giving a temperature compensated voltage output proportional to the sum of the strain gauge outputs. Ideally this output should be insensitive to the mechanical arrangement by which the load cell is introduced into the load path. However, in practice their outputs are dependent, not only on the force applied, but also on the distributions of contact stress (Debnam and Jenkins, 1972; Robinson, 1989). Ideally, the force should be distributed uniformly over the load cell's contact surfaces. However, in practice, contact stresses are unlikely to be uniform and may differ significantly from those applied during calibration. Common causes of such variations are (fig. 6.5):

- The surfaces in contact with the load cell may not have been machined perfectly flat or may have ridges and depressions as a result of damage during use.
- The surfaces in contact with the load cell may differ in flexural stiffness.
- The surfaces the load cell contacts may differ in peripheral stiffness.
- The contact coefficient of friction may vary from one surface to another.

The European standard for the calibration of load cells, EN10002–3, specifies a test method for evaluating the sensitivity of load cells to these so-called end effects. The test requires the load cell to be loaded via plane, conically raised and conically depressed surfaces. The centres of the conical surfaces are respectively raised and depressed by 1/1000th of their radius, an angle of 0.06°. The standard specifies limits for the maximum output variation at the

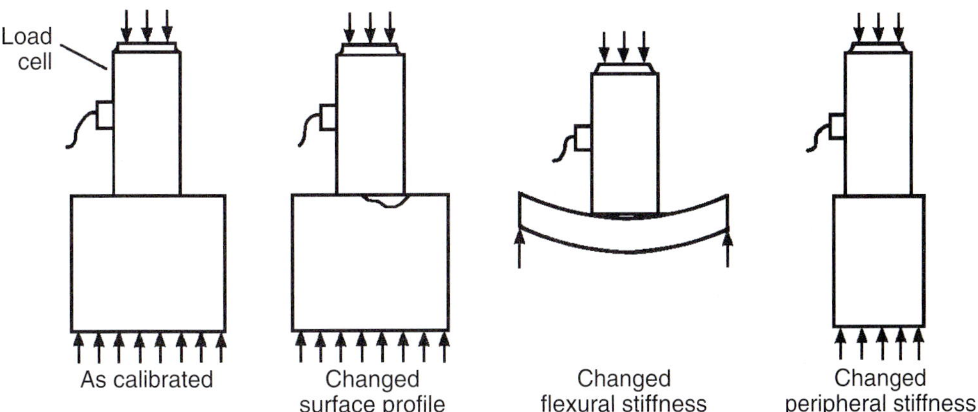

Figure 6.5 Variation of load cell contact conditions.

maximum and minimum loads of its calibration range. The load cell designer's task is to select an elastic element geometry and strain gauge configuration which minimizes the sensitivity of the output to these end effects. The reduction of end effects to acceptable levels relies on the rapid spatial decay of non-uniform stress distributions. Despite the simplicity of St Venant's principle, the decay of stress distributions within elastic bodies is complex, general analytic solutions being unavailable for even the simplest of bodies. This complexity has led to load cell designers placing high reliance on simple design rules. These ensure the strain gauges are sufficiently far from the contact surfaces for the non-uniform contact stress components to have decayed to insignificant levels. However, in some important applications it is not possible to accommodate the physical dimensions of devices conforming to the rules. Traditionally, development of load cells for these applications has required many hours of experimental testing of prototypes. Much of the experimental testing has now been replaced by finite element modelling. However, the complexity of deriving a geometry with specific decay characteristics still makes for an unpredictable design process which is exceptionally time consuming and expensive. Optimization methods offer the potential to exploit the complexity which frustrates human designers to produce superior designs at reduced cost.

The work detailed in this second case study concerns the development of a program for the optimization of load cell elements for reduced end loading sensitivity (Robinson, 1995). The development of the program consisted of the following stages. First, the load cell geometry was represented as a set of parameters and an algorithm for the automatic generation of a finite element mesh of the geometry from these parameters developed. Next, a computationally efficient method for solution of the finite element contact problem was developed. Finally a genetic algorithm was interfaced to the finite element analysis code and used to minimize the variation in bridge output over a representative set of contact conditions.

6.3.1 Parameterization

Program development was initially limited to column compression load cells, the geometry being defined by the following (see fig. 6.6):

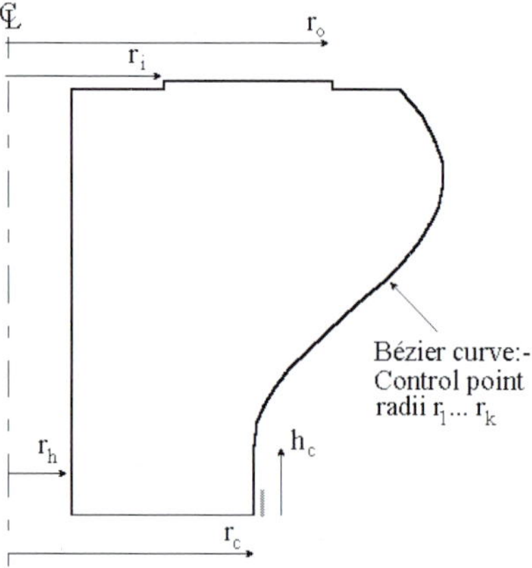

Figure 6.6 Parameterization of load cell geometry.

- The elastic element is axisymmetric, of height h, with strain gauges located at mid-height on a plane of mirror symmetry.
- A plane hole of radius r_h is bored down the centre of the load cell. The possibility of this radius being zero, the element therefore being solid, is not excluded.
- A slightly raised area is machined on both the upper and lower surfaces and defines the contact surfaces of the load cell. The inner and outer radii of these surface are r_i and r_o respectively. The possibilities that $r_i = 0$ or that r_o is equal to the radius of the end faces are not excluded.
- The central portion of the load cell is a cylindrical section of height h_c, and radius r_c. The remainder of the lateral surface is represented as a Bézier curve with typically 12 control points equispaced in height.

The global influence of the control points of the Bézier curve decouples them from the effect of distortions of the finite element mesh, avoiding convergence on geometries containing badly distorted elements which can otherwise occur when parameters have more local influence (Shyy *et al.*, 1988).

As three of the boundaries are straight lines, automatic meshing of the load cell shape is a relatively simple problem. An algorithm was developed for automatic creation of axisymmetric finite element models from the parameter values using a method based on that of Kela *et al.*, (1987).

6.3.2 Analysis

Finite element analysis routines were developed around the NAg finite element library using a frictional contact algorithm similar to that described by Sachdeva and Ramakrishnan (1981). As the non-linearity of the contact problem is resolved by iteration, and each geometry requires solution for a number of contact conditions, the solution is potentially computationally costly. However, in this case it was possible to exploit an unusual nature of the problem to carry out the analysis at reduced cost.

Typically, finite element analyses are carried out to determine maximum stress and strain values. As the locations of these maxima are not known a priori, a full field solution is required. In contrast, the load cell analyses required strain values to be determined at the strain gauge positions only. This allowed solutions to be calculated by the use of influence factors relating the strain at the gauge positions to the nodal forces at the contact surfaces. The influence factors were calculated by application of Maxwell's reciprocal theorem; a single solution of the finite element equations with unit strain imposed at the gauge positions giving the influence surface for all the contact nodes. Strain gauge strains could then be obtained by multiplication of the nodal contact forces by these influence factors. The contact force values were calculated using contact stiffness matrices, condensed from the full stiffness matrices by elimination of all degrees of freedom except those associated with the contact nodes. The relatively small size of these contact matrices allowed iterative solution at low cost. This algorithm allowed the calculation of gauge outputs over seven representative contact conditions for approximately 10% of the cost of a conventional non-linear solution.

6.3.3 Optimization

Having developed a computationally efficient analysis code, GA optimization was added, implemented as a set of Fortran routines. The resulting program was christened POGLE (Program for Optimizing the Geometry of Load cell Elements). The GA was binary coded, with linear fitness scaling and roulette wheel selection. It was anticipated that some parameters might interact non-linearly. In order to allow for this, crossover was carried out using a partially matched crossover operator (Goldberg, 1989). This ensures that offspring inherit the loci of their alleles as well as allele values from their parents. The string order therefore evolves simultaneously with the allele values allowing complementary alleles to be located at nearby loci. Most of the constraints were geometric and were imposed in the mapping of the parameter values. Each of the typically 18 parameters was encoded as 12 bits. The values of the GA parameters, $N = 100$, $P_c = 0.6$, $P_m = 0.03$, were set after trials on test problems.

In order to demonstrate the program's capabilities it was used to optimize a low-profile 3 MN (~300 tonf) load cell. This problem is of practical interest in the calibration of machines used for the testing of concrete samples. The working volume of typical concrete cube testing machines imposes a height limit of 200 mm. Reducing the height of conventional 3 MN load cells to 200 mm leads to unacceptably high sensitivity to end effects. Plate 1 shows the strain distributions in a low-profile conventional design when 3 MN is applied via the EN10002–3 contact conditions. The large variation of gauge output with contact condition is apparent in the strain contours at the gauge location (gauge shown exaggerated). There is therefore a requirement for an improved design meeting the height restriction.

The strain contours in the POGLE optimized design are shown in Plate 2 for the same loading conditions as the conventional design. It is apparent that the variation of strain at the gauge positions in the optimized design is much reduced, the analysis predicting an end effect sensitivity less than one tenth that of the conventional design. In order to test this prediction a prototype load cell was manufactured to the optimized shape. The prototype, shown in Plate 3, was manufactured from 826M40 steel using a copy lathe to follow a template machined using a numerically controlled spark erosion machine. Tests on the prototype over the EN10002-3 contact conditions confirmed the finite element predictions, the performance of the 185 mm high prototype being superior to any previous 3 MN load cell less than 500 mm in height.

6.3.4 Discussion

Successful development and testing of the 3 MN load cell design has demonstrated the potential of optimizing the shape of load cells using a combination of non-linear finite element analysis and genetic algorithm optimization. Analysis of the optimized load cell revealed that very small changes in the parameters result in a much degraded performance. For example, changes to the lateral surface of the order of 0.5 mm are sufficient to completely negate the performance improvement of the optimized design. Is therefore unlikely that such a design could have been developed using traditional design methods. The POGLE program has since been used to develop several other novel load cell designs.

The authors believe this case study to be typical of the current application of GAs to real engineering problems where, because of the finite computational resources, much greater effort must be devoted to development of the analysis code than to the GA itself. This is in contrast to more typical GA research where although the objective function may be chosen for its difficulty, its coding and evaluation is trivial. The optimization in this case study was made tractable only by use of a customized analysis code exploiting the special nature of the problem. The application of such genetic algorithms to more general non-linear finite element analysis problems will remain limited by available computer resources for the foreseeable future.

6.4 A Way Forward: Multi-level Design Techniques

6.4.1 A Case for Multi-level Optimization in Engineering Design

The optimizations in the case studies presented here were feasible only because the problems were such as to allow use of analyses of reduced cost, in one case a receptance method and in the other an influence surface approach. This illustrates the main difference between the use of optimization methods on test problems and their use in practical engineering design. In engineering design, the choice of analysis method has at least as much influence on the feasibility of the search as the details of the actual optimization algorithm used.

The constant improvement in computer performance allows use of increasingly sophisticated models. However, the available computational effort will always be finite, placing limits on the sophistication of the models used. With current optimization algorithms, there is a lag between the analysis methods used within optimizers and those used by human designers. For example, in aircraft design, while aerodynamicists make use of Euler and Navier–Stokes CFD codes requiring hours per solution, optimization studies are generally carried out using empirical models with solution times measured in tens of milliseconds. The take-up of optimization in engineering design will be limited while there is such a large disparity in the sophistication of the models used. To become more generally applicable, improved optimization algorithms are required which make use of the available analysis methods in ways more like human designers.

The key to designers' effective use of costly sophisticated analysis methods is their co-ordinated use with cheaper less sophisticated models. In a typical design process, preliminary design exploration is carried out using cheap analyses, perhaps as simple as 'back of envelope' calculations. As the design progresses, occasional use is made of more sophisticated analyses to guide the exploration and reduce the number of candidate designs. Finally the designs are refined using the most costly tools. However, practical design is not exclusively a one way process in the direction of increasingly sophisticated models. Designers also use the simpler models to make 'reality checks' on the results of the sophisticated models. The differences in analysis sophistication may result from switches in solution method, for example between full potential, Euler and Navier–Stokes solutions in CFD. Alternately, the trade off between accuracy and cost may take place within a single analysis method by switching between problem representations, for example between beam and shell models and full solid models in finite element analysis.

Designers therefore switch naturally between analyses at different 'levels' of accuracy and cost. In doing so they balance the computational cost of each method with the confidence they can place in the results. It is the authors' opinion that if optimization algorithms are to become practical everyday tools in engineering design, they must adopt a similar 'multi-level' approach. The ultimate aim must therefore be to develop algorithms which achieve the performance of the most sophisticated models at computational costs approaching those of the simplest models.

We would perhaps expect that a multi-level GA would initially use mainly cheap evaluations with occasional calls to more expensive methods. As the optimization progresses we would expect interleaving of an increasing proportion of more expensive solutions until, at convergence, almost all evaluations would use the sophisticated model, with perhaps occasional use of a simple model as a reality check.

Some simple schemes of this type are applied in the third case study discussed here. Although they show some moderate improvement over the direct application of search methods at the most expensive level, these gains are modest. It is therefore interesting to speculate on alternative approaches.

All genetic algorithms developed to date are based on the assumption that evaluations of the objective function are either cost free, or are all of equal cost. No explicit allowance is made for the finite computational resources available for a particular problem. It is also assumed that all evaluations are of equal accuracy. If multiple analysis levels are to be incorporated in a single algorithm, the cost and uncertainty of each evaluation must be considered explicitly. Selection is currently made solely on the basis of objective function value. One approach to making GAs multi-level would be for selection to take into consideration the cost and uncertainty of each evaluation. The evaluation cost can be predicted with reasonable accuracy and is known retrospectively. Uncertainty is more problematic. The relative accuracy of different methods is frequently not known explicitly and may vary over the design space. It would therefore be necessary to assign accuracy values to different levels based on experience of similar problems.

6.4.2 A Role for Ecology in Genetic Algorithms?

Some insight into the issues involved in the development of multi-level GAs might be obtained by reference back to their biological roots. It is the authors' belief that GAs have reached a stage in their development analogous to that of biology prior to the emergence of ecology as a separate discipline, little consideration being given to the finite character of natural resources. The relatively new field of ecology, the study of organisms in their natural environment, has since established the explicit study of intra- and inter-specific competition for resources as central to evolutionary biology. Development of multi-level GAs requires theory and practice to be similarly extended to account for the finite computational resources available to real applications. The emergence of the study of the 'ecology of genetic algorithms' is therefore anticipated.

In studying the ecology of GAs we might expect to be able to draw on the work of evolutionary ecologists. For example ecologists study 'life history' (e.g. McNamara and Houston, 1996; Partridge and Harvey, 1988). This concerns the balance between the probabilities of survival and rates of reproduction at each age in the life span and their affects on the optimal allocation of resources between reproduction and growth. Some comparisons between life history considerations in biology and GAs are straightforward. For example GA individuals become sexually mature (i.e. able to reproduce) as soon as they have been evaluated. The time taken in evaluating an individual is therefore analogous to the age at sexual maturity in biology; i.e. in some cases increases in time to reach maturity may lead to more useful members of the population. Less obvious is the drawing of parallels between the cost of reproduction. In simple GAs, reproduction is effectively cost free. However, in multi-level GAs where different individual's offspring may consume different resources, it may be appropriate to artificially impose a cost of reproduction on parents so as to allow trade-off between production of many cheap and fewer expensive offspring.

Further parallels may be drawn with the mechanisms of r- and K-selection (MacArthur and Wilson, 1967; Pianka, 1977). This concerns the relative importance of different selection modes between colonizing and established populations. In the former, r-selection is favoured, (r referring to the maximum rate of natural increase), whereas in the latter K-selection is favoured (K referring to carrying capacity). Pure r-selection represents existence in an ecological vacuum in which there is no competition. The optimal strategy is then to allocate resources to producing as many individuals as possible with each individual using a minimum of resources. Pure K-selection represents existence in an environment saturated with competitors. The optimal strategy is then to allocate resources to production of a few extremely fit offspring. These two modes, representing extremes of the selection continuum, have parallels in the exploration and exploitation phases of GA searches. In the exploration phase, individuals are likely to find niches which are uncolonized. The optimal strategy at this stage might be production of many cheap offspring. During the later exploration phase, all niches in the design space are likely to be already populated. Offspring would then be required to be more competitive, which in a multi-level GA would result from more accurate evaluation. The available resources would therefore be used to produce fewer more costly offspring.

Further parallels between the ecology of biological and GA populations could be drawn. To what extent such analogies are valid and applicable to GAs is an open question. However, the authors believe that any ecological theories developed for GAs will have significant commonality with their biological predecessors.

6.5 Case Study 3: The use of Multi-level Optimization on a Test Problem

Having set out the need to develop an optimization strategy that can combine a significant number of less accurate evaluations with a few accurate ones to arrive at an optimum design this final case study illustrates some preliminary work in this area. In it a number of different stochastic search methods have been studied when multi-level combinations are attempted.

A modified Keane 'bump' test problem was used for this study (El-Beltagy and Keane, 1998). It is defined as

$$\text{maximize} \frac{\text{abs}\left(\sum_{i=1}^{n} \cos^4(\alpha(x_i+\beta)) - 2\prod_{i=1}^{n} \cos^2(\alpha(x_i+\beta))\right)}{\sqrt{\sum_{i=1}^{n} i(x_i+\beta)^2}} \quad \text{for } 0 < x_i < 10 \quad i = 1, \ldots, n$$

$$\text{subject to } \prod_{i=1}^{n} x_i > 0.75 \text{ and } \sum_{i=1}^{n} x_i < \frac{15n}{2} \text{ starting from } x_i = 5, i = 1, \ldots, n.$$

Here the α and β parameters are used to describe the different degrees of distortion. The undistorted bump in which $\alpha = 1$ and $\beta = 0$ is illustrated in fig. 6.7. The α parameter spreads out the peaks ($\alpha < 1$) or makes them closer together ($\alpha > 1$), while β just shifts the peaks of bump in x_i.

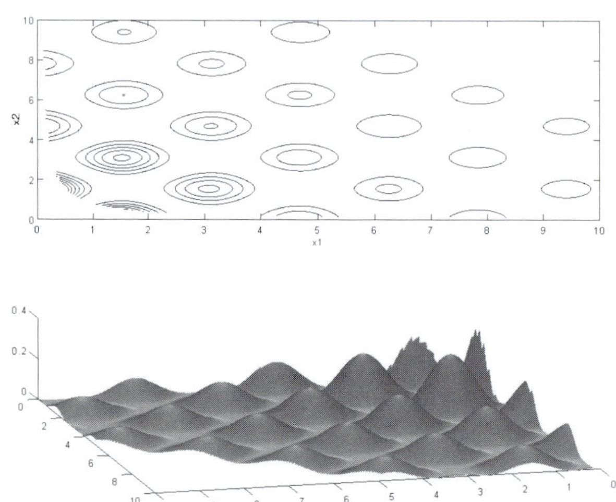

Figure 6.7 Contour map and 3D plot of undistorted bump function for $n = 2$.

Seven stochastic optimization methods were applied to the modified 'bump' with variable distortions representing the different levels in the problem and using three different multi-level strategies. All of these are available in the OPTIONS design exploration system (Keane, 1994b). The methods used are:

A genetic algorithm based on clustering and sharing (GACS) (Yin and Germay, 1993).
A bit climbing algorithm (BClimb) (Davis, 1991).
A dynamic hill climbing algorithm (DHClimb) (Yuret and de la Maza, 1993).
A population-based incremental learning algorithm (PBIL) (Baluja, 1994).
Simulated annealing (SA) (Kirkpatrick *et al.*, 1983).
Evolutionary programming (EP) (Fogel, 1993).
Evolution strategy (ES) (Back *et al.*, 1991).

In the next section three multi-level optimization strategies are set out: sequential, gradually mixed, and totally mixed strategies.

6.5.1 Sequential Multi-level Optimization

In this approach, the optimization is started using the least accurate level of representation; then, after a predetermined number of function evaluations, the optimization on this level is stopped and the results used as starting points for the next more accurate level. This is carried on sequentially and the number of function evaluations is decreased from one level to the next until the most accurate level is reached where fewest function evaluations are carried out. The number of function evaluations carried out at each level would ordinarily be chosen to roughly equalize the computational effort expended at each level. For the bump problem the first less accurate level corresponds to maximum distortion (high values of α and/or β). The optimization then proceeds through an intermediate level ($\alpha \to 1$ and $\beta \to 0$) after which the final accurate representation is reached ($\alpha = 1$ and $\beta = 0$).

The reduction in the number of evaluations mimics the situation where more refined models become more computationally expensive and hence only a more limited number of evaluations can be afforded. Details of the number of generations used here for each level are shown in table 6.1. Assuming that an equal amount of effort were expended at each level, this supposes the true function evaluation to be 25 times more expensive than that for $\alpha = 1.5$ and/or $\beta = 0.5$ and five times more expensive than for $\alpha = 1.1$ and/or $\beta = 0.1$.

Table 6.1 Number of evaluations at each level and corresponding distortion parameters.

Optimization level	1	2	3
Number of evaluations	12500	2500	500
α	1.5	1.1	1
β	0.5	0.1	0

Experiments were performed using both the 2D and 20D bump functions. The optimization was carried out for: (1) varying α; (2) varying β; (3) varying both α and β using the values and limit on function evaluations for the levels as shown in table 6.1. The results were averaged over thirty optimization runs. The initial population was randomly selected, but contained the point $x_i = 5$ for $i = 1, \ldots, n$.

6.5.2 Gradually Mixed Multi-level Optimization

Here the optimization procedure is carried out with three levels which are heterogeneously mixed throughout the optimization process. The probability of using a particular level varies with the number of function evaluations as shown in fig. 6.11.

Using this scheme the first 10 200 evaluations were carried out using the 1st level. In the next 4600 evaluations the 1st and 2nd levels were mixed gradually. This was followed by 400 evaluations, where the 2nd and 3rd levels were mixed, finally the last 300 evaluations were carried out solely at the third and most accurate level. The scheme was chosen such that the overall notional computational cost was equal to that in the sequential mixing scheme, on average the number of evaluations used at each level being equal to that in table 6.1.

6.5.3 Totally Mixed Multi-level Optimization

In totally mixed multi-level optimization the probability of using a particular level is constant throughout most of the optimization process. Towards the very end of the optimization only the most accurate level is used. In our case the probability of evaluation at the 1st level was 82.2%, at the 2nd level 16.4%, and the probability of evaluation at the 3rd and most accurate

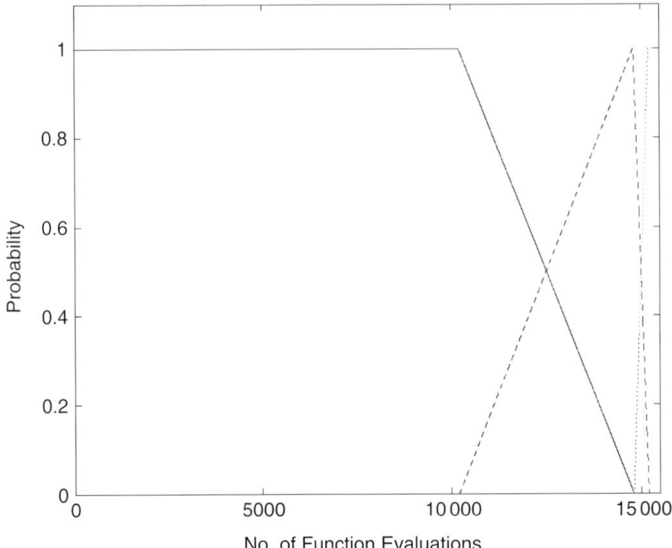

Figure 6.11 Probability of selecting a level after a given number of function evaluations. The 1st level is solid, the 2nd dashed, and the 3rd dotted.

level 1.32%. In the last 300 evaluations the 3rd level probability became 100%. This scheme was set up such that the notional computational cost on average was the same as in the previous two schemes.

6.5.4 Discussion

To gain a basis of comparison it is also useful to consider the case where the entire computational time is dedicated to using the most accurate level (i.e. 1500 such evaluations assuming the same notional costs as in the previous sections). Using this approach, the performance of the stochastic optimizers is as in table 6.2. Shown are the averaged (AVG) and best ever obtained results (BST) over 30 runs for each optimizer.

Table 6.2 Results for a single level optimization using the accurate bump.

	2 D AVG	20 D AVG	2 D BST	20 D BST
GACS	0.312	0.473	0.364	0.597
DHClimb	0.281	0.397	0.358	0.589
PBIL	0.293	0.224	0.358	0.296
EP	0.311	0.311	0.363	0.397
SA	0.301	0.394	0.364	0.482
Bclimb	0.262	0.451	0.363	0.591
ES	0.273	0.183	0.358	0.211

The comparative improvement of each method using any of the three proposed strategies may then be calculated, see table 6.3. Here the results are normalized by dividing the average performance of each method by the values in table 6.2. The results may also be normalized by dividing by the best known results for the accurate function evaluation (0.3650 and 0.8035, respectively, for the 2D and 20D cases), see table 6.4.

Table 6.3 Comparative improvements using the three mixing strategies.

	Sequential Mixing		Gradual Mixing		Total Mixing		Average	
	2 D	*20 D*	*2 D*	*20 D*	*2 D*	*20 D*	*2 D*	*20 D*
GACS	0.918	1.162	0.918	1.086	0.758	0.840	0.865	1.030
DHClimb	0.993	1.329	0.536	0.710	0.532	0.699	0.687	0.912
PBIL	0.812	2.145	0.706	1.736	0.661	2.136	0.726	2.006
EP	0.878	1.422	0.433	0.859	0.469	0.912	0.594	1.064
SA	0.942	1.014	0.831	1.061	0.411	0.676	0.728	0.917
Bclimb	0.983	0.858	0.426	0.468	0.495	0.699	0.635	0.675
ES	0.779	0.954	0.467	0.744	0.484	0.751	0.576	0.816
Average	0.901	1.269	0.617	0.952	0.544	0.959	0.687	1.060

Table 6.4 Absolute performance using the three mixing strategies.

	Sequential Mixing		Gradual Mixing		Total Mixing		Average	
	2 D	*20 D*	*2 D*	*20 D*	*2 D*	*20 D*	*2 D*	*20 D*
GACS	0.784	0.684	0.784	0.639	0.648	0.494	0.739	0.606
DHClimb	0.765	0.656	0.413	0.350	0.410	0.345	0.529	0.450
PBIL	0.652	0.599	0.567	0.484	0.531	0.596	0.583	0.556
EP	0.749	0.550	0.369	0.332	0.400	0.353	0.506	0.412
SA	0.776	0.496	0.684	0.520	0.339	0.331	0.600	0.449
Bclimb	0.706	0.481	0.306	0.263	0.356	0.392	0.456	0.379
ES	0.584	0.218	0.350	0.170	0.362	0.171	0.432	0.186
Average	0.716	0.526	0.496	0.394	0.435	0.383	0.549	0.434

The results in the tables indicate that:

- Sequential mixing is a better strategy when averaged across all methods.
- None of the three proposed strategies provide any improvement for the 2D case.
- For the 20D case, when averaged across all mixing strategies, only GACS, PBIL, and EP demonstrated an improved relative performance.
- In terms of absolute performance, the overall best combination for the 20D case was use of GACS with the sequential strategy. This gives an average final objective function on the three tests (a only, b only, a plus b) of 0.550. However, this final value is only 16% better than a straightforward use of GACS on the accurate function for 1500 steps.
- Although PBIL and EP showed improvements in the mixed methods (with a factor of 2.006 for PBIL and 1.064 for EP), their objective function values were generally lower

than GACS (the exception being PBIL on the 20D totally mixed case). Their performance was also rather erratic between runs.

These observations indicate that simple schemes, such as those described in this case study, are likely to give only minimal improvement over single level optimizations. To fully realize the potential of mixed method environments, new optimization algorithms are required which have been specifically designed to exploit multi-level evaluations.

6.6 Concluding Remarks

In this brief discussion the application of genetic algorithm optimization to two very different engineering structures has been presented. In each case the optimized design has actually been manufactured and the predictions of the computational modelling verified by experiment. Both case studies were atypical in being susceptible to analysis by relatively cheap analysis methods, whereas in the majority of engineering design problems the central difficulty is posed by the inevitably limited computing resources that can be deployed. It is noted that the belief that faster computers will make this problem go away is a mirage: as faster computers emerge, designers inevitably adopt more sophisticated models and see no reason why search engines should use out-moded design methods when searching for better results.

This requirement for the most sophisticated design methods to be applied by evaluation hungry evolutionary search engines leads naturally to the multi-level optimization problem where few expensive design calculations are augmented by many more cheaper, but less accurate methods. This paradigm fits naturally into a number of evolutionary search methods and the subject of ecology and opens the prospect of real progress in the applications of such methods to difficult real-world problems.

References

Anderberg, M. R. (1975). *Cluster Analysis for Applications*, Academic Press.

Bäck, T., Hoffmeister, F. and Schwefel, H. P. (1991). A survey of evolution strategies, *Proceedings of The Fourth International Conference on Genetic Algorithms*, Morgan Kaufmann, pp. 2–9.

Baluja, S. (1994). *A Method for Integrating Genetic Search Based Function Optimization and Competitive Learning*, Report CMU-CS-94-163, Carnegie Mellon University.

Davis, L. (1991). Bit-climbing, representational bias, and test suite design, *Proceedings of The Fourth International Conference on Genetic Algorithms*, Morgan Kaufmann, pp. 18–23.

Debnam, R. C. and Jenkins, R. F. (1972). The influence of end loading conditions on the performance of strain gauge load cells, *VDI-Berichte*, No 176, pp. 53–60.

El-Beltagy, M. A. and Keane, A. J. (1998). A comparison of genetic algorithms with various optimization methods for multilevel problems, *Engineering Applications of Artificial Intelligence* (Submitted).

Fiacco, A. V. and McCormick, G. P. (1968). *Nonlinear Programming: Sequential Unconstrained Minimization Techniques*, J. Wiley.

Fogel, D. B. (1993). Applying evolutionary programming to selected travelling salesman problems, *Cybernetics and Systems*, **24(1)**; 27–36.

Goldberg, D. E. (1989). *Genetic Algorithms in Search, Optimization and Machine Learning*, Addison-Wesley.

Igusa, T. (1994). *I-DEAS Master Series Reference Manual*, S.D.R.C.

Keane, A. J. (1994a). Experiences with optimizers in structural design, *Proc.of the Conf. on Adaptive Computing in Engineering Design and Control 94*, Parmee, I. C. (ed.), P.E.D.C., University of Plymouth, Plymouth, pp. 14–27.

Keane, A. J. (1994b). *The OPTIONS Design Exploration System User Guide and Reference Manual*, http://www.soton.ac.uk/~ajk/options.ps.

Keane, A. J. (1995). Passive vibration control via unusual geometries: the application of genetic algorithm optimization to structural design, *J. Sound Vib.*, **185**(3), pp. 441–453.

Keane, A. J. and Bright, A. P. (1996). Passive vibration control via unusual geometries: experiments on model aerospace structures, *J. Sound Vib.* **190**(4), pp. 713–719.

Keane, A. J. and Brown, S. M. (1996). The design of a satellite boom with enhanced vibration performance using genetic algorithm techniques, *Proc. of the Conf. on Adaptive Computing in Engineering Design and Control 96*, Parmee, I. C. (ed.), ISBN 0 905227 61 1, University of Plymouth, Plymouth, pp. 107–113.

Kela, A., Saxena, M. and Perucchio, R. (1987). A hierarchical structure for automatic meshing and adaptive FEM analysis, *Eng. Comp.*, **4**; 104–111.

Kirkpatrick, S., Gelatt, C. D. and Vecchi, M. P. (1983). Optimization by simulated annealing, *Science*, **220**(4598); 671–680.

MacArthur, R. H. and Wilson, E. O. (1967). *The Theory of Island Biogeography*, Princeton Univ. Press, Princeton, N.J.

McNamara, J. and Houston, A. I. (1996). State dependent life histories, *Nature*, **380**; 215–221.

Partridge, L. and Harvey, P. (1988). The ecological context of life history evolution, *Science*, **241**; 1449–1455.

Pianka, E. R. (1977), On r- and K- selection, *The American Naturalist*, **104**; 592–597.

Robinson, G. M. (1989). Errors due to axisymmetric non-uniform loading of column load cells, *Measurement*, **7**(1); 30–34.

Robinson, G. M. (1995). Load cell shape optimisation using genetic algorithms and finite element analysis, *Proceedings of the 14th IMEKO TC3 Conference*, Warsaw, Poland, pp. 167–172.

Sachdeva, T. D. and Ramakrishnan, C. V. (1981). A finite element solution for the two dimensional elastic contact problem with friction, *Int. J. Num. Meth. Eng.*, **17**; 1257–1271.

Shankar, K. and Keane, A. J., (1995). Energy flow predictions in a structure of rigidly joined beams using receptance theory, *J. Sound Vib.* **185**(5); 867–890.

Shyy, Y. K., Fleury, C. and Izadpanah, K. (1988). Shape optimal design using high order elements, *Comp. Meth. in Appl. Mechanics and Eng.*, **71**; 99–116.

Yin, X. and Germay, N. (1993). A fast genetic algorithm with sharing scheme using cluster methods in multimodal function optimization, *Proceedings of the International Conference on Artificial Neural Nets and Genetic Algorithms*, Springer-Verlag, Innsbruck, pp. 450–457.

Yuret, D. and de la Maza, M. (1993). Dynamic hill climbing: overcoming the limitations of optimization techniques, *Proceedings of the 2nd Turkish Symposium of AI and ANN*, pp. 254–260.

Chapter 7

The Optimization of Flywheels using an Injection Island Genetic Algorithm

By David Eby, R. C. Averill, William F. Punch III, and Erik D. Goodman

7.1 Introduction

New optimization problems arise every day — for instance, what is the quickest path to work? Where and how congested is the road construction? Am I better off riding my bike? If so, what is the shortest path? Sometimes these problems are easily solved, but many engineering problems cannot be handled satisfactorily using traditional optimization methods. Engineering involves a wide class of problems and optimization techniques. Many engineering design approaches such as 'make-it-and-break-it' are simply out-of-date, and have been replaced by computer simulations that exploit various mathematical methods such as the finite element method to avoid costly design iterations. However, even with high-speed supercomputers, this design process can still be hindersome, producing designs that evolve slowly over a long period of time. The next step in the engineering of systems is the automation of optimization through computer simulation. If the desired performance factors for the system can be appropriately captured, then optimization over them is simply engineering on a grander scale.

Shape optimization of flywheels for the maximization of specific energy density (SED, rotational energy per unit weight) is an appealing thought that has received its fair attention by researchers. The concept of a flywheel is as old as the axe grinder's wheel, but could very well hold the key to tomorrow's problems of efficient energy storage. The flywheel has a bright outlook because of the recent achievement of high specific energy densities. A simple example of a flywheel is a solid, flat rotating disc. The SED of a flat solid disc can be increased by varying the shape of the disc to redistribute the inertial forces induced from rotation. A flywheel stores kinetic energy by rotating a mass about a constant axis, which makes it easy to integrate flywheels into energy conservation systems. Some vehicles currently use flywheels during braking for regenerating energy lost during deceleration. Another practical application is energy storage in low earth orbit satellites, where photoelectric cells are exposed to 60 minutes of light to charge, followed by 30 minutes of darkness when stored energy must be used. Electrochemical energy storage (e.g., in batteries) is limited by low cyclic lifetimes, low longtime reliability and low specific energies, all major concerns in satellite applications. The flywheel is well suited for this application due to high cyclic lifetimes, longtime reliability and high specific energies. Also, large-scale flywheels could be used in energy plants to store huge amounts of energy. Finding practical applications for flywheels is not a problem, but optimizing the

EVOLUTIONARY DESIGN BY COMPUTERS
ISBN 1-55860-605-X

SED of flywheels, given a problem-specific set of parameters and constraints, provides a challenge.

This chapter steps through various approaches that have been designed to optimize elastic flywheels. First, a simple genetic algorithm (sGA) searches for the well-known constant stress flywheel profile while measuring fitness with a plane stress finite element analysis. Shortcomings of the plane stress analysis are demonstrated via the sGA discovering solutions that are *artifacts* of the simplified plane stress analysis. Concepts of simulated annealing (SA) and threshold accepting (TA) are presented. The description of an injection island genetic algorithm (iiGA) is given for the optimization of flywheels. An iiGA in combination with a finite element code is used to search for shape variations to optimize the specific energy density of flywheels. iiGAs seek solutions simultaneously at different levels of refinement of the problem representation (and correspondingly different definitions of the fitness function) in separate subpopulations (islands). Solutions are sought first at low levels of refinement with an axisymmetric plane stress finite element code for high-speed exploration of the coarse design space. Next, individuals are injected into populations with a higher level of resolution that measures fitness with an axisymmetric three-dimensional finite element model to 'fine-tune' the flywheel designs. Solutions found for these various 'coarse' fitness functions on various nodes are injected into nodes that evaluate the ultimate fitness to be optimized. Allowing subpopulations to explore different regions of the fitness space simultaneously allows relatively robust and efficient exploration in problems for which fitness evaluations are costly.

For the flywheel problem treated here, the lowest level of the iiGA searches with a simple axisymmetric plane stress finite element model (with a 'sub-fitness' function), which quickly finds 'building blocks' to inject into a series of GA populations using several more refined, axisymmetric, three-dimensional finite element models. The flywheel is modelled as a series of concentric rings (see fig. 7.1). The thickness within each ring varies linearly in the radial direction. A diverse set of material choices is provided for each ring. Figure 7.2 shows a typical planar finite element model used to represent a flywheel, in which symmetry about the transverse normal direction and about the axis of rotation is used to increase computational efficiency. The overall fitness function for the genetic algorithm GALOPPS (Goodman, 1996) was the specific energy density (SED) of the flywheel, which is defined as:

$$SED = \frac{\frac{1}{2} Ix^2}{mass} \tag{1}$$

where ω is the angular velocity of the flywheel ('sub-fitness' function), I is the mass moment of inertia defined by:

$$I = \int_V q \cdot r^2 dV \tag{2}$$

and ρ is the density of the material.

A greatly simplified design space (containing two million possible solutions) will be examined. The search space was enumerated, yielding the global optimum. The success and speed of many methods, including several variations of an iiGA can now be compared. The iiGA methods always locate the global optimum while other methods never locate the global optimum. Hybridizing the iiGA with a local search operator and a threshold accepting (TA)

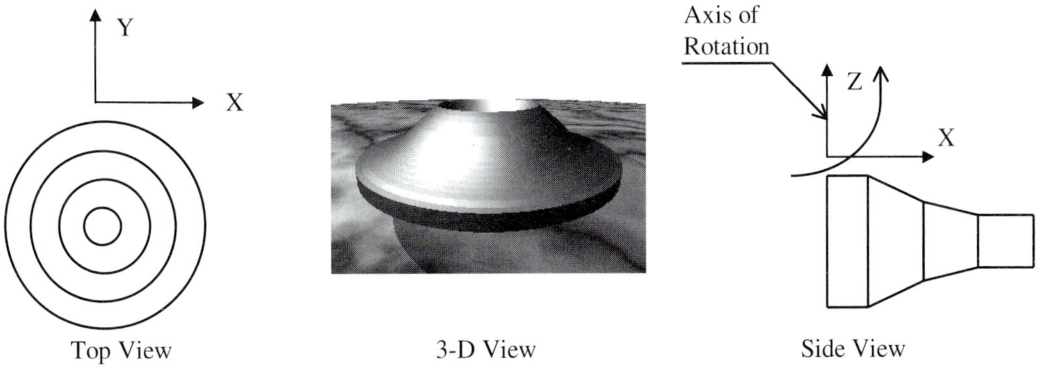

Figure 7.1 Visual display of flywheel.

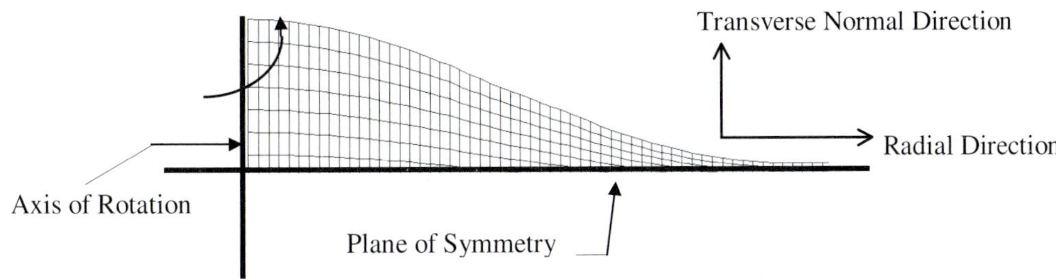

Figure 7.2 Typical flywheel model.

search at the end of each generation provide the fastest solutions, without sacrificing robustness. Results from an unconstrained optimization problem with a larger design space will be presented. Finally, a constraint will be placed on the maximum allowable angular velocity of the flywheel to create a more challenging optimization problem. Results from this more challenging problem are compared for various optimization approaches that include: Parallel GAs (PGAs) that have various topological structures, iiGAs and hybrid iiGAs. The hybrid iiGA greatly outperforms the PGA in terms of fitness and search efficiency for this given problem.

7.2 Optimization Methods

Optimization approaches include hill climbing, stochastic search, directed stochastic search and hybrid methods. Hill climbing or gradient-based methods are single-point search methods that have been applied successfully to many shape optimization problems (Soto and Diaz, 1993; Suzuki and Kikuchi, 1990; Suzuki and Kikuchi, 1991), and are extensible via neighbourhood sampling even to cases in which derivatives are not analytically given. However, these methods are severely restricted in their application due to the likelihood of quickly converging to local extrema (Sangren et al., 1990). Random search methods simply evaluate randomly sampled designs in the search space, and are therefore generally limited to problems that have small search spaces, if practical search times are required. A directed random search method, such as a genetic algorithm (GA), is a multiple-point, directed stochastic search method that can be an effective optimization approach to a broad class of problems. The use of GAs for optimal design requires that a large number of possible designs be analysed, even though this number generally still represents only a miniscule fraction of the total design space. When each evaluation is computationally intensive, a traditional simple or parallel GA can thus be difficult to apply. Injection island genetic algorithms (iiGAs) can help reduce the computational intensity associated with typical GAs by searching at various levels of resolution within the search space using multiple analyses that can vary in levels of complexity, accuracy and computational efficiency.

Structural optimization via GAs is the main topic of this chapter: for other examples, see Hajela and Lee, (1997), Mares and Surace (1996), Chapman and Jakiela (1996), Rajan (1995), Keane (1995), Nakaishi and Nakagiri (1996), Queipo *et al.* (1994), Flynn and Sherman (1995), Furuya and Haftka (1995). Recently, GAs have been successfully applied in the optimization of laminated composite materials (Punch *et al.*, 1994; Punch *et al.*, 1995; Kosigo *et al.*, 1993; Le Riche and Haftka, 1993; Todoroki *et al.*, 1995). The authors of this chapter have used an iiGA in the design of laminated composite structures; and others have applied the iiGA to other engineering problems (e.g., Parmee and Vekeria, 1997). Others use different GA approaches (see Le Riche and Haftka, 1993; Todoroki *et al.*, 1995). Several authors have dealt with the application of GAs to shape optimization problems. Fabbri (1997) and Foster and Dulikravich (1997) used GAs to find optimal shapes based on various polynomials, while Haslinger and Jedelsky (1996) present the concept of fictitious domains to generate new shapes. Wolfersdorf *et al.* (1997) reduced computational costs associated with generating meshes for finite element evaluations by a point heat sink approach. Genta and Bassani (1995) modeled flywheels as a series of concentric rings (see fig. 7.1) using a simple GA measuring fitness with a plane stress finite difference model. Although Genta and Bassani have already performed optimization of flywheels using a simple GA, this chapter differs in many respects: Genta and Bassani *seeded* the initial population with flywheels that varied linearly in thickness from the inner to outer radii, allowing genetic operators to find new shapes, while this chapter allows for ring thickness to be *randomly* chosen in the initial population; Genta and Bassani searched for shapes using a simple GA while this chapter will present various optimization approaches such as threshold accepting (TA), GAs, iiGAs and hybrid techniques; Genta and Bassani-based fitness on a *single objective* in each run while *multiple fitness* definitions where used *concurrently* in each iiGA run for this chapter; Genta and Bassani measures fitness only with a *plane stress evaluation* while the current chapter presents techniques that *concurrently* use *multiple evaluations* that vary in levels of complexity, accuracy and computational efficiency.

Combining a GA with the finite element method is by now a familiar approach in the optimization of structures, but using an iiGA with multiple evaluation tools and with different fitness functions is a new approach aimed at decreasing computational time while increasing the robustness of a typical GA. Typically, a useful approximation to the overall response of most structures can be captured with a computationally efficient, simplified model, but often, these simplified models cannot capture all complex structural behaviors. If the model does not accurately capture the physics of the problem, then the results of any optimization technique will be an *artifact* of the simplified analysis, dooming the solution(s) to be incorrect. This forces the designer to use a more refined model, which can be computationally demanding, sometimes leading to evaluation times too long to be practical for use in a GA search. These obstacles are nearly always present in interesting structural optimization problems. This chapter will show how an efficient, simplified axisymmetric plane stress finite element model, when used to evaluate fitness in an optimization problem, produces solutions that are *artifacts* of the simplified analysis. The chapter will also show that an ordinary parallel GA using the refined axisymmetric three-dimensional finite element model requires excessively long search times, in comparison to an iiGA approach which employs both the axisymmetric plane stress and three-dimensional finite element models.

An eventual goal of this effort is to develop tools for multi-criterion optimization of large-scale, three-dimensional composite structures, using an iiGA that searches at various levels of resolution and model realism. This technique incorporates several simultaneous and interconnected searches, including some that are faster (but often less accurate). This approach is constructed to spend less time evaluating poor designs with computationally intensive fitness functions (this is to be done with the efficient, less accurate evaluations) and to spend more time evaluating potentially good designs with the computationally intensive fitness evaluation.

7.2.1 Simulated Annealing

Simulated annealing (SA) is a combinatorial optimization technique that is based on the statistical mechanics of annealing of solids (Ruthenbar, 1989). To understand how such an approach can be used as an optimization tool, one must consider how to coerce a solid into a low energy state. Annealing is a process typically applied to solid materials to force the atomic structure of the material into a highly ordered state. Atomic structures that maintain a highly ordered state are also at a low energy state. In an annealing process, a material is heated to a temperature that allows many atomic arrangements, then cooled slowly, minimizing energy, while statistically allowing an occasional increase in atomic energy. When the material is extremely hot, the probability of an increase in atomic energy is very high. As the cooling continues, the probability of an increase in atomic energy decreases. Similarly, SA methods use an analogous set of parameters that simulate controlled cooling effects found in the annealing of materials.

SA methods begin with an initial solution that is often generated randomly, and try to perturb the solution to improve it. If the perturbation improves the solution then it is accepted and the process of perturbing continues. In this manner, SA methods are like iterative methods that climb hills. As with hill-climbing methods, this process of searching just for a better solution tends to force the process to a local optimum. However, SA methods are different in this respect: annealing occasionally allows perturbations that are harmful to the solution to be accepted. This allows SA methods to 'climb out' of local optima to search for a global optimum. In real physical systems, jumps to a higher ('worse') state of energy actually do occur. The probability of these jumps is reflected in the current temperature. As the annealing process (cooling) continues, the probability that only better solutions will be accepted increases. At the beginning of the annealing process (associated with a high temperature), the chance that a worse solution is accepted is greater, while later in the annealing process (at a lower temperature), the chance that a worse solution is accepted is small. This probability of accepting worse solutions is based on a Boltzman distribution:

$$\Pr[Accept] = e^{-\Delta E/T} \tag{3}$$

By successively lowering the temperature *T*, the simulation of material coming into equilibrium at each newly reduced temperature can effectively simulate physical annealing.

7.2.2 Threshold Accepting

Threshold accepting (TA) is a simplified version of simulated annealing. The probability of accepting a worse solution is governed by the Boltzmann distribution for SA applications and the TA algorithm, but the TA algorithm is not dependent upon a specified temperature. Instead, the TA algorithm rate of cooling is based on a specified percentage of the current solution fitness. This percentage decreases over the set of generations. This causes the TA in earlier generations to have a higher probability of accepting a worse individual, while later generations in the optimization are less likely to accept a worse solution.

7.2.3 Parallel Genetic Algorithms

Two problems associated with GAs are their need for many fitness evaluations and their propensity to converge prematurely. An approach that ameliorates both of these problems is a parallel GA (PGA), which also produces a more realistic model of nature than a single large population. PGAs typically decrease processing time to a given solution quality, even when executed on a single processor, and better explore the search space. If they are executed using parallel processors, an additional speed-up (in wall clock time) nearly linear with processor number may be achieved.

Two primary classes of parallel GAs are in common usage: coarse grain and fine grain. Coarse-grain PGAs divide the total population into independently breeding subpopulations with occasional migration among them. Fine-grain PGAs typically distribute individuals in a multidimensional space (2-D or 3-D) and allow breeding only among near neighbors. Unlike some specialized sequential GAs which may pay a nontrivial computational cost for maintaining a structured population (demes, etc.) based on similarity comparisons (niching techniques, etc.), coarse-grain PGAs maintain multiple, separate subpopulations which are allowed to evolve nearly independently. This allows each subpopulation to explore different parts of the search space, each maintaining its own high-fitness individuals and each controlling how mixing occurs with other subpopulations, if at all. Note that this advantage is NOT shared by approaches (which we label 'micro-grain' parallelism) which execute a sequential GA (i.e., perform exactly the same calculations) but distribute individuals among multiple processors for fitness evaluation – such an approach produces at best linear speed-up.

7.2.4 Injection Island GAs

In Lin *et al.* (1994), we extended the notion of a coarse-grain (or island-) parallel GA to the iiGA (injection island GA), allowing each subpopulation to search at different levels of resolution within a given space, or to search using representations or fitness functions which differ in some other way among subpopulations. This often includes searching at low levels of resolution on some nodes (islands) and injecting their highest-performance individuals into islands of higher resolution for 'fine-tuning'. This injection occurs while all islands continue to search simultaneously, although it is also possible to stop or to re-assign low-resolution islands once

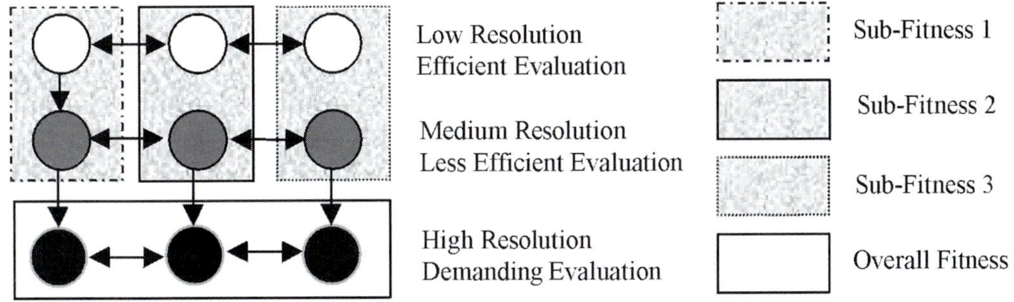

Figure 7.3 An iiGA that searches with multiple fitness definitions at various levels of resolution with evaluations that vary in levels of complexity, accuracy and computational efficiency.

they have converged. The parallel GA environment in which the iiGA is run is based on the GALOPPS toolkit developed by Goodman (1996). The software can be run on one or multiple workstations (a single processor was used for all runs reported here). Islands with different levels of resolution evaluate fitness using either a simplified analysis that is computationally cheaper or a refined, computationally expensive analysis (see fig. 7.3). Different GA parameters can be used for each population. The rates of crossover, mutation, and island interaction can all vary from island to island. For example, an island can exploit a simplified evaluation tool that is computationally cheap by increasing the island's population size. Also, islands using a computationally cheap evaluation function can be allowed to evaluate more generations before injecting their results into other islands. This will be demonstrated later in the chapter.

Many engineering problems require satisfying multiple fitness criteria in some sort of weighted overall fitness function to find an optimal design, if not actually requiring multi-criterion optimization. Each individual fitness measure may have its own optimal or suboptimal solutions. In an iiGA, it may be useful to use each individual criterion as the fitness function for some subpopulations, allowing them to seek 'good' designs with respect to each individual criterion, as potential building blocks for the more difficult weighted fitness function, or as useful points for assessment of Pareto optimality (see fig. 7.3). iiGAs take advantage of the low communications bandwidth required to migrate individuals from island to island. Often, only the best individual in a population migrates to allow 'good' ideas (building blocks) to be combined with other 'good' ideas to find 'better' ideas amongst islands using different 'sub-fitness' functions. Finally, for weighted fitness evaluation, individuals may be injected into a set of nodes where the evaluation of an overall weighted fitness function is employed. This search method facilitates robust exploration of the search space for all aspects of the overall fitness. Of course, many variations on these injection island architectures can be custom tailored for specific problems.

iiGAs using islands of different resolutions have the following advantages over other PGAs:

(i) Building blocks of lower resolution can be directly found by search at that resolution. After receiving lower resolution solutions from its parent island(s), an island of higher resolution can 'fine-tune' these solutions, but may also reject those inferior to better solution regions already located.

(ii) The search space in islands with lower resolution is proportionally smaller. This typically results in finding 'fit' solutions more quickly, which are injected into higher resolution islands for refinement.

(iii) Islands connected in the hierarchy (islands with a parent–child relationship) share portions of the same search space, since the search space of the parent is typically contained in the search space of the child. Fast search at low resolution by the parent can potentially help the child find fitter individuals.

(iv) iiGAs embody a divide-and-conquer and partitioning strategy which has been successfully applied to many problems. In iiGAs, the search space is usually fundamentally divided into hierarchical levels with well-defined overlap (the search space of the parent is contained in the search space of the child).

(v) In iiGAs, nodes with smaller block size can find the solutions with higher resolution. Although dynamic parameter encoding (DPE) (Schraudolph and Belew, 1991) and ARGOT (Schaefer, 1987) also deal with the resolution problem, using a zoom or inverse zoom operator, they are different from iiGAs. First, they are working at the phenotype level and only for real-valued parameters. iiGAs typically divide the string into small blocks regardless of the meaning of each bit. Second, it is difficult to establish a well-founded, general trigger criterion for zoom or inverse zoom operators in DPE and ARGOT. Furthermore, the sampling error can fool them into prematurely converging on suboptimal regions. Unlike DPE and ARGOT, iiGAs search different resolution levels in parallel and may reduce the risk of zooming into the wrong target interval, although there remains, of course, a risk that search will prematurely converge on a suboptimal region.

7.3 Finite Element Models of Flywheels

Two axisymmetric finite element models were developed to predict planar and three-dimensional stresses that occur in flywheels composed of orthotropic materials undergoing a constant angular velocity. Both finite element models were developed applying the principle of minimum potential energy. The finite element model that assumes a plane stress state is truly a one-dimensional finite element model, and is accurate when the gradient of the flywheel thickness is small. The finite element model that yields a three-dimensional stress state is truly a two-dimensional finite element model, and is accurate for all shapes. An automated mesh generator was written to allow for mesh refinement through the transverse normal and the radial directions. Therefore, the finite element code that predicts three-dimensional stresses can have various levels of refinement. A coarse mesh with a small number of degrees of freedom will be less accurate but more efficient than a refined mesh that contains more degrees of freedom. The mesh was also generated to minimize the time required to solve the set of linear equations created by the finite element code. By first assuming an initial angular velocity, the stresses and strains were calculated. Next, the initial angular velocity was scaled to the maximum failure angular velocity. The maximum stress failure criterion was used to predict the maximum failure angular velocity in the analysis of isotropic flywheels, while the maximum strain criterion was used for composite flywheels.

7.4 Searching for the Constant Stress Profile

A simple approach was first taken using a sGA to search for the well-known constant stress profile (Ugural, 1995) for a solid isotropic flywheel measuring fitness with a plane stress finite element model. The fitness function was defined as SED (amount of rotational energy stored per unit mass). The constant stress profile requires a natural boundary condition placed at the end of the disc (this can be accomplished for example by placing a metal 'band' around the end of the flywheel). sGA runs had a population size of 300 and a 75% crossover rate. All GA runs used elitism (guaranteed survival of best individual) and one-point crossover with a 1% mutation rate.

Figure 7.4 shows the best solution in the 400th generation. The simplified plane stress evaluation ignores in-plane shearing and transverse normal stresses and will not capture the variation of radial and tangential stresses through the thickness of the flywheel. Thus, the GA places a large volume of mass near the end of the flywheel to increase the mass moment of inertia (equation (2)) in the fitness (equation (1)). This large volume of mass at the end of the flywheel causes gross variations in ring thickness near the end of the flywheel which give rise to substantial through-thickness variations in stress. Because this is a violation of the plane stress assumption, the design is an *artifact* of the simplified plane stress evaluation. To help overcome this, the fitness was based on a 'sub-fitness' function defined by the failure angular velocity of the flywheel. SED is dependent upon the square of the failure angular velocity (equation (1)), so the search space defined by the failure angular velocity could contain potentially good designs that would be found in the search space based on SED. Also, basing fitness on angular velocity (not explicitly SED) eliminates the sGAs drive to find flywheels designed as in fig. 7.4. Figure 7.5 displays the evolution of the constant stress flywheel basing fitness on angular velocity while fig. 7.6 compares the theoretical constant stress profile to the constant stress profile found by the sGA. This demonstrates that the search space defined by the 'sub-fitness' function (failure angular velocity) provided not only potentially good designs, but fruitful designs. The sGA spent less than 5 minutes (on a SUN SPARC Ultra) searching for the constant stress profile.

Next, the natural boundary condition at the outer radius of the flywheel was made homogeneous to design a flywheel that does not require a prescribed force at the outer radius of the

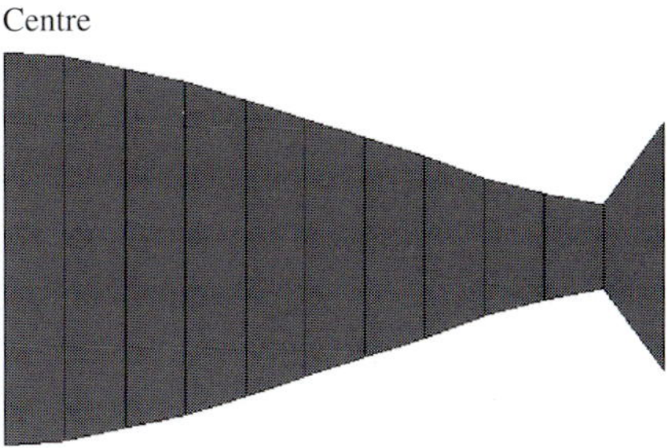

Figure 7.4 Typical example of a solution that is an artifact of a simplified plane stress evaluation. The sGA places a large volume of mass near the end of the flywheel to increase the mass moment of inertia in the definition of the fitness (SED).

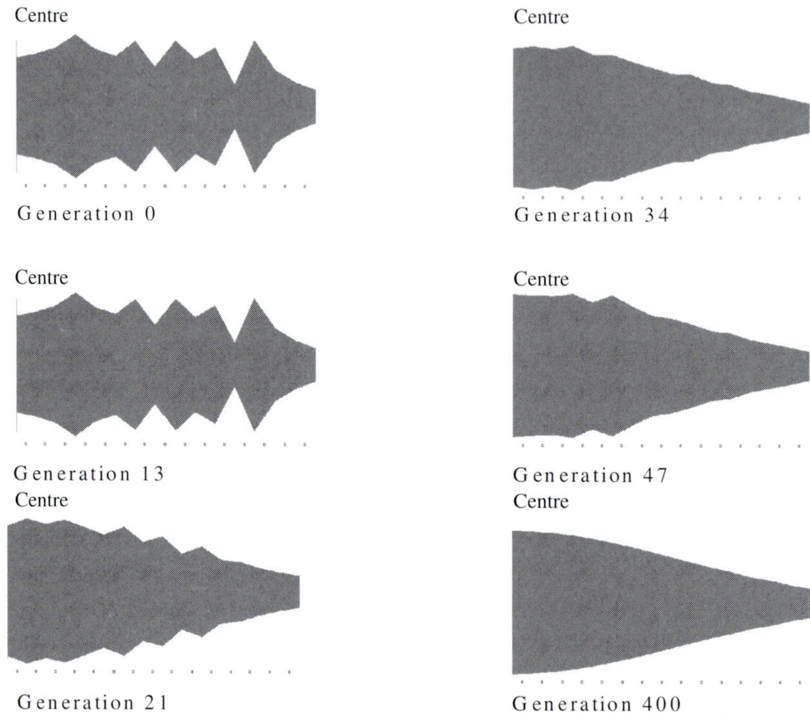

Figure 7.5 The evolution of the constant stress flywheel. Fitness was measured with a plane stress finite element evaluation while maximizing angular velocity.

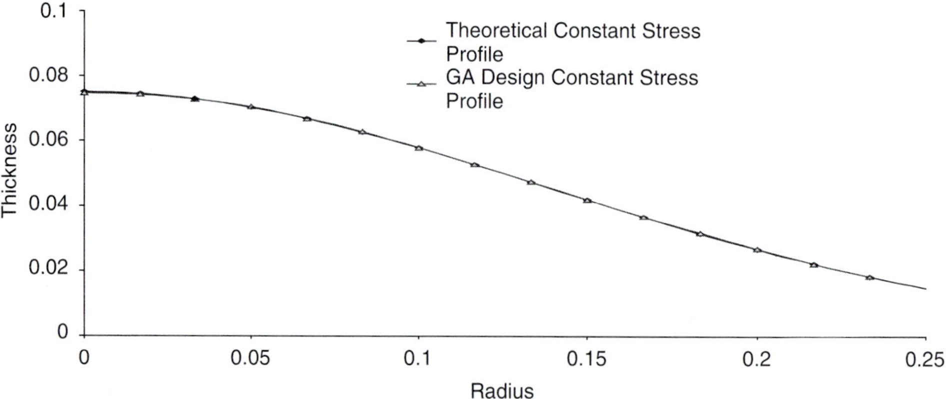

Figure 7.6 Comparison of theoretical to the GA-designed constant stress profile.

flywheel. Figure 7.7 displays a GA-designed flywheel profile that has a 55% increase in SED when compared to the theoretical constant stress flywheel.

Finally, an optimal profile for an annular isotropic flywheel was sought with the sGA measuring fitness with the plane stress finite element evaluation while basing fitness on (a) SED and (b) the 'sub-fitness' function (failure angular velocity) in two independent runs.

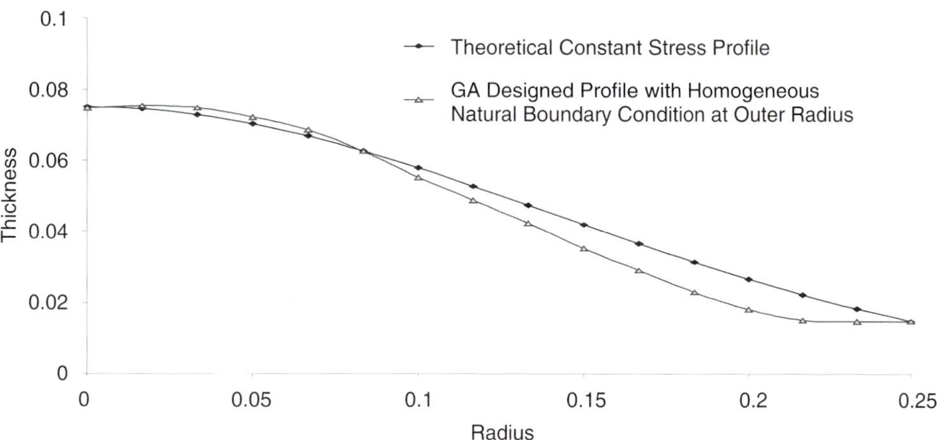

Figure 7.7 Comparison of theoretical constant stress profile to the GA-designed profile (homogeneous natural boundary condition). A 55% increase in SED was achieved in the GA-designed flywheel.

Figure 7.8a and b display the best flywheel found in the 400th generation basing fitness on SED and angular velocity, respectively. The sGA has discovered designs that have steep gradients in ring thickness, which violate the condition of plane stress. The flywheel profile in fig. 7.8a and b are artifacts of the plane stress analysis. These artifacts (fig. 7.4, 7.8a and b) are motivations to utilize a more refined analysis. A more refined analysis will be more robust and also allow the fitness to be based on SED (rather than a 'subfitness' function).

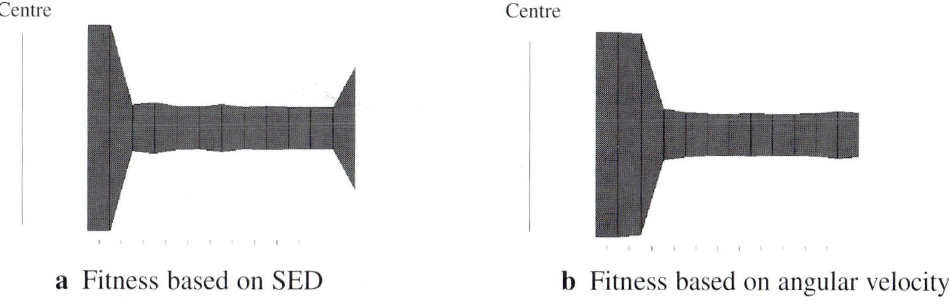

a Fitness based on SED

b Fitness based on angular velocity

Figure 7.8 The best solutions found by two separate sGA runs in the 400th generation. These illustrate typical examples of artifacts (steep gradients in ring thickness) which violate the assumed condition of plane stress.

7.5 Global Optima for a Simplified Flywheel

In order to explore how effective the iiGA search is in finding the global optimum for this sort of problem, and to compare the speed of finding it using iiGAs with various enhancements, a simplified flywheel problem was posed. A solid isotropic flywheel that contains six concentric rings (i.e., seven heights) with eight possible values for each height (see fig. 7.9b) created a design space of 8^7 or about 2 million possible designs. Using a coarse (962 DOF), axisymmetric finite element model, it was possible to calculate the SED of all of these designs, in about 50 hours on a SPARC Ultra processor. With the global optimum design known from exhaustive search, other search methods could be judged as to robustness and efficiency.

The TA algorithm alone began its search with a randomly initiated design. All hybrid algorithms that incorporated the TA algorithm were initiated with the best individual of the current generation, performing at most 10 TA operations, with the resulting solution always replacing the worst in the population. The local search method took the best individual of each generation and varied the thickness profile of whichever ring the FEA code found to fail first. The inner and outer thickness were increased and decreased independently, so a total of four evaluations occurred. When incorporating the local search method in any algorithm, the worst solution in the population was replaced only when a better solution was found by the local search. All multipoint search methods used the same total population size, 2200 individuals. Typically, for larger, computationally expensive problems, each island would be located on a separate processor, but for this problem, only a single Sun Sparc Ultra workstation was used.

The motivation for the particular iiGA topology used here requires some explanation. The search space for the plane stress finite element model evaluation contains good building blocks for the iiGA. Also, the plane stress evaluation (0.001 seconds per evaluation) is up to 1000 times faster than the most refined three-dimensional evaluation of stress (for this analysis). To make the iiGA search less computationally intensive and more robust, the iiGA shown in fig. 7.9a was designed to exploit these facts. A full cycle in an iiGA consists of evaluating a specified number of generations (which varies from island to island) in each island. Genetic operations can also be varied from island to island. Islands 0 through 1 had a 75% rate of crossover, population size of 300, and completed 12 generations per cycle before migrating 3 individuals in accordance with fig. 7.9a. Islands 0 and 1 measured fitness with plane stress finite element code, basing fitness on the subfitness function (angular velocity alone). Islands 0 and 1 contained designs with 3 and 6 rings with 7 and 13 DOF, respectively. A high crossover rate was chosen to motivate those particular islands to discover new designs. A large population size and high number of generations per cycle was used due to the computational efficiency of the plane stress evaluation and to force the islands to converge quickly to potentially productive regions of the design space, presumably containing useful building blocks. Islands 2 and 3 had a crossover rate of 70%, population size of 200, and completed six generations per cycle before migrating three individuals, evaluating fitness with the three-dimensional axisymmetric finite element code basing fitness on SED (130 DOF). Islands 4 and 5 had a 65% crossover rate, population size of 200 and completed four generations before migrating individuals, measuring fitness with the three-dimensional axisymmetric finite element code basing fitness on SED (430 DOF). Islands 6 through 8 had a crossover rate of 60%, population size of 100, and received migrated individuals every two generations, measuring fitness with the three-dimensional axisymmetric finite element code basing fitness on SED (962 DOF). Islands 6 through 8 have a lower population size and number of generations per cycle to explore the space more slowly and to avoid a large number of costly evaluations. Islands 6 through 8 should fine tune potentially good designs (building blocks) received from the islands at a lower resolution. Figure 7.9a also displays a hybrid iiGA design that groups the islands

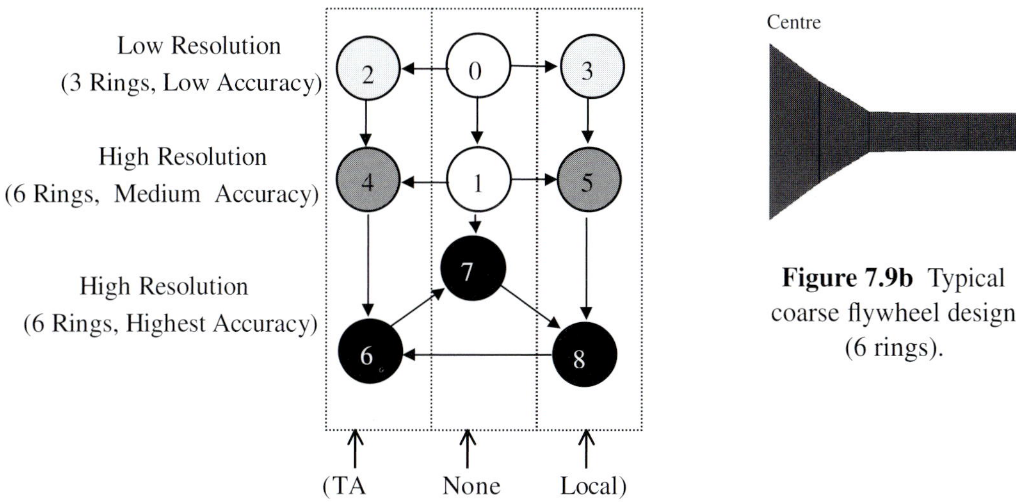

Figure 7.9a Simplified iiGA topology.

Figure 7.9b Typical coarse flywheel design (6 rings).

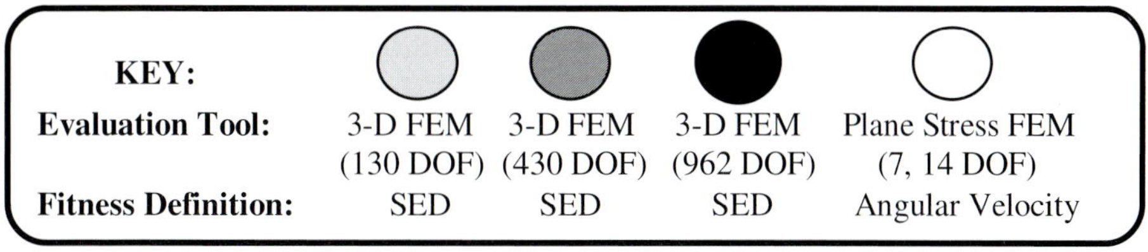

Figure 7.9b Simplified injection island GA topology with coarse flywheel representation.

according to the method by which they perform their specialized heuristic search (if any) at the end of each generation. Of course, many variations on these hybrid iiGA designs can be custom tailored for specific problems. The authors believe that the process is not very sensitive to the particular parameters (such as genetic operator rates and number of migrants) chosen, and did not find it necessary to tune the parameters – they were set a priori based on the intuitions described above. Of course, the number of generations per cycle per island could increase overall run time if this parameter is significantly increased in islands that measure fitness with a computationally expensive analysis.

7.6 Results of Global Optimization Study

Table 7.1 shows the results of the various methods. Each run lasted 6000 seconds on the same processor. In five runs of each method, the simple GA, with and without TA and local search heuristics, and the ring topology parallel GA, never found the global optimum. Figure 7.10 displays the fitness as a function of time of a typical run for a TA algorithm, simple GA and a simple GA that incorporated either a TA algorithm or a local search method. Elitism was used in all GA runs, so solutions are only plotted when better solutions are found, which leads to the appearance of different run lengths.

Table 7.1 Comparison of results of various optimization approaches.

Optimization technique	Average time to find global solution (5 Runs)
TA	Never Found
Simple GA	Never Found
Simple GA with Local Search	Never Found
Simple GA with TA	Never Found
Ring Topology GA	Never Found
iiGA	Always Found, 768 Seconds
Hybrid iiGA with Local Search	Always Found, 715 Seconds
Hybrid iiGA with TA	Always Found, 674 Seconds
Hybrid iiGA with Local Search and TA	Always Found, 417 Seconds

Other hybrid iiGA topologies were tested that incorporated either threshold accepting or local search methods. Without the local search or TA heuristics, the iiGA took an average of 768 seconds to find the global optimum. The hybrid iiGA that also used local search found the global optimum in 715 seconds (average) while the iiGA that incorporated the TA found the global solution in 674 seconds (average). Figures 7.11 and 7.12 display the fitness as a function of time for the iiGA (same topology as fig. 7.9a) and hybrid iiGA (fig. 7.9a, TA/None/local), respectively. All figures that display fitness as a function of time are reevaluated with the most accurate three-dimensional finite element model (962 DOF) to insure that all solutions are compared with the same 'measuring stick' (the plane stress analysis will predict an overly optimistic fitness when compared to the more refined analysis). The iiGA alone found the global solution in 768 seconds (average), while the hybrid iiGA (fig. 7.9a, TA/None/Local) found the global optimum in 417 seconds (average). The hybrid iiGA that used the TA algorithm and local search method evaluated less than 5% of the entire search space, taking less than 0.5% of the time needed to enumerate the entire search space, measuring more than half of the

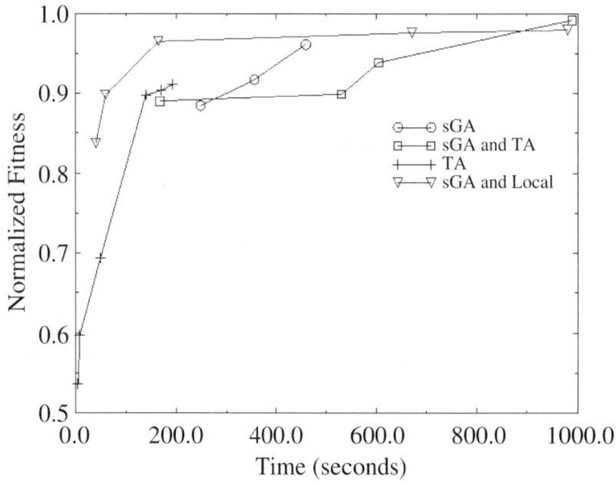

Figure 7.10 Fitness as a function of time on a single processor for a typical run of a simple GA, GA with TA, and simple GA.

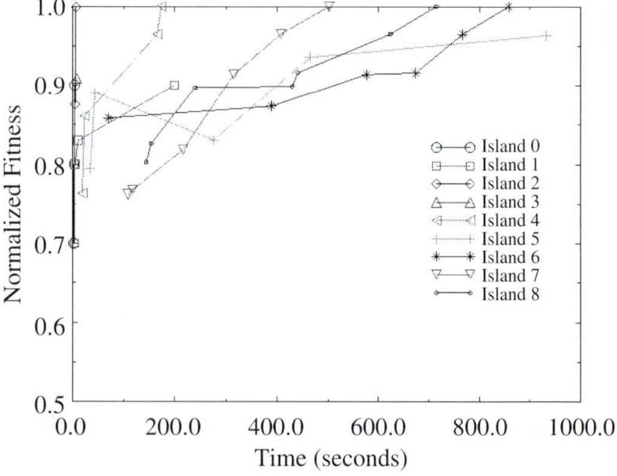

Figure 7.11 Fitness as a function of time on a single processor for a typical iiGA run.

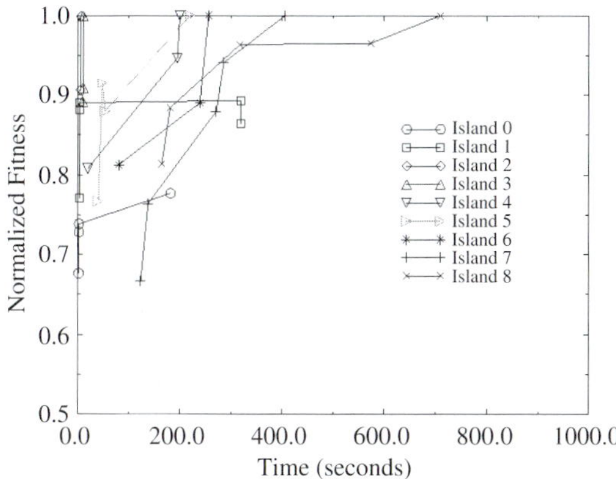

Figure 7.12 Fitness as a function of time on a single processor for a typical hybrid iiGA that incorporated TA and local search methods.

evaluations with the plane stress finite element model to find the global optimum. Examination of fig. 7.10, shows that the local search and the TA help the simple GA find better solutions. Also, the TA alone quickly climbs to a suboptimal solution. Figure 7.10 shows the iiGA quickly finding 'building blocks' at low levels of resolution that are injected into islands of higher resolution. Figure 7.11 displays the hybrid iiGA (fig. 7.9a, TA/none/Local) benefiting from the combination of TA and local search heuristics. Figures 7.10–12 only display the first 1000 seconds because no better solutions were ever found thereafter.

7.7 Searching Larger Design Spaces using iiGAs and PGAs

In this section, a much harder flywheel optimization problem is defined in order to compare results from PGAs (that have various topological structures), iiGAs and hybrid iiGAs. Two main changes were made to increase the problem difficulty: various constraints were added and a much larger search space was defined.

Often it is desirable to have an upper bound on the maximum allowable angular velocity of the flywheel in the design search space. Another possible goal might be to reduce 'air gap' growth in annular flywheels (displacement of the inner radius due to forces induced from rotation). Constraints on a maximum allowable angular velocity and 'air gap' growth will be developed by first considering the unconstrained version of the optimization problem with a hybrid iiGA.

A much larger search domain was created to increase the problem difficulty. A 24-ring flywheel with 1024 heights per thickness with 32 material choices created a huge design space. Table 7.2 lists all isotropic material properties, materials 1–3 have their Young's modulus, density and strength recombined, representing 3^3 (27) materials with materials 4–8 representing the final five materials.

7.7.1 The Unconstrained Optimization Problem

Since no previous numerical information is known about typical ranges of angular velocities and 'air gap' growth, the unconstrained problem will be first approached with a hybrid iiGA

Table 7.2 Material Properties

Material	Young's modulus (GPa)	Density (kg/m3)	Strength (MPa)	Poisson's ratio
1*	10	1.5	100	0.25
2*	75	3.0	250	0.25
3*	200	9.0	400	0.25
4	140	1.5	1500	0.25
5	50	1.5	1600	0.25
6	15	1.5	250	0.25
7	45	1.5	150	0.25
8	3	1.5	85	0.25

basing overall fitness on SED. Again, to make the GA search less computationally intensive and more robust, a hybrid iiGA as shown in fig. 7.13 was designed. Islands that use similar special search heuristics (local, TA or none) are grouped together. Islands 0 through 2 evaluate fitness based on angular velocity with a simplified plane stress finite element model with varying geometric resolutions (3, 6 and 12 rings). Islands 0 through 2 have 7, 13 and 25 computational degrees of freedom, respectively. Islands 3 through 11 measure fitness based on SED using the three-dimensional axisymmetric finite element model. Islands 3 and 4 are low in geometric resolution (3 rings), but have 104 degrees of freedom. Islands 5 and 6 are medium in geometric resolution (6 rings), containing 372 degrees of freedom. Islands 7 and 8 are high in geometric resolution (12 rings), having 2606 degrees of freedom. Islands 9 through 11 are the highest in geometric resolution (24 rings) with 13 250 degrees of freedom.

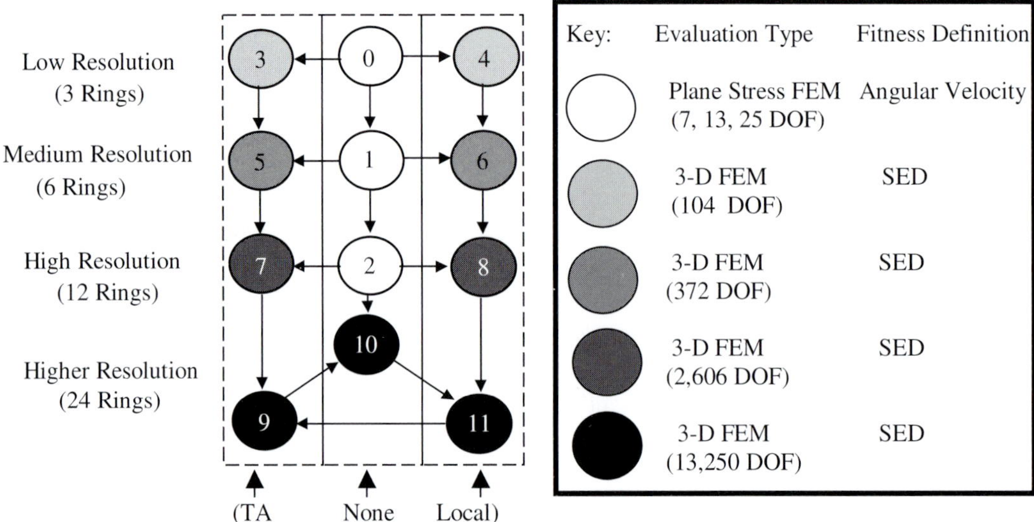

Figure 7.13 Hybrid injection island GA topology.

A full cycle consists of evaluating a specified number of generations (which varies from island to island) in the injection island topology. Islands 0 through 2 had a 75% rate of crossover, population size of 300, and completed 12 generations per cycle before migrating the island's best individual in accordance with Figure 7.13. Islands 3 and 4 had a crossover rate of 70%, population size of 200, and completed 8 generations per cycle before migrating the island's best individual. Islands 5 and 6 had a 65% crossover rate, population size of 150 and completed 4 generations before migrating the island's best individual. Islands 7 and 8 had a crossover rate of 60%, population size of 120 and the island's best individual after evaluating 4 generations. Islands 9 through 11 had a crossover rate of 60%, population size of 86 and received migrated individuals every 3 generations. Islands 0 through 2 can converge much faster to 'good' building blocks when compared to the rest of the islands due to the simplification of the plane stress evaluation and the level of resolution. The iiGA topology design in the iiGA in fig. 7.13 uses this as an advantage because the topology injects building blocks from the simplified plane stress evaluation based on angular velocity into two isolated islands that evolve independently, searching separate spaces efficiently using the axisymmetric three-dimensional finite element model to evaluate SED.

Figure 7.14 displays the 'best ever' annular composite flywheel at all the levels of geometric resolution for the unconstrained optimization problem. Also, Figure 7.14 compares the three-dimensional to the plane stress axisymmetric results. The plane stress results based on angular velocity are exaggerated shapes that are *artifacts* of the analysis. However, the plane stress results cannot be dismissed because they are the building blocks that helped rapidly form the final 'finely tuned' flywheels.

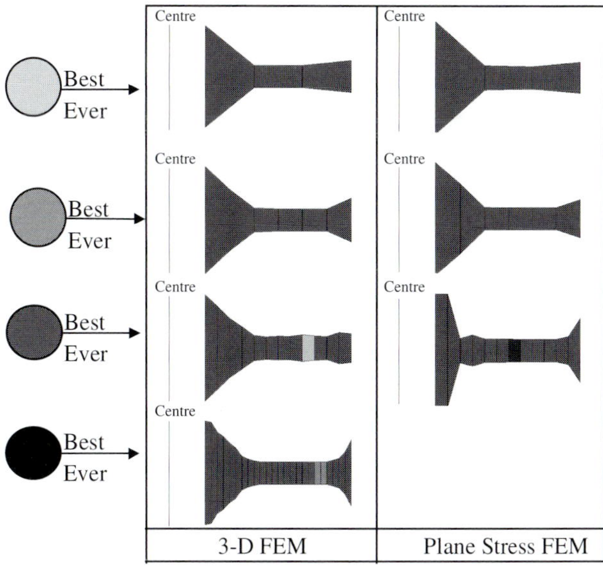

Figure 7.14 Best flywheel discovered at each level of resolution with a comparison of three-dimensional and plane stress solutions. The plane stress solutions are exaggerated variations of the three-dimensional counterparts.

Figure 7.15 displays the 'raw' fitness of each island as a function of time for the unconstrained problem. The 'raw' fitness is the actual SED measured by each island's specific finite element evaluation. Islands 0–2 measure 'raw' fitness with an approximate but efficient evaluation based on angular velocity. The plane stress evaluation predicts fitness accurately for flywheels that have small gradients in ring thickness, but predicts excessively optimistic fitness values for designs that violate the plane stress assumption. Islands 3–8 evaluate fitness with a reduced number of degrees-of-freedom when compared to the refined evaluation in islands 9–11. Therefore we can expect discrepancies in the fitness values for islands 3–8 when reevaluating the designs with the most refined three-dimensional finite element model.

Figure 7.16 displays the fitness of annular multi-material flywheels as a function of time (reevaluated at the highest level of accuracy with the three-dimensional finite element model containing 13 250 degrees-of freedom). Figure 7.16 displays an expected response; islands 0–8 initially find good solutions but begin to find worse solutions as time progresses. These solutions contain building blocks that are used to help evolve islands at higher levels of resolution through injection and therefore cannot be discarded even though they have a low fitness when evaluated with the most refined finite element model. We can expect, but cannot discard what appears to be 'noise' in the search. 'Noise' occurs when the iiGA cannot decipher the differences between a solution that does or does not violate an assumption of the fitness evaluation (for example a plane stress finite element evaluation). If a high fitness is associated with solutions that violate the fitness evaluation, expect the iiGA to sooner or later exploit the evaluation's 'Achilles heel' to improve the existing solutions in the population. This 'noise' is typically more dominate near the end of a long run, where the design space is less 'exciting' and more sensitive to slight variations in fitness because there is little more to gain in the designer's intended fitness definition. This effect can be seen in islands 0–8 in Figure 7.16,

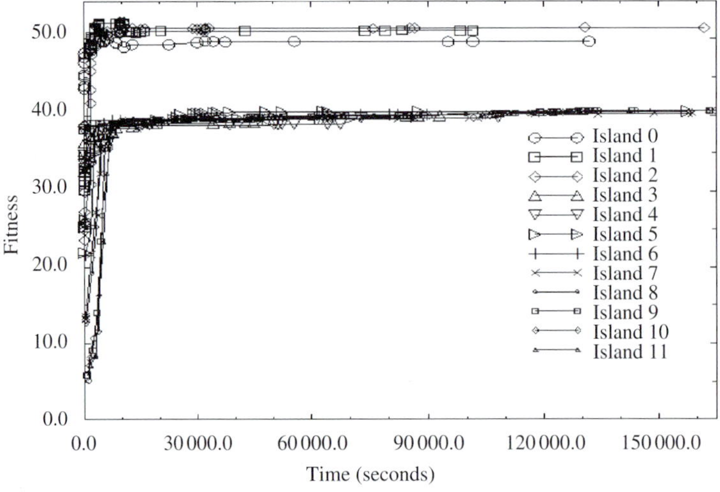

Figure 7.15 'Raw' fitness of each island as a function of time. Islands 0–2 predict excessively optimistic fitness values for designs that violate the plane stress evaluation while all other islands have realistic fitness values.

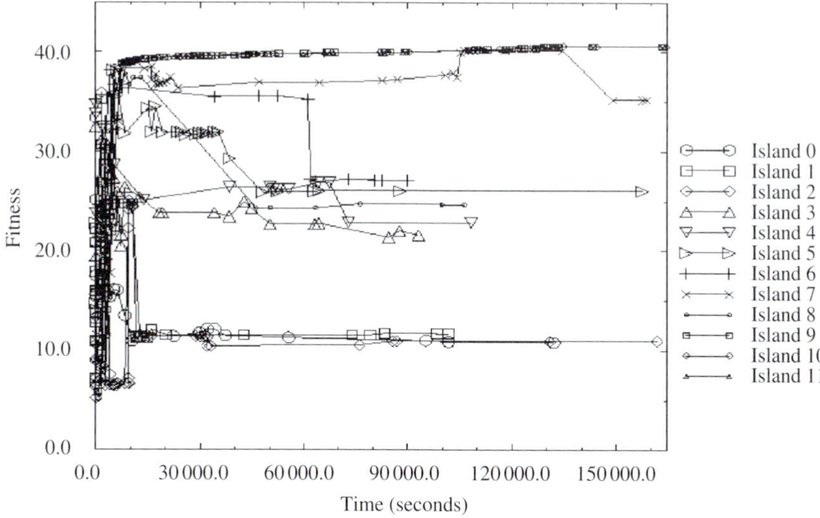

Figure 7.16 Reevaluated fitness (with most accurate evaluation) of each island as a function of time. Islands 0–8 display 'noise' that develops from modelling complex structural response with less accurate evaluations.

where the iiGA instantly finds good designs with the plane stress evaluation and then the designs progressively worsen as time progresses.

7.7.2 The Constrained Optimization Problem

This section compares a constrained problem (with a huge search space) using PGAs (with various topological structures), iiGAs and hybrid iiGAs. The constrained optimization problem can be defined from numerical information based on the best design's maximum SED, angular velocity and 'air gap' growth from the unconstrained problem. In no way is there a guarantee on discovering the global unconstrained solution with the hybrid iiGA, but rather the information gained from the unconstrained optimization problem is understood to be relative (possibly near global) and used as an estimate on constraint parameters in order to define a more difficult optimization problem. Constraints were enforced by the penalty method to ensure that designs not contained in the feasible set were still considered (but penalized).

The maximum values of SED, 'air-gap' growth and angular velocity from the unconstrained problem were used to normalize the fitness function in the following manner:

$$\text{Fitness}_{\text{norm}} = C_1 \frac{SED}{SED_{\text{max}}} - C_2 \frac{airgap}{airgap_{\text{max}}} - C_3 \frac{x}{x_{\text{max}}} \tag{4}$$

C_1, C_2 and C_3 are weighting coefficients and are given in table 7.3. The constraint C_3 was set to zero when the angular velocity of the design was below the maximum allowable angular velocity (which was chosen to be 75% of the angular velocity found in the best solution of the unconstrained problem). Also, equation 4 slightly penalizes flywheels that have large 'air gap' growths.

Table 7.3 Weighting coefficient values.

C1	C2	C3
250	40	20

Table 7.4 contains average (found over five independent runs) fitness values with computation times for various GA runs that include: a PGA with a topological 'ring' structure (fig. 7.17a), a PGA with a topological 'matrix' or 'toroid' structure (fig. 7.17b, similar numbers connect the structured migration) and some variations of the heuristic searches found in the hybrid iiGA depicted in fig. 7.12. Due to constraints on angular velocity, all islands in the iiGA (fig. 7.12) based fitness on equation 4. All PGAs measured fitness at the highest level of resolution (24 rings) with the most refined three-dimensional finite element model. All PGAs migrated the best solution every 3 generations and used a 65% crossover rate with 1% mutation with the same total number of individuals as the iiGA dispersed equally amongst 12 islands.

Figure 7.18 compares the fitness as a function of time for a typical island for the 'ring' PGA, 'matrix' PGA, iiGA and various hybrid iiGAs. The PGAs display excessive computational effort when compared to all forms of the iiGA.

Figure 7.19 displays typical annular flywheels found by the iiGA, all hybrid iiGAs, topological 'ring' and 'matrix' PGAs. All designs are in the feasible set (satisfied the constraints).

Table 7.4 Average fitness (five independent runs) for various GA approaches

	Ring PGA	Matrix PGA	iiGA (none)	iiGA (TA)	iiGA (local)	iiGA (local/none/TA)
Fitness (Average over 5 runs)	200.8	194.4	206.1	212.3	199.1	205.4
Time (Days)	10	10	2	2	2	2

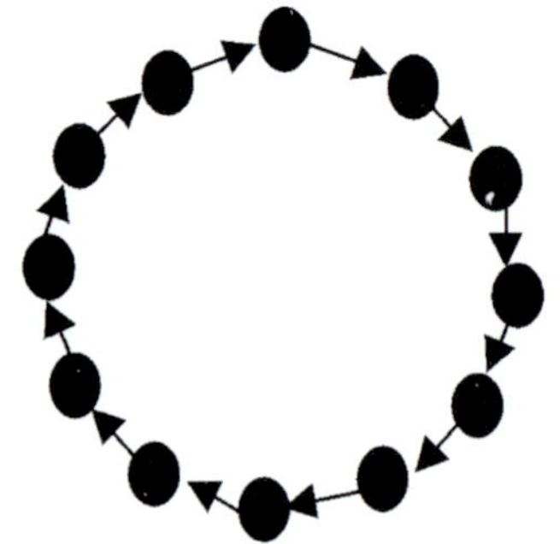

Figure 7.17a 'Ring' PGA topology.

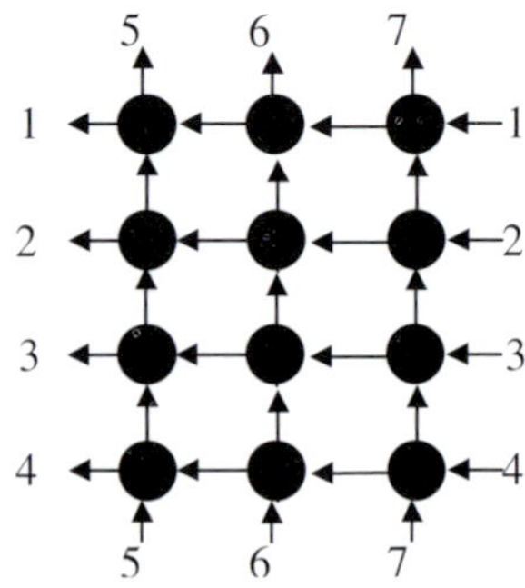

Figure 7.17b 'Matrix' PGA topology.

Figure 7.17 'Ring' and 'matrix' PGA topologies. All evaluations performed by the highest level of finite element accuracy and resolution.

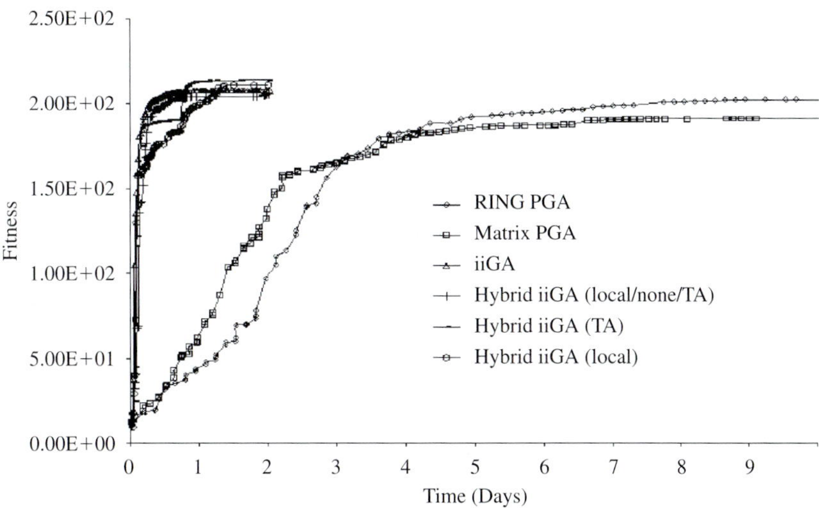

Figure 7.18 Comparison of fitness as a function of time for typical single island for a 'ring' PGA, 'matrix' PGA, iiGA and various hybrid iiGAs ran on a single processor. PGA displays excessive computational efforts when compared to all forms of the iiGA.

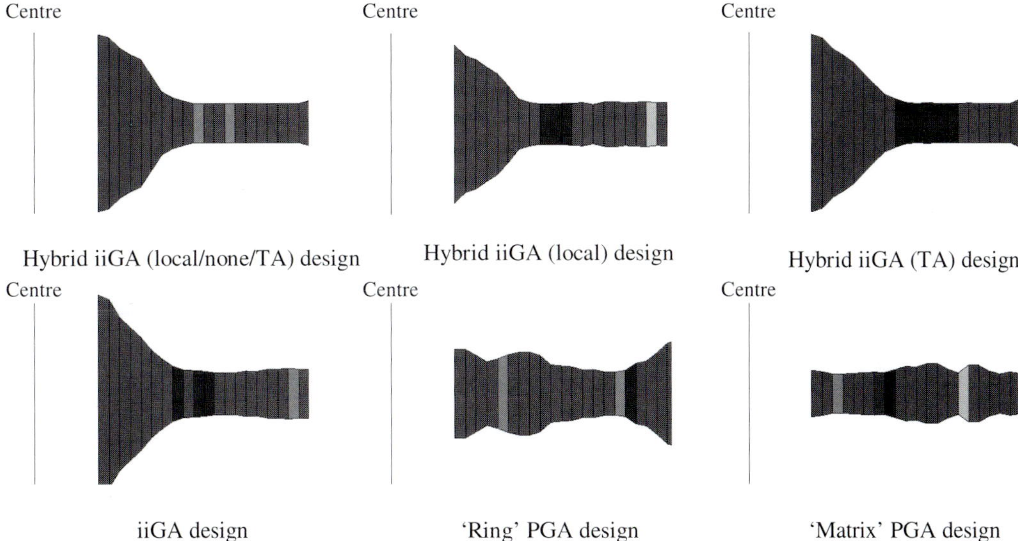

Figure 7.19 Typical designs found by all GA techniques. All iiGA flywheel designs are of similar shape with some variations in material placement. PGA and iiGA designed flywheels have noticeably different shapes near the inner radius.

All designs display an increase in thickness at the end of the radius, which helps increase the mass moment of inertia in the SED term (equation (1)) for the normalized fitness definition (equation (4)) due to the constraint placed on angular velocity. All iiGA designs are similar in shape but have slight variations in material placement. The PGA designs are not as refined as the iiGA designs. The iiGA designs in fig. 7.18 have fitness values that are about 5% higher than the PGA designs, but the PGAs designs required excessive computational effort.

7.8 Discussion and Conclusions

The iiGA offers some new tools for approaching difficult optimization problems. For many problems, the iiGA can be used to break down a complex fitness function into 'subfitness' functions, which represent 'good' aspects of the overall fitness. The iiGA can build solutions in a sequence of increasingly refined representations, spatially or according to some other metric. The iiGA can also use differing evaluation tools, even with the same representation. A simplified analysis tool can be used to quickly search for good building blocks. This, in combination with searching at various levels of resolution, makes the iiGA efficient and robust. Mimicking a smart engineer, the iiGA can first quickly evaluate the overall response of a structure with a coarse representation of the design and finish the job off by slowly increasing the levels of refinement until a 'finely tuned' structure has been evolved. This approach allows the iiGA to decrease computational time and increase robustness in comparison with a typical GA, or even a typical parallel GA. This was demonstrated with the results for the simple problem with the known global optimum, in which all variants of iiGA found the solution unerringly and rapidly, and all variants of the sGA with local search and threshold accepting heuristics, and the parallel ring GA, never found the solution. Of course, finding the global optimum for a problem with a reduced search space does not guarantee that the iiGA will find the global optimum for more complex cases, but it at least lends plausibility to the idea that the iiGA methods are helpful in searching such spaces relatively efficiently for near-optimal solutions. This was also demonstrated with the considerably more difficult constrained optimization problem where all topological versions of the PGA required excessive computational effort when compared to all versions of the iiGA. In many engineering domains in which each design evaluation may take many minutes (or hours), the availability of such a method, parallelizable with minimal communication workload, could make good solutions attainable for problems not previously addressable.

References

Chapman, C. and Jakiela, M. (1996). 'Genetic Algorithm-Based Structural Topology Design with Compliance and Topology Simplification Considerations,' *Journal of Mechanical Design*, **118**; 89–98.

Fabbri, G., 1997, 'A Genetic Algorithm for Fin Profile Optimization,' *Int. J. of Heat and Mass Transfer*, **40**; 2165–2172.

Flynn, R. and Sherman, P. (1995). 'Multi-Criteria Optimization of Aircraft Panels: Determining Viable Genetic Algorithm Configurations,' *International J of Intelligent Systems*, **10**; 987–999.

Foster, N. and Dulikravich, G. (1997). 'Three-Dimensional Aerodynamic Shape Optimization Using Genetic and Gradient Search Algorithms,' *Journal of Spacecraft and Rockets*, **34**; 36–42.

Furuya, H. and Haftka, R. (1995). 'Placing Actuators on Space Structures by Genetic Algorithms and Effective Indices,' *Structural Optimization*, **9**; 69–75.

Genta, G. and Bassani, D. (1995). 'Use of Genetic Algorithms for the Design of Rotors,' *Meccanica*, **30**; 707–717.

Goodman, E. (1996). 'GALOPPS, The Genetic Algorithm Optimized for Portability and Parallelism System, Release 3.2, User's Guide,' Technical Report, Genetic Algorithms Research and Applications Group (GARAGe), Michigan State University, East Lansing, July (1996). 100 pp.

Goodman, E., Averill, R., Punch, W. and Eby, D. (1997). 'Parallel Genetic Algorithms in the Optimization of Composite Structures,' in *Soft Computing in Engineering Design and Manufacture*, Chawdry, P. K., Roy, R. and Pant, R. K. (eds), Springer Verlag, 1998.

Hajela P. and Lee, E. (1997). 'Topological Optimization of Rotorcraft Subfloor Structures for Crashworthiness Considerations,' *Computers and Structures*, **64**; 65–76.

Haslinger, J. and Jedelsky, D. (1996). 'Genetic Algorithms and Fictitious Domain Based Approaches in Shape Optimization,' *Structural Optimization*, **12**; 257–264.

Keane, A. (1995). 'Passive Vibration Control via Unusual Geometries: The Application of Genetic Algorithm Optimization to Structural Design,' *Journal of Sound and Vibration*, **185**; 441–453.

Kosigo, N., Watson, L., Gurdal, Z. and Haftka, R. (1993). 'Genetic Algorithms with Local Improvement for Composite Laminate Design,' *Struct. & Controls Opt.*, ASME, Aero. Div., **38**; 13–28.

Le Riche, T. and Haftka, R. (1993). 'Optimization of Laminate Stacking Sequence for Buckling Load Maximization by Genetic Algorithm,' *AIAA J*, **31**; 951–956.

Lin, S.-C., Goodman, E. D. and Punch, W. F. (1994). 'Coarse-Grain Parallel Genetic Algorithms: Categorization and New Approach,' *IEEE Conf. on Parallel & Distributed Processing*, Nov., 1994.

Mares, C. and Surace, C. (1996). 'An Application of Genetic Algorithms to Identify Damage in Elastic Structures' *Journal of Sound and Vibration*, **195**; 195–215.

Nakaishi, Y. and Nakagiri, S. (1996). 'Optimization of Frame Topology Using Boundary Cycle and Genetic Algorithm,' *JSME International Journal*, **39**; 279–285.

Parmee, I. and Vekeria, H. (1997). 'Co-Operative Evolutionary Strategies for Single Component Design,' *Proc. 7th Int. Conf. Genetic Alg.*, Baeck, T. (ed.), Morgan Kaufmann, San Francisco, 529–536.

Punch, W., Averill, R., Goodman, E., Lin, S.-C., Ding, Y. and Yip, Y. (1994). 'Optimal Design of Laminated Composite Structures using Coarse-Grain Parallel Genetic Algorithms,' *Computing Systems in Eng.*, **5**; 414–423.

Punch, W., Averill, R., Goodman, E., Lin, S.-C. and Ding, Y. (1995). 'Design Using Genetic Algorithms – Some Results for Laminated Composite Structures,' *IEEE Expert*, **10**; 42–49.

Queipo, N., Devarakonda, R. and Humphrey, J. (1994). 'Genetic Algorithms for Thermosciences Research: Application to the Optimized Cooling of Electronic Components,' *Int. J. of Heat and Mass Transfer*, **37**; 893–908.

Rajan, S. (1995). 'Sizing, Shape and Topology Design Optimization of Trusses using Genetic Algorithms,' *Journal of Structural Engineering*, **121**; 1480–1487.

Ruthenbar, R. (1989). 'Simulated Annealing Algorithms: An Overview,' *IEEE Circuits and Devices Magazine*, **5**; 19–26.

Schaefer, C. (1987). 'The ARGOT Strategy: Adaptive Representation Genetic Optimized Technique', *Proc. 2nd Intl. Conf. on Genetic Alg.*, Grefenstette, J. (ed.), Lawrence Erlbaum, Cambridge, MA, 50–58.

Schraudolph, N. and Belew, R. (1991). 'Dynamic Parameter Encoding for Genetic Algorithms,' Technical Report LAUR 90–2795 (revised), Los Alamos National Laboratories.

Sangren, E., Jensen, E. and Welton, J. (1990). 'Topological Design of Structural Components using Genetic Optimization Methods,' *Sensitivity Analysis and Optimiz. with Num. Methods*, **115**; 31–43.

Soto, C. and Diaz, A. (1993). Optimum Layout and Shape of Plate Structures using Homogenization. In *NATO Advanced Research Workshop on Topology Design of Structures*, 1992, Sesimbra, Portugal, pp. 407–420.

Suzuki, K. and Kikuchi, N. (1990). 'Shape and Topology Optimization by a Homogenization Method,' *Sensitivity Analysis and Optimization with Numerical Methods*, **115**; 15–30.

Suzuki, K. and Kikuchi, N. (1991). 'A Homogenization Method for Shape and Topology Optimization,' *Computational Methods in Applied Mechanics in Engineering*, **93**; 291–318.

Todoroki, A., Watanabe K. and Kobayashi, H. (1995). 'Application of Genetic Algorithms to Stiffness Optimization of Laminated Composite Plates with Stress-Concentrated Open Holes,' *JSME Internat. Journal*, **38**(4); 458–464.

Ugural, A. and Fenster, S. (1995). *Advanced Strength and Applied Elasticity*, 3rd Edition, PTR Prentice Hall, Englewood Cliffs, NJ.

Wolfersdorf, J., Achermann, E. and Weigand, B. (1997). 'Shape Optimization of Cooling Channels Using Genetic Algorithms,' *J. of Heat Transfer*, **119**; 380–388.

Chapter 8

A GA-based Approach to Reliability Design

By Mitsuo Gen and Jong Ryul Kim

8.1 Introduction

In the broadest sense, *reliability* is a *measure of performance* of systems. As systems have grown more complex, the consequences of their unreliable behaviour have become severe in terms of cost, effort, lives, etc., and the interest in accessing system reliability and the need for improving the reliability of products and systems has become very important. The reliability of a system can be defined as the probability that the system has operated successfully over a specified interval of time under stated conditions. In the past few decades, the field of reliability has grown sufficiently large to include separate specialised subtopics, such as reliability analysis, failure modelling, reliability optimisation, reliability growth and its modelling, reliability testing, reliability data analysis, accelerated testing, and life cycle costing (Ramakumar, 1993).

Numerous reliability design techniques have been proposed in the last twenty years. Generally, these techniques can be classified as linear programming, dynamic programming, integer programming, geometric programming, heuristic methods, Lagrangean multiplier methods and so on (Rai and Agrawal, 1990). A good review of optimisation techniques for system reliability can be found in the book by Tillman, Hwang, and Kuo (Tillman *et al.*, 1980).

Most of these techniques transform the original problems, formulated as non-linear integer programming problems, into 0–1 linear programming problems. However, this transformation can increase the number of variables and constraints to be considered, making the problem more difficult in sense of the computation time and memory spaces needed. Therefore, it is better to solve the original reliability design problems without any transformation.

A *genetic algorithm* (GA) (Gen and Cheng, 1997) is a powerful tool for solving various optimal design problems and can handle any kind of non-linear objective functions and constraints without any transformation. In this chapter, we describe five reliability design models as follows:

(1) reliability design problems of redundant systems, which are formulated as non-linear integer programming (NIP) problems and involve the maximisation of system reliability when parallel redundant units in subsystems fail in several modes

(2) reliability design problems with alternatives, where design alternatives are selected and the number of redundant units to use is determined, in order to maximise the system reliability

EVOLUTIONARY DESIGN BY COMPUTERS
ISBN 1-55860-605-X

(3) reliability design problems with time-dependent reliability, which involve finding the optimal level of subsystem reliability as well as an integer solution for the number of redundant subsystems
(4) reliability design problems with uncertain coefficients, which are given as the intervals of confidence, i.e. these models are formulated as interval programming problems, and
(5) reliable network design problems, which involve devising local area networks (LANs), being used as communication infrastructures, to meet the demands of use in local environments.

Such network design problems, which consider system reliability constraints or objectives, have been the subject of many research efforts and have many applications in telecommunications and computer networking and related domains in electric, gas and sewer networks (Dengiz, Altiparmak and Smith, 1997).

This chapter begins by describing how the reliability of complex systems can be calculated. Following this, seven GA-based approaches for reliability design problems are described:

- GA-based reliability design of redundant systems (Gen *et al.*, 1993)
- GA-based reliability design with alternative designs (Gen *et al.*, 1993, Yokota *et al.*, 1995a)
- GA-based reliability design with time-dependent reliability (Yokota *et al.*, 1996)
- GA-based reliability design with interval coefficients (Gen and Cheng, 1996)
- GA-based bicriteria reliability design (Li, 1996)
- GA-based reliability design with fuzzy goals (Gen *et al.*, 1998)
- GA-based bicriteria LAN design with tree reliability and message delay (Kim, 1998; Gen, Ida, Kim and Lee, 1998).

8.2 Combinatorial Aspects of System Reliability

Complex systems are usually decomposed into functional entities composed of units, subsystems, or components, for the purpose of reliability analysis. Network modelling techniques and combinatorial aspects of reliability analysis are employed to connect the components in series, parallel, a meshed structure, or in any combination of these. Probability concepts are then employed to compute the reliability of the system in terms of the reliabilities of its components.

8.2.1 Series Structure

From a reliability point of view, a set of n components is said to be *in series* if the success of the system depends on the success of all the components. The components themselves need not be physically or topologically in series; what is relevant is only the fact that all of them must succeed for the system to succeed. Such a system is also known as a *non-redundant* system. Let x_i denote the event that the i-th unit is successful and x'_i denote the event that the i-th unit is not successful. Then the system reliability is defined as the probability of system success as follows:

$$R = P(x_1 x_2 \cdots x_n) = P(x_1)P(x_2|x_1)P(x_3|x_1 x_2) \cdots P(x_n|x_1 x_2 \cdots x_{n-1}) \tag{8.1}$$

If the unit failures are independent, then we have

$$R = P(x_1)P(x_2) \cdots P(x_n) = \prod_{i=1}^{n} P(x_i) \equiv \prod_{i=1}^{n} R_i \tag{8.2}$$

and the system unreliability Q can be expressed as follows:

$$Q = P(x'_1 + x'_2 + \cdots + x'_n) = 1 - P(x_1 x_2 \cdots x_n) = 1 - \prod_{i=1}^{n} R_i = 1 - \prod_{i=1}^{n} (1 - Q_i) \tag{8.3}$$

8.2.2 Parallel Structure

From a reliability point of view, a set of components is said to be in *parallel* if the system can succeed when at least one component succeeds. Such a system is also known as a *fully* or *completely redundant* system. The system reliability is defined as the probability of system success as follows:

$$\begin{aligned} R &= P(x_1 + x_2 + \cdots + x_n) \\ &= 1 - P(x'_1 x'_2 \cdots x'_n) \\ &= 1 - P(x'_1)P(x'_2|x'_1)P(x'_3|x'_1 x'_2) \cdots P(x'_n|x'_1 x'_2 \cdots x'_{n-1}) \end{aligned} \tag{8.4}$$

If the unit failures are independent, then we have

$$R = 1 - \prod_{i=1}^{n} P(x'_i) = 1 - \prod_{i=1}^{n} Q_i \tag{8.5}$$

and the system unreliability Q can be expressed as follows:

$$Q = \prod_{i=1}^{n} Q_i = \prod_{i=1}^{n} (1 - R_i) \tag{8.6}$$

8.2.3 *k*-out-of-*n* Structure

Such a subsystem consists of n identical independent components of which at least $k < n$ of the components should succeed in order for the subsystem to succeed. If p_i is the probability of success of a component, the probability of exactly k successes and $(n - k)$ failures in n components should be:

$$R_i = \binom{n}{k} p_i^k (1 - p_i)^{n-k} \tag{8.7}$$

Such subsystems are said to have *redundancy*. For $k = 1$, they become truly parallel (fully redundant) subsystems, and for $k = n$, they become serial (non-redundant) subsystems.

8.3 Single Objective Reliability Design Problems

We first consider four reliability design problems which have one objective function: redundant systems, alternative design, time-dependent reliability, and interval coefficients. We also briefly survey the GAs which are used for solving reliability design problems.

8.3.1 Reliability Design of a Redundant System (NIP-1)

Using redundant components is well accepted as a technique to improve the reliability of systems. Usually this problem can be formulated as a non-linear integer programming (NIP) model (Barlow, Hunter and Proschan, 1963; Tillman, 1969).

Problem Formulation

The reliability optimisation problem of a redundant system can be mathematically formulated as follows:

$$\max \; R(\boldsymbol{m}) = \prod_{i=1}^{3}\left[1 - \{1 - (1 - q_i)^{m_i+1}\} - \sum_{u=2}^{4}(q_{iu})^{m_i+1}\right]$$

$$\text{s. t.} \quad G_1(\boldsymbol{m}) = (m_1 + 3)^2 + (m_2)^2 + (m_3)^2 \leq 51$$

$$G_2(\boldsymbol{m}) = 20\sum_{i=1}^{3}(m_i + \exp(-m_i)) \geq 120$$

$$G_3(\boldsymbol{m}) = 20\sum_{i=1}^{3}(m_i \cdot \exp(-m_i/4)) \geq 65$$

$$1 \leq m_1 \leq 4, \; 1 \leq m_2, \; m_3 \leq 7$$

$$m_i \geq 0: \text{ integer}, \; i = 1, 2, 3$$

where: m_i is the number of elements in subsystem i and $\boldsymbol{m} = [m_1 \; m_2 \; m_3]$,
$R(\boldsymbol{m})$ is the reliability of the system when the element allocation is $\boldsymbol{m}$,
$G_t(\boldsymbol{m})$ is the system which requires this amount of resource t ($t = 1, 2, 3$) when the element allocation is $\boldsymbol{m}$.

More detailed data for this problem is shown in the reference (Tillman, 1969).

Genetic Algorithm

Gen, Ida and Yokata first proposed a simple genetic algorithm to solve reliability optimisation (Gen *et al.*, 1993; Ida *et al.*, 1994; Yokota *et al.*, 1995a). They considered the reliability optimisation problem of redundant systems with several failure modes given by Tillman (Tillman, 1969), which is used as a benchmark problem by many researchers (Gen, 1975; Gen, Ida, Sasaki and Lee, 1989).

Chromosome Representation: In the simple genetic algorithm, the chromosome is represented as a binary string. For this problem, the integer value of each variable m_i is represented as a binary string. We used the following chromosome:

$$v = [x_{33}x_{32}x_{31}x_{23}x_{22}x_{21}x_{13}x_{12}x_{11}]$$

where x_{ij} is the symbol of the j-th binary bit for variable m_i.

Initial Population: The initial population of chromosomes is generated randomly. Each chromosome is a binary string containing 9 bits. Unfortunately, such a random approach can yield illegal chromosomes in two ways: by violating the system constraints and/or by violating the upper bounds. Consequently, a *feasible checking* step is performed to guarantee that all chromosomes are legal.

Evaluation of Chromosome: When evaluating chromosomes, each legal one is assigned the value of the objective function $R(m)$ and each illegal chromosome is assigned a big penalty as follows:

$$eval(\boldsymbol{v}_k) = \begin{cases} R(\boldsymbol{m}), G_t(\boldsymbol{m}) \le b_t \quad \forall_t \text{ and } 1 \le m_i \le u_i \ \forall_i \\ -M, \quad \text{otherwise} \end{cases}$$

where $\boldsymbol{v}_k$ represents the k-th chromosome. M is a positive large integer number.

Crossover: One-point crossover is used here. If the random number $r < p_c$, relative chromosomes are selected for crossover. For example, the chromosomes $\boldsymbol{v}_2$ and $\boldsymbol{v}_3$ might be selected for crossover.

Mutation: Mutation is performed on a bit-by-bit basis. This operation randomly alters a gene selected for mutation.

Selection: A deterministic approach is adopted as the selection strategy, that is, sort all of the parents and offspring in descending order and select the first *pop_size* chromosomes as the new population.

Numerical Example and Result

The best solution from a random run of the genetic algorithm with 50 generations was:

$$v^* = [0\ 1\ 1\ 0\ 0\ 1\ 0\ 1\ 0], \qquad eval(\boldsymbol{v}^*) = 0.679722$$

The corresponding integer values of the offspring were:

$$[\ m_3\ \ m_2\ \ m_1\ ] = [\ 3\ \ 1\ \ 2\ ]$$

This result is identical to (and hence corroborated by) Tillman and Gen (Tillman, 1969; Gen, 1975). The statistical data over 30 runs is shown in Table 8.1.

8.3.2 Reliability Design with Alternative Design (NIP-2)

Another way to improve the reliability of a system is by using alternative designs having greater reliability but perhaps higher costs. Fyffe *et al.* formulated the reliability optimisation problem with redundant units and alternative design as a non-linear integer programming problem (Fyffe, Hines and Lee, 1968).

Table 8.1 Statistical data over 30 trials.

Total runs:	30
Frequency for obtaining optima:	0.933
Earliest generation for obtaining optima:	1
Latest generation for obtaining optima:	44
Average generation for obtaining optima:	13.4
Standard deviation[a]:	0.00093

[a] Standard deviation: $(x^* - \Sigma x_i/N)/x^*$.

Problem Formulation

The example used here was first given by Fyffe *et al.* (Fyffe, Hines and Lee, 1968):

$$\max \; R(\boldsymbol{m}, \boldsymbol{a}) = \prod_{i=1}^{14} (1 - (1 - R_i(a_i))^{m_i})$$

$$\text{s. t.} \; G_1(\boldsymbol{m}, \boldsymbol{a}) = \sum_{i=1}^{14} c_i(a_i) m_i \leq 130$$

$$G_2(\boldsymbol{m}, \boldsymbol{a}) = \sum_{i=1}^{14} w_i(a_i) m_i \leq 170$$

$$1 \leq m_i \leq u_i, \qquad i = 1, 2, \ldots, 14$$

$$1 \leq \alpha_i \leq \beta_i, \qquad i = 1, 2, \ldots, 14$$

$$m_i, \alpha_i \geq 0 : \text{integer} \qquad i = 1, 2, \ldots, 14$$

where: a_i is the design alternative available for the i-th subsystem and $\boldsymbol{a} = [a_1 \; a_2 \; \ldots \; a_{14}]$
u_i is the upper bound of m_i elements in subsystem i,
β_i is the upper bound of alternative design for the i-th subsystem,
$R(\boldsymbol{m}, \boldsymbol{a})$ is the reliability of the system with redundant units $\boldsymbol{m}$ and alternative design $\boldsymbol{a}$,
$G_t(\boldsymbol{m}, \boldsymbol{a})$ means the system requires this amount of resource t ($t = 1, 2$) when redundant units are $\boldsymbol{m}$ and the alternative design is $\boldsymbol{a}$.

The problem is then to determine which design alternative to select, and how many redundant units to use in order to achieve the greatest reliability while keeping the total system cost and weight within the allowable amounts. Further data are given in the reference (Yokota *et al.*, 1995).

Genetic Algorithm

Gen, Yokota, Ida and Taguchi further extended their work on reliability optimisation problems under the consideration of both redundant units and alternative design (Gen, Ida, and Taguchi, 1993; Yokota *et al.*, 1995b). As it is much more complex than the problem discussed in the last section, the classic approach of the genetic algorithm cannot be applied without modification.

Chromosome Representation: A gene is defined as an ordered couple of design alternatives a_{ki} and redundant units m_{ki} shown as follows:

$$v_{ki} = (a_{ki}, m_{ki})$$

where the subscript k is the index of the chromosome the gene belongs to and subscript i indicates the subsystem i. A chromosome is an ordered list of such genes as follows:

$$\boldsymbol{v}_k = [v_{k1}v_{k2} \cdots v_{k14}] = [(\alpha_{k1}, m_{k1})(\alpha_{k2}, m_{k2}) \cdots (\alpha_{k14}, m_{k14})]$$

where a_{ki} takes a value in the range $[1, \beta_i]$ and m_{ki} in the range $[1, u_i]$ ($i = 1, 2, 3, 4$).

Evaluation of Chromosome: The random approach to generate an initial population may yield illegal chromosomes, which violate system constraints. A ready way to handle such unfeasibility is to give a big penalty to each illegal chromosome. This approach will essentially narrow the search space by eliminating all illegal ones from the evolutionary process. In such a case, it is very hard to find better candidates for the global optimum with any selection mechanisms and the genetic search tends to be inefficient. To overcome this problem, a special measure function is introduced to evaluate illegal chromosomes by how far they separate from the feasible region. Usually the optimum occurs at the boundary between the feasible and infeasible areas. If the information of the degree of infallibility of solutions is embedded in the fitness evaluation, a genetic search will approach the optimum from both feasible and infeasible sides. The measure of the degree of infallibility for an illegal chromosome is given as follows:

$$d_{kt} = \begin{cases} 0, & G_t(\mathbf{m}, \cdot\,) \leq b_t \\ (G_t(\boldsymbol{m}, \cdot\,) - b_t)/b_t, & \text{otherwise} \end{cases}$$

where the subscript k indicates the k-th chromosome and i indicates the i-th constraint. Then the fitness function is given as follows:

$$eval(\boldsymbol{v}_k) = R(\boldsymbol{m}, \boldsymbol{a})\left(1 - \frac{1}{T}\sum_{i=1}^{T} d_{kt}\right)$$

where T is the total number of constraints.

Crossover: The uniform crossover operator given by Syswerda is used here, which has been shown to be superior to traditional crossover strategies for combinatorial problems (Syswerda, 1989). This operation is illustrated in fig. 8.1.

Mutation: Mutation is performed as a random perturbation. For a selected gene $\boldsymbol{v}_{ki} = (a_{ki}, m_{ki})$, a_{ki} will be replaced by a random integer within the range $[1, \beta_i]$ and m_{ki} will be replaced by a random integer within the range $[1, u_i]$.

Selection: A deterministic approach is adopted as the selection strategy, that is, sort all of the parents and offspring in descending order and select the first *pop_size* chromosomes as the new population.

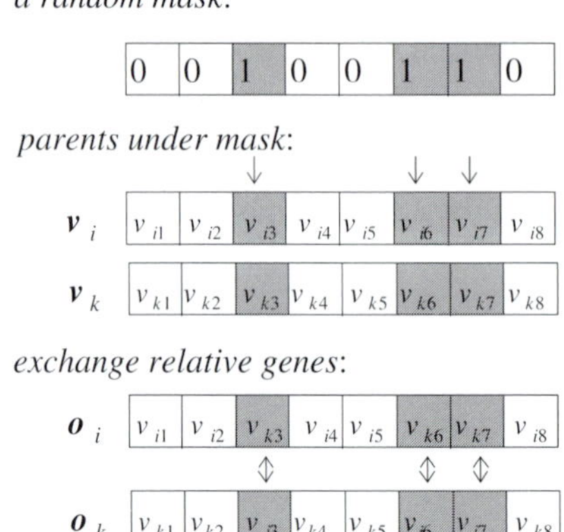

Figure 8.1 Illustration of the uniform crossover operation.

Numerical Example and Result

The best chromosome at the 623rd generation from a random run was:

$$v^* = [(3,3)(1,2)(4,3)(3,3)(2,3)(2,2)(1,2)(1,4)(3,2)(2,3)(1,2)(1,4)(2,2)(3,2)]$$

The reliability of the systems is 0.970015. This result is identical with the one given by Nakagawa *et al.* (Nakagawa and Miyazaki, 1981) and Gen *et al.* (Gen, Ida and Lee, 1988). The statistical data over 30 runs are shown in Table 8.2.

Table 8.2 Statistical data over 30 trials.

Total runs:	30
Frequency for obtaining optima	0.170
Earliest generation for obtaining optima	161
Latest generation for obtaining optima	975
Average generation for obtaining optima	423.8
Standard deviation[a]	0.002375

[a] Standard deviation: $(x^* - \Sigma x_i/N)/x^*$.

Coit and Smith have examined the reliability design problem with mixing components redundant in subsystems and developed GA-based reliability design with mixing components (Coit and Smith, 1996a,b).

8.3.3 Reliability Design with Time-dependent Reliability (nMIP)

The reliability of a multistage series system can be improved in two ways: (a) by using more reliable components, or (b) by adding redundant components in parallel. However, most previous research on allocation of redundancy has assumed that the reliability of the subsystems is fixed, and the optimal number of redundancies is determined where the system is subject to constraints. Therefore we consider the case when either of the two methods can be used at each stage to improve system reliability. Usually this reliability design problem for a series system with time-dependent reliability can be formulated as a non-linear mixed integer programming problem subject to several design constraints. The problem is then to determine the optimum level of component reliability and the number of redundant components at each stage (Dhingra, 1992; Yokota, Gen and Li, 1996).

Problem Formulation

Dhingra further researched the reliability apportionment problem for a series system with time-dependent reliability (Dhingra, 1992). Jacobson and Arora (Jacobson and Arora, 1996) proposed a solving method of problems which require finding the optimal level of subsystem reliability as well as an integer solution for the number of redundant subsystems combining the simplex searching method and heuristic approach developed by Aggarwal *et al.* (Aggarwal, Gupta and Misra, 1975). This is a non-linear mixed integer programming (nMIP) problem and is formulated as follows:

$$\max\ R(\boldsymbol{m}, \boldsymbol{x}) = \prod_{i=1}^{4}(1-(1-x_i)^{m_i})$$

$$\text{s. t.}\ G_1(\boldsymbol{m}, \boldsymbol{x}) = \sum_{i=1}^{4} C(x_i)\cdot\left(m_i + \exp\left(\frac{m_i}{4}\right)\right) \leq 400$$

$$G_2(\boldsymbol{m}) = \sum_{i=1}^{4} w_i \cdot m_i \cdot \exp\left(\frac{m_i}{4}\right) \leq 500$$

$$G_3(\boldsymbol{m}) = \sum_{i=1}^{4} v_i \cdot m_i^2 \leq 250$$

$$1 \leq m_i \leq 10\text{: integer} \quad i = 1, 2, 3, 4$$

$$0.5 \leq x_i \leq 1 - 10^{-6}\text{: real number}$$

where: x_i is the level of component reliability for the i-th subsystem and $\boldsymbol{x} = [x_1\ x_2 \ldots x_N]$,
$R(\boldsymbol{m}, \boldsymbol{x})$ is the reliability of the system with redundant components $\boldsymbol{m}$ and component reliabilities $\boldsymbol{x}$,
$G_t(\boldsymbol{m}, \boldsymbol{x})$ means the system requires this amount of resource t ($t = 1, 2, 3$) when the component allocation is $\boldsymbol{m}$ and the allocation of component reliability is $\boldsymbol{x}$,
v_i is the product of weight and volume per element at stage i,
w_i is the weight of each components at the stage i, and
$C(x_i)$ is the cost of each component with reliability x_i at stage i as follows:

$$C(x_i) = \alpha_i \cdot \left(\frac{-O_T}{ln(x_i)}\right)^{\beta_i} \quad i = 1, \ldots, 4$$

where α_i, β_i are constants representing the physical characteristics of each component at stage i, and O_T is the operating time during which the component must not fail.

The design data for this problem is shown in table 8.3.

Table 8.3 Constant coefficients for reliability apportionment problem

Number of subsystems			4	
Operation time O_T			1000 h	
Subsystem	$10^5\alpha_i$	β_i	v_i	w_i
1	1.0	1.5	1	6
2	2.3	1.5	2	6
3	0.3	1.5	3	8
4	2.3	1.5	2	7

Genetic Algorithm

Yokota *et al.* proposed a genetic algorithm to determine the optimum level of component reliability and the number of redundant components at each stage (Yokota, Gen and Li, 1996).

Representation and Initialisation: A gene is defined as an ordered couple of the number of redundant subsystems m_{ki} and the level of subsystem reliability x_{ki} shown as follows:

$$v_{ki} = (m_{ki}, x_{ki})$$

where the subscript k is the index of the chromosome the gene belongs to and the subscript i indicate the subsystem i. A chromosome is an ordered list of such genes as follows:

$$\boldsymbol{v}_k = [v_{k1}v_{k2}v_{k3}v_{k4}] = [(m_{k1}, x_{k1})(m_{k2}, x_{k2})(m_{k3}, x_{k3})(m_{k4}, x_{k4})]$$

where m_{ki} takes a random integer within the range [1, 10] and x_{ki} takes a random real number within the range $[0.5, 1\text{–}10^{-6}]$ ($i = 1, 2, 3, 4$).

Evaluation of Chromosome: To create an evaluation function $eval(\boldsymbol{v}_k)$, we first introduce the following scale for system constraints t ($t = 1, 2, 3$),

$$d_{kt} = \begin{cases} 0, & g_i(\boldsymbol{m}, \boldsymbol{x}) \leq b_i \\ (g_i(\boldsymbol{m}, \boldsymbol{x}) - b_i)/b_i, & \text{otherwise} \end{cases}$$

where d_{kt} is the scale for describing the exceeded resource rate in the t-th constraint of the k-th chromosome. Using the above scale, we define the evaluation function as follows:

$$eval(\boldsymbol{v}_k) = \begin{cases} R(\boldsymbol{m}, \boldsymbol{x}), & \text{if a chromosome is feasible} \\ R(\boldsymbol{m}, \boldsymbol{x})\left(1 - \left(\sum_{t \in T_c} d_{kt}\right)/n_c\right), & \text{if a chromosome is infeasible} \end{cases}$$

$$T_c = \{t | g_i(\boldsymbol{m}, \boldsymbol{x}) > b_i, t = 1, 2, \ldots, T\}$$

where n_c is the number of exceeded system constraints.

Crossover: We use an arithmetic crossover operator which is defined as a linear combination of two chromosomes (Michalewicz, 1994; Gen and Cheng, 1997). Let us denote the two chromosomes selected randomly for crossover in generation k as $\boldsymbol{v}_{k1}$ and $\boldsymbol{v}_{k2}$; the offspring will be:

$$\begin{aligned} \boldsymbol{O}_{k1} &= \lfloor c \ \ \boldsymbol{v}_{k1} + (1-c)\boldsymbol{v}_{k2} \rfloor \\ \boldsymbol{O}_{k2} &= \lfloor c \ \ \boldsymbol{v}_{k2} + (1-c)\boldsymbol{v}_{k1} \rfloor \end{aligned}$$

where $\lfloor x \rfloor$ is defined as the maximum integer smaller than the real number x.
c is a random number in the range [0, 1].

Mutation: We also incorporate a local search scheme for the mutation operator to find a better point near the current point undergoing mutation. The general procedure is as follows: select a chromosome $\boldsymbol{v}_k$ randomly for mutation, and denote a gene in this chromosome being mutated with $\boldsymbol{v}_{ki}$ $(i = 1, \ldots, 4)$. Then the gene will be replaced by a value in its domain which makes the fitness of the offspring greatest than other alternatives.

Selection: The selection operator uses the elitist model (Michalewicz, 1994; Gen and Cheng, 1997). The procedure can be stated as follows: calculate the evaluation function $eval(\boldsymbol{v}_k)$, and select the chromosome among the parents and the offspring in the way that is superior to others. The number to be selected is *pop_size* and let these chromosomes enter the next generation. The duplication of selection is prohibited.

Numerical Example and Result

For this problem, the parameters were set as *pop_size* = 14, $p_C = 0.4$, $p_M = 0.1$ and *max_gen* = 1000. The best solution by the GA with arithmetic crossover and penalties was found in the 875-th generation with the objective function value $R(\boldsymbol{m}, \boldsymbol{x}) = 0.999468$, $\boldsymbol{m} = [3\ 6\ 3\ 5]$ and $\boldsymbol{x} = [0.965993\ \ 0.760592\ \ 0.972646\ \ 0.804660]$.

The optimal solution (Dhingra, 1992) of this problem is $R(\boldsymbol{m}, \boldsymbol{x}) = 0.99961$ with $\boldsymbol{m} = [6\ 6\ 3\ 5]$ and $\boldsymbol{x} = [0.81604\ \ 0.80309\ \ 0.98364\ \ 0.80373]$. The objective value obtained by our method was considered to be acceptable.

8.3.4 Reliability Design with Interval Coefficients

In many application cases of real-world problems, it is not so easy for decision-makers to specify either probability distributions or membership functions; however, such uncertainty can be easily represented as an *interval of confidence*. This was the motivation to develop interval arithmetic and interval programming (Ishibuchi and Tanaka, 1990; Nakahara, Sasaki and Gen, 1992).

Gen and Cheng (1997) have examined the optimal design problem of system reliability with uncertain coefficients. These coefficients can be roughly given as intervals of confidence. This problem is then formulated as an interval programming model.

Problem Formulation

In practice, it is usually very difficult to determine the precise values for the coefficients of the above models. For these uncertain circumstances, all such parameters are replaced by interval numbers and the problem can be formulated as the following interval programming model (Gen and Cheng, 1996):

$$\max \quad R(\boldsymbol{m}, \alpha) = \prod_{i=1}^{14} (1 - (1 - R_i(\alpha_i))^{m_i}) \tag{8.8}$$

$$\text{s. t.} \quad G_1(\boldsymbol{m}, \alpha) = \sum_{i=1}^{14} C_i(\alpha_i) m_i \leq C \tag{8.9}$$

$$G_2(\boldsymbol{m}, \alpha) = \sum_{i=1}^{14} W_i(\alpha_i) m_i \leq W \tag{8.10}$$

$$1 \leq m_i \leq u_i, : \text{ integer}, \; i = 1, 2, \ldots, 14 \tag{8.11}$$

$$1 \leq \alpha_i \leq \beta_i, : \text{ integer}, \; i = 1, 2, \ldots, 14 \tag{8.12}$$

where: $R_i(a_i)$ is the interval reliability $R_i(a_i) = [r_i^L(a_i), r_i^R(a_i)]$, $C_i(a_i)$, $W_i(a_i)$ are the interval coefficients ($C_i(a_i) = [c_i^L(a_i), c_i^R(a_i)]$, $W_i(a_i) = [w_i^L(a_i), w_i^R(a_i)]$),
C is the interval overall constraint on the system cost $C = [c^L, c^R]$, and
W is the interval overall constraint on the system weight $W = [w^L, w^R]$.

The problem then can be transformed into an equivalent crisp bicriteria programming problem. For more detailed information, see (Gen and Cheng, 1997; Nakahara, Sasaki, Ida and Gen, 1991; Ishibuchi and Tanaka, 1990). The problem (8.8)–(8.12) can be transformed into the following problem:

$$\max \quad z^L(\boldsymbol{m}, \alpha) = \sum_{i=1}^{14} d_i^L(m_i, \alpha_i) \tag{8.13}$$

$$\max \quad z^C(\boldsymbol{m}, \alpha) = \sum_{i=1}^{14} \frac{d_i^L(m_i, \alpha_i) + d_i^R(m_i, \alpha_i)}{2} \tag{8.14}$$

$$\text{s. t.} \quad g_1(\boldsymbol{m}, \alpha) = \sum_{i=1}^{14} c_i(\alpha_i) m_i \leq c \tag{8.15}$$

$$g_2(\boldsymbol{m}, \alpha) = \sum_{i=1}^{1N} w_i(\alpha_i) m_i \leq w \tag{8.16}$$

$$1 \leq m_i \leq u_i, : \text{ integer}, \; i = 1, 2, \ldots, 14 \tag{8.17}$$

$$1 \leq \alpha_i \leq \beta_i, : \text{ integer}, \; i = 1, 2, \ldots, 14 \tag{8.18}$$

If readers wish to know the transformation of this problem in more detail, they can see the references (Gen and Cheng, 1996; Nakahara, Sasaki, Ida and Gen, 1991; Ishibuchi and Tanaka, 1990). If readers need information about the reliability design model of bicriteria non-linear integer programming, they can see the references (Gen and Cheng, 1997; Li, 1996).

The recent research results of reliability design with fuzzy goals and fuzzy constraints can be found in the references (Gen and Cheng, 1997; Sasaki, Yokota and Gen, 1995).

Genetic Algorithm

Gen and Cheng proposed a genetic algorithm to solve the optimal design problem of system reliability with interval coefficients, which is formulated as an interval programming model (Gen and Cheng, 1997; Gen and Cheng, 1996).

Representation and Initialisation: A chromosome is defined as follows:

$$\boldsymbol{v}_k = [(\alpha_{k1}, m_{k1})(\alpha_{k2}, m_{k2}) \ldots (\alpha_{k14}, m_{k14})]$$

where the subscript k is the index of the chromosome, a_{ki} is the design alternative for sub-system i, and m_{ki} represents the redundant units.

The initial population is generated randomly within the range $[1, u_i]$ for all m_{ki} and the range $[1, \beta_i]$ for all a_{ki}.

Crossover and Mutation: Crossover is implemented with the uniform crossover operator (Syswerda, 1989) and mutation is performed as a random perturbation within the permissive range of integer variables.

Selection: Deterministic selection is used, that is, we delete all duplicates among parents and offspring and then sort them in descending order and select the first *pop_size* chromosomes as the new population.

Evaluation: There are two main tasks involved in this phase: (a) how to handle infeasible chromosomes and (b) how to determine fitness values of chromosomes according to the two criteria. Let $\boldsymbol{v}_k$ be the k-th chromosome in the current generation. The evaluation function is defined as follows:

$$eval(\boldsymbol{v}_k) = w_1 z^L(\boldsymbol{m}_k, \boldsymbol{f}\langle ¿_k) + w_2 z^C(\boldsymbol{m}_k, \boldsymbol{f}\langle ¿_k).$$

The evaluation function contains two terms: a *weighted-sum objective* and a *penalty* (Gen and Cheng, 1997). The weighted-sum objective term tries to induce a selection pressure to force genetic search towards exploiting the set of Pareto solutions and the penalty term tries to force genetic search to approach Pareto solutions from both sides of the feasible and infeasible regions.

Table 8.4 Pareto solution.

n	z^L	z^R
1	0.97801	0.98758
2	0.97826	0.98660
3	0.97832	0.98647

Table 8.5 Optimal design of system reliability

Subsystem	Pareto solutions					
	1		2		3	
i	Design	Units	Design	Units	Design	Units
1	1	5	3	5	1	5
2	1	5	1	5	1	5
3	1	4	2	4	1	4
4	1	5	1	4	1	5
5	2	3	1	3	2	3
6	3	3	2	3	3	3
7	2	5	2	3	2	5
8	1	4	1	5	2	3
9	2	4	1	2	2	4
10	1	4	1	5	1	4
11	2	2	1	5	2	3
12	3	4	2	4	3	4
13	1	4	1	2	1	4
14	3	4	3	5	3	4

Numerical Example and Result

The numerical example used to test the GA is an extension of the problem given by Fyffe *et al.* (Fyffe, Hines and Lee, 1968). The system consists of 14 subsystems. Each subsystem has three or four alternative designs and the possible maximum of redundant units for each subsystem is six. The interval coefficients of the problem are shown in reference (Gen and Cheng, 1997). The parameters for the genetic algorithm were set as follows: population size, *pop_size* = 40; crossover probability, $p_c = 0.4$; mutation probability, $p_m = 0.4$; maximum generation, *max_gen* = 2000. The values of h_1 and h_2 were set as $h_1 = 0.5$ and $h_2 = 0.5$.

The Pareto solutions found by the proposed algorithm are listed in Table 8.4. The corresponding solutions (the optimal designs) are given in Table 8.5.

8.4 Multi-objective Reliability Design Problems

In this section, we discuss two multi-objective reliability design problems: bicriteria reliability design and reliability design with fuzzy goals. The resulting mathematical formulations determine the optimal level of component reliability and redundant components at each stage to optimise several objectives under design constraints. These problems are multiple-objective, non-linear and mixed integer programming problems. We also describe the GAs used for solving multi-objective reliability design problems.

8.4.1 Bicriteria Reliability Design

Problem Formulation

The problem of bicriteria reliability design is a variation of the optimal reliability allocation problem (Dhingra, 1992) and an example of the non-linear mixed integer programming problems. This problem includes not only reliability maximisation but also cost minimisation and weight minimisation. The bicriteria reliability design problem can be formulated as follows (Li, 1996):

$$\max \quad R(\boldsymbol{m}, \boldsymbol{x}) = \prod_{i=1}^{4} (1 - (1 - x_i)^{m_i})$$

$$\max \quad C(\boldsymbol{m}, \boldsymbol{x}) = \sum_{i=1}^{4} C(x_i) \cdot \left(m_i + \exp\left(\frac{m_i}{4}\right)\right)$$

$$\text{s. t.} \quad G_1(\boldsymbol{m}) = \sum_{i=1}^{4} w_i \cdot m_i \cdot \exp\left(\frac{m_i}{4}\right) \le 500$$

$$G_2(\boldsymbol{m}) = \sum_{i=1}^{4} v_i \cdot m_i^2 \le 250$$

$$1 \le m_i \le 10\text{: integer} \quad i = 1, 2, 3, 4$$

$$0.5 \le x_i \le 1 - 10^{-6}\text{:} \quad \text{real number}$$

where v_i, w_i, and $C(x_i)$ have the same meaning as before. The design data for this problem is in Table 8.3.

Genetic Algorithm

Li proposed a GA for bicriteria reliability design problems to maximise the reliability of the system and minimise the total cost of the system. Li also proposed the use of the sum of rank-based order of each objective as each chromosome's fitness and storing the Pareto solutions by updating it at the generation level (Li, 1996).

Representations and Initialisation: Let v_k denote the k-th chromosome in a population as follows:

$$v_k = [(m_{k1}, x_{k1})(m_{k2}, x_{k2})(m_{k3}, x_{k3})(m_{k4}, x_{k4})] \quad k = 1, 2, \ldots, pop\_size.$$

The initialisation process randomly generates t genes for a chromosome.

Evaluation and Selection: We use the sum of the rank-based order of each objective function as each chromosome's fitness and store the Pareto solutions by updating them at the generation level. The procedure of this fitness assignment is as follows:

Procedure: Rank-based Order Number Evaluation

Step 1: Calculate each objective value for each chromosome.

Step 2: Rank chromosomes based on their objective function values and obtain the order $r_i(\boldsymbol{v}_k)$.

Step 3: Calculate the fitness value using the following equation:

$$eval(\boldsymbol{v}_k) = \sum_{i=1}^{Q} \boldsymbol{r}_i(\boldsymbol{v}_k)$$

where Q is the number of objective functions.

We employ elitist selection to determine the next generation.

Crossover and Mutation: The arithmetic crossover operator and uniform mutation are used here. For a chosen parent $\boldsymbol{v}_k$, if its element x_{k3} is randomly selected for mutation, the resulted offspring is $\boldsymbol{v}'_k = [(m_{k1}, x_{k1})\ (m_{k2}, x_{k2})\ (m_{k3}, x'_{k3})\ (m_{k4}, x_{k4})]$, where x'_{k3} is a random (uniform probability distribution) value from $[0.5, 1-10^{-6}]$. If m_{k3} is selected then the algorithm returns the integer random number within its domain.

Numerical Example and Result

For this problem, when the parameters were set as $pop\_size = 200$, $p_C = 0.4$, $p_M = 0.6$, and $max\_gen = 1000$, the Pareto solutions obtained were as shown in Table 8.6.

Table 8.6 The Pareto solutions

$R(\boldsymbol{m}, \boldsymbol{x})$	$C(\boldsymbol{m}, \boldsymbol{x})$	$G_1(\boldsymbol{m})$	$G_2(\boldsymbol{m})$	Chromosome
0.998395	398.559	396.25	217.00	[(0.777820, 5), (0.697710, 6), (0.916213, 4), (0.748629, 6)]
0.995562	313.737	391.43	244.00	[(0.791324, 6), (0.705309, 5), (0.682558, 6), (0.743228, 5)]
0.992422	253.985	369.69	235.00	[(0.764636, 4), (0.607286, 6), (0.801730, 5), (0.713641, 6)]
0.989157	206.800	364.25	206.00	[(0.670458, 6), (0.689409, 5), (0.832996, 4), (0.574555, 6)]
0.987813	186.650	386.00	244.00	[(0.694460, 5), (0.649614, 6), (0.769595, 5), (0.561921, 6)]
0.972312	136.093	386.00	244.00	[(0.602327, 5), (0.576630, 6), (0.729846, 5), (0.529785, 6)]

8.4.2 Reliability Design with Fuzzy Goals

Problem Formulation

The problem of reliability design with fuzzy goals is a variation of the optimal reliability allocation problem (Dhingra, 1992) and an example of a non-linear mixed integer programming problem. This problem includes not only reliability maximisation but also cost minimisation and weight minimisation. The reliability design problem with fuzzy goals can be formulated as follows (Gen, Ida and Kim, 1998):

$$\max\ R(\boldsymbol{m}, \boldsymbol{x}) = \prod_{i=1}^{4} (1 - (1 - x_i)^{m_i}) \gtrsim b_1$$

Plate 4 Nine Mutations. (Ribbed Branched Structure).
Latham 1991. Computer/Cibachrome. 4'x4'.

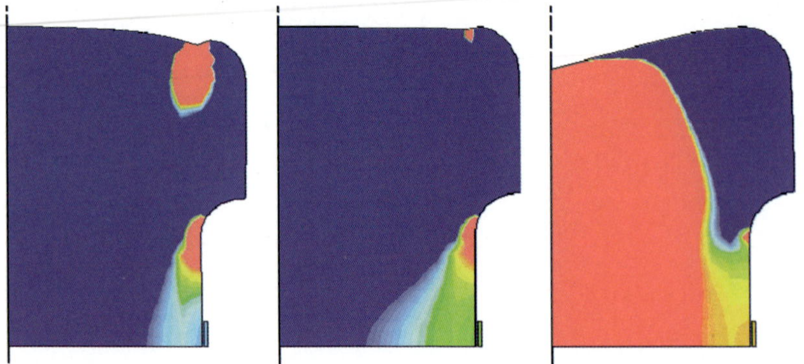

Plate 1 Strain in upper radial cross section of conventional low-profile 3 MN load cell.

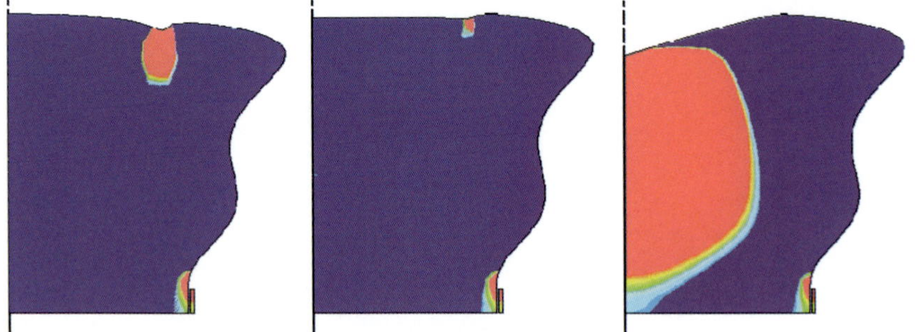

Plate 2 Strain in upper radial cross section of GA optimized 3 MN load cell.

Plate 3 The GA optimized 3 MN load cell.

$$\min \ C(\boldsymbol{m}, \boldsymbol{x}) = \sum_{i=1}^{4} C(x_i) \cdot \left(m_i + \exp\left(\frac{m_i}{4}\right)\right) \lesssim b_2$$

$$\min \ W(\boldsymbol{m}) = \sum_{i=1}^{4} w_i \cdot m_i \cdot \exp\left(\frac{m_i}{4}\right) \lesssim b_3$$

$$\text{s. t.} \ G_1(\boldsymbol{m}) = \sum_{i=1}^{4} v_i \cdot m_i^2 \leq 250$$

$$1 \leq m_i \leq 10\text{: integer} \quad i = 1, 2, 3, 4$$
$$0.5 \leq x_i \leq 1 - 10^{-6}\text{:} \quad \text{real number}$$

where v_i, w_i, and $C(x_i)$ have the same meaning as before, and
F_1 is equal to $b_1 - t_1^L$, F_2 is equal to $b_2 + t_2^R$, and F_3 is equal to $b_3 + t_3^R$.

As given by Tiwari *et al.* and Chu (Tiwari, Dharmar and Rao, 1986; Chu, 1993), we can transform the above problem into the following non-linear mixed integer programming problem:

$$\begin{aligned}
\max \quad & q_R k_R + q_C k_C + q_W k_W \\
\text{s. t.} \quad & k_R = l_R(R(\boldsymbol{m}, \boldsymbol{x})) \\
& k_C = l_C(C(\boldsymbol{m}, \boldsymbol{x})) \\
& k_W = l_W(W(\boldsymbol{m})) \\
& G_1(\boldsymbol{m}) = \sum_{i=1}^{4} v_i \cdot m_i^2 \leq 250 \\
& 0 \leq k_R \leq 1, \ 0 \leq k_C \leq 1, \ 0 \leq k_W \leq 1
\end{aligned}$$

where q_R, q_C, and q_w are suitable weight factors which are assigned by the decision maker.

The membership functions (Zimmerman, 1978; Gen, Ida and Kim, 1998) of the fuzzy goals can be defined as follows:

$$1_R(R(\boldsymbol{m}, \boldsymbol{x})) = \begin{cases} 0 & \text{if } R(\boldsymbol{m}, \boldsymbol{x}) < b_1 - t_1^L, \\ \dfrac{R(\boldsymbol{m}, \boldsymbol{x}) - (b_1 - t_1^L)}{t_1^L} & \text{if } b_1 - t_1^L \leq R(\boldsymbol{m}, \boldsymbol{x}) \leq b_1, \\ 1 & \text{if } R(\boldsymbol{m}, \boldsymbol{x}) > b_1, \end{cases}$$

$$1_C(C(\boldsymbol{m}, \boldsymbol{x})) = \begin{cases} 1 & \text{if } C(\boldsymbol{m}, \boldsymbol{x}) < b_2, \\ 1 - \dfrac{C(\boldsymbol{m}, \boldsymbol{x}) - b_2}{t_2^R} & \text{if } b_2 \leq C(\boldsymbol{m}, \boldsymbol{x}) \leq b_2 + t_2^R, \\ 0 & \text{if } C(\boldsymbol{m}, \boldsymbol{x}) > b_2 + t_2^R, \end{cases}$$

$$1_W(W(\boldsymbol{m})) = \begin{cases} 1 & \text{if } W(\boldsymbol{m}) < b_3, \\ 1 - \dfrac{W(\boldsymbol{m}) - b_3}{t_3^R} & \text{if } b_3 \le W(\boldsymbol{m}) \le b_3 + t_3^R, \\ 0 & \text{if } W(\boldsymbol{m}) > b_3 + t_3^R, \end{cases}$$

The constant coefficients for this problem are given in Table 8.7.

Table 8.7 Constant coefficients for reliability design with fuzzy goals

Number of subsystems	4
Limit on F_1	0.75
Limit on F_2	400
Limit on F_3	500
Operation time O_T	1000 h

Subsystem	$10^5 \alpha_i$	β_i	v_i	w_i
1	1.0	1.5	1	6
2	2.3	1.5	2	6
3	0.3	1.5	3	8
4	2.3	1.5	2	7

Evaluation of Chromosome: The evaluation function is defined in consideration of a weight factor as follows:

$$eval(\boldsymbol{v}_k) = q_R \kappa_R + q_C \kappa_C + q_w \kappa_w, \quad k = 1, 2, \ldots, pop\_size.$$

From the following equations, we can keep the best chromosome $\boldsymbol{v}^*$ with the largest fitness value at each generation:

$$\boldsymbol{v}^* = \text{argmax}\{eval(\boldsymbol{v}_k) | k = 1, 2, \ldots, pop\_size.\}$$

Crossover and Mutation: We use the arithmetic crossover operator for the crossover operation. Here, we manipulate two kinds of variables, i.e. real variables and integer variables. For integer variables, we need to consider integer variables as real variables in order to carry out the arithmetical crossover operation. Then we truncate the decimals for integer variables after the crossover operation and save only the integer part. Uniform mutation is used.

Selection: The selection used here is a method which combines the *roulette wheel* and *elitist* approach. Roulette wheel selection, which is one of the fitness-proportional methods, is used to create the new generation randomly, and the elitist method is employed to preserve the best chromosome for the next generation and overcome the stochastic errors of sampling.

Numerical Example and Result

The parameters were set as follows: $pop\_size = 20$, $p_c = 0.4$, $p_m = 0.1$, and $T = 2000$. Also we set the parameters as $t_1^L = 0.25$, $t_2^R = 300$, $t_3^R = 360$ and selected the relative weights of

Plate 5 Breeding Forms on the Infinite Plane.
Latham 1992. Computer Image.

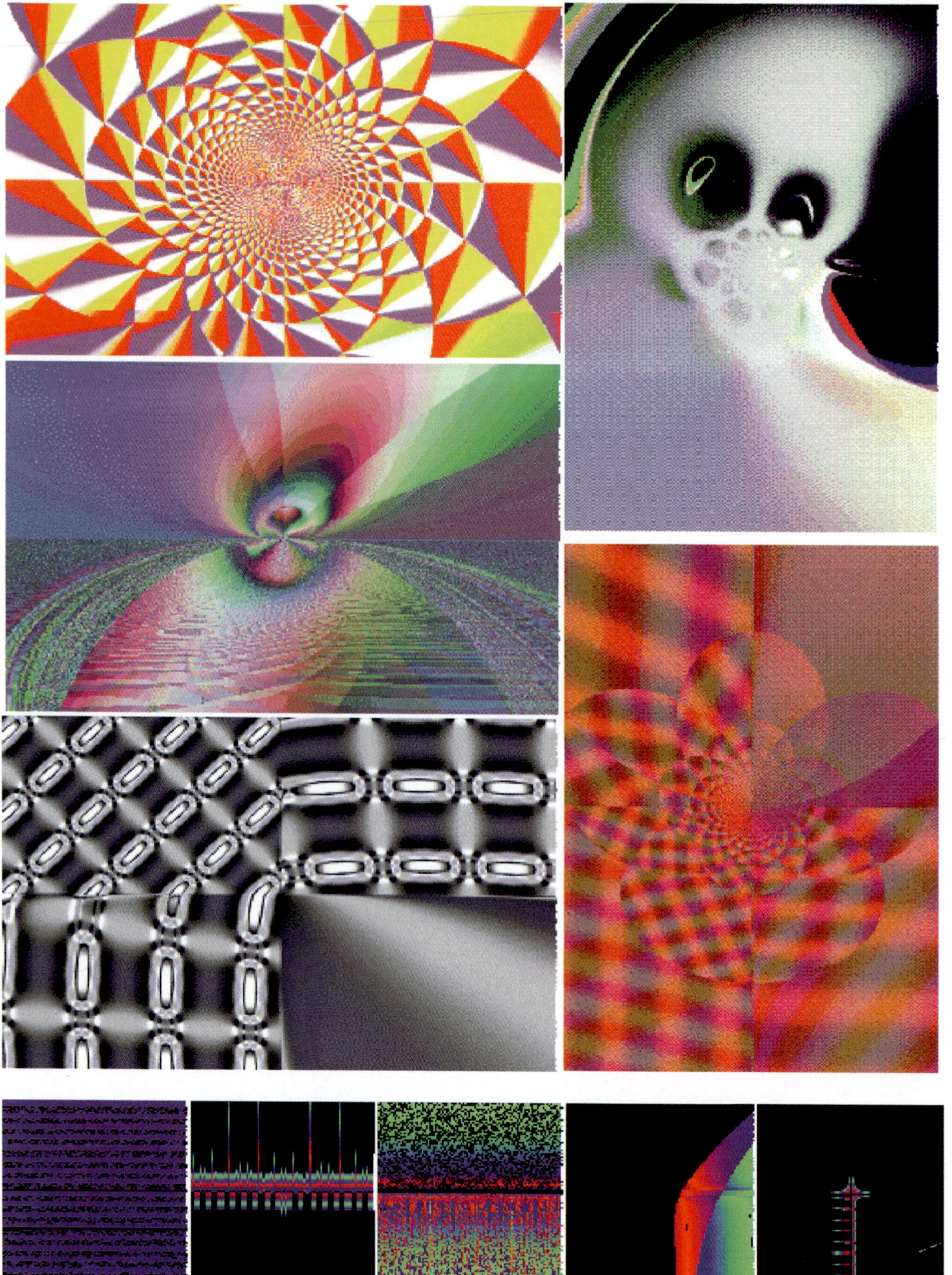

Plate 6 Examples from the genetic art projects. The top five images are from the second generation system, IIGA2. The lower five were produced by IIGA1. Many hundreds of other images can be viewed at http://www.geneticart.org

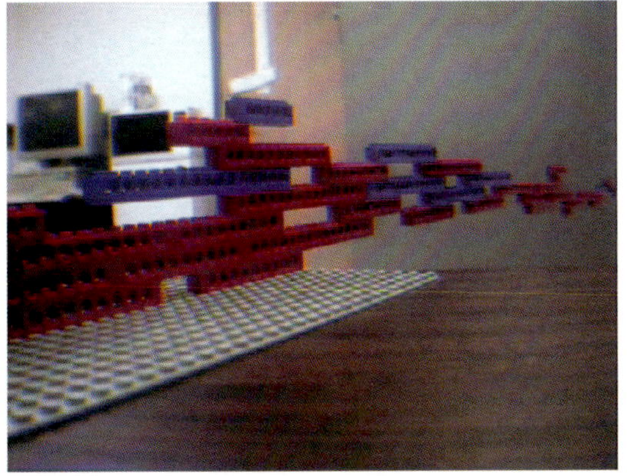

Plate 7 The "Lego bridge" defined by the scheme of fig. 17.1, built on our lab table.*

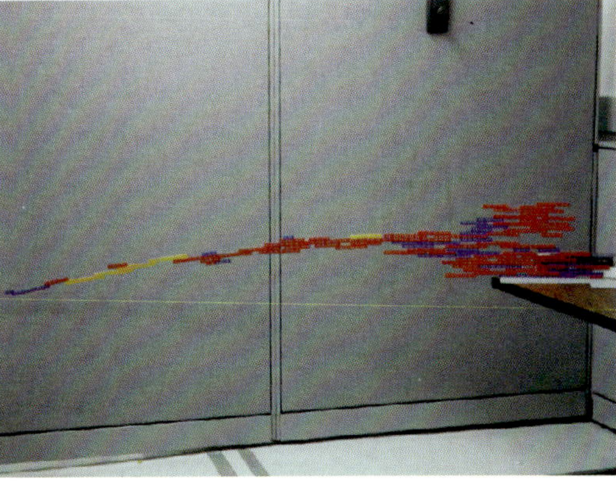

Plate 8 Long Bridge.*

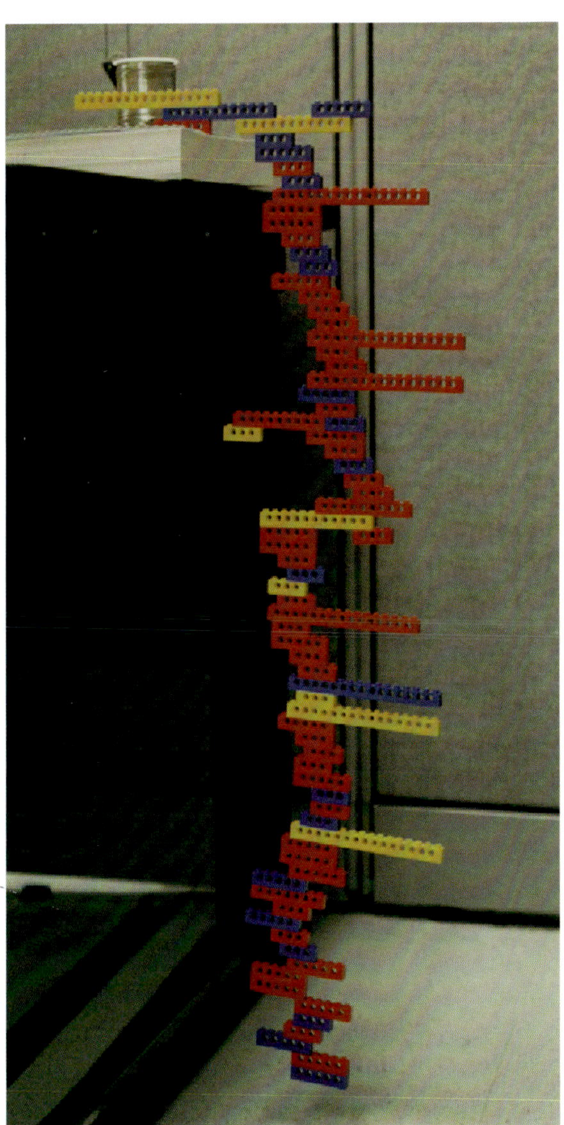

Plate 9 Scaffold.*

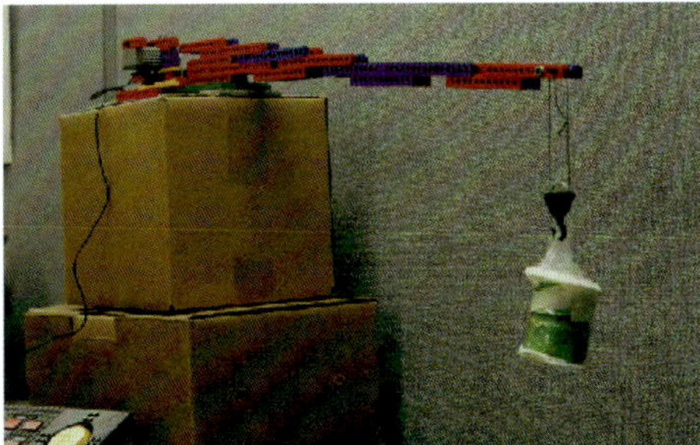

Plate 10 Crane with evolved horizontal crane arm.*

Plate 11 Crane with diagonal crane arm.*

Plate 12 Lego table as specified by the diagram of fig. 17.5, holding a 50g weight.*

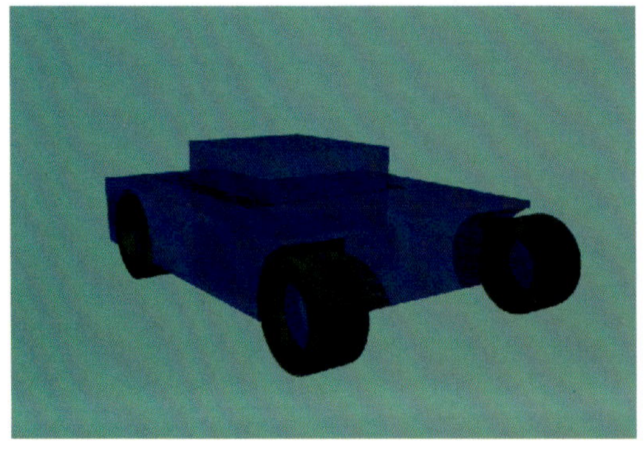

Fixed, inflexible skeleton of sports car.

A random initial design of sports car.

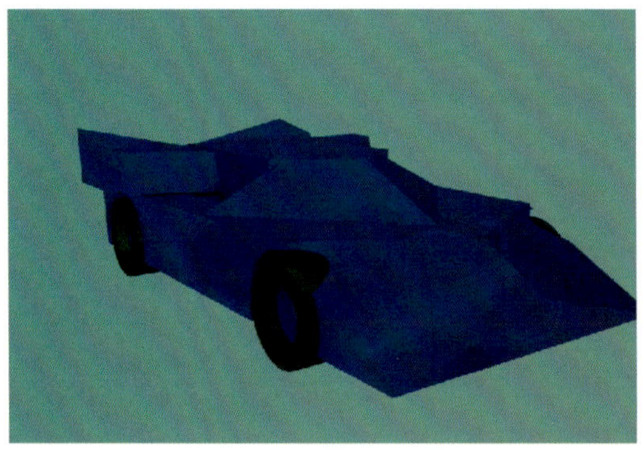

Best evolved sports car after 20 generations.

Best sports car after 100 generations.

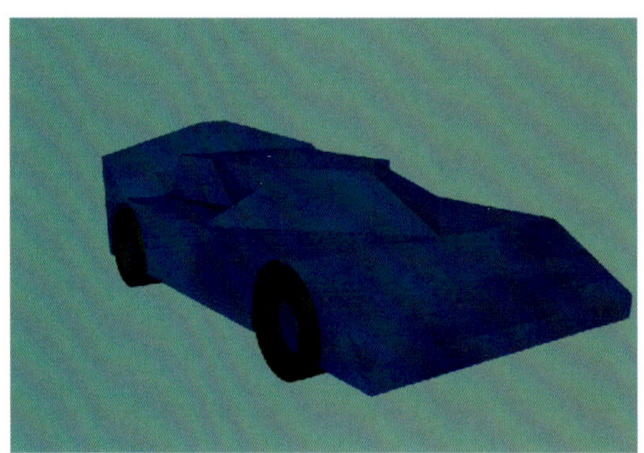

Best sports car after re-evolving the rear.

The final evolved sports car design.

Plate 13 The evolution of an aerodynamic sports car around a fixed chassis by the Generic Evolutionary Design system (wheels added).

objectives (0.5, 0.25, 0.25), in order to make the first objective twice as important as other objectives.

The best solution of the proposed GA was found in the 1923-th generation with objectives $R(\boldsymbol{m}, \boldsymbol{x}) = 0.982335$, $C(\boldsymbol{m}, \boldsymbol{x}) = 135.001259$, $W(\boldsymbol{m}) = 147.048541$, and solution:

[(3, 0.853070), (3, 0.821421), (2, 0.939903), (3, 0.825620)].

The optimal solution (Dhingra, 1992) has objectives: $R(\boldsymbol{m},\boldsymbol{x}) = 0.94478$, $C(\boldsymbol{m},\boldsymbol{x}) = 104.472$, $W(\boldsymbol{m}) = 128.727$ and solution:

[(2, 0.86504), (3, 0.81814), (2, 0.84253), (3, 0.80645)].

8.5 Reliable Network Design Problems

The problem of optimal design of network topology considering reliability can be formulated as a combinatorial problem where the selection of components either maximises reliability or minimises cost. The combinatorial problem of optimal reliability design of networks is NP-hard, and further compounding this is the computation required to calculate or estimate network reliability.

The reliabilities related for network design problems can be classified into the following two:

- All-terminal network reliability (also called overall network reliability): every node in the network can communicate with every other node over a specified mission time.
- Source–sink network reliability: the source node in the network can communicate with the sink node over a specified mission time.

We propose three approaches for optimal reliability network design problems as follows: the enumerative-based approach, the heuristic-based approach, and the GA-based approach.

Enumerative-based approaches are applicable only for small network sizes. They are founded on the enumeration of states, minpaths or mincuts. Roughly speaking these methods use some combination of enumerative and reduction techniques. Heuristic-based approaches, such as Tabu search, simulated annealing, and so on, can be applied to larger networks but do not guarantee optimality.

Recently, GA-based approaches have taken attention as the tool of the solution method for the optimal design of networks considering reliability. Kumar *et al.* (Kumar, Pathak, Gupta and Parsaei, 1995) proposed a GA to design the distributed system topology. Kumar *et al.* (Kumar, Pathak and Gupta, 1995) developed a GA considering diameter, distance, and reliability to design and expand computer networks. Walters and Smith (Walters and Smith, 1995) proposed an evolutionary algorithm for the optimal layout design of networks with tree structure. Deeter and Smith (Deeter and Smith, 1997) presented a GA-based approach to the design of networks considering all-terminal reliability with alternative link options, allowing links to be chosen from different components with different costs and reliabilities. Dengiz *et al.* (Dengiz, Altiparmak and Smith, 1995) attempted to apply a genetic algorithm to the optimal design of networks considering all terminals. Dengiz, *et al.* (Dengiz, Altiparmak and Smith, 1997) focused on large backbone communication network design considering the all-terminal network reliability and used a GA, but appreciably customised it to the all-terminal design problem to give an effective, efficient optimisation methodology. We define the following notations to describe the design problem of all-terminal reliable networks.

8.5.1 Bicriteria LAN Design with Tree Reliability and Message Delay

Large networks usually comprise a collection of LANs tied together by a backbone. The LANs are often spanning trees. Thus, the evaluation of the reliability of a large network can often be accomplished by breaking down the problem into several problems on trees, and a single problem into a relatively small mesh backbone. Most of the nodes in the network are in the local access portion. Also, centralised networks, where all nodes communicate to or through a single central point, are often entirely trees. It is therefore important to be able to analyse the reliability of tree networks efficiently (Kershenbaum, 1993).

We consider, as a reliability measure, the probability of all operative nodes being connected. Now we want to calculate the reliability of a spanning tree network assuming the reliability of its elements, nodes and links, are known. Considering the tree to be a rooted tree, we associate a state vector with the root of each of the subtrees. The state vector associated with a root node contains all the information about that node relevant to our calculation. We then define a set of recursion relations which yield the state vector of a rooted tree given the state of its subtrees. For subtrees consisting of single nodes the state is obvious. Then we join the rooted subtrees into larger and larger rooted subtrees using the recursion relations until the state of the entire network is obtained (Kershenbaum and van Slyke, 1973).

Deriving the recurrence relations is somewhat mechanical. It comes simply from considering the situation depicted in fig. 8.2. We have two subtrees, one with root i and the other having as its root j. We assume the state of node i and node j are known and we wish to compute the state of j relative to the tree obtained by joining node i into node j with the link (i, j), where node j is the father node of node i.

We assume we have associated with each node i a probability of node failure p_i^f and a probability $p_i^o = 1 - p_i^f$ of the node being operative. Similarly, for the link (i, j) we have probabilities l_i^f and l_i^o of the link (i, j) failing and being operative respectively. We also define the following state vectors for each subtree: b_i means the probability that all nodes in the subtree

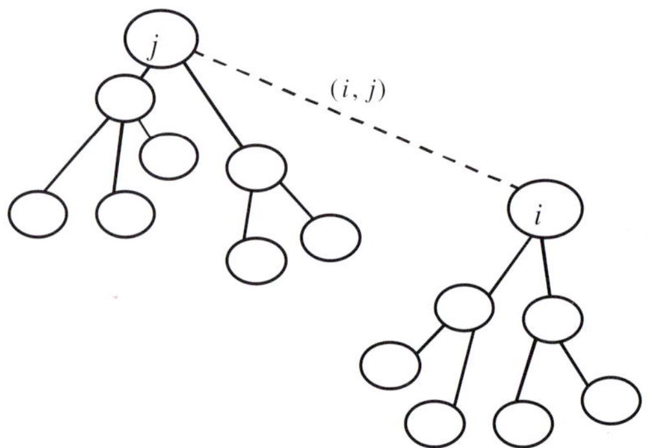

Figure 8.2 The recurrence relation of a tree.

have failed, o_i means the probability that the set of operative nodes, including the root of the subtree, are connected, and r_i means the probability that the root of the subtree has failed and the set of operative nodes in the subtree is connected.

For the tree with root node 1 and n nodes, we can calculate the reliability of the tree, i.e. the probability of all operating nodes communicating as follows:

Procedure: Tree Reliability Calculation

Step 1: Set $r_i = 0$, $o_i = p_i$, $b_i = p_i^f$, $i = 1, 2, \ldots, n$. Set $i = n$. Go to step 2.

Step 2: If node j is the father node of node i, using the following recurrence relations, recalculate r_j, o_j, b_j:

$$r'_j = r_j \cdot b_i + r_i \cdot b_j + o_i \cdot b_j$$
$$o'_j = o_i \cdot o_j \cdot l_i^o + o_j \cdot b_i$$
$$b'_j = b_i \cdot b_j$$

Go to step 3.

Step 3: Set $i = i - 1$. If $i = 1$, go to step 4; otherwise go to step 2.

Step 4: Return $r_1 + o_1 + b_1$.

Problem Formulation

Consider LANs that connect m users. The communication traffic demand between the users is given by an $m \times m$ matrix U which is called the *users traffic matrix*. An element u_{ij} of matrix U represents the traffic from user i to user j. We shall assume that the traffic characteristics are known and have summarised in the users traffic matrix U. Also we define the $n \times n$ service centre topology matrix X_1 which represents the connected appearance of service centres. An element x_{1ij} represents whether the centres i and j are connected. We further assume that LANs are partitioned into n segments (service centres). The users are distributed over those n service centres. The $n \times m$ clustering matrix X_2 specifies which user belongs to which centre. An element x_{2ij} means that user j belongs to centre i. We define the $n \times (n + m)$ matrix X, called the *spanning tree matrix* ($[X_1X_2]$), and define the $n \times n$ matrix T, called the *service centre traffic matrix*. An element t_{ij} of this matrix represents the traffic forwarded from users in centre i to users in centre j. We can calculate the service centre traffic matrix T as follows: $T = X_2^T\, U\, X_2$. The total offered traffic Γ is represented by

$$\Gamma = \sum_{i=1}^{n} \sum_{j=l}^{n} t_{ij}.$$

The total traffic at centre k, $c_k(X)$, is represented as follows:

$$c_k(X) = \sum_{i=1}^{n} \sum_{j=1}^{n} t_{ij} \cdot a_{ij}^{k}(X), \qquad k = 1, 2, \ldots, n.$$

where $\boldsymbol{a}_{ij}^{k}(X)$ means whether traffic from centre i to centre j through centre k exists. The total traffic through link (k, l), $F_{kl}(X)$, is represented as follows:

$$f_{kl}(X) = \sum_{i=1}^{n} \sum_{j=1}^{n} t_{ij} \cdot b_{ij}^{(k,l)}(X), \qquad k = 1, 2, \ldots, n,\ l = 1, 2, \ldots, n.$$

where $b_{ij}^{(k,l)}(X)$ means whether traffic from centre i through centre j passes through the existing link connecting centres k and l exists.

An M/M/1 model (Bertsekas and Gallager, 1992) is used here to describe a single LAN segment behaviour. Recently Gen *et al.* formulated the bicriteria LAN topology design problem (Gen, Ida, Kim and Lee, 1998). The bicriteria LAN topology design problem maximising network reliability and minimising average message delay is formulated as follows (Kim, 1998):

$$\max \quad f_1(X) = R(X)$$

$$\min \quad f_2(X) = \frac{1}{\Gamma}\left[\sum_{i=1}^{n} \frac{c_i(X)}{C_i - c_i(X)} + \sum_{i=1}^{n}\sum_{j=1}^{n} \clubsuit_{ij} \cdot d_{ij}(X)\right]$$

$$\text{s. t.} \quad \sum_{j=1}^{m} x_{2ij} \leq g_i, \quad i = 1, 2, \ldots, n$$

$$\sum_{j=1}^{n} x_{2ij} = 1, \quad j = 1, 2, \ldots, m$$

$$c_i(X) < C_i, \quad i = 1, 2, \ldots, n$$

where C_i is the traffic capacity of centre i, β_{ij} is the delay per bit due to the link between centres i and j, and g_i is the maximum number which is capable of connecting to centre i.

Genetic Algorithm

Gen *et al.* proposed a GA for bicriteria network design problems (Gen, Ida, Kim and Lee, 1998). Kim also proposed a GA for bicriteria network topology design problems maximising network reliability and minimising the average network message delay (Kim, 1998).

Representations and Initialisation: Here we employ the spanning tree representation using *Prüfer* numbers in order to represent active LAN configurations.

One of the classical theorems in graphical enumeration is Cayley's theorem that there are $k^{(k-2)}$ distinct labelled trees on a complete graph with k nodes. Prüfer provided a constructive proof of Cayley's theorem by establishing a one-to-one correspondence between such trees and the set of all strings of $(k-2)$ digits (Zhou and Gen, 1997a,b). This means that we can use just a $(k-2)$ digit permutation to uniquely represent a tree where each digit is an integer between 1 and k inclusive. This permutation is usually known as the Prüfer number.

To illustrate this kind of encoding, consider the following example: the Prüfer number (1 1 2 2) of a spanning tree on a six node complete graph represented in fig. 8.3. The construction of the Prüfer number is described as follows: Locate the leaf node having the smallest label. In this case, it is node 3. Since node 1 is adjacent to node 3 in the tree, assign 1 to the first digit in the Prüfer number, and then remove node 3 and the link (3, 1). Repeat the process on the subtree until link (2, 6) is left and the Prüfer number of this tree with four digits is finally produced.

Alternatively, for the Prüfer number $P = (1\ 1\ 2\ 2)$, the nodes 3, 4, 5, and 6 are eligible and set as $\bar{P} = \{3, 4, 5, 6\}$. Node 3 is the eligible node with the smallest label; node 1 is the leftmost digit in P. Add link (3, 1) to the tree, remove node 3 from $\bar{P}$ for further consideration,

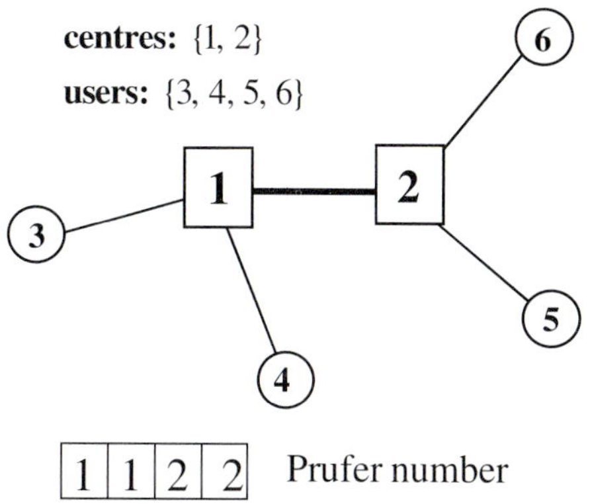

Figure 8.3 A tree and its Prüfer number.

and remove the leftmost digit 1 of P leaving $P = (1\ 2\ 2)$. Node 4 is now the eligible element with the smallest label and the second node 1 is the leftmost digit in the remaining P. Then add link (4, 1) to the tree, remove node 4 from $\bar{P}$ for further consideration, and remove the digit 1 from P leaving $P = (2\ 2)$. Because node 1 is now no longer in the remaining P, it becomes eligible and is put into $\bar{P} = \{1, 5, 6\}$. Repeat the above procedure until P is empty and only nodes 2 and 6 are eligible in $\bar{P}$. Then add link (2, 6) to the tree and stop. The tree is formed as shown in fig. 8.3.

The Prüfer number is more suitable for encoding a spanning tree, especially in some research fields, such as transportation problems, minimum spanning problems, and so on. Also, the verification for the excellence of Prüfer number is addressed by Zhou and Gen (1997b).

From fig. 8.3, we can see that all digits of the Prüfer number are the figures of the centres displayed in boxes. Therefore, the initialisation of a chromosome $\boldsymbol{v}$ (i.e., a Prüfer number) is performed from the randomly generated $n + m - 2$ digits in the range $[1, n]$. In a chromosome, the centre is represented but the user does not appear in a chromosome and is only used as elements of the set $\bar{P}$. Here the centres are represented by the number from 1 to n and the users are represented by the number from $n + 1$ to $n + m$.

Evaluation of Chromosome: We employ the weighted sums method to construct the fitness function. Then we use the following evaluation for combining the bicriteria objective functions into one overall fitness function and evaluate each chromosome.

Procedure: Evaluation

Step 1: Convert chromosome $\boldsymbol{v}$ represented by Prüfer number to spanning matrix $\boldsymbol{x}$.

Step 2: Calculate the objective values ($f_i(\boldsymbol{v})$, $i = 1, 2$).

Step 3: Choose the solution points which contain the minimum $f_i^{\min}$ (or the maximum $f_i^{\max}$) corresponding to each objective function value, and then compare with the stored solution points of the previous generation and select the best points to save again.

$$f_i^{\min(t)} = \min\{f_i^{\min(t-1)}, f_i^{(t)}(v_k)\}$$
$$f_i^{\max(t)} = \max\{f_i^{\max(t-1)}, f_i^{(t)}(v_k)\} \quad i = 1, 2, \quad k = 1, 2, \ldots, chr\_size.$$

where $f_i^{\min(t)}, f_i^{\max(t)}$ is the minimum value and the maximum value of i-th objective function at generation t respectively, $f_1^{(t)}(v_k)$ is the i-th objective function value of the k-th chromosome at generation t, and chr_size is equal to the pop_size plus the offspring generated after genetic operations.

Step 4: Solve the following equation to get weights for the fitness function:

$$\alpha_i = (f_i^{\max(t)} - f_i^{\min(t)})/f_i^{\max(t)}, \qquad i = 1, 2$$
$$\kappa_i = \frac{\alpha_i}{\sum_{i=1}^{2} \alpha_i}, \qquad i = 1, 2$$

Step 5: Calculate the evaluation function value for each chromosome as follows:

$$eval(v_k) = \sum_{i=1}^{2} \kappa_i \cdot f_i(v_k), \quad k = 1, 2, \ldots, chr\_size.$$

Step 6: Convert the evaluation function value to fitness as in the following equation:

$$fit(v_k) = \frac{1}{eval(v_k)}, \quad k = 1, 2, \ldots, chr\_size.$$

where $fit\,(v_k)$ means a fitness value for the k-th chromosome

Crossover and Mutation: We employ the uniform crossover. Mutation simply selects two positions at random and swaps their contents.

Selection: The selection used here combines the roulette wheel and elitist approach, in order to allow the GA to search the solution space freely. Roulette wheel selection is used to create the new generation and the elitist method is employed to preserve the best chromosome for the next generation and overcome stochastic errors of sampling.

Modification of Chromosome: Because of the existence of the maximum number which is capable of connecting on each centre, the chromosomes generated randomly in the initial population and the offspring produced by crossover may be illegal in the sense of violating the maximum number of connections for each centre. In such cases we adopt the repairing strategy to modify the connection number.

Let $\bar{G}$ be the set of centres whose maximum number of connections has not been checked and modified in a chromosome. If a centre i violates the constraint with the maximum number g_i of connections for centre i, this means that the number of this centre in the chromosome is more than $(g_i - 1)$. Decrease the number of the centre by checking the extra centre and randomly replace it with another centre from $\bar{G}$.

Numerical Example and Result

We applied the problem with $n = 6$, $m = 30$, $g_i = 10$, $C_i = 300$, and $\beta_{ij} = 0.1$. The user matrix $\boldsymbol{u}$ is described by Kim (1998). We also set the operative probability of centres as 0.95, the operative probability of users as 0.9, the operative probability between centres as 0.9, and the operative probability between centre and user as 0.85. The parameters for the genetic algorithm were set as follows: *pop_size* = 10, *max_gen* = 500, $p_c = 0.4$, $p_m = 0.1$ and centre 2 was considered as the root node of the tree. Twenty experiments were preformed for this problem. Most results generated by the GA were Pareto optimal, as shown in fig. 8.4.

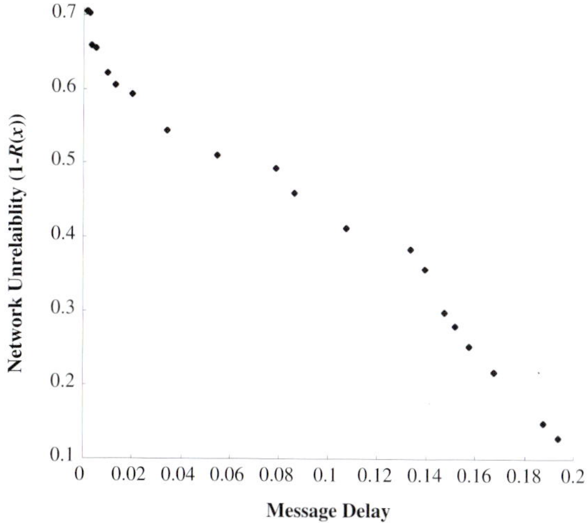

Figure 8.4 The Pareto solutions

8.6 Conclusions

In this chapter, we introduced the idea of optimising the reliability of designs. These reliability design problems are usually formulated as non-linear integer programming problems with some constraints. Generally, these problems are not easy to solve without any transformation. Therefore, many methods, which first transform these problems into 0–1 linear programming problems and solve them based on traditional methods, are proposed in the literature. But when these reliability design problems are transformed into 0–1 linear programming problems, the number of variables and constraints to be treated increases and their manipulation becomes more difficult in the sense of the computation time and memory spaces needed. For this reason, it is more desirable to solve untransformed reliability design problems. This is the motivation for using GAs – one of the features of the GA is the ability to solve the non-linear integer programming problems without any transformation.

We described seven GA-based approaches for reliability design problems: redundant systems, alternative designs, time-dependent reliability, interval coefficients, bicriteria reliability design, fuzzy goals, bicriteria LAN design with tree reliability and message delay. From this chapter, we can see that GAs are powerful tools for solving reliability design problems and GAs can be easily used to solve various reliability design problems, without any transformation.

Acknowledgements

This chapter was supported by the International Scientific Research Program, the Grant-in-Aid for Scientific Research (No.10044173: 1998.4–2001.3) by the Ministry of Education, Science and Culture, the Japanese Government. Also, we gratefully acknowledge valuable discussions with Dr. Yasuhiro Tsujimura, Ashigaka Institute of Technology and for exchanging research work with Dr. Alice E. Smith, University of Pittsburgh.

References

Aggarawal. K. K., Gupta, J. S. and Misra, K. B. (1975). A New Heuristic Criterion for Solving a Redundancy Optimization Problem, *IEEE Transactions on Reliability*, Vol. R-24, No. 1, pp. 86–87.

Barlow, R., Hunter, L. and Proschan, F. (1963). Optimum Redundancy When Components Are Subject To Two Kinds of Failure, *Journal of SIAM*, **11**; 64–73.

Bertsekas, D. and Gallager, R. (1992). *Data Networks*, 2nd ed., Prentice-Hall, Englewood Cliffs, New Jersey.

Chu, T. C. (1993). Some Problems in Fuzzy Decision Making, Ph.D Dissertation, University of Texas at Arlington.

Coit, D. and Smith, A. (1996a). Penalty Guided Genetic Search for Reliability Design Optimization, *International Journal of Computers and Industrial Engineering*, **30**; No. 4, 895–904.

Coit, D. and Smith, A. (1996b). Reliability Optimization of Series-Parallel Systems using a Genetic Algorithm, *IEEE Transactions on Reliability*, **45**; No. 2, 254–260.

Deeter, D. L. and Smith, A. E. (1997). Heuristic Optimisation of Network Design considering All-Terminal Reliability, *Proceedings of Annual Reliability and Maintainability Symposium*, pp. 194–199.

Dengiz, B., Altiparmak, F. and Smith, A. E. (1995). A Genetic Algorithm Approach to Optimal Topology Design of All Terminal Networks, *Intelligent Engineering Systems Through Artificial Neural Network*, **5**; 405–410.

Dengiz, B., Altiparmak, F. and Smith, A. E. (1997). Efficient Optimisation of All-terminal Reliable Networks Using Evolutionary Approach, *IEEE Transactions on Reliability*, **46**; No. 1, 18–26.

Dhingra, A. K. (1992). Optimal Apportionment of Reliability and Redundancy in Series Systems under Multiple Objectives, *IEEE Transaction on Reliability*, **41**; No. 4, 576–582.

Fyffe, D., Hines, W. and Lee, N. (1968). System Reliability Allocation and a Computational Algorithm, *IEEE Transactions on Reliability*, Vol. R-17, pp. 64–69.

Gen, M. (1975). Reliability Optimisation by 0–1 Programming for a System with Several Failure Modes, IEEE Transactions on Reliability, Vol. R-24, pp. 206–210, also in Rai, S. and D. P. Agrawal, (eds) (1990), *Distributed Computing Network Reliability*, IEEE Comp. Soc. Press, pp. 252–256.

Gen, M., Ida, K. and Lee, J. (1988). Optimal Selection and Allocation of a System Availability using 0–1 Linear Programming with GUB Structure, *Transactions of Institute of Electronics, Information and Communication Engineers*, Vol. J71–D, pp. 2140–2147 (in Japanese).

Gen, M., Ida, K. Sasaki, M. and Lee, J. (1989). Algorithm for Solving Large-Scale 0–1 Goal Programming and its Application to Reliability Optimisation Problem, *International Journal of Computers and Industrial Engineering*, **17**; 525–530.

Gen, M., K. Ida and T. Taguchi (1993). Reliability Optimisation Problems: a Novel Genetic Algorithm Approach, Technical Report, ISE93–5, Ashikaga Institute of Technology, Ashikaga, Japan.

Gen, M. and Cheng, R. (1996). Optimal Design of System Reliability using Interval Programming and Genetic Algorithm, *International Journal of Computers and Industrial Engineering*, **31**; No. 1, 237–240.

Gen, M. and Cheng, R. (1997). *Genetic Algorithms and Engineering Design*. John Wiley & Sons, New York.

Gen, M., Ida, K., Kim, J. R. and Lee, J. (1998). Bicriteria Network Design using Spanning Tree-based Genetic Algorithm, *Proceedings of the 3rd International Symposium on Artificial Life and Robotics*, No. 1, pp. 43–46.

Gen, M., Ida, K. and Kim, J. R. (1998). System Reliability Optimization with Fuzzy Goals using Genetic Algorithm, *Japanese Journal of Fuzzy Theory and Systems,* **10**; No. 2, 356–365.

Goldberg, D. E. (1989). *Genetic Algorithms in Search, Optimisation, and Machine Learning*. Addison-Wesley.

Holland, J. (1975). *Adaptation in Natural and Artificial Systems*. University of Michigan Press, Ann Arbor.

Ida, K., Gen, M. and Yokota, T. (1994). System Reliability Optimisation with Several Failure Modes by Genetic Algorithm, In Gen, M. and Kobayashi, T. (eds.), *Proceedings of the 16th International Conference on Computer and Industrial Engineering*, pp. 349–352.

Ishibuchi, H. and Tanaka, H. (1990). Multiobjective Programming in Optimisation of the Interval Objective Function, *European Journal of Operational Research*, **48**; 219–225.

Jacobson, D. W. and Arora, S. R. (1996). Simultaneous allocation of reliability and redundancy using simplex search, *Proceedings of Annual Reliability and Maintainability Symposium*, pp. 243–250.

Kershenbaum, A. and Van Slyke, R. (1973) Recursive Analysis of Network Reliability, *Networks*, **3**; 81–94.

Kershenbaum, A. (1993). *Telecommunication Network Design Algorithms*, McGraw-Hill, Inc., New York.

Kim, J. R. (1998). Study on Genetic Algorithms-based Multiobjective Computer Network Design Problems, Master's Thesis, Dept. of Industrial and Information Systems Engg., Ashikaga Institute of Technology.

Kumar, A., R., Pathak, M., Gupta, Y. P. and Parsaei, H. R. (1995). A Genetic Algorithm for Distributed System Topology Design, *International Journal of Computers and Industrial Engineering*, **28**; No. 3, 659–670.

Kumar, A., R., Pathak, M. and Gupta, Y. P. (1995). Genetic-Algorithm-Based Reliability Optimisation for Computer Network Expansion, *IEEE Transactions on Reliability*, **44**; No. 1, 63–72.

Kuo, W., Prasad, V. R., Tillman, F. A. and Hwang, C. L. (1999). *Fundamentals and Applications of Reliability Optimization*, submitted.

Li, Y. X. (1996). Multi-criteria Optimization Techniques and Its Application to Engineering Design Problems, Master's Thesis, Dept. of Industrial and Information Systems Engg., Ashikaga Institute of Technology.

Michalewicz, Z. (1994). *Genetic Algorithms + Data Structures = Evolution Programs*, 2nd ed., Springer-Verlag, Berlin.

Nakagawa, Y. and Miyazaki, S. (1981). Surrogate Constraints Algorithm for Reliability Optimisation Problems with Two Constraints, *IEEE Transactions on Reliabilty*, **30**; No. 2, 175–180.

Nakahara, Y., Sasaki, M. Ida, K. and Gen, M. (1991). A Method for Solving 0–1 Linear Programming Problem with Interval Coefficients, *Journal of Japan Industrial Management Association*, **42**; No. 5, 345–351 (in Japanese).

Nakahara, Y., Sasaki, M. and Gen, M. (1992). On the Linear Programming with Interval Coefficients, *International Journal of Computers and Industrial Engineering*, **23**; 301–304.

Rai, S. and D. Agrawal (1990). *Distributed Computing Network Reliability*, IEEE Computer Society Press, Los Alamitos, California.

Ramakumar, R. (1993). *Engineering Reliability: Fundamentals and Applications*, Prentice-Hall, Englewood Cliffs, New Jersey.

Sasaki, M., Yokota, T. and Gen, M. (1995). A Method for Solving Fuzzy Optimal Reliability Design Problem by Genetic Algorithms, *Japanese Journal of Fuzzy Theory and Systems*, **7**; No. 5, 1062–1072 (in Japanese).

Syswerda, G. (1989). Uniform Crossover in Genetic Algorithms, in Schaffer, J. (ed.), *Proceedings of the 3rd International Conference on Genetic Algorithms*. Morgan Kaufmann, pp. 2–9.

Tillman, F. (1969). Optimisation by Integer Programming of Constrained Reliability Problems with Several Modes of Failure, *IEEE Transactions on Reliability*, Vol. R-18, pp. 47–53.

Tillman, F., Hwang, C. and Kuo, W. (1980). *Optimisation of Systems Reliability*, Marcel Dekker, New York.

Tiwari, R. N., Dharmar, S. and Rao, J. R. (1986). Priority Structure in Fuzzy Goal Programming, *Fuzzy Sets and Systems*, **19**; 251–259.

Walters, G. A. and D. K. Smith (1995). Evolutionary Design Algorithm for Optimal Layout of Tree Networks, *Engineering Optimisation*, **24**; 261–281.

Yokota, T., Gen, M. and Ida, K. (1995a). System Reliability of Optimisation Problems with Several Failure Modes by Genetic Algorithm, *Japanese Journal of Fuzzy Theory and Systems*, **7**; No. 1, 117–185.

Yokota, T., Gen, M. Ida, K. and Taguchi, T. (1995b). Optimal Design of System Reliability by an Approved Genetic Algorithm, *Transactions on Institute of Electronics, Information and Communication Engineers*, **J78A**; No. 6, 702–709 (in Japanese).

Yokota, T., Gen, M. and Li, Y. (1996). Genetic Algorithm for Non-linear Mixed Integer Programming Problems and Its Applications, *International Journal of Computers and Industrial Engineering*, **30**; No. 4, 905–917.

Zhou, G. and Gen, M. (1997a). Approach to Degree-constrained Minimum Spanning Tree Problem Using Genetic Algorithm, *Engineering Design and Automation*, **3**; No. 2, 157–165.

Zhou, G. and Gen, M. (1997b). A Note on Genetic Algorithms for Degree-Constrained Spanning Tree Problems, *Networks*, **30**; 91–95.

Zimmerman, H. J. (1978). Fuzzy Programming and Linear Programming with Several Objective Functions, *Fuzzy Sets and Systems*, **1**; 45–55.

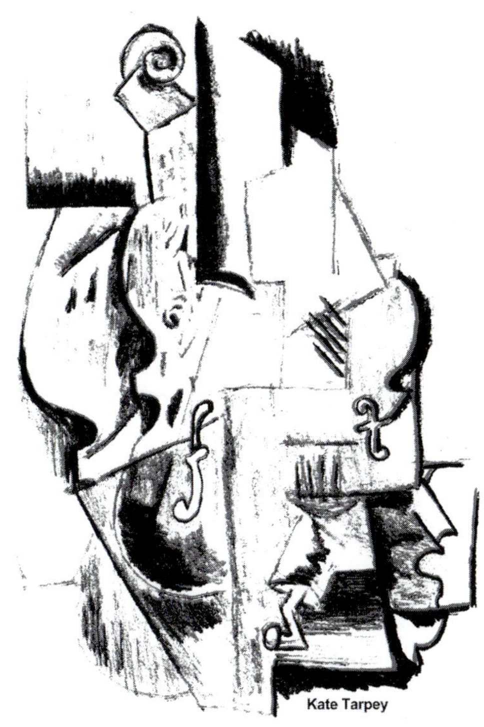

3 EVOLUTIONARY ART

How can a computer generate art? The three chapters in this section answer this question by providing detailed descriptions of every significant evolutionary art system developed to date. ***The Mutation and Growth of Art by Computers*** describes the renowned work of Prof. Stephen Todd, of *IBM Research Labs*, and William Latham, the internationally respected artist and managing director of *Computer Artworks Ltd.* They describe how a computer can be used to breed three-dimensional forms, and also provide details of how this same technology can be employed for other applications. ***Evolving Genetic Art*** by Scott Neil-Rielly of *Zoesis Inc.* and Michael Witbrock of *Justresearch* describe academic research in this area and outline their own well-known on-line evolutionary art system. This pioneering system was the first to appear on the internet, and permitted the general public to guide the evolution of art *en masse*. Finally, ***Evolutionary Art and Form*** by Andrew Rowbottom of *Geoworks Limited* provides a review of evolutionary art software currently available, and describes the development of Andrew's own evolutionary art system (which is included on the CD-ROM).

Chapter 9

The Mutation and Growth of Art by Computers

By Stephen Todd and William Latham*

9.1 Introduction

In this chapter we describe the artistic system *Mutator*, a computer program based on mutation and natural selection which helps an artist explore the world of three-dimensional forms. *Mutator* controls the *Form Grow* system, which produces horns, pumpkins, shells, mathematical shapes and many other shapes as yet unseen and unnamed.

Art created using this type of system has a distinctive philosophy, and generates unique results with a distinctive artistic style, which we call *evolutionism*.

	IMPRESSIONISM
	CUBISM
	REALISM
Art Style =	SURREALISM
	POP ART
	↓
	EVOLUTIONISM

The initial concepts for *Mutator* came from *Formsynth* (Latham 1989; Todd and Latham, 1992) combined with the two-dimensional *Biomorph* system (Dawkins, 1986). Biomorph demonstrates in zoological terms the power of natural selection. *Mutator* harnesses this power, and extends it with the controls described below to make a fast and effective exploration tool. It is these extra features which provide the precision required to make *Mutator* a valuable tool for the artist:

structure	=	expression defining configuration of forms
genotype	=	parameter values defining the number, shape and relationships of elements in the structure
phenotype	=	computer form 'grown' from the structure and genotype.

Each new *structure* expression defines a different family of forms and artworks, each with its family style. The choice of families defines the virtual world of the animation.

* Chapter prepared by Peter Bentley using material provided by Stephen Todd and William Latham

EVOLUTIONARY DESIGN BY COMPUTERS
ISBN 1-55860-605-X

Each family has countless members laid out in a multidimensional form space, and the artist is faced with the problem of searching for the most aesthetic forms in this space. Form space may be explored in contrasting ways. In one traditional approach the artist consciously analyses what it is that makes forms the way they are and acts based on the analysis: 'I think this object needs more bend, I will connect the bend gene to a slider and experiment'.

Mutator provides a second way for an artist to explore form space. The artist makes subjective decisions about the quality of forms. Not only does the artist not *need* to think in terms of the structure definition, *Mutator* does not *permit* changes based on such analytic knowledge. This contrasts with almost all other interfaces used in computer art: they make analytic use easier; *Mutator* escapes from it completely.

The following sections of this chapter describe *Mutator* and how it is used to search for interesting forms and to save their genes in a gene bank (fig. 9.1). The next section summarises *Form Grow*, the artificial embryogeny used to generate forms from the structure and genotype. The basic *Mutator* mechanism is then described, random mutation of the genes by the computer, and selection of forms by the artist. The following sections deal with various enhancements: controlling the mutation rate, steering the progress of the *Mutator* session to speed up the search, and marrying forms. It then describes the various control structures to view the evolutionary progress and to output genes and forms for use by other systems. Lastly, we discuss some ideas for future work.

9.2 Form Grow

Form Grow employs the ideas of iteration, recursion and conditionals, to allow forms to be built using a set of rules or 'growing instructions' (fig. 9.2). Forms are constructed from

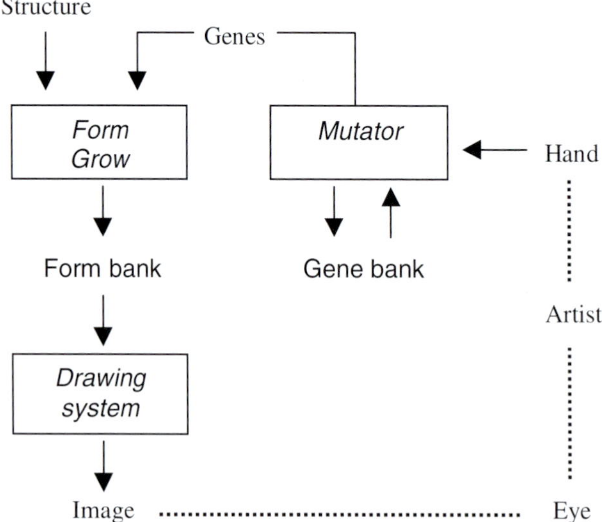

Figure 9.1 *Mutator* keeps a bank of genes and their forms (generated by *Form Grow*), which it displays to the artist. Based on judgements made by the artist, *Mutator* generates and displays new forms, assisting the artist to search for interesting forms and bank the results.

- **basic horn options**

inform	define sub-object from which horn is to be built (e.g. sphere, torus, other_horn)
ribs	number of the last sub-object (e.g. 40)
start	number of the first sub-object (e.g. 3)
head	object to place at head of horn
tail	object to place at tail of horn
fulltail	automatic generation of tail to hide animation popping
parttail	automatic generation of growing tail to hide animation popping
texture	define texture for a horn
tranrule1	define transforms for a horn (pre-texture)
tranrule2	define transforms for a horn (post-texture)
build	control detail of the way transforms are specified
skip	skip some sub-objects for faster display

- **fractal horn options**

fracnum	number of objects at each recursion level
fraccol	colour and texture of objects at each recursion level
fractstart	for constructing lower level details only
orient	for orientation of subhorns to main horn

- **transform construction**

stack	with numeric parameter, stack vertically
stack	with vector parameter, stack in any direction
side	stack to right
back	stack backwards
twist	with numeric parameter, twist about vertical axis
twist	with two numeric parameters, twist angle and offset
twist	with vector parameter, twist about any axis
bend	bend to left or right
grow	grow objects along horn
branch	branch objects out in all directions

- **fractal irregularity**

fractal	uses the transform rule as a fractal irregularity

- **extensions to basic horns**

ribcage	generate a symmetric 'rib cage' along horn skeleton
hornweb	generate a web shaped form

Figure 9.2 Summary of rules of *Form Grow*.

ribs (where a rib is a primitive shape such as a sphere or ellipsoid) and *horns* (collections of ribs).

The keywords used are descriptive of the effect they were originally intended to produce. For example the first objects looked like animal horns and the individual components that made up the horn looked like ribs, and so we used the words 'horn' and 'ribs' in the language to help the artist reliably use the operations. The language often looks like a list of commands that the computer is to follow, and forms a bridge between the underlying code and the artist's perception of *Form Grow*. Most of the operations can be used to achieve many different effects. The keywords sometimes seem rather strange when operations are used outside their original purpose, but we do not generally change them once the artist is used to them. The requirements of animation have in particular shaped the details of *Form Grow* and meant repeated extension (Todd and Latham, 1992).

9.2.1 Constructing Horns

The basic construction of a horn takes a number (*ribs*) of input forms, an input form (*inform*) and a list (*tranrule*) of transform rules. *ribs* defines how many times the input form should appear in the horn. *inform* defines the objects out of which the horn is to be built, either primitive or compound CSG objects, or other horns. (Alternatively, a list of objects may be given. Where a list is used, elements from the list are taken in turn as ribs of the horn, giving greater visual variety.) Lastly, the transform rules (*tranrule*) define how and where each rib should be arranged in the horn, using operations such as *twist*, *bend*, *stack* and *grow*. Figures 9.3 and 9.4 give some examples of *Form Grow* instructions and their corresponding forms.

9.2.2 Drawing Horns

Form Grow turns horns into computer forms when the artist uses the *csg* function. This usually produces a full CSG model that may be displayed in either wire frame or rendered. There are various options for producing simplified output for special purposes, for example to get a quick impression of a form which the artist can rotate for three dimensional information or to give a fast animation preview. These simplified methods are akin to an artist drawing preparatory quick sketches, and these computer sketches often have an artistic interest of their own, much as hand-drawn sketches do. We developed the hidden line drawing options for the production of our book (Todd and Latham, 1992), though we expect to use them for other purposes. Some of the options control *Form Grow* and others the underlying ESME drawing system, but the options are all packaged into a function *drawstyle* for ease of use by the artist.

The low level drawing style controls the way each primitive is drawn:

Wire draws in simple wire frame, best for fast interaction.

Hline draws in wire frame with hidden line removal.

Nurb draws rendered solids using the rendering power of the display device. Nurbs are only available on high-powered display devices. They give quite good pictures that are properly lit and shaded, but with limited texturing capability. Each redraw takes from well under a second to several seconds depending on complexity.

Render calls Winsom for full rendering, including texturing and raytracing if required. Each frame takes from well under a minute to several minutes depending on complexity.

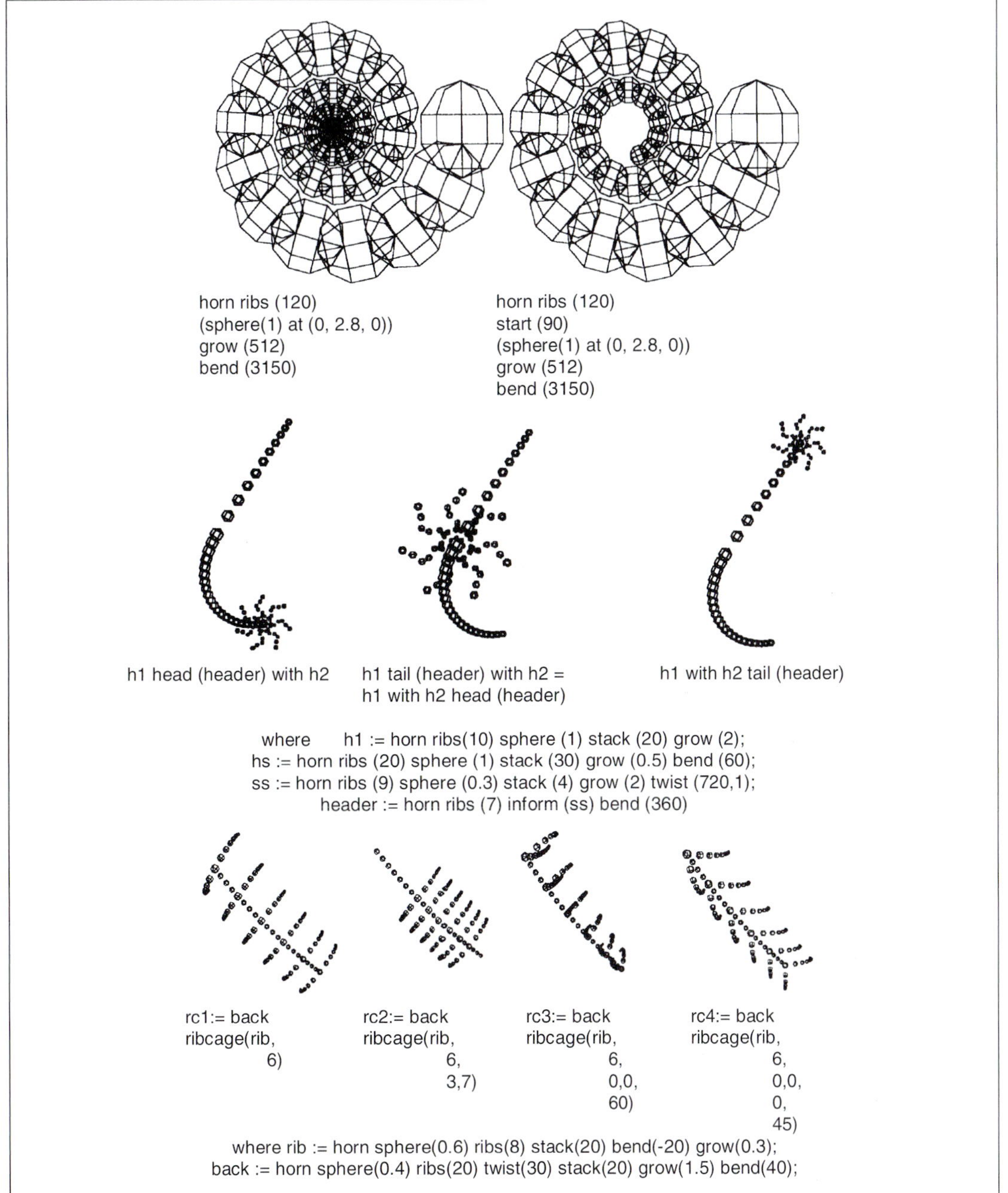

Figure 9.3 Examples of *Form Grow* rules and their corresponding forms. The 'with' operator is used to concatenate horns end to end.

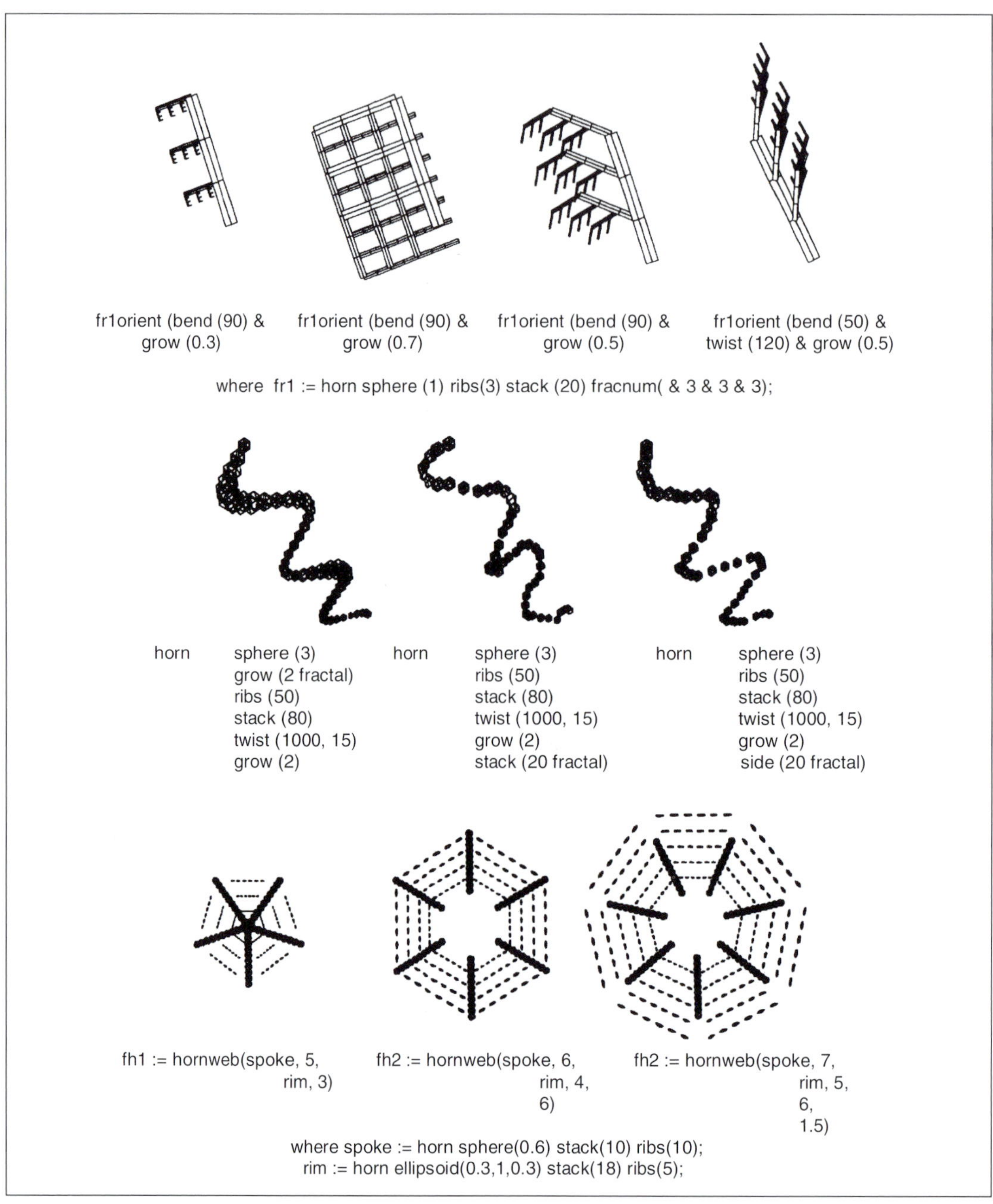

Figure 9.4 Examples of *Form Grow* rules and their corresponding forms. The '&' operator is used here to generate lists.

9.3 Mutator

This section describes our original *Mutator.* The following sections describe various refinements, and a later PC version of *Mutator.* The basic *Mutator* operates by taking a structure expression and generating a corresponding starting gene vector (fig. 9.5). *Mutator* then generates eight mutated gene vectors, and places them into the gene bank. *Form Grow* is used to generate a form from each gene vector and the structure expression, and the nine forms are displayed by the *Mutator* layout component. This group of nine forms is called a *Mutator frame* (fig. 9.6)

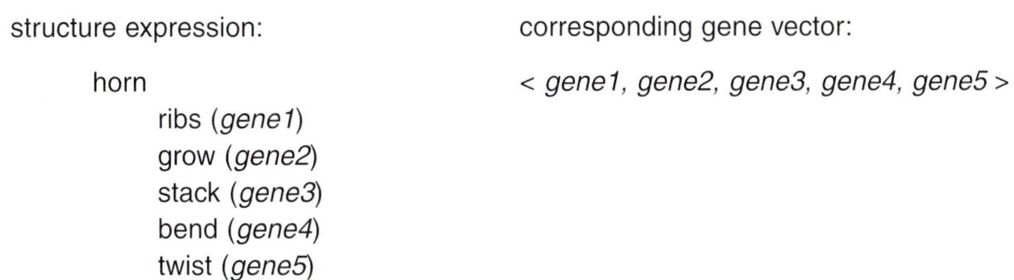

Figure 9.5 An example of a structure expression (created by the artist) and its corresponding gene vector (to be evolved by *Mutator*).

Figure 9.6 A frame of nine mutations. The parent is in the centre surrounded by offspring.

The artist chooses his favourite displayed form as the current form by selecting it with the mouse. The menu item **breed** uses the current form as the start for a new mutation iteration. The genes of this form are used as a new state, and a new frame with mutations from this state is created and banked. Iteration of the generation and selection processes continues until the artist is satisfied with one of the forms (fig. 9.7).

Our original *Mutator* displays the form based on the current position in the centre of the frame.

The other forms are arranged in pairs, displayed opposite each other. The members of each pair use the same mutation vector with opposite orientations (fig. 9.8). This has some attraction, but reduces the number of independent mutations available. *Mutator* can work with any number of forms per frame, but experience shows that nine forms are generally suitable.

The scale of forms generated by *Form Grow* from the same structure varies by a huge amount as the parameters change: a single family can easily include both whales and insects. This is inconvenient when viewed on the *Mutator* screen, and also for animation. *Mutator* and the animation software automatically scales all computer forms to fit into a standard size box, and the artist has no idea how big the forms are prior to this scaling.

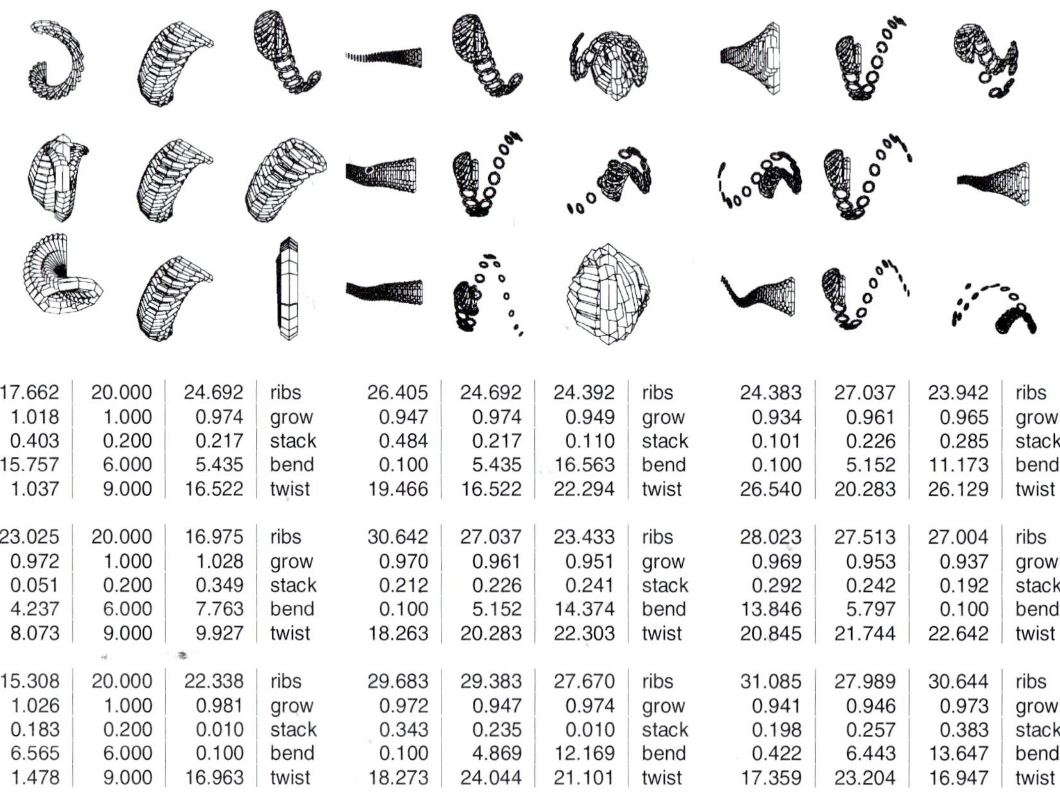

17.662	20.000	24.692	ribs	26.405	24.692	24.392	ribs	24.383	27.037	23.942	ribs
1.018	1.000	0.974	grow	0.947	0.974	0.949	grow	0.934	0.961	0.965	grow
0.403	0.200	0.217	stack	0.484	0.217	0.110	stack	0.101	0.226	0.285	stack
15.757	6.000	5.435	bend	0.100	5.435	16.563	bend	0.100	5.152	11.173	bend
1.037	9.000	16.522	twist	19.466	16.522	22.294	twist	26.540	20.283	26.129	twist

23.025	20.000	16.975	ribs	30.642	27.037	23.433	ribs	28.023	27.513	27.004	ribs
0.972	1.000	1.028	grow	0.970	0.961	0.951	grow	0.969	0.953	0.937	grow
0.051	0.200	0.349	stack	0.212	0.226	0.241	stack	0.292	0.242	0.192	stack
4.237	6.000	7.763	bend	0.100	5.152	14.374	bend	13.846	5.797	0.100	bend
8.073	9.000	9.927	twist	18.263	20.283	22.303	twist	20.845	21.744	22.642	twist

15.308	20.000	22.338	ribs	29.683	29.383	27.670	ribs	31.085	27.989	30.644	ribs
1.026	1.000	0.981	grow	0.972	0.947	0.974	grow	0.941	0.946	0.973	grow
0.183	0.200	0.010	stack	0.343	0.235	0.010	stack	0.198	0.257	0.383	stack
6.565	6.000	0.100	bend	0.100	4.869	12.169	bend	0.422	6.443	13.647	bend
1.478	9.000	16.963	twist	18.273	24.044	21.101	twist	17.359	23.204	16.947	twist

Figure 9.7 Three successive *Mutator* steps with the genes of the forms. The five genes for each form (ribs, grow, stack, bend, twist) are printed vertically.

s+r1	s	s+r2
s+r3	s	s−r3
s−r2	s	s−r1

Figure 9.8 Layout of forms in a *Mutator* frame. **s** is the gene vector for the starting form, and *r1*, *r2* and *r3* are random mutation vectors. The form for **s** is repeated for consistency with the layout used with steering.

9.4 Control of Gene Space

9.4.1 Distance in Gene Space

Different genes naturally have different ranges. For example, a typical horn has sphere radius around 0.5 to 2 acus,[1] whereas twist is measured in hundreds of degrees. *Mutator* naturally adapts itself where these differences are not too great, a factor of two for example, but it does not behave well with large factors. *Mutator* uses a vector *vdiff* that sets a reasonable value for random changes to each gene: thus a sphere radius may reasonably change by 0.1 in a single mutation, but a twist value of 720 degrees may change by 50 degrees (fig. 9.9).[2]

Gene space is not always regular – some discontinuities in the space can occur. A highly stacked form is very sensitive to changes in bend, whereas a squat form is not so sensitive.

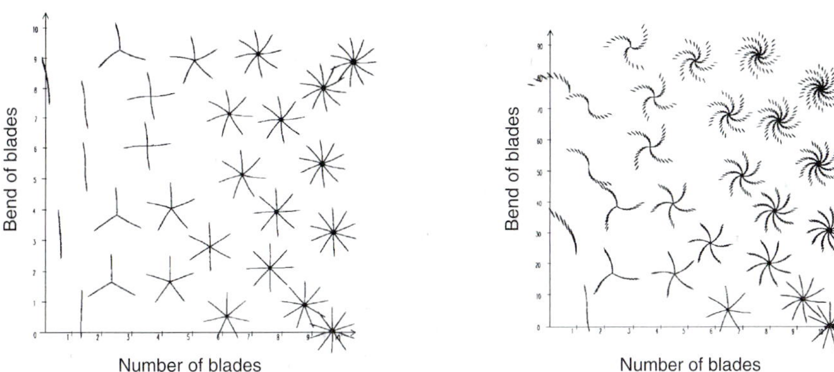

Figure 9.9 Distance in gene space. There are two genes for these forms, number of blades increasing to the right, and the bend of each blade increasing vertically. The group on the left uses the same scaling for each gene giving very little visual change for the bend. The group on the right uses a much greater range for bend genes than for blade genes to give a more even visual change.

---

[1] acu: artist's creative unit

[2] *vdiff* effectively defines a transformation between gene space and Cartesian space. The Cartesian metric corresponds roughly to the perpetual difference between forms. Extending *vdiff* to a matrix permits the designer to indicate that genes are not independent. For example, increasing the stack height and decreasing the sphere size have similar visual effects, so these genes are not independent. The use of *vdiff* as a matrix was suggested by the mathematical uncleanliness of distributing * over a vector.

Depending how the structure is set up there may be unstable volumes of space in which tiny changes to the genes make a huge change to the computer form. We have not had any problems for the structures we use, but it is possible that *Mutator* could become very awkward in unstable parts of gene space.

Small irregularities of gene space do not affect the operation of *Mutator*, and the artist can make use of them to get unexpected results, a creative use of chaos.

9.4.2 Boundary of Gene Space

Some genes may not validly take on certain values, for example a growth value may not be negative. There may be other values that the artist does not wish to use, for example horns with too many ribs or deep fractal recursion may be too expensive to process. Vectors *vmin* and *vmax* define limits in gene space to which *Mutator* confines itself.

These limits should only be used to mark off no-go areas that are in some way dangerous to explore. It is not worth setting limits to impose soft constraints such as 'I do not think that I want to explore this part of space', because the artist's directions will naturally make *Mutator* avoid them.

The function *eg* provides a convenient way to set up a starting default value for a gene, and if required its rate of change, and minimum and maximum permissible values (fig. 9.10). The change rate defaults to ten percent of the initial value, and minimum and maximum values to the largest negative and positive real numbers.

9.4.3 Implementation

Mutator uses five global vectors: *vstate* for the vector of the 'main' form from which others have been mutated, *vinit* for the initial state using the default gene values, *vdiff* to control the rate of change for each slot, *vmin* and *vmax* for the minimum and maximum allowable values. To create each mutated vector *vmut*, *Mutator* makes a vector (*vrand*) of the appropriate width with each slot a random number in the range $[-1 \ldots 1]$, and applies

```
vmut: = vstate + randrate * vdiff * vrand;
vmut: = (vmut max vmin) min vmax;
```

The global variable *randrate* controls the overall degree of mutation. A high value gives widely differing mutations, and is suitable at the start of a *Mutator* session to travel across a

```
horn                                  // define a horn
    sphere (3)                        // made of spheres of radius 3
    ribs (eg (20, 2, 10))             // number of items
    grow (eg (1.4, 0.1, 0.5, 3))      // shrinkage or expansion of elements
    stack (eg (20))                   // raise elements up to for stack
    bend (eg (90))                    // bend it
    twist (eg (720), eg (1))          // and twist, amount and radius
```

Figure 9.10 Using 'eg' to define a structure and control *Mutator*. The structure designer has specified that the horn will be made up of spheres. Initially there will be 20 spheres, and never fewer than 10. The designer considers adding two spheres will make a similar amount of visual difference as changing the growth factor by 0.1, or twisting by an extra 72 degrees.

wide volume of search space. As mutation continues and approaches a 'good' form, lower mutation rates give more sensitive control (fig. 9.11).

Menu options give the artist means to alter the mutation rate as required. In early experiments, the rate was automatically lowered as the session continued. No formula was found that performed this automatic lowering of rate in a convenient way, and so *Mutator* reverted to the manual method.

9.5 Good Forms, Bad Forms, and Steering

When the artist is presented with several mutations, just to choose the best one is in some sense a waste of the other mutations. *Mutator* presents the artist with the opportunity to make subjective judgements on all mutations before moving to the next iteration. From the artist's point of view this captures the idea of judgement, and from the system point of view it considerably speeds up the search of form space as it allows the artist to steer the navigation and reduces the

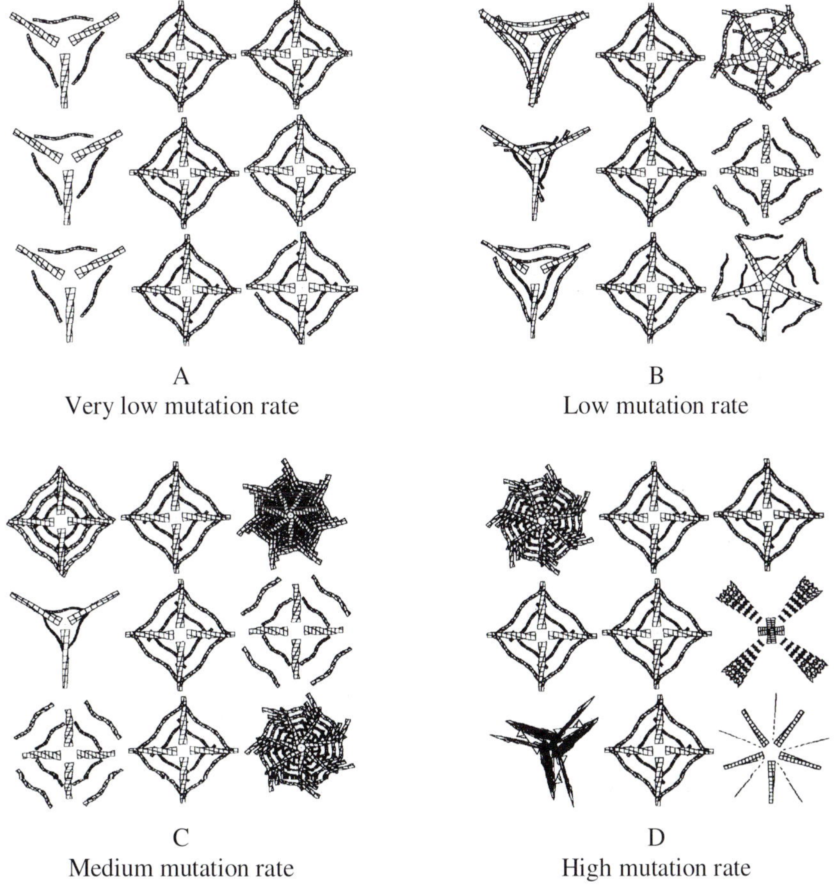

Figure 9.11 The artist uses a high mutation rate at the start of the session quickly to search the form space. As he nears an acceptable form, he moves to lower mutation rates to 'hone' the details of the form.

number of jumps to reach a target. We do not have millions of years to spare selecting from completely random mutations, so these techniques for accelerated evolution are important.

Judgement is made by selecting a mutation, and then making menu choice **very good**, **good**, **bad** or **very bad**. Feedback is provided by a tick or cross against each form, scaled to indicate goodness or badness. When the artist selects **breed**, the next mutation step occurs, based on the mutation chosen as best during judgement.

The implementation of this judgement is based on a global state direction vector *vdir*, that indicates the general direction the artist is steering in state space. Selections of **good** and **bad** on a mutation with vector *vmut* invoke respectively:

vdir: = beta * vdir + alpha * (vmut − vstate)
vdir: = beta * vdir − alpha * (vmut − vstate)

When the next mutation step occurs, it establishes the new state *vstate* from the vector *vbest* for the best mutation using:

vstate: = vbest + vdir

Mutations are made from the new *vstate*. Our current values for *alpha* and *beta* are 0.9 and 0.5. As *beta* + *alpha* is greater than 1, this means that as *vdir* is changed, its length is likely to increase. *vdir* represents a rate of travel as well as a direction, and this rate increases as a good direction is established. As the artist nears a good form and manually reduces *randrate*, *vdir* is also reduced more quickly to prevent overshooting the form.

The form for vector *vbest* from the old frame is displayed top centre in the new frame to provide a visual link between them. The form for the new state *vstate* is displayed in the centre of the frame, and the form for vector *vstate* + *vdir* is displayed bottom centre. This last form goes twice as far from *vbest* along the steering direction as does *vstate* (see central frame of fig. 9.7).

Another way to exploit **good** and **bad** decisions is to use particular forms as attractors and repellers in gene space that affect the generation of future mutations.

9.6 Marriage

A user of *Mutator* arranges a marriage by selecting two parents. Menu choice **other_parent** selects the first parent of a marriage. Menu choice **marry** makes a marriage between this first parent and the current form. Seven children are created by **marry** (all one operation, we do not follow nature here), and the new frame of parents and children is displayed. Inbreeding between two mutations in the same frame is useful for honing or enhancing a particular characteristic of a form. Marriage between distantly related mutations generates interesting new forms which inherit some characteristics from each parent (fig. 9.12).

Child creation shares mixtures of genes from the parents. There are various mixing algorithms (fig. 9.13). Each mixing algorithm is chosen by its own menu item. This is an undesirable expedient to help experimentation with the algorithms. It imposes on the artist an additional analytic decision: ‘What kind of marriage do I want?’ (fig. 9.13).

There is no theoretical reason to limit *Mutator* marriages to two parents. A five-parent marriage is possible for example. We have experimented with multi-parent marriages which look like being a very powerful tool.

As mentioned above, *Mutator* automatically rescales objects to a standard size. Not only

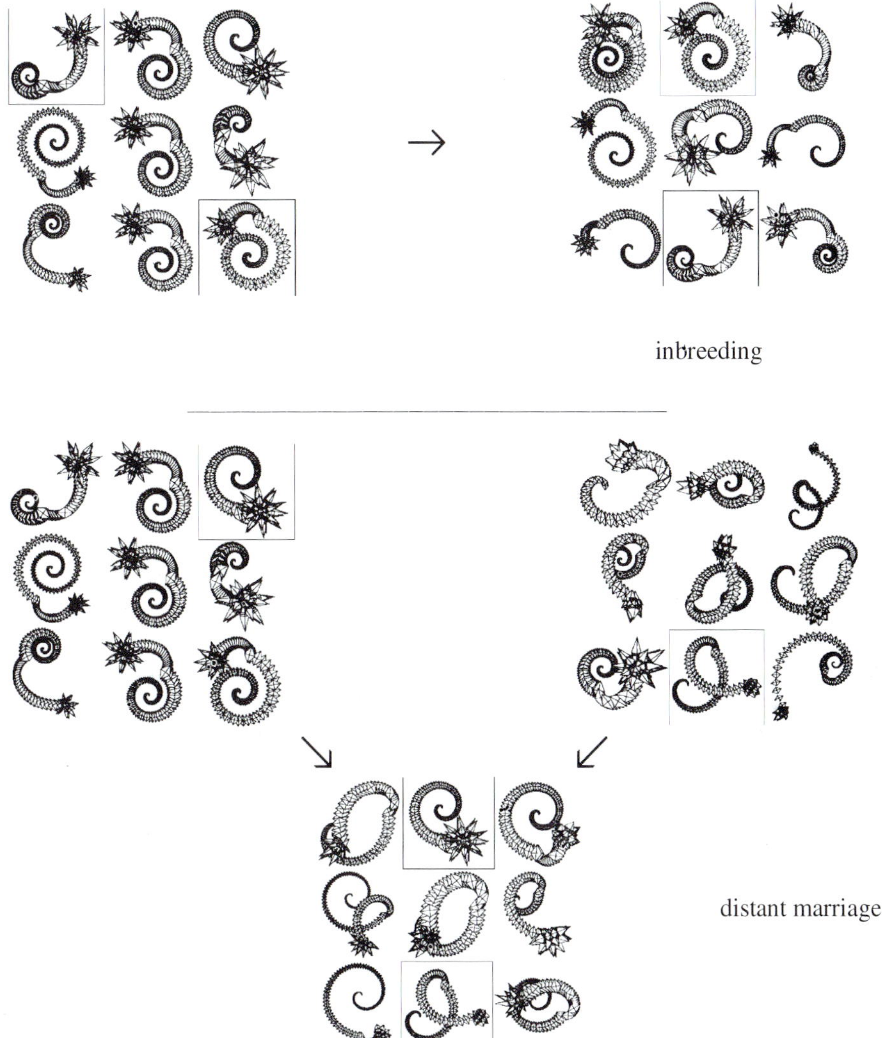

Figure 9.12 Random inbreeding and distant marriage. At the top we see the results of inbreeding. Two similar parent forms are taken from the same *Mutator* frame (left) resulting in a frame (right) of similar inbred forms. Inbreeding is used for fine tuning forms. At the bottom we see the results of marriage of distant cousins, drawn from two different *Mutator* frames (above). The result (below) is a much more varied frame of forms, useful for fast but controlled exploration of form space. Both examples use random gene selection for breeding offspring. The parents are displayed at the top and bottom of the breeding frame and are both highlighted by boxes.

spliced
weighted average

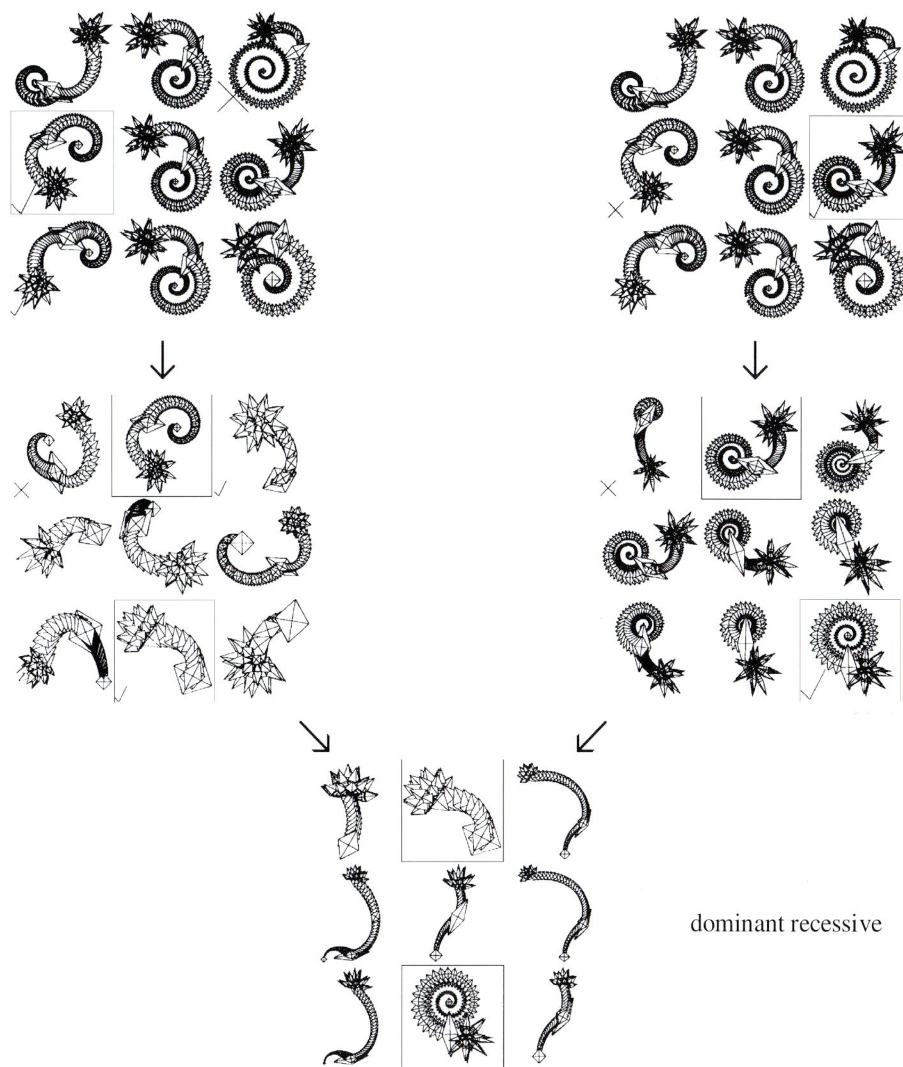

Figure 9.13 Spliced (left above), weighted average (left below) and dominant recessive (right) marriage. The spliced and weighted average marriages give the frames of the two parents (above) and the breeding frame (below). The dominant recessive breeding rule depends on the judgements used in creating the parent forms. The diagram shows two generations above the marriage with an indication (tick=good, cross=bad) of the judgements made. The 180 degree mace form has been very favourably judged in deriving the parent on the left. Its genes have therefore become dominant, and all the offspring include a similar mace form. No strong judgements have been made in deriving the left parent, and so it does not impose any dominant characteristics on the children. In all three examples the parents are located in the top centre and bottom centre of the lower boxes.

can whales and insects easily coexist under these circumstances, they can breed and produce offspring as easily as two forms that would naturally be of the same size.

9.6.1 Random Selection Marriage

Random selection generates children by setting each vector slot from the corresponding slot of one of the parents' vectors. The choice of parent is made randomly for each vector slot. Thus vectors (1,1,1) and (2,2,2) might create children (1,2,1), (1,2,2) and so on (Figure 9.14).

9.6.2 Weighted Average Marriage

In-betweening takes a weighted average of the two parent vectors. Vectors (1,1,1) and (2,2,2) might create children (1.3,1.3,1.3) and (1.6,1.6,1.6). Random weighted average works slot by slot, using a different weight in each slot. Thus vectors (1,1,1) and (2,2,2) might create children (1.3,1.7,1.4) and (1.5,1.2,1.9).

Experience shows that averages are not usually good at producing radically different forms, but very useful for fine tuning (fig. 9.15).

9.6.3 Grouping of Genes

The genes for a structure are often naturally grouped. For example: when a form consists of many subforms it is reasonable to group the genes of each subform. Grouped gene child generation uses the same random number (for selection or weighting) for all slots in a group.

One grouping *Mutator* supports is splicing, which relies on the ordering of the genes. The first n genes are chosen from one parent, and the remainder from the other. Thus vectors (1,1,1,1,1) and (2,2,2,2,2) might create children (1,1,1,2,2), (2,1,1,1,1) and (1,1,2,2,2).

Splicing has the opposite effect to unbiased random selection. It extracts more information rather than less from the precise way in which the structure is written. The children created derive more obviously recognisable features from their parents.

9.6.4 Dominant and Recessive Genes

The *Mutator* algorithm picks up the strongest characteristics of each parent. It uses the direction of travel when a form is generated to highlight slot values with which the artist is not fully

(11,22,13)	(11,12,13)	(11,22,23)
(11,12,23)	(11,12,13)	(21,22,13)
(21,12,23)	(21,22,23)	(21,12,23)

Figure 9.14 Arrangement of child forms. When the new frame of forms is displayed, one parent is displayed top centre and the other parent bottom centre. These have genes (11,12,13) and (21,22,23) in the example. Other children are arranged in opposite pairs, so if a gene is chosen from one parent by one child, it is chosen from the other parent in the opposite child. Random selection is biased towards the axis of the form space imposed by the genes in the structure. This bias is removed by unbiased random selection, which performs random selection in a rotated gene space. It places child vectors on the hypersphere that passes through the two parents, and has its centre halfway between them. Thus parents (−0.7,−0.7,0) and (0.7,0,0.7) can produce children (0,1,0) and (0,−0.5,0.866).

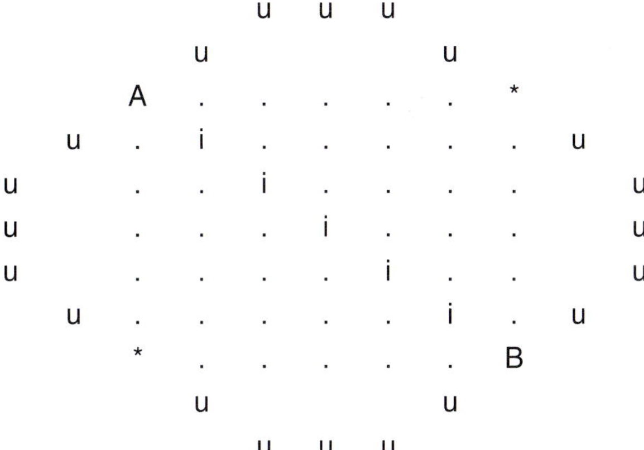

Figure 9.15 Form space accessed by different kinds of marriage. The figure shows a fragment of two dimensional gene space, and points that may be reached from parents *A* and *B* by random selection (*), by unbiased random selection (u), random weighted average (.) and in-betweening (i).

satisfied. A fast moving gene is assumed to be a gene with which the artist is not happy and so is still experimenting, and so the gene is made *recessive* with a reduced chance of selection. Conversely, a slow moving value is taken to be dominant.

The formula used is shown below. The idea is powerful, but the details of the formula may require some improvement.

```
d1:= abs (vvdir1[i]);            // rate of movement of i'th gene for mother
d2:= abs(vvdir2[i]);             // rate of movement of i'th gene for father
if (d1+d2) < 0.01
  break := 0.5;                  // if both are slow moving, split 50:50
else
  break := d1/(d1+d2);           // break is high if mother gene recessive
if random(0,1) < break then      // compare with a random number
  choice := 2;
else
  choice := 1;
```

For example, suppose the ith gene is moving fast in the mother (recessive), and slowly in the father (dominant). Then *d1* is greater than *d2*, and so break is greater than 0.5. The *if* clause is likely to be true, and so *choice* is likely to be set to 2, giving the dominant father gene value.

9.7 Evolutionary Tree

As the mutation session continues it creates an evolutionary history of the genes and forms in its bank which the layout component displays in various ways controlled by its associated sub-menu. Menu item **up** moves to past frames. If **breed** is selected against a frame that already has mutated subframes, the session forms a tree. The artist may navigate the tree with menu items **up**, **down**, **left** and **right**.

Mutator normally shows just one frame. Menu item **tree** displays the entire tree, and **single** reverts to single frame display. *Mutator* normally shows all forms in each frame. Menu item **see1** displays just the initial form for each frame, and **see9** reverts to display of all forms in each frame.

The artist may **jump** to any form in the bank either by pointing with the mouse if the form is in the current display, or by entering the gene bank code, which consists of frame number and mutation number. *Jump* helps the artist to move to other forms anywhere in the tree and to prepare marriages between distantly related forms. When arranging a marriage between distant cousins, the artist jumps around the tree searching for a suitable mate.

Tree display may be simplified by a (temporary) **hide** of the current subtree, or a (permanent) **delete** which is like a lumber jack removing a branch of a tree for ever. As trees get large, tree display becomes more important, so we have options to control the number of generations displayed above and below the current frame (fig. 9.16).

9.8 Saving

The results of *Mutator* may be saved in various ways. The entire session is always logged, and may be restarted later. The current display may be saved as a WINSOM model file at any time for high quality batch rendering, whether display mode is **single** or **tree**, and **see1** or **see9**. Genes for a favoured form or the entire bank may be dumped into a named gene file for later use as key forms in an animation. Naming conventions prevent the application of a gene vector to an inappropriate structure.

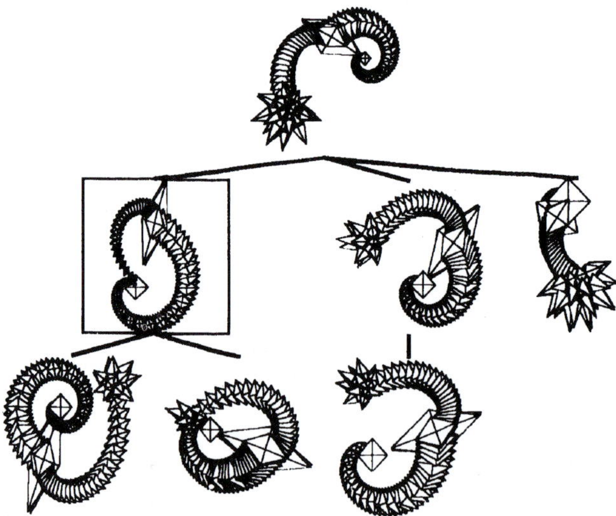

Figure 9.16 Extract from an evolutionary tree. The tree has become too large to display clearly, so the artist has restricted the display to include only frames between one level above and one level below the current frame. Cousin frames are not displayed.

There is potential to use artificial intelligence techniques such as neural networks to classify the gene vectors in named gene files. This would try to capture the nature of *gothicness* from the gene file *gothic*. Similar work has already been done, but this sets itself the even more difficult task of analysis at the image level. Work by Voss[3] on the fractal dimension of images may well be a suitable tool for analysis.

9.9 Nature, Mutator and Optimisation

Mutator was designed to help artists explore form space by means of subjective decisions. The marriage algorithm and other enhancements were suggested as simulations of nature, and implemented to reduce the number of steps needed to find a required form. In nature, new forms of life are created by mutation and marriage. The fittest survive in a process of natural selection. In *Mutator*, the computer generates new forms, and the artist's judgements drive selection. Steering is one of the features that makes *Mutator* effective at searching form space quickly. Steering was implemented to meet the artist's wish to be able to make judgements on forms independently of breeding from them, and was not derived from a biological analogue. However, recent papers in biology suggest that real life mutation is quicker than would be expected for a purely random system, and that there is some mechanism other than natural selection steering intelligent mutation.

Another view of *Mutator* is as an optimisation system. Both *Mutator* and optimisation systems use the computer to generate alternative solutions, but the cost function in optimisation is replaced by the artist's choice in *Mutator*. The basic random mutation algorithm corresponds to Monte Carlo optimisation (Metropolis et al., 1953). The reduction of mutation rate as interaction continues is like the lowering of temperature in simulated annealing (Kirkpatrick et al., 1983). Making judgements of forms to define a steering direction in form space is analogous to steepest ascent optimisation (Dixon and Szego, 1978), and *Mutator* marriage corresponds to genetic optimisation. The problems *Mutator* encounters in irregular parts of gene space are like the instabilities found when optimising badly behaved functions.

These analogies are not precise, and *Mutator* has not capitalised on them. Features of *Mutator* such as steering, inbreeding and the control of mutation rate already permit *Mutator* to be used artistically for honing in on a form. Future work will apply optimisation techniques to Mutator, with the aim of improving its speed, accuracy and stability.

9.10 Further examples

Examples of *Mutator* being used on other aspects of artistic design are shown in: colour (Plates 4 and 5), texture (fig. 9.17) and mathematical equations (fig. 9.18).

9.11 Structure Mutation

Mutator as described so far only changes genes and not the underlying structure. Many of the principles also apply to structure mutation (fig. 9.19), in particular the method of random mutation.

---

[3] private communication

Figure 9.17 Mutation of texture. Various parameters of the texture such as the thickness and brightness of each band have been used as the genes of the structure.

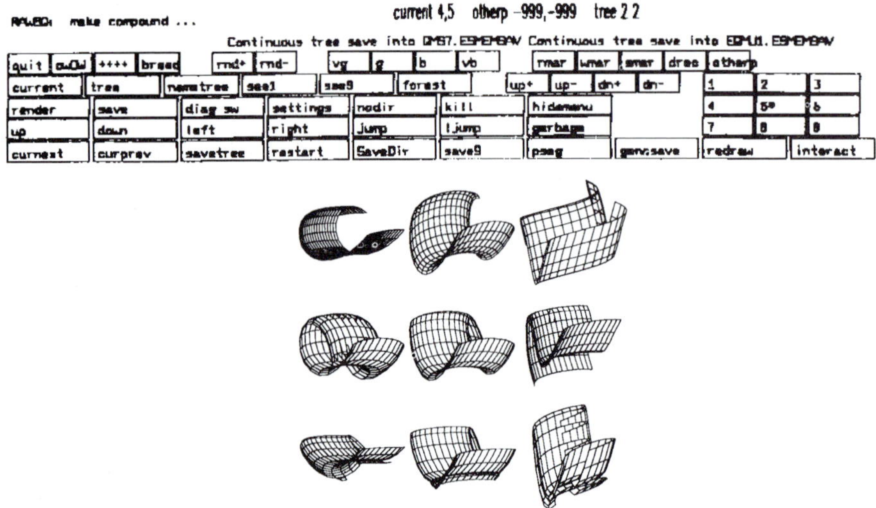

Figure 9.18 Mutation of mathematical equations. The equations are generated by interacting sine and cosine waves, with the genes controlling the 'constants' of the equations.

9.11.1 Steering with Mutated Structures

Many of the more sophisticated aspects of *Mutator* are an important part of the fine control in its artistic use and are more difficult to define with structure mutation. For example, steering requires not only the mutation of gene values at a given instant in time, but also the comparison of different sets of gene values. Structure mutation changes the position of genes, in the example the 'grow' gene moves from position 5 to position 6. It is thus no longer adequate to keep a simple vector of genes, but the genes must be flagged by some position independent identifier (fig. 9.20).

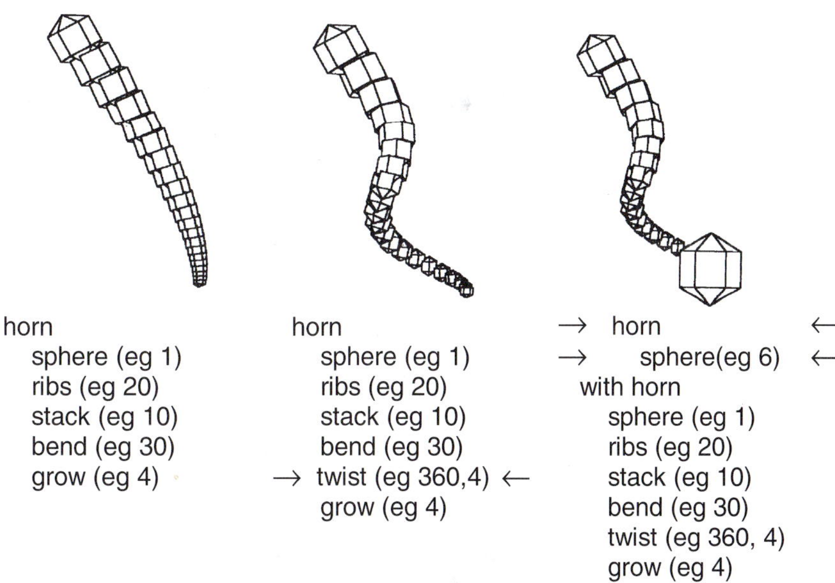

Figure 9.19 Structure mutation. The left hand structure is mutated to the middle one by adding an extra transform rule, and this is mutated to the the right-hand one by the addition of an extra horn segment. Mutation can also shorten structures or interchange elements. In this example the genes are frozen, but it is possible simultaneously to mutate structure and genes.

horn	horn	→ horn
sphere (eg r = 1)	sphere (eg r = 1)	→ sphere(eg rx = 6)
ribs (eg n = 20)	ribs (eg n = 20)	with horn
stack (eg st = 10)	stack (eg st = 10)	sphere (eg r = 1)
bend (eg be = 30)	bend (eg be = 30)	ribs (eg n = 20)
	→ twist (eg tw = 360,4)	stack (eg st = 10)
grow (eg gr = 4)	grow (eg gr = 4)	bend (eg be = 30)
		twist (eg tw = 360, 4)
		grow (eg gr = 4)

Figure 9.20 This indicates how genes are tagged. In practice the tag names are being applied automatically by *Mutator* and do *not* impose an extra burden on the structure designer.

9.11.2 Marriage and Structure Matching

Similarly, if breeding two forms with different structures is to have controlled results, the newly bred structure must preserve as much as possible of the parent structures. This requires an algorithm rather like a file compare algorithm to find a best match of the parent structures. Where both parents are descended from some common ancestor and flagged genes are used, then the flags that are common between the parents help guide the structure matching algorithm (fig. 9.21).

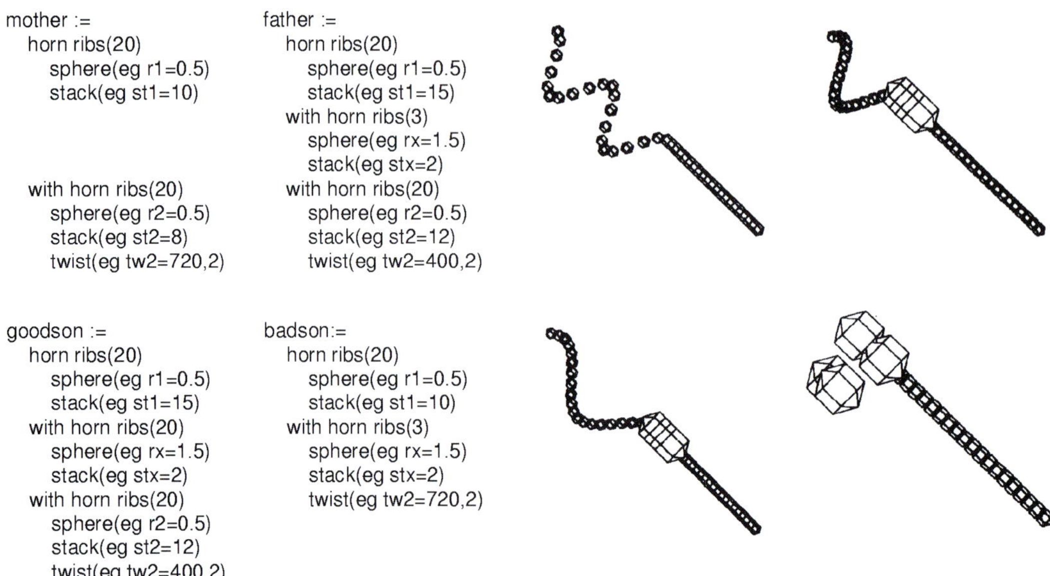

Figure 9.21 Structure matching and marriage. The father and mother are both derived from the same structure, and so share tags *r1*, *st1*, *r2* and *st2*. The goodson structure respects these tags, and produces a controlled result. The badson structure mixes the structures to give a structure not sensibly related to the parents with corrupt mixture of the stubby middle segment and long end segment. In this simple example the structures for both children are the same as the structure for one of the parents. This is not generally true when more complex structures are merged in marriage.

9.11.3 Simulated Structure Mutation

Structure mutation can be simulated by designing a complex structure and using conditional structure programming (Todd and Latham, 1992) to make some gene values switch different substructures on and off. The genes for the substructures are always there in a fixed position in the gene vector, but are not always used (fig. 9.22).

Sims has implemented a system that uses the ideas of Biomorph and *Mutator* and permits structure mutation, and has applied it to a wide variety of computer graphics techniques with very interesting results (Sims, 1991). However, his system does not allow for steering, and the structure matching algorithm used in marriage can give rather wild results, and so we do not consider that this implementation yet gives enough control for artistic applications.

9.12 Grouped genes

The artist usually uses *Mutator* to change all aspects of a sculpture simultaneously. He may identify certain aspects of a sculpture to work on at a given time, for example first the basic body shape of the lobster, then the ribcage, and then the head. Work on the ribcage and head may lead the artist back to consider further tuning of the basic body shape, and so on.

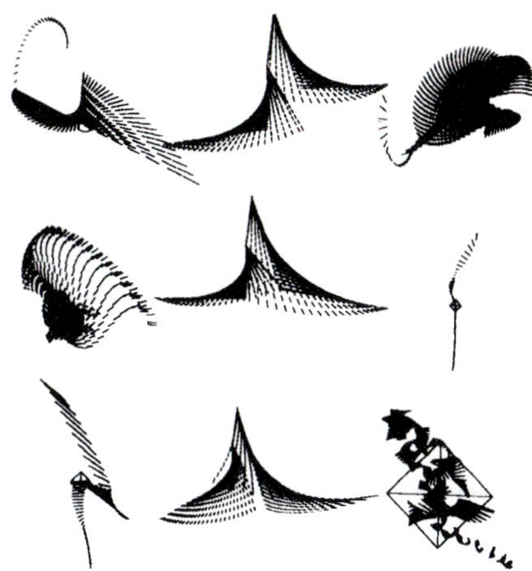

Figure 9.22 A *Mutator* frame in which the structure as well as the genes have been mutated.

9.12.1 Frozen Genes

The identification of the different parts of the structure is done by naming groups of genes in the structure file. Sometimes we identify a substructure because we are happy with it, and we wish mutation to continue on the remaining genes with the genes of the identified substructure frozen. Alternatively, we identify a substructure because it is poor, and so mutate genes in the identified group only and freeze the remaining genes.

9.12.2 Grafting

Form Grow automatically groups genes by horn segment, with a segment identified by pointing at it with the mouse. This is also useful for highly controlled marriages (fig. 9.23) and for

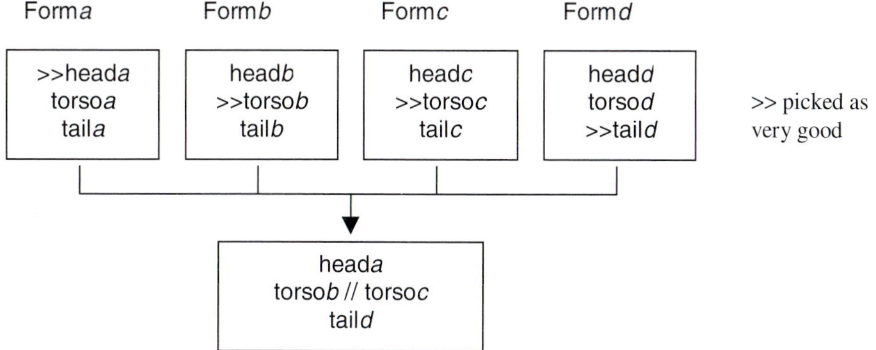

Figure 9.23 Highly controlled marriage. There are four computer forms visible: form*a*, form*b*, form*c* and form*d*, each with the same head, torso and tail structure. The artist points in turn at head*a*, torso*b*, torso*c* and tail*d*, indicating that they are good features. The result of the marriage produces forms which all have the head of form*a* and the tail of form*d*. The torsos are made by marrying the genes of torso*b* and torso*c*.

interactively constructing new structures from fragments of old ones. The artist gardener can now use new splicing tools in his exploration and exploitation of form space. This artistic gene splicing is like a real gardener grafting the stem of a decorative rose onto strong root stock, though with *Mutator* there are no problems with further breeding from the hybrid.

Grafting and the use of a mouse for substructure selection also helps an artist to assemble new structures in a very direct and graphical manner. This is an example of the mixing of subjective mutation with analytic working.

9.13 Ideas for Future Work

9.13.1 Continuous Evolution

The current version of *Mutator* works very much in two phases. In the first phase, the computer creates and displays the mutations for a new frame, and the artist waits. In the second, the artist interacts with the frame, and the computer is more or less idle. This is no problem for simple forms, for which a new frame is created and displayed very quickly. Where each form contains several thousand primitives the artist must wait many seconds for the display of a complete frame which reduces the benefits of *Mutator*.

An alternative is for the computer continuously to prepare new forms, some by mutation and some as children of a marriage. New forms are displayed as they complete. Old forms are allowed to age and die. Mutation continues even without interaction, but interaction directs the exploration as with the implemented system. Such a system should improve the friendliness of *Mutator*, and also its 'natural' feel as an independent evolution of forms from which the user selects. It will also increase its impact as an artwork that could be shown continuously in a gallery being used by the artist.

The continuous version of *Mutator* will not place forms into nine regular boxes, but place them more or less at random on the screen or in three dimensional space (fig. 9.24). Old forms will move to the back, with new ones being created at the front. Alternatively, forms may be laid out according to their position in gene space, with a continuously tumbling multidimensional viewing transform.

9.13.2 SAFARI and virtual reality

In the world of artificial reality the process of interaction becomes more like hunting than gardening. We are combining the natural representation of evolution depicted in our animations with the interactive selection processes of *Mutator* in a system called *SAFARI* (Selection of Artistic Forms with an Artificial Reality Interface). We need considerably more computer power before *SAFARI* becomes effective. *SAFARI* is a virtual reality system in which the artist hunts in the artificial sculpture garden.

artist = hunter

The rifle fires many kinds of shot that correspond to the items on the *Mutator* menu: bullets to inject mutation causing drugs, deadly poison, love potions and so on.

A destructive user hunts to kill, but an artist uses *SAFARI* to hunt for exciting new forms of life and control an evolving population of sculptures in an accelerated evolution environ-

Figure 9.24 The forms layed out in a continuous *Mutator* session much as they would be in an animation such as the film '*Mutations*'.

ment. Another possibility is to let several hunters loose at once, each with a different idea of what the hunt is about and to include predators which automatically kill forms under certain circumstances, such as when the screen is too full or the horns are too complex.

9.13.3 Autonomous mutation

One of the purposes of artistic systems is to allow the artist to express general ideas and to have the computer undertake much of the hard work. Autonomous mutation operates by the artist initially identifying features such as surface area, and the computer measures these features and performs selections based on them, for example 'select forms with the largest surface area'. In real life, lung shapes evolve to maximise surface area and so improve breathing ability and survival, and the results have very interesting and sometimes artistic shapes. We will experiment to see whether the simulation of these evolution processes on the computer will help the artist to derive new and interesting forms.

From the computer science point of view, autonomous mutation replaces *Mutator* with a standard system to optimise a stated function. The interesting task is to combine autonomous mutation with artist-controlled mutation. For example, a jeweller wishes to use as little silver as possible but not at the expense of the artistic design. The system may highlight forms that are most economical, but leave the artistic decision to the jeweller.

9.14 A PC-based *Mutator* system

A major addition since we wrote our book *Evolutionary Art and Computers* is a PC-based *Mutator* system. This has a much simplified and more attractive interface than our original system, see fig. 9.25. It has been successfully used by 5 year olds in a public exhibition in the Royal Festival Hall; we think it could even be used by managers and professors.

The basic user option in *PC Mutator* is the selection of 'good' items. The user identifies a good object by dropping the butterfly tool onto it; multiple clicks for very good objects. Alternatively, the user can drag favoured items to the top of the *Mutator* window. The user then asks the computer to breed the next generation from the good objects using the babies tool.

PC Mutator gives the user no control over the details of the mutation. It automatically uses a hybrid of mutation, steering and various marriage types. It automatically adjusts the proportion of different mechanisms according to those that give results chosen by the user. The only user control is a slider for mutation rate. This interface simplification permits the user to concentrate on the real task; judgement of the best objects. In technical jargon, the interface minimizes cognitive overload.

PC Mutator permits the use of independent mutation in multiple windows. The user can breed for different desired attributes in different windows, and then cross breed by dragging and dropping objects between the windows. A genetic engineering window shows a table of genes for different objects from which the user creates new objects by gene splicing. A freezer window allows the user to freeze the values of selected genes.

PC Mutator includes key-frame animation. Key-frame objects are dropped onto the animation window. The genes of the key objects are used in a splining algorithm to generate genes and thus pictures for the inbetween frames.

A different way to mix new objects is to drop selected objects into position on the Rover window. This implements a kind of two dimensional animation space. As the user moves the mouse or joystick over the window, Rover interpolates between neighbouring objects. Rover

Figure 9.25 PC-based *Mutator*.

was suggested to us by Luc at CIRM in Nice for use with music applications. It is used for underwater concerts, with the mouse replaced by a swimmer detection device.

9.15 Mutator Applications

The most important aspect of the *PC Mutator* system is its ability to talk to any generation system by DDE or OLE. This allows us easily to experiment with *Mutator* in a variety of applications. We have tried many visual applications such as cartoon faces (programmed by Ralph Bruno), fount design, architecture and page layout, using programs such as CorelDraw, Freelance Graphics and Painter. The use of *Mutator* for less naturally visual applications is even more interesting. The rest of this section describes what makes for a suitable *Mutator* application, and describes examples in games, financial planning and music.

9.15.1 What Makes a Good Application for Mutator?

A good *Mutator* application must satisfy four requirements:

- Someone must be able to define a parameterised model. The model definer will not usually be the end user.
- The model must have an output that the end user can judge subjectively. This is typically in the form of a picture or graph, but sound, smell, touch or taste are all possible.
- It should not take too long to run the model and for the user to judge the output. How long is acceptable depends on the user's patience. William often waited overnight for each Mutation step with *Form Grow*, but this would not be acceptable for most applications.
- There should not be an easily defined formal objective. If there is, this objective can be programmed in to the computer together with the model, and standard (possibly genetic) optimisation techniques used. There are cases where a hybrid of user and machine-defined objectives can reach a result more flexibly than pure optimization, and more quickly than pure subjective mutation.

9.15.2 Computer Artworks

William Latham's art, generated by *Mutator*, is known throughout the art and computer worlds, and has been featured in numerous newspapers, magazines and TV programmes. More recently, growing dissatisfied with the 'high art' and 'research world', William started to think about how to embody the ideas, technology and art in a popular form for the mass market. PCs were getting faster and 3D games and entertainment software seemed the way forward. In 1993 he met Mark Atkinson and together they founded *Computer Artworks Ltd.*

Computer Artworks has taken ideas developed for *Mutator*, and has developed commercially successful products in a number of areas, including: computer games, computer screen savers, CD album covers, clothing patterns, and cinema special effects.

One of the most successful products to date has been *Organic Art*, the 3D screen-saver which has similar functionality to *Mutator* and *Form Grow*. *Organic Art* contains over 100 3D screen saver scenes that generate in real time, continually creating new mutations for the user to discover. *Organic Art* is also fully interactive, letting the user design virtual scenes with its Evolutionary Generator. There are over 400 million combinations to explore!

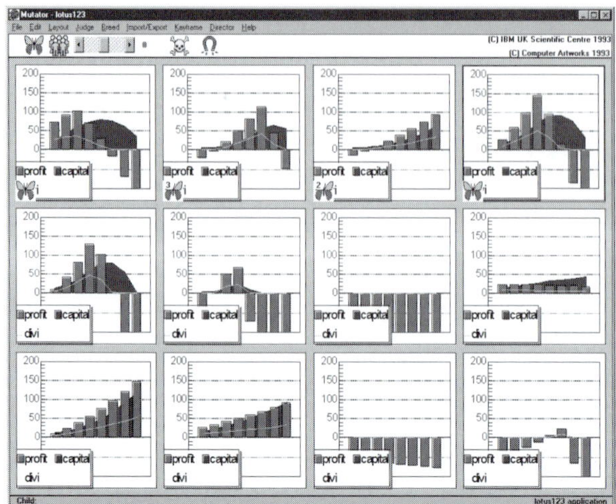

Figure 9.26 Predicted profits of a simulated company.

9.15.3 Financial Planning

Financial planning is the application of *Mutator* most removed from its original artistic use. The model for financial planning is typically a prediction model. What if I change my stock portfolio? Will the likely yield and capital gain go up or down? What are the risks involved?

Figure 9.26 shows results from a model of a company. The model is implemented in Lotus123, with input genes for parameters such as investment in production, price charged for goods, and amount spent on advertising. The model predicts likely market share and sales, other costs, and thus predicted profit. The output graph shows this predicted profit over the next few quarters; in a real application it would also show many other output factors.

It is easy for an experienced user to judge the desirability of different outputs; and thus the merit of the strategies they represent. However, the output is not suitable for pure optimisation as it depends on a balance of items. Even with just the single profit line there is the balance between short-term profit and longer-term growth; with added imponderables such as the user's view of the accuracy of the model, particularly the long-term predictions.

In cases with a very clear objective function optimisation is excellent. In less precise areas the commonest result of an optimisation run is that the user discovers why the formal objective function was inappropriate. *Mutator* provides continuous feedback to the user, who reconsiders informal objectives as a result of the session. It permits what formal methods often discourage: gut feel and common sense. Often, the major benefit of the session is not the final mutation result, but the greater understanding by the user of the model and its implications.

Syd Chapman, a colleague at IBM, likes the collaborative aspects of *Mutator*. People using it together (maybe a research director and a financial director) have different objectives. *Mutator* shows scenarios where different users choose different results. Cross breeding may help them find a result acceptable to both. More important, the concrete scenarios help users discuss their differences, to understand and maybe even reconcile their different implicit objectives.

9.15.4 Music

We have made several experiments in music mutation, especially in collaboration with Michel Redolfi at CIRM in Nice. Models for music operate at several levels, from the tone, through the texture of note patterns to larger scale tune construction. Mutation is most successful at the lower levels; at higher levels it is too slow to sample and compare different mutations.

We have tried two versions of sound modelling. In one, the genes are synthesiser parameters such as attack rate, decay rate and harmonic mix. Where we have access only to MIDI parameters the sound is made by mixing different instruments; each note played causes several MIDI notes to fire on different channels. The genes control the relative volume of each instrument, slight variations in start time and end time, and possibly detuning of some instruments. Sound modelling gave immediately interesting results with surprising variation. This application suggested the Rover window mentioned earlier.

Musical textures can be made by algorithmic generation of notes. Several lines of music intertwine. Genes for each line control features such as the average length of notes, the gaps between them, the pitch range, and the pitch difference between adjacent notes. Global genes control the degree of rhythm and pitch synchronisation between the lines.

Musical mutation requires significant changes to the user interface, as alternatives must be heard and compared sequentially. We have tried various techniques. Some adjust the details of the *Mutator* interface for the non-visual and sequential aspect of music mutation.

A greater variation eliminates the visual aspects of mutation. A set of keys is allocated to *Mutator* control, for example the bottom octave of the music keyboard. *Mutator* selects the current object; the user plays (if appropriate), listens and makes a judgement pressing a *Mutator* control key. *Mutator* then selects another object; sometimes a newly generated mutation and sometimes an older one. Revisiting older mutations permits the user to re-evaluate them relative to more recent ones; if mutation is working well a mutation that was good when it was first created is poor when compared to later improved ones. This variation of the interface lets a music user really concentrate on the sound. It is appropriate even for blind users; a radical change from the original interface for visual forms.

9.15.5 Practical Limitations

We have found two major limitations to the application of *Mutator*. The first is the practical problem of programming interaction between *Mutator* and other applications. This has improved over the last few years as more applications such as CorelDraw acquire scripting interfaces with almost the full power available to the interactive user.

The more fundamental limitation is the difficulty of building models. Most graphical users are trained to create finished results, not parameterised models. Even in financial areas we have found model building is much less common than we anticipated. This is partly due to the inherent difficulty in any model building. It is also due to the limitations of tools for using imprecise models. If you cannot build a precise model, and have no use for an imprecise one, why build a model at all?

9.16 Conclusion

Mutator is a general-purpose interface that assists exploration of multidimensional gene spaces. It relies on the definition of a structure which produces a form or other visible result for any position in gene space. The structure is defined using conventional programming, though *Mutator* is beginning to help here too.

Mutator is driven by subjective user choices such as **good** and **bad**. Different *Mutator* algorithms support random exploration of space, directed steering, and generation of hybrid children of a marriage.

Mutator derives its methods from processes of nature, and was partly inspired by a simulation of natural selection. These methods are related to Monte Carlo, simulated annealing and genetic optimisation techniques.

Use of *Mutator* for the design of forms and animations has already produced very promising results. Some artists feel that it provides a genuinely a new way of working, and it has certainly led to the creation of forms that would not have been created by other methods (Plates 4 and 5).

References

Dawkins, R. (1986). *The Blind Watchmaker*. Longman Scientific and Technical, Harlow.

Dixon L. C. W. and Szego, G. P. (eds) (1978). *Towards Global Optimization 2*. North Holland, New York, 1–18.

Kirkpatrick, S., Gelatt Jr, C. D. and Vecchi, M. P. (1983). 'Optimization by Simulated Annealing', *Science*, **220**(4598); 671–679.

Latham, W. (1989). 'FormSynth: The Rule-based Evolution of Complex Forms from Geometric Primitives', Lansdown, J. and Earnshaw, R. A. (eds), *Computers in Art, Design and Animation*. Springer-Verlag, Berlin.

Metropolis, N., Rosenbluth, A. W., Teller A. H. and Teller, E. (1953). 'Equations of State Calculations by Fast Computing Machines', *Journal of Chemical Physics* **21**(6); 1087–1089.

Sims, K. (1991). 'Artificial Evolution for Computer Graphics', *ACM Siggraph Conference Proceedings, Computer Graphics*, **25**(4); 319–328.

Todd, S. and Latham, W. (1992). *Evolutionary Art and Computers*. Academic Press, London.

Chapter 10

Evolving Genetic Art

By Michael Witbrock and Scott Neil-Reilly

10.1 Introduction

The basic purpose of a genetic algorithm (GA) is to search efficiently through a large space of possible solutions in an attempt to maximize a complex function. While this function can be a reasonably straightforward mathematical formulation, one of the advantages of using GAs is that this need not necessarily be the case. In biological evolution, the 'fitness function' is based on the ability of a given organism to survive and reproduce in a given environment. Similarly, with GAs the fitness function can be a characteristic of the environment and does not have to be expressible mathematically. In 1991, Karl Sims (Sims, 1991) showed that genetic algorithms can also use fitness functions, based on the subjective aesthetic of a human, to produce complex and beautiful images.

In this chapter we look in depth at the idea of using genetic algorithms to create artistic images (or, at least, 'pretty pictures'). We start with a brief look at some related work. We then give a concrete description of a simple system that can run on almost any computer. We conclude with a discussion of a number of variations that can be made on this simple system, including some of the features that Karl Sims used to produce his spectacular images.

10.2 Background

As can be seen elsewhere in this book, there is a good deal of work in the area of genetically evolved art. Two examples are the continued work of Sims in the domain of evolving agents and their behaviours, and the work of Latham and Todd in creating genetically evolved 3D sculptures (in addition to the chapters in this book, see also Sims (1994) and Todd and Latham (1992)).

Dawkins (1987) first described a computer program to genetically evolve visually interesting 'bug-like' structures. Though the work was not artistic in intent, it still served as the inspiration for most of the work described in this chapter.

The work of Baluja *et al.* (1993) attempted to automate the role of the human in the types of systems described here. They built a neural network that learns the preferences of the user by 'watching' the user choose from sets of images. This network can then stand in for the human and work with the genetic program to produce the kinds of images that the human might like. The systems Baluja *et al.* have built in this fashion tend to have fairly high error rates when guessing human ratings, which is not particularly surprising given the difficulty of

EVOLUTIONARY DESIGN BY COMPUTERS
ISBN 1-55860-605-X

the task of learning to emulate human aesthetic judgements. Nevertheless, the systems have produced a number of very complex and interesting images.

Baker and Seltzer (1993) created two systems that use genetic techniques to produce and modify line drawings. The genotypes in these systems encode information about a series of line segments, including the co-ordinates of the endpoints and whether the segments are connected to other segments. A drawing program created using this technique allows users to interactively generate interesting line drawings. They have also used this technique to allow users to interactively modify line drawings of human faces and used this system to produce a suspect sketch system for police. While they have not yet reported much success with being able to control the system well enough to create a desired face, they do point to the intriguing possibility of practical applications for genetically generated images.

10.3 Description of IIGA1

In this section, we describe a genetic art system called *International Interactive Genetic Art I* (IIGA1), which has been running on the web, on and off, for 4 years. This system was inspired by the work of Sims (1991) and Baluja *et al.* (1993). The system can currently be found at http://www.geneticart.org/.

10.3.1 Genetic Programming Primitives

Karl Sims's proposal for creating genetic images was to use genetic programming techniques rather than straight genetic algorithms. In other words, instead of trying to map strings of bits directly into pixel colours and locations, he genetically generated functions that mapped X and Y coordinates into pixel colours. We took a similar approach, though we used a reduced set of functions as genetic material. The set of primitives used by IIGA1 is given in Table 10.1. For each function, x and y are the coordinates of a pixel and the value of the function, evaluated at (x,y), is used to determine the colour of the pixel, as described below.

Table 10.1 The operators used by International Genetic Art 1. These functions were combined, using a genetic algorithm, into expressions determining the pixel values in images.

Monadic		Diadic		
($\log_{10}$ x)	(sqrt x)	(rand x y)	(pow x y)	(+ x y)
(sqr x)	(sin x)	(mod x y)	(min x y)	(− x y)
(exp x)	(cos x)	(avg x y)	(max x y)	(* x y)
(/ 1 x)	(ln x)			(/ x y)

10.3.2 Placing the Origin and Labelling the Coordinates

The centre of the image is set as the origin and the edges of the image are described as being 1 unit away. The pixels, then, all have x and y coordinates ranging from -1 to 1. Another approach would have been to use integer coordinates for pixels, so a 1000×1000 pixel image would have x and y coordinates ranging from -500 to 500. The former approach has the advantage that the resolution of the image can be changed without changing its content.

Of course, the origin could just as well have been placed at, say, the bottom left of the image, with coordinate values ranging from 0 to 1. This scheme should work just as well as placing the origin at the centre of the image.

10.3.3 Generating the Initial Images

A randomized algorithm was used to create an initial set of nine genetic programs. The particular algorithm is described in fig. 10.1.

This method yielded initial functions like those seen in figs 10.2 and 10.3,[1] which will be used for examples later in this section.

```
function create_random_function_tree (depth)
  returns function_tree

  if depth > 0                                   not at root node
    and random [0; 7-depth] = 0                  and we choose to stop
    return 'x' or 'y' at random                  finish with a leaf symbol
  otherwise                                      elaborate the function
    choose a function, fun, from Table
    foreach argument v of fun
      replace v with create_random_function_tree (depth+1)
    return fun
```

Figure 10.1 This algorithm creates a random initial function. It operates recursively. At each level of recursion, it decides whether to further elaborate the function or stop. If it is at the root, it always elaborates the function. Otherwise, it chooses to use the leaf functions, x or y, with probability that increases with depth. If it reaches depth 7 it always uses a leaf function. To elaborate the function, the algorithm simply replaces each argument of a randomly chosen function with the result of a recursive call to itself.

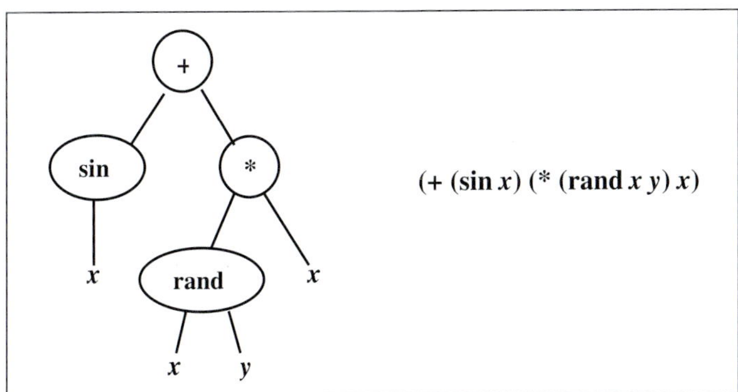

Figure 10.2 Sample function tree 1.

[1] Actually, the initial functions tend to be more complex than these, but these make nice examples. Here is an actual initial function: *(+ (/ 1 (sqr (sqr y))) (ln (sin (* (mod x y) x))))*.

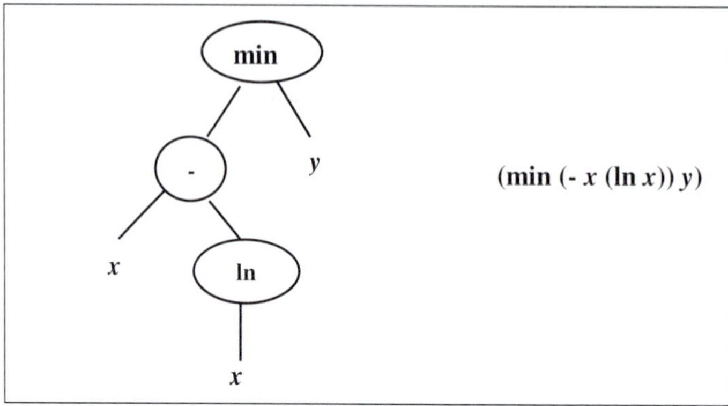

Figure 10.3 Sample function tree 2.

10.3.4 Mapping from Genotype to Phenotype

The formulas represented by function trees were used to map x-y coordinates to a single value corresponding to the colour of the image at that coordinate. There is no single best way to take a scalar and turn it immediately into a screen colour. The basic scheme adopted for IIGA1 was to map various combinations of red, green and blue, defining various colours, on to a line, and to use the colour scalar to index along this line. A number of mappings from colour scalars to RGB values were tried.[2] Each such mapping has a unique feel to it. For instance, one mapping goes smoothly from red to blue to green to blue to red with black at either end. This gives bright primary colours and a sort of 'techno' feel. Another goes around a colour wheel at an approximately constant level of saturation, making more colourful images.

A much better mapping scheme, based on quaternions, was used in the IIGA2 system that John Mount derived from IIGA1. This system is described later in the chapter.

10.3.5 Evaluation Function

The evaluation function determining the fitness of images in the system was composed of the subjective aesthetic preferences of users accessing the system through the web. Each of the nine images in a particular generation was shown and the user provided a rating for each image from 1 to 10. The interface for this process is shown in fig. 10.4. In our web-based system, we collected ratings from ten users before producing a new generation. Once these were available, the users' votes were summed to produce a rating. The final fitness evaluation of an image was the rating of that image, divided by the sum of the ratings of all of the images. That is:

$$eval_i = \frac{r_i}{\sum_{j=1}^{n\ images} r_j}.$$

[2] We used RGB instead of, say HSV, because it was trivial to write out PPM (portable pixmap file format) files which are simply a header followed by RGB values. Using standard Unix utilities (such as ppmquant and ppmtogif) these were then easily converted to other formats, like GIF, which are suitable for displaying on the web. It is likely, though, that a good mapping to an HSV colour space would have produced attractive images.

10.3.6 Procreation

We used two methods for passing the genetic material from one generation to the next. First, the winner of each generation was passed unchanged to the next generation. This meant that the current best image could not be randomly lost from one generation to the next. While one might have hoped that an even better image would always have been generated in the next generation, this often turns out not to be the case, particularly for the very small population sizes that we used.

The second mode of passing down genetic material was sexual reproduction. Each image was assigned $eval_i$ probability of being one of the parents for any particular image in the next generation. Once the first parent was chosen, the system continued to pick images with probability $eval_i$ until a second parent had been chosen that differed from the first.

We could have allowed the parents to be the same, and thus permitted asexual reproduction, but this tended to remove too much variation from the gene pool. We could also have allowed the ratings for images to range from 0 to 9 (or 0 to 10) instead of starting at 1. By starting at 1, we assured that even poorly rated images had some chance of passing their genetic material on to the next generation. This is another way of keeping the gene pool varied and of giving images with interesting genotypes but uninteresting phenotypes the chance to pass on their genes. This is done in the hope that the gene will, at some later point, be expressed in a more interesting manner.

The two important issues related to passing along genetic material from one generation to the next are determining the method for reproduction, and determining the method for mutation. We will look at each of these issues in turn.

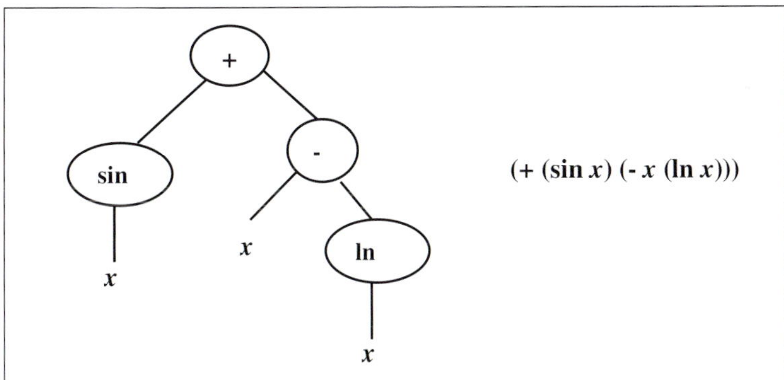

Figure 10.4 Possible result of crossover between Tree 1 and Tree 2.

10.3.7 Crossover

Sexual reproduction in a system where the genes are functions is necessarily going to be somewhat different from reproduction where the genes are strings of bits. In particular, applying the clean idea of crossover becomes a little less straightforward when the genes are trees rather than sequences. There is, however, an approach for handling crossover in function trees that Sims used in his system (Sims, 1991) and that we adopted for IIGA1.

When performing a crossover on two function trees, one subtree from one parent is chosen at random and is used to replace a random subtree from the other parent. For example, if the two functions in figs 10.2 and 10.3 were to mate, the system might randomly choose the subtree rooted at the multiplication, in fig. 10.2, and replace it with the subtree in fig. 10.3 rooted at the subtraction operator. This would produce the child tree shown in fig. 10.4.

The other constraint on this process, in IIGA1, ensures that the subtree to be replaced in the second parent cannot be the full tree. The first parent can be chosen in its entirety to be the replacement tree. This constraint ensures that neither parent provides all of the genetic material for the child.

10.3.8 Mutation

An important part of evolving interesting images is the ability to mutate current images. This allows new genetic material to be added to the pool on a regular basis. It will often provide uninteresting, or even harmful, variation, but it can also provide very interesting variation that would not be possible through crossover alone. In IIGA1, the amount of mutation can be set at will. Too little mutation tends to result in a system that gets bogged down in the production of large numbers of similar images. Too much variation makes it hard to explore interesting variations on appealing images, since they are radically changed by mutation too quickly.

Our approach has been to assign some probability to the case that a child image in a newly generated generation is not the product of the mating of two parents, but the result of random mutation. In this case, the word *mutation* is being used rather loosely as we do not create a minor variation of an existing image, but rather create an entirely new randomly generated image as was described above. It is certainly possible to use a more standard mutation scheme, replacing individual functions with other random functions, with the only complexity being that replacing an n-ary function with an m-ary function (where $n <> m$) would require special handling. Either ensuring that this doesn't happen or providing code to handle the $n > m$ and $m > n$ cases would be reasonable. The only advantages of our approach are that it was simpler to code and that it provides radically different images to the population, which we have found to be a useful feature in practice.

Our system has a population size of nine, so an 11% mutation rate results in roughly one completely new image per generation. This rate seemed to be high enough to provide enough fresh genetic material to keep the population from stagnating, but low enough to provide stability and consistence from generation to generation.

10.3.9 Results

IIGA1 and its derivative systems were very successful, if popularity is used as a criterion for success. We set this system up on the web and received tens of thousand of visits to the site and a great deal of positive feedback, including a mention in *Wired* magazine (Spence, 1995). While detailed access records were not kept for the first implementation (IIGA1), the second version (IIGA2) described below, using quaternions, went through 3853 generations prior to the move to the new 'geneticart.org' web site. This required the generation of 34 677 images, and the submission of 38 530 votes. Since there was an approximately 3:1 visit to vote ratio on the site (Mount, 1998), the web pages of images were viewed around 115 590 times. The genetic movies, also described below, which were considerably more trouble to view, went through 715 generations and received 7150 votes.

The crossover of functions worked surprisingly well, with the children of each generation tending to be closely and visibly related to the parent generation, but different enough to allow users to slowly explore the space of images.

One of the engaging features of the system, for the participant audience, was mutation. We found that the ability of the system to occasionally produce something radically different from what had come before was very important. Without it, the images tended to vary somewhat slowly and cluster around one or two interesting images. Mutation allowed users to stop exploring a particular set of images and to quickly jump to a different part of image space to continue their exploration.

One of the weaknesses of the system was the static and somewhat uninteresting colour mapping that we used. By choosing one mapping from scalar function values to colours, we constrained all of the images to have a similar feel to them. It would have been nice to be able to support a wider range of colour mappings. We would like to extend the system by exploring ways of making the colour map richer or of making it possible to evolve it, as well, over time.

10.4 Variations on the Theme

The system described in the previous section is just a simple place to start; there are numerous variations on the theme that all produce interesting images. In many cases, the amount of computation power required increases, but results may be correspondingly more spectacular.

10.4.1 Other Image Processing Functions

The pictures generated by Sims' system showed considerably more variation than those created by the simple system IIGA1 described here. He accomplished this not so much by having a larger set of functions as genetic material, but by having a set of functions that was better suited to the task of image generation and manipulation. Whereas the list for IIGA1, presented in table 10.1, includes simple mathematical functions, Sims also used noise functions, warping functions, image processing functions such as blur, vector functions, band-pass convolutions, gradient functions, and interactive function systems. The complete list of these functions can be found in Sims (1991).

While adding such functions adds considerable power to the system, it also adds considerable computation demands. Sims was working with a Connection Machine CM-2 parallel supercomputer. For those with less computing power available, simpler functions also create very appealing images in much less time. The ever-increasing power of low priced computers should allow more widespread experimentation with novel and sophisticated image generation operators in the future.

10.4.2 Other Mathematical Functions

The set of functions used as the genetic material of the images obviously has a profound influence on the types of images generated. One way to produce very different kinds of images is to use more complex mathematical functions in addition to, or instead of, the ones listed above.

One example of this approach is the work of Mount and Witbrock who built a web-based system called *International Interactive Genetic Art II* (IIGA2), which is similar to the one described above, but used quaternions as the basic functions. Quaternions are 4-dimensional vectors of real numbers with a particular set of operations defined for them. They were invented by Sir William Rowan Hamilton in the 19th century in the course of his attempt to develop a three-dimensional algebra (Ebbinghaus *et al.*, 1988).[3]

In IIGA2, each point in the image plane was turned into a quaternion and had a number of operations applied to it. These operations are stored as trees and manipulated just as the functions described earlier. The first three values of the resulting 4-valued vector were used as the RGB values for the point. The last value was discarded.

This particular system also included a non-standard quaternion *mod* operation that provided periodic visual effects. Some of the most interesting images from IIGA2 were variations of *mod*(1/*point*), which produces increasing detail towards the origin. The system is now on-line at http://www.geneticart.com/ and sample images from this system are displayed in Plate 6.

10.4.3 Genetic Movies

Another variation on genetic art is the addition of a third dimension, time, to the image coordinate system. By producing functions mapping (x,y,t) triples into to RGB colour descriptions, the system can produce an image at each time t, thus creating simple movies. This idea was first proposed by Sims (1991) and was used by Mount and Witbrock to build the third web-based exhibit in the IIGA series, called *International Interactive Genetic Movies*. This exhibit was built on top of the work with quaternions described in the previous section, using simple, publicly available MPEG encoding tools.

10.4.4 Genetic Image Processing

Anyone who has had the chance to play with software like Adobe's Photoshop knows how much fun it can be to take a picture and apply various image-processing operations to it. As well as using GAs to create images from scratch, Sims (1991) used the same sorts of techniques described in this chapter to control the manipulation of naturally occurring images. Instead of simply having functions take x and y locations as inputs, he created variations that could take input from image pixel values, as well as x and y positions. We would like to explore the same kind of image manipulations in future work.

10.4.5 Distributed Image Generation

Since the era of IIGA1, a great deal has changed about the nature of the web. Perhaps the most important change, at least from a theoretical point of view, results from the development of the Java language and its use in web browser applets. We envision a future interactive genetic art exhibit that, instead of producing a small set of images at the server, and delivering them identically to all visitors within a generation, simply uses the server to store the 'genetic material' for a large population of images. Each new visitor would receive a randomly chosen

[3] Lord Kelvin is also reported as having said that '*Quaternions came from Hamilton after his really good work had been done; and though beautifully ingenious, have been an unmixed evil to those which have touched them in any way.*' Nevertheless, we think they make nice pictures.

set of function trees from the current population, from which images would be rendered by an applet running in their browser. Their aesthetic judgements about these images would be fed back to the population for use in reproduction.

By distributing the computational costs of image generation in this way, larger and more diverse populations could be maintained, and the huge populations of users possible with today's expanded web could be served by a relatively small central site.

10.5 Summary

In this chapter we described the use of genetic algorithms to evolve artistic images (or, at least, 'pretty pictures'). Three internet-based systems were outlined: *International Interactive Genetic Art I, II*, and *International Interactive Genetic Movies*. All three generated considerable interest, with over a hundred thousand visits and tens of thousands of votes being registered, and hundreds of different images being evolved.

Acknowledgements

We would like to thank John Mount for his help explaining his work with quaternions and providing us with code to generate images from his work. We would also like to thank Carnegie Mellon University, for the computing resources on which much of this work was carried out, and for having provided us with the freedom to pursue diversions such as these.

References

Baker, E. and Seltzer, M. (1993). *Evolving Line Drawings*. Technical Report TR-21–93, centre for Research in Computing Technology, Harvard University, Cambridge, MA.

Baluja, S., Pomerleau, D. and Jochem, T. (1993). *Simulating User's Preferences: Towards Automated Artificial Evolution for Computer Generated Images*. Technical Report CMU-CS-93–198, School of Computer Science, Carnegie Mellon University, Pittsburgh, PA. October 1993.

Dawkins, R. (1987). *The Blind Watchmaker*. W. W. Norton and Company, New York.

Ebbinghaus *et al.* (1988). *Numbers*, 2nd edition. Springer-Verlag.

Mount, J. A. (1998). Personal Communication.

Sims, K. (1991). Artificial Evolution for Computer Graphics. *Computer Graphics*, **25**(4); 319–328.

Sims, K. (1994). Evolving 3D Morphology and Behavior by Competition. *Artificial Life IV Proceedings*.

Spence, K, (Ed). (1995). Genetic Exhibitionism, *Wired*, p. 148.

Todd, S. and Latham, W. (1992). *Evolutionary Art and Computers*. Academic Press, London.

Chapter 11

Evolutionary Art and Form

by Andrew Rowbottom

11.1 Introduction

Computers have been used to produce art almost as long as they have had output devices. Evolutionary art – the use of computers to evolve artistic images – is a much more recent development, relying as it does on several physical aspects of computing such as 'real-time' displays as well as developments in computer science such as genetic programming.

There are now a number of evolutionary art (or *evoart*) packages available, most of which use surprisingly similar user interfaces. Typically a grid of cells forms the main front-end of these systems. Each cell within the grid contains a representation of an individual (a two-dimensional image or three-dimensional sculpture) and some of these cells may contain ancestors of the current generation.

Computer generated evolutionary art programs can be divided into the two types: 'mutating' and 'breeding'. In 'mutating' programs all children are derived in incremental steps from a single parent, while 'breeding' programs employ genetic programming techniques coupled with mutation to produce the next generation of individuals. However, most 'breeding' programs can also be used in a 'mutate only' mode.

This chapter presents a review of several of these programs, and then goes on to describe *Form*, a program which evolves and displays three-dimensional forms, inspired by the work of Richard Dawkins and William Latham (Dawkins, 1986; Todd and Latham, 1992).

11.2 Evolutionary Art Programs

11.2.1 Biomorphs

No collection of evolutionary art programs would be complete without this grand daddy of all evoart programs. Although perhaps not strictly evoart, Richard Dawkins' creation of his 'Biomorphs' program and his publication of its output in *The Blind Watchmaker* (Dawkins, 1986) caused many people to rethink the way that computers could be used in art. Dawkins' program provided perhaps the first illustration that computers could be used for creating unique works in the virtual space of the computer screen, see fig. 11.1.

All Biomorph variations can be categorised as 2D mutating 'drawing' programs. The control of the images is based on a fixed number of 'genes' which are used as parameters to produce tree branches of varying numbers and dimensions. Several variations on this program

EVOLUTIONARY DESIGN BY COMPUTERS
ISBN 1-55860-605-X

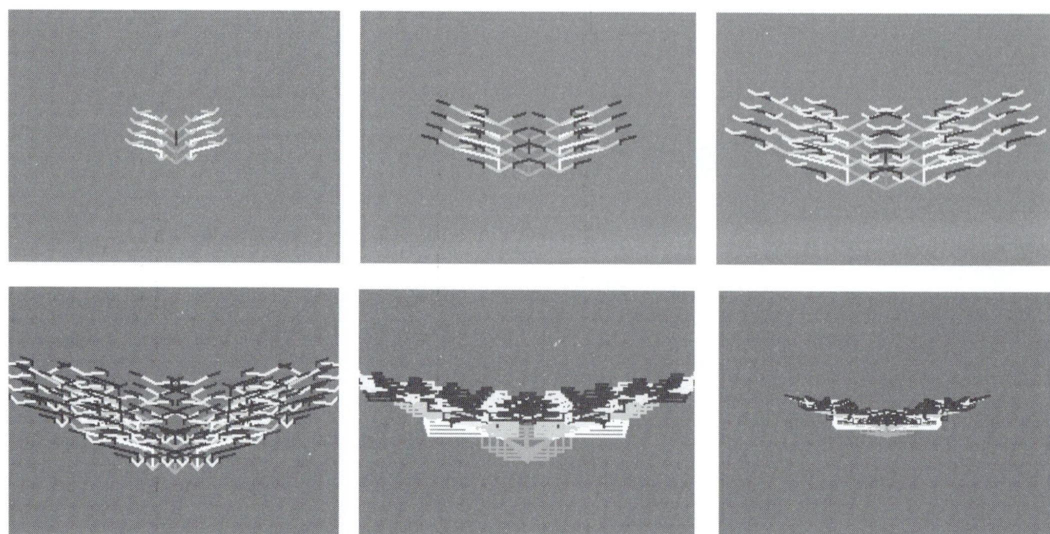

Figure 11.1 Images by Dawkins' colour watchmaker (see CD-ROM).

have been implemented in Java, most extending Dawkins' original implementation slightly by adding colour or new shapes – something that he later did himself, fig. 11.1 (Dawkins, 1989). This program and its variants are available on several platforms, from palmtop computers to web based Java applets.

11.2.2 Sbart

Author:	*Tatsuo Unemi*
Platforms:	*UNIX/X-Windows (SGI, LINUX)* *Microsoft® NT™ with X-Windows server*
Version:	*2.2b*
URL:	*http://www.intlab.soka.ac.jp/~unemi/sbart/*

Developed between 1993 and late 1996, Sbart is probably the most complete evolutionary art program available for free. It is a two-dimensional formula-based 'breeding' type, and like most of this type of evolutionary art programs, it was inspired by the work of Karl Sims (Sims, 1991).

On starting Sbart, the user is presented with a fairly standard five by four grid of cells containing fairly simple random patterns. The visual representation of each individual is created by evaluating a function for each pixel in the window and then assigning a colour to that pixel based on the result. In Sbart the functions are created by tree-like expressions created from a range of mathematical functions, see Table 11.1. The functions operate on three values in the HSV colour space.

From the starting point you can opt to load a previously saved session, or begin to evolve your own forms. Basic use is simple: cells to be cross-bred are selected by the user and the

Table 11.1 Sbart functions

Unary	Binary
	+
–	–
abs	*
sin	/
cos	pow
log	hypot
exp	max
sqrt	min
sign	and
image	mdist
	mix

'Next' button pressed (if only one cell is selected then it will be mutated). The mutation and crossbreeding rates are preset with fixed values so that there are usually a couple of individuals which represent the parents. Because of this, the 'undo' function is not usually needed, but it is nevertheless available. Populations can be saved and re-loaded, and individuals can be dragged from one window to another to introduce new species for crossbreeding. This is a very powerful technique, and is also useful for compiling a 'zoo' of favourites.

A particularly nice feature of Sbart is the gene editor. This allows you to see, and edit, the function tree that makes up an individual. It is possible to copy and paste subsections of the genes, and individually replace a node in the gene tree with functions, constants and variables. It is possible to use this window to play genetic engineer, but caution is needed: it is difficult to change just a single element of the image, without changing the rest of the image.

Sbart also provides a Zoom window where you can view an individual at any resolution

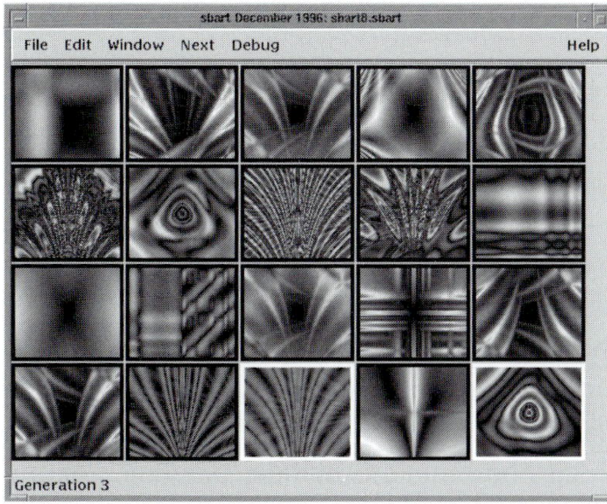

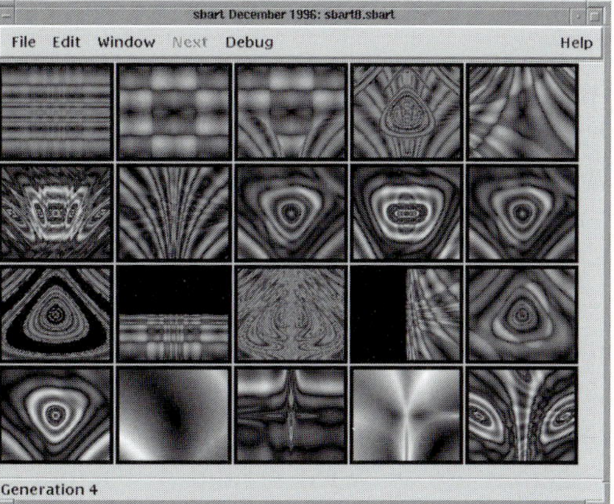

Figure 11.2 Two successive generations from Sbart. The parents are shown highlighted at the far right and middle of the bottom row in the first screen.

Figure 11.3 Example Sbart image.

up to full screen, revealing detail hidden at the lower preview resolutions. It is from this window that you can print, or save the image to GIF, EPSF, XWD, JPEG or TGA formats. The save as GIF capability is hampered by GIF's 256 colour limitation, which causes unpleasant artefacts.

Overall this program appears well implemented, with many good features making it one of the best evolutionary art programs currently available. One of the few limitations of the program is that there is no mechanism to control the degree of mutation and crossover.

11.2.3 Kai Power Tools™

Author:	*MetaTools Inc ®.*
Platforms:	*Apple Macintosh™, Windows™*
Version:	*3*
URL:	*http://www.metatools.com*

The Kai Power Tools™ are primarily 'plugins' for image manipulation tools such as Adobe Photoshop™, however there are several evolutionary tools included in the package. These include the Texture Explorer, which is a mutating program.

This program makes use of a very polished but unusual user interface. Since this tool is primarily a design tool as well as an evolutionary tool, many of the features are under direct user control and are responsible for several of the controls that can be seen. As can be seen from the screen shot shown in fig. 11.4, the 'parent' is displayed in the large central window with the mutations around it. The curved series of spheres are used like a 'slider bar' to control the amount of mutation involved. As usual, clicking on a mutation selects a new parent and mutations are spawned around it. Factors which can be mutated include: panning, rotation, scale, zoom, colour, blending, opacity and the texture itself. These can all be mutated individually or in combinations. This tool makes the production of acceptable textures quick and easy, although the full gamut of textures seems to be fairly limited.

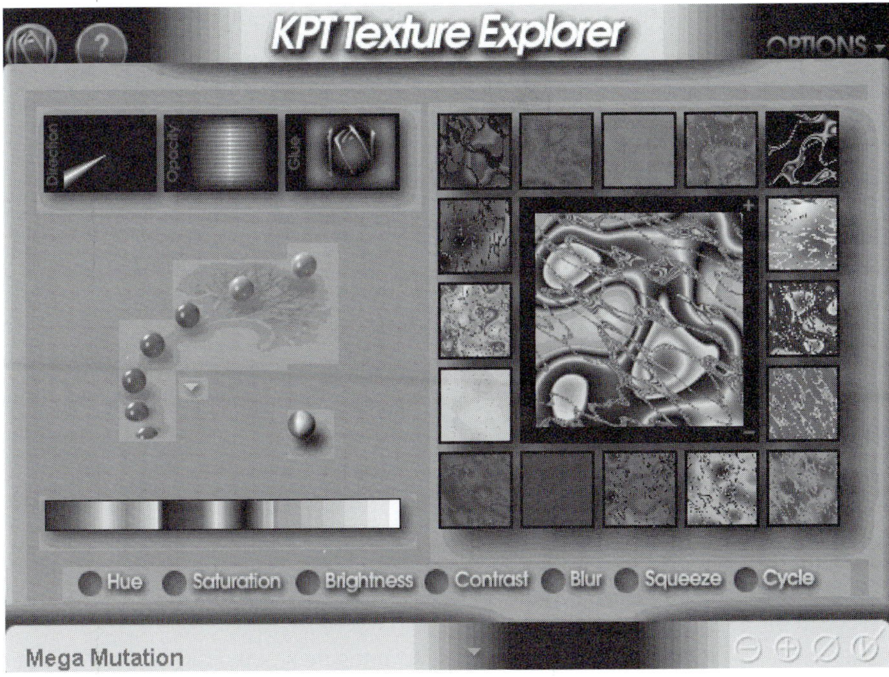

Figure 11.4 The KPT Texture Explorer user interface.

11.2.4 Imogenes

Author:	*Harley Davis*
Platforms:	*Windows*
Version:	*1.0*
URL:	*ftp://bells.cs.ucl.ac.uk/genetic/ftp.io.com/code/imogenes.zip*

Imogenes is a 2D functional genetic art program, with a very rich function set. The display is produced by mapping a single value modulo 256 through a user defined loadable colour-map, and provides a population of nine individuals arranged in a three by three grid of cells, see fig. 11.5. Unlike Sbart, Imogenes allows the user to assign fitness to each individual by clicking several times on that cell. The next generation is produced using these fitness ratings.

The cells are resizable so an enlarged image of an individual can be produced, although the display must be refreshed for this to work properly. The image in a cell can be saved as a bitmap, and in this way it is possible to produce an almost full screen image. Unfortunately this is as far as save and load functions go for this program, and although source code is available no-one has yet taken up Harley's mantle and provided the extra functionality.

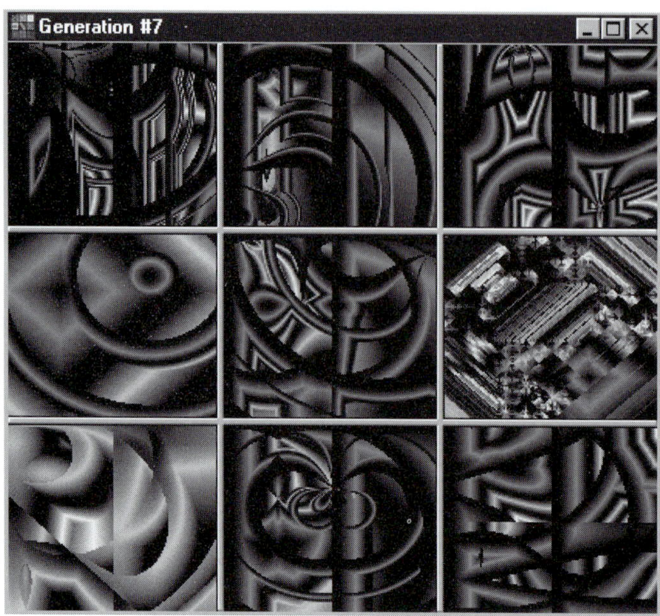

Figure 11.5 A lightly evolved imogenes population.

11.2.5 Artificial Painter

Author:	*L. Pagliarini, H. H. Lund and O. Miglino*
Platforms:	*DOS*
Version:	*1.0*
URL:	*http://www.daimi.aau.dk/~hhl/ap.html*

Artificial Painter is a 2D genetic art program. On entry, the user is presented with a selection of twelve images, and to produce the next generation of images, four of the current generation must be ranked (it is possible to rank the same image more than once). Degree of mutation is set through a simple on-screen control. The program uses only sixteen colours and has an unusual interface where the 'Next generation' option must be selected first and then the four images ranked. Apparently a new Windows 95 version of the program is in the pipeline, with a user-interface revamp.

11.2.6 Interactive Genetic Art

Author:	*John Mount, Michael Witbrock and Scott Neil Reilly*
Platforms:	*Web*
Version:	*2*
URL:	*http://www.geneticart.org/cgi-bin/mwgenformII*

John Mount's Interactive Genetic Art was the first Web-based evolutionary art program, allowing images to be generated collaboratively. It had produced several thousand generations, but is not currently available on-line. The basis is a standard 2D functional genetic system, using functions which operate in a four-dimensional space. The resulting components are then used to produce the red, green and blue (RGB) outputs. The interface displays several images, which the user rates from one to nine. When all images have been rated, the vote is submitted, and after ten votes have been submitted the next generation is produced and displayed.

A complete description of this system is given in the chapter *Evolving Genetic Art*, by Witbrock and Reilly.

11.2.7 Henry Rowley's Genetic Art

Author:	*Henry Rowley*
Platforms:	*Web*
Version:	
URL:	*http://www.cs.cmu.edu/~har/GeneticArt.html*

This 2D Java applet is a mutation-driven drawing program. The displays are based on Iterated Functional Systems (IFSystems), using contractive affine transforms. A contractive affine transform is a simple rotation and scaling matrix, where the scaling is one or less. IFSystems repeatedly iterate a single point through one or more affine transforms, plotting its location after each iteration. In Henry's implementation the order in which these functions are applied is selected randomly; this does not affect output except to even out the pixel density. The interface is a four by four grid, the parent is kept, and control over mutation-rate and stability is provided.

While in theory, IFSystems are capable of producing everything from ferns to mock Julia sets, it does seem difficult to produce anything except ink blots with this program, fig. 11.6.

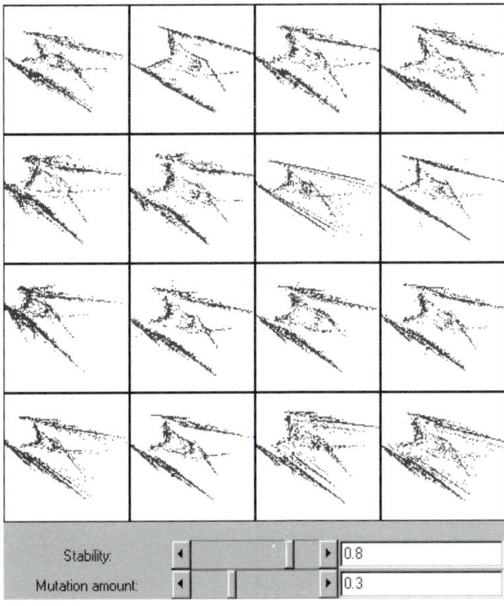

Figure 11.6 Henry Rowley's genetic Art Java Program in action.

11.2.8 Doodle Garden

Author:	*Andy Singleton*
Platforms:	*Windows 3.x*
Version:	
URL:	*http://www.cinteractive.com/andy/andy02.htm*

Andy Singleton's Doodle Garden is a 2D breeding and mutating drawing program, based on a logo-like language. The user is able to load and save collections of drawings and hand-edit programs. Cells can be protected, mutated individually, or cross-bred with each other, see fig. 11.7. An unusual aspect of this program is the provision of a screen-saver module which will read a population file and randomly cross-breed them.

11.2.9 Mutator and Form Grow

Author:	*Stephen Todd and William Latham*
Platforms:	*IBM workstation and PC*
Version:	
URL:	*http://www.artworks.co.uk/*

Mutator is a fully blown 3D mutation and genetic program, developed by Todd and Latham at IBM®. In order to give Latham as strong an artistic control as possible the core shape is designed using a simple 'description' language, and this can then be evolved and can be cross bred with other forms. The program includes texturing (for completeness the textures are also evolvable) and animation. It is this last feature that has perhaps produced the most media coverage, being

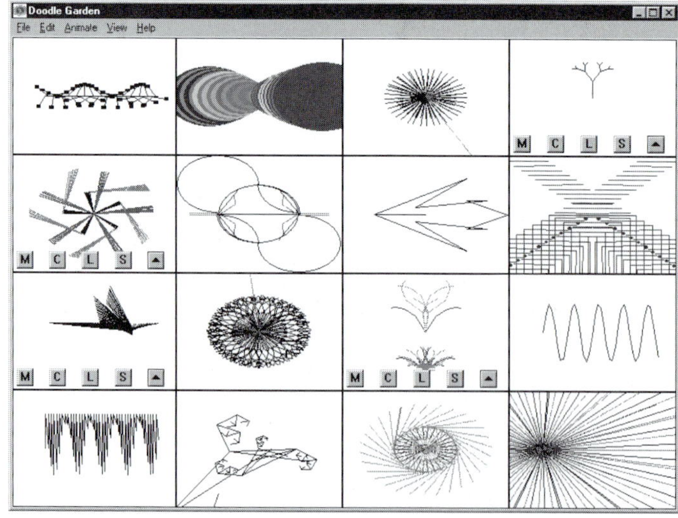

Figure 11.7 Doodle Garden's initial display.

particularly suited to television. Animations and imagery from this program have been used by musicians as the basis for album artwork and videos. This program is not freely available, although it has been exhibited several times around the country, and the resultant artforms have been widely seen both on television and at museums and other exhibitions. The design concepts and specific details of the Mutator program, along with numerous colour plates of the output are documented in Todd and Latham (1992).

A description of this work is given in the chapter *The Mutation and Growth of Art by Computers*, by Todd and Latham.

11.2.10 Cybertation

Author:	*Homer Perry, Jonathon Weinreich*
Platforms:	*Windows*
Version:	*1.0*
URL:	*http://www.nottinghill.com/cyber/index.html*

Cybertation is a good example of the three-dimensional evolutionary art programs currently available. The forms are based on a 3D turtle-like language with colour and texture capability. The program is capable of mutating and breeding individuals, and there is an adjustable evolutionary-rate slider bar for fine-tuning at the later stages of creation. The program, like Sbart, allows multiple windows to be opened containing different populations, and individuals can be cut or copied from one window and pasted into another. The rendering quality can be changed, from wire-frame to Phong, and the degree of complexity can also be limited, so that rendering time is not overly compromised. Rendering is performed in real-time with the individuals being created as you watch, see fig. 11.8.

Several fully evolved individuals as well as 'seeds' are provided as starting points, and a web site exists for exchanging these virtual creations. A particularly nice aspect of this program is its use of a 3D-rendering engine to allow you to view the creations from all sides.

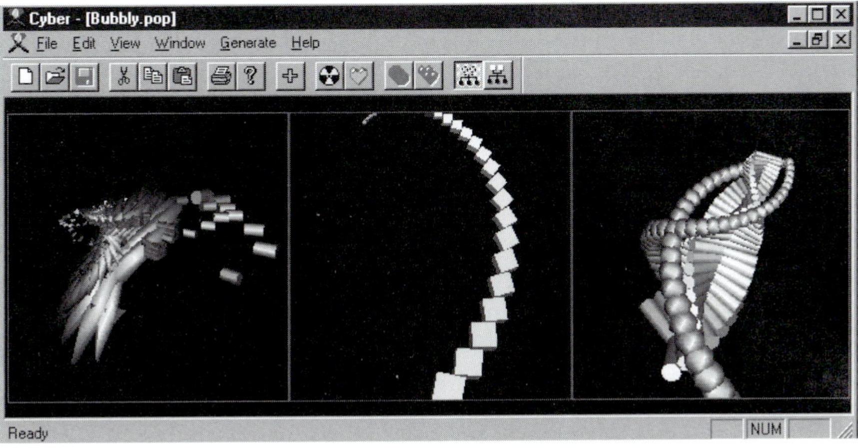

Figure 11.8 Cybertation, showing two pre-evolved 'life forms'.

However, some problems with the user-interface are evident: to rotate a creature it must be selected, and after viewing an entire population, all the cells are inconveniently left selected.

11.2.11 Morphogenesis

Author:	*Bernd Lintermann*
Platforms:	*Web*
Version:	
URL:	*http://i31www.ira.uka.de/~linter/morphogenesis.html*

Morphogenesis is a 3D mutation-based system, installed at the ZKM Media Museum in Karlsruhe Germany, running on an SGI Onyx2, but Bernd Lintermann has now provided it with a web interface. Morphogenesis is based in part on an earlier 3D modeller called xfrog in which the user constructs objects from primitives, textures and actions. Bernd has extended the capabilities of xfrog immensely in this project. The web user interface is of necessity very simple, though adequate, allowing you to select a mutation rate from one to six, or to simplify your creation. The quality of the output is very high, producing organic looking creatures complete with colour and texturing, you may even download a VRML representation of your creation and so view it in all three-dimensions. Once you are happy with your creation you can 'contribute' to a public collection of evolved creatures. At the time of writing this is a project under development, so some of the contributions do not have images.

11.2.12 Lparser

Author:	*Laurens Lapre*
Platforms:	*MS-DOS*
Version:	*4*
URL:	*http://www.xs4all.nl/~ljlapre/*

Lparser is a borderline evoart program. Using a 3D L-systems language to produce its output, the program itself comes in two parts: a compiler and a previewer. The compiler can output RenderStar compatible files, which is used in the previewer as well as DXF, raw triangle, VRML, and POV formats.

To use this program in an evolutionary manner, the user first creates a progenitor, and then runs Lparser multiple times to produce multiple offspring. These must then be viewed, a suitable one selected and the process repeated. Control of the mutation rate is provided by a command-line parameter, this controls the number of individual mutations that are applied to the parent to produce the offspring. A simple Microsoft Windows™ shell is available which allows the user to view a single mutation at a time. Source code to Lparser is now available, perhaps someone will produce a more comprehensive evolutionary interface to this powerful language.

(Chapter 14 *Exploring Three-Dimensional Design Worlds* by Broughton, Coates and Jackson describes the use of Lindenmayer Systems and genetic programming in design.)

11.2.13 GA music

Author:	*Jason H. Moore*
Platforms:	*Windows*
Version:	*1.0*
URL:	*http://www-ks.rus.uni-stuttgart.de/people/schulz/fmusic/gamusic.html*

This program stands out from the others in that it is used to evolve music rather than visual art. It uses genetic algorithms to manipulate a 128 bit string which controls the pitch and duration of, at most, thirty note melodies, fig. 11.9. A 'palette' of twelve melodies is provided and the user can rate these as poor, average or good. Control is provided over mutation and recombination factors. Like much evoart it takes several generations to produce acceptable results. On the downside everyone in the room has to experience the selection process since it uses a full volume PC speaker to produce output. Early generations produce pure cacophony and can be quite annoying to the uninvolved; my cat was particularly critical of some of these.

Figure 11.9 The GA music user interface, showing some of the melodies after rating.

11.3 FORM

Author:	*Andrew Rowbottom*
Platforms:	*Windows/DOS*
Version:	*6*
URL:	*http://www.netlink.co.uk/~snaffle/form/form.html*

11.3.1 Inspiration

Form was inspired by the work of Richard Dawkins and William Latham (Dawkins, 1986; Todd and Latham, 1992). I found the visual complexity overlying the clearly simple construction of both Dawkins' Biomorphs and Latham's evolved forms to be the solution to creating visually exciting objects without having to work in the difficult interface of a traditional 3D CAD environment. The program would be released as freeware, both as a contribution to the freeware already available on the Internet, and, more pragmatically, because this would not cause a conflict of interests with my employers.

11.3.2 Version Two

The initial aim was for *Form* to be a simple compiler-like system, used to directly compile form scripts to produce output suitable for rendering using a third party program. Version One was abandoned owing to compiler problems, and so the first full version was version two. The display programs initially chosen were REND386 – a small, fast polygonal-based real-time renderer for the IBM-PC, and POVRay – a respected raytracer. Rend386 would be used to generate a quick preview, and POVRay would be used to render high quality output. However, I rapidly discovered that all except the simplest forms were too complex for Rend386 to display, as internal limits of 64K per data structure were frequently violated. I had clearly achieved my first aim to produce complex forms from simple scripts!

Figure 11.10 'Blobhead' – the first 'complex' form, raytraced as there was no preview mode, texturing was hand edited into the output POV Ray script.

```
l = torus ( 0.14 , 0.7 );
stem = l stack 20 in 10 twist 360 , 0.5 grow 0.7;
s = sphere stack 10 in 3 twist 360 , 0.3 bend 30 grow 0.3;
head = s fan 10 , 90;
stem & head;
end
```

Figure 11.11 The script for 'Blobhead' shown in fig. 11.10.

11.3.3 Version Three

Having reached the limits of Rend386 so rapidly, it was clear that a new previewer needed to be built. This turned out to be the longest single part of the *Form* project.

Although I had previously written simple polygonal renderers based on a painters algorithm, it was clear that *Form* was going to produce quantities of data that was going to outstrip the humble memory capabilities of my computer. For this reason I chose to implement a simple Z-Buffer algorithm which would allow objects to be drawn in a random order, for a constant memory usage, and fairly linear relationship between time and complexity. The memory and speed constraints of an Intel 386 clocked at 16Mhz with only 2Mb of RAM became the prime criteria at this point and influenced almost every aspect of the rendering engine. The Z-buffer was written using 2 byte integers rather than floating point number which occupy twice the memory space, and it was written with paging modules to allow it to page to DOS EMS where possible, and to disk if that wasn't available. The speed constraints forced me to use simple Gouraud shading (Foley et al., 1990), but using an integer linear interpolation algorithm at every stage. This does lead to imperfections in the previewed image, but a speed improvement of least one order of magnitude made this acceptable. The Gouraud shading code was optimized until the screen access time became the limiting factor. This meant that Gouraud shading was now as fast as the 'flat' shading code. This version became the first public release.

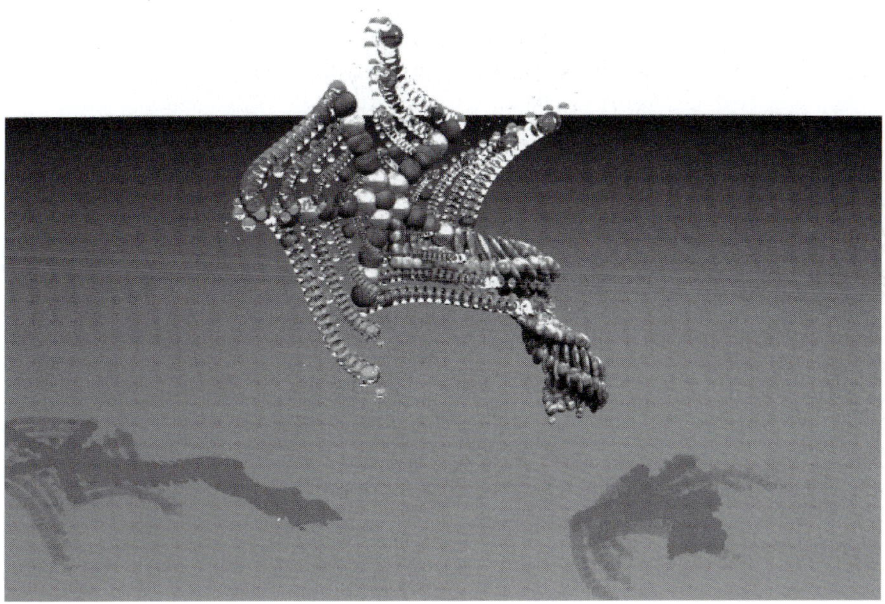

Figure 11.12 'Webgood'.

11.3.4 Version Four

Now that *Form* had a built-in previewer, I began the next stage: adding the ability to mutate and select from those mutations. Rather than be over-ambitious I opted to apply a

Biomorphs-like strategy of leaving the structure of the *Form* unaltered, and to merely modify the parameters applied to that structure. These parameters are simple integer numbers. Initially, the mutation rate was applied in terms of a multiplier. For example, under a mutation rate of 10% a stack of ten spheres would be likely to mutate to 9 or 11 spheres. Although in practice this mechanism works fairly well it fails for the simple case of 0, so a simple 'jitter' factor was added.

At the suggestion of Matt Haiken, a 'steering' factor was added, using a simple mechanism for pre-selecting the next generation. The computer tries to predict in a very simplistic manner what the user is 'aiming' for and attempts to produce more forms like the predicted than any other. The prediction is a simple linear method, if the parent form had ten spheres, and the user selects a new parent with 12 spheres, then the next generation will contain forms with roughly 14 spheres. However, I soon found that if all forms were 'centred' around the predicted form too much variation was lost, so the steering is adjustable, and by default only a fraction of it is used; the forms produced would probably be centred around having 12½ spheres.

Once complete I was amazed at the intricate complexity that was being produced from the simplest Forms.

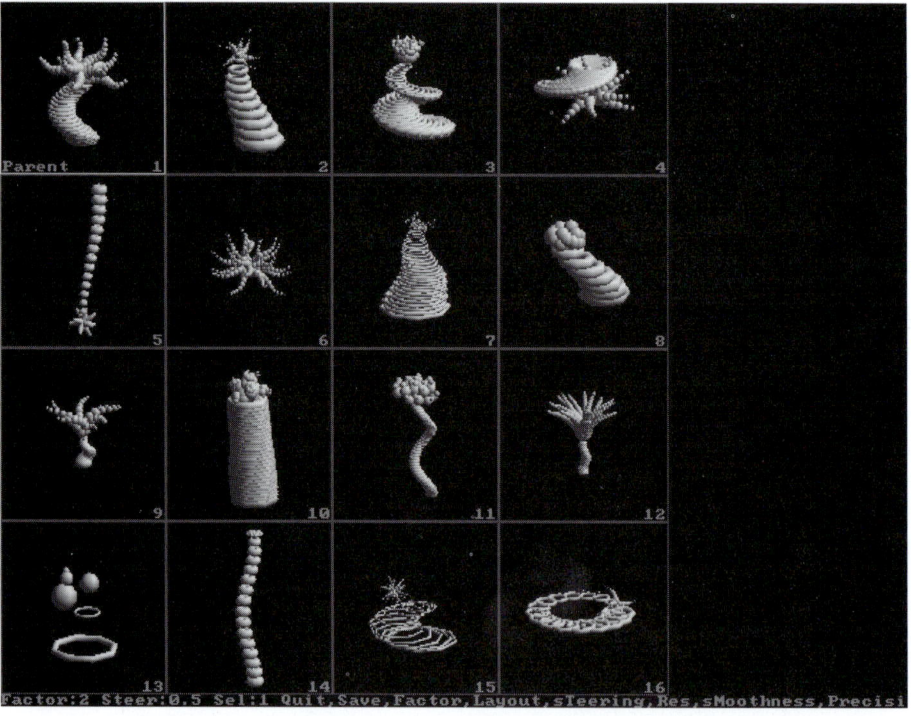

Figure 11.13 Snapshot of an active mutation screen.

11.3.5 Version Five

The next version of *Form* was to include animation, the ability to smoothly interpolate between two mutations sharing the same progenitor. This appeared to be simple to implement, each form would have exactly the same basic structure, just the parameters would be interpolated linearly. The first attempts revealed that my program had been written for integers, not floating point numbers. This produced 'jumping' – when a new primitive appeared on the end of a stack it appeared complete, changing the size of the object, and causing a sudden re-scaling between one frame and another. My initial solution was to add the final object, but to scale its size from nothing to full sized, when the next object would start to appear. This revealed more problems: the orientation of the final object affects the angle at which further objects attach, so this too had to be smoothed. More and more problems like this occurred, I would find a solution, try it out, and a few days later spot another 'jump'. Eventually, I found a solution that worked for a set of clearly defined cases:

1. First the final object is placed in the position it would assume when complete.
2. It is then rescaled so it grows from nothing to fill size.
3. It is positioned so that its 'attachment' point moves from the surface of the previous object to its final position.
4. Finally it is orientated between the orientation of the last whole object and its final orientation.

This appeared to work for all cases but produced unpleasant transitions when there is less than a single object in a construction; these were dealt with explicitly in each language construction.

Another problem encountered during animation was the size of the 'tweened' forms. It was clear that smoothing was needed to allow even changes in scale from one form to another, It had been assumed that most of the in-between forms would change in scale fairly linearly. It wasn't too long before I discovered that if form A is 100 units tall and form B was also 100 units tall it did not mean that the form half way between A and B was also 100 units tall. I have seen several cases where the 'tweened' forms were many times larger than either end point.

There are several solutions to this problem:

- Perform no scaling at all. This would result in forms growing outside the screen, or shrinking to tiny dots. This also prevents the creation of looping animations.
- Scale each and every intermediate to fit. This works, but leads to rapid jumps of scale during certain phases. Visually it is bearable but unattractive.
- Apply some smoothing to the changes in scale.

The latter is the option that was implemented. The scale of the intermediate forms is sampled; for perfect results every frame should be sampled for scale, but for speed fewer than that are. The number of samples is then reduced to just a few keyframes and the scale is interpolated between these keyframes using cardinal interpolation, the end points being duplicated to ensure that they are reached. Cardinal curves are used for smoothing rather than B-spline curves because although both produce smooth curves cardinal curves pass through the nodes, unlike B-spline curves.

There are two mechanism for selecting these keyframes automatically: the user can specify the number of keyframes they want, and the computer selects the best, or the user can provide an 'error' factor.

Initially just two keyframes are selected, the first and last frame. All intermediate frames are then scanned and the frame with the largest deviation of scale is chosen. If this deviation (as a percentage) is larger than the supplied error factor it is added to the keyframes list. The process is then repeated until all frames have been added as keyframes (a very poor solution), or there are no more keyframes which deviate enough from the calculated curve. If the user has supplied a number of keyframes to add then this number of keyframes is used, selected in the same manner as previously.

Thus I was able to produce animations. Selecting several forms all with a common progenitor it was possible to produce looping animations where the form evolved smoothly from A to B to C to A.

11.3.6 Version Five

A version of *Form* for windows was produced, using a similar interface to the DOS version.

11.3.7 Work in Progress

A new version is being prepared, with better GUI integration, and a more consistent output structure allowing export to many more file formats and devices. I am planning to add some cross platform independence, and may use OpenGL to enable 3D graphics acceleration. Other less likely additions are colour, perspective, user definable construction keywords, and possibly to provide a uniform interface to multiple creation systems such as L-systems, Biomorphs, 2D Functional, and others. A 'leave overnight' running feature to produce a larger selection of forms is also a possibility.

11.4 Conclusions

Clearly evolutionary art is here, and is being incorporated into serious products. However, the take-off of evoart has been slow, due in no small part to the computational power required. In addition, as my own experience in developing Form has shown, a significant effort is required to produce an acceptable evolutionary art program, requiring knowledge in several areas of computer science.

Another aspect which may well have contributed to the slow uptake is that virtually all of these systems produce output which carries a certain 'signature' that identifies the program far more than the artist. This 'signature' effect is stronger in the 2D evoart programs than the 3D ones, excusable in part perhaps due to the post texturing and rendering applied to the 3D forms. Karl Sims' program seems to have the weakest signature of all the programs listed here. Perhaps further advances in evolutionary art will provide the artist with the means to remove these signatures, just as the computer graphics industry has now largely removed the 'too perfect' signature of its earlier attempts at modelling reality.

Acknowledgements

My thanks to Pantek Ltd., Andy Pearmund, Matt Haiken, Dan Farmer, Laurens Lapre, Bob Galka, Sue Cunningham and the authors who provided evaluation copies of their programs for the review.

References

Arvo, J. (ed.). Graphics Gems II, Academic Press.

Dawkins, R. (1986). *The Blind Watchmaker*. Penguin Books.

Dawkins, R. (1989). The Evolution of Evolvability. *Artificial Life. The Proceedings of an Interdisciplinary Workshop on the Synthesis and Simulation of Living Systems*, Vol. VI, Langton, C. G. (ed.), September 1987, Los Alamos, New Mexico, Addison-Wesley, pp. 201–220.

Foley, J., van Dam, A., Feiner, S. and Hughes, J. (1990). *Computer Graphics Principles and Practice*, 2nd edn. Addison-Wesley.

Glassner, A. S. (ed). *Graphics Gems*, Academic Press.

Kirk, D. (ed). *Graphics Gems III*, Academic Press.

Sims, K. (1991). Artificial Evolution for Computer Graphics. *Computer Graphics*, **25**(4); 319–328.

Todd, S. and Latham, W. (1992). *Evolutionary Art and Computers*. Academic Press.

Watt, A. *Fundamentals of Three-Dimensional Computer Graphics*, Addison-Wesley.

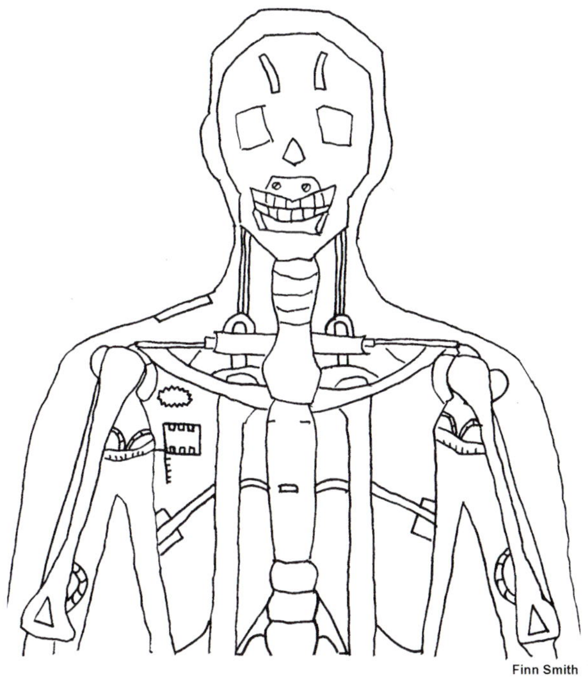

4 EVOLUTIONARY ARTIFICIAL LIFE FORMS

Can we evolve embryogenies similar to those defined by the DNA of living creatures? Is it possible to evolve forms that are constructed from cellular structures and grow in a similar way to plants in nature? Are our computers capable of evolving artificial 'brains' in addition to forms? Can our computers really evolve artificial life?

The three chapters in this section describe some of the most significant work to date in this fascinating area. The first chapter, ***Artificial Embryology and Cellular Differentiation***, is by Dr. Hugo de Garis, head of the famous *Brain Builder Group*, of *ATR Human Information Processing Research Labs*. Hugo describes some of his pioneering work in the evolution of embryogenies with cellular automata to evolve shapes, and provides his vision of the future of work in this area. ***Evolving Three-Dimensional Morphology and Behaviour*** by Karl Sims, of *Thinking Machines Corp.*, gives a complete description of Karl's very impressive evolved virtual creatures. These astonishing computer beasts have both brain and body evolved to allow them to walk, jump, swim and compete with each other. Finally, ***Exploring Three-Dimensional Design Worlds using Lindenmeyer Systems and Genetic Programming***, by Dr. Paul Coates and his team at the *Centre for Environment and Computing in Architecture, University of East London*, describes how 3D space and forms can be evolved and grown in a plant-like manner.

Chapter 12

Artificial Embryology and Cellular Differentiation

by Hugo de Garis

12.1 Introduction

The broad aim of this chapter is to create an awareness that self-assembling, 'artificial embryological'-type systems need to be studied, so that future molecular scale technologies (Drexler, 1992) will be able to build machines which have too many components for sequential mechanical assembly. With this broader aim in mind, a more concrete aim is to introduce the concept of embryological differentiation into genetic algorithms. Traditionally, GAs have contained such ideas as reproductive fitness, crossover, mutation, etc. but nothing equivalent to the way genes switch on and off in natural embryogenesis. The ideas of differentiation are used in this chapter to try to grow non-convex artificial shapes of colonies of cells in reproductive cellular automata. Earlier publications aimed at creating an 'artificial embryology' resulted in the growth of successful convex shapes but non-convex shapes failed to evolve (e.g. de Garis, 1992b).

The new field of artificial embryology (or at least the self-assembly of complex systems) is felt to be important for the future development of complex system design. New technologies, such as WSI (wafer scale integration), molecular electronics (Carter *et al.*, 1988), and nanotechnology (Schneiker, 1989), promise to allow the construction of devices with a huge number of components (e.g. billions, trillions, and up to Avogadro's number). This in turn will create problems for the design and construction of these devices. If a device contains literally trillions of components, it cannot be built by a machine which positions one component at a time, because such a machine would be too slow. The device will either have to be built by positioning many components simultaneously (which will become increasingly difficult as the number of components to be simultaneously placed increases), or, the device will have to build itself in a form of embryological self-assembly.

It is this second option which is of interest to the author. It is also the solution employed by nature to build its (hyper) complex systems, such as embryos and brains. However, if one is to employ self-assembly techniques to build complex systems, how can one be sure that the self-assembled product is useful to human beings? The self-assembly will need to be tested for its quality of performance. Those self-assemblies which do poorly can be abandoned. Those that do well, may be used. But what if all the initial attempts at self-assembly do poorly? How is progress in the design to be made when the self-assembled device is massively complex?

EVOLUTIONARY DESIGN BY COMPUTERS
ISBN 1-55860-605-X

The answer to this question may be to mimic nature by using a form of applied evolution called evolutionary engineering (EE), i.e. using GAs to build/evolve complex systems (de Garis, 1990, 1991, 1992). Improvement in a hypercomplex system may be achieved blindly by randomly mutating linearly coded instructions for self-assembling devices. Those mutations which are 'positive' will produce devices with superior performance values. The linear codes which contain these positive mutations can be allowed to produce more offspring in the next generation of a population of such codes.

The author feels that it is important to begin investigating how to build and evolve (EE style) self-assembling devices. This chapter is an attempt in this direction. It is part of a general vision that future devices may be used to *grow* complex systems, such as electronic circuits at various levels of granularity. At a very basic level, simple RLC circuits could be coded and grown on an electronic substrate in a special hardware device called a 'Darwin machine'. At a higher level of granularity, circuits of component parts such as flip-flops and amplifiers could be grown. At a still higher level of granularity, circuits of artificial neurons and synapses could be grown. Thus self-assembling (and self-testing) artificial nervous systems might be grown in these Darwin machines. This is the vision and the longer-term direction in which the work of this chapter is aimed.

With this vision in mind, present day computer technology should begin raising its sights beyond the usual style of 'homogeneous' architectures. A homogeneous architecture is defined to be one which contains a large number of copies of a small number of relatively simple (i.e. humanly understandable) components or modular designs, which are then connected using simple rules to make the whole. The net result is a machine whose functioning is humanly understandable, because it is built according to a plan, a blueprint. Obvious examples are mass computer memories, von Neumann computers, the Connection Machine (Hillis, 1985), etc. A 'heterogeneous' computer architecture is non-homogeneous, e.g. it may contain complex modules which differ greatly one from another, and be connected in very complex ways. The paradigm example of such an architecture is the human brain.

If, for example, one is attempting to build a million or a billion processor machine (assuming that the underlying technologies allow such a thing), then why restrict oneself to a homogeneous architecture, when one could almost as easily (in purely technological implementation terms) build a heterogeneous machine, with all its greater sophistication and subtlety of behavior. Of course, the obvious answer to this question is that a million (or billion) processor heterogeneous machine would be hyper-complex and would compare to the complexity level of simple biological nervous systems, in terms of dynamics, structure and most importantly, 'un-understandability'.

Traditionally, engineers and scientists have shied away from building hyper-complex machines, because of this 'un-understandability', i.e. a lack of theoretical principles to explain their structures or functions. However, recently, a new approach to building complex systems has been demonstrated. It is called *evolutionary engineering* (EE) (de Garis, 1990, 1991, 1992), and uses genetic algorithms (GAs) as a tool to build things, where the internal complexity of the system being built/evolved is (within certain limits) irrelevant to its successful construction. So long as the GA being used gets a fitness value which continues to increase over the generations, then a steady improvement in the system being evolved will result. One does not care about the internal complexity. The system is in effect, a 'black box'.

It is possible that this EE approach to building complex systems may have a strong future, and play a vital role in 21st-century technology and engineering. It is essentially the approach taken by nature to build/evolve such hyper-complex systems as ourselves.

If the prospect of a one million (or billion) processor computer raises the issue of homogeneous vs. heterogeneous architectures and the problem of complexity of heterogeneous machines, then this level of complexity pales into insignificance when one considers the molecular scale technologies now exploding in research labs around the world. The author's previous lab (ETL) has whole sections of people devoted to building and testing devices which can pick up atoms at one point and place them at some other point to build desired molecular scale structures or tools. Molecular scale technologies ('nanotech' (Drexler, 1992)) offer the long-term prospect of building Avogadro machines, i.e. machines containing an Avogadro number (i.e. of the order of a trillion trillion) components. With such a huge number, it will obviously be impossible to assemble them one by one. Thus the reasoning behind the need for self-assembling, self-testing, EE-style design and construction techniques, will be all the more compelling when it comes to 21st-century nanotechnology.

This chapter describes the initial steps at using EE techniques to build/grow structures in an embryological-like manner, and in particular to use ideas analogous to the phenomenon of 'differentiation' in the biological world. It is hoped that the initial ideas presented in this chapter will inspire other researchers to work on the embryological 'growth' of (neuro) electronic circuits, thus creating a new speciality called 'Embryonics' (Embryological Electronics). A device which evolves a complex (neuro) electronic circuit has been called a Darwin machine (de Garis, 1991a) by the author. It is envisioned that such machines may play a role in building artificial nervous systems for future artificial creatures (e.g. biological robots, or biots).

The artificial 'embryos' presented in this chapter are two-dimensional shapes formed by a colony of 'cells' in reproductive cellular automata. The basic idea is that a GA is used to evolve sets of reproduction rules of these cells. These rule-sets are spread out (one set per 'operon') along a bit string GA chromosome, and are switched on and off according to whether the state of a cell matches the 'condition' field of the operon, and if so, the corresponding 'action' field controls the reproduction (or not) of the cell. One has in effect a type of production system on a chromosome.

The remainder of this chapter is structured as follows. Section 12.2 provides a more general introduction to differentiable chromosomes and shape genes. Section 12.3 contains a more detailed description of the algorithms used in this chapter to grow non-convex shapes. Section 12.4 presents some results of experiments using the ideas of the previous section.

12.2 Differentiable Chromosomes and Shape Genes

Figure 12.1 illustrates a *differentiable chromosome*, which in this particular example, consists of four genes (or *operons*, a term taken from molecular biology), where each operon (separated by double vertical lines) contains a condition field C and an action field A. These operons switch on and off over time, as in nature. The actions of earlier operons cause other operons to switch on and off. The desired net result of this sequential operon switching is the controlled growth of an artificial embryo.

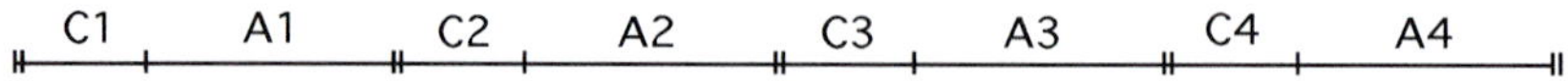

Figure 12.1 A differentiable chromosome.

Each cell of a particular cellular automaton described in this chapter contains the same chromosome. At each stroke of a clock (where the cellular automata are assumed to be synchronous or clocked), each cell calculates its present state by observing the states of its neighbouring cells at the end of the previous cycle (where a cycle is the time between two clock strokes). Each cell then compares its present state with all the coded condition fields C_i of its genes (or operons). If one of the conditions (e.g. C_m) matches, then the corresponding action field A_m is activated, and the instructions coded in that action field are executed. The activation of these instructions may change the state of some of the cells, and thus activate new instructions, which in turn may change further states. Thus it is possible to generate a time sequence of state-changes and execution of instructions, which result in some final desired product, e.g. an embryo or colony of cells having a desired shape.

The ideas contained in the previous paragraph are very general, and may be applicable to many kinds of concrete situations. The above ideas have similarities with the traditional production systems of artificial intelligence and Holland's classifier systems (Holland, 1986). Perhaps future research might be able to incorporate ideas from the extensive work already done on production and classifier systems into differentiable chromosomes.

In order to give a more concrete example of what coded instructions might be like, a brief introduction to some earlier work of the author on artificial embryology will now be given (de Garis, 1991a, 1992b). Basically, the main idea of this work was to evolve reproduction rules for cellular automata (CA), such that the final shape of a colony of cells attained, as closely as possible, some desired shape, such as a square, triangle, ellipsoid, tadpole, etc. The state of a cell in one of these experiments was defined in terms of the configuration of its neighbourless sides. Assuming only edge cells can reproduce (where reproduction is defined as putting a daughter cell in a vacant square contiguous with the parent cell) there are fourteen possible states, as shown in fig. 12.2.

For a 2D cellular automaton, each cell has one of the above fourteen states (assuming only edge cells can reproduce, and that no isolated cells are generated). For each cell, for each cycle, a cell may reproduce or not, hence fourteen bits (one per state) are needed to specify which cells in a given cycle will reproduce, as shown in fig. 12.3 with the REPRO? fields (one per cycle). If a cell is to reproduce, it needs to know in which direction (E, N, W, or S). If there is only one neighbourless side, then no R DIRNS (reproduction directions) field bits are needed to specify the side for the daughter cell, because there can only be one choice.

For two neighbourless sides, one bit is needed (for six such states). For three neighbourless sides, two bits are needed (for four such states). If an occupied side is specified with these two bits, it is ignored. Hence to specify the reproduction directions, 4C2*1 + 4C3*2 = 14 bits are needed, as shown in fig. 12.3 by the R DIRNSi fields. Thus, 14 + 14 = 28 bits per cycle are used, with separate REPRO? and R DIRNS fields for each cycle. The number of cycles (or iterations) NI is also coded onto the bitstring chromosome and evolves along with the other fields.

These chromosomes are then evolved using a genetic algorithm (Goldberg, 1989), such that the resulting colony of cells attains as closely as possible some desired or target shape. The

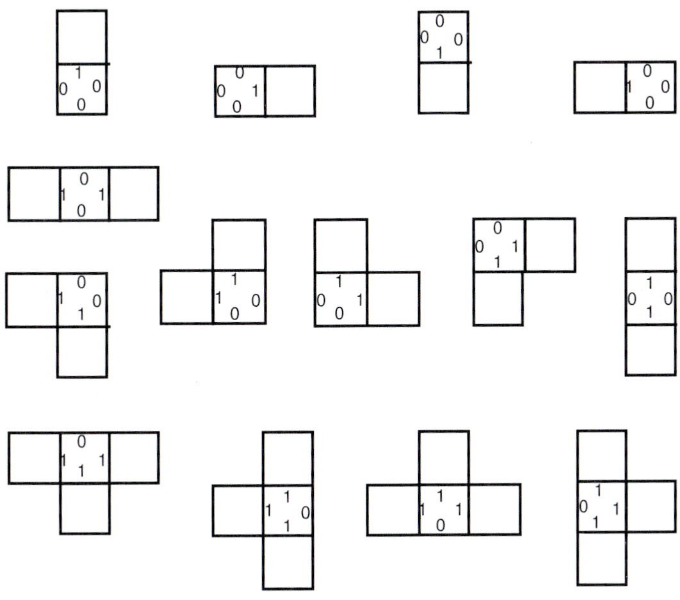

Figure 12.2 The 14 neighbourless states for 2D cells.

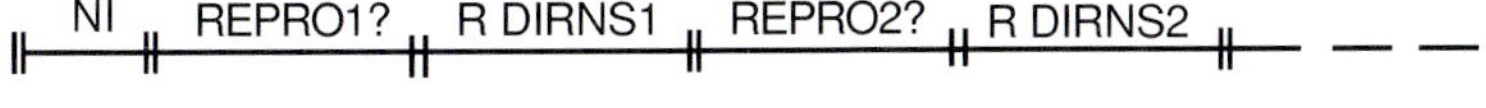

NI = NUMBER OF ITERATIONS
REPRO1? = WHICH STATES CAN REPRODUCE IN ITERATION 1
R DIRNS1 = REPRODUCTION DIRECTIONS IN ITERATION 1
REPRO2? = WHICH STATES CAN REPRODUCE IN ITERATION 2
R DIRNS2 = REPRODUCTION DIRECTIONS IN ITERATION 2

Figure 12.3 Format of a simplified chromosome.

fitness of the chromosome (i.e. the measure of closeness of the final and the target shapes) was defined as follows:

Fitness = (#ins − 0.5*#outs)/(#des) where:

#ins = the number of filled cells inside the desired shape
#outs = the number of filled cells outside the desired shape
#des = the number of cells inside the desired shape

Some examples of this type of evolution (for triangular and rectangular target shapes) are shown in fig. 12.4, with one frame per cycle or iteration. Note that NI evolved to be 4, for both shapes.

The above ideas were tested on various shapes (de Garis 1992b), both convex and non-convex. The convex shapes worked well (with fitness values around 95%, e.g. fig. 12.4), but

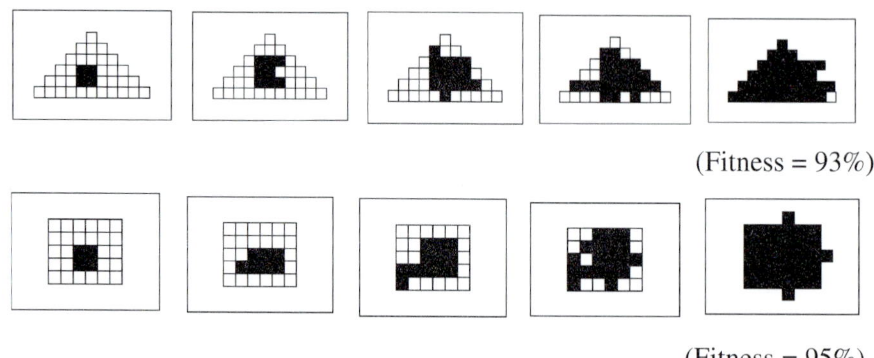

Figure 12.4 Triangular and rectangular target shapes.

non-convex shapes evolved poorly, with low fitness values (e.g. as low as 20% for an arch shape). The challenge then was to evolve arbitrary non-convex shapes, e.g. 3D embryo shapes with a head, body, limbs, fingers and toes, etc. Evolving such an artificial embryo implies a type of sequential, time dependent unfolding of shapes, e.g. first the body is grown, then the limbs and head emerge from the body, then the fingers and toes emerge from the limbs, etc. It appears that one needs some means of switching on and off shape-forming instructions for the various components.

12.3 Evolving a (Non-convex) 'L' Shape

To illustrate the ideas contained in the above section, a concrete example is now introduced, which is to 'grow' a simple nonconvex target shape in the form of the letter 'L'. Figure 12.5 shows the set-up. To keep things simple, it is assumed that there are only two operons in the 'L chromosome', and that the first operon is used to code for instructions to grow region A, and the second operon is used to code for region B. The trick then is to decide how to define the state of a cell, plus the nature of the condition fields, so that operon 'A' switches off at the appropriate time and operon 'B' switches on. What is required is that once the region A has been filled, all the edge cells (except those in region R) stop reproducing. The R cells then grow region B. Hence we need some means to distinguish the R region from the rest of the edge cells of region A (assuming only edge cells reproduce). The R region lies south-east of the A region, so one idea might be to let the A region grow for a given number of iterations (as in the above section) and then let only the south-east cells reproduce beyond that number. So, the condition for region A might be simply:

[number of iterations < X]

where X needs to be evolved. The conditions(s) for region B might be:

[number of iterations = X] & [cell region type = south-east]

OR

[X < number of iterations <= X+Y]

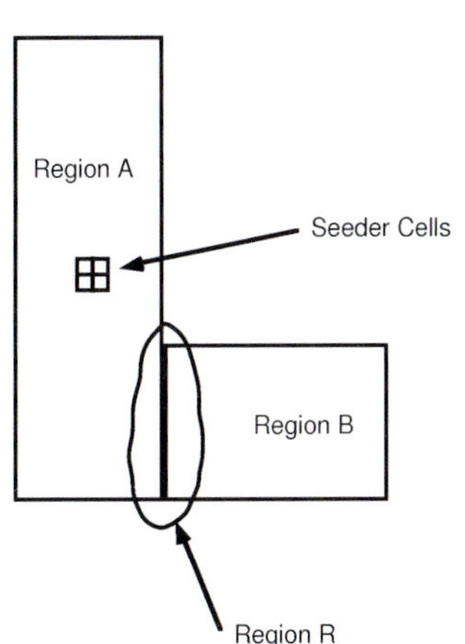

Figure 12.5 Target shape 'L'.

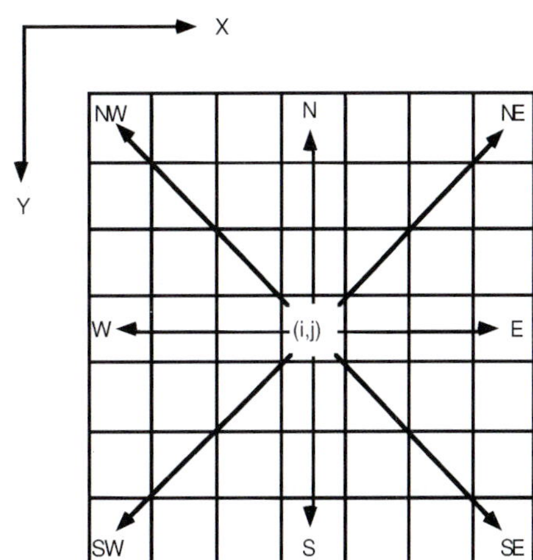

Figure 12.6 Cell neighbourhood.

Alternatively, the region B operon could be split into two operons B1 and B2, where the condition for B1 would be the first disjunct, and the condition for B2 would be the second disjunct. What are needed now are means to specify the number of iterations, and 'south-east-ness'. (Note that in an iteration, all edge cells in a colony of cells which are allowed to reproduce, do so.) One idea to specify something similar to the number of iterations (in cellular terms), might be to give each cell a generation count (GC), such that a parent cell with a GC of 'g', would have a daughter cell with a GC of '$g + 1$'.

To specify 'south-east-ness', one might use a concentration gradient of some 'chemical', which is passed in fractionally decreasing quantities from parent to daughter cell, e.g. a parent cell may have a quantity q of this chemical, which is fractionally reproduced and transmitted to the daughter cell which receives, say, a quantity $0.95q$ of this chemical. Assume that each cell uses this chemical to create another chemical which is diffused into the intercellular environment. By measuring the q value of neighbouring cells, each cell can determine the q gradient, and hence determine its position.

To calculate the q gradient at each cell, the following approach is suggested, as shown in fig. 12.6. A square block of 49 cells, i.e. the 7 by 7 'neighbourhood' of a cell is used. The average 'q value' over four cells is calculated (i.e. over the 'middle' cell, and the other three cells in the same direction). For example, if the middle cell is given coordinates (i,j) then the average 'q value' in the north-west direction (Q_{nw}) would be:

$$Q_{nw} = 0.25*[q(i,j) + q(i-1,j-1) + q(i-2,j-2) + q(i-3,j-3)]$$

Similar q values are calculated for all eight directions (i.e. E, NE, N, NW, W, SW, S, SE). Since these calculations are only performed at the edge cells, about half of these eight directions will involve empty cell positions. Hence the average q value in such directions will be low. The high q value directions are likely to be towards the center of a colony of cells, i.e. perpendicular to the edge of the colony at the point (i,j). The q gradient (QG) at a cell, is defined to be the direction (one of the eight possible) which has the largest q value. For example, those cells lying at the south-east edge of a colony of cells, will have their q gradients pointing north-west.

The notions of generation count and q gradient can be used to decide when cells should switch from their first operon to their second. What now needs to be discussed is how these notions can be coded on the operon (i.e. how to express the condition part of the operon) and how the cells are to reproduce (i.e. how to express the action part of the operon).

Figure 12.7 shows the suggested chromosome format.

This format requires some explanation. X is the iteration count (IC) when operon 1 switches off and operon 2 switches on. When the iteration count is X + Y, operon 2 switches off. Note, in one iteration, all edge cells which can reproduce, do so synchronously.

The NEWS DIRNS field is 8 bits long, and is used to specify which cells can reproduce beyond X iterations. Only those cells whose q gradients have their corresponding bits set in this field can reproduce further. For example, if a cell's q gradient is NE, and the bit corresponding to NE is set (i.e. the second bit), and the iteration count is X, then that cell can use operon 2 when the iteration count IC obeys $X =< IC =< X + Y$.

REPRO?/DIRN PAIRS (or RD Pairs) are the pairs of fields shown in fig. 12.3. The ith pair of fields in operon 1 applies to cells when the IC is i. The jth pair in operon 2 applies to cells when the IC is $X + j$.

If m bits are reserved for the X field, then $2m$ RD pairs are needed in operon 1. Similarly, if n bits are reserved for the Y field, $2n$ RD pairs are needed in operon 2. Hence the length of the chromosome can be calculated as $(m + 28*2m + n + 8 + 28*2n)$ bits. The fitness definition is the same as defined earlier, i.e. Fitness = (#ins − 0.5*#outs)/(#des), where the target shape is the 'L' (double rectangle) of fig. 12.5.

12.4 Experimental Results

This section presents some experimental results of the ideas introduced in earlier sections. These results were obtained from programs run on a MAC IIci computer, designed in 'C'. Two general approaches to the evolution were usually taken. In the first approach, both operons were switchable during a run (i.e. the second operon was able to switch on later in the run). In the second approach, so called 'shaping' techniques were used. The concept of shaping has been defined in earlier publications (de Garis, 1991a,b, 1992a). Shaping is simply splitting up an evolutionary process into intermediate phases, with intermediate targets. The results of a previous phase (i.e. the population of evolved chromosomes), are fed as the starting conditions (i.e. initial chromosomes) for the next phase. This is done to push the evolution in a desired direction by suitable choices of intermediate targets. When shaping is used, the behavior or structure evolved in phase A carries over into phase B. By suitable choice of A, a desired B (or

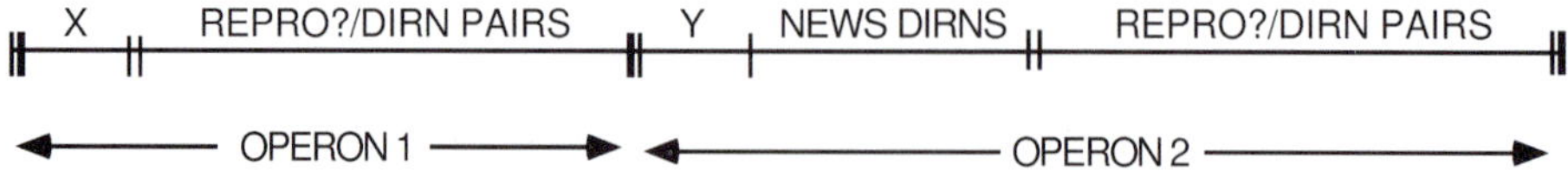

Figure 12.7 Two-operon chromosome format.

C, etc.) can often be attained. Shaping can increase the odds of obtaining a desired result, by reducing the size of the search space, thus accelerating the evolution. In some cases, shaping is needed just to get a required evolution.

In a first experiment, no shaping was used, i.e. both operons were allowed to be active, starting with random chromosomes. Figure 12.8 shows the results after 600 generations, and little further fitness growth. The X and Y values evolved to be 13 and 15 respectively, the NEWS DIRNS were [00100010]. The fitness was about 80%. Figure 12.8a shows the colony of cells grown using the instructions of the first operon (i.e. before the switching to the second operon). Figure 12.8b shows the final result after both operons have finished, i.e. after X + Y iterations. An 80% result was not thought to be particularly impressive, although at least a definite 'L' shape began to emerge. A second experiment was undertaken using shaping techniques to see if a better result could be obtained. In this second experiment, initially only operon 1 was allowed to evolve (using the L target shape). Operon 2 was switched permanently off. In a second phase of evolution, the resulting chromosome population from the evolution of operon 1 was used as a starting set of chromosomes, in an evolutionary phase in which operon 2 was able to switch on.

Figure 12.9 shows the results using shaping techniques. Figure 12.9a resulted from 1200 generations of evolution of operon 1 alone. Figure 12.9b resulted from taking operon 1 from fig. 12.9a and allowing it to evolve a further 1500 generations with both operons. Figure 12.9b shows that a definite turning occurred before fitness values stagnated, and that a non-convex shape was being formed. For fig. 12.9a, the X value evolved to be 15, and in fig. 12.9b, both the X and Y values evolved to be 15. For fig. 12.9a, the NEWS DIRNS were [11000110], which evolved to [01000100] for fig. 12.9b.

The final fitness value of fig. 12.9b was also about 80%, so shaping did not seem to have much of an effect. The vertical part of fig. 12.9a is deeper and 'cleaner' than in 12.8a, as one would expect, but the net result in 12.9b is not particularly praiseworthy.

These 80% results were rather disappointing, and showed the difficulty of the task. With convex shapes (circles, squares, rectangles, ellipses) in earlier experiments (de Garis, 1992b)

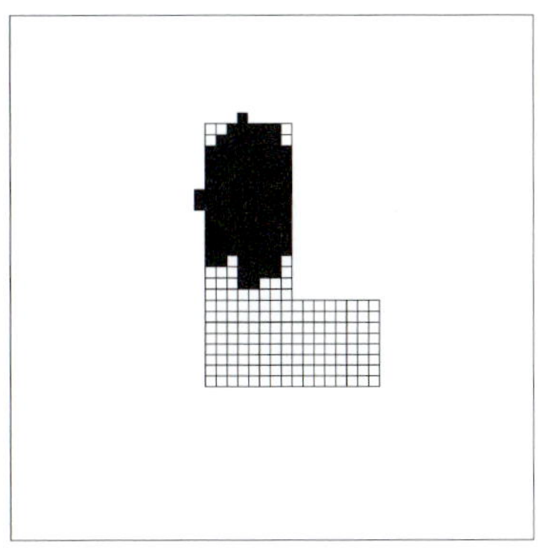

(a) AFTER OPERON 1

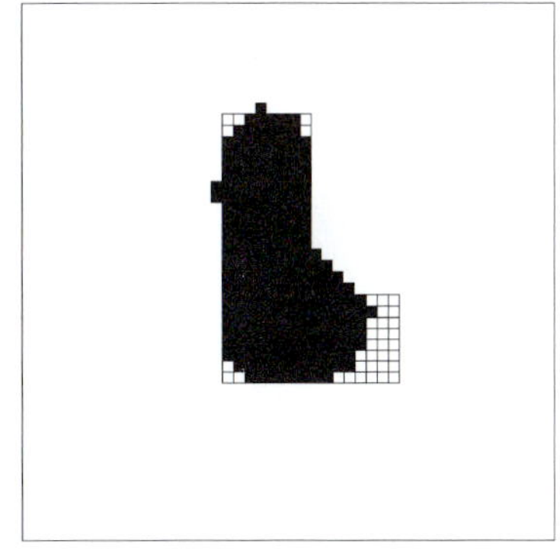

(b) AFTER OPERONS 1 & 2

Figure 12.8 'L' shape results using both operons.

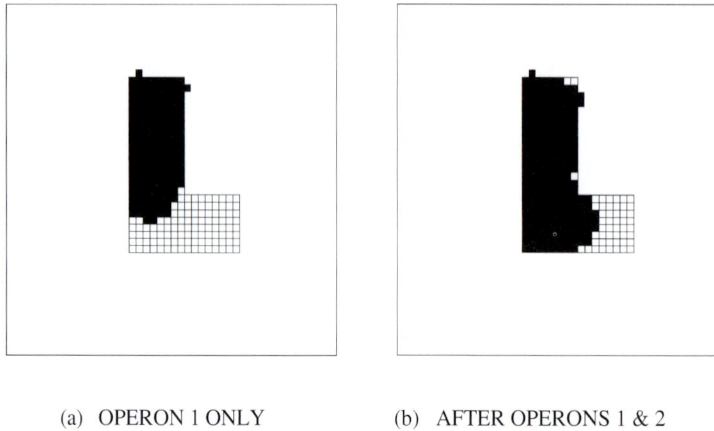

Figure 12.9 'L' shape results using shaping techniques.

fitness values around 95% (using the same fitness definition as in this chapter) were typically obtained, but non-convex shapes failed badly. The results of figs 12.8 and 12.9 show that at least non-convex shapes can be obtained, but not yet to high quality. This relative failure is probably not surprising with hindsight. The algorithm as presented in this chapter, effectively causes one convex shape to grow out of a subset of edge cells of a previous convex shape. By having a series of switch-ons and offs, one could probably generate some interesting shapes, but fully random shapes will probably require new kinds of algorithms.

A third experiment using the 'L' target shape was undertaken, which gave better results. The four seeder cells were moved down six squares, so that they were positioned more centrally relative to the vertical part of the L. This seemed to constrain the evolutionary path less. The X and Y values which evolved in fig. 12.10 were 10 and 15 respectively, and the NEWS DIRNS were [01100011]. Note that figs 12.10a and 12.10b are from the same run, with no shaping. The resulting fitness value was 87%.

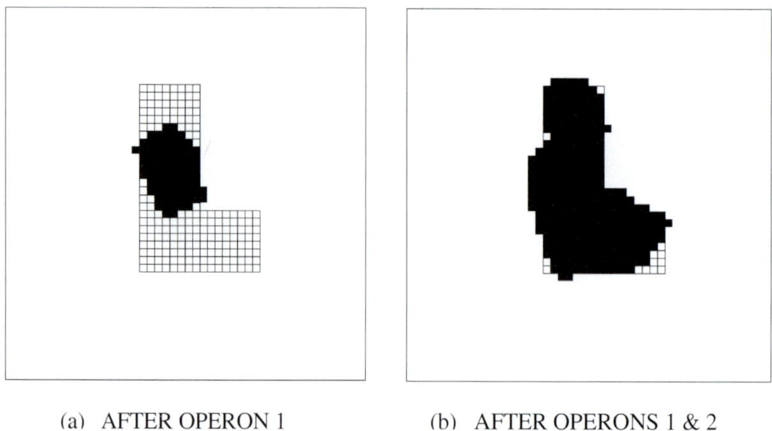

Figure 12.10 'L' shape results with more central seeder cells.

The parameter values used for the above experiments were as follows :-

Population size	20 chromosomes
Chromosome length	1810 bits
MaxX	32
MaxY	32
Max number of bits for X field	5
Max number of bits for Y field	5
Seeder cells chemical Q value	1.0
Chemical transmission coefficient	0.95
Cell grid size	48*48 cells
Seeder cell coords (figs 12.8, 12.9)	(20,14), (21,14), (20,15), (21,15)
Seeder cell coords (fig. 12.10)	(20,20), (21,20), (20,21), (21,21)
(Uniform) crossover probability	0.6
Mutation probability	0.005/bit
Linear scaling constant	2.0

The relative success of fig. 12.10 suggested trying a more complex non-convex shape. A turtle shape, consisting of five circles (body, head, and four limbs) was attempted (de Garis, 1992b). However, results were not good, with at best a blob with four limb buds being evolved. It appears that the target shape of a turtle is too ambitious for the two-operon algorithm.

In all of these experiments, there was only one switching, and many iterations. Perhaps one could increase the number of switchings and thus obtain better shapes (i.e. shapes with higher fitness values). It seems that once a cell becomes reproductive, it and its descendants will form a circular colony of cells (in 2D), with the original cell roughly at its center. If a cell (which lies along a long straight edge of cells) becomes reproductive, its descendants will form a colony which will be roughly semicircular and lie against the original edge of cells. Perhaps the art of growing arbitrary shapes is to use multiple switchings, and to select a subset of edge cells recursively, to be the reproductive cells in the next iteration of switching.

With this idea in mind, an experiment with two switchings was undertaken, using a target shape that was thought to be more realistic, i.e. it consisted of agglomerations of crescent shaped regions. Figure 12.11 shows an example of such a shape. It looks like a snowman, where the first operon is supposed to grow the body A (where Xa is the position of the original seeder cells). The second operon is supposed to grow the neck B (where Xb is the position of the edge cells of body A, which switch on), and the third operon is supposed to grow the head C (where Xc is the position of the edge cells of the neck B, which switch on). This shape is less ambitious in some ways than a turtle. If a body, neck and head can be grown, then at a later stage, perhaps four limbs can be grown as well. The actual target shape based on fig. 12.11 is shown in fig. 12.12.

We assume that cells which are switched on for the third operon can only be descendants of those cells which were switched on for the second operon. This type of 'embryological chaining' allows a certain degree of morphogenetic control. One can add layers of cells progressively to form desired shapes. The chromosome format for these double-switching (triple operon) experiments is shown in fig. 12.13. This format is a simple extension of fig. 12.7. The

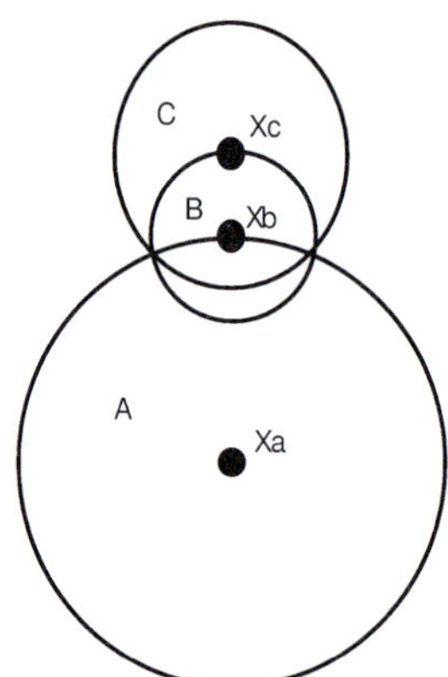

Figure 12.11 Snowman shape.

Figure 12.12 Snowman target shape.

results of the three-operon snowman shape, where all three operons were switchable (i.e. there was no shaping) are shown in fig. 12.14. To highlight which operons generated which cells, a grey coding is used. The four seeder cells are shown in light grey. Cells generated under control of operon 1 are shown in black. Cells generated under control of operon 2 are shown in light grey. Cells generated under control of operon 3 are shown in dark grey. The X, Y and Z values for fig. 12.14 were 30, 3 and 15 respectively. The NEWS DIRNS Y and NEWS DIRNS Z were [00100010] and [01000111]. The number of generations used for the evolution of fig. 12.14 was 100. The other parameter values were as in the above experiments.

Figure 12.14 was thought to be reasonably successful. The resulting figure does look a bit like a snowman, with a body and a head. The overall shape is also non-convex. Encouraged by this result, an attempt was made to see whether a three-operon chromosome could generate a better turtle shape (de Garis, 1992b). The results were better, but still not recognizably turtle-like. With longer evolution times on a more powerful computer, better results would probably be obtainable.

12.5 Conclusions

The above results show that it is possible to apply genetic algorithms to the growth of reproducible cellular automata to produce desired final shapes. The above work also shows that time sequential, switchable genes or instruction subsets can be used in an 'embryological' way. The author is now using such ideas to build artificial brains using evolvable electronic neural network modules, rather than evolvable shapes. Perhaps one day it might be possible to combine both by creating a form of neuro-embryology directly in electronics at electronic speeds,

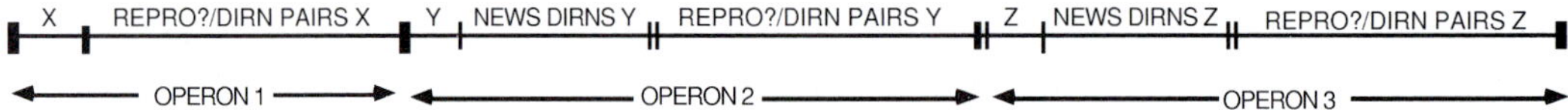

Figure 12.13 Three-operon chromosome format.

Figure 12.14 Three-operon snowman results.

using cellular automata equivalents of time switchable and multivaried NGFs (neural growth factors) and concentration gradients which neurites (baby neurons) follow in their wiring up phase. For the moment, however, such dreams are beyond state-of-the-art electronics. At the time of writing, the author knows of no real applications of the above techniques, but still dreams that someone will use similar ideas to grow artificial brains in 'embryo-electronics'.

Further down the road, molecular scale technologies will be capable of building devices with a huge number of components (Drexler, 1992). It will be totally impractical to build these devices one component at a time. They will probably have to self-assemble in an embryological-like way. However, due to the large number of components and the complexity of their connections, the global behaviour of the device will be too complex to be predictable, i.e. one will not be able to map its structure to its performance. Under such circumstances, the only way to proceed may be to use an EE approach, i.e. to imitate nature's method of building complex devices (creatures). However, very little is known about how to self-assemble devices artificially in an embryological-like manner. This chapter has made some initial attempts at providing some solutions to this problem, and has contributed towards the creation of an 'artificial embryology'.

It is hoped that the challenge to 'grow' artificial embryos will appeal to other ALife researchers, so that some real progress can be made in this field in the next few years. If so, it is possible that ALife's algorithmic engineering approach to embryology may even generate clues as to how nature performs its morphogenesis, and hence be of interest to the biologists. However, such interest need not be confined to the biologists. Electronic and molecular engineers may also be interested. The author intends to direct his future work in the field he calls 'embryonics', i.e. 'embryological electronics', which will attempt to 'grow' electronic circuits, using EE techniques. Hopefully this approach will allow extremely complex yet functional electronic (neural) circuits to be built/evolved, using special hardware devices called Darwin machines. Darwin machines may accelerate the evolution of artificial nervous systems for artificial creatures.

Once it is possible to evolve arbitrary shapes successfully, the next step might be to add extra operons which switch internal cells to give them the ability to move, or act as muscles, etc. so that the colony of cells can perform some useful function. Later, it might be possible to evolve systems which act as tools to help build other systems. It might even be possible to evolve systems which build copies of themselves, which later work together to build some larger system. These ideas might be implemented on 'cellular automata Darwin machines' (CADMs). At a later date, when nanoscale technologies come on line, it might be possible to carry over these ideas to molecular scale devices.

A Note on the Term 'Evolutionary Engineering'

Until a few years ago, I used to use the term 'genetic programming', instead of my current term of 'evolutionary engineering', to describe what I do. This created so much confusion with John Koza's use of the term with a different definition, that I abandoned my use of it. Hence do not be confused to find the term genetic programming in many of my papers in the references. Simply substitute the term evolutionary engineering in your mind and do not be confused with Koza's definition (i.e. evolving tree structured software programs).

References

Carter F.L., Siatkowski H., Wohltjen H., (eds) (1988). *Molecular Electronic Devices*, North Holland.

de Garis, H. (1990a). 'Genetic Programming: Modular Evolution for Darwin Machines', *IJCNN-90-WASH-DC, Int. Joint Conf. on Neural Networks*, January 1990, Washington DC, USA.

de Garis, H. (1990b). 'Genetic Programming: Building Nanobrains with Genetically Programmed Neural Network Modules', *IJCNN-90 San Diego, Int. Joint Conf. on Neural Networks*, June 1990, San Diego, California, USA.

de Garis, H. (1990c). 'Genetic Programming: Building Artificial Nervous Systems Using Genetically Programmed Neural Network Modules', in Porter, B. W. and Mooney, R. J. (eds), *Proc. 7th. Int. Conf. on Machine Learning*, pp. 132–139, Morgan Kaufmann.

de Garis, H. (1990d) 'Genetic Programming: Evolution of a Time Dependent Neural Network Module Which Teaches a Pair of Stick Legs to Walk', *ECAI-90, 9th European Conf. on Artificial Intelligence*, August 1990, Stockholm, Sweden.

de Garis, H. (1991a). 'Genetic Programming: Artificial Nervous Systems, Artificial Embryos and Embryological Electronics', in *Parallel Problem Solving from Nature*, Lecture Notes in Computer Science 496, Springer-Verlag.

de Garis, H. (1991b). 'LIZZY: The Genetic Programming of an Artificial Nervous System', *ICANN91, Int. Conf. on Artificial Neural Networks*, June 1991, Espoo, Finland.

de Garis, H. (1991c). 'GenNETS: Genetically Programmed Neural Nets: Using the Genetic Algorithm to Train Neural Nets Whose Inputs and/or Outputs Vary in Time', *IJCNN91 Singapore, Int. Joint Conf. on Neural Networks*, November 1991, Singapore.

de Garis, H. (1991d). 'Genetic Programming', Ch. 8 in *Neural and Intelligent Systems Integration*, Branko Soucek (ed.), Wiley.

de Garis, H. (1992a). 'Steerable GenNETS: The Genetic Programming of Controllable Behaviors in GenNets', *ECAL91 Paris, Proceedings of the 1st European Conference on Artificial Life*, MIT Press.

de Garis, H. (1992b). 'Artificial Embryology: The Genetic Programming of an Artificial Embryo', Ch.14 in *Dynamic, Genetic, and Chaotic Programming*, ed. Branko Soucek and the IRIS Group, Wiley.

de Garis, H. (1992c). 'Exploring GenNet Behaviors: Using Genetic Programming to Explore Qualitatively New Behaviors in Recurrent Neural Networks', *IJCNN-92-Baltimore, Int. Joint Conf. on Neural Networks*, June 1992, Baltimore, USA.

de Garis, H. (1992d). 'Genetic Programming: Evolutionary Approaches to Multistrategy Learning', ch. 21 in *Machine Learning: A Multistrategy Approach*, Vol. 4, Michalski, R.S. and Tecuci, G. (eds), Morgan Kauffmann.

de Garis, H. (1993). *Genetic Programming: GenNets, Artificial Nervous Systems, Artificial Embryos*, Wiley, in press.

Drexler, K. E. (1992). *Nanosystems: Molecular Machinery, Manufacturing and Computation*, Wiley.

Goldberg, D. E. (1989). *Genetic Algorithms in Search, Optimization, and Machine Learning*, Addison-Wesley.

Hillis, W. D. (1985). *The Connection Machine*, MIT Press.

Holland, J. (1986). 'Escaping Brittleness: The Possibilities of General Purpose Learning Algorithms Applied to Parallel Rule-Bases Systems', chapter 20 of, *Machine Learning: An Artificial Intelligence Approach*, vol. 2, Michalski, R. S., Carbonell, J. G. and Mitchell T. M., (eds), Morgan Kauffmann.

Koza, J. R. (1990). 'Genetic Programming: A Paradigm for Genetically Breeding Populations of Computer Programs to Solve Problems', Stanford University Comp. Sci. Dept. Technical Report, STAN-CS-90-1314.

Koza, J. R. (1992). *Genetic Programming*, MIT Press.

Schneiker, C. (1989). 'Nano Technology with Feynman Machines: Scanning Tunneling Engineering and Artificial Life', in *Artificial Life*, Langton, C. G. (ed.), Addison-Wesley.

Wolfram, S. (ed.) (1986). *Theory and Applications of Cellular Automata*, World Scientific.

Chapter 13

Evolving Three-Dimensional Morphology and Behaviour

By Karl Sims*

13.1 Introduction

A classic trade-off in the fields of artificial life and computer animation is that of complexity vs. control. It is often difficult to build interesting or realistic virtual entities and still maintain control over them. Sometimes it is difficult to build a complex virtual world at all, if it is necessary to conceive, design, and assemble each component. An example of this trade-off is that of kinematic control vs. dynamic simulation. If we directly provide the positions and angles for moving objects, we can control each detail of their behaviour, but it might be difficult to achieve physically plausible motions. If we instead provide forces and torques and simulate the resulting dynamics, the result will probably look correct, but then it can be very difficult to achieve the desired behaviour, especially as the objects we want to control become more complex. Methods have been developed for dynamically controlling specific objects to successfully crawl, walk, or even run (McKenna and Zeltzer, 1990; Miller, 1988; Raibert and Hodgins, 1991), but a new control algorithm must be carefully designed each time a new behaviour or morphology is desired.

Optimization techniques offer possibilities for the automatic generation of complexity. The genetic algorithm is a form of artificial evolution, and is a commonly used method for optimization. A Darwinian 'survival of the fittest' approach is employed to search for optima in large multidimensional spaces (Goldberg, 1989; Holland, 1975). Genetic algorithms permit virtual entities to be created without requiring an understanding of the procedures or parameters used to generate them. The measure of success, or *fitness*, of each individual can be calculated automatically, or it can instead be provided interactively by a user. Interactive evolution allows procedurally generated results to be explored by simply choosing those that are the most aesthetically desirable for each generation (Dawkins, 1986; Sims, 1991; Sims, 1992; Todd and Latham, 1992).

The user sacrifices some control when using these methods, especially when the fitness is procedurally defined. However, the potential gain in automating the creation of complexity can

* Chapter produced and edited with permission by Peter Bentley from the two papers: *Evolving Virtual Creatures* and *Evolving 3D Morphology and Behavior by Competition* by Karl Sims. Reprinted with permission.

EVOLUTIONARY DESIGN BY COMPUTERS
ISBN 1-55860-605-X

often compensate for this loss of control, and a higher level of user influence is still maintained by the fitness criteria specification.

In several cases, optimization has been used to automatically generate dynamic control systems for given articulated structures: de Garis has evolved weight values for neural networks (de Garis, 1990), Ngo and Marks have performed genetic algorithms on stimulus-response pairs (Ngo and Marks, 1993), and van de Panne and Fiume have optimized sensor-actuator networks (van de Panne and Fiume, 1993). Each of these methods has resulted in successful locomotion of two-dimensional stick figures.

The work presented here is related to these projects, but differs in several respects. In previous work, control systems were generated for fixed structures that were user-designed, but here entire creatures are evolved: the optimization determines the creature morphologies as well as their control systems. Also, here the creatures' bodies are three-dimensional and fully physically based. The three-dimensional physical structure of a creature can adapt to its control system, and vice versa, as they evolve together. The 'nervous systems' of creatures are also completely determined by the optimization: the number of internal nodes, the connectivity, and the type of function each neural node performs are included in the genetic description of each creature, and can grow in complexity as an evolution proceeds. Together, these remove the necessity for a user to provide any specific creature information such as shape, size, joint constraints, sensors, actuators, or internal neural parameters. Finally, here a developmental process is used to generate the creatures and their control systems, and allows similar components including their local neural circuitry to be defined once and then replicated, instead of requiring each to be separately specified. This approach is related to L-systems, graftal grammars, and object instancing techniques (Hart, 1992; Kitano, 1990; Lindenmayer, 1968; Mjolsness *et al.* 1989; Smith, 1984).

It is convenient to use the biological terms *genotype* and *phenotype* when discussing artificial evolution. A *genotype* is a coded representation of a possible individual or problem solution. In biological systems, a genotype is usually composed of DNA and contains the instructions for the development of an organism. Genetic algorithms typically use populations of genotypes consisting of strings of binary digits or parameters. These are mapped to produce *phenotypes* which are then evaluated according to some fitness criteria and selectively reproduced. New genotypes are generated by copying, mutating, and/or combining the genotypes of the most fit individuals, and as the cycle repeats the population should ascend to higher and higher levels of fitness.

Variable length genotypes such as hierarchical Lisp expressions or other computer programs can be useful in expanding the set of possible results beyond a predefined genetic space of fixed dimensions. Genetic languages such as these allow new parameters and new dimensions to be added to the genetic space as an evolution proceeds, and therefore define rather a *hyperspace* of possible results. This approach has been used to genetically program solutions to a variety of problems (Cramer, 1985; Koza, 1992), as well as to explore procedurally generated images and dynamical systems (Sims, 1991; Sims, 1992).

In the spirit of unbounded genetic languages, directed graphs are presented here as an appropriate basis for a grammar that can be used to describe both the morphology and nervous systems of virtual creatures. New features and functions can be added to creatures, or existing ones removed, so the levels of complexity can also evolve.

13.2 Creature Morphology

In this work, the phenotype embodiment of a virtual creature is a hierarchy of articulated three-dimensional rigid parts. The genetic representation of this morphology is a directed graph of nodes and connections. Each graph contains the developmental instructions for growing a creature, and provides a way of reusing instructions to make similar or recursive components within the creature. A phenotype hierarchy of parts is made from a graph by starting at a defined *root-node* and synthesizing parts from the node information while tracing through the connections of the graph. The graph can be recurrent. Nodes can connect to themselves or in cycles to form recursive or fractal like structures. They can also connect to the same child multiple times to make duplicate instances of the same appendage.

Each node in the graph contains information describing a rigid part. The *dimensions* determine the physical shape of the part. A *joint-type* determines the constraints on the relative motion between this part and its parent by defining the number of degrees of freedom of the joint and the movement allowed for each degree of freedom. The different joint-types allowed are: *rigid*, *revolute*, *twist*, *universal*, *bend-twist*, *twist-bend*, or *spherical*. *Joint-limits* determine the point beyond which restoring spring forces will be exerted for each degree of freedom. A *recursive-limit* parameter determines how many times this node should generate a phenotype part when in a recursive cycle. A set of local *neurons* is also included in each node, and will

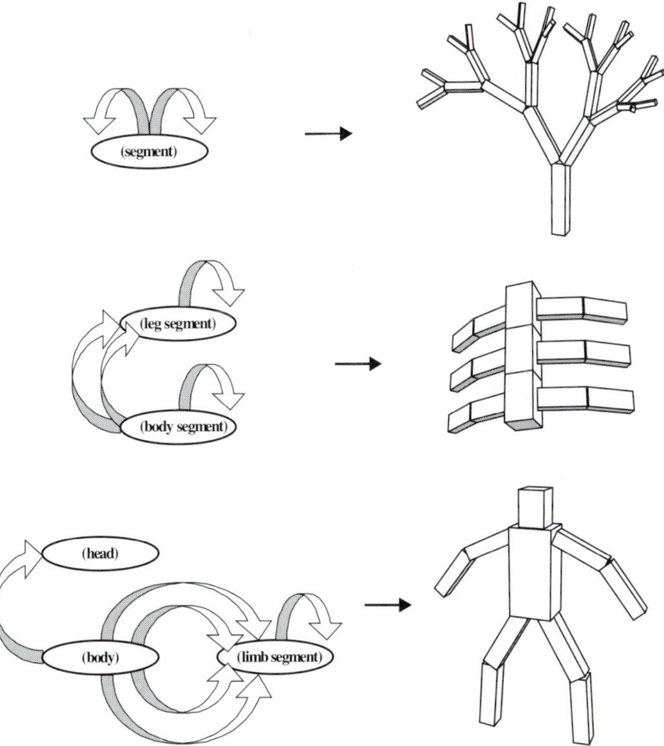

Figure 13.1 Hand-designed examples of genotype graphs and corresponding creature morphologies.

be explained further in the next section. Finally, a node contains a set of *connections* to other nodes.

Each connection also contains information. The placement of a child part relative to its parent is decomposed into *position*, *orientation*, *scale*, and *reflection*, so each can be mutated independently. The position of attachment is constrained to be on the surface of the parent part. Reflections cause negative scaling, and allow similar but symmetrical subtrees to be described. A *terminal-only* flag can cause a connection to be applied only when the *recursive limit* is reached, and permits tail or hand-like components to occur at the end of chains or repeating units.

Figure 13.1 shows some simple hand-designed graph topologies and resulting phenotype morphologies. Note that the parameters in the nodes and connections such as recursive-limit are not shown for the genotype even though they affect the morphology of the phenotype. The nodes are anthropomorphically labelled as 'body', 'leg', etc., but the genetic descriptions actually have no concept of specific categories of functional components.

13.3 Creature Control

A virtual 'brain' determines the behaviour of a creature. The brain is a dynamical system that accepts input sensor values and provides output effector values. The output values are applied as forces or torques at the degrees of freedom of the body's joints. This cycle of effects is shown in fig. 13.2.

Sensor, effector, and internal neuron signals are represented here by continuously variable scalars that may be positive or negative. Allowing negative values permits the implementation of single effectors that can both push and pull. Although this may not be biologically realistic, it simplifies the more natural development of muscle pairs.

13.3.1 Sensors

Each sensor is contained within a specific part of the body, and measures either aspects of that part or aspects of the world relative to that part. Three different types of sensors were used for these experiments:

1. *Joint angle sensors* give the current value for each degree of freedom of each joint.
2. *Contact sensors* activate (1.0) if a contact is made, and negatively activate (−1.0) if not.

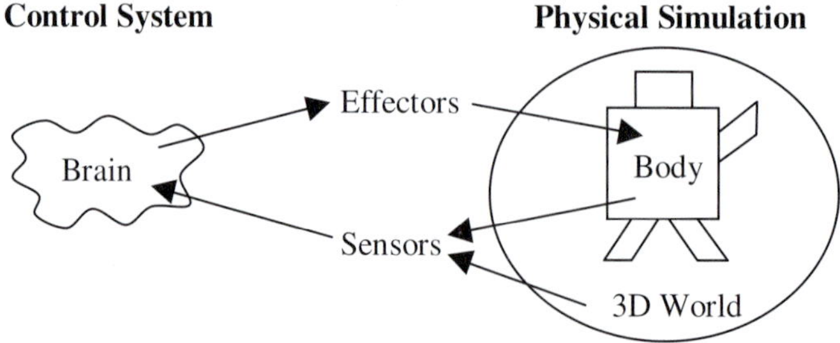

Figure 13.2 The cycle of effects between brain, body and world.

Each contact sensor has a sensitive region within a part's shape and activates when any contacts occur in that area. In this work, contact sensors are made available for each face of each part. No distinction is made between self-contact and environmental contact.

3. *Photosensors* react to a global light source position. Three photosensor signals provide the coordinates of the normalized light source direction relative to the orientation of the part. This is the same as having pairs of opposing photosensitive surfaces in which the left side negates its response and adds it to the right side for the total response.

Other types of sensors, such as accelerometers, additional proprioceptors, or even sound or smell detectors could also be implemented, but these basic three are enough to allow interesting and adaptive behaviours to occur. The inclusion of the different types of sensors in an evolving virtual brain can be enabled or disabled as appropriate depending on the physical environment and behaviour goals. For example, contact sensors are enabled for land environments, and photosensors are enabled for following behaviours.

13.3.2 Neurons

Internal neural nodes are used to give virtual creatures the possibility of arbitrary behaviour. Ideally a creature should be able to have an internal state beyond its sensor values, or be affected by its history.

In this work, different neural nodes can perform diverse functions on their inputs to generate their output signals. Because of this, a creature's brain might resemble a dataflow computer program more than a typical neural network. This approach is probably less biologically realistic than just using sum and threshold functions, but it is hoped that it makes the evolution of interesting behaviours more likely. The set of functions that neural nodes can have is: *sum*, *product*, *divide*, *sum-threshold*, *greater-than*, *sign-of*, *min*, *max*, *abs*, *if*, *interpolate*, *sin*, *cos*, *atan*, *log*, *expt*, *sigmoid*, *integrate*, *differentiate*, *smooth*, *memory*, *oscillate-wave*, and *oscillate-saw*.

Some functions compute an output directly from their inputs, while others such as the oscillators retain some state and can give time varying outputs even when their inputs are constant. The number of inputs to a neuron depends on its function, and here is at most three. Each input contains a connection to another neuron or a sensor from which to receive a value. Alternatively, an input can simply receive a constant value. The input values are first scaled by weights before being operated on. The genetic parameters for each neural node include these weights as well as the function type and the connection information. For each simulated time interval, every neuron computes its output value from its inputs. In this work, two brain time steps are performed for each dynamic simulation time step so signals can propagate through multiple neurons with less delay.

13.3.3 Effectors

Each effector simply contains a connection to a neuron or a sensor from which to receive a value. This input value is scaled by a constant weight, and then exerted as a joint force which affects the dynamic simulation and the resulting behaviour of the creature. Different types of effectors, such as sound or scent emitters, might also be interesting, but only effectors that exert simulated muscle forces are used here.

Each effector controls a degree of freedom of a joint. The effectors for a given joint connecting two parts are contained in the part further out in the hierarchy, so that each non-root part operates only a single joint connecting it to its parent. The angle sensors for that joint are also contained in this part.

Each effector is given a *maximum-strength* proportional to the maximum cross-sectional area of the two parts it joins. Effector forces are scaled by these strengths and not permitted to exceed them. Since strength scales with area, but mass scales with volume, as in nature, behaviour does not always scale uniformly.

13.3.4 Combining Morphology and Control

The genotype descriptions of virtual brains and the actual phenotype brains are both directed graphs of nodes and connections. The nodes contain the sensors, neurons, and effectors, and the connections define the flow of signals between these nodes. These graphs can also be recurrent, and as a result the final control system can have feedback loops and cycles.

However, most of these neural elements exist within a specific part of the creature. Thus the genotype for the nervous system is a nested graph: the morphological nodes each contain graphs of the neural nodes and connections.

When a creature is synthesized from its genetic description, the neural components described within each part are generated along with the morphological structure. This causes blocks of neural control circuitry to be replicated along with each instanced part, so each duplicated segment or appendage of a creature can have a similar but independent local control system.

These local control systems can be connected to enable the possibility of coordinated control. Connections are allowed between adjacent parts in the hierarchy: the neurons and effectors within a part can receive signals from sensors or neurons in their parent part or in their child parts.

Creatures are also given a set of neurons that are not associated with a specific part, and are copied only once into the phenotype. This gives the opportunity for the development of global synchronization or centralized control. These neurons can receive signals from each other or from sensors or neurons in specific instances of any of the creature's parts, and the neurons and effectors within the parts can optionally receive signals from these unassociated-neuron outputs.

In this way the genetic language for morphology and control is merged. A local control system is described for each type of part, and these are copied and connected into the hierarchy of the creature's body to make a complete distributed nervous system. Figure 13.3b shows the creature morphology resulting from the genotype in fig. 13.3a. Again, parameters describing shapes, recursive-limits, and weights are not shown for the genotype even though they affect the phenotype. Figure 13.3c shows the corresponding brain of this creature. The brackets on the left side of fig. 13.3c group the neural components of each part. Some groups have similar neural systems because they are copies from the same genetic description. This creature can swim by making cyclic paddling motions with four similar flippers. Note that it can be difficult to analyze exactly how a control system such as this works, and some components may not actually be used at all. Fortunately, a primary benefit of using artificial evolution is that understanding these representations is not necessary.

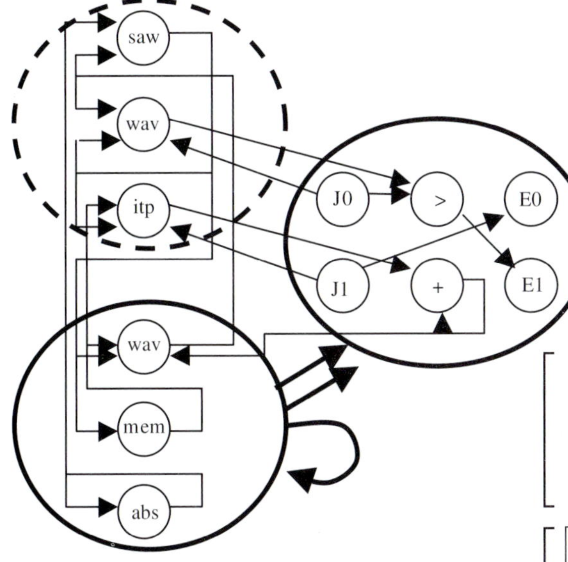

Figure 13.3a Example of evolved nested graph genotype. The outer graph in bold describes a creature's morphology.The inner graph describes its neural circuitry. J0 and J1 are joint angle sensors, and E0 and E1 are effector outputs. The dashed node contains centralized neurons that are not associated with any part.

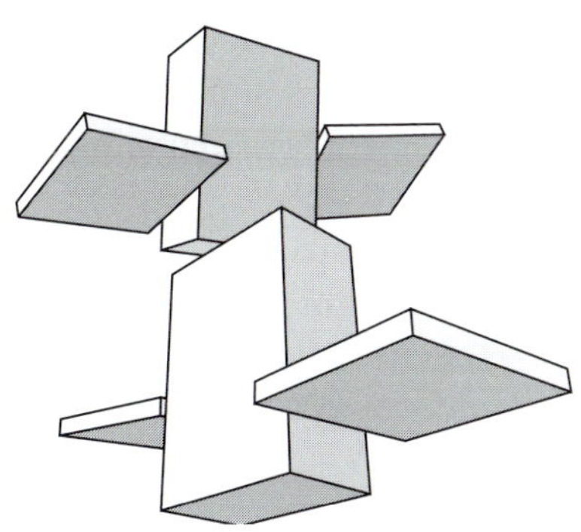

Figure 13.3b The phenotype morphology generated from the evolved genotype shown in figure 13.3a.

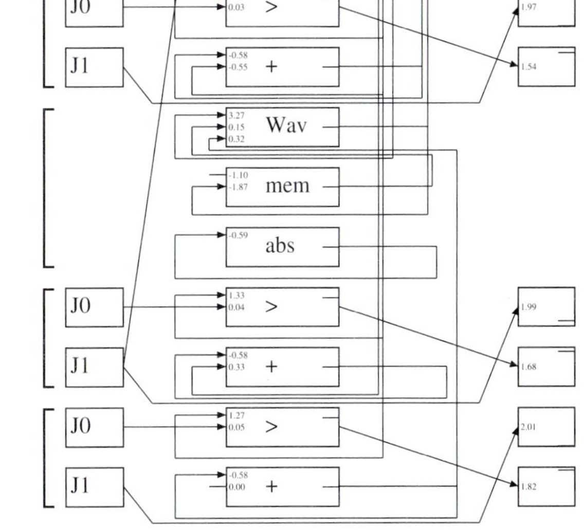

Figure 13.3c The phenotype 'brain' generated from the evolved genotype shown in figure 13.3a. The effector outputs of this control system cause paddling motions in the four flippers of the morphology shown in 13.3b.

13.4 Physical Simulation

Dynamics simulation is used to calculate the movement of creatures resulting from their interaction with a virtual three-dimensional world. There are several components of the physical simulation used in this work: articulated body dynamics, numerical integration, collision detection, collision response, friction, and an optional viscous fluid effect. These are only briefly summarized here, since physical simulation is not the emphasis of this chapter.

Featherstone's recursive O(N) articulated body method is used to calculate the accelerations from the velocities and external forces of each hierarchy of connected rigid parts (Featherstone, 1987). Integration determines the resulting motions from these accelerations and is performed by a Runge–Kutta–Fehlberg method which is a fourth order Runge–Kutta with an additional evaluation to estimate the error and adapt the step size. Typically between 1 and 5 integration time steps are performed for each animation frame of 1/30 second.

The shapes of parts are represented here by simple rectangular solids. Bounding box hierarchies are used to reduce the number of collision tests between parts from $O(N^2)$. Pairs whose world-space bounding boxes intersect are tested for penetrations, and collisions with a ground plane are also tested if one exists. If necessary, the previous time-step is reduced to keep any new penetrations below a certain tolerance. Connected parts are permitted to interpenetrate but not rotate completely through each other. This is achieved by using adjusted shapes when testing for collisions between connected parts. The shape of the smaller part is clipped halfway back from its point of attachment so it can swing freely until its remote end makes contact.

Collision response is accomplished by a hybrid model using both impulses and penalty spring forces. At high velocities, instantaneous impulse forces are used, and at low velocities springs are used, to simulate collisions and contacts with arbitrary elasticity and friction parameters.

A viscosity effect is used for the simulations in underwater environments. For each exposed moving surface, a viscous force resists the normal component of its velocity, proportional to its surface area and normal velocity magnitude. This is a simple approximation that does not include the motion of the fluid itself, but is still sufficient for simulating realistic looking swimming and paddling dynamics.

It is important that the physical simulation be reasonably accurate when optimizing for creatures that can move within it. Any bugs that allow energy leaks from non-conservation, or even round-off errors, will inevitably be discovered and exploited by the evolving creatures. Although this can be a lazy and often amusing approach for debugging a physical modelling system, it is not necessarily the most practical.

13.5 Behaviour Selection

In this work, virtual creatures are evolved by optimizing for a specific task or behaviour. A creature is grown from its genetic description as previously explained, and then it is placed in a dynamically simulated virtual world. The brain provides effector forces which move parts of the creature, the sensors report aspects of the world and the creature's body back to the brain, and the resulting physical behaviour of the creature is evaluated. After a certain duration of virtual time (perhaps 10 seconds), a *fitness* value is assigned that corresponds to the success level of that behaviour. If a creature has a high fitness relative to the rest of the population, it will be selected for survival and reproduction as described in the next section.

Before creatures are simulated for fitness evaluation, some simple viability checks are performed, and inappropriate creatures are removed from the population by giving them zero fitness values. Those that have more than a specified number of parts are removed. A subset of genotypes will generate creatures whose parts initially interpenetrate. A short simulation with collision detection and response attempts to repel any intersecting parts, but those creatures with persistent interpenetrations are also discarded.

Computation can be conserved for most fitness methods by discontinuing the simulations of individuals that are predicted to be unlikely to survive the next generation. The fitness is periodically estimated for each simulation as it proceeds. Those are stopped that are either not moving at all or are doing somewhat worse than the minimum fitness of the previously surviving individuals.

Many different types of fitness measures can be used to perform evolutions of virtual creatures. Four examples of fitness methods are described here.

13.5.1 Swimming

Physical simulation of a water environment is achieved by turning off gravity and adding the viscous water resistance effect as described. Swimming speed is used as the fitness value and is measured by the distance travelled by the creature's centre of mass per unit time. Straight swimming is rewarded over circling by using the maximum distance from the initial centre of mass. Continuing movement is rewarded over that from a single initial push, by giving the velocities during the final phase of the test period a stronger relative weight in the total fitness value.

13.5.2 Walking

The term *walking* is used loosely here to indicate any form of land locomotion. A land environment is simulated by including gravity, turning off the viscous water effect, and adding a static ground plane with friction. Additional inanimate objects can be placed in the world for more complex environments. Again, speed is used as the selection criterion, but the vertical component of velocity is ignored.

For land environments, it can be necessary to prevent creatures from generating high velocities by simply falling over. This is accomplished by first running the simulation with no friction and no effector forces until the height of the centre of mass reaches a stable minimum.

13.5.3 Jumping

Jumping behaviour can be selected for by measuring the maximum height above the ground of the lowest part of the creature. An alternative method is to use the average height of the lowest part of the creature during the duration of simulation.

13.5.4 Following

Another evaluation method is used to select for creatures that can adaptively follow a light source. Photosensors are enabled, so the effector output forces and resulting behaviour can depend on the relative direction of a light source to the creature. Several trials are run with the light source in different locations, and the speeds at which a creature moves toward it are averaged for the fitness value. Following behaviours can be evolved for both water and land environments.

Fleeing creatures can also be generated in a similar manner, or following behaviour can be transformed into fleeing behaviour by simply negating a creature's photo sensor signals.

Once creatures are found that exhibit successful following behaviours, they can be led around in arbitrary paths by movement of the light sources.

13.6 Creature Evolution

An evolution of virtual creatures is begun by first creating an initial population of genotypes. Seed genotypes are synthesized 'from scratch' by random generation of sets of nodes and connections. Alternatively, an existing genotype from a previous evolution can be used to seed an initial population.

A *survival-ratio* determines the percentage of the population that will survive each generation. In this work, population sizes were typically 300, and the survival ratio was 1/5. If the initially generated population has fewer individuals with positive fitness than the number that should survive, another round of seed genotypes is generated to replace those with zero fitness.

For each generation, creatures are grown from their genetic descriptions, and their fitness values are measured by a method such as those described in the previous section. The individuals whose fitnesses fall within the survival percentile are then reproduced, and their offspring fill the slots of those individuals that did not survive. The survivors are kept in the population for the next generation, and the total size of the population is maintained. The number of offspring that each surviving individual generates is proportional to its fitness – the most successful creatures make the most children.

Offspring are generated from the surviving creatures by copying and combining their directed graph genotypes. When these graphs are reproduced they are subjected to probabilistic variation or mutation, so the corresponding phenotypes are similar to their parents but have been altered or adjusted in random ways.

13.6.1 Mutating Directed Graphs

A directed graph is mutated by the following sequence of steps:

1. The internal parameters of each node are subjected to possible alterations. A mutation frequency for each parameter type determines the probability that a mutation will be applied to it at all. Boolean values are mutated by simply flipping their state. Scalar values are mutated by adding several random numbers to them for a Gaussian-like distribution so small adjustments are more likely than drastic ones. The scale of an adjustment is relative to the original value, so large quantities can be varied more easily and small ones can be carefully tuned. A scalar can also be negated. After a mutation occurs, values are clamped to their legal bounds. Some parameters that only have a limited number of legal values are mutated by simply picking a new value at random from the set of possibilities.
2. A new random node is added to the graph. A new node normally has no effect on the phenotype unless a connection also mutates a pointer to it. Therefore a new node is always

initially added, but then garbage collected later (in step 5) if it does not become connected. This type of mutation allows the complexity of the graph to grow as an evolution proceeds.

3. The parameters of each connection are subjected to possible mutations, in the same way the node parameters were in step 1. With some frequency the connection pointer is moved to point to a different node which is chosen at random.
4. New random connections are added and existing ones are removed. In the case of the neural graphs these operations are not performed because the number of inputs for each element is fixed, but the morphological graphs can have a variable number of connections per node. Each existing node is subject to having a new random connection added to it, and each existing connection is subject to possible removal.
5. Unconnected elements are garbage collected. Connectedness is propagated outwards through the connections of the graph, starting from the root node of the morphology, or from the effector nodes of neural graphs. Although leaving the disconnected nodes for possible reconnection might be advantageous, and is probably biologically analogous, at least the unconnected newly added ones are removed to prevent unnecessary growth in graph size.

Since mutations are performed on a per element basis, genotypes with only a few elements might not receive any mutations, where genotypes with many elements would receive enough mutations that they rarely resemble their parents. This is compensated for by temporarily scaling the mutation frequencies by an amount inversely proportional to the size of the current graph being mutated, such that on the average, at least one mutation occurs in the entire graph.

Mutation of nested directed graphs, as are used here to represent creatures, is performed by first mutating the outer graph and then mutating the inner layer of graphs. The inner graphs are mutated last because legal values for some of their parameters (inter-node neural input sources) can depend on the topology of the outer graph.

13.6.2 Mating Directed Graphs

Sexual reproduction allows components from more than one parent to be combined into new offspring. This permits features to evolve independently and later be merged into a single individual. Two different methods for mating directed graphs are used in this work.

The first is a *crossover* operation (see fig. 13.4a). The nodes of two parents are each aligned in a row as they are stored, and the nodes of the first parent are copied to make the child, but one or more crossover points determine when the copying source should switch to the other parent. The connections of a node are copied with it and simply point to the same relative node locations as before. If the copied connections now point out of bounds because of varying node numbers they are randomly reassigned.

A second mating method *grafts* two genotypes together by connecting a node of one parent to a node of another (see fig. 13.4b). The first parent is copied, and one of its connections is chosen at random and adjusted to point to a random node in the second parent. Newly unconnected nodes of the first parent are removed and the newly connected node of the second parent and any of its descendants are appended to the new graph.

A new directed graph can be produced by either of these two mating methods, or asexually by using only mutations. Offspring from matings are sometimes subjected to mutations afterwards, but with reduced mutation frequencies. In this work a reproduction method is chosen at

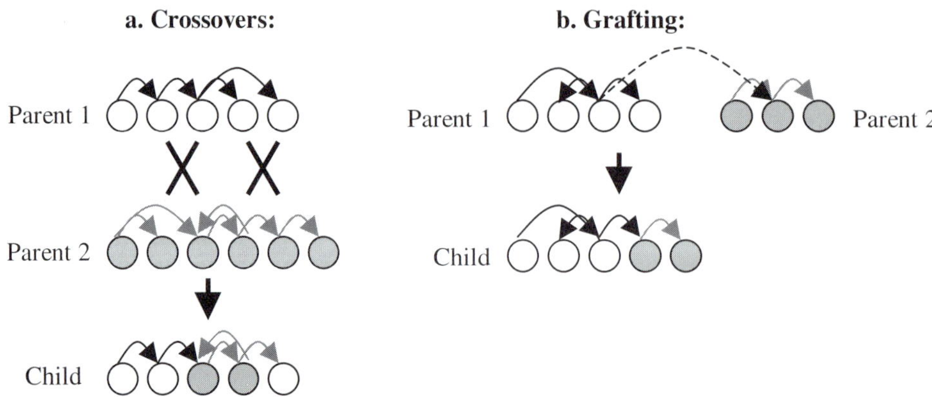

Figure 13.4 Two methods for mating directed graphs.

random for each child to be produced by the surviving individuals using the ratios: 40% asexual, 30% crossovers, and 30% grafting. A second parent is chosen from the survivors if necessary, and a new genotype is produced from the parent or parents.

After a new generation of genotypes is created, a phenotype creature is generated from each, and again their fitness levels are evaluated. As this cycle of variation and selection continues, the population is directed towards creatures with higher and higher fitness.

13.6.3 Parallel Implementation

This genetic algorithm has been implemented to run in parallel on a Connection Machine® CM-5 in a master/slave message passing model. A single processing node performs the genetic algorithm. It farms out genotypes to the other nodes to be fitness tested, and gathers back the fitness values after they have been determined. The fitness tests each include a dynamics simulation and although most can execute in nearly real-time, they are still the dominant computational requirement of the system. Performing a fitness test per processor is a simple but effective way to parallelize this genetic algorithm, and the overall performance scales quite linearly with the number of processors, as long as the population size is somewhat larger than the number of processors.

Each fitness test takes a different amount of time to compute depending on the complexity of the creature and how it attempts to move. To prevent idle processors from just waiting for others to finish, new generations are started before the fitness tests have been completed for all individuals. Those slower simulations are simply skipped during that reproductive cycle, so all processors remain active. With this approach, an evolution with population size 300, run for 100 generations, might take around 3 or 4 hours to complete on a 32 processor CM-5.

13.7 Evolved Results

Evolutions were performed for each of the behaviour selection methods described in section 13.5. A population of interbreeding creatures often converges toward homogeneity, but each separately run evolution can produce completely different locomotion strategies that satisfy the requested behaviour. For this reason, many separate evolutions were performed, each for 50 to 100 generations, and the most successful creatures of each evolution were inspected. A selection of these is shown in figs 13.5 to 13.8. In a few cases, genotypes resulting from one evolution were used as seed genotypes for a second evolution.

The swimming fitness measure produced a large number of simple paddling and tail wagging creatures. A variety of more complex strategies also emerged from some evolutions. A few creatures pulled themselves through the water with specialized sculling appendages. Some used two symmetrical flippers or even large numbers of similar flippers to propel themselves, and several multi-segmented watersnake creatures evolved that wind through the water with sinusoidal motions.

The walking fitness measure also produced a surprising number of simple creatures that could shuffle or hobble along at fairly high speeds. Some walk with lizard-like gaits using the corners of their parts. Some simply wag an appendage in the air to rock back and forth in just the right manner to move forward. A number of more complex creatures emerged that push or pull themselves along, inchworm style. Others use one or more leg-like appendages to successfully crawl or walk. Some hopping creatures even emerged that raise and lower arm-like structures to bound along at fairly high speeds.

The jumping fitness measure did not seem to produce as many different strategies as the swimming and walking optimizations, but a number of simple jumping creatures did emerge.

The light-following fitness measure was used in both water and land environments, and produced a wide variety of creatures that can swim or walk towards a light source. Some consistently and successfully follow the light source at different locations. Others can follow it some of the time, but then at certain relative locations fail to turn towards it. In the water environment, some developed steering fins that turn them towards the light using photosensor inputs. Others adjust the angle of their paddles appropriately as they oscillate along.

Sometimes a user may want to exert more control on the results of this process instead of simply letting creatures evolve entirely automatically. Aesthetic selection is a possible way to achieve this, but observation of the trial simulations of every creature and providing every fitness value interactively would require too much patience on the part of the user. A convenient way of mixing automatic selection with aesthetic selection is to observe the final successful results of a number of evolutions, and then start new evolutions with those that are aesthetically preferred. Although the control may be limited, this gives the user some influence on the creatures that are developed.

Another method of evolving creatures is to interactively evolve a morphology based on looks only, or alternatively hand design the morphology, and then automatically evolve a brain for that morphology that results in a desirable behaviour.

Creatures that evolved in one physical world can be placed in another and evolved further. An evolved watersnake, for example, was placed on land and then evolved to crawl instead of swim.

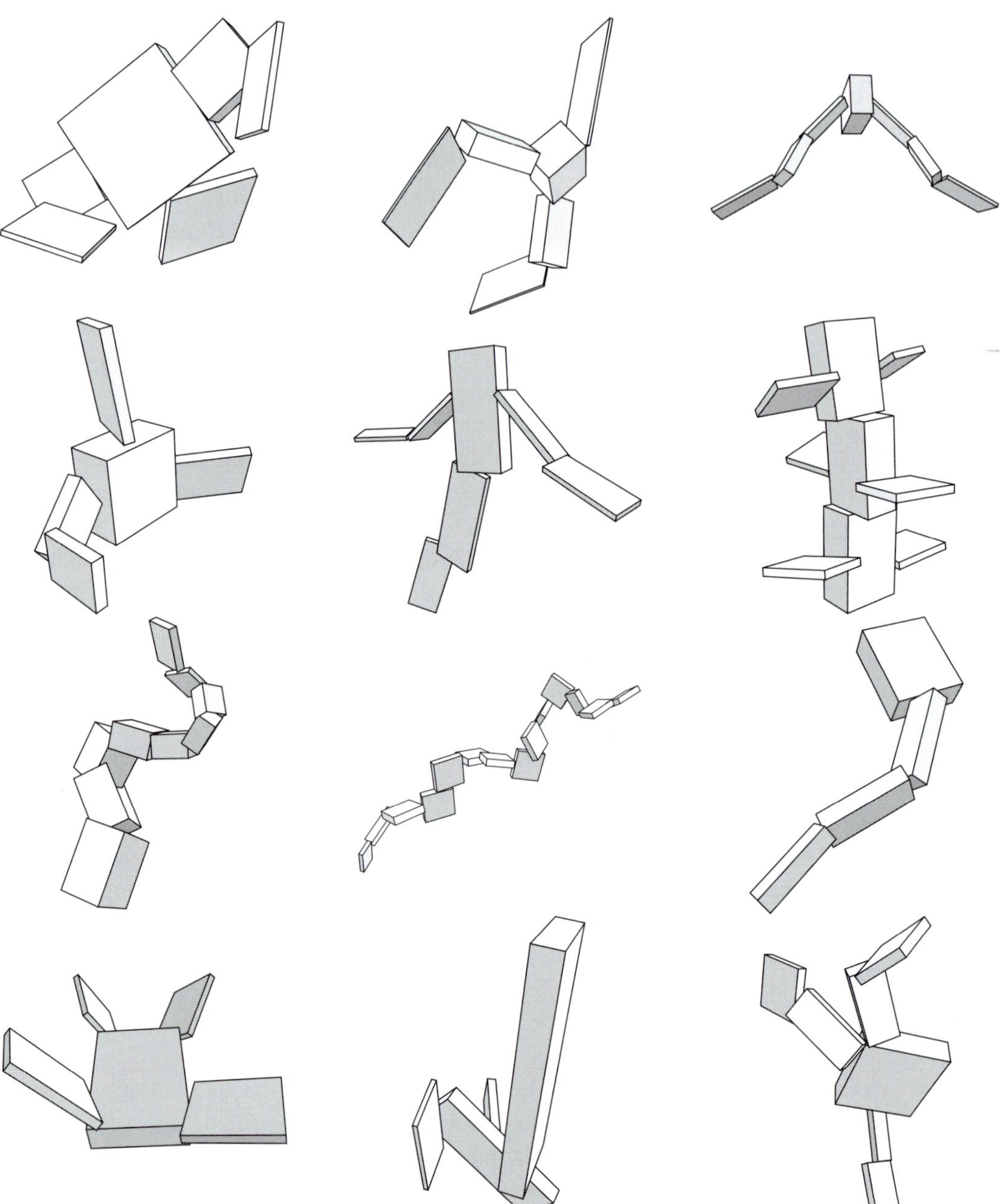

Figure 13.5 Creatures evolved for swimming.

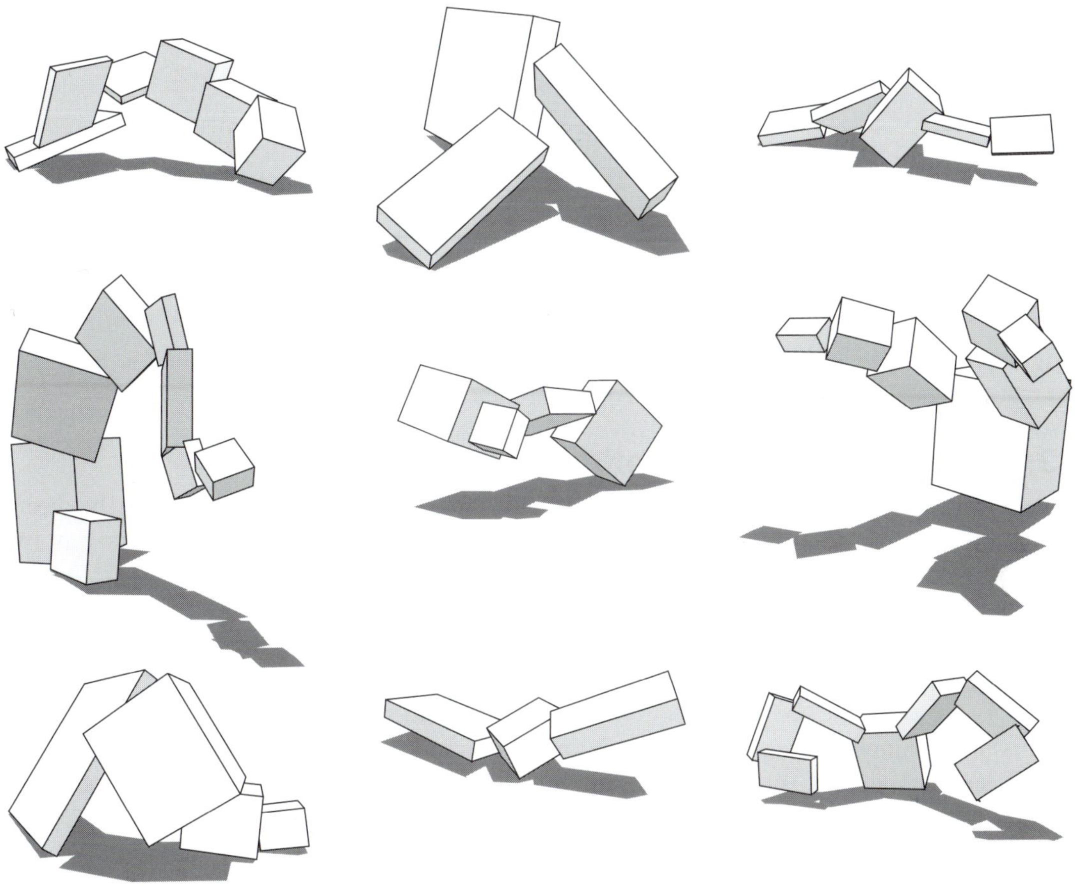

Figure 13.6 Creatures evolved for walking.

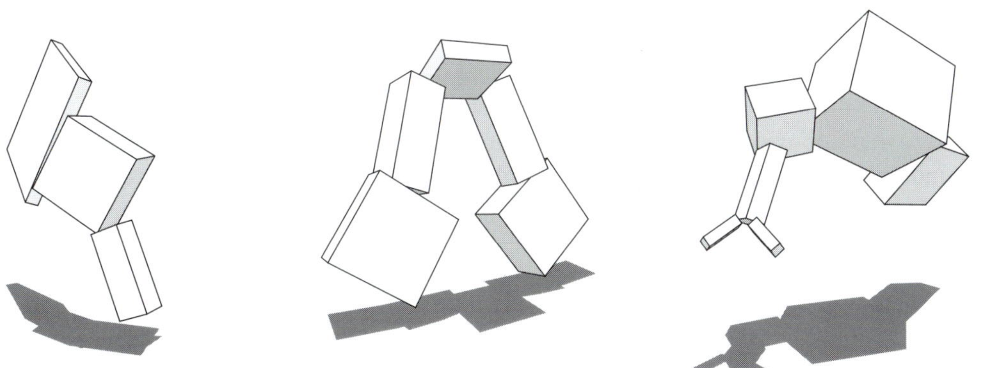

Figure 13.7 Creatures evolved for jumping.

Figure 13.8 Following behaviour. For each creature, four separate trials are shown for the same starting point towards different light source goal locations.

13.8 Evolution by Competition

An alternative way to evolve morphology and behaviour is to allow competition between virtual creatures. In this way, fitness can be defined in a more biologically realistic way by allowing populations of virtual creatures to compete against each other within a physically simulated changing world.

Interactions between evolving organisms are generally believed to have a strong influence on their resulting complexity and diversity. In natural evolutionary systems the measure of fitness is not constant: the reproducibility of an organism depends on many environmental factors including other evolving organisms, and is continuously in flux. Competition between organisms is thought to play a significant role in preventing static fitness landscapes and sustaining evolutionary change.

These effects are a distinguishing difference between natural evolution and optimization. Evolution proceeds with no explicit goal, but optimization, including the genetic algorithm, usually aims to search for individuals with the highest possible fitness values where the fitness measure has been predefined, remains constant, and depends only on the individual being tested.

The work described next takes the former approach. The fitness of an individual is highly dependent on the specific behaviours of other individuals currently in the population. The hope is that virtual creatures with higher complexity and more interesting behaviour will evolve than when applying the selection pressures of optimization alone.

Many simulations of co-evolving populations have been performed which involve competing individuals (Angeline and Pollack, 1993; Axelrod, 1989). As examples, Lindgren has studied the evolutionary dynamics of competing game strategy rules (Lindgren, 1991), Hillis has demonstrated that co-evolving parasites can enhance evolutionary optimization (Hillis, 1991), and Reynolds evolves vehicles for competition in the game of tag (Reynolds, 1994). The work presented next involves similar evolutionary dynamics to help achieve interesting results when phenotypes have three-dimensional bodies and compete in physically simulated worlds.

13.9 The Contest

Figure 13.9 shows the arena in which two virtual creatures will compete to gain control of a single cube. The cube is placed in the centre of the world, and the creatures start on opposite

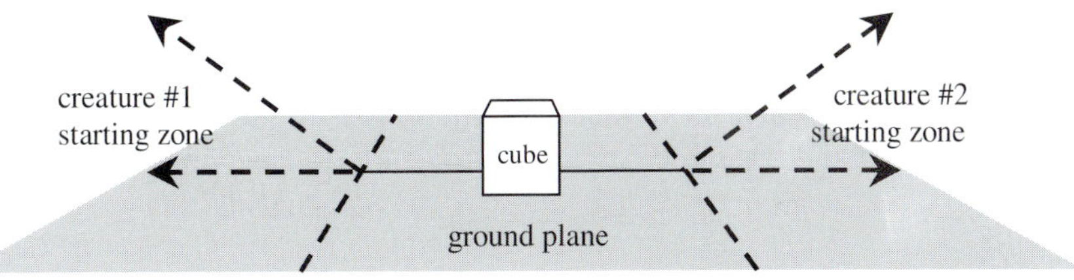

Figure 13.9 The arena.

sides of the cube. The second contestant is initially turned by 180° so the relative position of the cube to the creature is consistent from contest to contest no matter which starting side it is assigned. Each creature starts on the ground and behind a diagonal plane slanting up and away from the cube. Creatures are wedged into these 'starting zones' until they contact both the ground plane and the diagonal plane, so taller creatures must start further back. This helps prevent the inelegant strategy of simply falling over onto the cube. Strategies like this that utilize only potential energy are further discouraged by relaxing a creature's body before it is placed in the starting zone. The effect of gravity is simulated until the creature reaches a stable minimum state.

At the start of the contest the creatures' nervous systems are activated, and a physical simulation of the creatures' bodies, the cube, and the ground plane begins. The winner is the creature that has the most control over the cube after a certain duration of simulated time (8 seconds were given). Instead of just defining a winner and loser, the margin of victory is determined in the form of a relative fitness value, so there is selection pressure not just to win, but to win by the largest possible margin.

The creatures' final distances to the cube are used to calculate their fitness scores. The shortest distance from any point on the surface of a creature's parts to the centre of the cube is used as its distance value. A creature gets a higher score by being closer to the cube, but also gets a higher score when its opponent is further away. This encourages creatures to reach the cube, but also gives points for keeping the opponent away from it. If d_1 and d_2 are the final shortest distances of each creature to the cube, then the fitnesses for each creature, f_1 and f_2, are given by:

$$f_1 = 1.0 + \frac{d_2 - d_1}{d_1 + d_2}$$

$$f_2 = 1.0 + \frac{d_1 - d_2}{d_1 + d_2}.$$

This formulation puts all fitness values in the limited range of 0.0 to 2.0. If the two distances are equal the contestants receive tie scores of 1.0 each, and in all cases the scores will average 1.0.

Credit is also given for having 'control' over the cube, beyond just as measured by the minimum distance to it. If both creatures end up contacting the cube, the winner is the one that surrounds it the most. This is approximated by further decreasing the distance value, as used above, when a creature is touching the cube on the side that opposes its centre of mass. Since the initial distances are measured from the centre of the cube they can be adjusted in this way and still remain positive.

During the simulated contest, if neither creature shows any movement for a full second, the simulation is stopped and the scores are evaluated early to save unnecessary computation.

13.10 Approximating Competitive Environments

There are many trade-offs to consider when simulating an evolution in which fitness is determined by discrete competitions between individuals. In this work, pairs of individuals compete one-on-one. At every generation of a simulated evolution the individuals in the population are paired up by some pattern and a number of competitions are performed to eventually determine a fitness value for every individual. The simulations of the competitions are by far the dominant computational requirement of the process, so the total number of competitions performed for each generation and the effectiveness of the pattern of competitions are important considerations.

In one extreme, each individual competes with all the others in the population and the average score determines the fitness (fig. 13.10a). However, this requires $(N^2 - N)/2$ total competitions for a single-species population of N individuals. For large populations this is often unacceptable, especially if the competition time is significant, as it is in this work.

In the other extreme, each individual competes with just a single opponent (fig. 13.10e). This requires only N/2 total competitions, but can cause inconsistency in the fitness values since each fitness is often highly dependent on the specific individual that happens to be

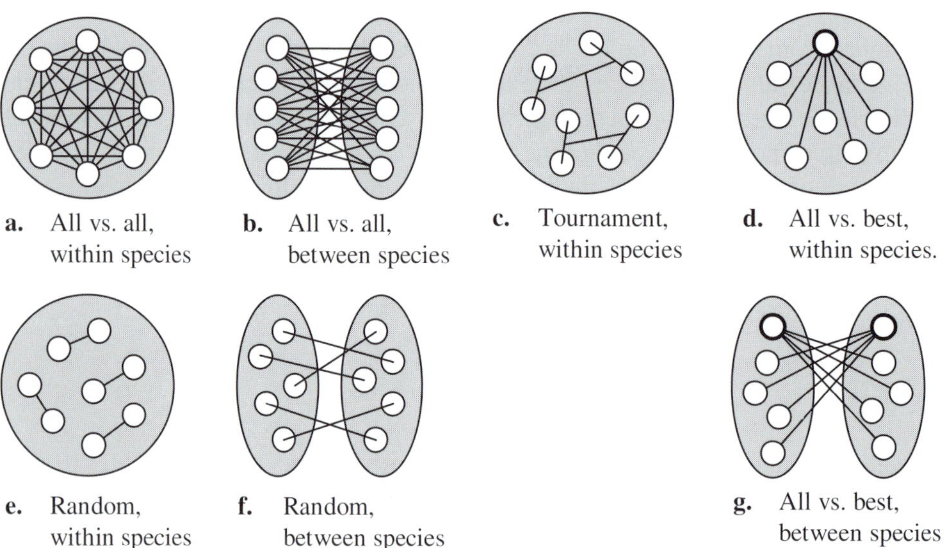

Figure 13.10 Different pair-wise competition patterns for one and two species. The grey areas represent species of interbreeding individuals, and lines indicate competition performed between individuals.

assigned as the opponent. If the pairing is done at random, and especially if the mutation rate is high, fitness can be more dependent on the luck of receiving a poor opponent than on an individual's actual ability.

One compromise between these extremes is for each individual to compete against several opponents chosen at random for each generation. This can somewhat dilute the fitness inconsistency problem, but at the expense of more competition simulations.

A second compromise is a tournament pattern (fig. 13.10c) which can efficiently determine a single overall winner with N − 1 competitions. But this also does not necessarily give all individuals fair scores because of the random initial opponent assignments. Also, this pattern does not easily apply to multi-species evolutions where competitions are not performed between individuals within the same species.

A third compromise is for each individual to compete once per generation, but all against the same opponent. The individual with the highest fitness from the previous generation is chosen as this one-to-beat (fig. 13.10d). This also requires N − 1 competitions per generation, but effectively gives fair relative fitness values since all are playing against the same opponent which has proven to be competent. Various interesting instabilities can still occur over generations however, since the strategy of the 'best' individual can change suddenly between generations.

The number of species in the population is another element to consider when simulating evolutions involving competition. A species may be described as an interbreeding subset of individuals in the population. In single-species evolutions individuals will compete against their relatives, but in multi-species evolutions individuals can optionally compete only against individuals from other species. Figure 13.10 shows graphical representations of some of the different competition patterns described above for both one and two species.

The resulting effects of using these different competition patterns is unfortunately difficult to quantify in this work, since by its nature a simple overall measure of success is absent. Evolutions were performed using several of the methods described above with both one and two species, and the results were subjectively judged. The most 'interesting' results occurred when the all vs. best competition pattern was used. Both one and two species evolutions produced some intriguing strategies, but the multi-species simulations tended to produce more interesting interactions between the evolving creatures.

13.11 Results Evolved by Competition

Many independent evolutions were performed using the 'all vs. best' competition pattern as described previously. Some single-species evolutions were performed in which all individuals both compete and breed with each other, but most included two species where individuals only compete with members of the opponent species.

Some examples of resulting two-species evolutionary dynamics are shown in fig. 13.11. The relative fitnesses of the best individuals of each species are plotted over 100 generations. The rate of evolutionary progress varied widely in different runs. Some species took many generations before they could even reach the cube at all, while others discovered a fairly successful strategy in the first 10 or 20 generations. Figure 13.11c shows an example where one species was successful fairly quickly and the other species never evolved an effective strategy to challenge it. The other three graphs in fig. 13.11 show evolutions where more interactions occurred between the evolving species.

A variety of methods for reaching the cube were discovered. Some extended arms out onto the cube, and some reached out while falling forward to land on top of it. Others could crawl inch-worm style or roll towards the cube, and a few even developed leg-like appendages that they used to walk towards it.

The most interesting results often occurred when both species discovered methods for reaching the cube and then further evolved strategies to counter the opponent's behaviour. Some creatures pushed their opponent away from the cube, some moved the cube away from its initial location and then followed it, and others simply covered up the cube to block the opponent's access. Some counter-strategies took advantage of a specific weakness in the original strategy and could be easily foiled in a few generations by a minor adaptation to the original strategy. Others permanently defeated the original strategy and required the first species to evolve another level of counter-counter-strategy to regain the lead. In some evolutions the winners alternated between species many times with new strategies and counter-strategies. In other runs one species kept a consistent lead with the other species only providing temporary challenges.

After the results from many simulations were observed, the best were collected and then played against each other in additional competitions. The different strategies were compared, and the behaviour and adaptability of creatures were observed as they faced new types of opponents that were not encountered during their evolutions. A few evolutions were also performed starting with an existing creature as a seed genotype for each species so they could further evolve to compete against a new type of opponent.

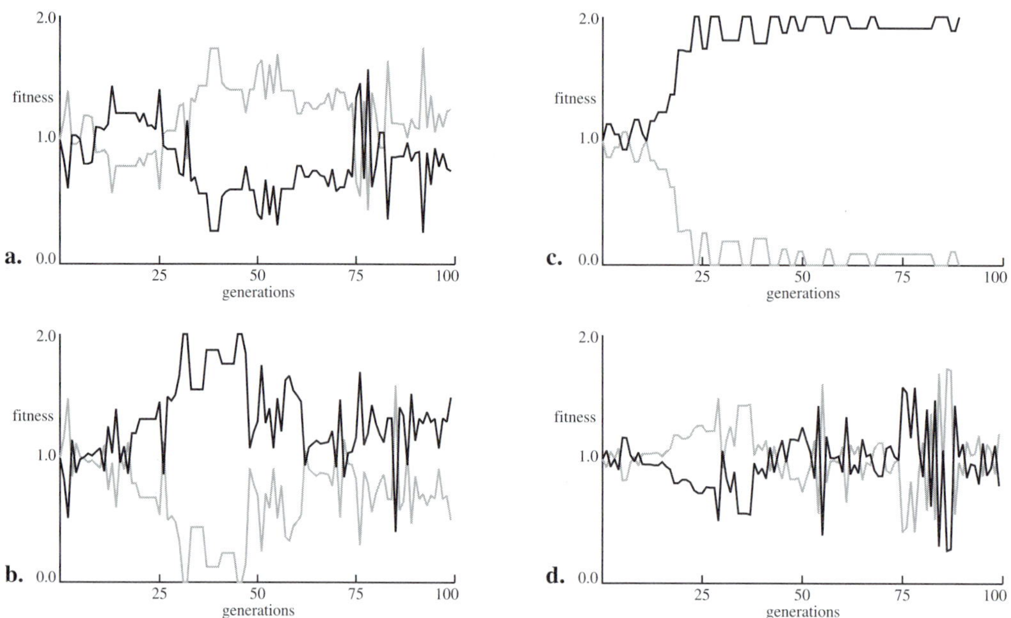

Figure 13.11 Relative fitness between two co-evolving and competing species, from four independent simulations.

Figure 13.12 shows some examples of evolved competing creatures and demonstrates the diversity of the different strategies that emerged. Some of the behaviours and interactions of these specific creatures are described briefly here. The larger creature in fig. 13.12b nudges the cube aside and then pins down his smaller opponent. The crab-like creature in 13.12c can successfully walk forward, but then continues blindly past the cube and over the opponent.

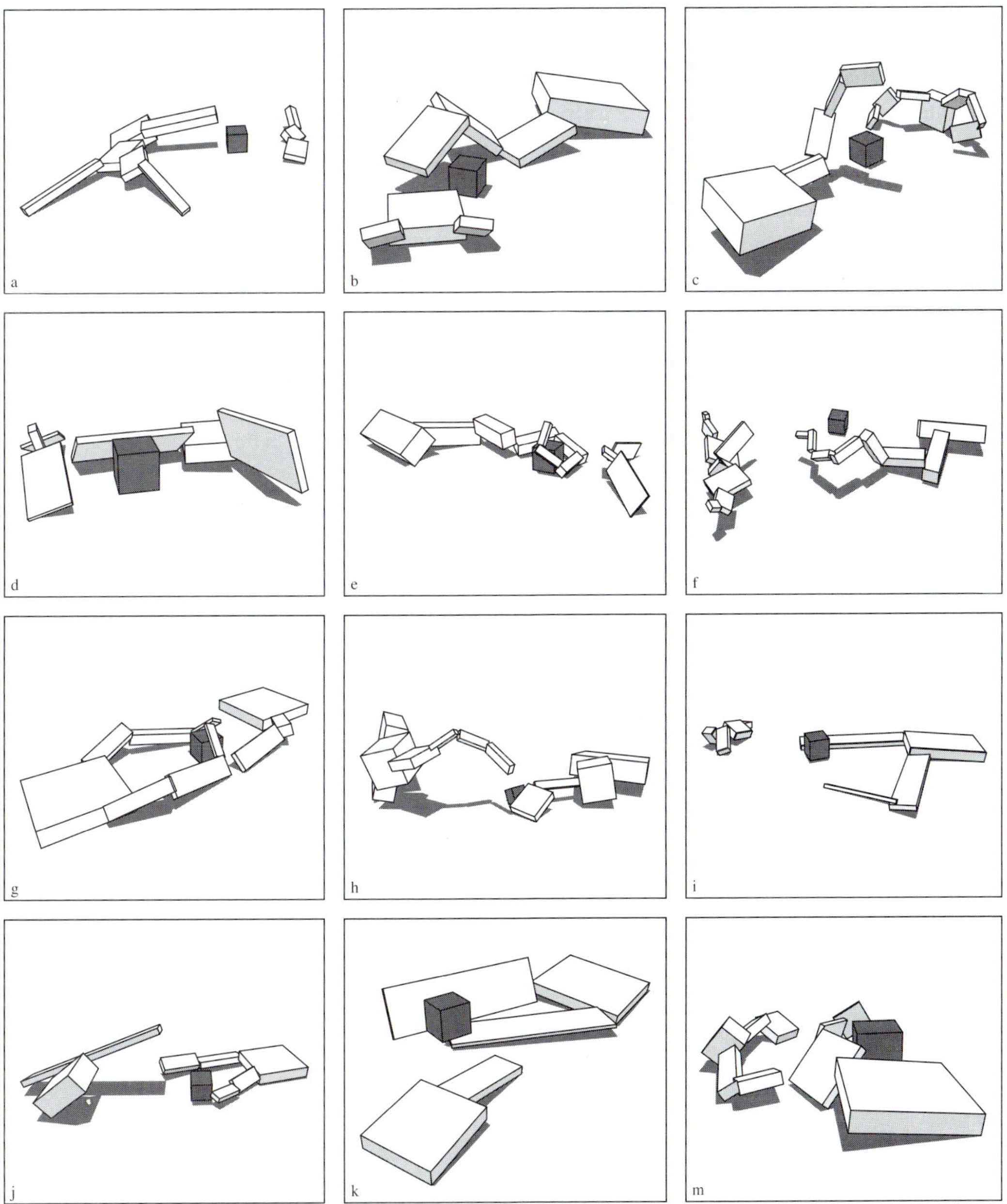

Figure 13.12 Evolved competing creatures.

Figure 13.12d shows a creature that has just pushed its opponent away from the cube, and the arm-like creature in 13.12e also jabs at its opponent before curling around the cube.

Most creatures perform similar behaviour independently of the opponent's actions, but a few are adaptive in that they can reach towards the cube wherever it moves. For example the arm-like creature in fig. 13.12f pushes the cube aside and then uses photosensors to adaptively follow it. If its opponent moves the cube in a different direction it will successfully grope towards the new location.

The two-armed creature in fig. 13.12g blocks access to the cube by covering it up. Several other two-armed creatures in 13.12i, j, and k use the strategy of batting the cube to the side with one arm and catching it with the other arm. This seemed to be the most successful strategy of the creatures in this group, and the one in 13.12k was actually the overall winner because it could whisk the cube aside very quickly. However, it was a near tie between this and the photosensitive arm in 13.12f. The larger creature in fig. 13.12m wins by a large margin against some opponents because it can literally walk away with the cube, but it does not initially reach the cube very quickly and tends to lose against faster opponents.

It is possible that adaptation on an evolutionary scale occurred more easily than the evolution of individuals that were themselves adaptive. Perhaps individuals with adaptive behaviour would be significantly more rewarded if evolutions were performed with many species instead of just one or two. To be successful, a single individual would then need to defeat a larger number of different opposing strategies.

13.12 Future Work

One direction of future work would be to experiment with additional types of fitness evaluation methods. More complex behaviours might be evolved by defining fitness functions that could measure the level of success at performing more difficult tasks, or even multiple tasks. Fitness could also include the efficiency at which a behaviour was achieved. For example, a fitness measure might be the distance traveled divided by the amount of energy consumed to move that distance.

Alternatively, other types of contests could be defined in which creatures compete in different environments and different rules determine the winners. Creatures might also be rewarded for cooperative behaviour somehow as well as competitive, and teams of interacting creatures could be simulated.

Evolutions containing larger numbers of species should certainly be performed, with the hope of increasing the chances for emergence of more adaptive individuals as hypothesized above.

An additional extension to this work would be to simulate a more complex but more realistic environment in which many creatures simultaneously compete and/or cooperate with each another, instead of pairing off in one-on-one contests. Speciation, mating patterns, competing patterns, and even offspring production could all be determined by one long ecological simulation. Experiments like this have been performed with simpler organisms and have produced interesting results including specialization and various social interactions (Ray, 1991; Yaeger, 1994).

Another direction of future work might be to adjust the genetic language of possible creatures to describe only those that could actually be built as real robots. The virtual robots that can best perform a given task in simulation would then be assembled, and would hopefully also perform well in reality.

Much work could be done to dress up these virtual creatures to give them different shapes and improved rendered looks. Flexible skin could surround or be controlled by the rigid components. Various materials could be added such as scales, hair, fur, eyes, or tentacles, and they might flow or bounce using simple local dynamic simulations, even if they did not influence the overall dynamics. The shape details and external materials could also be included in the creatures' genetic descriptions and be determined by artificial evolution.

Perhaps the techniques presented here should be considered as an approach toward creating artificial intelligence. When a genetic language allows virtual entities to evolve with increasing complexity, it is common for the resulting system to be difficult to understand in detail. In many cases it would also be difficult to design a similar system using traditional methods. Techniques such as these have the potential of surpassing those limits that are often imposed when human understanding and design is required. The examples presented here suggest that it might be easier to evolve virtual entities exhibiting intelligent behaviour than it would be for humans to design and build them.

13.13 Conclusions

In summary, a system has been described that can generate autonomous three-dimensional virtual creatures without requiring cumbersome user specifications, design efforts, or knowledge of algorithmic details. These creatures exhibit surprisingly diverse behaviours and competitive strategies in physically simulated worlds.

A genetic language that uses directed graphs to describe both morphology and behaviour defines an unlimited hyperspace of possible results, and a variety of interesting virtual creatures have been shown to emerge when this hyperspace is explored by populations of evolving and competing individuals. It is believed that these methods have potential as a powerful tool for the creation of desirable complexity.

As computers become more powerful, the creation of virtual actors, whether animal, human, or machines, may be limited mainly by our ability to design them, rather than our ability to satisfy their computational requirements. A control system that someday actually generates 'intelligent' behaviour might tend to be a complex mess beyond our understanding. Artificial evolution permits the generation of complicated virtual systems without requiring design, and the use of unbounded genetic languages allows evolving systems to increase in complexity beyond our understanding. Perhaps methods such as those presented here will provide a practical pathway toward the creation of novel morphologies with intelligent behaviour.

Acknowledgements

Thanks to Gary Oberbrunner and Matt Fitzgibbon for Connection Machine and software support. Thanks to Thinking Machines Corporation and Lew Tucker for supporting this research. Thanks to Bruce Blumberg and Peter Schröder for dynamic simulation help and suggestions. And special thanks to Pattie Maes.

References

Angeline, P. J. and Pollack, J. B. (1993). Competitive Environments Evolve Better Solutions for Complex Tasks, *Proceedings of the 5th International Conference on Genetic Algorithms*, ed. by S. Forrest, Morgan Kaufmann, Urbana-Champaign, pp. 264–270.

Axelrod, R. (1989) Evolution of Strategies in the Iterated Prisoner's Dilemma, *Genetic Algorithms and Simulated Annealing*, ed. by L. Davis, Morgan Kaufmann.

Cramer, N. L. (1985). A Representation for the Adaptive Generation of Simple Sequential Programs, *Proceedings of the First International Conference on Genetic Algorithms*, ed. by J. Grefenstette, pp. 183–187.

Dawkins, R. (1986). *The Blind Watchmaker*, Longman, Harlow.

de Garis, H. (1990). Genetic Programming: Building Artificial Nervous Systems Using Genetically Programmed Neural Network Modules, *Proceedings of the 7th International Conference on Machine Learning*, pp. 132–139.

Featherstone, R. (1987). *Robot Dynamics Algorithms*, Kluwer Academic Publishers, Norwell, MA.

Goldberg, D. E. (1989). *Genetic Algorithms in Search, Optimization, and Machine Learning*, Addison-Wesley.

Hart, J. (1992). The Object Instancing Paradigm for Linear Fractal Modeling, *Graphics Interface*, pp. 224–231.

Hillis, W. D. (1991). Co-evolving Parasites Improve Simulated Evolution as an Optimization Procedure, *Artificial Life II*, ed. by Langton, Taylor, Farmer and Rasmussen, Addison-Wesley, pp. 313–324.

Holland, J. H. (1975). *Adaptation in Natural and Artificial Systems*, University of Michigan Press, Ann Arbor.

Kitano, H. (1990) Designing Neural Networks Using Genetic Algorithms with Graph Generation Aystem, *Complex Systems* **4**; 461–476.

Koza, J. (1992). *Genetic Programming: on the Programming of Computers by Means of Natural Selection*, MIT Press, Cambridge, MA.

Lindenmayer, A. (1968). Mathematical Models for Cellular Interactions in Development, Parts I and II, *Journal of Theoretical Biology* **18**; 280–315.

Lindgren, K. (1991). Evolutionary Phenomena in Simple Dynamics, *Artificial Life II*, ed. by Langton, Taylor, Farmer and Rasmussen, Addison-Wesley, Santa Fe, NM, pp. 295–312.

McKenna, M. and Zeltzer, D. (1990). Dynamic Simulation of Autonomous Legged Locomotion, *Computer Graphics* **24**(4); 29–38.

Miller, G. (1988). The Motion Dynamics of Snakes and Worms, *Computer Graphics* **22**(4); 169–178.

Mjolsness, E., Sharp, D. and Alpert, B. (1989). Scaling, Machine Learning, and Genetic Neural Nets, *Advances in Applied Mathematics* **10**; 137–163.

Ngo, J. T. and Marks, J. (1993). Spacetime Constraints Revisited, *Computer Graphics, Annual Conference Series*, pp. 343–350.

van de Panne, M. and Fiume, E. (1993). Sensor-Actuator Networks, *Computer Graphics, Annual Conference Series*, pp. 335–342.

Raibert, M. and Hodgins, J. K. (1991). Animation of Dynamic Legged Locomotion, *Computer Graphics* **25**(4); 349–358.

Ray, T. (1991). An Approach to the Synthesis of Life, *Artificial Life II*, ed. by Langton, Taylor, Farmer and Rasmussen, Addison-Wesley, Santa Fe, NM, pp. 371–408.

Reynolds, C. (1994). Competition, Coevolution and the Game of Tag, *Artificial Life IV Proceedings*, ed. by R. Brooks and P. Maes, MIT Press, Cambridge, MA.

Sims, K. (1991). Artificial Evolution for Computer Graphics, *Computer Graphics* **25**(4); 319–328.

Sims, K. (1992). Interactive Evolution of Dynamical Systems, *Toward a Practice of Autonomous Systems: Proceedings of the First European Conference on Artificial Life*, ed. by Varela, Francisco and Bourgine, MIT Press, Cambridge, MA, pp. 171–178.

Smith, A. R. (1984). Plants, Fractals, and Formal Languages, *Computer Graphics* **18**(3); 1–10.

Todd, S. and Latham, W. (1992). *Evolutionary Art and Computers*, Academic Press, London.

Yaeger, L. (1994). Computational Genetics, Physiology, Metabolism, Neural Systems, Learning, Vision, and Behavior or PolyWorld: Life in a New Context, *Artificial Life III Proceedings Vol. XVII*, ed. by C. Langton, Santa Fe Institute Studies in the Sciences of Complexity, Addison-Wesley, pp. 263–298.

Chapter 14

Exploring Three-Dimensional Design Worlds using Lindenmayer Systems and Genetic Programming

By Paul Coates, Terence Broughton and Helen Jackson

14.1 Introduction: Architecture, Aesthetics and the Utilitarian Tradition

Since the end of the last century it has commonly been seen as decadent to simply apply aesthetics to the structure of a building to make it beautiful (with the exception of the deliberately ironic, although irony itself would have been thought decadent by the stern moralists of the modern movement).

Architects such as Louis Sullivan, Mies Van der Rohe, Le Corbusier and so on used the example of engineering to help to explain the relationship between form and function. Based on the simplistic assumption that engineers do not design form, but that it emerges from the correct solution to mechanical realities (cf. the Eiffel tower, Brunel's bridges and the 'dom-ino' concrete frame) the modern movement declared such objects as *pure* and *right*. The functionalist tradition has suffered many blows in the last 50 years, partly because it was always an oversimplification, and partly because technology has now reached a point where the constraints of structure have almost vanished, with form becoming the precursor of function rather than its determinant, i.e. anything is possible (cf. Utzon's Sydney Opera House, Frank Gehry's new Bilbao gallery, etc.)

The study of evolutionary algorithms allows us to get back to a more rigorous analysis of the basic determinants of form, where the global form of an object not only should not but actually cannot be predetermined on an aesthetic whim. Thus with genetic algorithms we have an opportunity to experiment with the true determinants of form in a way that the pioneers of the modern movement would have relished – an aesthetic of pure function whose outcome is totally embedded in the problem to be solved.

14.1.1 What this Chapter is About

This chapter explains the recent experiments at the University of East London School of Architecture using genetic programming (GP) and Lindenmayer systems, which use production systems to make recursively defined three-dimensional objects. The chapter starts with objects evolving in simple environments, the flytrap, sun trap and wind tunnel experiments,

EVOLUTIONARY DESIGN BY COMPUTERS
ISBN 1-55860-605-X

then covers space and enclosure, looking at slightly more architectural examples. The final part covers some different ways of measuring spatial fitness, in particular the use of turtles and connectivity measures to measure spatial properties in evolving configurations, and the use of single and multi-goal evolutionary fitness tests.

14.2 Genetic Programming, L-systems and the Isospatial Grid

14.2.1 Why Lindenmayer Systems and Genetic Programming?

In order to explain the choice of L systems and the use of the isospatial array, one must make a distinction between the use of genetic algorithms to optimise parameters to a given geometry, and the use of evolutionary algorithms to generate form.

In the case of the optimising approach (used for the past twenty years by engineers) the macro decisions about form, and the fundamental design decisions are already taken. For instance, in the well-documented procedures for developing the hull of a boat, while the algorithm can develop a set of appropriate spline curves to make up the shape, using random perturbations of spline curves and a model of hydraulic drag on the developed surface, it would not be possible for such an algorithm to generate a multi-hulled solution (catamaran) since the initial problem description has specified a solution space that only includes single hulled morphologies.

The problem with such attempts is that nothing more than fine-tuning can take place. The aim of the current research is to try as far as possible to avoid over-specifying the problem domain, in the hope that the evolutionary algorithm will be able to search over a wider area of possible solutions. In order to do this we have to find a neutral description of three dimensional form, which is capable of embodying the widest possible range of objects and a methodology of form generation which is responsive to evolution and not predefined by a particular technology.

14.2.2 The Isospatial Grid

The fact that the Cartesian coordinate system is so universally adopted in mathematics, software design and the design professions generally has led to an over reliance on orthogonal geometry and a tendency to assume that cubic tessellations are the *natural* way to represent three-dimensional form. The Cartesian grid with its three planes and three major axes per point, while capable of representing any arbitrary object, is nevertheless fundamentally aligned to the idea that the three-dimensional objects are just projections of the two-dimensional plane, which in CAD terms are usually defined as two-and-a-half dimensional. Things which are not projections of the plane are much more difficult to model than simple orthogonal objects.

The orthogonal grid also has built in to it a lack of homogeneity (and a bias in favour of orthogonality) because the orthogonal distances between points are not the same as the diagonal differences. In the Cartesian grid, the distance between a point and its 27 neighbours (plus or minus one cell away in all directions) varies between the unit distance along the three axes, the distance to edge joining cells, and the distance to vertex joining cells. In cellular automata (CA) for instance, where neighbour counting is the basis of state change rules, it is necessary to build in weighting factors to overcome the problem of the three different distances between the neighbours of a point (face, edge and vertex).

The isospatial grid, on the other hand, is defined as a point and its twelve neighbours are defined by a dodecahedron. This repeats across three-dimensional space just as the orthogonal grid does, but without the three different point to point distances of the orthogonal grid. Carter Bays and John Fraser (Bays, 1987, 1988; Fraser, 1995) have both used this grid in cellular automata in place of the cubic grid. The isospatial grid, with its twelve equidistant neighbours from any point would seem to represent a more 'neutral' method of representing spatial objects and in particular offers generative algorithms a simpler and more robust set of relationships between particles of the system. With six axes and four planes of symmetry it is a superset of the Cartesian grid, and can accommodate orthogonal relationships, but does not presume them.

In a project where the aim is to work towards the evolution of form with the minimum of preconceived notions of what constitutes it, this geometry seems more appropriate than many, hopefully leading to novel objects where the form could truly be said to emerge from the process of fitness testing, rather than being an artifact of the method of representation.

14.2.3 L-systems as a Generative Method

Various computer-generated models of morphogenesis have been used to help understand the emergence of complex forms in living organisms since Turing proposed the reaction-diffusion process in 1952. Diffusion limited aggregation models have been used to simulate crystal formation in supersaturated solutions and J. Kaandorp in *Fractal Modelling: Growth and Form in Biology* (Kaandorp, 1994) uses an aggregation model to investigate the growth of corals. L-systems were developed by Aristid Lindenmayer in 1968 to model the morphology of organisms using string-rewriting techniques (Lindenmayer and Prusinkiewicz, 1988). These techniques have been applied in a variety of studies to the production of abstract models of biological forms as an aid to interspecies comparison and classification (see deBoer, Fracchia and Prusinkiewicz, 1992).

As well as settling on a representational method, any evolutionary design algorithm needs a generating engine whose parameters are subject to evolutionary pressure. One of the factors which can militate against an open-ended process is the separation of the phenotype development process from the genotype description. That is to say, the genotype only describes parameters to the phenotype construction process, whose fundamental operation remains the same. This must of course always be the case, but in general it would seem to be better to make the genotype be as complete a description of the phenotype as possible, so that as many aspects of its behaviour are under evolutionary pressure as possible.

14.2.4 Genetic Programming as an Apt Approach

The development of genetic programming provides a clue as to how this could be achieved. GP was developed as part of the attempt to use the genotype as – literally – a code system for evolving software where the genotype maps very specifically onto the phenotype. The original attempts to use crossover on the code expressed as an undifferentiated list resulted in 100% failure, as random chunks of code recombined always resulted in a crash of the phenotype.

By defining the code as a tree structure of s-expressions and only allowing crossover/

replication and mutation to take place on the subtrees, sexual reproduction could take place and the resulting code trees would always be syntactically correct – so no crashes.

This use of s-expressions to represent recursively defined algorithms can be parallelled in the productions found in branching Lindenmayer systems. L-systems have been used to demonstrate a wide range of recursively defined objects since being originally defined as a formalism for describing botanical systems. They work using turtle geometry with polar rather than Cartesian coordinates and the production system itself forms a very compact description of a wide variety of forms. The productions themselves are s-expressions and can be manipulated using GP just like the programming examples of Koza *et al.* (Koza, 1992).

Using L-systems in the isospatial array combines two ideas both concerned with minimising the number of 'givens' for a form evolving system:

1. It provides as far as possible a neutral description of space.
2. It reduces the number of arbitrary mappings between the genotype and the phenotype.

14.2.5 Using L-systems and the Isospatial Array in Architectural Modelling

The simple string rewriting systems used here are restricted to branching tree systems and, while not wanting to suggest that such systems are generally applicable, they have useful attributes in the architectural context for at least the following reasons:

1. Since no part of the configuration can exist without having grown from an existing component the branching tree structure is useful for modelling structural/frame systems.
2. The necessary connectedness of these configurations can be used to model space systems since, like pieces of a branching structure, spaces are only viable if connected via other spaces to the outside world.
3. Because of the recursive nature of the string rewriting system, the three dimensional objects are also recursive in structure, exhibiting self-similarity over scale and displacement. These are useful properties when modelling structures, with often self-similar hierarchical arrangements of parts (main space, ante space, broom cupboard; main beam, subbeam, floor covering).

14.3 Three-Dimensional L-systems, Production Rules and s-expressions

14.3.1 L-systems Experiments

An L-system model starts with an initial axiom and one or more production rules. Axioms and production rules consist of symbol strings whereby individual symbols in the axiom are replaced by a string of symbols designated by the production rule. This process of character recognition and string substitution is carried out iteratively with each successive iteration producing a symbol string of greater complexity.

The resultant symbol string is interpreted as a series of drawing instructions which produce an abstract representation of the desired organism. The success of the L-system model lies in the self-similarity of cell structure that many biological systems exhibit, which is mirrored in the grammar-based string-rewriting process.

The L-system method of modelling developmental processes has been the subject of considerable research. Our approach is to use the L-system biological model in conjunction with an evolutionary algorithm and is an area which has seen relatively little investigation, recent work is reported in (Jacob, 1996; Horling, 1996).

A standard genetic algorithm and the associated genetic programming strategy are models which utilise the processes involved in the evolution of biological organisms.

Visualisation of the growth model was carried out in Autocad, a three-dimensional modelling application using the Autolisp programming language.

The twelve neighbours of any given point – 'apoint' – are given by the Autolisp function 'getneighbours', see fig. 14.1. The method of representing form is through the insertion of spheres drawn and saved in separate drawing files. Different shaded spheres represent different levels of recursive branching, see fig. 14.2. Spheres can only be inserted at the vertices of the isospatial grid so each sphere has twelve equally spaced neighbours.

```
(defun getneighbours ( apoint / neighbours offsets p np )
(setq neighbours '()
offsets(list '(1 1 0)
             '( 1 -1 0)
             '( -1 1 0)
             '(-1 -1 0)
             '(1 0 1)
             '(0 1 1)
             '(-1 0 1)
             '(0 -1 1)
             '(1 0 -1)
             '(0 1 -1)
             '(-1 0 -1)
             '(0 -1 -1)))
(foreach p offsets
(setq np (mapcar '+ a point p)
neighbours (cons np neighbours)))
```

Figure 14.1 The twelve balls of the isospatial array.

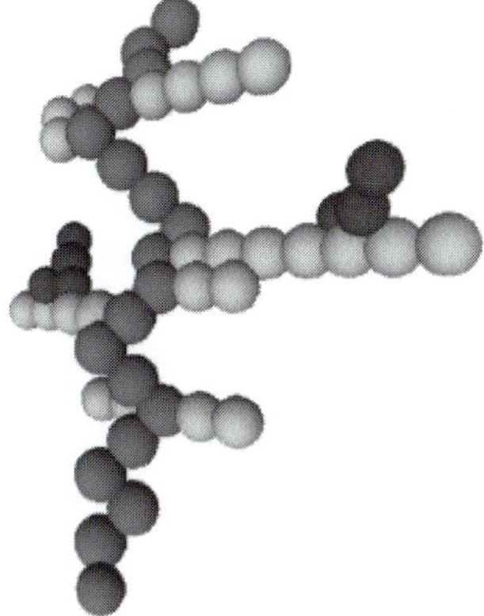

Figure 14.2 Branching tree structure.

A variation on this geometry is the one used by Carter Bays in *Patterns for Simple Cellular Automata in a Universe of Dense-Packed Spheres* which has a four axial system where twelve neighbouring points are the vertices of a dodecahedron (Bays, 1987).

There are three primary genetic operators used in this experiment: initialisation, crossover and mutation.

14.3.2 Initialisation

The first stage of the program is initialisation where a function is called to produce an initial gene pool. The genes are a randomly generated series of nested brackets containing three types of symbols:

1. An instruction to insert a sphere: represented by the symbol ***F*** (for 'forward').
2. A positional variable which refers to where to place the next ball: these are given in the symbology as *POS1 . . . POSn* for each of the *n* possible headings from any sphere. L-systems use turtle graphics (polar as opposed to Cartesian coordinates) so the POS function should be thought of as a 'turn' instruction, where the actual direction taken depends on the current heading. Early experiments used six possible turns, later ones reduced this to four.
3. A bracket: an open one '(' indicates a branching point, a closed one ')' is an instruction to return to a position on a lower 'limb' where it last branched.

These symbol strings which make up the gene pool are the production rules of the L-system.

14.3.3 Production Rule

The next stage of the program is to iteratively apply a production rule to the initial axiom – in this experiment a simple ***F*** symbol. It only requires three or four iterations to generate a symbol string of considerable length as every instance of ***F*** is substituted by the production rule which itself is made up largely of ***F***s:

F ->
(F(F POS1(F F POS2)F)F) ->
(F(F POS1(F F POS2)F)F)((F(F POS1(F F POS2)F)F) POS1(F(F POS1(F F POS2)F)F) (F(F POS1(F F POS2)F)F)POS2)(F(F POS1(F F POS2)F)F)(F(F POS1(F F POS2)F)F))

The rewritten symbol string is passed to a function for interpretation of the symbols, i.e. its genetic code and the realisation of the artificial organism in the drawing database. Every symbol in the string is evaluated and the corresponding function is called which carries the instruction for either:

1. changing the positional variable, or
2. inserting a sphere at a point on the grid.

Before a sphere is inserted, clash detection is carried out and if a collision is imminent the insertion command is ignored and the next symbol evaluated.

14.3.4 Genetic Programming Operations on Productions

The L-system productions can be seen as nested bracketed s-expressions with operations carried out on the nodes, just like Koza's examples, but with the functions *F* and *POS1 . . . n* rather than the arithmetic functions of classic GP (Koza 92).

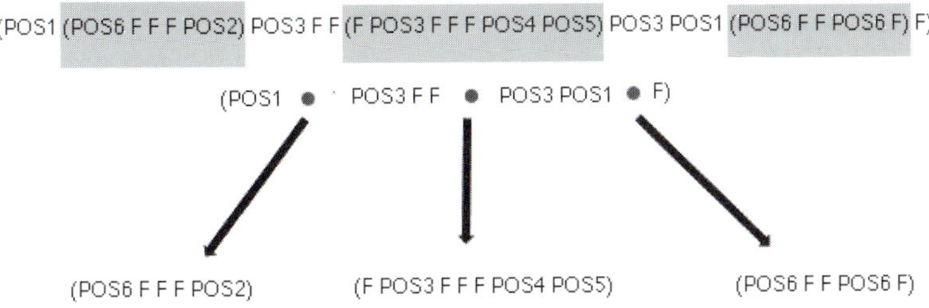

Figure 14.3 Productions as trees of s-expressions.

In the example shown in fig. 14.3, the three shaded components can be seen as subtrees from the main rule and can be isolated as candidates for mutation or crossover. A fully developed tree is shown in fig. 14.4.

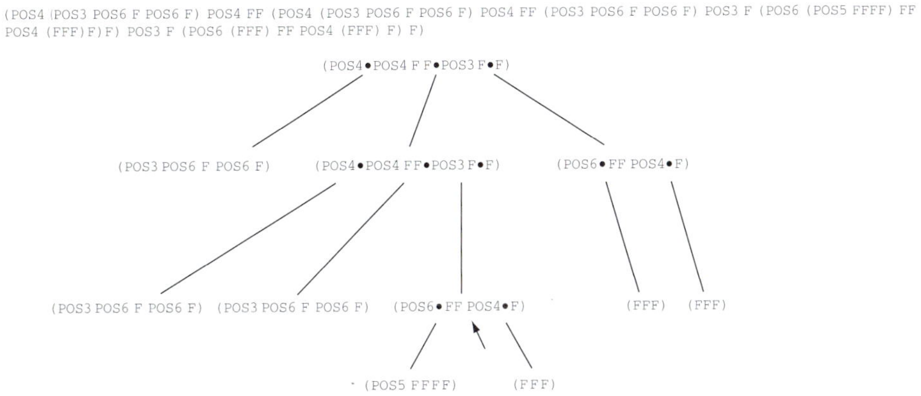

Figure 14.4 Example of a genotype generated by the L-system, drawn as a tree of functions.

14.3.5 Mutation

The mutation genetic operator works by counting the levels of recursion or nested brackets in an individual's genetic code and selecting, at random, a self-contained balanced chunk of code to be replaced by a similar, randomly generated, chunk. The chunk of code selected always starts with a branching bracket symbol and ends with a closed bracket. The symbol string is not of fixed length so mutated organisms can have varying lengths of genetic material.

14.3.6 Crossover

Crossover works by choosing two organisms, selecting suitably balanced sections of code and swapping them. As in mutation, the amount of genetic material an individual has can change, producing differences in generations ranging from slight to radical.

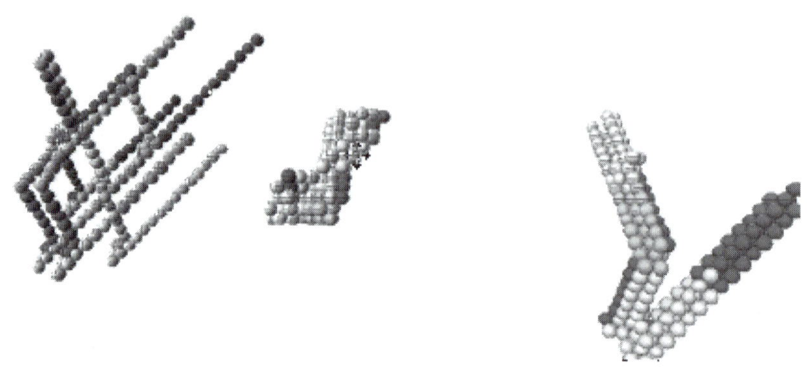

Figure 14.5 Example of phenotypes demonstrating crossover.

Initial experiments were carried out to test the crossover function. In fig. 14.5, the left-hand and centre configurations are two objects generated from a random production rule, the right-hand object is generated from the resulting rule after crossover of the other two rule sets.

14.3.7 Objective function

After choosing a data structure and method of representation and defining the type of genetic operators to be used, the third element of the algorithm is defining the objective function or 'fitness' function.

The work described here is introduced as an exploration of design worlds. What we mean by this is an n-dimensional search space of three-dimensional objects which evolution searches with its pursuit of the survival of fittest phenotypes. One can imagine a countless arrangement of phenotypes which the evolutionary algorithm moves around, sometimes in jumps, sometimes gradually.

In these experiments the idea was to see what three-dimensional objects resulted from various evolutionary pressures resulting from setting up a survival 'efficiency' test. The object of the exercise is to show how global form can be made to emerge from a 'blind' bottom-up generative process. For reasons outlined above, design worlds described here are restricted to:

1. The interaction of a branching tree structure and a directional supply of nutrients/pathogens. This was conceptualised as evolving 3D structures to either avoid or catch the supply, provided as a directed parallel stream of particles.
2. The interaction between two populations of branching tree structures 'enclosure' and 'permeability' with the evolutionary pressure of space construction.

14.4 Evolutionary Experiments in Simple Environments

14.4.1 Artificial Selection

Our immediate goal was to develop a model which would respond to the user's selection of the characteristics of two individuals which would survive and combine and become accentuated over successive generations – the 'eyeball' test as used in Dawkins' Biomorph program (Dawkins, 1990). Figure 14.6 shows screen shots of one experiment.

The mechanism used here is to display in three dimensions the members of the isospatial grid occupied by balls. The breeder can view the nine individuals rendered in isometric and make a judgement as to how appropriate each candidate is to their preconceived goal shape. For each generation the user chooses two parents from which to breed the next generation. These two candidates' production rules (genetic material) are then crossed over nine times to create the nine genotypes for the next generation, which are then developed into the nine phenotypes for display.

In the example shown in fig. 14.6, the user was selecting for length and regular branching, which rapidly evolved to the collection of pipe cleaner like objects in the lower right panel.

Such systems as this are already in use in the two dimensional world (Kais power tools for Photoshop) and allow the user to search through a potentially infinite set of forms.

14.4.2 Natural Selection

Simple one-goal natural selection was used in the following five experiments. The L-systems were developed in an environment with a stream of particles moving across the area where the phenotypes were constructed. Each phenotype was bombarded with particles, which were tracked across the universe and the number of hits counted.

The Windtunnel Experiment

In the first experiment using natural selection, the fitness function was to reward those individuals which avoided being hit by the 'wind particles'. The outcome after twenty generations is a flat sheet of balls where only those on the leading edge are hit, the rest sheltering behind them, see fig. 14.7.

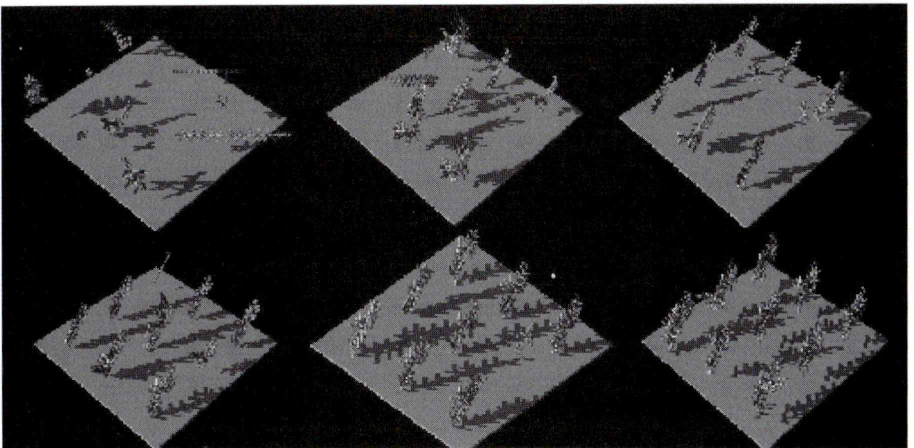

Figure 14.6 Artificial selection: starting population at top left, final evolved population bottom right.

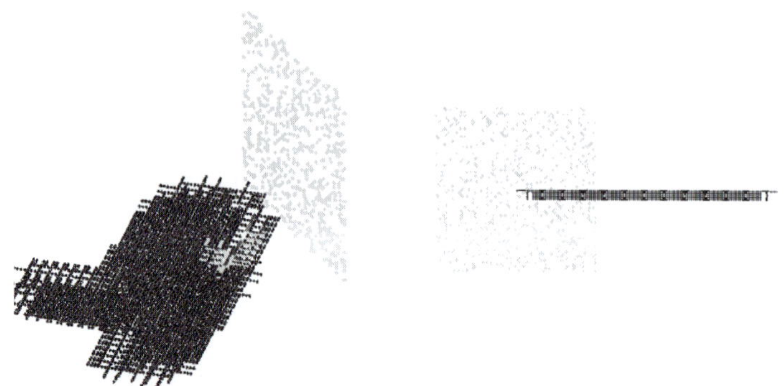

Figure 14.7 Windtunnel experiment – phenotype evolved as a flat sheet (foreground); particle screen shown in light grey.

The Flytrap Experiment

The exact opposite of the windtunnel, the fitness function for this experiment rewarded individuals for capturing the most particles. Early experiments were disappointing, with large negative scores and very little growth, often with the best individuals being reduced to a single ball. This turned out to be because the default cost of constructing an object was too high making it impossible to grow a big enough configuration to take enough hits to promote development. Once the ratio between the cost of a ball and the cost of a hit was altered to be more like 1:20 positive scores and useful shapes emerged.

This parallels Dawkins' work with spider webs (Dawkins, 1996), where a fly is seen as food and web construction is a cost to the fly. Our early experiments made it impossible to survive: since a fly was only worth one ball the developing phenotypes ran out of energy before being able to catch any flies. With a ratio of 1:20 or thereabouts each hit can justify more building and evolution can take place. The configuration evolved into a flat sheet, oriented towards the particle origin. In fig. 14.8 the evolved individual is on the right, the particle sheet on the left. Particles travel diagonally across the environment. The example shown here used hit cost of 20 and ballcost of 0.2.

Further flytrap experiments were undertaken using Macintosh Common Lisp (MCL) with the ball data exported to Microstation for rendering. Longer runs were attempted, usually 40 or 80 generations, with similar results, see fig. 14.9 (left). The chart in fig. 14.9 (right) shows the gradual evolution of the fitness over time.

Suntrap

The flytrap results were extended with experiments to explore the effect of evolving configurations to catch vertically moving particles. These individuals were mainly horizontal configurations, but unlike the windtunnel experiments there are many spikes growing up from the surface. This can be explained by noting that a ball can catch a particle whatever Z height it is at, the only condition being that it should not overshadow balls below it. A more open lattice evolves, rather than the flat windtunnel shape, see fig. 14.10.

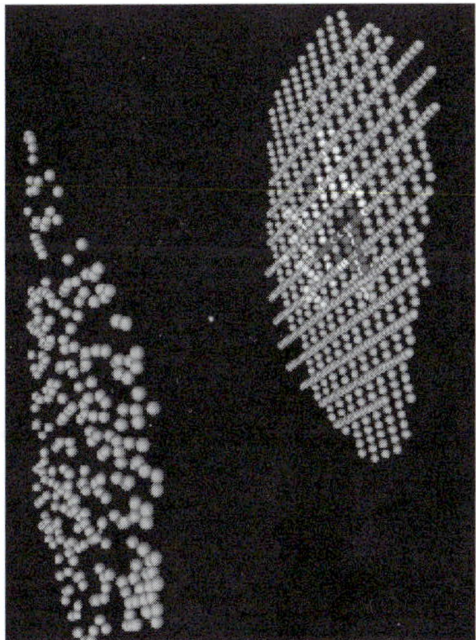

Figure 14.8 Flytrap with particle screen in foreground.

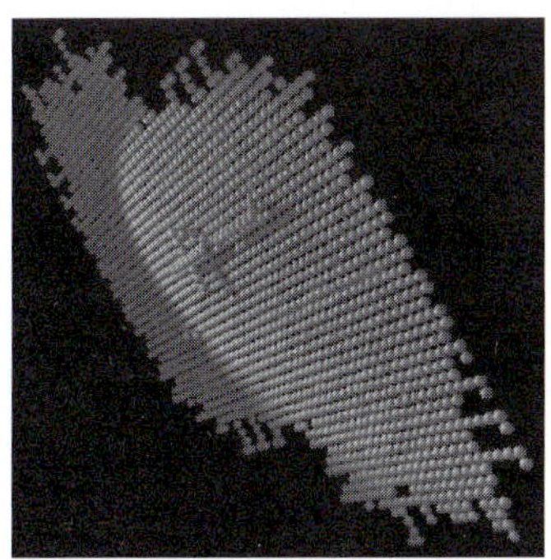

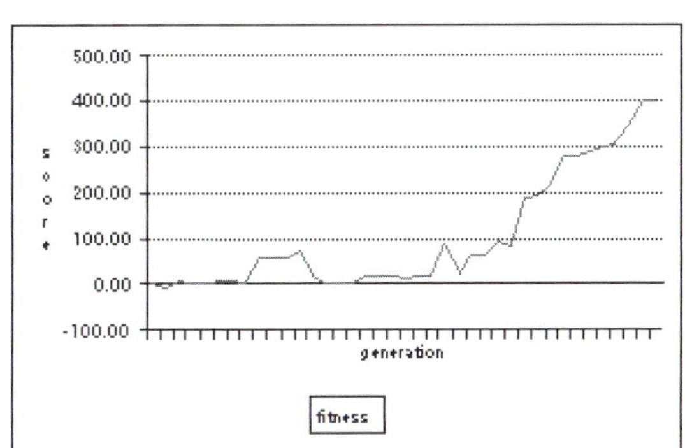

*Fitness function = number_of_hits*hit_cost-number_of_balls*balls cost*

Figure 14.9 Flytrap after 40 generations, graph showing increase in fitness over time.

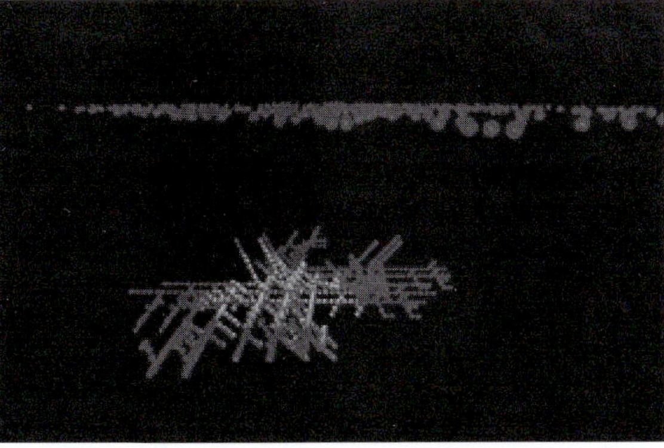

Figure 14.10 The evolved lattice, with the particle screen shown above.

Sun and Flies

Using both horizontal and vertical particle screens leads to the evolution of individuals with combinations of both types of configuration seen separately in the flytrap and suntrap examples. Figure 14.11 shows a form consisting of a central vertical sheet surrounded by horizontal extensions, evolved to catch these horizontal and vertical particles.

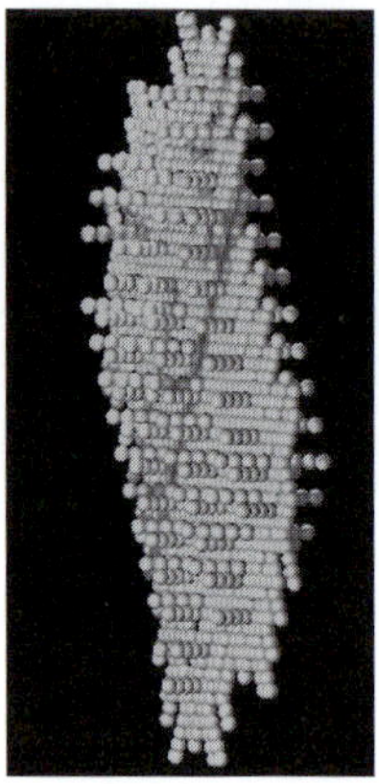

Figure 14.11 Object generated using a low ball cost, with (in this case) a much higher success in catching horizontal balls than vertical ones.

In an attempt to discourage the evolution of these spiky vertical sheets, the ball cost was increased and the vertical hits were weighted at twice the value of horizontal ones. This allowed the evolution of a range of more balanced objects. One such form is shown in figs. 14.12 and 14.13.

Figure 14.12 Sun and flytrap perspective view from the front.

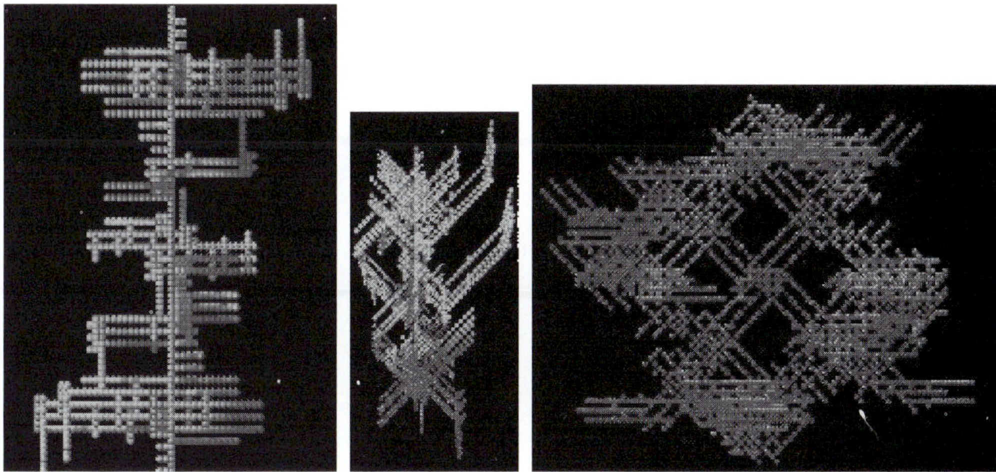

Figures 14.13 Front, top and right views of same object.

Enclosure

After these initial abstract experiments, the remainder are concerned with evolving shapes that might be useful as configurations of space. Our use of the term 'space' and the methods of analysis derive from the Space Syntax research at University College London (Hillier and Leaman, 1976; Hillier and Hanson, 1984), particularly calculation of accessibility indices of the justified graph of spaces. Space in buildings, in our definition, must be permeable (one must be able to get to all the spaces) and has to be separated from the outside by some kind of enclosure.

An early attempt to evolve for a single characteristic useful within the sphere of architectural design led to experimentation with the definition of enclosure. An architectural form is the enclosure of a system of space that is intended to serve some purpose. The internal space can be defined as that part of the universe that cannot be seen from the edges of the universe due to the position of an opaque building form, see fig. 14.14.

In terms of configurations of solid matter, a good enclosure form is one with a high volume enclosed compared to the volume of the configuration. This criterion is the fitness function for a simple, single-goal genetic program. An individual's score is the ratio internal-volume: wall-volume expressed as a percentage. The minimum score is 0%, but there is no specified

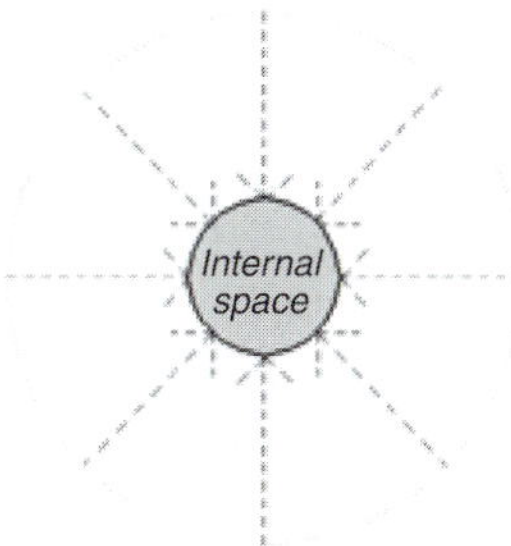

Figure 14.14 The internal space is that part of the universe invisible from outside.

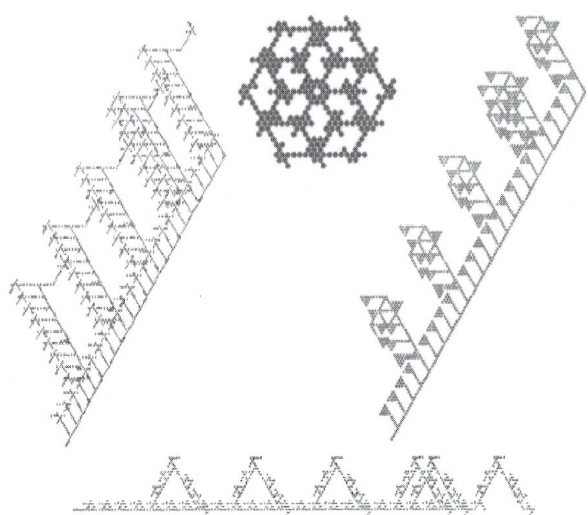

Figure 14.15 High scoring individuals using the space enclosure criterion.

maximum. GP operates equally well in two or three dimensions, but results are quicker to obtain and easier to read as diagrams in two dimensions.

Figure 14.15 shows the highest scoring configurations from an evolutionary run using this GP. It can been seen that the simple fitness function produces recognisable space enclosures which can begin to be viewed architecturally.

14.5 Symbiotic Coevolution

Basic single-goal, single-species evolution as demonstrated is an established process in evolutionary computation. The development of techniques for dual-species and multi-goal evolution from this basis is currently being explored.

14.5.1 Symbiosis

Symbiosis in the natural world is now recognised as a powerful force for evolutionary change. The full understanding of symbiotic relationships is a relatively recent development in biology, but its importance is now clearly recognised. Albert Schneider, an early pioneer of mutualism, stated that: 'Theoretically, there is no limit to the degree of specialisation and perfection that this form of symbiosis may attain. In fact, mutualistic symbiosis implies that there is a higher specialisation and greater fitness to enter into the struggle for existence.' (Schneider, 1897).

The evolution of two species towards mutual benefit produces lifecycles linked at all levels. Any specific design problem requires the identification of two interlinked systems and analysis of the relationship between the two. Testing based on project-specific criteria can then be developed and carried out.

The evolutionary impetus given by a mutualistic coevolutionary system allows both species to gain advantage through the evolution of characteristics which benefit the partnership.

14.5.2 Coevolution of Space and Enclosure

Symbiosis within architectural genetic programming requires the identification of two related systems. In this case the basic pairing is the association of enclosure and space. This combination provides a way of assessing a GP symbiotic methodology via a simple example.

The genotypes of both species – empty space and solid enclosure – are L-system production rules, giving phenotypes that consist of a list of grid positions. Testing of the phenotypes is carried out on pairs of individuals, one of each species. Crossover of successful individuals is also carried out between pairs: the 'space individuals' crossing over or mutating at the same time as their partner 'enclosure individuals'. The nature of symbiosis only allows individual's fitness to be discussed in relation to a particular partner. A good enclosure is defined as one which surrounds a maximum of its space individual, while a good space is an individual with a maximum of itself inside the enclosure. Each individual can therefore be given a percentage score; the overall symbiotic score is the mean of these two percentages (fig. 14.16). Using this fitness criterion, a GP has been developed to evolve symbiotically linked pairs of space and enclosure individuals.

The evolved pairs of configurations become enclosures of space through the simple symbiotic need to act together to obtain a high fitness score, see fig. 14.17.

14.5.3 Coevolution of Enclosure and Circulation

A slightly more complex relationship than that between space and enclosure is the one between enclosed spaces ('rooms') and the circulation routes between them. In this case the two species being evolved are the enclosure and circulation forms, both of which are continuous systems and thus can be represented using L-system production rules. The enclosed space is important and is defined, as before, as those grid positions invisible from the outside due to the enclosure form.

Fitness Criteria

There are a number of criteria which must be met by enclosure/circulation partnerships:

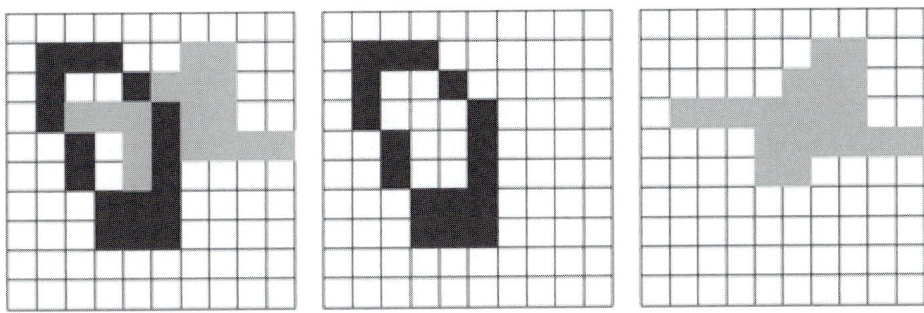

Figure 14.16 Fitness calculation – of the nine grid spaces inside the black enclosure individual, five are filled by the grey space configuration. This gives the enclosure a score of 5/9 or 55.6%. The space individual has five of its twenty grid spaces inside the enclosure, giving it a score of 5/20 (25%). The overall score is therefore 40.3%.

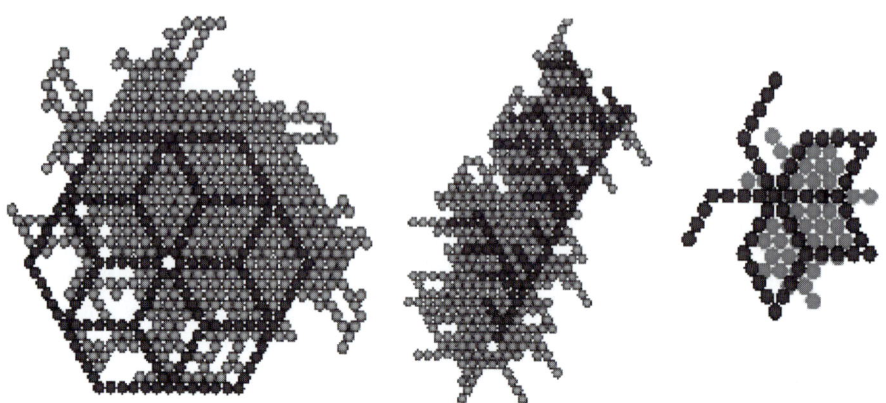

Figure 14.17 Evolved high scoring two-dimensional space: enclosure partnerships (enclosure shown in black, space in grey).

1. The enclosure must contain a certain number of 'rooms', specified by the user.
2. The circulation must allow all rooms to be accessed.
3. The combined configuration must evolve towards a mean depth (Hillier and Hanson, 1984) specified by the user.

Fitness Testing

Investigation of the configuration of an enclosure/circulation partnership is carried out in a series of tests. The first test identifies separate internal spaces, storing a list of the grid positions in each room. Once the individual rooms have been identified, the enclosure individual can be given a score reflecting whether it has the correct number of rooms. It is then necessary to discover whether the rooms are connected. The circulation individual is compared with the lists of inside space, resulting in a score showing how many of the rooms are connected. In order to calculate the mean depth a 'turtle' begins a random walk at some point on the circulation individual, building up a list of the rooms she has visited. This list records which rooms are directly connected. For example, a list running [1 2 3 2] demonstrates that room one is connected to room two which in turn is connected to room three.

A justified graph (j-graph) is a simple representation of the configuration of a series of spaces showing how the spaces are connected to one another. Each room in a configuration will have an individual j-graph. The depth of each j-graph configuration can be found allowing the combined mean depth of the complete enclosure/circulation partnership to be calculated.

Experimental Results

The images in fig. 14.18 show the results of a two-dimensional run of evolution for diagrammatic purposes. The evolutionary criteria were intended to produce a configuration containing ten highly connected rooms. The j-graph for each room is identical and is shown in fig. 14.19. As can be seen, each room is connected to all of the other rooms, minimising the mean depth. The total depth for each room is nine, thus the mean depth is nine also – the minimum for a ten room configuration.

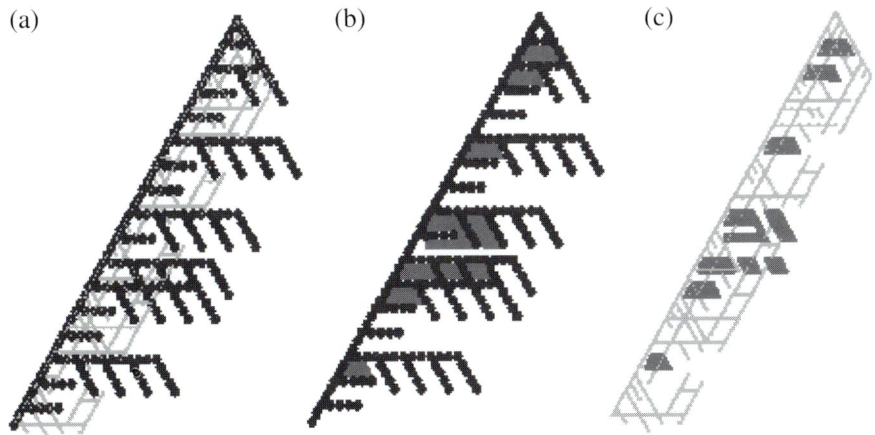

Figure 14.18 (a) The enclosure/circulation partnership (enclosure in black, circulation in light grey); (b) Rooms shades in mid grey; (c) Relationship between rooms and circulation.

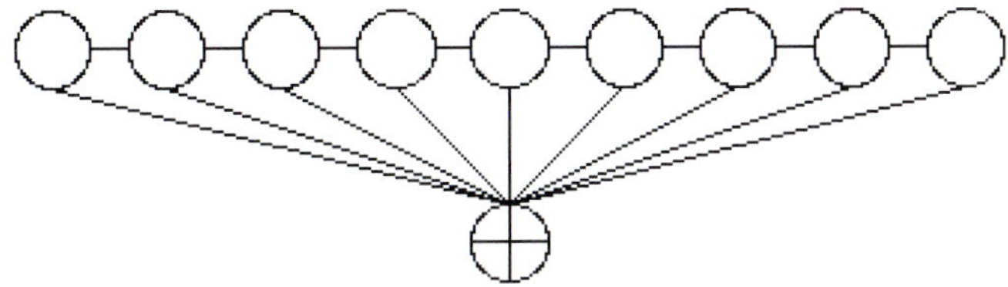

Figure 14.19 Justified graph for each room in the configuration shown in figure 14.18.

16.6 Conclusions

This chapter has shown that global form can be made to emerge from the interaction of 'blind' generative systems evolving within a set of environmental constraints. The architectural aim of research such as this is to try to get the computer to 'come across' otherwise unexplored alternatives to designs, and shifts the burden from defining the phenotype (what my building will look like) to defining the performance criteria (how will my building work). The major difficulty lies in the development of good (computable) performance indicators to be used as fitness functions. In addition, as this work has discovered, the development and improvement of the artificial embryogeny is crucial.

Further work in this area will develop new representations of architectural objects with expanded function sets and primitive components, and we hope to include more aspects of the string rewriting system under the control of evolution, in particular the branching and rewriting parameters and the ratios between the primitive functions/objects.

References

Bays, C. (1987). Patterns for Simple Cellular Automata in a Universe of Dense-Packed Spheres. In *Proceedings of Complex Systems Summer School University of Santa Fe, vol. I.* Addison-Wesley, Bucks.

Bays, C. (1988). Classification of Semi-Totalistic Cellular Automata in 3-D. In *Proceedings of Complex Systems Summer School University of Santa Fe, vol. II*. Addison-Wesley, Bucks.

Broughton, T., Tan, A. and Coates, P. S. (1997). 'The Use of Genetic Programming in Exploring 3d Design Worlds', *CAAD Futures 1997*, ed. Richard Junge, Kluwer Academic Publishers.

Das, S., Franguiadakis, T., Papka, M., DeFanti, T. A. and Sandin, D. J. (1994). 'A Genetic Programming Application in Virtual Reality', *IEEE Computational Intelligence Evolutionary Computation Conference Proceedings*. IEEE.

D'arcy Wentworth, Thomson (1917/61). *On Growth and Form*, Tyler Bonner, J. (ed.) abridged edn, Cambridge University Press.

Dawkins, R. (1990). 'Evolving Evolvability', *Artificial Life II, Proceedings of the Workshop on Artificial Life*, Langton, C. (ed.). Addison-Wesley.

Dawkins, R. (1991). *The Blind Watchmaker*, Penguin.

Dawkins, R. (1996). *Climbing Mount Improbable*, Viking.

DeBoer Fracchia Prusinkiewicz (1992). 'Analysis and Simulation of the Development of Cellular Layers', *Artificial Life II*, Langton, C. (ed.), Addison-Wesley.

Fraser, J. (1995). *An Evolutionary Architecture*, Architectural Association.

Gero, J. S. and Schnier, T. (1995). *Evolving Representations of Designcases and their Use in Creative Design*, Key Centre of Design Computing.

Goldberg, D. E. (1989). *Genetic Algorithms in Search, Optimization, and Machine Learning*, Addison-Wesley.

Hillier, W. (1996). *Space is the Machine*, Cambridge University Press.

Hillier, W. and Leaman, A. (1976). *Space Syntax, Environment and Planning B.*

Hillier, W. and Hanson, J (1984). *The Social Logic of Space*, Cambridge University Press.

Holland, J. (1975). *Adaptation in Natural and Artificial Systems*, MIT Press.

Horling, B. (1996). 'Implementation of a Context-Sensitive Lindenmayer-system Modeller', Dept Engineering and Computer Science Trinity College Hartford, USA.

Jacob, C. (1996). 'Evolving Evolution Programs:Genetic Programs and L-Systems', *Proceedings of the First Annual Conference on Genetic Programming*, Stanford, MIT Press, pp. 107–115.

Jo, H. and Gero, J. (1995). 'Representation and Use of Design Knowledge in Evolutionary Design', *CAAD Futures '95*, Kluwer, Singapore.

Kaandorp, J. (1994). *Fractal Modelling: Growth and Form in Biology*, Springer-Verlag.

Koza, J. R. (1992). *Genetic Programming, or the Programming of Computers by Means of Natural Selection*, MIT Press.

Lindenmayer, A. and Prusinkiewicz, P. (1988). *The Algorithmic Beauty of Plants*, Springer-Verlag.

Sapp, J. (1994). *Evolution by Association, A History of Symbiosis*, Oxford University Press.

Schneider, A. (1897). 'The Phenomena of Symbiosis', *Minnesota Botanical Studies*, 1, p. 940, quoted in Sapp (1994).

Schnier, T. and Gero, J. (1995). 'Learning Representations for Evolutionary Computation', *8th Australian Joint Conference on Artificial Intelligence, AI '95*, pp. 387–394.

Schnier, T. and Gero, J. (1996). 'Learning Genetic Representations as Alternative to Hand-Coded Shape Grammars', *Artificial Intelligence in Design '96*. Kluwer, pp. 35–57.

Steadman, P. (1979). *The Evolution of Designs*, Cambridge University Press.

Todd, S. and Latham, W. (1992). *Evolutionary Art and Computers,* Academic Press.

Walker, M. (1993). Digital Evolutions, M.Sc. Thesis, University of East London, UK.

Tom Caumont

5 CREATIVE EVOLUTIONARY DESIGN

Can a computer evolve good designs from scratch, given very little knowledge about what the form of the design should be? Is it possible for a computer to discover new design concepts? How creative is creative evolutionary design?

The four chapters in the final section of the book provide the best answers to date to these questions. ***Evolving Designs by Generating Useful Complex Gene Structures*** by Prof. John Gero and Dr. Mike Rosenman of the *Key Centre of Design Computing, University of Sydney* describe two approaches to the evolution of architecture. They show how new representations can be evolved, and how hierarchical structures can help in the evolution of floor-plans. Prof. John Koza (the creator of genetic programming) of *Stanford University*, provides the second chapter in this section: ***The Design of Analog Circuits by Means of Genetic Programming***. He describes how novel analogue circuits can be evolved to perform a variety of functions. The third chapter, ***Computer Evolution of Buildable Objects*** by Pablo Funes and Prof. Jordan Pollack, of *Brandeis University*, provides a fascinating description of how very original designs of scaffolding, cranes and bridges can be evolved and built as models. Finally, the last chapter of the book, ***From Coffee Tables to Hospitals: Generic Evolutionary Design***, provides a description of my own work in this area. The chapter outlines *GADES*, a generic evolutionary design system, which has been used to evolve a wide variety of different and novel designs.

Chapter 15

Evolving Designs by Generating Useful Complex Gene Structures

By Mike Rosenman and John Gero

15.1 Introduction

This chapter presents two examples of work for evolving designs by generating useful complex gene structures. The first example uses a genetic engineering approach, the second uses a growth model of form. Both examples have as their motivation to overcome the combinatorial effect of large design spaces by focusing the search in useful areas. This focusing is achieved by starting with design spaces defined by low-level basic genes and creating design spaces defined by increasingly more complex gene structures. In both cases the low-level basic genes represent simple design actions which when executed produce parts of design solutions. Both works are exemplified in the domain of architectural floor plans.

15.2 Example 1: Evolving Complex Design Genes Using a Genetic Engineering Approach

Evolutionary systems are often superior to other search algorithms for problems consisting of large unstructured search spaces, where no heuristic exists to guide the search. However, the search time for evolutionary systems depends greatly on efficient codings. Since the search time grows exponentially with the size of the genotype, one way to reduce the search time is to have the system learn more efficient problem specific coding containing the minimal genotype size while at the same time not excluding potential solutions and producing small numbers of illegal solutions. To achieve this, an evolutionary system which identifies successful combinations of low-level (basic) genes and combines them into higher-level (complex) genes is presented. Genes evolve in ever-increasing complexity, thus encoding a higher number of the original basic genes. This results in a continuous restructuring of the search space, allowing potential successful solutions to be found in much shorter search time. This restructuring changes the landscape by changing the probabilities of particular parts of the space being located. It increases the probability of finding those solutions which contain combinations of genes which contribute to good solutions and, as a consequence, reduces the probability of landing on those solutions which contain combinations which do not contribute to good solutions. The evolved coding can then be used to solve other related problems. These concepts are demonstrated by an example from the design of two-dimensional architectural floor plans.

EVOLUTIONARY DESIGN BY COMPUTERS
ISBN 1-55860-605-X

15.2.1 Basic and Complex Genes

Let us take an example where solutions are coded as strings of 19 different integer numbers from the range [0; 18]. Some fitness function is defined over the phenotype where higher values are better. Mutation here is defined as a pair-wise swap of two randomly picked genes. Assume that a standard GA is running for a predefined number of generations. Let us examine the genotypes of the evolved population. First, we classify each genotype as being either high fit or low fit, if the fitness of its phenotype is above or below some threshold. Then we try to identify features which distinguish the genotypes of the high fit phenotypes from the genotypes of the low fit phenotypes, fig. 15.1. Here it is easy to see that the fittest genotypes all contain the string of genes A = {0; 1; 2; 8; 4; 3} and all that are less fit lack it.

Hence, we can assume that A is an evolved gene and that its presence in a genotype leads to a high level of fitness. This hypothesis can be tested by generating two random sets of genotypes: one with and one without this evolved gene and using statistical tests to check if the former one is fitter than the latter one. If A withstands this testing we declare it our current evolved gene. Now we operate under the assumption that the presence of high levels of A in the genetic pool leads to a fitter population. Hence, we want to increase the presence of A in the population. The first step is to encapsulate A into an evolved gene, and protect it from disturbance by genetic operations like crossover and mutation. This can be done by marking the sections in the genotypes that contain the evolved gene, fig. 15.2, or by introducing a new

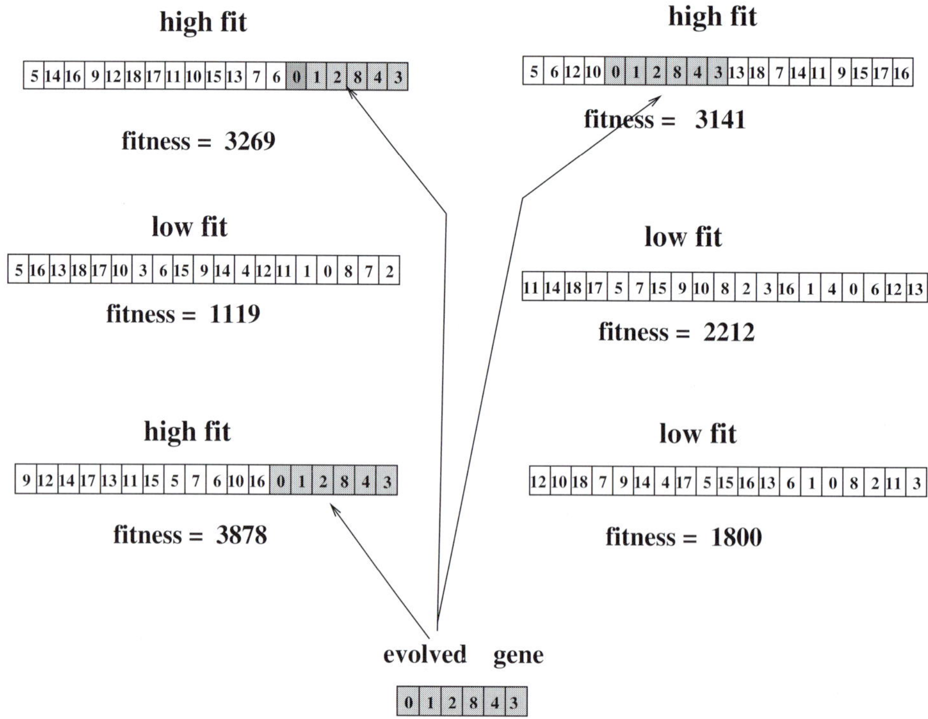

Figure 15.1 The identification of the evolved gene A = {0; 1; 2; 8; 4; 3} based on distinguishing between high and low fitness phenotypes.

symbol and replacing all or a high percentage of the occurrences of the evolved gene with the new symbol, fig. 15.3. In the first case, the length of the genotype does not change, and a fixed-length representation can be used. In the second case, a new symbol is added to the alphabet used in the genotypes and the genotypes may change length. The encapsulated evolved genes function as fixed subassembled genetic blocks in the population.

15.2.2 Evolving a Representation

The starting point for evolving complex genes is a population of randomly created individuals using a coding with basic genes. This coding has to allow for genotypes of variable lengths.

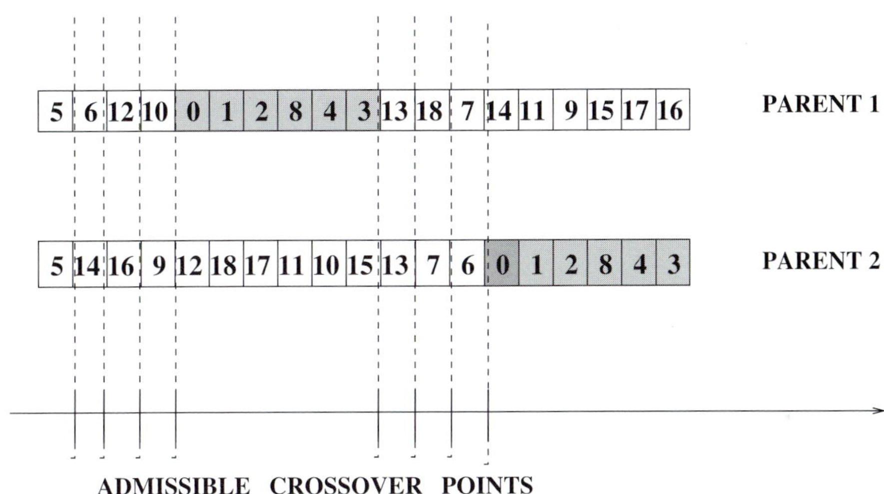

Figure 15.2 Encapsulating evolved genes by restricting the choice of crossover points to regions not occupied by evolved genes (for a fixed length genotype).

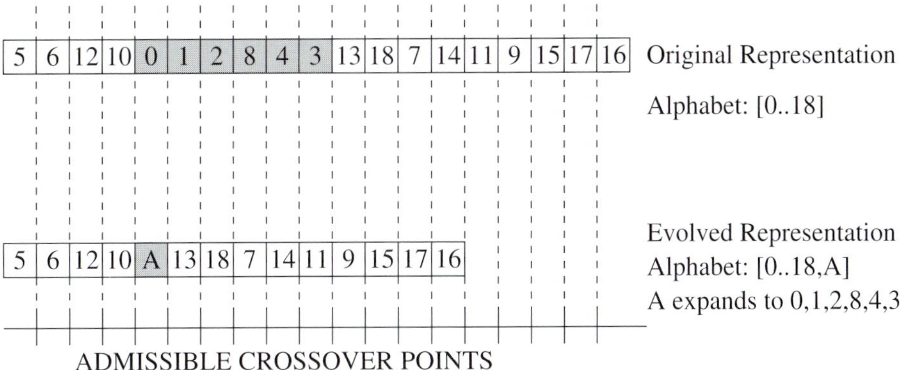

Figure 15.3 Encapsulating evolved genes by replacing them with a newly introduced symbol (Gero and Kazakov, 1996).

The individuals are evolved through a number of generations using a given fitness function. At the same time an additional operation identifies particularly successful combinations of genes. For every such gene combination, a new evolved gene is created that represents this combination and is then introduced into the population. At first, the evolved genes are composed of basic genes but in later cycles most evolved genes are composed of combinations of other, lower-level, evolved genes or combinations of these with basic genes. This growing hierarchy of representations gives rise to a more complex and abstract coding which contains domain specific knowledge that is 'learnt' by the system.

An evolved complex gene subsequently becomes an 'atom' in a new coding and hence the lower-level genes that are represented by it are protected from disturbance from genetic operations such as crossover and mutation. An effect of replacing a number of lower-level genes with evolved genes is that variable-length genotypes have to be catered for, even if the 'unpacked' individuals were to be of the same length.

Since the length of any genotype may not be restricted, the search space is infinitely large. It can be illustrated by an (infinite) number of concentric circles, each defining the space of solutions that can be defined by genotypes of different lengths. Solutions produced by genotypes of length one (the basic genes) are in the centre. The further away a solution is from the centre, the more complex it is and the larger the space that has to be searched to find it. Each time a complex gene is evolved, the structure of the search space changes. The solution that is created from it is moved into the centre and all solutions that can be derived from it move towards the centre accordingly, fig. 15.4.

15.2.3 Using the Evolved Representation – a Genetic Engineering Approach

The evolved representation can be now used to solve other, similar, problems. The initial population is generated using both the original basic genes and the evolved genes. The presence of the original basic genes ensures that the whole original search space can still be searched while the evolved genes restructure the search space in favour of structures that were established as useful when the complex genes were evolved.

The introduction of evolved genes obviously changes the probability that a part of a genotype maps onto a useful feature. While the number of different genes that can be used in the genotypes expands, the length of the genotype that is required to describe a feature shrinks. The net effect is that a smaller space has to be searched. If, for example, we want to find the window-like shape composed of four squares that was used in the example above, and assume we already know how long the genotypes have to be to find it, then the original search space would have a size of about $4^{14} = 2^{28}$, while with the evolved representation, only a space of $6^5 = \sim 2^{13}$ possible genotypes has to be searched.

To further increase the proportion of the fit evolved genes in the population, the evolved genes can be artificially introduced into genotypes lacking it, as it is done in genetic engineering. We try to make our trial population fitter before further reproduction by changing (the majority of) these genotypes which lack evolved genes in such a way that they acquire them with minimal changes. It can be done using a 'directed' macromutation, a sequence of mutations which leads to the creation of a previously evolved gene, for example A = {0,1,2,8,4,3} in fig. 15.5. Minimal changes to genetic material here mean that a number of elementary

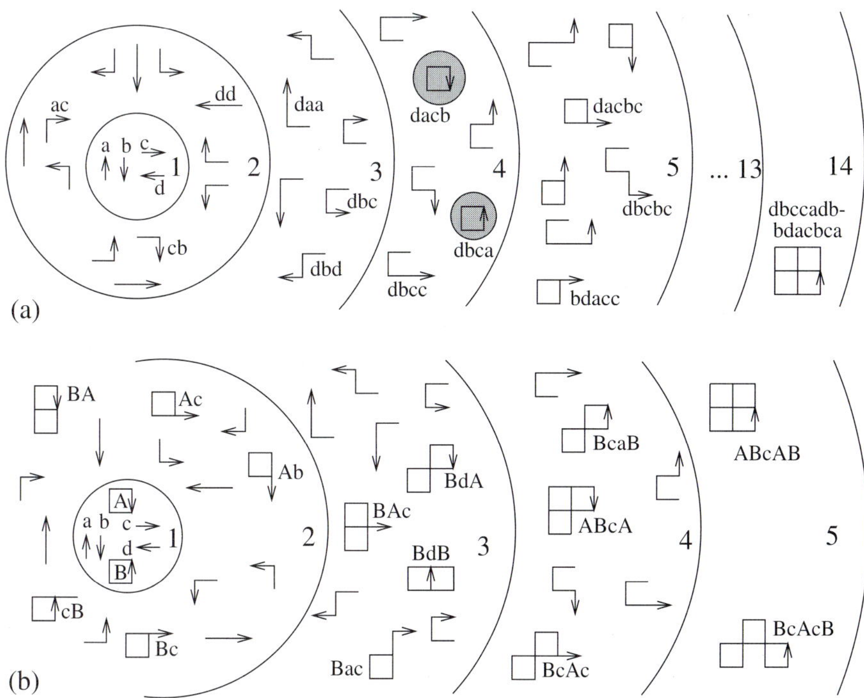

Figure 15.4 Example of an evolving representation: (a) original representation and (b) representation with evolved genes. Some of the corresponding genotypes are given, capital letters denote evolved genes. The transformation from phenotype to genotype is not always unique, e.g. the genotypes 'ABc' and 'BAc' produce the same phenotype. Arc segments indicate that only part of the space is shown (Schnier and Gero, 1996).

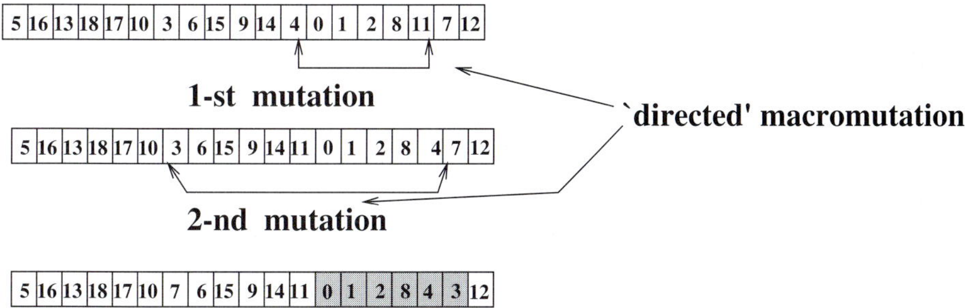

Figure 15.5 The genetic 'operation' to create evolved gene A = {0, 1, 2, 8, 4, 3} using directed macromutation (Gero *et al.*, 1997).

mutations in a macromutation should be minimal. As a result of the introduction of evolved genes and the measures which ensure their survival at above the natural rate, the evolutionary path of a standard GA is shortcut. If the genetic encoding is fixed-length and position-dependent then the evolved genes are just building blocks of a standard GA theory, and the genetic engineering extension of GA can be viewed as a way of explicitly handling such blocks. If the coding is position-independent and variable-length then it is clear that the effect of evolved genes usage instead of original genes is twofold: first, it allows the sampling of larger areas of a search space subject to the same computational resources; and second, it allows the searching of a particular partition of the search space which contains the fittest points more thoroughly, again subject to the same computational resources.

After we have identified newly evolved genes and made the population genetically healthier by 'operating' on those genotypes which lack the evolved genes using directed macromutations, we run a standard GA for a predetermined number of generations. We set the mutation rate of the evolved gene's components at a much lower level than the standard mutation rate level. Then we again analyse the genetic material of the evolved population, identify newly evolved genes, test them together with previously evolved genes to produce the current set of evolved genes and 'operate' on those genotypes which lack these genes. The cycle is then repeated. In practice, the analysis of genetic material is not carried out 'manually' as we did in our illustrative example but automatically, by using one of several string analysis techniques developed in genetic engineering and speech processing (Collins and Coulson, 1987; Karlin *et al.*, 1990; Needleman and Wunsch, 1970; Sankoff and Kruskal, 1983; Schuler *et al.*, 1991). In the general case, the type of evolved genes naturally developing is problem and encoding dependent. It could be any arbitrary feature of a genotype, not necessarily a substring (fixed group of genes with arbitrary ordering, periodic pattern, etc.) (Gero and Ding, 1997). If the type of evolved gene's characteristic for a particular type of problem is known then it is possible to design a much more efficient method for genetic analysis. Techniques employed during genetic 'operations' could also be designed differently. It should produce a particular type of evolved gene in a particular encoded (position-dependent, position-independent, order-based, fixed length, variable length, etc.) genotype and still lead to as little change of genetic material as possible. These conditions still leave a significant freedom of choice. The simplest way of designing such an 'operation' technique is to use macromutation (directed sequence of standard mutations) similar to the example. Usually one of the techniques of genetic engineering of natural organisms (genetic surgery, genetic therapy, etc.) is used as a template to design a particular operation technique. If one chooses genetic surgery as a model then the genetic 'operation' changes only the genotype's pieces which are similar enough (according to some measure) to the evolved genes and not the whole trial genotype. If genetic therapy is chosen as a model of genetic 'operation' then the evolved genes are inserted into trial genotypes in variable-length genotypes or they replace pieces of equal length in fixed-length genotypes, fig. 15.6. Usually, a random position for this insertion or replacement is chosen. Related ideas have been developed in genetic programming (Angeline, 1994). The main differences between the ideas developed in genetic programming and those in genetic engineering GAs include the way evolved genes are identified and their ultimate use. Genetic engineering uses the fitness function associated with partial genotypes, and evolved genes are re-used in related problems.

15.2.4 The Design of Architectural Floor Plans

In this example, we show how the idea can be used in the design of architectural floor plans. (This example is described in more detail in Schnier and Gero (1995).) As the basic coding,

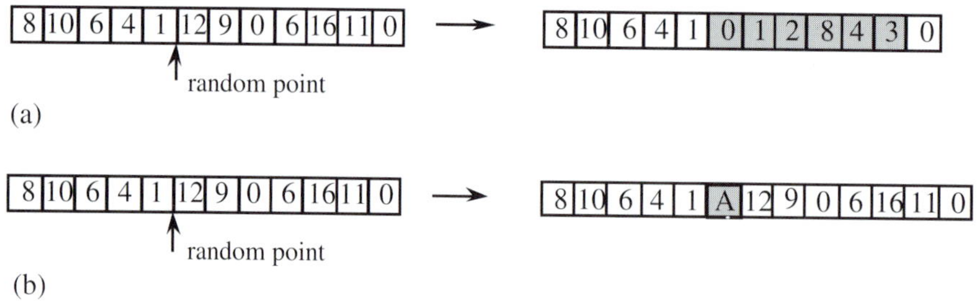

Figure 15.6 Genetic therapy model: (a) evolved gene A = {0,1,2,8,4,3} replaces randomly selected part of equal length in a fixed-length genotype; (b) evolved gene A = {0,1,2,8,4,3} is inserted at a random position into a variable-length genotype (Gero and Kazakov, 1996).

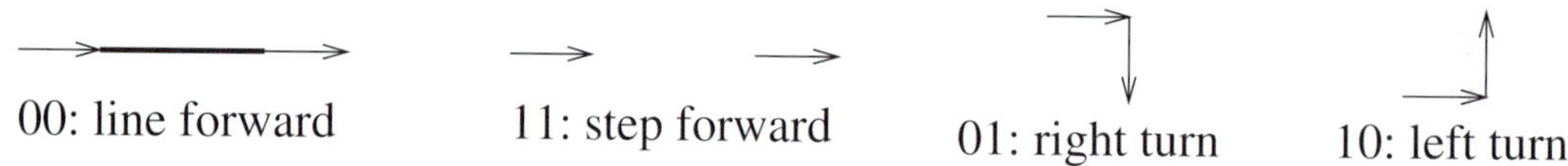

Figure 15.7 Basic coding, arrows show pen position and current direction before and after the gene is drawn.

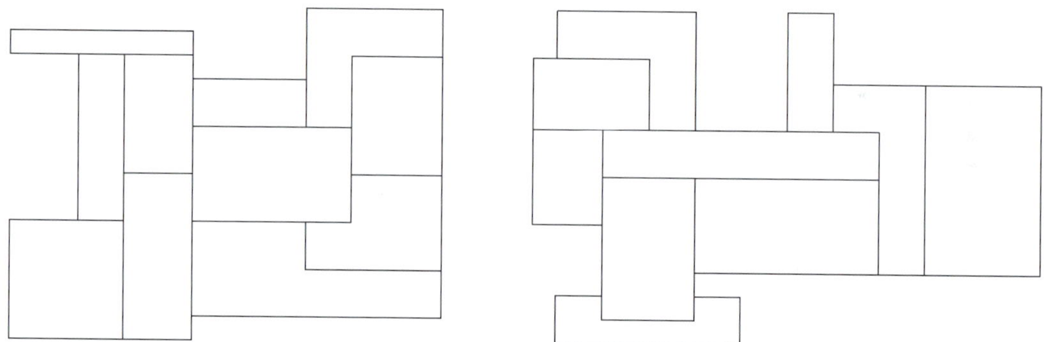

Figure 15.8 Room plans used as example cases (Schnier and Gero, 1995; Gero and Schnier, 1995).

we use a turtle graphics-like coding with only four different basic genes, that either draw a line in the current direction, move the pen ahead, or change the current direction, fig. 15.7. This coding constitutes a simple grammar for constructing orthographic shapes.

An Implementation for Evolving the Representation

The two floor plans shown in fig. 15.8 are used together as the designs to be represented. The fitness function compares individuals with this drawing, and rewards individuals depending on how much of the drawing they fit.

To create evolved genes, successful combinations of genes in the population have to be identified. We will only consider pairs of successive genes in the creation of evolved genes, using the following algorithm:

1. Create a table of all different pairs of successive genes that occur in the population.
2. For all individuals in the population divide the fitness by the length of the individual. In the table, add this value to all pairs occurring in the genotype of that individual.
3. Find the pair with the highest sum of fitnesses in the table.
4. Create a new evolved gene with a unique designator, and replace all occurrences of the pair in the population with the new evolved gene. The number of evolved genes is kept to a certain percentage of the population (3% in the examples shown). Figure 15.9(a) shows a branch of the hierarchical composition of one of the evolved genes (no. 363) from lower-level evolved genes and basic genes (numbers in brackets). Figure 15.9(b) shows how an individual is composed from six evolved genes.

Using the Representation

After a representation based on the examples in fig. 15.8 has been developed, it is used for new different fitness requirements. A standard evolutionary algorithm is used, where the fitness requirements are coded into the fitness function. The representation is not evolved further, instead the set of evolved genes learned from the examples is used, together with the original basic genes. As an example, the new requirement was to create a floor plan with minimal overall wall length, while at the same time fulfilling the following additional requirements:

1. No walls with 'open ends', that is, no walls that do not build a closed room;
2. Six rooms; and
3. Room sizes 300, 300, 200, 200, 100 and 100 units.

The additional requirements were given higher priority than the minimization of the wall length.

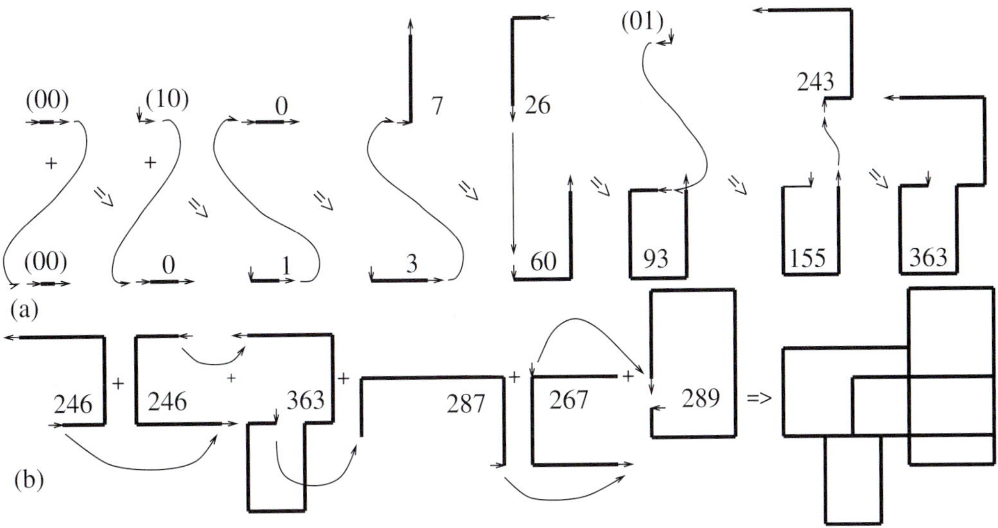

Figure 15.9 Evolved representation: (a) part of the hierarchical composition of the evolved gene 363; and (b) composition of the individual with the genotype (289 267 287 363 246 246) (Schnier and Gero, 1995; Gero and Schnier, 1995).

Results

Figure 15.10(a) shows the result of one run, after 150 000 crossovers were performed. The population size was 1000 individuals. 320 evolved genes created from the examples in fig. 15.8 were introduced into the population by using them with equal probability in the generation of the initial random population, and by the mutation operator. Shown are the best individuals (rotated copies have been omitted). To compare the performance with a standard genetic algorithm without evolving coding, fig. 15.10(b) shows the results of a run with only the basic coding, but identical fitness conditions. No rooms of more than unit size were produced. More than two thirds of the 15 400 genes used in the genotypes of the final population are evolved genes, encoding between 2 and 45 low-level genes. This shows that the new results indeed make use of the evolved representation to a very large degree, but at the same time use basic genes to 'fill in the holes' between evolved genes.

15.3 Example 2: Evolving Complex Design Genes Using a Hierarchical Growth Approach

While the previous example used a genetic engineering approach in which useful combinations of genes in existing solutions are found and subsequently used, the following example investigates how complex genes can be evolved through a bottom-up hierarchical growth approach. The evolutionary approach for synthesizing design solutions is based on a genotype which represents design grammar rules for instructions on locating appropriate building blocks. A decomposition/aggregation hierarchical organization of the design object is used to overcome combinatorial problems and to maximize parallelism in implementation.

15.3.1 An Evolutionary Model Of Design

Whereas the process of generation of form in living systems involves the placement of different kinds of protein in particular locations, we can describe the process of generation of form as involving the placement of units of different kinds of material in particular locations. An object can be 'grown' by locating a required number of such units, i.e. cells or building blocks, one at a time in sequence. The form produced will depend on the form of the building block and the location procedures, i.e. rules of growth, used. The genotype for a homogeneous object is thus the sequence of coded instructions for selecting and locating material units. When this

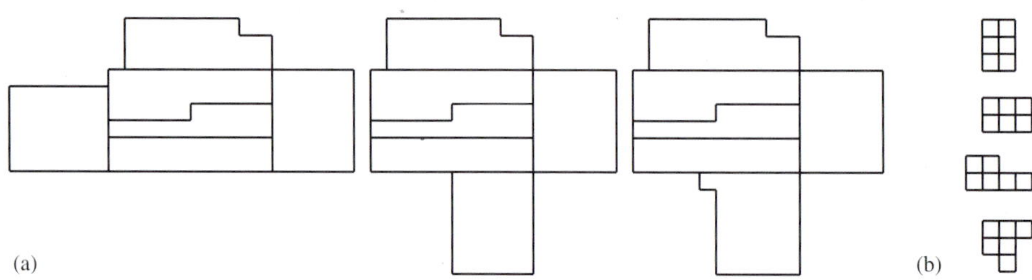

Figure 15.10 New floor plans, using coding knowledge from the example cases (see text for fitness requirements): (a) using 320 evolved genes; (b) using only the basic genes (Schnier and Gero, 1995).

code is interpreted and executed, the phenotype, i.e. the object (or rather its representation) will be generated. A general model of form growth can be proposed as:

For given total units of material required:
SELECT a unit of material, Mm
LOCATE unit of material, Mm relative to other units

A gene in such a model becomes (Ot, Mm, L(Mm)), where L(Mm) is the instruction for locating the unit of material Mm relative to the generated object at each step, Ot. Initially Ot is a single unit. The genotype is a sequence of such genes. Where a homogenous object is considered, the material identification is constant and the gene is basically a sequence of location operators.

Design Through Hierarchical Decomposition/Aggregation

Simon (1969) points out that it is only possible for complex organisms to evolve if their structure is organized hierarchically. The generation of an object can be achieved through the recursive generation of its components until a level is reached where the generation becomes one of generating an element which is composed of basic units. Such an approach assumes a formulation of the decomposition structure of an object.

A top-down hierarchical approach is used in genetic programming (Koza, 1992; Rosca and Ballard, 1994). The approach used here is a bottom-up multi-level approach where, at each level, a component is generated from a combination of components from the level immediately below, fig. 15.11.

At each level, an initial population is generated and then evolved over a number of generations until a satisfactory population of objects at that level is obtained. Members of that population are then selected as suitable components for generating the initial population at the next level. The process is repeated for all levels.

The advantages of such a hierarchical approach are that only those factors relevant to the design of that component are considered and factors relevant to the relationships between components are treated at their assembly level. Instead of a single long genotype consisting of a large number of basic genes, the genotype is composed of a set of chromosomes relevant to their particular level. In addition to reducing the combinatorial problem substantially, parallelism is supported since all the different chromosomes (components) at a particular level can be generated in parallel. If the set of possible alternatives of component types is sufficiently large and varied, then many different combinations of members of different such sets are possible, at the next level, with a good chance of satisfying the criteria and constraints at that level. Only when no such possible combination satisfies such criteria is there a need for some generation of new alternatives at the lower level.

In a flat model of form generation, a genotype will consist of a string of a large number of basic genes. In a hierarchical model, there are a number of component chromosomes, at different levels, consisting of much shorter strings of genes which are the chromosomes at the next lower level. All in all, the total number of basic genes will be the same in the flat and hierarchical models.

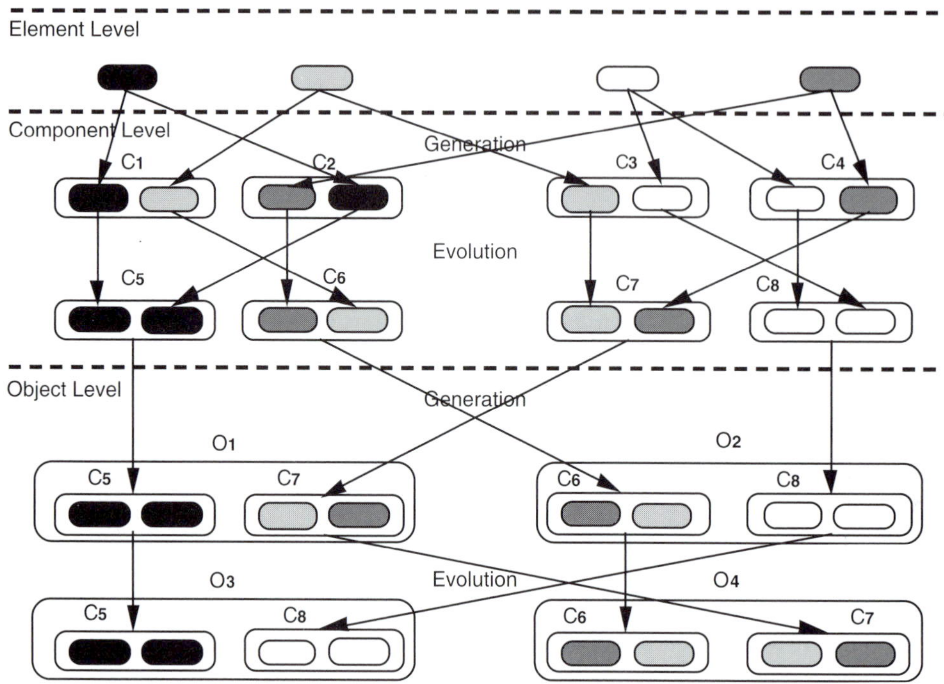

Figure 15.11 Multi-level combination and propagation.

Design Grammars for Genotype Representation

Design grammars deal with a vocabulary of design elements and transformation on these elements and hence define a design space (Stiny and Mitchell, 1978; Stiny, 1980). While design grammars provide a syntactic generative capability, they lack the evaluative mechanisms for directing the generation towards meaningful solutions. Using a design grammar as the genotype representation in an evolutionary approach allows for the generation of meaningful solutions with regard to some requirements formulated in a fitness function (Woodbury, 1993).

The aim of the design process, in this evolutionary approach, is the attainment of a set of instructions, a genotype, that when executed, yields a design description of a product, a phenotype, whose interpreted behaviours satisfy a set of required behaviours, the fitness function. In this approach, a grammar rule is a gene, the plan (sequence of rules) is the genotype and the design solution is the phenotype. The approach taken here is based on the premise that the grammar rules are fundamental operators, which cannot be decomposed or recomposed, that the particular grammar contains all required rules and that the aim of the design process is to find satisfactory sequences of such rules.

A General Model for a Hierarchical Evolutionary Approach to Design

The general model of design using a hierarchical evolutionary approach may be stated as follows:

for all levels in the object hierarchy
    for all components at that level
        GENERATE initial population of members by synthesizing lower level units through random application of rules
        EVOLVE population until satisfactory

15.3.2 A House Design Example – Space Generation

The above concepts can be exemplified through the generation of 2-D plans for single-storey houses. Previous work demonstrated that a single-level approach was not able to converge towards satisfactory solutions mainly due to the interactions of the various factors of the fitness function required for the various elements (Jo, 1993; Jo and Gero, 1995). A more detailed presentation of this work can be found in Rosenman (1996).

A house can be considered to be composed of a number of zones, such as living zone, entertainment zone, bed zone, utility zone, etc. Each zone is composed of a number of rooms (or spaces), such as living room, dining-room, bedroom, hall, bathroom, etc. Different houses are composed of different zones where each zone may be composed of different rooms. Each room is composed of a number of space units. Generally, in a design such as a house, the space unit will be constant. The scale (level of abstraction) of the space unit depends on the precision required in differences between various possible room sizes. The smaller the unit, the longer the genotype for a given size of room but the greater the shape alternatives.

The Design Grammar

In the above formulation, the generation of spaces basically comes down to locating spatial component units for that level. At the room level, the component unit is a fundamental unit of space. At the zone level, the component unit is a room and at the house level the component unit is a zone.

The design grammar used here is based on the method for constructing polygonal shapes represented as closed loops of edge vectors (Rosenman, 1995). The grammar is based on a single fundamental rule which states that any two polygons, Pi and Pj, may be joined through the conjunction of negative edge vectors, V_1 and V_2 (equal in magnitude and opposite in direction). The conjoining of these vectors results in an internal edge and a new polygon, Pk. This rule ensure that new cells are always added at the perimeter of the new resultant shape.

The fundamental conjoining rule can be specialized for different types of geometries. Orthogonal geometries are based on the following four vectors of unit length: W = (1, 90), N = (1, 0), E = (1, 270), S= (1, 180) so that the two pairs of negative vectors are N – S and E – W. These two pairs of negative vectors allow for the generation of all polyminoes. Orthogonal geometries will be used in this example without loss of generality. Other (sub)rules may be formed for other geometries (Rosenman, 1995).

Genotype and Phenotype

A polygon is described by its sequence of edge vectors. A suffix is used to identify individual edges of the same vector type. Thus the square cell of fig. 15.12 is described as (W1, N1, E1, S1). The sequence of edge vectors for a shape is the phenotype providing the description of that shape's structure. The genotype for any generated polymino is the sequence of the two

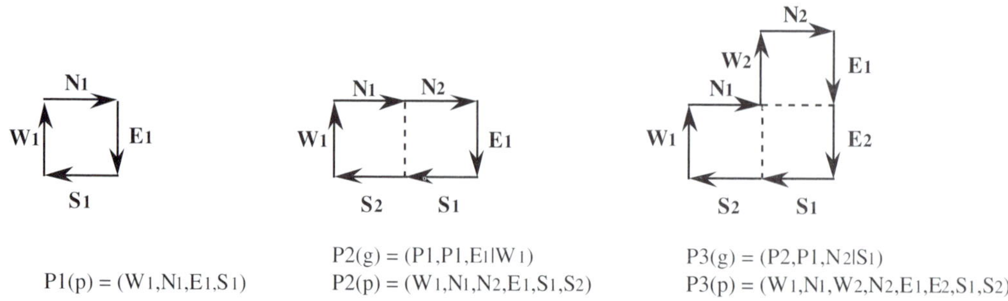

Figure 15.12 Generation of a trimino.

subshapes (polyminoes) used and the two edges joined. An example of the generation of a trimino is shown in fig. 15.12. Figure 15.12 shows a basic unit or cell, P1, which provides a starting point for the generation of polyminoes. Each generated shape is accompanied by its genotype and phenotype. The generation of these polyminoes occurs from a random selection of edges in the first shape conjoined with a random selection from equal and opposite edges in the second shape. At each step in the generation, the phenotype is reinterpreted to generate a new edge vector description and the conjoining (sub)rules applied. The genotype for the generated trimino is given as (P2, P1, N2|S1). This can be expanded as ((P1, P1, E1|W1), P1, N2|S1). When the same units are used for generation, the unit can be omitted and the genotype represented as the sequence of edge vector conjoinings. That is P3(g) = (E1|W1, N2|S1). The length of the genotype depends on the size of the polymino to be generated, that is on the area of the polymino. This corresponds to required room sizes.

Once a population of different rooms is generated for each room type in a given zone, the zone can be generated through the conjoining of rooms in a progressive fashion. Because of the cell-type structure of the polygons, the conjoining may occur at any appropriate pair of cell edges. Therefore, a large number of possible zone forms can be generated from two rooms. An example of some possibilities arising from the conjoining of two polyminoes is given in fig. 15.13.

The two polyminoes, P1 and P2, represent instances of two different room types and the polyminoes resulting from the joining of the two rooms represent instances of a particular zone type. When one pair of edges is conjoined other edges may also be conjoined, e.g. P4, P5 and P6. In the case of overlap, as in P6, the resultant shape is discarded.

The same process used for generating zones is used to generate houses. The joining of different instances of different zone types generates different instances of houses.

15.3.3 The Evolution Of House Designs

The above grammar can be used to generate initial populations for each level in the spatial hierarchy. Each such initial population is then evolved, as necessary, so that solutions are 'adapted' to design requirements.

The Evaluation Criteria – Fitness Functions

At each level, different fitness functions apply according to the requirements for that level. While the requirements for designs of houses involve many factors, many of which cannot be

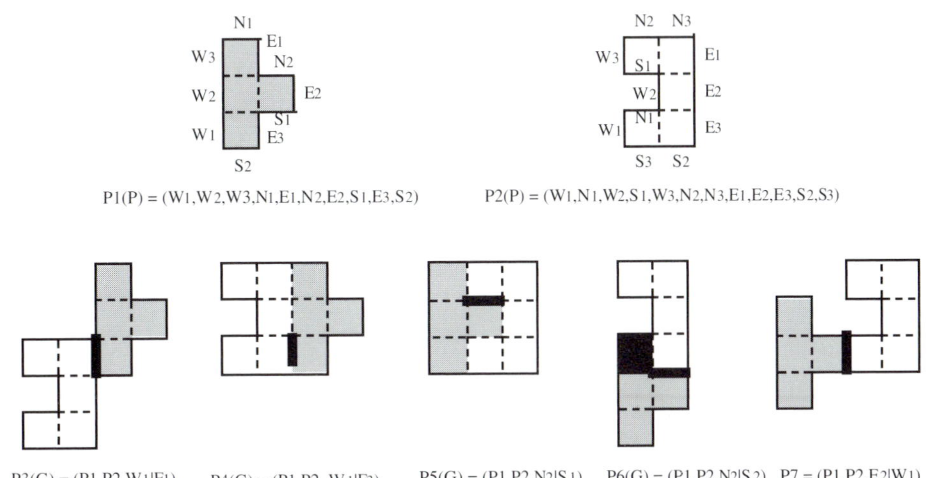

Figure 15.13 Some examples of conjoining two polyminoes. The thick lines show the conjoined edges. The black square shows an example of overlap.

quantified or adequately formulated in a fitness function, some simple factors have been used initially to test the feasibility of the approach. For this example, the fitness function for rooms consists of minimizing the perimeter to area ratio and the number of angles. This requirement tends to produce compact forms, useful as rooms. For zones, the fitness function consists of minimizing a sum of adjacency requirements between rooms reflecting functional requirements. At the house level, the fitness function consists of minimizing a sum of adjacency requirements between rooms in one zone and rooms in other zones. This has the tendency to select those arrangements of zones where adjacency interrelations are required between rooms of different zones. In addition to these quantitative assessments, qualitative assessments will be made subjectively and interactively by a user/designer.

Although the above criteria have been described in terms of optimizing functions, the aim is not to produce global optimum solutions but rather to direct the evolutionary process to produce populations of good solutions either as components for higher levels or at the final level itself. So that, even though the global optimum solution for the shape of a room using the above criteria, may be known, this may not be the optimum solution at the zone and house levels. By selecting other non-optimal but good solutions, according to the given criteria, good unexpected results may be achieved for the overall design.

Propagation – Crossover

Simple crossover is used for the production of 'child' members during the evolution process. Looking first at the room level to see the effect of such a crossover process, crossover can occur at any of the four sites as shown in fig. 15.14(a) with two results as shown in fig. 15.14(b). Since we are always dealing with cells of the same space unit, the cell identification in the genotype representation has been omitted for simplicity.

At the zone level, crossover occurs as shown in fig. 15.15. Two initial instances of living zones, Z1 and Z2 are shown in fig. 15.15(a). Each zone has one instance of each of living room,

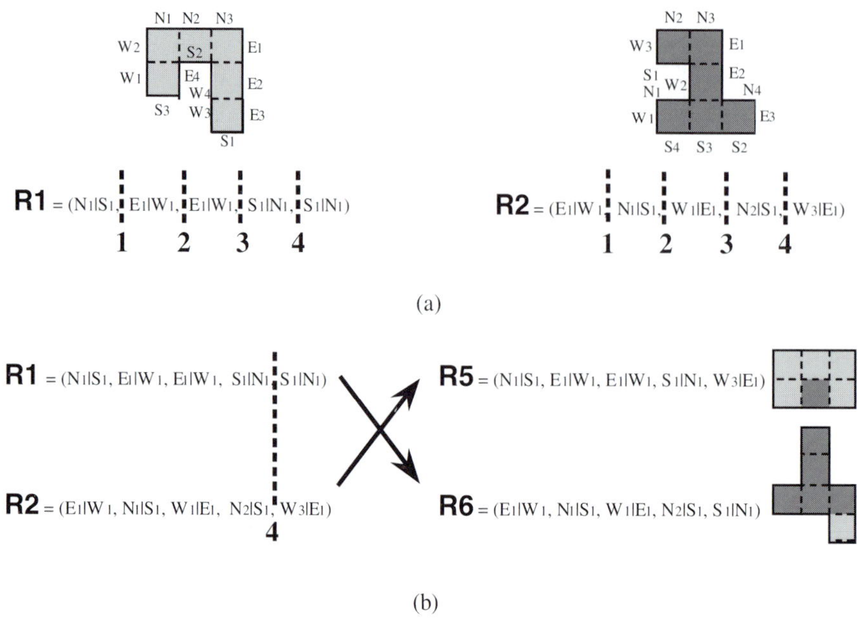

Figure 15.14 Crossover at room level: (a) initial rooms R1 and R2 generated from unit square cell U1; (b) crossover at site 4.

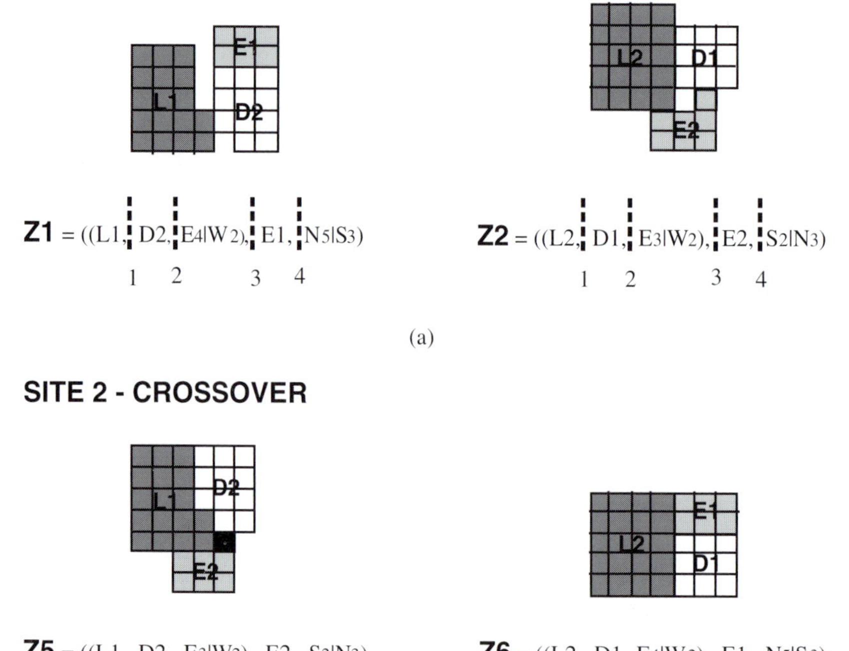

Figure 15.15 Examples of zone crossover: (a) rooms and initial zones, Z1 and Z2; (b) crossover at Site 2.

dining-room and entrance. Figure 15.15(b) shows crossover for one of the four possible sites. A similar process is followed at the house level.

Implementation and Results

A computer program written in C++ and Tcl-Tk under the Sun Solaris environment has been implemented using the simple criteria described previously. Each evolution run, for all levels, tends to converge fairly quickly to some dominant solution. Rather than use a mutation operator to break out of such convergence, it was found that a more efficient strategy was to generate multiple runs with different initial randomly generated populations. This produces a variety of gene pools thus covering a more diverse area of the possible design space. Moreover, such runs can be generated in parallel. Users can nominate the population size, number of generations for each run and select rooms, zones and houses from any generation in any run as suitable for final room, zone or house populations. These selections are made interactively by users as solutions appear which are judged favourable, based perhaps on factors not included in the fitness function. Such selections may therefore not be optimal according to the given fitness function.

Results are shown in figs 15.16 to 15.19 for room, zone and house solutions.

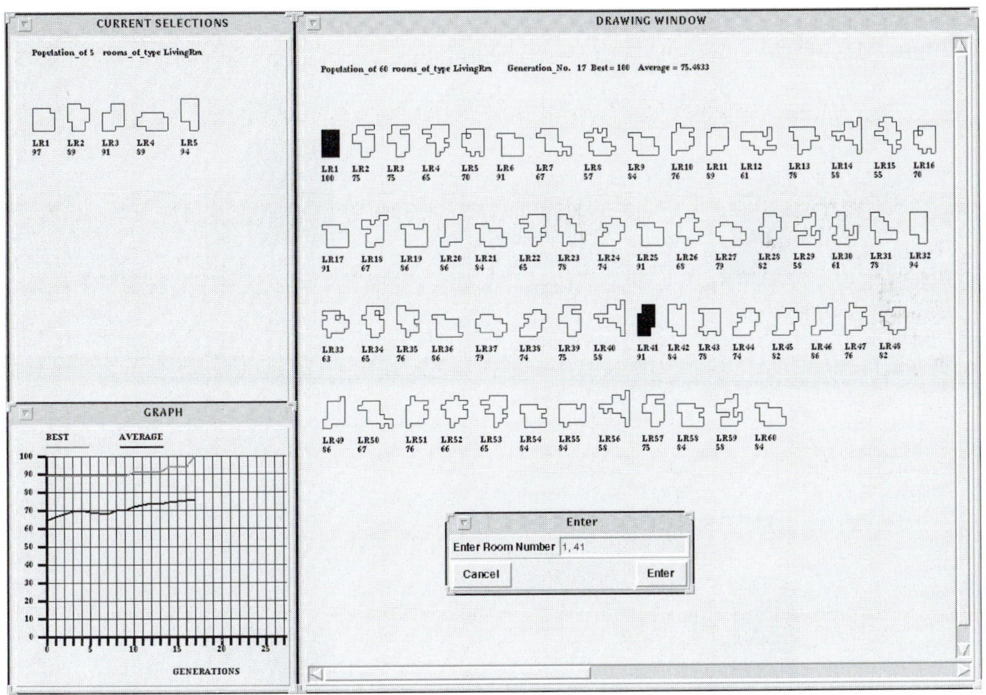

Figure 15.16 Results of living room generation after the 17th generation.

Figure 15.16 shows the results of the 8th run of the generation of Living Rooms where the first 4 room shapes were selected from 7 previous runs. Figure 15.16 shows the 17th generation of the evolution of this population of 60 members. A fifth room shape was selected at the

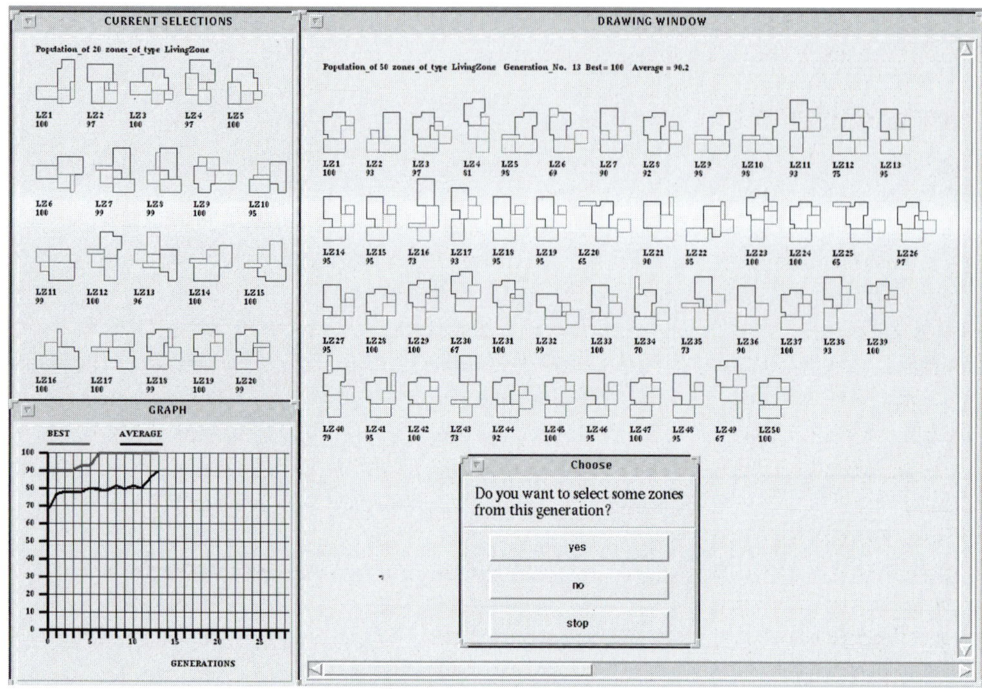

Figure 15.17 Results of living zone generation.

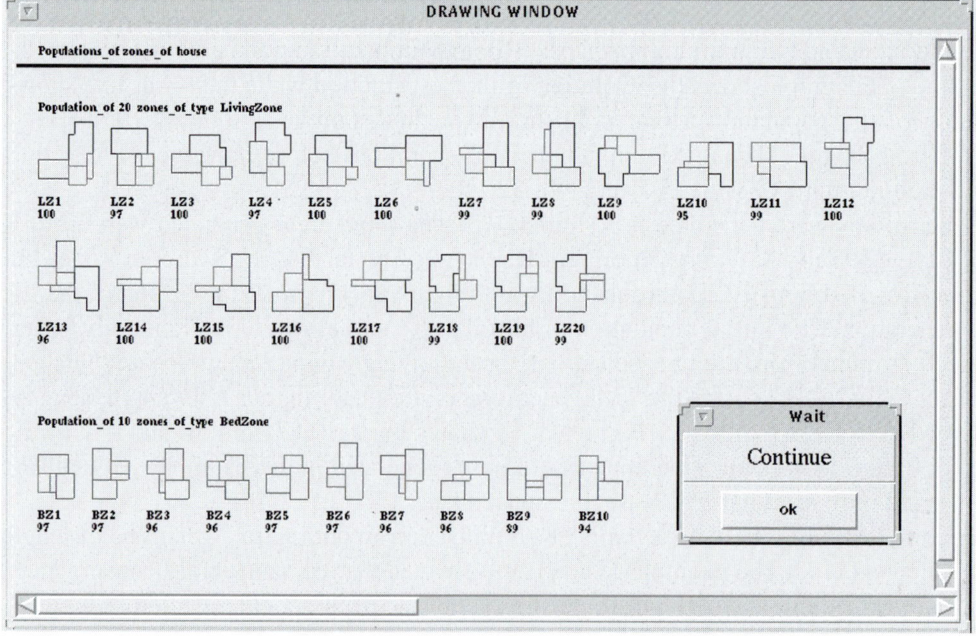

Figure 15.18 Results of bed and living zones generation.

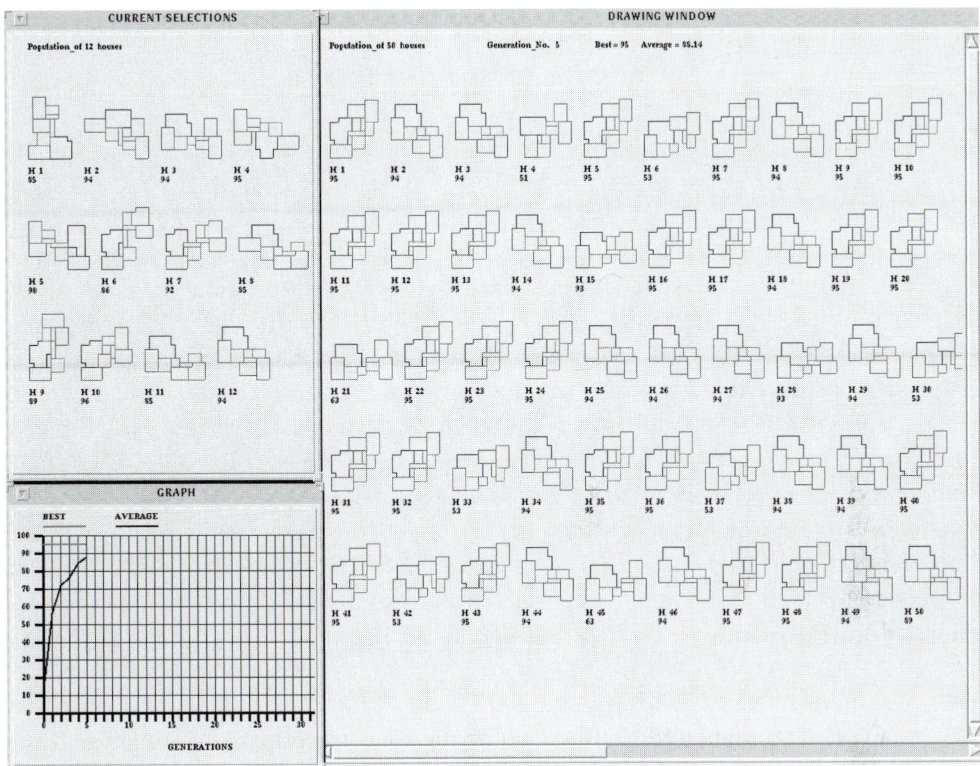

Figure 15.19 Results of house generation.

14th generation and two more room shapes (Room Numbers 1 and 41) are being selected. The upper line in the graph shows the evolution of the best solution while the lower line shows the evolution of the population average. All in all for this example, a total of 10 shapes were selected from 13 runs. The maximum number of generations before convergence for a run was 50 and the minimum 19 with an average of 32.

Other rooms were generated in a similar way. The room areas generated were: (a) Living Zone: Living Room 24; Dining Room 15; Kitchen 9; Entrance 4; (b) Bedroom Zone: Master Bedroom 15; Bedroom 12; Bathroom 6; Hall 3. Figure 15.17 shows the results of the Living Zone generation. The initial population of 50 Living Zones at run 1 was randomly generated by selecting rooms from the final selections for the Living Room, Dining Room, Kitchen and Entrance. Figure 15.17 shows the 13th generation of the final run, run 7. Twenty Living Zones have been selected by the user. Figure 15.18 shows the set of Bedroom and Living Zones selected. Figure 15.19 shows the final set of houses generated in this example. All in all 7 runs were carried out for a total of 12 suitable house plans.

The total area of this house type is 88 sq units, corresponding to a genotype of length 87 in a single genotype. The example of Jo (1993) showed that no satisfactory convergence was obtained with a single genotype of this length. The size of the population and the number of generations and runs required to generate a satisfactory number of members depends on the genotype length. The longest genotype was of length 23, for the Living Room. The addition of

more zones and rooms presents no problem for the hierarchical approach used here although it would present extra combinatorial problems for the single genotype approach.

15.4 Summary

This chapter presented two approaches to the evolution of architectural designs, one using a learning approach to evolving complex gene structures from a given population of design solutions while the other uses a hierarchical growth approach. Each approach identifies or creates complex building blocks which are then treated as individual components of the overall design solution or of a higher-level component assembly. The growth approach uses a more strictly ordered hierarchical approach in which components are generated for the next level in the component/assembly hierarchy whereas the learning approach is able to use any level of component. The growth approach explicitly generates recognizably meaningful component building blocks whereas the learning approach generates component building blocks which may not be recognizable as entities. In general, the hierarchical growth approach is not necessarily restricted to component/assembly structures using the same gene codings and, in addition, the fitness functions used for the various components and assemblies are different reflecting relevant requirements. In the learning approach presented, the one fitness function is used to determine the evolved genes at all levels, although multiple fitnesses can be used (Gero and Ding, 1997).

What both approaches have in common is that they demonstrate the advantages of shortening the genotype representation by creating hierarchies of increasingly complex gene structures and restructuring the search space thus focusing the search for useful solutions much more efficiently. The advantage gained is that a linear increase in genotype representation is obtained as against an exponential increase, similar to that gained by stage-state decomposition optimization methods, such as dynamic programming.

These approaches lay the foundations for the development of tools to aid designers to arrive at unexpected solutions for those classes of design problems for which evolved complex genes are beneficial, namely those design problems for which a hierarchical structure of components can be formulated.

Acknowledgements

This work is supported by the Australian Research Council Large Grant Scheme. Part of the work reported here was done in collaboration with Vladimir Kazakov and Thorsten Schnier.

References

Angeline, P. (1994). Genetic programming and emergent intelligence, in Kinnear, K. (ed.), *Advances in Genetic Programming*, MIT Press, Cambridge, MA, pp. 75–98.

Collins, J. and Coulson, A. (1987). Molecular sequence comparison and alignment, *Nucleic Acid and Protein Sequence Analysis: A Practical Approach*, IRL Press, Washington DC, pp. 323–358.

Gero, J. S. and Ding, L. (1997). Learning emergent style using an evolutionary approach, in Varma, B. and Yao, X. (eds), *ICCIMA '97*, Griffith University, Gold Coast, Queensland, Australia, pp. 171–175.

Gero, J. S. and Kazakov, V. (1996). A genetic engineering extension to genetic algorithms, Working Paper, Key Centre of Design Computing, University of Sydney.

Gero, J. S. and Schnier, T. (1995). Evolving representations of design cases and their use in creative design, in Gero, J. S., Maher, M. L. and Sudweeks, F. (eds), *Preprints Computational Models of Creative Design*, Key Centre of Design Computing, University of Sydney, pp. 343–368.

Gero, J. S., Kazakov, V. A. and Schnier, T. (1997). Genetic engineering and design problems, in Dasgupta, D. and Michalewicz, Z. (eds), *Evolutionary Algorithms in Engineering Applications*, Springer-Verlag, Berlin, pp. 47–68.

Jo, J. H. (1993). A computational design process model using a genetic evolution approach, Ph.D. Thesis, Department of Architectural and Design Science, University of Sydney (unpublished).

Jo, J. H. and Gero, J. S. (1995). A genetic search approach to space layout planning, *Architectural Science Review*, **38**(1); 37–46.

Karlin, S., Dembo, A. and Kawabata, T. (1990). Methods for assessing the statistical significance of molecular sequence features by using general scoring scheme, *Proceedings of the National Academy of Science USA*, **87**; 5509–5513.

Koza, J. R. (1992). *Genetic Programming: On the Programming of Computers by Means of Natural Selection*, MIT Press, Cambridge, MA.

Needleman, S. and Wunsch, C. (1970). A general method applicable to the search for similarities in the amino acid sequence of two proteins, *Journal of Molecular Biology*, **48**; 443–453.

Rosca, J. P. and Ballard, D. H. (1994). Hierarchical self-organization in genetic programming, *Proc. of the Eleventh Int. Conf. on Machine Learning*, Morgan-Kaufmann, San Mateo, CA, pp. 252–258.

Rosenman, M. A. (1995). An edge vector representation for the construction of 2–dimensional shapes, *Environment and Planning B: Planning and Design*, **22**; 191–212.

Rosenman, M. A. (1996). The generation of form using an evolutionary approach, in Gero, J. S. and Sudweeks, F. (eds), *Artificial Intelligence '96*, Kluwer Academic, Dordrecht, The Netherlands, pp. 643–662.

Sankoff, D. and Kruskal, J. (eds) (1983). *Time Warps, String and Macro-molecules: The Theory and Practice of Sequence Comparison*, Addison-Wesley, Reading, MA.

Schnier, T. and Gero, J. S. (1995). Learning representations for evolutionary computation, in Yao, X. (ed.), *AI '95 Eighth Australian Joint Conference on Artificial Intelligence*, World Scientific, Singapore, pp. 387–394.

Schnier, T. and Gero, J. S. (1996). Learning genetic representations as alternative to hand-coded shape grammars, in Gero, J. S. and Sudweeks, F. (eds), *Artificial Intelligence in Design '96*, Kluwer, Dordrecht, pp. 39–57.

Schuler, G., Altschul, S. F. and Lipman, D. J. (1991). A workbench for multiple alignment construction and analysis, *PROTEINS: Structure, Function, and Genetics*, **9**; 180–190.

Simon, H. A. (1969). *The Sciences of the Artificial*, MIT Press, Cambridge, MA.

Stiny, G. (1980). Introduction to shape and shape grammars, *Environment and Planning B*, **7**; 343–351.

Stiny, G. and Mitchell, W. (1978). The Palladian grammar, *Environment and Planning B*, **5**; 5–18.

Woodbury, R. F. (1993). A genetic approach to creative design, in Gero, J. S. and Maher, M. L. (eds), *Modeling Creativity and Knowledge-Based Creative Design*, Lawrence Erlbaum, Hillsdale, NJ, pp. 211–232.

Chapter 16

The Design of Analogue Circuits by Means of Genetic Programming

by John Koza, Forrest H Bennett III, David Andre and Martin A. Keane

16.1 Introduction

The design process entails creation of a complex structure to satisfy user-defined requirements. The design of analogue electrical circuits is particularly challenging because it is generally viewed as requiring human intelligence and because it is a major activity of practising analogue electrical engineers.

The design process for analogue circuits begins with a high-level description of the circuit's desired behaviour and entails creation of both the topology and the sizing of a satisfactory circuit. The topology comprises the gross number of components in the circuit, the type of each component (e.g., a resistor), and a list of all connections between the components. The sizing involves specifying the values (typically numerical) of each of the circuit's components.

Considerable progress has been made in automating the design of certain categories of purely digital circuits; however, the design of analogue circuits and mixed analogue-digital circuits has not proved as amenable to automation (Rutenbar, 1993). Describing 'the analogue dilemma,' Aaserud and Nielsen (1995) noted:

Analogue designers are few and far between. In contrast to digital design, most of the analogue circuits are still handcrafted by the experts or so-called 'zahs' of analogue design. The design process is characterized by a combination of experience and intuition and requires a thorough knowledge of the process characteristics and the detailed specifications of the actual product.

Analogue circuit design is known to be a knowledge-intensive, multiphase, iterative task, which usually stretches over a significant period of time and is performed by designers with a large portfolio of skills. It is therefore considered by many to be a form of art rather than a science.

There has been extensive previous work on the problem of circuit design (synthesis) using simulated annealing, artificial intelligence, and other techniques as outlined by Koza, Bennett, Andre, Keane and Dunlap (1997), including work using genetic algorithms (Kruiskamp and Leenaerts, 1995; Grimbleby 1995; Thompson 1996). However, there has previously been no general automated technique for synthesizing an analogue electrical circuit from a high-level statement of the circuit's desired behaviour.

EVOLUTIONARY DESIGN BY COMPUTERS
ISBN 1-55860-605-X

This chapter presents a uniform approach to the automatic design of both the topology and sizing of analogue electrical circuits. Section 16.2 presents design problems involving six prototypical analogue circuits. Section 16.3 describes the method. Section 16.4 details required preparatory steps. Section 16.5 shows the results for the six problems. Section 16.6 cites other circuits that have been designed by genetic programming.

16.2 Six Problems of Analogue Design

This chapter applies genetic programming to an illustrative suite of six problems of analogue circuit design. The circuits comprise a variety of types of components, including transistors, diodes, resistors, inductors, and capacitors. The circuits have varying numbers of inputs and outputs.

(1) Design a one-input, one-output low-pass filter composed of capacitors and inductors that passes all frequencies below 1000 Hz and suppresses all frequencies above 2000 Hz.
(2) Design a one-input, one-output high-pass filter composed of capacitors and inductors that suppresses all frequencies below 1000 Hz and passes all frequencies above 2000 Hz.
(3) Design a one-input, one-output tri-state frequency discriminator (source identification) circuit that is composed of resistors, capacitors, and inductors and that produces an output of 1/2 volt and 1 volt for incoming signals whose frequencies are within 10% of 256 Hz and within 10% of 2560 Hz, respectively, but produces an output of 0 volts otherwise.
(4) Design a one-input, one-output computational circuit that is composed of transistors, diodes, resistors, and capacitors and that produces an output voltage equal to the square root of its input voltage.
(5) Design a two-input, one-output time-optimal robot controller circuit that is composed of the above components and that navigates a constant-speed autonomous mobile robot (with nonzero turning radius) to an arbitrary destination in minimal time.
(6) Design a one-input, one-output amplifier composed of the above components and that delivers amplification of 60 dB (i.e., 1000 to 1) with low distortion and low bias.

The above six prototypical circuits are representative of analogue circuits that are in widespread use. Filters extract specified ranges from frequencies from electrical signals and amplifiers enhance the amplitude of the signal. Frequency discriminators are used in source identification and signal recognition. Analogue computational circuits are used to perform real-time mathematical calculations on signals. Embedded controllers are used to control the operation of numerous automatic devices.

The techniques illustrated for these six prototypical circuits can be applied to numerous other circuits, including an asymmetric band-pass filter (Koza, Bennett, Andre and Keane, 1996c), a crossover filter (Koza, Bennett, Andre and Keane, 1996a), a double pass-band filter (Koza, Andre, Bennett and Keane, 1996), other amplifiers (Koza, Bennett, Andre and Keane, 1997), a temperature-sensing circuit, and a voltage reference circuit (Koza, Bennett, Andre, Keane and Dunlap, 1997).

16.3 Design by Genetic Programming

The circuits are developed using genetic programming (Koza, 1992; Koza and Rice, 1992), an extension of the genetic algorithm (Holland, 1975) in which the population consists of computer programs. Multipart programs consisting of a main program and one or more reusable, parameterized, hierarchically-called subprograms can be evolved using automatically defined functions (Koza, 1994a,b). Architecture-altering operations (Koza, 1995) automatically determine the number of such subprograms, the number of arguments that each possesses, and the nature of the hierarchical references, if any, among such automatically defined functions. For current research in genetic programming, see (Kinnear, 1994; Angeline and Kinnear, 1996; Koza, Goldberg, Fogel and Riolo, 1996; Koza et al., 1997a; Banzhaf, Nordin, Keller and Francone, 1998).

A computer program is not a circuit design. Genetic programming can be applied to circuits if a mapping is established between the program trees (rooted, point-labelled trees – that is, acyclic graphs – with ordered branches) used in genetic programming and the labelled cyclic graphs germane to electrical circuits. The principles of developmental biology, the creative work of Kitano (1990) on using genetic algorithms to evolve neural networks, and the innovative work of Gruau (1992) on using genetic programming to evolve neural networks provide the motivation for mapping trees into circuits by means of a growth process that begins with an embryo. For circuits, the embryonic circuit typically includes fixed wires that connect the inputs and outputs of the particular circuit being designed and certain fixed components (such as source and load resistors). Until these wires are modified, the circuit does not produce interesting output. An electrical circuit is developed by progressively applying the functions in a circuit-constructing program tree to the modifiable wires of the embryonic circuit (and, during the developmental process, to new components and modifiable wires).

The functions in the circuit-constructing program trees are divided into four categories:

(1) topology-modifying functions that alter the circuit topology
(2) component-creating functions that insert components into the circuit
(3) arithmetic-performing functions that appear in subtrees as argument(s) to the component-creating functions and specify the numerical value of the component, and
(4) automatically defined functions that appear in the function-defining branches and potentially enable certain substructures of the circuit to be reused (with parameterization).

Each branch of the program tree is created in accordance with a constrained syntactic structure. Branches are composed of construction-continuing subtrees that continue the developmental process and arithmetic-performing subtrees that determine the numerical value of components. Topology-modifying functions have one or more construction-continuing subtrees, but no arithmetic-performing subtree. Component-creating functions have one or more construction-continuing subtrees and typically have one arithmetic-performing subtree. This constrained syntactic structure is preserved using structure-preserving crossover with point typing (see Koza, 1994a).

16.3.1 The Embryonic Circuit

An electrical circuit is created by executing a circuit-constructing program tree that contains various component-creating and topology-modifying functions. Each tree in the population

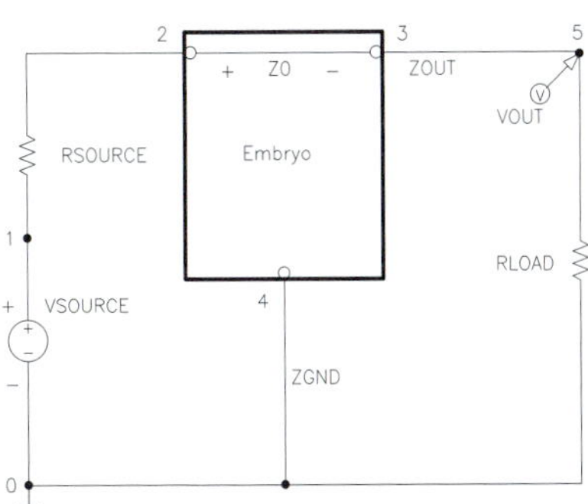

Figure 16.1 One-input, one-output embryonic circuit.

creates one circuit. The specific embryo used depends on the number of inputs and outputs.

Figure 16.1 shows a one-input, one-output embryonic circuit in which VSOURCE is the input signal and VOUT is the output signal (the probe point). The circuit is driven by an incoming alternating circuit source VSOURCE. There is a fixed load resistor RLOAD and a fixed source resistor RSOURCE in the embryo. In addition to the fixed components, there is a modifiable wire Z0 between nodes 2 and 3. All development originates from this modifiable wire.

16.3.2 Component-creating Functions

Each program tree contains component-creating functions and topology-modifying functions. The component-creating functions insert a component into the developing circuit and assign component value(s) to the component.

Each component-creating function has a writing head that points to an associated highlighted component in the developing circuit and modifies that component in a specified manner. The construction-continuing subtree of each component-creating function points to a successor function or terminal in the circuit-constructing program tree.

The arithmetic-performing subtree of a component-creating function consists of a composition of arithmetic functions (addition and subtraction) and random constants (in the range −1.000 to +1.000). The arithmetic-performing subtree specifies the numerical value of a component by returning a floating-point value that is interpreted on a logarithmic scale as the value for the component in a range of 10 orders of magnitude (using a unit of measure that is appropriate for the particular type of component).

The two-argument resistor-creating R function causes the highlighted component to be changed into a resistor. The value of the resistor in kilo ohms is specified by its arithmetic-performing subtree.

Figure 16.2 shows a modifiable wire Z0 connecting nodes 1 and 2 of a partial circuit containing four capacitors (C2, C3, C4, and C5). Z0 has a writing head and is subject to subsequent modification). Figure 16.3 shows the result of applying the R function to the modifiable wire Z0 of fig. 16.2. The newly created R1 has a writing head so that R1 remains subject to subsequent modification.

Similarly, the two-argument capacitor-creating C function causes the highlighted component to be changed into a capacitor whose value in microfarads is specified by its arithmetic-

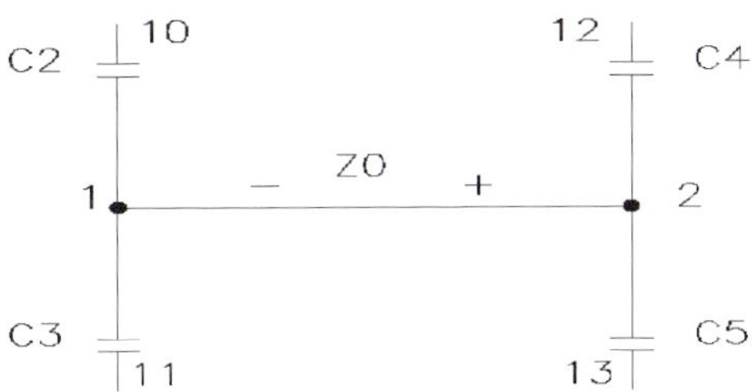

Figure 16.2 Modifiable wire Z0.

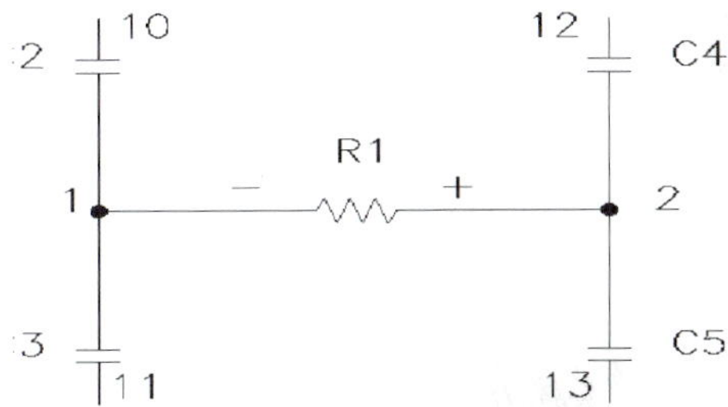

Figure 16.3 Result of applying the R function.

performing subtree. In addition, the two-argument inductor-creating L function causes the highlighted component to be changed into an inductor whose value in microhenrys is specified by its arithmetic-performing subtree.

The one-argument Q_D_PNP diode-creating function causes a diode to be inserted in lieu of the highlighted component. This function has only one argument because there is no numerical value associated with a diode and thus no arithmetic-performing subtree. In practice, the diode is implemented here using a pnp transistor whose collector and base are connected to each other. The Q_D_NPN function inserts a diode using an npn transistor in a similar manner.

There are also six one-argument transistor-creating functions (Q_POS_COLL_NPN, Q_GND_EMIT_NPN, Q_NEG_EMIT_NPN, Q_GND_EMIT_PNP, Q_POS_EMIT_PNP, Q_NEG_COLL_PNP) that insert a bipolar junction transistor in lieu of the highlighted component and that directly connect the collector or emitter of the newly created transistor to a fixed point of the circuit (the positive power supply, ground, or the negative power supply). For example, the Q_POS_COLL_NPN function inserts a bipolar junction transistor whose collector is connected to the positive power supply.

Each of the functions in the family of six different three-argument transistor-creating Q_3_NPN functions causes an npn bipolar junction transistor to be inserted in place of the highlighted component and one of the nodes to which the highlighted component is connected. The Q_3_NPN function creates five new nodes and three modifiable wires. There is no writing head on the new transistor, but there is a writing head on each of the three new modifiable wires. There are 12 members (called Q_3_NPN0, . . . , Q_3_NPN11) in this family of functions because there are two choices of nodes (1 and 2) to be bifurcated and then there are six ways of attaching the transistor's base, collector, and emitter after the bifurcation. Similarly the family of 12 Q_3_PNP functions causes a pnp bipolar junction transistor to be inserted.

16.3.3 Topology-modifying Functions

Each topology-modifying function in a program tree points to an associated highlighted component and modifies the topology of the developing circuit.

The three-argument SERIES division function creates a series composition of the highlighted component (with a writing head), a copy of it (with a writing head), one new modifiable wire (with a writing head), and two new nodes.

The four-argument PARALLEL0 parallel division function creates a parallel composition consisting of the original highlighted component (with a writing head), a copy of it (with a writing head), two new modifiable wires (each with a writing head), and two new nodes. Figure 16.4 shows the result of applying PARALLEL0 to the resistor R1 from fig. 16.3.

The one-argument polarity-reversing FLIP function reverses the polarity of the highlighted component. There are six three-argument functions (T_GND_0, T_GND_1, T_POS_0, T_POS_1, T_NEG_0, T_NEG_1) that insert two new nodes and two new modifiable wires, and then make a connection to ground, positive power supply, or negative power supply, respectively.

There are two three-argument functions (PAIR_CONNECT_0 and PAIR_CONNECT_1) that enable distant parts of a circuit to be connected together. The first PAIR_CONNECT to occur in the development of a circuit creates two new wires, two new nodes, and one temporary port. The next PAIR_CONNECT creates two new wires and one new node, connects the temporary port to the end of one of these new wires, and then removes the temporary port.

The one-argument NOOP function has no effect on the highlighted component; however, it delays activity on the developmental path on which it appears in relation to other developmental paths in the overall program tree.

The zero-argument END function causes the highlighted component to lose its writing head, thereby ending that particular developmental path.

The zero-argument SAFE_CUT function causes the highlighted component to be removed from the circuit provided that the degree of the nodes at both ends of the highlighted component is three (i.e., no dangling components or wires are created).

An electrical circuit is created by executing the functions in a circuit-constructing program tree. The functions are progressively applied in a developmental process to the embryonic circuit and its successors until all of the functions in the program tree are executed. That is, the functions in the circuit-constructing program tree progressively side-effect the embryonic

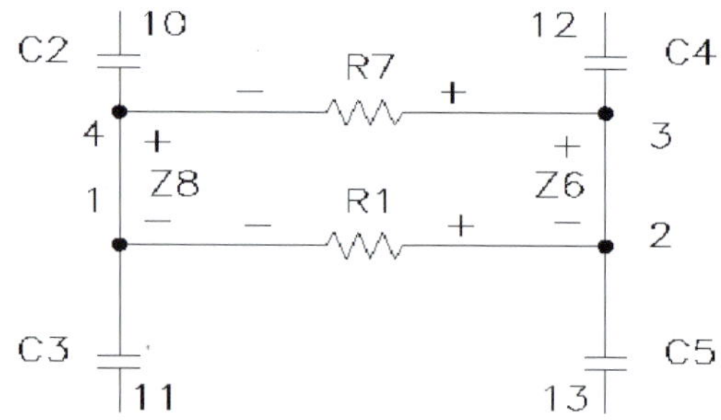

Figure 16.4 Result of the PARALLEL0 function.

circuit and its successors until a fully developed circuit eventually emerges. The functions are applied in a breadth-first order.

Figure 16.5 is an illustrative circuit-constructing program tree shown as a rooted, point-labelled tree with ordered branches. The overall program consists of two main result-producing branches joined by a connective LIST function (labelled 1). The first (left) result-producing branch is rooted at the capacitor-creating C function (labelled 2). The second result-producing branch is rooted at the polarity-reversing FLIP function (labelled 3). This figure also contains four occurrences of the inductor-creating L function (at 17, 11, 20, and 12). The figure contains two occurrences of the topology-modifying SERIES function (at 5 and 10). The figure also contains five occurrences of the development-controlling END function (at 15, 25, 27, 31, and 22) and one occurrence of the development-controlling 'no operation' NOP function (at 6). There is a seven-point arithmetic-performing subtree at 4 under the capacitor-creating C function at 4. Similarly, there is a three-point arithmetic-performing subtree at 19 under the inductor-creating L function at 11, and one-point arithmetic-performing subtrees (i.e., constants) at 26, 30, and 21. Additional details can be found in (Koza, Bennett, Andre and Keane, 1999).

16.4 Preparatory Steps

Before applying genetic programming to a problem of circuit design, seven major preparatory steps are required: (1) identify the suitable embryonic circuit; (2) determine the architecture of the overall circuit-constructing program trees; (3) identify the terminals of the program trees; (4) identify the primitive functions of the program trees; (5) create the fitness measure; (6) choose parameters; and (7) determine the termination criterion and method of result designation.

16.4.1 Embryonic Circuit

The embryonic circuit used on a particular problem depends on the circuit's number of inputs and outputs. For example, an embryonic circuit with two modifiable wires (Z0 and Z1) was used for the low-pass and high-pass filters (which each have one input and one output). However, the robot controller circuit has two inputs (VSOURCE1 and VSOURCE2), not just one. Each input needs its own separate source resistor (RSOURCE1 and RSOURCE2). Thus, the

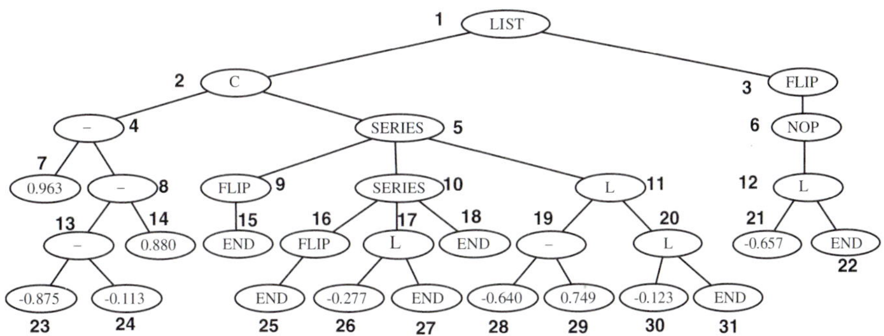

Figure 16.5 Illustrative circuit-constructing program tree.

embryonic circuit for the robot controller circuit has three modifiable wires (Z0, Z1, and Z2) in order to provide full connectivity between the two inputs and the one output.

All development originates from the modifiable wires.

In some problems, such as the amplifier, the embryonic circuit contains additional fixed components (as described by Koza, Bennett, Andre and Keane (1997)).

16.4.2 Program Architecture

Since there is one result-producing branch in the program tree for each modifiable wire in the embryo, the architecture of each circuit-constructing program tree depends on the embryonic circuit. One result-producing branch was used for the frequency discriminator and the computational circuit; two were used for low-pass and high-pass filter problems; and three were used for the robot controller and amplifier.

The architecture of each circuit-constructing program tree also depends on the use, if any, of automatically defined functions. Automatically defined functions provide a mechanism enabling certain substructures to be reused and are described in detail by (Koza, Bennett, Andre and Keane, 1999). Automatically defined functions and architecture-altering operations were used in the frequency discriminator, robot controller, and amplifier. For these problems, each program in the initial population of programs had a uniform architecture with no automatically defined functions. In later generations, the number of automatically defined functions, if any, emerged as a consequence of the architecture-altering operations (also described in Koza, Bennett, Andre and Keane, 1999).

16.4.3 Function and Terminal Sets

The function set for each design problem depended on the type of electrical components that were used to construct the circuit. Inductors and capacitors were used for the low-pass and high-pass filter problems. Capacitors, diodes, and transistors were used for the computational circuit, the robot controller, and the amplifier. Resistors (in addition to inductors and capacitors) were used for the frequency discriminator. When transistors were used, functions to provide connectivity to the positive and negative power supplies were also included.

For the computational circuit, the robot controller, and the amplifier, the function set, $\mathcal{F}_{ccs\text{-}initial}$, for each construction-continuing subtree was:

$\mathcal{F}_{ccs\text{-}initial}$ = {R, C, SERIES, PARALLEL0, PARALLEL1, FLIP, NOOP, T_GND_0, T_GND_1, T_POS_0, T_POS_1, T_NEG_0, T_NEG_1, PAIR_CONNECT_0, PAIR_CONNECT_1, Q_D_NPN, Q_D_PNP, Q_3_NPN0, . . . , Q_3_NPN11, Q_3_PNP0, . . . , Q_3_PNP11, Q_POS_COLL_NPN, Q_GND_EMIT_NPN, Q_NEG_EMIT_NPN, Q_GND_EMIT_PNP, Q_POS_EMIT_PNP, Q_NEG_COLL_PNP}.

For the *npn* transistors, the Q2N3904 model was used. For *pnp* transistors, the Q2N3906 model was used. The initial terminal set, $\mathcal{T}_{ccs\text{-}initial}$, for each construction-continuing subtree was:

$\mathcal{T}_{ccs\text{-}initial}$ = {END, SAFE_CUT}.

The initial terminal set, $\mathcal{T}_{aps\text{-}initial}$, for each arithmetic-performing subtree consisted of:

$\mathcal{T}_{aps\text{-}initial} = \{\mathcal{R}\}$,

where $\mathcal{R}$ represents floating-point random constants from -1.0 to $+1.0$.

The function set, $\mathcal{F}_{aps}$, for each arithmetic-performing subtree was:

$\mathcal{F}_{aps} = \{+, -\}$.

The terminal and function sets were identical for all result-producing branches for a particular problem. For the low-pass filter, high-pass filter, and frequency discriminator, there was no need for functions to provide connectivity to the positive and negative power supplies. For the frequency discriminator, the robot controller, and the amplifier, the architecture-altering operations were used and the set of potential new functions, $F_{potential}$, was:

$\mathcal{F}_{potential} = \{\text{ADF0, ADF1}, \ldots\}$.

The set of potential new terminals, $\mathcal{T}_{potential}$, for the automatically defined functions was

$\mathcal{T}_{potential} = \{\text{ARG0}\}$.

The architecture-altering operations change the function sets and terminal sets, $\mathcal{F}_{ccs}$, for each construction-continuing subtree of all three result-producing branches and the function-defining branches.

16.4.4 Fitness Measure

The fitness measure varies for each problem. The high-level statement of desired circuit behaviour is translated into a well-defined measurable quantity that can be used by genetic programming to guide the evolutionary process. The evaluation of each individual circuit-constructing program tree in the population begins with its execution. This execution progressively applies the functions in each program tree to an embryonic circuit, thereby creating a fully developed circuit. A netlist is created that identifies each component of the developed circuit, the nodes to which each component is connected, and the value of each component. The netlist becomes the input to our modified version of the 217 000–line SPICE (Simulation Program with Integrated Circuit Emphasis) simulation program (Quarles, Newton, Pederson and Sangiovanni-Vincentelli, 1994). SPICE then determines the behaviour of the circuit. It was necessary to make considerable modifications in SPICE so that it could run as a submodule within the genetic programming system.

Fitness Measure for the Low-pass Filter

A simple *filter* is a one-input, one-output electronic circuit that receives a signal as its input and passes the frequency components of the incoming signal that lie in a specified range (called the *pass-band*) while suppressing the frequency components that lie in all other frequency ranges (the *stop-band*).

The desired low-pass LC filter has a pass-band below 1000 Hz and a stop-band above 2000 Hz. The circuit is driven by an incoming AC voltage source with a 2 volt amplitude.

The *attenuation* of the filter is defined in terms of the output signal relative to the reference voltage (one volt here). A *decibel* is a unitless measure of relative voltage that is defined as 20 times the common (base 10) logarithm of the ratio between the voltage at a particular probe point and a reference voltage.

In this problem, a voltage in the pass-band of exactly 1 volt and a voltage in the stop-band of exactly 0 volts is regarded as ideal. The (preferably small) variation within the pass-band is called the *pass-band ripple*. Similarly, the incoming signal is never fully reduced to zero in the stop-band of an actual filter. The (preferably small) variation within the stop-band is called the stop-band ripple. A voltage in the pass-band of between 970 millivolts and 1 volt (i.e. a pass-band ripple of 30 millivolts or less) and a voltage in the stop-band of between 0 volts and 1 millivolts (i.e. a stop-band ripple of 1 millivolts or less) is regarded as acceptable. Any voltage lower than 970 millivolts in the pass-band and any voltage above 1 millivolt in the stop-band is regarded as unacceptable.

A fifth-order *elliptic* (*Cauer*) *filter* with a modular angle Θ of 30 degrees (i.e., the arcsine of the ratio of the boundaries of the pass-band and stop-band) and a reflection coefficient ρ of 24.3% is required to satisfy these design goals (Williams and Taylor, 1995).

Since the high-level statement of behaviour for the desired circuit is expressed in terms of frequencies, the voltage VOUT is measured in the frequency domain. SPICE performs an AC small signal analysis and reports the circuit's behaviour over 5 decades (between 1 Hz and 100 000 Hz) with each decade being divided into 20 parts (using a logarithmic scale), so that there are a total of 101 fitness cases.

Fitness is measured in terms of the sum over these cases of the absolute weighted deviation between the actual value of the voltage that is produced by the circuit at the probe point VOUT and the target value for voltage. The smaller the value of fitness, the better. A fitness of zero represents an (unattainable) ideal filter.

Specifically, the standardized fitness is:

$$F(t) = \sum_{i=0}^{100} (W(d(f_i), f_i)d(f_i))$$

where f_i is the frequency of fitness case i; $d(x)$ is the absolute value of the difference between the target and observed values at frequency x; and $W(y, x)$ is the weighting for difference y at frequency x.

The fitness measure is designed to not penalize ideal values, to slightly penalize every acceptable deviation, and to heavily penalize every unacceptable deviation. Specifically, the procedure for each of the 61 points in the 3-decade interval between 1 Hz and 1000 Hz for the intended pass-band is as follows:

- If the voltage equals the ideal value of 1.0 volt in this interval, the deviation is 0.0.
- If the voltage is between 970 millivolts and 1 volt, the absolute value of the deviation from 1 volt is weighted by a factor of 1.0.
- If the voltage is less than 970 millivolts, the absolute value of the deviation from 1 volt is weighted by a factor of 10.0.

The acceptable and unacceptable deviations for each of the 35 points from 2000 Hz to 100 000 Hz in the intended stop-band are similarly weighed (by 1.0 or 10.0) based on the amount of deviation from the ideal voltage of 0 volts and the acceptable deviation of 1 millivolt.

For each of the five 'don't care' points between 1000 and 2000 Hz, the deviation is deemed to be zero. The number of 'hits' for this problem (and all other problems herein) is defined as the number of fitness cases for which the voltage is acceptable or ideal or that lie in the 'don't care' band (for a filter).

Many of the random initial circuits and many that are created by the crossover and mutation operations in subsequent generations cannot be simulated by SPICE. These circuits receive a high penalty value of fitness (10^8) and become the worst-of-generation programs for each generation.

For further details, see (Koza, Bennett, Andre and Keane, 1996b).

Fitness Measure for the High-pass Filter

The fitness cases for the high-pass filter are the same 101 points in the 5 decades of frequency between 1 Hz and 100 000 Hz as for the low-pass filter. The fitness measure is substantially the same as that for the low-pass filter problem above, except that the locations of the pass-band and stop-band are reversed.

Fitness Measure for the Tri-state Frequency Discriminator

Fitness is the sum, over 101 fitness cases, of the absolute weighted deviation between the actual value of the voltage that is produced by the circuit and the target value.

The three points that are closest to the band located within 10% of 256 Hz are 229.1 Hz, 251.2 Hz, and 275.4 Hz. The procedure for each of these three points is as follows: If the voltage equals the ideal value of 1/2 volts in this interval, the deviation is 0.0. If the voltage is more than 240 millivolts from 1/2 volts, the absolute value of the deviation from 1/2 volts is weighted by a factor of 20. If the voltage is more than 240 millivolts from 1/2 volts, the absolute value of the deviation from 1/2 volts is weighted by a factor of 200. This arrangement reflects the fact that the ideal output voltage for this range of frequencies is 1/2 volts, the fact that a 240-millivolt discrepancy is acceptable, and the fact that a larger discrepancy is not acceptable.

Similar weighting was used for the three points (2291 Hz, 2512 Hz, and 2754 Hz) that are closest to the band located within 10% of 2560 Hz.

The procedure for each of the remaining 95 points is as follows: If the voltage equals the ideal value of 0 volts, the deviation is 0.0. If the voltage is within 240 millivolts of 0 volts, the absolute value of the deviation from 0 volts is weighted by a factor of 1.0. If the voltage is more than 240 millivolts from 0 volts, the absolute value of the deviation from 0 volts is weighted by a factor of 10. For further details, see (Koza, Bennett, Lohn, Dunlap, Andre and Keane, 1997b).

Fitness Measure for the Computational Circuit

SPICE is called to perform a DC sweep analysis at 21 equidistant voltages between −250 millivolts and +250 millivolts. Fitness is the sum, over these 21 fitness cases, of the absolute weighted deviation between the actual value of the voltage that is produced by the circuit and the target value for voltage. For more details, see (Koza, Bennett, Lohn, Dunlap, Andre and Keane, 1997a).

Fitness Measure for the Robot Controller Circuit

The fitness of a robot controller was evaluated using 72 randomly chosen fitness cases each representing a different target point. Fitness is the sum, over the 72 fitness cases, of the travel times. If the robot came within a capture radius of 0.28 metres of its target point before the end of the 80 time steps allowed for a particular fitness case, the contribution to fitness for that fitness case was the actual time. However, if the robot failed to come within the capture radius during the 80 time steps, the contribution to fitness was 0.160 hours (i.e. double the worst possible time).

SPICE performs a nested DC sweep, which provides a way to simulate the DC behaviour of a circuit with two inputs. It resembles a nested pair of FOR loops in a computer program in that both of the loops have a starting value for the voltage, an increment, and an ending value for the voltage. For each voltage value in the outer loop, the inner loop simulates the behaviour of the circuit by stepping through its range of voltages. Specifically, the starting value for voltage is −4 volts, the step size is 0.2 volts, and the ending value is +4 volts. These values correspond to the dimensions of the robot's world of 64 square metres extending 4 metres in each of the four directions from the origin of a coordinate system (i.e. 1 volt equals 1 metre). For details, see (Koza, Bennett, Keane and Andre, 1997).

Fitness Measure for the 60 dB Amplifier

SPICE was requested to perform a DC sweep analysis to determine the circuit's response for several different DC input voltages. An ideal inverting amplifier circuit would receive the DC input, invert it, and multiply it by the amplification factor. A circuit is flawed to the extent that it does not achieve the desired amplification, the output signal is not perfectly centered on 0 volts (i.e. it is biased), or the DC response is not linear. Fitness is calculated by summing an amplification penalty, a bias penalty, and two non-linearity penalties – each derived from these five DC outputs. For further details, see Bennett, Koza, Andre and Keane (1996).

16.4.5 Control Parameters

The population size, M, was 640 000 for all problems. Other parameters were substantially the same for each of the six problems and can be found in the references cited above.

16.4.6 Implementation on Parallel Computer

Each problem was run on a medium-grained parallel Parsytec computer system (Andre and Koza, 1996) consisting of 64 80-MHz PowerPC 601 processors arranged in an 8 by 8 toroidal mesh with a host PC Pentium type computer. The distributed genetic algorithm was used with a population size of Q = 10 000 at each of the D = 64 demes (semi-isolated subpopulations). On each generation, four boatloads of emigrants, each consisting of B = 2% (the migration rate) of the node's subpopulation (selected on the basis of fitness) were dispatched to each of the four adjacent processing nodes.

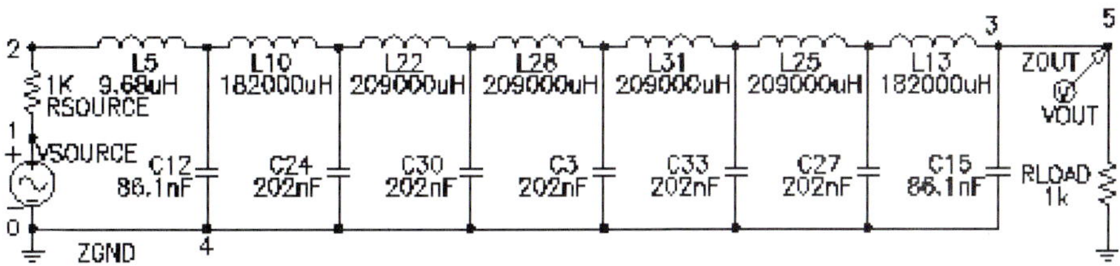

Figure 16.6 Evolved seven-rung ladder low-pass filter.

16.5 Results

In all six problems, fitness was observed to improve over successive generations. A large majority of the randomly created initial circuits of generation 0 were not able to be simulated by SPICE; however, most were simulatable after only a few generations. Satisfactory results were generated in every case on the first or second trial. When two runs were required, the first produced an almost satisfactory result. This rate of success suggests that the capabilities of the approach and current computing system have not been fully exploited.

16.5.1 Low-pass Filter

Many of the runs produced low-pass filters having a topology similar to that employed by human engineers. For example, in generation 32 of one run, a circuit (fig. 16.6) was evolved with a near-zero fitness of 0.00781. The circuit was 100% compliant with the design requirements in that it scored 101 hits (out of 101). After the evolutionary run, this circuit (and all evolved circuits herein) were simulated anew using the commercially available MicroSim circuit simulator to verify performance. As can be seen, inductors appear in series horizontally across the top of the figure, while capacitors appear vertically as shunts to ground. This circuit had the recognizable ladder topology of a Butterworth or Chebychev low-pass filter (Williams and Taylor, 1995).

Figure 16.7 shows the behaviour in the frequency domain of this evolved low-pass filter. As can be seen, the evolved circuit delivers about 1 volt for all frequencies up to 1000 Hz and about 0 volts for all frequencies above 2000 Hz.

In another run, a 100% compliant recognizable 'bridged T' arrangement was evolved. In yet another run using automatically defined functions, a 100% compliant circuit emerged with the recognizable elliptic topology that was invented and patented by Cauer. When invented, the Cauer filter was a significant advance (both theoretically and commercially) over the Butterworth and Chebychev filters.

Thus, genetic programming rediscovered the ladder topology of the Butterworth and Chebychev filters, the 'bridged T' topology, and the elliptic topology.

It is important to note that when we performed the preparatory steps for applying genetic programming to the problem of synthesizing a low-pass filter, we did not employ any significant domain knowledge from the field of electrical engineering. We did not incorporate knowledge of Kirchhoff's laws, integro-differential equations, Laplace transforms, poles, zeroes, or the other mathematical techniques and insights about filters that are known to electrical engineers who design analogue filters. In spite of this absence of explicit domain

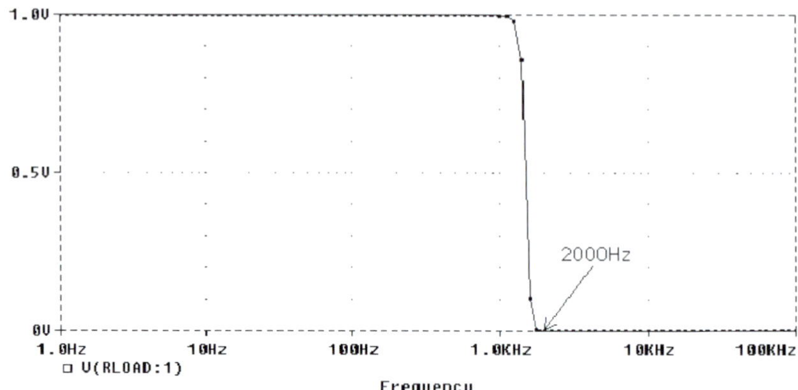

Figure 16.7 Frequency domain behaviour of genetically evolved seven-rung ladder low-pass filter.

knowledge, genetic programming evolved a 100% compliant circuit for the problem of designing an LC low-pass filter that embodied the ladder topology that is well known in the field of electrical engineering.

The reinvention by genetic programming of the recognizable ladder topology of Butterworth or Chebychev low-pass filters is an instance where genetic programming has produced a result that is competitive with those created by inventive and knowledgeable humans. It satisfies Arthur Samuel's criterion (1983) for artificial intelligence and machine learning, namely

The aim [is] . . . to get machines to exhibit behaviour which if done by humans would be assumed to involve the use of intelligence.

16.5.2 High-pass Filter

In generation 27 of one run, a 100% compliant circuit (fig. 16.8) was evolved with a near-zero fitness of 0.213. This circuit has four capacitors and five inductors (in addition to the fixed components of the embryo). As can be seen, capacitors appear in series horizontally across the top of the figure, while inductors appear vertically as shunts to ground.

Figure 16.9 shows the behaviour in the frequency domain of this evolved high-pass filter. As desired, the evolved high-pass delivers about 0 volts for all frequencies up to 1000 Hz and about 1 volt for all frequencies above 2000 Hz.

The reversal of roles for the capacitors and inductors in low-pass and high-pass ladder filters is well known to electrical engineers. It arises because of the duality of the single terms (derivatives versus integrals) in the integro-differential equations that represent the voltages and currents of the inductors and capacitors in the loops and nodes of a circuit. However, genetic programming was not given any domain knowledge concerning this duality. In fact, the fitness measure was the only difference in the preparatory steps for the problem of synthesizing the high-pass filter versus the problem of synthesizing the low-pass filter. In spite of the absence of explicit domain knowledge about electrical engineering in general or duality in particular, genetic programming evolved a 100% compliant high-pass filter embodying the well-known high-pass ladder topology. Using the fitness measure appropriate for high-pass filters, genetic programming searched the same space (i.e. the space of circuit-constructing program

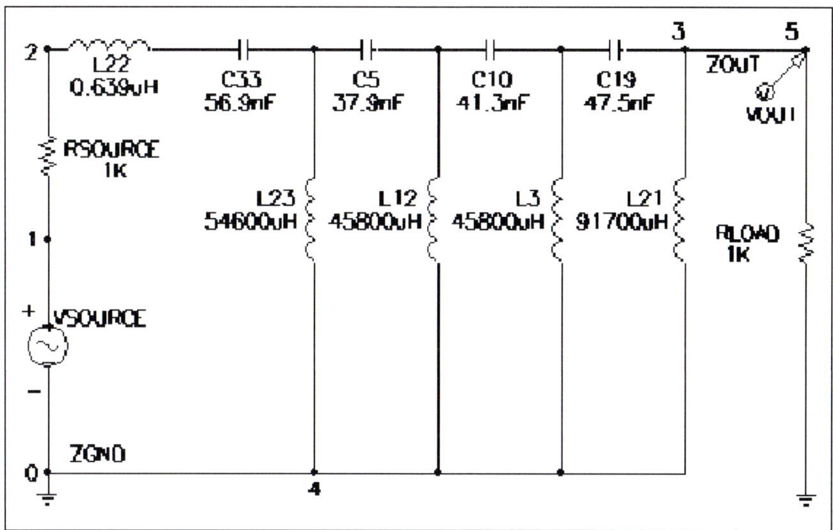

Figure 16.8 Evolved four-rung ladder high-pass filter.

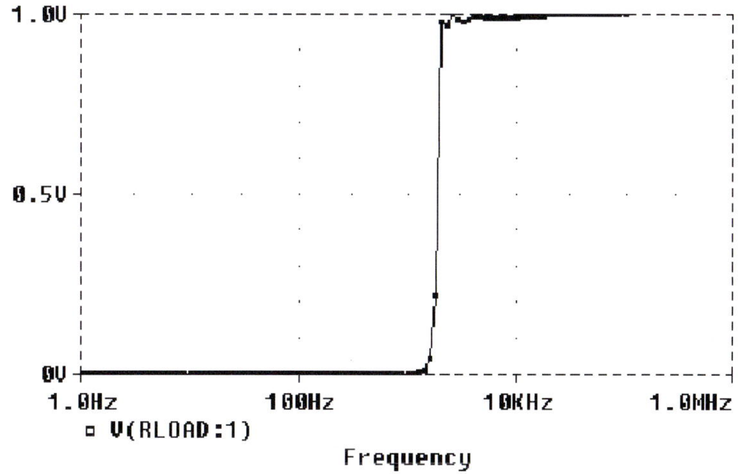

Figure 16.9 Frequency domain behaviour of evolved four-rung ladder high-pass filter.

trees composed of the same component-creating functions and the same topology-modifying functions) and discovered a circuit-constructing program tree that yielded a 100%-complaint high-pass filter.

The rediscovery by genetic programming of the reversal of roles of capacitors and inductors in low-pass and filters is an instance where genetic programming has produced a result that is competitive with those created by inventive and knowledgeable humans. This result (and all of the succeeding results in this chapter) satisfies Arthur Samuel's criterion (1983) for success in artificial intelligence and machine learning.

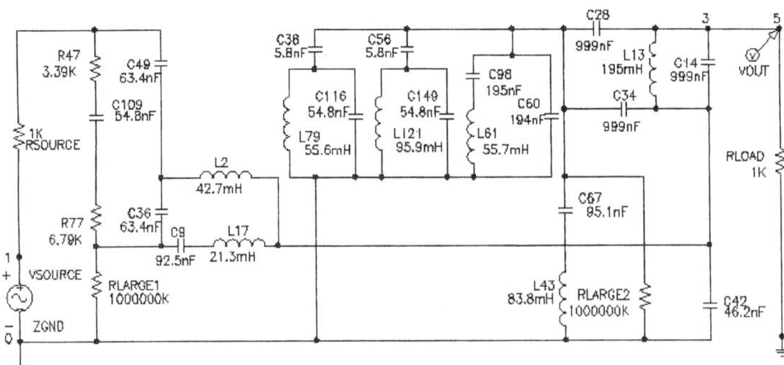

Figure 16.10 Evolved frequency discriminator.

16.5.3 Tri-state Frequency Discriminator

The evolved three-way tri-state frequency discriminator circuit from generation 106 scores 101 hits (out of 101). Figure 16.10 shows this circuit (after expansion of its automatically defined functions). The circuit produces the desired outputs of 1 volt and 1/2 volts (each within the allowable tolerance) for the two specified bands of frequencies and the desired near-zero signal for all other frequencies.

16.5.4 Computational Circuit

The genetically evolved computational circuit for the square root from generation 60 (fig. 16.11), achieves a fitness of 1.68, and has 36 transistors, two diodes, no capacitors, and 12 resistors (in addition to the source and load resistors in the embryo). The output voltages produced by this best-of-run circuit are almost exactly the required values.

16.5.5 Robot Controller Circuit

The best-of-run time-optimal robot controller circuit (fig. 16.12) appeared in generation 31, scores 72 hits, and achieves a near-optimal fitness of 1.541 hours. In comparison, the optimal value of fitness for this problem is known to be 1.518 hours. This best-of-run circuit has 10 transistors and 4 resistors. The program has one automatically defined function that is called twice (incorporated into the figure).

This problem entails navigating a robot to a destination in minimum time, so its fitness measure (section 4.4.5) is expressed in terms of elapsed time. The fitness measure is a high-level description of 'what needs to be done' – namely, get the robot to the destination in a time-optimal way. However, the fitness measure does not specify 'how to do it.' In particular, the fitness measure conveys no hint about the critical (and counterintuitive) tactic needed to minimize elapsed time in time-optimal control problems – namely, that it is sometimes necessary to veer away from the destination in order to reach it in minimal time. None the less, the evolved time-optimal robot controller embodies this counterintuitive tactic. For example, fig. 16.13 shows the trajectory for the fitness case where the destination is (0.409, −0.892). Correct time-optimal handling of this difficult destination point requires a trajectory that begins by veering away from the destination (thereby increasing the distance to the destination)

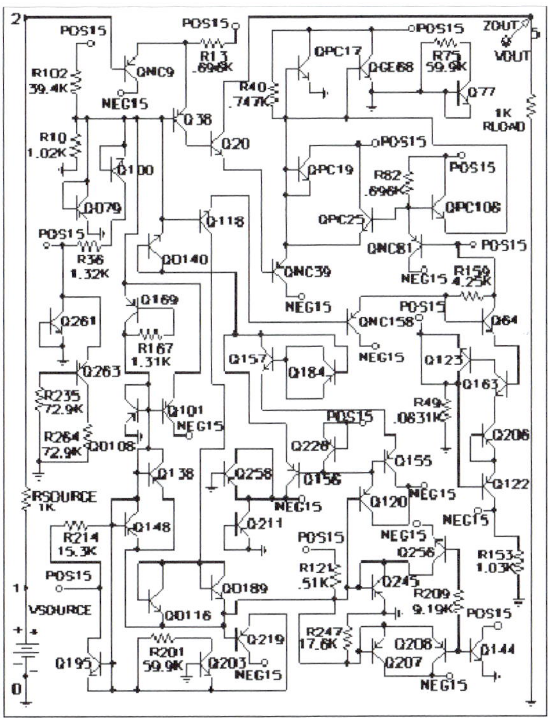

Figure 16.11 Evolved square root circuit.

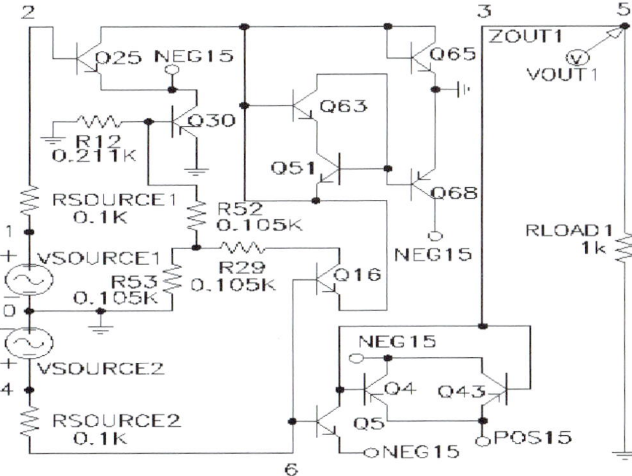

Figure 16.12 Evolved robot controller.

followed by a circular trajectory to the destination. The small circle in the figure represents the capture radius of 0.28 metres around the destination point.

The evolved time-optimal robot controller generalizes so as to correctly handle all other possible destinations in the plane.

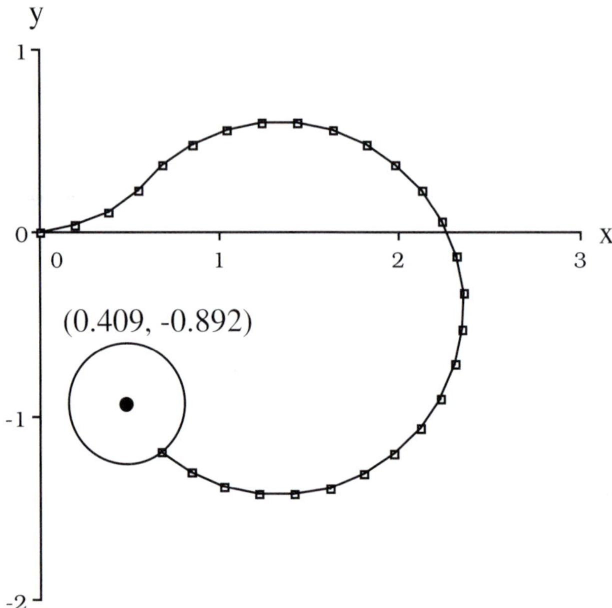

Figure 16.13 Evolved time-optimal trajectory to destination point (0.409, −0.892).

16.5.6 60 dB Amplifier

The best circuit from generation 109 (fig. 16.14) achieves a fitness of 0.178. Based on a DC sweep, the amplification is 60 dB here (i.e. 1,000-to-1 ratio) and the bias is 0.2 volts. Based on a transient analysis at 1000 Hz, the amplification is 59.7 dB; the bias is 0.18 volts; and the total harmonic distortion is very low (0.17%). Based on an AC sweep, the amplification at 1000 Hz is 59.7 dB; the flat-band gain is 60 dB; and the 3 dB bandwidth is 79 333 Hz. Thus, a high-gain amplifier with low distortion and acceptable bias has been evolved.

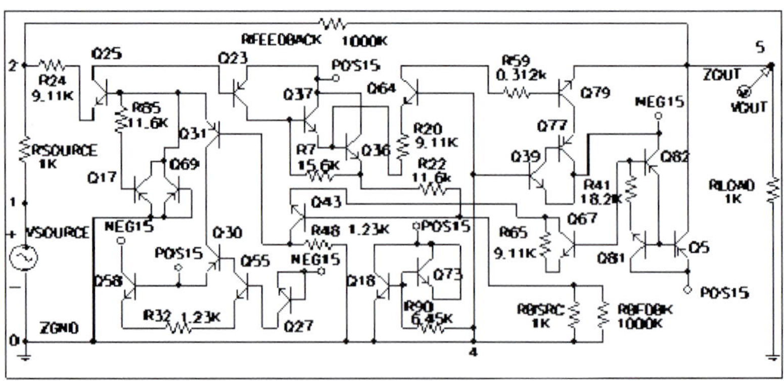

Figure 16.14 Genetically evolved amplifier.

16.6 Conclusion

In this chapter, genetic programming succeeded in evolving both the topology and sizing of six different prototypical analogue electrical circuits, including a low-pass filter, a high-pass filter, a tri-state frequency discriminator circuit, a 60 dB amplifier, a computational circuit for the square root, and a time-optimal robot controller circuit. All six of these genetically evolved circuits constitute instances of an evolutionary computation technique solving a problem that is usually thought to require human intelligence.

There has previously been no general automated technique for synthesizing an analogue electrical circuit from a high-level statement of the circuit's desired behaviour. The approach using genetic programming to the problem of analogue circuit synthesis is general; it can be directly applied to other problems of analogue circuit synthesis.

In fact, this same approach is even more general and can be applied to the problem of automatic programming (i.e. the challenge of getting a computer to solve a problem without explicitly programming it). Paraphrasing Arthur Samuel (1959), the challenge of automatic programming is:

How can computers be made to do what needs to be done, without being told exactly how to do it?

Each of the problems in this chapter illustrates the automatic creation of a satisfactory way of 'how to do it' from a high-level statement of 'what needs to be done.'

References

Aaserud, O. and Nielsen, I. Ring. (1995). Trends in current analogue design: A panel debate. *Analogue Integrated Circuits and Signal Processing*, **7**(1); 5–9.

Andre, D. and Koza, J. R. (1996). Parallel genetic programming: A scalable implementation using the transputer architecture. In Angeline, P. J. and Kinnear, K. E. Jr. (eds), *Advances in Genetic Programming 2*. Cambridge, MA: MIT Press.

Angeline, P. J. and Kinnear, K. E. Jr. (eds). (1996). *Advances in Genetic Programming 2*. Cambridge, MA: MIT Press.

Banzhaf, W., Nordin, P., Keller, R. E. and Francone, F. D. (1998). *Genetic Programming – An Introduction*. San Francisco, CA: Morgan Kaufmann and Heidelberg: dpunkt.

Bennett III, F. H., Koza, J. R., Andre, D. and Keane, M. A. (1996). Evolution of a 60 Decibel op amp using genetic programming. In Higuchi, T., Iwata, M. and Lui, W. (eds), *Proceedings of International Conference on Evolvable Systems: From Biology to Hardware (ICES-96)*. Lecture Notes in Computer Science, Volume 1259. Berlin: Springer-Verlag, pp. 455–469.

Grimbleby, J. B. (1995). Automatic analogueue network synthesis using genetic algorithms. *Proceedings of the First International Conference on Genetic Algorithms in Engineering Systems: Innovations and Applications*. London: Institution of Electrical Engineers, pp. 53–58.

Gruau, F. (1992). *Cellular Encoding of Genetic Neural Networks*. Technical report 92-21. Laboratoire de l'Informatique du Parallélisme. Ecole Normale Supérieure de Lyon. May (1992).

Holland, J. H. (1975). *Adaptation in Natural and Artificial Systems*. Ann Arbor, MI: University of Michigan Press.

Kinnear, K. E. Jr. (ed.) (1994). *Advances in Genetic Programming*. Cambridge, MA: MIT Press.

Kitano, H. (1990). Designing neural networks using genetic algorithms with graph generation system. *Complex Systems*, **4**(1990); 461–476.

Koza, J. R. (1992). *Genetic Programming: On the Programming of Computers by Means of Natural Selection*. Cambridge, MA: MIT Press.

Koza, J. R. (1994a). *Genetic Programming II: Automatic Discovery of Reusable Programs*. Cambridge, MA: MIT Press.

Koza, J. R. (1994b). *Genetic Programming II Videotape: The Next Generation*. Cambridge, MA: MIT Press.

Koza, J. R. (1995). Evolving the architecture of a multi-part program in genetic programming using architecture-altering operations. In McDonnell, J. R., Reynolds, R. G. and Fogel, D. B. (eds) (1995). *Evolutionary Programming IV: Proceedings of the Fourth Annual Conference on Evolutionary Programming*. Cambridge, MA: MIT Press, pp. 695–717.

Koza, J. R., Andre, D., Bennett III, F. H and Keane, M. A. (1996). Use of automatically defined functions and architecture-altering operations in automated circuit synthesis using genetic programming. In Koza, J. R., Goldberg, D. E., Fogel, D. B. and Riolo, R. L. (eds), *Genetic Programming 1996: Proceedings of the First Annual Conference*. Cambridge, MA: MIT Press.

Koza, J. R., Bennett III, F. H, Andre, D. and Keane, M. A. (1999). *Genetic Programming III: Darwian Invention and Problem Solving*. San Francisco, CA: Morgan Kaufmann.

Koza, J. R., Bennett III, F. H, Andre, D. and Keane, M. A. (1996a). Four problems for which a computer program evolved by genetic programming is competitive with human performance. *Proceedings of the 1996 IEEE International Conference on Evolutionary Computation*. IEEE Press, pp. 1–10.

Koza, J. R., Bennett III, F. H, Andre, D. and Keane, M. A. (1996b). Automated design of both the topology and sizing of analogue electrical circuits using genetic programming. In Gero, J. S. and Sudweeks, F. (eds), *Artificial Intelligence in Design '96*. Dordrecht: Kluwer. pp. 151–170.

Koza, J. R., Bennett III, F. H, Andre, D. and Keane, M. A. (1996c). Automated WYWIWYG design of both the topology and component values of analogue electrical circuits using genetic programming. In Koza, J. R., Goldberg, D. E., Fogel, D. B. and Riolo, R. L. (eds), *Genetic Programming 1996: Proceedings of the First Annual Conference*. Cambridge, MA: MIT Press.

Koza, J. R., Bennett III, F. H., Andre, D. and Keane, M. A. (1997a). Evolution using genetic programming of a low-distortion 96 Decibel operational amplifier. *Proceedings of the 1997 ACM Symposium on Applied Computing, San Jose, California, February 28–March 2, 1997*. New York: Association for Computing Machinery, pp. 207–216.

Koza, J. R., Bennett III, F. H., Andre, D., Keane, M. A. and Dunlap, F. (1997). Automated synthesis of analogue electrical circuits by means of genetic programming. *IEEE Transactions on Evolutionary Computation*, **1**(2); 109–128.

Koza, J. R., Bennett III, F. H, Keane, M. A., and Andre, D. (1997). Automatic programming of a time-optimal robot controller and an analogue electrical circuit to implement the robot controller by means of genetic programming. *Proceedings of 1997 IEEE International Symposium on Computational Intelligence in Robotics and Automation*. Los Alamitos, CA; Computer Society Press, pp. 340–346.

Koza, J. R., Bennett III, F. H, Lohn, J., Dunlap, F., Andre, D. and Keane, M. A. (1997a). Automated synthesis of computational circuits using genetic programming. *Proceedings of the 1997 IEEE Conference on Evolutionary Computation*. Piscataway, NJ: IEEE Press, pp. 447–452.

Koza, J. R., Bennett III, F. H, Lohn, J., Dunlap, F., Andre, D. and Keane, M. A. (1997b). Use of architecture-altering operations to dynamically adapt a three-way analogue source identification circuit to accommodate a new source. In Koza, J. R., Deb, K., Dorigo, M., Fogel, D. B., Garzon, M., Iba, H. and Riolo, R. L. (eds), *Genetic Programming 1997: Proceedings of the Second Annual Conference*. San Francisco, CA: Morgan Kaufmann, pp. 213–221.

Koza, J. R., Deb, K., Dorigo, M., Fogel, D. B., Garzon, M., Iba, H. and Riolo, R. L. (eds) (1997). *Genetic Programming 1997: Proceedings of the Second Annual Conference*. San Francisco, CA: Morgan Kaufmann.

Koza, J. R., Goldberg, D. E., Fogel, D. B. and Riolo, R. L. (eds) (1996). *Genetic Programming 1996: Proceedings of the First Annual Conference*. Cambridge, MA: MIT Press.

Koza, J. R., and Rice, J. P. (1992). *Genetic Programming: The Movie*. Cambridge, MA: MIT Press.

Kruiskamp M. W. and Leenaerts, D. (1995). DARWIN: CMOS opamp synthesis by means of a genetic algorithm. *Proceedings of the 32nd Design Automation Conference*. New York: Association for Computing Machinery, pp. 433–438.

Quarles, T., Newton, A. R., Pederson, D. O. and Sangiovanni-Vincentelli, A. (1994). *SPICE 3 Version 3F5 User's Manual*. Department of Electrical Engineering and Computer Science, University of California, Berkeley, CA.

Rutenbar, R. A. (1993). Analogue design automation: Where are we? Where are we going? *Proceedings of the l5th IEEE CICC*. New York: IEEE.

Samuel, A. L. (1959). Some studies in machine learning using the game of checkers. *IBM Journal of Research and Development*, **3**(3): 210–229.

Samuel, A. L. (1983). AI: Where it has been and where it is going. *Proceedings of the Eighth International Joint Conference on Artificial Intelligence*. Los Altos, CA: Morgan Kaufmann, pp. 1152–1157.

Thompson, A. (1996). Silicon evolution. In Koza, J. R., Goldberg, D. E., Fogel, D. B. and Riolo, R. L. (eds), *Genetic Programming 1996: Proceedings of the First Annual Conference*. Cambridge, MA: MIT Press.

Williams, A. B. and Taylor, F. J. (1995). *Electronic Filter Design Handbook*, third edition. New York: McGraw-Hill.

Chapter 17

Computer Evolution of Buildable Objects

by Pablo Funes and Jordan Pollack

17.1 Introduction

This chapter describes our work in evolution of buildable designs using miniature plastic bricks as modular components. Lego[1] bricks are well known for their flexibility when it comes to creating low cost, handy designs of vehicles and structures. Their simple modular concept make toy bricks a good ground for doing evolution of computer simulated structures which can be built and deployed.

Instead of incorporating an expert system of engineering knowledge into the program, which would result in more familiar structures, we combined an evolutionary algorithm with a model of the physical reality and a purely utilitarian fitness function, providing measures of feasibility and functionality.

Our algorithms integrate a model of the physical properties of Lego structures with an evolutionary process that freely combines bricks of different shape and size into structures that are evaluated by how well they perform a desired function. The evolutionary process runs in an environment that has not been unnecessarily constrained by our own preconceptions on how to solve the problem.

The results are encouraging. The evolved structures have a surprisingly alien look: they are not based in common knowledge on how to build with brick toys; instead, the computer found ways of its own through the evolutionary search process. We were able to assemble the final designs manually and confirm that they accomplish the objectives introduced with our fitness functions.

This chapter discusses background and related work first (section 17.2), then goes on to describe our methods; first the model we use to simulate Lego structures (sections 17.3–17.4), then the representation and evolutionary algorithms (section 17.5). The results sections (17.6–17.7) discuss applications, showing the results of several evolutionary runs and illustrating with pictures of the final assembled Lego artifacts. Finally, on sections 17.8–17.9, current and future lines of work and conclusions are drawn.

17.2 Background

In order to evolve both the morphology and behavior of autonomous devices which can be manufactured, one must have adequate representations and simulations. The representation

[1] Lego is a registered trademark of the Lego group.

EVOLUTIONARY DESIGN BY COMPUTERS
ISBN 1-55860-605-X

must provide the computer with ways to create, manipulate and modify an infinite variety of virtual architectures to be tested in simulation. The objects being simulated need to be adaptive enough to cover the gap between simulated and real world, so they will perform correctly when built. Desirable features of a software engine for evolving morphology are:

- **Universal** – the simulator should cover an infinite general space of mechanisms.
- **Conservative** – because simulation is never perfect, it should preserve a margin of safety.
- **Efficient** – it should be quicker to test in simulation than through physical production and test.
- **Buildable** – results should be convertible from a simulation to a real object

With a representation and a physical simulation that follow these ideas, we have obtained some promising results. In a first stage we worked with two-dimensional structures only (Funes and Pollack, 1997). We have recently extended our framework to three dimensions; one 3D application is described here as well.

There are several fields which bear on these questions of representation and physical simulation, including qualitative physics and structural mechanics, computer graphics, evolutionary design and robotics.

17.2.1 Qualitative Physics

Qualitative physics is the subfield of artificial intelligence (AI) which deals with mechanical and physical knowledge representation. It starts with a logical representation of a mechanism, such as a heat pump (Forbus, 1984) or a string (Gardin and Meltzer, 1989), and produces simulations, or envisionments, of the future behaviour of the mechanism. QP has not to our knowledge been used as the simulator in an evolutionary design system.

17.2.2 Computer Graphics

The work of Karl Sims (Sims, 1994a,b) was seminal in the fields of evolutionary computation and artificial life. Following Ngo and Marks (1993), Sims evolved virtual creatures that have both physical architecture and control programs created by an evolutionary computation process (see Chapter 13 for full details).

Despite their beautiful realism, Sims' organisms are far from real. His simulations do not consider the mechanical feasibility of the articulations between different parts, which in fact overlap each other at the joints, nor the existence of real world mechanisms that could produce the forces responsible for their movements. There was no attempt to emulate a real environment that could house mechanical counterparts of those virtual creatures.

17.2.3 Structural Mechanics/Structural Topology

The engineering field of structural mechanics is based on methods, such as finite element modelling (Zienkiewicz, 1977) to construct computable models of continuous materials by approximating them with discrete networks. These tools are in broad use in the engineering community, carefully supervised and oriented towards particular product designs, and are often quite computationally intensive. Applications of genetic algorithms to structural topology optimization (Chapman *et al.*, 1993; Schoenauer, 1996) are related to our work. This type of application uses genetic algorithms as a search tool to optimize a shape under clearly defined preconditions. The GA is required, for example, to simultaneously maximize the stiffness and minimize the weight of a piece subject to external loads (Chapman *et al.*, 1993).

17.2.4 Evolutionary Design

Evolutionary design, the creation of new designs by computers, using evolutionary computation methods (Bentley, 1996), is a new research area with an enormous potential. Among the different approaches and techniques represented in the present volume, our direction is to exploit modular components to create complete functional structures.

While other research focuses in evolution of abstract shapes or optimization of one part or component, the line we are proposing is to let the evolutionary process take care of the entire design process by means of recombination of available components and evaluation of functionality through physics simulation.

17.2.5 Evolutionary Robotics

Work in evolutionary robotics has traditionally focused in the evolution of robot controllers to provide a given robot platform – either real or simulated – with a custom brain that, once downloaded, will produce an adequate behaviour (Mataric and Cliff, 1996). The process of adaptation through evolutionary search allows these artificial life forms with evolved brains to perform in the environments they inhabit. Some experiments rely on carefully designed simulations (Cliff *et al.*, 1996), while others apply evolution directly in the real robot (Floreano and Mondada, 1994). Hybrid techniques (Lund, 1995) are a mixture of the two.

Whereas some of the most interesting work in artificial life – Karl Sims' for example – involves evolution of morphology and control together, researchers in evolutionary robotics use human designed robot machines and try to evolve control programs for them. The observation can be made, however, that evolution of a creature's controlling brain addresses just one part of the problem of artificially evolving life forms: a creature that adapts to an environment needs an adequate body to inhabit. In nature, the brain for a body, and the body for a brain are exquisitely intertwined and co-adapted after millions of years of co-evolution.

The idea of co-evolving bodies and brains is becoming popular. Recent work by Lund, Hallam and Lee (Lund *et al.*, 1997; Lee *et al.*, 1996), for example, evolves in simulation a robot control program simultaneously with some parameters of its morphology such as sensor number and positioning and body size. Our work attempts to build from the opposite shore: we are using evolutionary techniques to create structures, physical forms, adapted to perform correctly in the physical world. This is a step on the way to the full co-evolution of morphology and behaviour we believe is necessary for the development of robots and brains with higher complexity than humans can engineer.

17.3 Modelling Lego Structures under Stress

We begin the description of our methods with the modelling procedure used to test in simulation the behaviour of virtual structures produced by an evolutionary process of genetic crossover and mutation.

The resistance of the plastic material (ABS-acrylonitrile butadiene styrene) of Lego bricks far surpasses the force necessary to either join two of them together or break their unions. This makes it possible to design a model that ignores the resistance of the material and evaluates the strain forces over a group of bricks only at their union areas. If a Lego structure fails, it will generally do so at the joints, but the actual bricks will not be damaged.

This characteristic of Lego structures makes their discretization for modelling an obvious step. Instead of imposing an artificial mesh for simulation purposes only – as in finite elements methods, for example – these structures are already made of relatively large discrete units.

17.3.1 Networks of Torque Propagation

We begin considering two-dimensional systems of forces. We measured the amount of stress that different linear (1×1, 2×1, 3×1, etc., as in fig. 17.2) unions of brick pairs can support (table 17.1). The main simplification comes from the observation that a 'fulcrum' effect, the angular torque exerted over such a joint, constitutes the principal cause for the breakage of a stressed pair of Lego bricks. Thus a critical abstraction for the purpose of modelling has come from disregarding radial forces such as vertical pulls, and describing the system of static forces inside a complex structure of Lego bricks as a network of 'rotational' joints located at each union between brick pairs and subject to loads coming from the weight of each brick (fig. 17.1).

Table 17.1 Estimated minimal torque capacities of the basic types of joints.

Joint size (knobs)	Approximate torque capacity (N-m $\times 10^{-6}$)
1	10.4
2	50.2
3	89.6
4	157.3
5	281.6
6	339.2
7	364.5

Given a structure formed by a combination of bricks, our model builds a network with joints of different capacities and external forces that must be in static equilibrium if the structure is not going to collapse. Each idealized joint is located at the center of the area of contact between a pair of bricks.

Each force applied to a brick, either its own weight or an external load, has to be cancelled by one or more reaction forces if the brick is stable – otherwise it would be falling. Such reaction forces can originate in any of the joints that connect it to neighbour bricks. In that case the force is transmitted through the joint to a connected brick. Thus a load is propagated through the network until finally absorbed by a fixed body – the 'ground'.

If a solution to this network exists, it means that there is a way to distribute all the forces along the structure. Our operating heuristic is this: As long as there is a way to distribute the weights among the network of bricks such that no joint is stressed beyond its maximum capacity, the structure will not break.

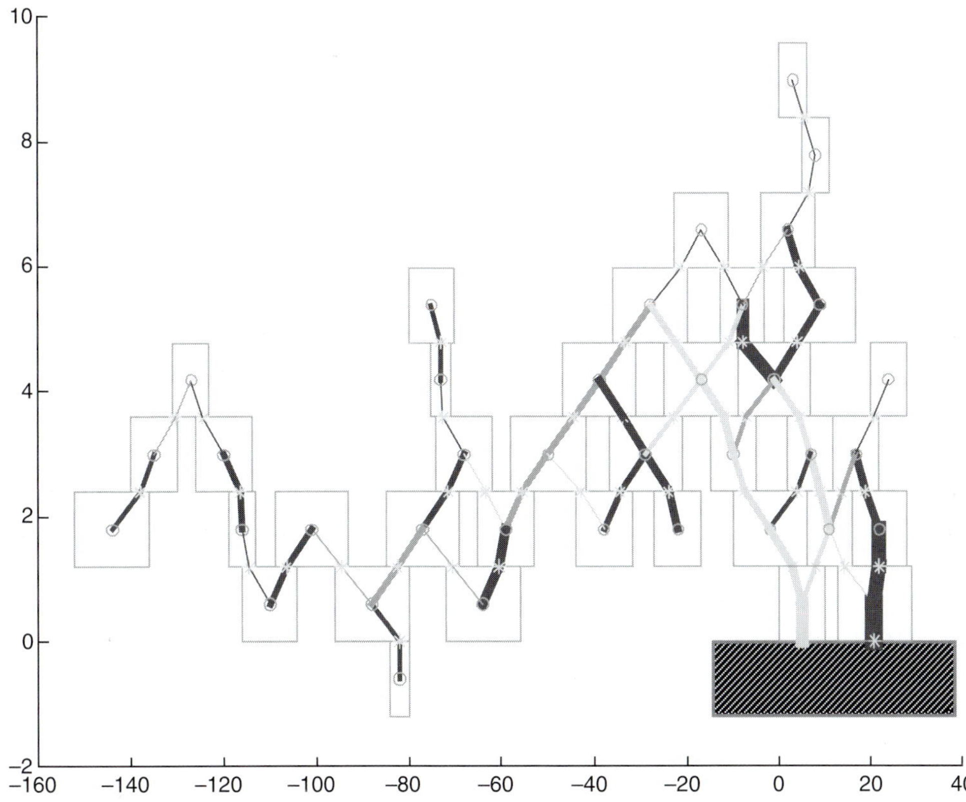

Figure 17.1 Model of a 2D lego structure showing the brick outlines (rectangles), centres of mass (circles), joints (diagonal lines, with axis located at the star), and 'ground' where the structure is attached (shaded area). The thickness of the joints' lines is proportional to the strength of the joint. A distribution of forces was calculated: highly stressed joints are shown in light colour, whereas those more relaxed are darker. Note that the x and y axis are in different scales.

From this strategy of modelling an algorithmic problem arises. Where nature simply distributes work dynamically through small deformations along the structure, our model needs an algorithm to determine the existence of solutions. We have not found a complete algorithm for this problem, but a greedy (Cormen *et al.*, 1989, p. 239) technique, not always capable of finding the solution when there is one, guarantees the stability of the structure in the numerous cases when a solution is actually found. Our model is thus conservative. It might be wrong in predicting the breakage of a structure, but any shape approved by it is guaranteed to resist the required loads.

17.3.2 From two- to three-dimensional Networks

To extend our model of networks of torque propagation to cover three-dimensional brick structures, our definition of joint needs to be extended. Where before all brick unions could be described with one integer quantity, the number of knobs that join two bricks, in the three-dimensional case these unions will be n-by-m rectangles. Two 2×4 bricks for example can

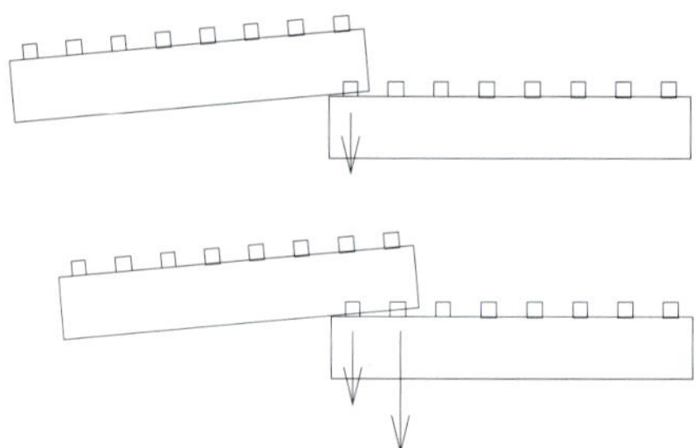

Figure 17.2 Fulcrum effect: a 1 × 2 union resists more than twice the load of a 1 × 1 because the second knob is farther away from the axis of rotation.

be stuck together in eight different types of joints: 1 × 1, 1 × 2, 1 × 3, 1 × 4, 2 × 1, 2 × 2, 2 × 3, 2 × 4. We know already, from the one-dimensional case, how $n \times 1$ unions respond to forces acting along the x-axis alone. A 2 × 1 union supports more than double the torque admitted by a 1 × 1, the reason being that the brick itself acts as a fulcrum (fig. 17.2). The distance from the border to the first knob is shorter than the distance to the second knob, resulting in a lower multiplication of the force for the second knob. This fulcrum effect does not happen when the force is orthogonal to the line of knobs. A 2 × 1 union can be considered as two 1 × 1 unions, or as one joint with double the strength of a 1 × 1 (fig. 17.3).

Following these ideas we enunciate the following rule: Two bricks united by $n \times m$ overlapping knobs will form a joint with a capacity Kx along the x axis equal to m times the capacity of one n-joint and Ky along the y axis equal to n times the capacity of an m-joint.

To test the resistance of this composite joint to any spatial force f we have to separate it into its two components, fx on the xz plane and fy on the yz plane. These components induce two torques tx, ty. To break the union either tx must be larger than Kx or ty larger than Ky. With this procedure we induce, from a three-dimensional brick structure, two separate two-dimensional systems of joints, one for the x components of torques and joints and the other for

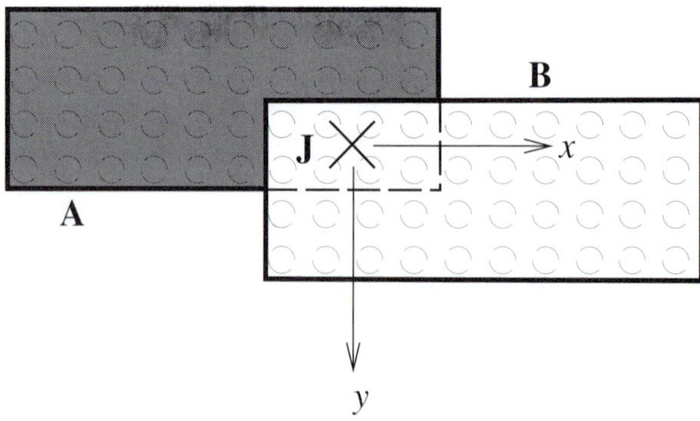

Figure 17.3 Two-dimensional brick joint: bricks A and B overlap in a 4 × 2 joint J. Along x the joint is a double 4 × 1 joint. Along the y axis it is a quadruple 2 × 1 joint.

the y components. The structure is stable if and only if both two-dimensional projections are stable networks (figs 17.5 and 17.6).

We are assuming that a dimensional independence hypothesis is true; it could be the case, however, that a force exerted along one axis will either weaken or strengthen the resistance in the orthogonal dimension. We made some exploratory experiments that suggested that the presence of stress along one axis does not modify the resistance along the other. It is probably the case that the rectangular shape of the joint makes it stronger for diagonal forces, justifying this simplification.

17.3.3 Limitations of Modelling

We know that this kind of naive modelling is not a complete description of the highly complex physical interactions that are taking place. However, we expect that considering an adequate margin of error we will be able to produce useful approximations to the true behaviour of actual Lego bricks.

The properties of Lego bricks are variable. Differences in construction, age, dirt, temperature, humidity and other unpredictable factors produce seemingly random variations on the measurements of their behaviour. These factors have to be taken into account in order to have buildable results.

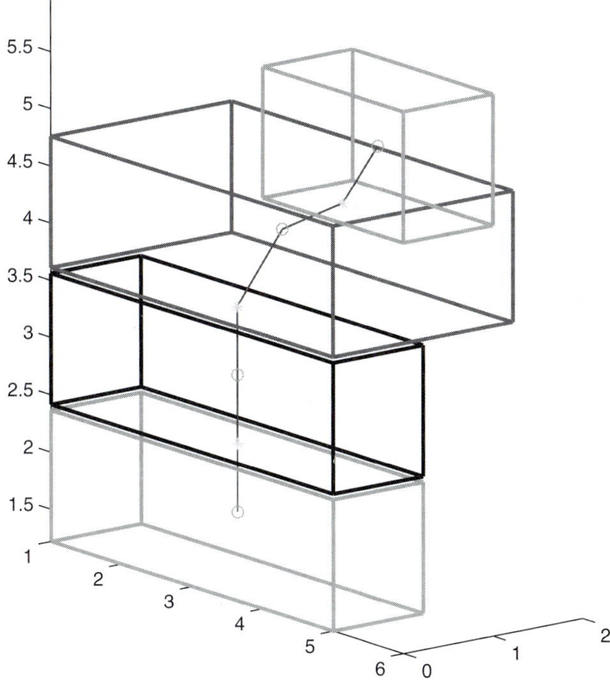

Figure 17.4 3D model for a few Lego bricks. For every pair of bricks we model a 'joint' located at the centre of the area of contact, whose resistance depends on its x and y dimensions (see fig. 17.3). Each joint is labelled with a star and each centre of mass with a circle.

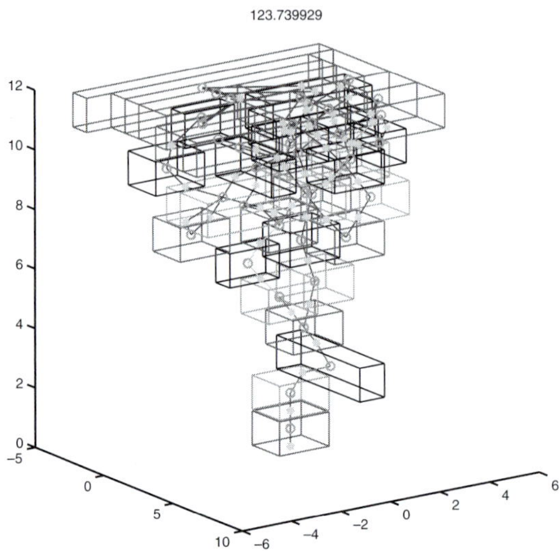

Figure 17.5 Structure of Lego bricks generated by our evolutionary process. The underlying physical model is shown.

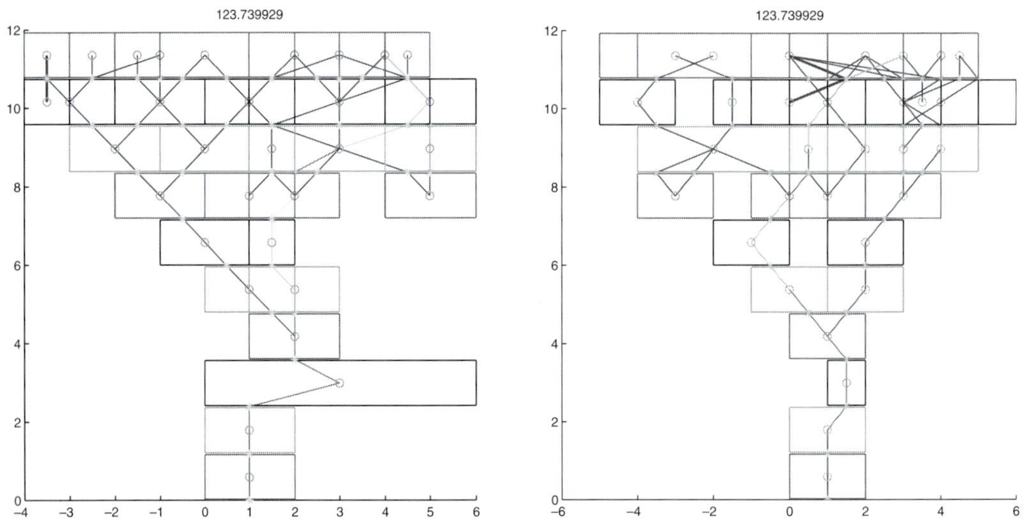

Figure 17.6 Projecting the 3D structure of fig. 17.5 to the *xz* and *yz* planes two 2D networks are obtained that can be solved independently.

So far we have accounted for this problem using a 'safety margin' of 20%. This means that our model actually assigns 20% less resistance to all the joints involved. Any model for modular structures will have to contemplate this kind of safety margin to compensate for the random variability of the generic properties of the average brick, but the value of 20% was set intuitively and may require further study, especially as our structures scale up in size and complexity.

Evolutionary roboticists have found similar unpredictabilities when attempting to simulate the environment for a real robot (Jakobi *et al.*, 1995). This has led to the incorporation of random noise to the simulators in order to generate robust behaviours suitable to be transferred to the real world.

Our model provides only an approximation to the complex physical properties of Lego. It may be possible to complicate it a great deal to have more accurate physics. But because of the variable, noisy properties of Lego, a highly accurate model would not remove the need for a safety margin. Noise means that real entities cannot be simulated beyond the limit of variability in the measurements of their physical parameters.

17.4 Solving a Model

Our model for a 2D structure of bricks generates a set of simultaneous interval equations that can be satisfied if and only if the structure is stable. Each force, either the weight of one of the bricks or an external load, will have to be absorbed by the joints in the structure and transmitted to the ground. The torque exerted by each joint must lie in the interval $[-K, K]$, where K represents its maximum capacity as deduced from the number and disposition of overlapping knobs between two bricks.

It is not clear to us yet which algorithm can solve the equations and find, for a given structure and set of forces, whether or not there is a valid distribution of loads such that all forces are in equilibrium and at the same time all torques lie inside the valid intervals of the joints. But in the case where only one force is present, the problem is describable as a network flow algorithm (NFA) (Cormen *et al.*, 1989, ch. 12) and can be solved by known methods. The possibility of adapting generalized versions of network flow algorithms (Iusem and Zenios, 1995; Leighton *et al.*, 1995) to our problem remains to be explored.

By separating each 3D joint into two orthogonal and independent 2D joints, which receive the x and y components of each external force, we can project an entire 3D network model of a bricks and joints structure into two orthogonal planes, xz and yz, generating two 2D networks that can be solved separately (figs 17.5 and 17.6). Thus the problem of solving a 3D network does not add any more complexity to the existing problem of solving 2D networks of bricks and joints.

17.4.1 NFA for Solving a 2D Network with a Greedy Algorithm

For each given force we consider the network of all the joints in the structure as a flow network that will absorb it and transmit it to the ground. Each joint j can support a certain fraction α of such a force, given by the formula

$$\alpha_{j,F} = \frac{K_j}{d(j,F)f} \tag{1}$$

Where K_j is the maximum capacity of the joint, $d(j,F)$ is the distance between the line generated by the force vector and the joint, and f the magnitude of the force.

If a given force F is fixed and each edge on the graph is labelled with the corresponding $\alpha_{j,F}$ according to (1), a network flow problem is obtained where the source is the brick to which the force is applied and the sinks are all the connections to the ground. A net flow of 1 represents a valid distribution of the force F throughout the structure.

The complete problem is not reducible, however, to an NFA, due to the fact that there are multiple forces to be applied at different points, and the capacity of each joint relative to each one varies with the magnitude of the force and the orthogonal distance between force and joint.

Leaving aside the study of better algorithmic implementations, we are using a greedy algorithm: once a solution has been found for the distribution of the first mass, it is fixed, and a remaining capacity for each joint is computed that will conform a reduced network that must support the next force, and so on.

While there may be a better algorithm for solving the weight distribution for a stable Lego structure, an incomplete algorithm could be enough for many applications. Any structure that is approved as 'gravitationally correct' by our simulation possesses a load distribution that does not overstress any joint, and thus will not fall under its own weight. Our evolutionary algorithm might be limited by the simulation when it fails to approve a structure that was physically valid, but still may succeed working only in the space of 'provable' solutions.

17.5 Genetic Coding for Lego Structures

To evolve structures in the computer, a genetic representation is required. The evolutionary algorithm manipulates this genotype to create new alternatives by recombination and mutation of previous ones. The new variations are then tested with the simulation machinery, as described in the previous sections, to evaluate their properties and select or discard them accordingly.

Our representation borrows the standard tree mutation and crossover operators from genetic programming (Koza, 1992). We have implemented tree representations of 2D and 3D Lego structures. Each node on the tree represents a brick and has a size type parameter indicating the size of the brick and a list of descendants, which are new bricks physically attached to the parent. Each descendant node has positional parameters that describe the position of the new brick relative to the parent.

17.5.1 Coding for 2D and 3D Structures

In the 2D version each brick node has a size type parameter (4, 6, 8, 10, 12 or 16, corresponding to the Lego bricks of size 1×4 through 1×16) and four potential sons, each one representing a new brick linked at one of its four corners (lower left, lower right, upper right, upper left). Each non-nil descendant has a 'joint size' parameter indicating the number of overlapping knobs in the union.

The diagram in fig. 17.7 represents a 10-brick with its 4 joint sites labelled 0, 1, 2, 3, that is linked to a 6-brick by two overlapping knobs. The corresponding tree could be written in pseudo-Lisp notation as:

(10 nil (2 (6 nil nil nil)) nil nil) (2)

In the extension to 3D we add more size types to incorporate bricks other than $1 \times n$ (the bricks currently available are 1×2, 1×4, 1×6, 1×8, 1×10, 1×12, 1×16, 2×2, and

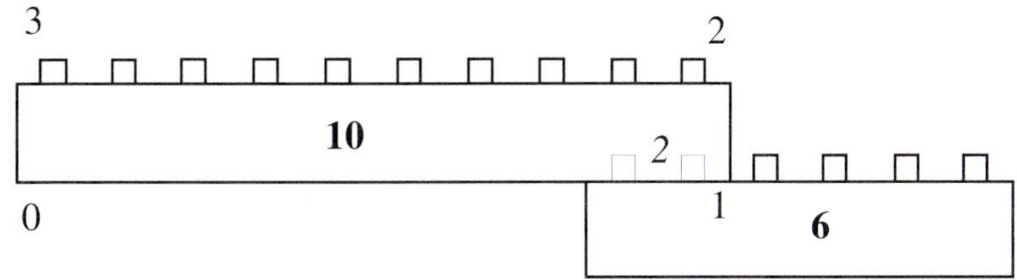

Figure 17.7 Example of 2D genetic encoding of bricks.

2×4), and use a list of descendants, each one representing a new brick to be plugged into the parent. Each descendant brick has three parameters: The integer (x, y, z) coordinates of the new brick (relative to its parent, so for a descendant of an $n \times m$ brick, $0 \leq x < n$, $0 \leq y < m$ and $z \in \{-1,1\}$); a rotation parameter that specifies the orientation of the descendant relative to the parent (0°, 90°, 180° or 270°), and the size of the descendant. As an example, the structure in fig. 17.4 can be codified as:

$$(1 \times 4\ ((0,0,1)\ 0°\ (1 \times 4\ ((0,0,1)\ 0°\ (2 \times 4\ ((3,0,1)\ 0°\ (1 \times 2)))))) \qquad (3)$$

17.5.2 Mutation and Crossover

Mutation operates by either random modification of a brick's parameters (size, position, orientation) or addition of a random brick. The basic crossover operator involves two parent trees out of which random subtrees are selected. The offspring generated has the first subtree removed and replaced by the second.

After mutation or crossover operators are applied, a new, possibly invalid specification tree is formed. The result is expanded one node at a time and overlapping is checked. Whenever an overlap is found the tree is truncated at that site. With this procedure, a maximum spatially valid subtree is built from a crossover or mutation. Branches that could not be expanded are discarded.

Once a valid tree has been obtained, the physical model is constructed and the structure tested for stress stability. If approved, fitness is evaluated and the new individual is added to the population.

A problem with our representations, similar in origin to the problem of valid function parameters in genetic programming, is that it is underconstrained: Only some trees will encode valid Lego structures. Many trees describe impossible, overlapping structures. The following mutation of (3), for example, is illegal because two bricks would share the same physical space ($z = -1$ after the second brick means that the third one goes below it, but the first brick is already there).

$$(1 \times 4\ ((0,0,1)\ 0°\ (1 \times 4\ ((0,0,-1)\ 0°\ (2 \times 4\ ((3,0,1)\ 0°\ (1 \times 2)))))) \qquad (4)$$

17.5.3 Evolutionary Algorithm

We use a straightforward steady-state genetic algorithm, initialized with a population of one single brick. Through mutation and crossovers a population of 1000 individuals is generated and then evolved:

1. While maximum fitness < Target fitness
2. Do Randomly select mutation or crossover.
3. Select 1 (2 for crossover) random individual(s) with fitness proportional probability.
4. Apply mutation or crossover operator.
5. Generate physical model and test for gravitational load.
6. If the new model will support its own weight.
7. Then replace a random individual with it (chosen with inverse fitness proportional probability).

17.6 Evolving Two-dimensional Lego Structures

In this section we summarize the experiments done and the Lego designs obtained. Our first assay was the 'Lego bridge': evolving a structure attached to a table to reach over the void to a neighbouring table. With appropriate fitness functions we went on to evolve other 2D structures, including longer bridges, scaffolds and cranes. Finally, our first 3D project is a table.

17.6.1 Reaching a Target Point: Bridges and Scaffolds

In our first experiments we conceived a Lego plate affixed to a table (fig. 17.8) and evolved 2D structures to reach a target point, using as fitness function a normalized distance to the target point,

$$Nd(S, T) = 1 - \frac{d(S, T)}{d(0, T)} \tag{5}$$

(where S is the structure, T the target point and d the euclidean distance).

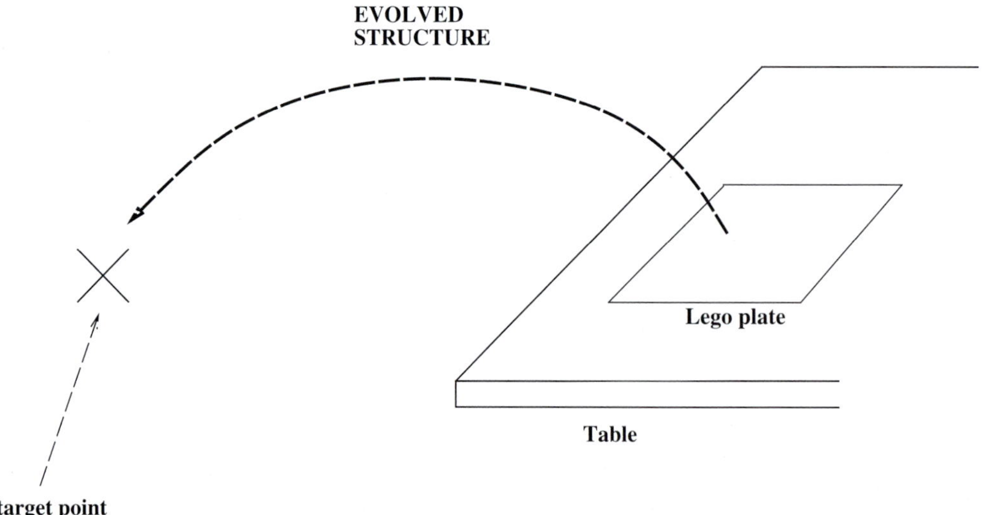

Figure 17.8 Basic set-up: The structure starts over a Lego plate affixed to a table and has to reach a target point supporting its own weight.

Structures not approved by the physical model were discarded. Those capable of supporting themselves – according to our simulation – were incorporated to the evolving population and selected according to this straightforward fitness measure.

With a target point located horizontally and away from the plate we generated a 'Lego Bridge' (fig. 17.1 and Plate 7), moving it to a remote position we obtained the 'long bridge' (Plate 8), and putting it below we generated a descending structure, a 'scaffold' (Plate 9).

17.6.2 External Loads: Horizontal Crane Arm

With a two-step fitness function that gives one point for reaching the target point as in equation (5) above and, if reached, additional points for supporting an external weight hanging from the last brick, we evolved a crane arm (Plate 10).

Since our algorithm gives a yes/no answer for the stability of a structure, we add the weight in small increments and test repeatedly to create a fitness function in this case. For example, for a target load m we can use the following fitness function:

1. For $i = 1$ to 100
2. Add a weight $m/100$ to the structure at T
3. If the structure does not resist, return $(i-1)/100$
4. Return 1.0

17.6.3 Constraining the Space: Diagonal Crane Arm

For a different type of crane we constrained the space where bricks can be located to the diagonal subspace $\{-x<y\}$. In order to evolve a crane arm that would support a weight of 250g we wrote a fitness function whose value is the fraction of 250g supported times the length of the arm along the x axis. Since no bricks can be placed below the diagonal, the resulting arm goes diagonally up and away (Plate 11 and fig. 17.9).

17.6.4 Optimization

A comment that we often received was that our final structures are not optimized: There have useless bricks that do not serve for any apparent purpose. Of course, these irregularities are useful during the search process. Since we are not rewarding nor punishing the number of bricks used, the evolutionary search will freely generate variations with different numbers of bricks. All of them are potentially useful in the process of finding new combinations with higher fitness.

In a new run of the diagonal crane arm experiment, we added a little reward for lightness, inversely proportional to the number of bricks, but three orders of magnitude smaller than the raw fitness function. Figure 17.9 shows two solutions for a crane arm the same length (a fitness value of 24). The second structure has a bigger premium, so we will prefer it.

There is a reason why the weight of the fitness of the 'simplicity' factor should be small compared with the raw fitness measure (length of the arm): we are willing to sacrifice everything else for the size of the crane, which is what we are really trying to maximize. Among cranes of the same size and resistance, however, we prefer those with a smaller number of bricks. The evolutionary process must not be biased against heavier versions of the crane. In the example shown in fig. 17.9, fitness values of 24.0029 and 24.0040 have nearly identical

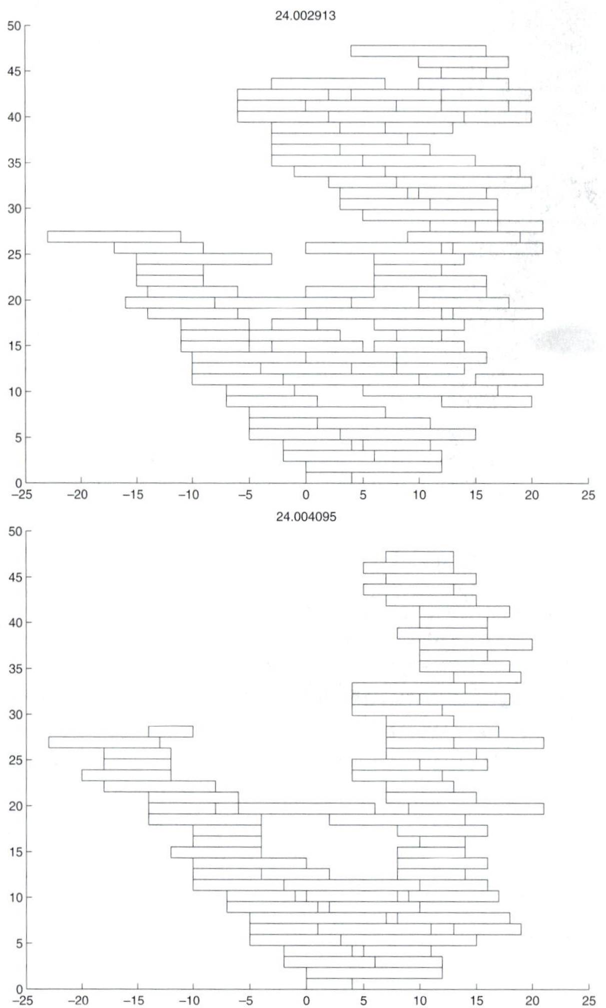

Figure 17.9 Optimization: Among several structures found with a raw fitness of 24, a small premium in the fitness function allows us to choose the one that uses less bricks (bottom). [Note that the tall column on the bottom cannot be eliminated because it acts as a counterbalance for the load that will be placed at the left tip of the crane].

chances of being selected in a fitness proportional selection scheme. But among otherwise identical cranes, the premium for optimality allows us to keep the one that is cleanest.

17.7 Evolving Three-dimensional Lego Structures

17.7.1 First Project: A Lego Table

We have run our first experiments in evolution of 3D Lego designs. Our initial project is a 'table'. We start with a fixed plate as in fig. 17.8, and want to obtain a table 10 bricks tall, with a support surface of 9×9 and capable of supporting a weight of 50 grams anywhere. There are four objectives to fulfill:

1. The height of the structure must be as required.
2. The surface most cover the target area.
3. The desired weight has to be supported all over the surface.
4. All other conditions met, a minimal number of bricks should be used.

To cover all the objectives we wrote a step fitness function that gives between 1 and 2 points for the first objective partially fulfilled, between 2 and 3 for the first objective completed and partial satisfaction of the second, and so on. With this set-up, the algorithm builds upwards first, then broadens to cover the surface, later secures that all points of the surface support a load of 50g and finally tries to reduce the number of bricks to a minimum.

One of the solutions we obtained is shown in figs. 17.5 and 17.6, and a picture of the Lego table built in Plate 12.

17.7.2 Problems Defining the Fitness Function

A first attempt to evolve a table failed to satisfy objective 2 (covering the entire surface). The reasons for this failure require further investigation. One problem with our representation is that the distance between genotype and phenotype is big, making most mutations too radical. Also, not providing 1×1 bricks complicates matters (but we did so because our current set of Lego does not include them). Finally, there is little selective pressure as fitness values between 1.9 and 2.0 are nearly identically selected. The raw value in the range [1, 5] was expanded by an exponential function to add selective pressure (so for example the fitness value of 123.74 in fig. 17.5 corresponds to a raw fitness of 4.8), but this did not solve the problem of full coverage. For the successful run pictured above the coverage objective was redefined as 'covering at least 96% of the target area'.

The use of stepped fitness functions might not be ideal; Pareto-optimality-aware GA techniques (Goldberg, 1989, ch. 5) should improve performance in multiobjective problems such as this one.

17.8 Problems and Future Research Directions

The algorithm being used to solve our models does not find all possible solutions. More sophisticated algorithmic tools may provide ways to fully solve the system of equations. The use of appropriate heuristics may in any case help a good deal. This is a critical factor as we may be wasting many plausible structures just because we are not capable of proving their stability.

The tree representation for Lego structures is a limiting factor. An improved description should bring genotype and phenotype closer, providing a better ground for evolution of objects of higher complexity.

The crossover operator provides a primitive way to reuse successful parts, modules, that may spread over the population. A better representation combined with modular recombination tools (Angeline and Pollack, 1994) could allow composite block structures – such as the bricklayers pattern which holds increased stress – to be discovered and replicated as new basic components.

We believe that we can reach some understanding of the dynamic stresses which would be involved in basic Lego mechanisms driven by Lego motors. This would open the field for evolving active pieces of machinery, including vehicles.

The use of more advanced evolutionary techniques including multiobjective optimization, speciation, automatic functional decomposition or landscape models (Goldberg, 1989; Darwen, 1996), may improve over the performance of our minimal steady-state GA.

17.9 Conclusions

We have shown that under some constraints, a simulator for objects can be used in an evolutionary computation, and then the objects can be built. Our belief is that in machine learning/evolving systems, the more interesting results, such as Sims' creatures or expert backgammon players (Tesauro, 1995; Pollack *et al.*, 1996), are due more to features of the learning environment than to any sophistication in the learning algorithm itself. By keeping inductive biases and *ad hoc* ingredients to a minimum, we have also demonstrated that interesting real-world behaviour can come from a simple virtual model of physics and a basic adaptive algorithm.

The use of modular building elements with predictable – within an error margin – properties allows evolutionary algorithms to manipulate physical entities in simulation in ways similar to what we have seen, for example, in the case of robot control software. The bits in our artificial chromosomes are not limited to codifying just bits; they are capable of representing the building blocks of an entire physical structure.

We believe to have only scratched the surface of what is achievable. Combined with suitable simulators, the recombination of modular components guided by an artificial selection algorithm is a powerful framework capable of designing complex architectures ready to be built and used.

References

Angeline, P. J. and Pollack, J. B. (1994). Coevolving High-Level Representations. In Langton, C. (ed.), *Proceedings of the Third Artificial Life Meeting*.

Bentley, P. J. (1996). Generic Evolutionary Design of Solid Objects using a Genetic Algorithm. Ph.D. thesis, Division of Computing and Control Systems, School of Engineering, University of Huddersfield.

Chapman, C. D., Saitou, K. and Jakiela, M. J. (1993). Genetic Algorithms as an Approach to Configuration and Topology Design. In *Proceedings of the 1993 Design Automation Conference*, DE-Vol. 65–1, Albuquerque, New Mexico: ASME, pp. 485–498.

Cliff, D., Harvey, I. and Husbands, P. (1996). Artificial Evolution of Visual Control Systems for Robots. In Srinivisan, M. and Venkatesh, S. (eds.), *From Living Eyes to Seeing Machines*. Oxford University Press.

Cormen, T. H., Leiserson, C. E. and Rivest, R. L. (1989). *Introduction to Algorithms*. McGraw Hill.

Darwen, P. J. (1996). Co-evolutionary Learning by Automatic Modularisation with Speciation. Thesis. University of New South Wales.

Floreano, D. and Mondada, F. (1994). Automatic Creation of an Autonomous Agent: Genetic Evolution of a Neural Network Driven Robot. In Cliff, D. Husbands, P. Meyer, J.-A. and Wilson, S. (eds), *From Animals to Animats III*. Cambridge, MA: MIT Press.

Forbus, K. (1984). Qualitative Process Theory. In *Artificial Intelligence* **24**; 85–168.

Funes, P. and Pollack, J. (1997). Computer Evolution of Buildable Objects. In Husbands, P. and Harvey, I. (eds), *Fourth European Conference on Artificial Life*, Cambridge, MA: MIT Press. pp. 358–367.

Gardin, F. and Meltzer, B. (1989). Analogical Representations of Naive Physics. *Artificial Life* **38**; 139–159.

Goldberg, D. E. (1989). *Genetic Algorithms in Search, Optimization, and Machine Learning*. Addison-Wesley.

Iusem, A. and Zenios, S. (1995). Interval Underrelaxed Bergman's method with an application. In *Optimization*, **35**(3); p. 227.

Jakobi, N., Husbands, P. and Harvey, I. (1995). Noise and the Reality Gap: The Use of Simulation in Evolutionary Robotics, in Moran, F., Moreno, A., Merelo, J., Chacon, P. (eds.), *Advances in Artificial Life: Proceedings of the 3rd European Conference on Artificial Life*, Springer-Verlag, Lecture Notes in Artificial Intelligence 929, pp. 704–720.

Koza, J. R. (1992). *Genetic Programming: On the Programming of Computers by Means of Natural Selection*. Cambridge, MA: MIT Press.

Lee, W., Hallam, J. and Lund, H. (1996). A Hybrid GP/GA Approach for Co-evolving Controllers and Robot Bodies to Achieve Fitness-Specified Tasks. In *Proceedings of IEEE 3rd International Conference on Evolutionary Computation*. IEEE Press.

Leighton, T., Makedon, F., Plotkin, S., Stein, C., Tardos, E. and Tragoudas, S. (1995). Fast Approximation Algorithms for Multicommodity Flow Problems. *Journal of Computer and Syst. Sciences*, **50**; 228–243.

Lund, H. (1995). Evolving Robot Control Systems. In Alander, J. T. (ed.), *Proceedings of 1NWGA*, University of Vaasa, Finland.

Lund, H., Hallam, J. and Lee, W. (1997). Evolving Robot Morphology. *Proceedings of IEEE Fourth International Conference on Evolutionary Computation*. NJ: IEEE Press.

Mataric, M and Cliff, D. (1996). Challenges In Evolving Controllers for Physical Robots. *Evolutional Robotics*, special issue of *Robotics and Autonomous Systems*, **19**(1). pp. 67–83.

Ngo, J. T. and Marks, J. (1993). Spacetime Constraints Revisited. *Computer Graphics*, Annual Conference Series, pp. 335–342.

Pollack, J. B., Blair, A. and Land, M. (1996). Coevolution of a Backgammon Player. In Langton, C. (ed.), *Proceedings of Artificial Life V*, Cambridge, MA: MIT Press.

Schoenauer, M. (1996). Shape Representations and Evolution Schemes. In Fogel, L. J. Angeline, P. J. and Back, T. (eds), *Proceedings of the 5th Annual Conference on Evolutionary Programming*, Cambridge, MA: MIT Press, pp. 121–129.

Sims, K. (1994a). Evolving Virtual Creatures. In *Computer Graphics*, Annual Conference Series (SIGGRAPH '94 Proceedings), July 1994, pp. 15–22.

Sims, K. (1994b). Evolving 3D Morphology and Behaviour by Competition. In Brooks, R. and Maes, P. (eds), *Artificial Life IV Proceedings*, Cambridge, MA: MIT Press, pp. 28–39.

Tesauro, G. (1995). Temporal Difference Learning and TD-Gammon. *Communications of the ACM*, **38**(3); 58–68.

Zienkiewicz, O.C. (1977). *The Finite Element Method in Engineering Science*. New York: McGraw-Hill, 3rd edition.

Chapter 18

From Coffee Tables to Hospitals: Generic Evolutionary Design

By Peter Bentley

'I wonder . . .', he mused to himself over breakfast. 'I wonder if I could do that . . .'.

The idea had come to him in the early hours of that Saturday, his mind wandering as he attempted to regain sleep. Not that he usually gave much thought to coffee tables.

The first idea had been predictable, if boring: spend Saturday wandering around the shops, and buy a new table. It was likely to take some time, cost a fair amount of money (for he wanted a nice *coffee table), and would probably end up being too big, too small, or too damaging to his favourite rug, which covered most of the living room floor.*

It was the second idea that he was currently concentrating upon that morning (with at least as much concentration as is possible to muster on a Saturday morning).

'It will probably take a while,' he muttered to himself, as he began browsing through a mail-order catalogue, studying the dimensions of coffee tables shown in the glossy pages, 'and my carpentry skills are rather limited . . .'.

He sat down on the couch and extended his legs in front of him, feet in the air, clumsily trying to gauge the distance from the floor and his heels with a tape measure. 'I'll probably have to choose one that's easy to build,' he considered, as he jotted down some figures on a pad. 'And it can be made from pine,' he decided, getting up and going over to his computer. He turned it on and launched a program.

For the last few days, he had been using this program to evolve preliminary floor plan designs for a new hospital building, to be built in a busy London site. 'Just a few minor changes,' he mumbled as he quickly moved a small initialisation file with his mouse, and then began writing a new version, glancing down at the figures scrawled messily on his pad every now and again. Ten minutes later he sat back in his chair, and pressed a single button. The program, now transformed from a hospital architect to a coffee table designer, quietly began its work, throwing mysterious lists of numbers onto the screen, and showing strange three-dimensional blobs rotating and changing. 'Just enough time to do some food shopping,' he murmured to himself, and after a brief glance around the kitchen in an entirely unsuccessful attempt to work out which supplies were needed, he left the apartment.

Alone, in the corner of the living room, the computer quietly continued to consider generation after generation of designs, occasionally saving a completed design on a different part of the whirring hard disk.

EVOLUTIONARY DESIGN BY COMPUTERS
ISBN 1-55860-605-X

Half an hour later, the sound of keys rattling in a lock could be heard. A door opened and closed, and soon the sounds of rustling bags and cupboard doors being opened and shut emanated from the kitchen. After a few muttered expletives about the three identical packets of cereal and the forgotten potatoes, he entered the living room and sat down in front of his computer.

For the next hour he viewed the twenty different coffee table designs that the computer had evolved. All were the right size, all were extremely sturdy, and all could be built without modification using standard sized pieces of pine available in the local DIY shop. The designs were also unusual and very creative. Some he dismissed instantly with an 'ugh', others he spent some time carefully examining, zooming in and out and rotating them in different directions on the screen. Eventually he chose a single design – still very distinctive and original, but not as outlandish as some of the others. Most importantly, he felt he could actually build it.

One phone call to a friend (with a car) later, and he was at a store picking out pine and having it cut to size, according to the plan generated by the computer. By Saturday evening, the wood had been planed, sanded, assembled, stained and oiled.

As his clock quietly chimed twelve, a custom-designed world-original coffee table stood drying in the middle of the living room floor. From conception to completion in less than a day. His distinctive new coffee table was finished!

'I wonder what I should try evolving tomorrow', he thought to himself as he prepared for bed.

18.1 Introduction

The previous passage may sound like science fiction, but it is not. It is an accurate description of my day on the 10th of January, 1998. The program referred to in the narrative is known as *GADES* – a genetic algorithm designer. *GADES* was created to evolve a range of different designs from scratch, i.e. it is a generic evolutionary design system. Referring back to the categorisation given in Chapter 1, the program performs integral evolutionary design (although the emphasis is more on the evolution of creativity than optimisation).

The purpose of this unconventional beginning has been to illustrate some important characteristics of *GADES*, by describing the use of the system to evolve a real design. These features can be summarised as follows:

- **Generic design capabilities.**
  GADES can evolve many different types of design (Bentley and Wakefield, 1997b).
- **Quick setting-up time.**
  The system is designed to cope automatically with multiple objectives, constraints and other problems. This means that the default parameter values for *GADES* ordinarily do not need modification for new problems (Bentley, 1996). Nevertheless, all values can be changed in an initialisation file, if necessary.
- **Quick and simple functional specification.**
  New design problems can be introduced to the system by rewriting a single initialisation file, to instruct *GADES* which evaluation modules (fitness functions) should be used in combination. Selecting which modules to use (from a library of such modules) can be

achieved surprisingly easily by trial and error, and with practice the appropriate modules can often be selected first time (Bentley and Wakefield, 1996a).

- **Minimal human supervision.**
  Once properly set up, the system can generate and store large numbers of different solutions to a problem, without any human intervention (Bentley, 1996).
- **Fast evolution.**
  The system uses a genetic algorithm which is designed to reduce the number of evaluations needed (Bentley and Wakefield, 1997b). (Inevitably, however, the speed of the system is determined by the complexity of the evaluations used for the problem.)
- **Reliable evolution of viable designs.**
  Once properly set up, the system is capable of consistently evolving good solutions to design problems (Bentley, 1996).
- **Easily viewed and analysed output.**
  The phenotype representation and output format allows designs to be analysed, evaluated, rendered and viewed with minimal computation (Bentley, 1996).

This work has been influenced by the related research in *evolutionary optimisation*, *creative evolutionary design*, *evolutionary art*, and *evolutionary artificial life forms* (see Chapter 1). However, the primary inspiration came from natural evolution – the original and best evolutionary design system. Nature shows us how a single evolutionary process can generate designs of astonishing variety and complexity (Dawkins, 1986). *GADES* was created in the hope that some of this awe-inspiring creative power could be harnessed and used to generate a diverse range of useful designs.

Most evolutionary design systems do not follow the example provided by natural evolution. Typically, researchers concentrate on building systems to tackle a specific stage of the human design process (e.g. conceptual design, detailed design or evaluation) or specific types of design (e.g. engineering designs, architecture or art). Natural evolution makes none of these distinctions – it uses the same genetic machinery to generate everything from bacteria to blue whales (Dawkins, 1986).

In order to explore the advantages and disadvantages of this highly generalised natural evolutionary approach, *GADES* makes no distinction between stages of design and is not limited to a single type of design. Instead, for every type of problem presented, the system simply evolves the form of new designs from random blobs to optimised shapes.

The following sections of this chapter will describe (with a little less narrative and a little more technical detail) how this computer program can evolve, from scratch, a range of very different types of design: literally from coffee tables to hospitals.

18.2 The Generic Evolutionary Design System

When applying an evolutionary algorithm (EA) to any new application, four main elements must be considered. First, the phenotype must be specified, i.e. the allowable solutions to the problem must be defined by the specification and enumeration of a *solution space*. Second, the genotype must be defined, i.e. the allowable coded solutions must be defined by the specification and enumeration of a *search space* (for some EAs, the search space may be the same as the solution space). Third, the type of evolutionary algorithm most suitable for the problem must be determined. Fourth, the fitness function must be created, in order to allow the evaluation of potential solutions of the problem for the EA.

Since a genetic algorithm (GA) was used to form the core of the generic evolutionary design system, these four elements can be identified in the system. Designs are searched for using a multiobjective genetic algorithm as the 'search-engine' to evolve solutions. To achieve this, the GA manipulates hierarchically-organised genotypes (or coded solutions). The genotypes are mapped to phenotypes (or designs) defined by a low-parameter spatial-partitioning representation. These phenotypes are analysed by modular evaluation software, which provides the GA with multiple fitness values for each design. Figure 18.1 illustrates how these four elements are combined to allow the evolution of a range of different designs from scratch.

18.2.1 Phenotypes

Evolving designs, or phenotypes, from scratch rather than optimising existing designs requires a very different approach to the representation of designs. When optimising an existing design, only selected parameters need have their values optimised (Bentley, 1998), e.g. for a jet-turbine blade, such parameters could define the length and cross-sectional area at specific parts of the blade. However, to allow a GA to create a new design, the GA must be able to modify more than a small selected part of that design – it must be able to modify every part of the design.

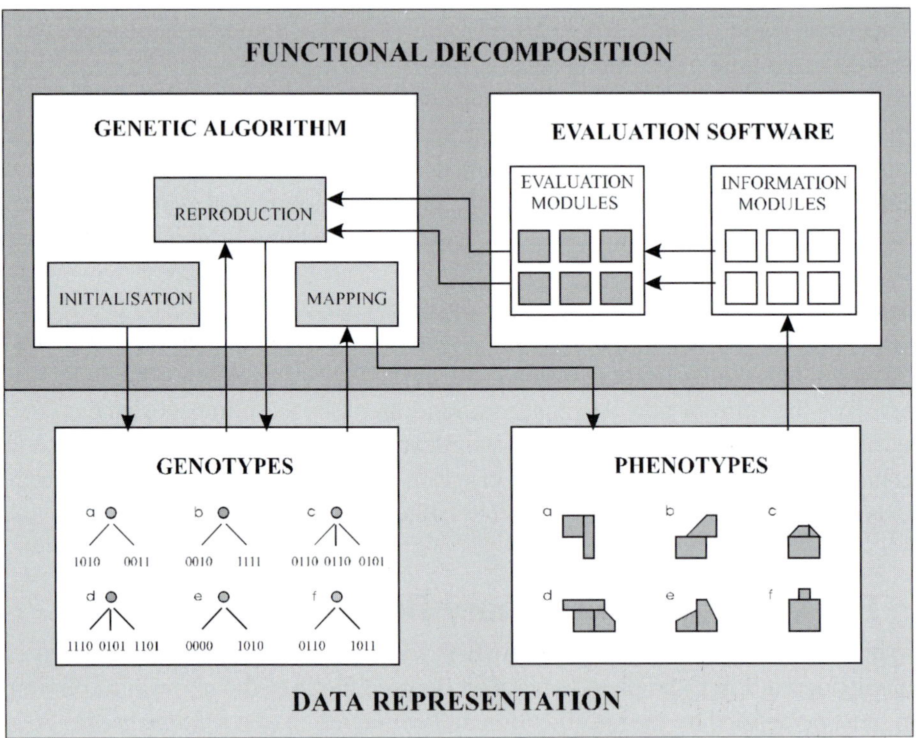

Figure 18.1 Block diagram of *GADES*.

This means that a representation capable of defining the entirety of designs is required, which is suitable for manipulation by GAs. Many possible representations exist, and some have been used by the evolutionary art systems: Todd and Latham (1992) used a variant of constructive solid geometry (CSG) (Foley et al., 1990), others have used fractal equations, and tree-like structures (Dawkins, 1986). However, for a system capable of designing a wide variety of different designs, a more generic representation is needed.

After some investigation, a new variant of spatial-partitioning representation (known as 'clipped stretched cuboids'), was developed for this work (Bentley and Wakefield, 1996b). This representation combines methods from CSG and traditional spatial partitioning representations, to allow the definition of a wide range of forms using a number of primitive shapes in combination. Primitive shapes consist of a rectangular block or cuboid with variable width, height and depth, and variable three-dimensional position. Every cuboid can also be intersected by a plane of variable orientation (see fig. 18.2), to allow the approximation of curved surfaces. Intersected cuboids, or primitives, require nine parameters to define their geometry. Designs are defined by a number of non-overlapping primitives.

This design representation is capable of the definition of a wide range of shapes using relatively few primitives to partition the space. Significantly, the fewer the primitives in a design, the fewer the number of parameters that need to be considered by the GA. Additionally, this representation helps to enumerate the search-space such that similar designs are placed close to each other, minimising discontinuities, and easing the task of finding an evolutionary path from a poor design to a better design (Bentley, 1996). In other words, it follows the rule of thumb that a small change of any parameter value should cause a small change to the design (see Chapter 1).

18.2.2 Genotypes

The genetic algorithm within the system never directly manipulates phenotypes. Only coded designs, or genotypes are actually modified by the genetic operators of the GA. Every genotype consists of a single chromosome arranged in a hierarchy consisting of multiple blocks of nine genes, each gene being defined by sixteen bits, see fig. 18.3. This arrangement corresponds to the spatial partitioning representation used to define the phenotypes, with each block of genes being a coded primitive shape and each gene being a coded parameter.

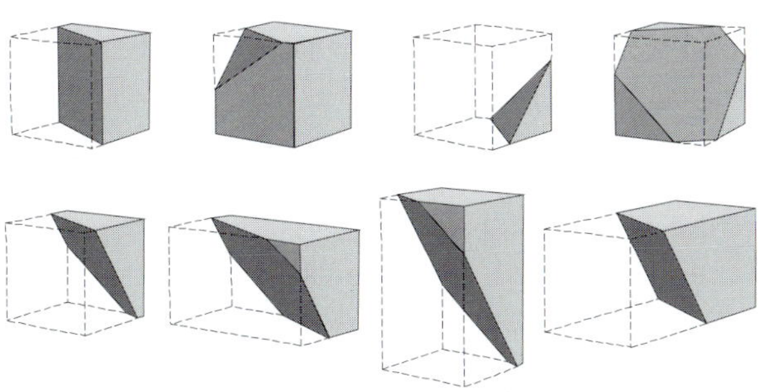

Figure 18.2 Examples of primitive shapes used to represent designs.

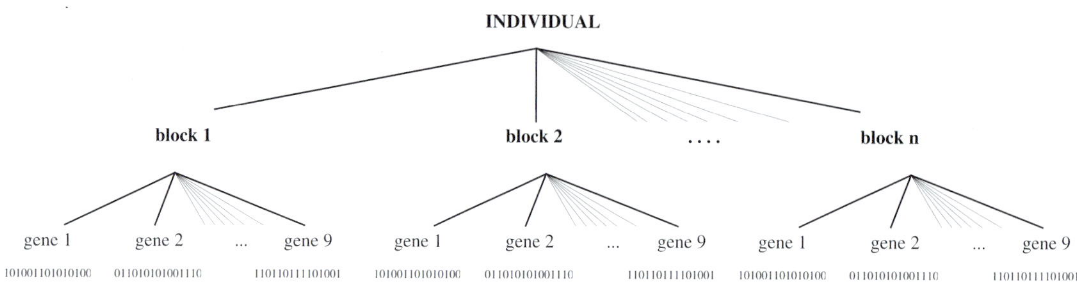

Figure 18.3 Hierarchically structured genotype of a design.

A mutation operator is used within the genetic algorithm to vary the number of primitives in a design by adding or removing new blocks of nine genes from chromosomes. This permits evolution to optimise the number of primitives in addition to the geometries of primitives in designs. (A new primitive is added to a design by splitting a randomly chosen primitive into two. A primitive is removed by simply deleting that primitive from the genotype.) However, varying the length of chromosomes in this way can cause the crossover operator to produce meaningless offspring. To overcome this, a new type of crossover operator, known as hierarchical crossover, was developed (Bentley and Wakefield, 1996c). This new version of crossover uses the hierarchical arrangement of the chromosomes to find points of similarity between two chromosomes of different sizes. Once such points are found, hierarchical crossover uses the tree-structure of the chromosomes to generate new offspring efficiently and without loss of meaning (Bentley and Wakefield, 1996c).

Hierarchical crossover is used by the GA to generate all offspring (i.e. with a probability of 1.0). Mutation is used to vary the number of primitives in a design with a default probability of 0.01 per primitive and a standard mutation operator is used to vary single bits within genes with a default probability of 0.001 per bit.

18.2.3 Genetic Algorithm

The genetic algorithm at the core of the system is more advanced than Goldberg's simple GA (Goldberg, 1989). For example, two populations of solutions are maintained: the main *external population*, and the smaller *internal population*. All new solutions are held in the internal population where they are evaluated. They are then moved into the external population (i.e. 'born' into the 'real world'), replacing only the weakest members of the external population. Other different features include the use of a mapping stage between genotypes and phenotypes, and the use of multiobjective techniques within the GA.

To begin with, the GA has the internal population of solutions initialised with random values to allow the evolution of designs from scratch (i.e., the GA begins with randomly shaped 'blobs'). However, if required, a combination of random values and user-specified values can be used to allow the evolution of pre-defined components of designs, or of selected parts of designs.

The GA then uses an external embryogeny (see Chapter 1) to map the genotypes to the phenotypes. This resembles nature, i.e., the DNA of an organism is never 'evaluated' directly;

first the phenotype must be grown from the 'instructions' given in the DNA, then the phenotype is evaluated. By performing this process explicitly, the system is able to gain some advantages. For example, should a symmetrical design be required, only half a design needs to be coded in the genotype and hence evolved by the GA. The partial design can then be reflected during the mapping stage to form a complete design, which is then evaluated (Bentley and Wakefield, 1995). This mapping stage is also used to enforce the constraints of the design representation, by ensuring that any designs with overlapping primitives are corrected so that their primitives touch rather than overlap (Bentley and Wakefield, 1996a).

Next, the GA calls user-specified modules of evaluation software to analyse the phenotypes and obtain multiple fitness values for each individual solution (most design problems are multiobjective problems). The GA must then determine from these multiple fitness values which phenotypes are fitter overall than others. In other words, the GA has to be able to place the phenotypes into order of overall fitness, using multiobjective optimisation techniques to handle the many separate fitness values produced by the evaluation software.

After performing comparisons between the performances of existing and new multiobjective ranking techniques, it was found that one of the new methods developed for this work allowed the GA to evolve the best designs most consistently. This multiobjective method automatically scales the separate fitness values of each phenotype, according to the effective ranges of the corresponding fitness functions, in order to make them commensurable (Bentley and Wakefield, 1997c). The fitness scores are then simply summed to provide a single, overall fitness value for each phenotype. In addition, by multiplying each scaled fitness value by a user-defined weighting value before aggregation, the new method also incorporates the concept of 'importance', allowing a user to increase or decrease the relative importance of any objective (Bentley and Wakefield, 1997c).

Once overall fitness values have been calculated for each individual solution, the GA moves the individuals from the internal population where all new individuals are held, into the main external population. However, unlike the simple GA, this GA does not replace an entire population of individuals with new individuals every generation. In a similar way to the steady-state GA, this GA only replaces the weakest (less fit) individuals in the external population with new individuals from the smaller internal population, allowing the fittest individuals to remain in the external population over multiple generations. Unusually, the GA also prevents very fit individuals from becoming immortal by giving every individual in the external population a pre-defined lifespan. Once the individual reaches this lifespan, they become very unfit and thus are quickly 'killed' by new individuals taking their places. This prevents poor individuals with high scores, caused by the random variations of noisy evaluation functions, from corrupting evolution (Bentley, 1996).

Finally, the GA favours individuals with higher overall fitnesses when picking 'parents' from the external population. The randomly chosen parent solutions (with fitter solutions preferentially selected) are then used to generate a new internal population of offspring using hierarchical crossover and the mutation operators.

The GA then maps the new genotypes to the phenotypes, evaluates the new phenotypes, and continues the same process as before. This iterative process continues until either a specified number of generations (i.e. loops) have passed, or until an acceptable solution has emerged.

18.2.4 Evaluation Software

All parts of the system described so far are generic, i.e. they can be applied to a wide range of different design problems. However, there is an element of the system that must inevitably be specific to individual design applications: the evaluation software. Designs must be evaluated to instruct the GA how fit they are, i.e. how well they perform the desired function described in the design specification. Hence, the evaluation software is a software version of the design specification, which must be changed for every new design task.

In an attempt to reduce the time needed to create evaluation software for a new design problem, all parts of the various different types of evaluation software created for this work have been implemented as re-usable modules. In other words, it is proposed that many designs can be specified by using a number of existing evaluation modules in combination. Moreover, wholly new design tasks will only require the creation of modules of evaluation software that do not already exist, thus dramatically shortening the time needed to apply the system to a new application. Over time a large library of such modules could be developed, to reduce the future need for new modules. Examples of the existing modules in the library of evaluation software developed as part of this research include: *minimum size*, *maximum size*, *specific mass*, *specific surface area*, *stability*, *supportiveness*, *ray-tracing*, and *particle-flow simulator*.

In addition to a library of different evaluation software modules (or fitness functions), a library of phenotype information modules is maintained. This is necessary because many modules of evaluation software require specific information about a design in order to calculate how fit that design is. Using a distinct information module to calculate, say, the mass of a design, allows all evaluation modules that need this value to share the information generated. Hence, such information on phenotypes need only be generated once, to supply all evaluation modules that require it. Examples of the information modules in the library developed as part of this work include: *vertices*, *mass*, *centre of mass*, *extents*, *primitive extents* and *surface area*.

Consequently, complete design applications are specified to *GADES* by the selection of a combination of modules of evaluation software, and their corresponding desired parameter values. The system then enables the appropriate information modules which supply all of the evaluation modules with the necessary information on the current phenotype. A number of separate fitness values is generated by the evaluation modules for each design, which is used by the GA to guide evolution to good solutions.

18.3 Designs Evolved by the System

To date, sixteen different design tasks have been presented to the system: tables, sets of steps, heatsinks, optical prisms (right-angle, roof, derotating, rhomboid, penta, abbe, porro), streamlined designs (train fronts, boat bows, boat hulls, saloon cars, sports cars) and floor-planning for a hospital building. Each of these tasks involved the evolution of a design with an entirely different shape, in order to allow that design to perform the desired function. Despite some of these problems being deceptive for the GA, this generic system was able to evolve not only fit, but acceptable designs (as judged by humans) for all sixteen problems (Bentley, 1996). Most designs took around 500 generations to evolve, using internal and external population sizes of 160 and 200 respectively.

18.3.1 Tables

The first task presented to *GADES* was to evolve the design of a table. This was specified by using five evaluation modules: *size*, *mass*, *flat upper surface*, *supportiveness* and *unfragmented*. These defined that good table designs should be an appropriate size and mass, should have a flat upper surface capable of supporting heavy objects without the table toppling over, and that the design should be whole (i.e. no part should 'float free' of the main design). The initial population was seeded with entirely random shapes.

Results were good: *GADES* consistently evolved very fit table designs, often with surprising creativity. Figure 18.4 shows four evolved designs, which use a variety of different concepts to increase the stability of the tables. For example, the top left design has a very low centre of mass to stop it from toppling over when heavy objects are placed on it. The top right table uses a wide base to provide good stability. The bottom two table designs (which were evolved to be symmetrical) use the more traditional approach of four legs to provide the required stability.

Further information on the evolution of tables is provided in (Bentley and Wakefield, 1996a) and (Bentley and Wakefield, 1995).

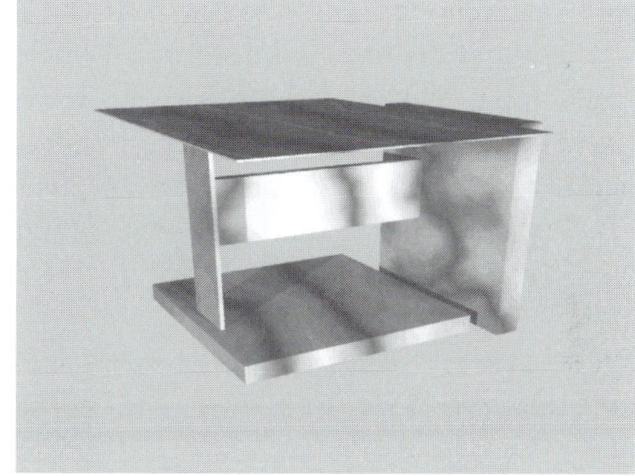
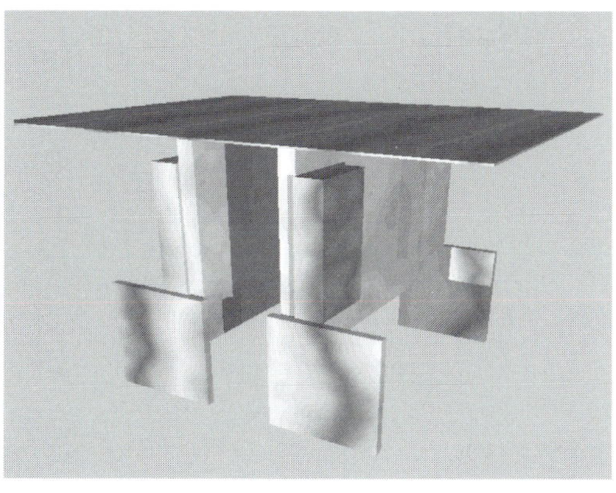
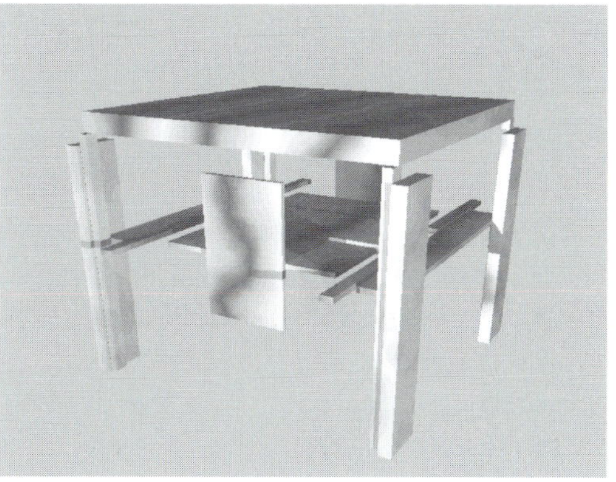

Figure 18.4 Tables evolved by the system. Asymmetrical tables (top), Symmetrical tables (bottom).

As was described in the introduction to this chapter, this design task has recently been reapplied to the current version of *GADES* with a more specific aim in mind: evolve the design of a coffee table, which can then be built and used.

To ensure that all designs would be easily buildable, the thickness of all 'blocks' used to define the shapes was fixed at two centimetres (the thickness of 'pine board' available at DIY stores). This was done by initialising the appropriate genes of the first population with this

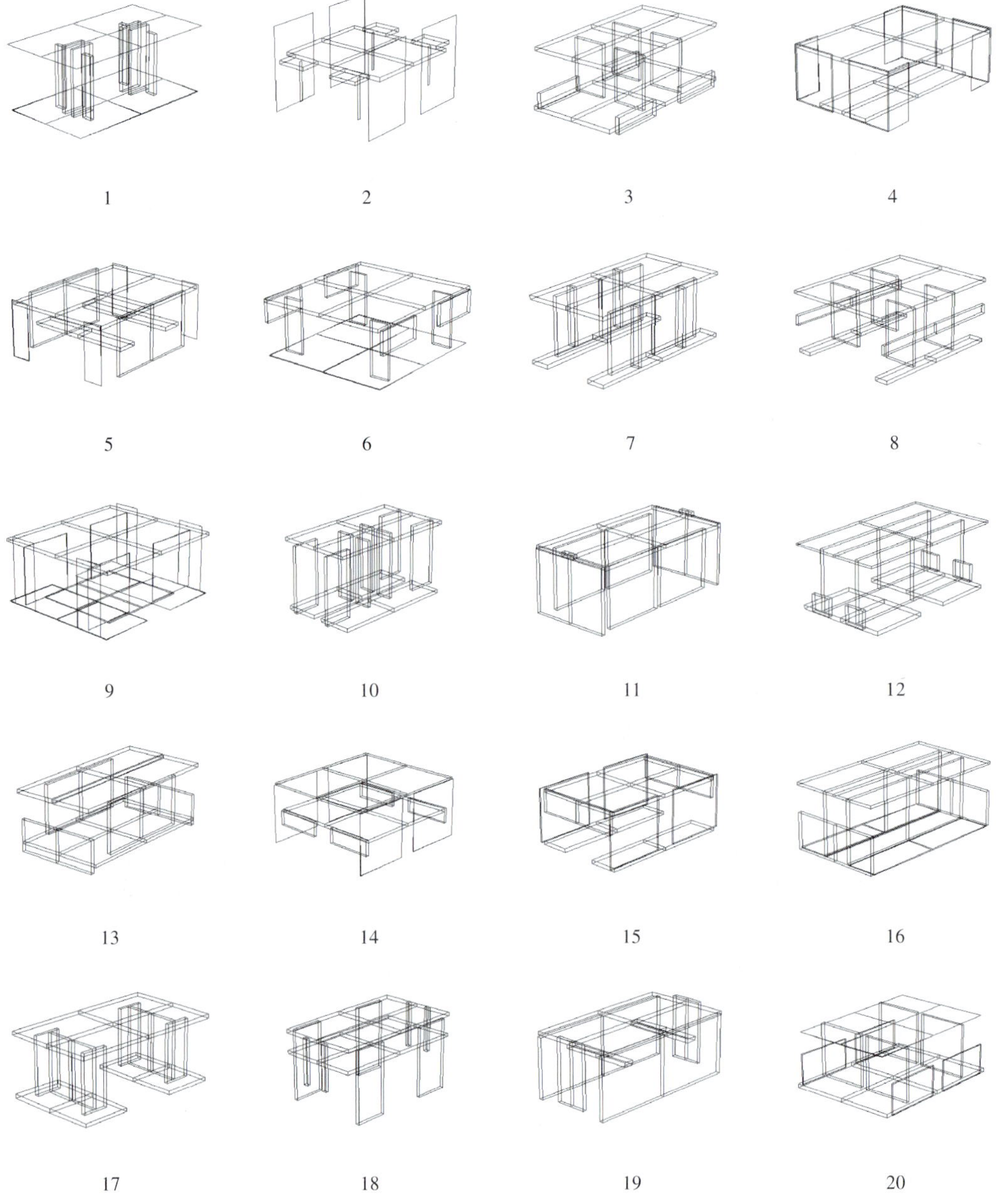

Figure 18.5 The 20 coffee table designs evolved by *GADES*.

value, then fixing those genes to become unchangeable by evolution (options built into the system). All other genes were initialised randomly. In addition, the desired minimum and maximum sizes, and the desired mass, were carefully specified in order to ensure the evolution of low and light tables.

GADES was set to run repeatedly until it had generated 20 coffee table designs (which took about 35 minutes). Figure 18.5 shows the 20 evolved designs. After some careful consideration, a suitable design was chosen from this collection. (Although all the designs performed the desired functions perfectly, some were more pleasing to the eye than others, and some were easier to construct than others. The chosen design, although still slightly unconventional, looked acceptable, and also looked simple enough for even the limited woodworking skills of the author to permit its construction.)

Having been chosen, the evolved output file was taken to a DIY store, where the 'pine board' was selected and cut into the specified dimensions. The table was then assembled, decorated, and is now in use by the author. Figure 18.6 (left) shows the evolved design, figure 18.6 (right) shows a photograph of the actual table.

18.3.2 Steps

The second task was to evolve the design of a small set of steps, specified with similar modules of evaluation software as used for the table problem, except that three flat surfaces at specified heights were desired (Bentley, 1996). Again, good results were obtained, often using a variety of different concepts. Figure 18.7 (left) shows an asymmetrical design which uses a large bottom step to provide a very low centre of mass, and hence greater stability. Figure 18.7 (right) shows an intricate design (evolved to be symmetrical) using two side supports for stability, with the top step being further supported by two columns at the rear. Behind the steps the design is hollow to reduce the mass.

18.3.3 Heatsinks

The third task was to evolve designs of heatsinks (to dissipate the heat of CPUs). The designs were defined to be symmetrical about the planes $x = 0$ and $z = 0$ and were evolved from an

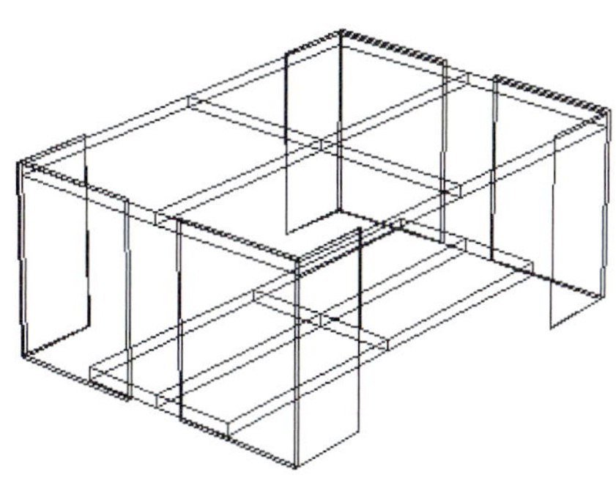

The chosen design (number 4)

Photo of actual table

Figure 18.6 The evolved design of a coffee table and a photo of the actual table.

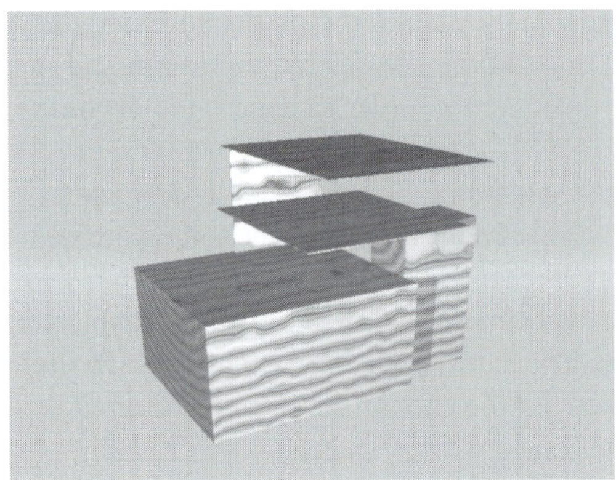
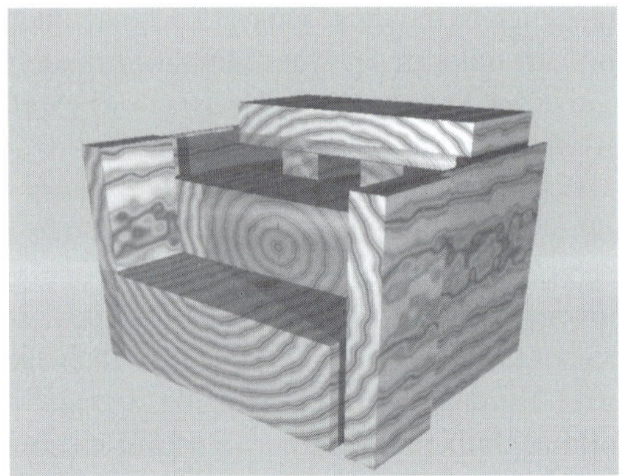

Figure 18.7 The evolved designs of two sets of steps.

initial population of entirely random shapes (on the top of a base of pre-defined size – the 'CPU'). The problem was specified using the evaluation modules: *size*, *mass*, *unfragmented*, and *surface area*. A very high value for the surface area was desired (to define, in effect, that the surface area, and hence the approximate ability of the heatsink to radiate heat, should be maximized).

The four designs shown in fig. 18.8 illustrate the variety of heatsink design that the computer created. The top two heatsinks resemble conventional heatsink designs, using a number of upright 'slats' to increase the surface area. The bottom two show the more typical sort of heatsink design evolved by *GADES*. These designs increase the surface area by creating heatsinks with detailed, uneven surfaces (in the same sort of way that nature increases the surface area of coral). To achieve this, the system 'decided to' add large numbers of primitive shapes to the designs. This in turn increased the number of parameters that the system needed to evolve. In other words, the system evolved the dimensions of the hyperspace it was searching in, while at the same time evolving the shape of the designs (Bentley, 1996).

18.3.4 Optical Prisms

The fourth type of problem was to evolve seven different kinds of optical prism. All of these problems were specified using the evaluation modules: *size*, *unfragmented*, and *ray-tracing*. The ray-tracing module was used to define the characteristics of light travelling into the prisms, and evaluate how well the characteristics of the emerging light matched the desired characteristics for each type of prism. This was achieved by specifying the initial position and direction of at least five light rays, and the desired final position and direction of these rays after passing through the design. The ability of designs to direct the light from source to required destination was then judged by raytracing software. In this way the desired optical function of the prism was defined without indirectly defining the shape of the prism.

Figure 18.9 shows some of the different kinds of prism evolved by *GADES*, and the path of the light through them. For most of these problems there were very few designs that could fulfil the desired function, so most designs strongly resemble human designs (and use the same concepts of total internal reflection). These problems were found to be more difficult for the system, often involving deceptive attractors (Bentley and Wakefield, 1997a) and relying on

Figure 18.8 Four evolved heat sink designs.

many interdependent and precisely optimised reflections. To help overcome such problems, additional guidance was given to *GADES* (such as enforcing symmetry, penalising the use of refraction, or evolving new designs from randomly placed collections of previously evolved right-angle prisms). Once properly set up, the system was able to consistently evolve good solutions for all of the different types of optical prism.

Full details on the application of *GADES* to the design of optical prisms are given in (Bentley and Wakefield, 1997a).

18.3.5 Streamlined Designs

The fifth type of problem was to evolve a number of different kinds of 'streamlined' designs. These were specified using the evaluation modules *size*, *unfragmented*, and *particle-flow simulator*. The 'particle-flow simulator' was used to provide an approximation of water and air-flow by firing particles at designs and calculating the forces generated when collisions with the designs occurred. By defining that minimal forces on the front of designs were required, designs with low water or air-resistance were specified (Bentley, 1996).

The two boat bows shown by fig. 18.10a and b were evolved in front of a fixed rectangular block. It should be clear that *GADES* has generated two designs which resemble a conventional hull and a twin-hulled catamaran, in order to allow the block to cut through the 'water'

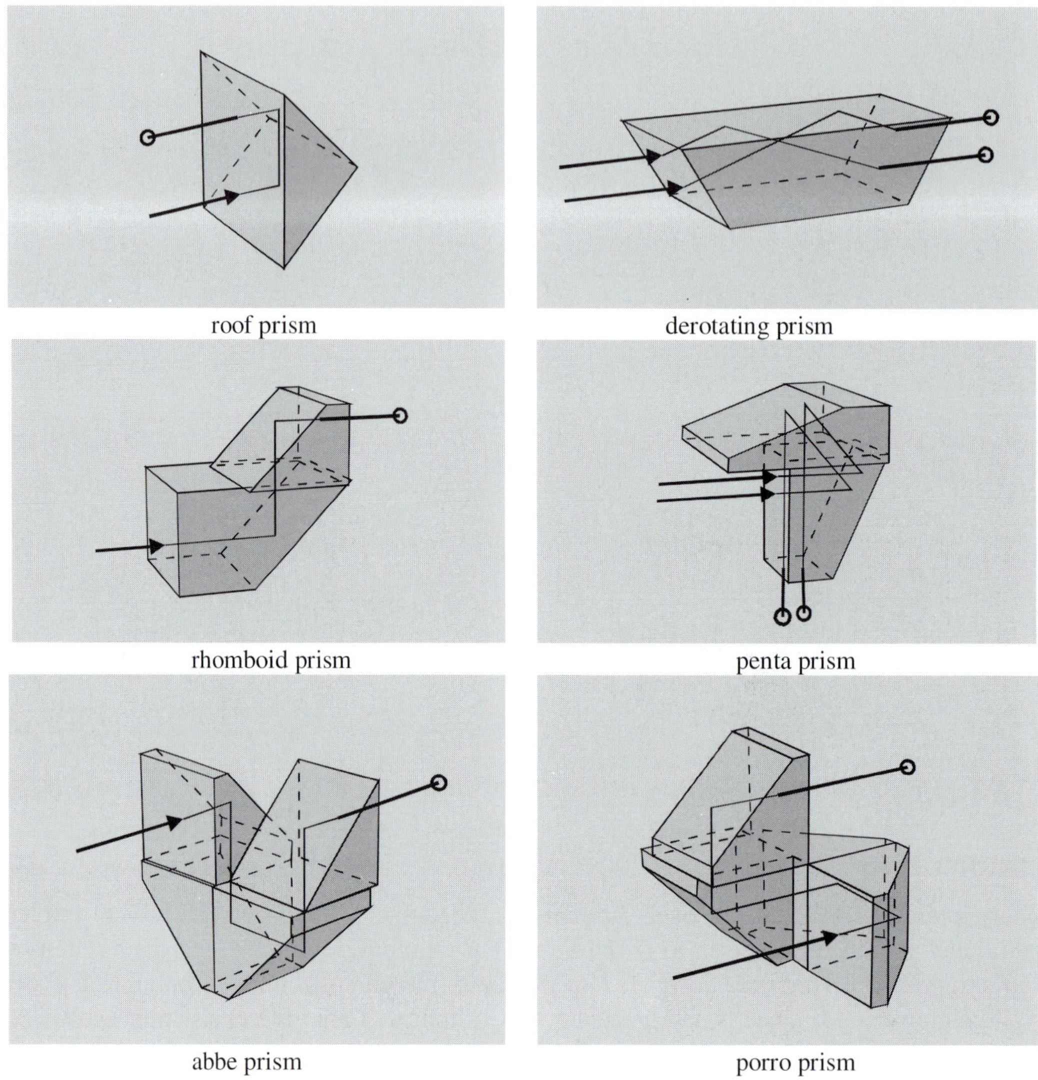

Figure 18.9 Six different kinds of evolved prism design.

cleanly, whilst generating an up-force. Figure 18.10c shows the front of a train with a pointed nose, shaped to minimise 'wind resistance' and generate an overall down-force. Figure 18.10d shows a design of a saloon car, evolved around a more complex fixed chassis, which uses a sloping windscreen and bonnet (windshield and hood) to reduce wind resistance and generate the desired down-force. Figure 18.10e shows the underside of a boat hull, angled to cut through water cleanly and provide the required amount of up-force. Finally, fig. 18.10f shows an evolved sports car that has a sloped bonnet, curved windscreen and large back spoiler which all work in unison to generate the required amount of force pushing down on each wheel, whilst minimising the air-resistance. Plate 13 shows the evolution of this design in more detail.

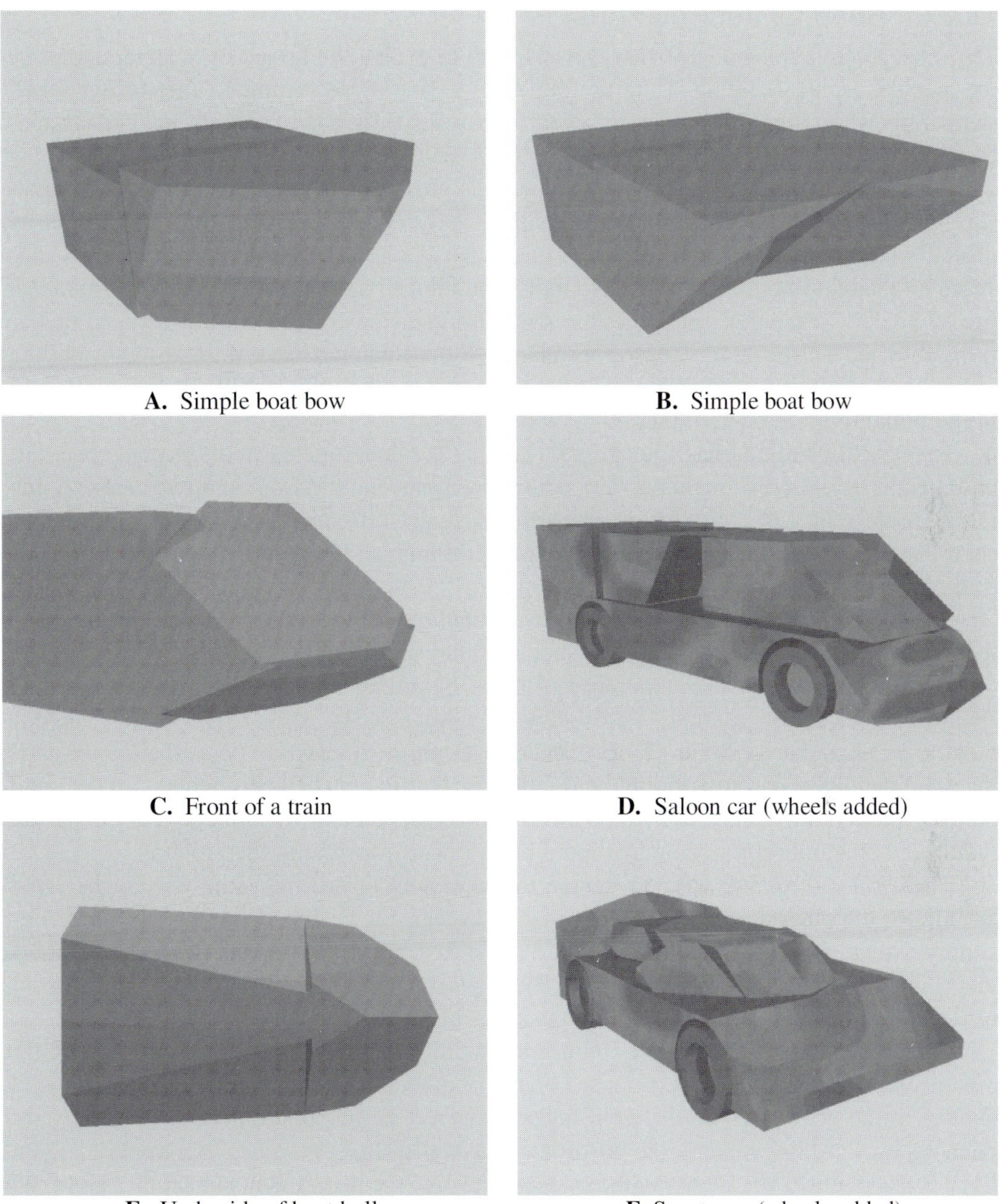

A. Simple boat bow

B. Simple boat bow

C. Front of a train

D. Saloon car (wheels added)

E. Underside of boat hull

F. Sports car (wheels added)

Figure 18.10 Evolved 'streamlined' designs.

18.3.6 Hospital floor-planning

The most recent application of *GADES* has been to evolve the layout of hospital departments for a real hospital building. Determining such a layout, according to the design schedule (which gives required floor areas for every department), is one of the normal early stages of hospital design.

For this problem, a real design schedule was provided. It describes the required areas of seventeen separate departments for a small, heavily constrained site (the building is to be placed within a tight space in a busy London hospital site). Because of the constraints on space and height imposed by the surrounding buildings, and because of the large numbers of fire and safety regulations in place, the overall dimensions of the building are, in this case, inevitable and unchangeable. Also, because of the available access ways to other buildings, and again because of various regulations, the position of entrances, lifts and main corridors in the building are predetermined.

In total, the building has four floors available for departments, with a small space in the basement. There are two main corridors, a main entrance at the front and two access points at the side and rear. Lifts are clustered in groups, in six different parts of the building, and a central atrium above the entranceway, extending through all floors, provides the required levels of light.

The problem presented to the system was then: evolve the size and location of the seventeen departments *within this structure*, such that they are suitably placed for staff and patients.

Architects typically use a number of rules of thumb to determine where departments should be placed. For example, wards should be organised in pairs, to allow staff and equipment to be shared across both. X-Ray and Eye Departments should be in the darker parts of the building, whereas wards should be brightly lit. Out-Patients Departments (OPD) should be on the ground floor, as near to the entrances as possible. Patient Records (a heavy department, requiring structural reinforcement) should be as low as possible in the building.

These rules of thumb were presented to the system in just the same way as the separate criteria for the other designs were specified. However, for this problem, the system could not simply evolve department 'blocks' (where a block denotes floor space for a specific department) in such an unconstrained manner. The departments had to fit within the given structure of the building, taking into account the positions of every element.

To achieve this, a new 'layers' concept was introduced to *GADES*. This permits three-dimensional designs to be superimposed on top of other designs, and be treated as independent entities in the genotypes (in different layers), and yet be mapped onto a single entity in the phenotypes. For this problem, the position of the walls, lifts, entrance, etc., were defined with fixed genes in one layer, allowing the system to evolve the departments in another layer. When combined into phenotypes, any part of a department intersected by the fixed elements of the design is removed, ensuring that all departments always fit within the structure of the building, without constraining evolution. Figure 18.12 shows an example of a hospital design evolved by the system, where dark grey elements are the fixed parts of the design in one layer, and light grey elements are the departments evolved by the system in another layer.

In addition to the new 'layers' option, a 'grid' option was also added to *GADES*. This operates in the mapping stage from genotypes to phenotypes, and forces the sides of all departments to lie on the structural grid for this problem. It also forces all departments to have the

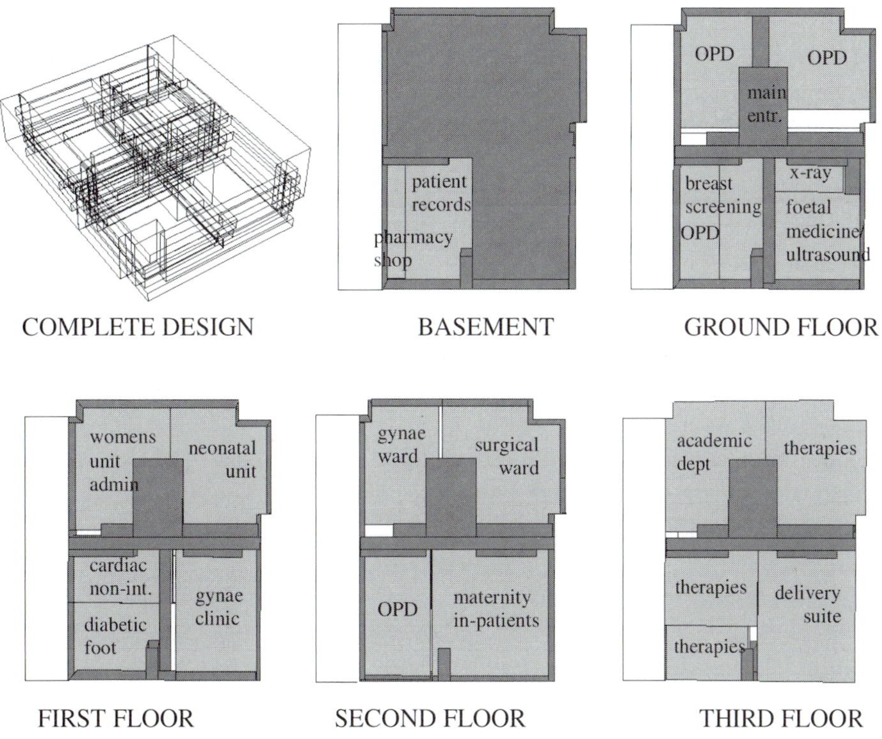

Figure 18.12 A hospital floor-plan design evolved by *GADES*.

appropriate ceiling height (without it, paper-thin departments were often evolved, stacked on top of each other, on a single floor).

As fig. 18.12 shows, *GADES* is capable of successfully evolving new hospital department layouts for this problem. It should be clear that *GADES* has placed Patient Records in the basement (where it will need no structural reinforcement), it has grouped the wards together and placed them in a brightly lit area of the building, it has placed the X-Ray department in a dark part of the building, next to the lifts and accessways, and so on. The advantage of using such a system to automate this process are numerous: firstly, the computer tends to assign each department the desired floor area with good accuracy. Secondly, the process of setting up the problem takes a single morning and once set up, new designs can be evolved in twenty minutes – compared to taking a professional architect two days for a single solution. Thirdly, this generic system has been proven to cope with many different types of design problem, and can be relied upon to tackle new designs of this nature successfully. Fourthly, by examining the fitness of final designs, the computer can explain to what extent each criterion has been satisfied to the clients (inevitably, many of the 'rules of thumb' will be partially contradictory).

18.4 Conclusions

This chapter has presented a new way of using computers in design. It has shown that it is possible, feasible and useful to produce a generic evolutionary design system capable of successfully creating a range of new and original designs.

This novel computer system has four main components:

- A new low-parameter spatial-partitioning representation, used to define the shape of designs.
- Hierarchically structured genotypes combined with a new hierarchical crossover operator, which allow child designs to be efficiently generated from parent designs with different sized genotypes without loss of meaning.
- A steady-state multiobjective genetic algorithm, using a mapping stage between genotypes and phenotypes, preferential selection of parents and a life-span operator, which forms the main search-engine at the core of the system.
- Modular evaluation software, which is used to guide evolution to functionally acceptable designs, with new design tasks being quickly specified by the user picking combinations of existing evaluation modules from a library.

The research described in this chapter has demonstrated the use of a computer to perform generic evolutionary design by evolving consistently acceptable designs for sixteen different design tasks. Designs evolved by the system were based on sound conceptual ideas, 'discovered' independently by the system. The shapes of designs were optimised in order to ensure that they performed the desired function accurately. The system evolved a range of conventional and unconventional designs for all problems presented to it.

In conclusion, evolutionary design has been performed in nature for millennia. This research has made the first steps towards harnessing the power of natural evolutionary design, by demonstrating that it is possible to use a single evolutionary design system to evolve a range of different designs from scratch: literally from coffee tables to hospitals.

Acknowledgements

Thanks to Jon Wakefield, and all the members of UCL's Design Group for their comments. Portions of this chapter appeared as the award-winning paper: Generic Evolutionary Design, in *Soft Computing in Engineering Design and Manfacturing*, Springer-Verlag, reprinted with permission. My thanks to *Nightingale & Associates Ltd* for their permission to publish details of the floor-planning work and for providing the hospital design schedule and their expertise, which was coded to the best of my ability within the evaluation software.

References

Bentley, P. J. (1996). *Generic Evolutionary Design of Solid Objects using a Genetic Algorithm*. Ph.D. Thesis, Division of Computing and Control Systems, School of Engineering, University of Huddersfield, UK.

Bentley, P. J. (1998). Aspects of Evolutionary Design by Computers. In *3rd On-line World Conference on Soft Computing in Engineering Design and Manufacturing (WSC3)*.

Bentley, P. J. and Wakefield, J. P. (1995). The Table: An Illustration of Evolutionary Design using Genetic Algorithms. In *Genetic Algorithms in Engineering Systems: Innovations and Applications (GALESIA '95)*, Sept. 1995, Sheffield, IEEE Press, London, pp. 412–418.

Bentley, P. J. and Wakefield, J. P. (1996a). The Evolution of Solid Object Designs using Genetic Algorithms. In Rayward-Smith, V. (ed.), *Modern Heuristic Search Methods*, Ch. 12, John Wiley, London, pp. 199–215.

Bentley, P. J. and Wakefield, J. P. (1996b). Generic Representation of Solid Geometry for Genetic Search. *Microcomputers in Civil Engineering* 11:3, Blackwell Publishers, pp. 153–161.

Bentley, P. J. and Wakefield, J. P. (1996c). Hierarchical Crossover in Genetic Algorithms. In *Proceedings of the 1st On-line Workshop on Soft Computing* (WSC1), Nagoya University, Japan, pp. 37–42.

Bentley, P. J. and Wakefield, J. P. (1997a). Conceptual Evolutionary Design by Genetic Algorithms. *Engineering Design and Automation Journal* 3:2, John Wiley & Sons Inc, pp. 119–131.

Bentley, P. J. and Wakefield, J. P. (1997b). Generic Evolutionary Design. In Chawdhry, P. K., Roy, R. and Pant, R. K. (eds), *Soft Computing in Engineering Design and Manufacturing*. Springer-Verlag, London, Part 6, pp. 289–298.

Bentley, P. J. and Wakefield, J. P. (1997c). Finding Acceptable Solutions in the Pareto-Optimal Range using Multiobjective Genetic Algorithms. In Chawdhry, P. K., Roy, R., and Pant, R. K. (eds), *Soft Computing in Engineering Design and Manufacturing*. Springer-Verlag, London, Part 5, pp. 231–240.

Dawkins, R. (1986). *The Blind Watchmaker*, Longman Scientific and Technical, Harlow.

Foley, J., van Dam, A., Feiner, S. and Hughes, J. (1990). *Computer Graphics Principles and Practice* (second edition). Addison-Wesley,

Goldberg, D. E., (1989). *Genetic Algorithms in Search, Optimization and Machine Learning*, Addison-Wesley,

Todd, S. and Latham, W. (1992). *Evolutionary Art and Computers*, Academic Press, London.

Glossary

Note that the terms defined here are specific to evolutionary computation and evolutionary design. Although most share the same meanings as the original terms from evolutionary biology, the meanings of some have been corrupted or extended.

Alleles [short for allelomorphs] Alternative forms or values that a gene can take.

Allelic coding Every coded value consists of a <gene, allele> pair, allowing reordering operators such as inversion to work without disruption of meaning.

Algorithm A human-readable description of the operation of a computer program which is independent of computer language.

Alphabet The allowable allelic characters, defined by the genetic coding. For example, a binary coded chromosome has a binary alphabet consisting of '1' and '0', with a cardinality of 2.

Artificial life (AL) The field of computer science devoted to the creation, simulation and investigation of artificial creatures or *animats*.

Artificial life forms (ALF) A subset of artificial life concerned with the creation of the external forms of animats in addition to their behaviour.

Artificial immune systems A new branch of evolutionary computation based on the working of our immune systems, which aims to evolve distributed solutions to problems (typically anomaly detection). Evolutionary pressure is exerted using negative selection.

Binary coding A type of genetic coding used in evolutionary algorithms; values are coded using a string of 1's and 0's.

Biomimetic Introduced by Prof. Schmitt, this term means 'the emulation of biology'.

Bloat The tendency for redundant genetic material (i.e., *junk*, or *junk DNA*) in the genome, which has no phenotypic effect, to increase.

Building block hypothesis This hypothesis suggests that genetic algorithms are able to evolve good solutions by combining building blocks to form better strings. (See Schema theorem.)

Child solution A solution (phenotype) mapped from the genotype, which was created by reproduction from two parent solutions.

Chromosome A collection of genes; may be a simple fixed-length string, may be a hierarchical tree or network.

Clone An individual which has an identical genome to another.

Co-evolution The evolution of solutions to two or more separate problems in parallel, where the fitness of the solutions depends on some interaction between them.

Conceptual evolutionary design A type of creative evolutionary design. New designs are evolved from building blocks of high-level design concepts.

Constraint A restriction or limit on the values a parameter can take, e.g. $0 < A < 32$; also can be a restriction on the algorithm as a whole, e.g. 0 < run-time < 10 min. Satisfying these constraints may involve the use of multiobjective algorithms.

Convergence The common phenomenon where the genotypes of all solutions in the population have evolved to become identical.

Creative evolutionary design The use of evolutionary algorithms to evolve new designs with a minimum of knowledge about existing relationships between the requirements and the form to satisfy those requirements.

Crossover A genetic operator used to generate new child genotypes which inherit 'shuffled' genes from their parents' genotypes.

Deceptive A type of fitness function which evolutionary algorithms find hard to evolve good solutions for, without a change of genetic representation.

Diploid A solution is diploid if its chromosomes are organised into pairs with the same genes (but different alleles). Only one gene in each pair exerts a phenotypic effect, determined by which allele is dominant and which allele is recessive.

Diversity The amount of different genetic material in the population. It is reduced to zero when the population converges.

Dominant A dominant allele of a gene in a diploid chromosome will always exert its phenotypic effect.

Elitism A method to preserve the best individuals in the population by inserting them into the following population if they are not already there.

Embryo Sometimes defined as the genotype before being mapped to a phenotype; alternatively used to mean a simplified or partially defined solution which will be subsequently improved by evolution.

Embryogeny (Often *artificial embryology*, or *mapping*). The process by which the genotype is mapped to the (child) phenotype. If the genotype representation uses a grammar or other indirect method, the embryogeny process 'grows' the phenotype from the instructions given in the genotype.

Epistasis The degree of dependency between separate genes in a chromosome for a specific phenotypic effect.

Evaluation The process which generates fitness value(s) for a solution, dependent on how well the phenotype fulfils the problem objective(s). Makes use of one or more fitness functions.

Evolution A gradual process of change, where alleles, genes, chromosomes, genetic structures and representations which enhance the probability of the individual's survival and reproduction tend to become more numerous in genomes. Requires reproduction, which must involve inheritance and variability. Also requires selection. Normally involves populations of individuals which reproduce for many generations.

Evolution strategies (ES) Rechenberg and Schwefel's evolutionary algorithm, which uses mostly mutation with self-adaptation to direct search. Early versions used only two individuals in a population.

Evolutionary algorithms (EAs) The search algorithms that make up evolutionary computation, e.g. genetic algorithms, evolutionary strategies, evolutionary programming.

Evolutionary art (evoart) (Or *genetic art*). The use of evolutionary algorithms to generate artistic images, guided by a human evaluator.

Evolutionary computation (EC) The field of computer science devoted to the study of evolving solutions to problems using computers.

Evolutionary design (ev. des.) The use of evolutionary computation for design problems.

Evolutionary pressure (Or *selection pressure*). Exerted by the selection, replacement, fertility and 'kill' operators in the evolutionary algorithm. High fitness-based evolutionary pressure means that fit parents propagate their genes faster and with higher probability (which can lead to premature convergence). Low evolutionary pressure will reduce convergence rates and preserve the diversity of the population.

Evolutionary programming (EP) Laurence Fogel and David Fogel's (father and son) evolutionary algorithm. EP only uses mutation with self-adaptation to perform search, and has no recombination operator at all.

Evolutionarily stable strategies (ESS) Used in analysis of evolution for problems with continuously changing fitness functions (e.g. a competitive environment). An ESS is an evolved strategy that does well in a population dominated by some other strategy. In such problems, populations can settle into evolutionary stable states.

Exon Genetic material which has a phenotypic effect. (Opposite of intron.)

Fertility The maximum number of offspring a parent is permitted to sire.

Fitness A score generated by the evaluation process.

Fitness function (Or *objective function*). The mathematical or logical function used in the evaluation process to generate fitness values. Phenotypes are the input to the function, the output is a positive real value. Typically, the closer this fitness value is to zero, the fitter the phenotype (i.e. the evolutionary algorithms are used to minimise fitness scores). If more than one fitness function is used, the problem becomes a multi-objective optimisation problem.

Fitness sharing Reduces the fitness of individuals in larger groups. Used to encourage speciation.

Gene A unit of heredity. May be a coded parameter value, a function, or an instruction, depending on the problem. (See alleles.)

Generation A cycle of population reproduction. If only one child solution is generated at a time (e.g. steady-state GAs), the concept of generations becomes a meaningless measure.

Generative evolutionary design (Or *genetic design*). A type of creative evolutionary design. The use of evolutionary algorithms to generate new designs from scratch.

Genetic algorithm (GA) John Holland's evolutionary search algorithm. One of the most widely used today.

Genetic coding The method used to convert the problem variables into genes in an individual's genotype. Examples of genetic coding are: binary coding and real coding.

Genetic drift Random fluctuations of genetic traits caused by mutation which may result in temporary fitness decreases.

Genetic operator A function applied to the genotypes of individuals to modify them. The genetic operators determine how and where the evolutionary algorithms will search in the search-space. Examples of genetic operators include: crossover, mutation, inversion.

Genetic programming (GP) John Koza's advanced type of GA which uses a tree-like genotype representation to evolve computer programs.

Genome The complete set of genetic material belonging to a single individual.

Genotype The specific versions of the genes, at specific loci, in an individual's genetic make-up. Usually used to mean the whole genetic counterpoint to phenotype.

Genotype representation The organisation and structure of an individual's genotype. May consist of one or more chromosomes organised as strings or in hierarchies. May use one or more types of genetic coding. Defines the search space.

Haploid A solution is haploid if it has a single set of chromosomes. (See diploid.)

Individual The collection of data which makes up each member of the population. Usually consists of genotype, phenotype, fitness value(s). May also contain values for life-span, age, species, fertility, etc.

Intron Or *intervening sequence*. Genetic material which has no effect on the phenotype, see exon.

Inversion Reverses the order of a random string of bits in a chromosome. To prevent disruption, allelic coding is required.

Lindenmayer system (L-system) A recursive string-rewriting grammar used to define the growth of plant and animal-like shapes.

Life span The maximum number of generations a solution is permitted to live for. Solutions which approach their life spans often have penalised fitnesses. Solutions which reach their life spans are declared totally unfit.

Locus The position of a gene (or set of alternative alleles) in the chromosome.

Meiosis Cell division where a cell (usually diploid) generates a child (usually haploid) with half as many chromosomes. Used to generate germ cells (gametes) during sexual reproduction. (See zygote and mitosis.)

Meme A unit of cultural inheritance (e.g., an idea, concept, song, religion).

Memetics The study of the evolution of ideas and concepts in society, from the perspective of the meme.

Mitosis Cell division where the child receives the full complement of chromosomes from the parent (see meiosis).

Multiobjective optimisation (MO) The optimisation of solutions for more than one objective. Involves specialised techniques for allowing an evolutionary algorithm to cope with multiple fitness values for each solution.

Mutation A random change in one or more genes of an individual, which is inherited by the offspring of that individual. For binary coded chromosomes, the most common type of mutation simply selects a random binary digit and inverts it.

Negative selection The opposite to selection – individuals are replaced or killed before they have a chance to reproduce. Typically the less-fit individuals are removed in preference to fit individuals.

Objective Functional criterion of the problem.

Ontogeny The process of development, usually culminating in the production of an adult solution.

Order (of schema) The order of a schema is the number of fixed characters in the template, e.g. the order of 1*1*0* is 4.

Parasite An individual which increases its own fitness at the expense of another individual's fitness. Usually the host and parasite species are co-evolved.

Parent solution A solution (phenotype) mapped from the genotype and evaluated, which is used by reproduction to generate child solutions.

Phenotype The solution, mapped from the genotype of the individual, consisting of the manifested attributes of activated genes.

Phenotypic effect The effect a gene has on the phenotype.

Phenotype representation The organisation and structure of the phenotype. Varies dramatically, depending on what type of evolutionary design is being performed, and what the problem is. Examples include: spatial partitioning, constructive solid geometry, L-systems. Custom-designed representations are common.

Pleiotropy The phenomenon in which changing the allele of a single gene causes multiple phenotypic changes.

Polygeny The combined influence of several genes on a single phenotypic trait.

Population The collection of individuals which is evolved in parallel by evolutionary algorithms.

Premature convergence The convergence of a population onto a sub-optimal solution, typically caused by problems with many local optima and over-strong evolutionary pressure.

Real coding A type of genetic coding used in evolutionary algorithms; values are coded using real numbers.

Recessive A recessive allele of a gene in a diploid chromosome will only exert its phenotypic effect if the paired gene also has the recessive allele.

Recombination A genetic operator used to 'shuffle together' genetic material from parents to generate the new genotypes of offspring. GAs and GP usually perform sexual recombination (two or more parents) with the crossover operator. ES uses panmictic or sexual recombination. EP does not use recombination.

Replacement The process whereby current individuals in the population are removed and new offspring inserted. Typically if this is performed at all, the least fit individuals are replaced with fitter offspring.

Reproduction A parent-copying stage in the simple GA. Today usually used to mean the process of generating child solutions, encompassing the selection, crossover and mutation operators.

Search space The space of all genotypes, defined by the genetic representation, in which the evolutionary algorithm must search using the genetic operators.

Self-adaptation A process in which probabilistic biases are evolved for genetic operators, usually mutation. Plays a fundamental role in ES, EP, and now being introduced into some GAs.

Schema (pl. schemata) A similarity template describing a set of chromosomes which match each other at certain positions. For example, the schema *10101 matches the two strings: {110101, 010101}.

Schema theorem Holland's schema theorem states that the action of reproduction, crossover and mutation within a genetic algorithm ensures that schemata of short defining length, low order and high fitness increase within a population. Such schemata are known as building blocks. (See building block hypothesis.)

Seed population The genotypes of individuals are given predetermined alleles. Normally performed during the initialisation of the evolutionary algorithm, populations are usually seeded with random alleles. However if the user wishes to add knowledge of previous solutions, populations can be partially seeded with previously evolved genotypes. More advanced algorithms may introduce such genetic material during evolution.

Segregation Promotes the evolution of linked genes in the same chromosome by randomly picking two haploid chromosomes from the parents' diploid chromosomes. Assumes the use of reordering operators such as translocation and allelic coding.

Selection The process whereby parents are selected for reproduction. Typically fitter individuals are chosen in preference to less fit individuals.

Solution The phenotype of an individual.

Solution space The space of all phenotypes which contains every solution that the phenotype representation is capable of defining.

Speciation (Or *Niching*). The process of evolving groups of individuals which do not (or rarely) interbreed. Speciation may be artificially enforced by the use of labelling, or may occur naturally in an environment with barriers to prevent interbreeding. Can be performed by random sampling in artificial immune systems; may involve fitness sharing.

Species A group of individuals that can potentially or actually interbreed, producing viable offspring, and that within the group may show gradual variations in genome but remain different to other groups.

Steady-state A type of GA in which a single child solution is generated at a time, replacing a single individual in the population.

Symbiosis The co-evolution of two species towards mutual benefit. Each individual's fitness depends on a co-evolving symbiont.

Termination criterion (TC) The criterion used to halt evolution (is often a threshold set at the desired fitness value or maximum number of generations). More advanced termination criteria halt evolution when convergence has occurred.

Translocation An interchromosomal crossover operator which allows genes to be shifted from one chromosome to another, over evolution.

Weak solution A solution with a low fitness score.

Zygote The immediate result of fusion of the parents' germ cells (gametes). If the gametes were haploid, the zygote will be diploid.

Index